Pacini
1-73

GENERAL THEORY OF VALUE

GENERAL THEORY OF VALUE

ITS MEANING AND BASIC PRINCIPLES
CONSTRUED IN TERMS OF INTEREST

BY

RALPH BARTON PERRY

CAMBRIDGE, MASSACHUSETTS
HARVARD UNIVERSITY PRESS

1967

PRINTED IN THE UNITED STATES OF AMERICA

PREFACE

There are two kinds of philosophy: that which cuts the Gordian knot, and that which attempts to untie it. The present book aims to exemplify the latter rather than the former method, and if it should prove tedious, that fault will be due in part, at least, to the fact that untying is a less swift and dramatic performance than a blow of the sword.

The philosophical method with which I should like to associate myself aims, furthermore, to bridge the gap between common-sense and science; by refining the former, and by extending the latter. The results are not likely to recommend themselves either to common-sense or to science, being too technical to please the one and not sufficiently technical to please the other. The range of the present topic is so broad as to touch almost every popular conviction and overlap almost every province of science. Believing that philosophy must face the facts of life and nature, taking them as both the point of departure and the touchstone of truth, I am perpetually haunted by the accusing presence of some expert who possesses in this or that special field a mastery which I can never attain. I have escaped some blunders through the friendly assistance of my colleagues Professor Walter B. Cannon and Professor Clarence I. Lewis. It would have taken an army of friends to have rid a book such as this of all blunders. But I know of no safe and prudent course for one who would be both an empiricist and a philosopher. He must run the risk of inaccuracy, or even court it, for the sake of that comprehensiveness of view, that tracing of connections and of contours, which is the only contribution to human wisdom which, as philosopher, he can hope to make.

Even so, one can never be comprehensive enough. I realize that what I have here in some measure set in order is adjoined on all sides by thickets abounding in monstrous doubts and difficulties.   There are complications which I have not followed out, assumptions which I have not followed back, and afterthoughts which I can already anticipate.   There are dawning ideas that one would feign take account of, new books that one would feign have read.   Hence that weakness so common among authors, which leads them to express the pious hope (not always shared by their readers) that the present fragment will be completed in a future work, and there rounded into a perfect whole.   Were it not for such a hope it is improbable that any philosophical work would reach the printer.   For philosophy is never finished,—it is only suspended.

The sequel of the present work has already received its title.   It is to be called "Realms of Value," and will deal with the varieties and types of that same "value" whose generic nature,—whose meaning and basic principles, are herein set forth.

Thus forewarned, but, I hope, not disheartened, my readers are invited to join me in obeying the biblical injunction:

"Whatsoever things are true, whatsoever things are honorable, whatsoever things are just, whatsoever things are pure, whatsoever things are lovely, whatsoever things are of good report; if there be any virtue, and if there be any praise, *think on these things.*"

RALPH BARTON PERRY

Cambridge, Massachusetts
  February, 1926.

CONTENTS

General Theory of Value

_____

CHAPTER I

THE PROBLEM AND ITS SCOPE

I. THE NEED FOR A GENERAL THEORY OF VALUE

§ 1. **Criticism versus Description.** If we open the *Century Dictionary* at the word "England," we read the following:

"A country of Europe, which forms with Wales the southern portion of the island of Great Britain. . . . The surface is generally level or undulating in the east, south and center. . . . The highest mountain is Scafell Pike (3,210) feet. The chief river-systems are those of the Thames, Humber and Severn. . . . Its capital is London and its government a constitutional hereditary monarchy. . . . Among the leading events in English history are invasions by Julius Caesar, 55 and 54 B.C. . . . Area, 50,867 square miles. Population (1901), with Wales, 32,526,075."

Compare with this the account of England in Shakespeare's *Richard II*:

"This royal throne of kings, this scepter'd isle,
This earth of majesty, this seat of Mars,
This other Eden, demi-paradise;
This fortress, built by Nature for herself,
Against infection and the hand of war;
This happy breed of men, this little world,
This precious stone set in the silver sea,
Which serves it in the office of a wall,
Or as a moat defensive to a house,
Against the envy of less happier lands;
This blessed plot, this earth, this realm, this England."

Compare, finally, the utterance of a later and lesser poet on the same theme,

"We have but one single hate;
We love as one, we hate as one;
We have but one single foe,
Whom you all know, whom you all know.
He sits crouched behind the gray flood,
Full of envy, full of fury, full of craft, full of guile,
Set apart by waters that are thicker than blood.
We wish to go before a seat of judgment
To swear an oath, face to face,
An oath of metal no wind can blow away,
An oath for children and children's children.
Hearken to the word, repeat the word,
It rolls on through all Germany;
We will not forbear from our hate;
We have all but one hate;
We love as one, we hate as one;
We have all but one foe—
                    England!" [1]

All three of these selections refer to the same object, namely, England. If, however, we compare the first with the second and third we remark a profound difference, the most profound and radical difference, perhaps, which appears in human discourse. The first selection purports to be a statement of fact. It is, as we say, a mere description of the object. It is colorless and unheated. The second and third, on the other hand, are critical and passionate. As compared with one another, furthermore, the second and third selections reveal a peculiar opposition, or difference of sense. The second is *for*, the third *against*, England. The first, in other words, is an unbiassed report; while the second and third are manifestations of friendly and hostile bias. Or, we may compare these selections from a different angle. All three characterize the object, England, but they qualify the object differently, that is, impute different characters to it. The first imputes to England a certain location in space, a certain epoch

[1] Lissauer's "Song of Hate" as translated in D. Appleton and Company's *Out of Their Own Mouths* (1917), p. 120.

in time, a certain magnitude of area and population. The second and third impute happiness, preciousness, blessedness, envy, craft and guile. Such a comparison brings to light two sets of characters or attributes, of which the second set again falls into two opposed groups, which we may term provisionally positive and negative. Theory of value as a separate branch of inquiry arises, then, from the difference between the first of these selections and the other two; and this difference may be regarded either as one of attitude on the part of the subject, or as one of character ascribed to the object.

The distinction may be made between the description of England and the criticism of England, whether favorable or unfavorable. In this case theory of value would undertake to discover the principles of criticism. It would distinguish between the act of description, and the act of criticism; and having defined the essential act of criticism, would then seek a systematic understanding of its modes, with special reference to the peculiar opposition of favor and disfavor. Theory of value would seek to define the radical difference between observing, noting, remarking, measuring, on the one hand; and loving, hating, approving, condemning, on the other hand; and would seek to understand the different attitudes comprised within the second set as variations of one attitude.

Or, one may distinguish between England as a geographical or ethnological entity, and England as an ideal or *bête noir*, assuming that the difference is one between two sets of characters. In this case theory of value would seek to bring to light the general character common to all members of the second set, and would employ the result for the purpose of a systematic classification of all members of the set. It would seek to understand the generic difference between position, area, date, duration, number, on the one hand; and happiness, preciousness, blessedness, envy, craft, guile, on the other hand; and would seek to understand the several members of the second set as variations of one character.

The task of the theory of value may thus be formulated either as the study of a peculiar kind of act, or as the study of a peculiar kind of predicate. It may be regarded as the study of the act of *valuing,* or as the study of the predicate *valuable.* But the theory of value is also compelled to judge between these two modes of formulating its own problem. As a branch of philosophy it must endeavor to see things in their right order. It must locate the seat or *root* of value. Is a thing valuable because it is valued? Is England valuable because Englishmen love it; and, in a negative sense, because Germans hate it? Or is a thing valued because it is valuable? Is England loved and hated because it is positively and negatively valuable? Even the formulation of this dilemma to some extent predetermines the answer. We must leave open the prior question, whether the predicate valuable may not be construed as a kind of act, or the act of valuing as a kind of predicate. This ulterior problem cannot be solved without an analysis of the fundamental act of judgment. Theory of value thus involves theory of knowledge, or epistemology; and must, for this reason also, be regarded as a branch of philosophy.

§ 2. **The Special Sciences of Value.** As a recognized and unified branch of philosophy theory of value is of recent origin. Its data, its special problems, and many of its rival doctrines have been familiar from antiquity. But until the present epoch they have been dispersed among the several philosophical and social sciences, such as *theory of knowledge, ethics, political science, economics, aesthetics,* and *philosophy of religion.* They have been treated one-sidedly and colored by a special context. Theory of value has thus, until recently, been a sort of by-product. The result has been both unduly to enlarge the scope of these special branches of knowledge, and also to lose sight of what they have in common. Each of them has been guilty of claiming too much for that variety of value with which it has been primarily occupied. There is promise of a better proportioned view of the matter if one takes up a position outside and draws them all to a new centre. No one would be disposed to deny that there is a common something in truth, goodness, legality, wealth, beauty and piety that distinguishes them from gravitation and chemical affinity. It is the express business of theory of value to discover what this something is; to define the genus, and discover the differentiae of the species. By means of such definitions and systematic connections theory of value may unify the special philosophical and social sciences enumerated above and arbitrate between them.[2]

The need of such a comprehensive inquiry is evident in each of these special sciences.

Theory of knowledge, for example, has found it necessary to trespass upon the fields of ethics, aesthetics and religion. Those idealists who find truth to consist in the right or obligatory judgment, and those pragmatists who find it to consist in the prudent or useful judgment, are evidently forced to employ ethical conceptions. And it often happens that they borrow such conceptions uncritically either from commonsense or from some ready-made body of doctrine.

Ethics has almost invariably found it necessary to refer beyond itself. Even those intuitional ethical theories which have professed to regard right or duty as irreducible, have attributed to them the force of self-evident truth, and thus virtually appealed to a "validity" which it should be the business of theory of knowledge to analyze. Other ethical theories appeal explicitly to religious or political sanctions. The type of ethical theory which has tended in the long run to prevail has defined right and duty in terms of an end defined as good." But whether regarded as happiness or as perfection, this more ultimate conception of good has evidently an extra-moral significance. The moral life is both bounded and permeated by the non-moral. It is preceded by sub-moral values, such as those of instinct or appetite; it is accompanied by un-moral values, such as are termed "mere considerations of expediency"; and it culminates in supermoral values, such as blessedness or holiness. Indeed, the

[2] Writing about 1885, Hermann Lotze said with reference to aesthetics and ethics, "and for these two investigations a third, common to both, may be conceived, which has hitherto never been carried out,—namely, an investigation concerning the nature of all determinations of value" (*Grundzüge der Logik und Encyclopädie der Philosophie,* trans. by G. T. Ladd, 1892, p. 154).

moral values are so inextricable that ethics has often assumed proprietorship of the whole field of values. But such an extension of the scope of ethics is by no means a satisfactory substitute for theory of value in the modern sense. Because it takes morality as its point of departure, ethics also employs morality as its centre of reference. It has slighted or subordinated other values. Furthermore, ethics has usually assumed a rôle of edification which has proved prejudicial to its scientific rigor. The word 'good,' which ethics commonly employs in a comprehensive sense, is thus so impregnated with an odor of sanctity that it will not serve the uses of an inquiry which proposes to regard morality as only one special division of its field.

The extra-legal implications of *political science* and *jurisprudence* are too familiar to require any proof. Underlying the question of the law as applied to a particular individual or act, is the question of the function of the law as a social institution. In what lies the difference between that of which the law takes cognizance and that of which conscience takes cognizance? To what ultimate principle is the judge to appeal in his interpretation of the law? Underlying the fact of sovereignty with its diverse organs and forms, there is the question of the validity of sovereignty. Is the state a delegation of divine authority, or an expression of the collective will, or merely a convenient instrument? These are questions which cannot be fairly answered without some such comprehensive survey as that which a general theory of value undertakes.

The case of *economics* is peculiarly instructive. In the first place, this science explicitly recognizes the logic of the situation. The type of value under examination in economics is defined by limiting and qualifying a more general conception. In his *Wealth of Nations*, Adam Smith wrote:

> "The word value has two different meanings, and sometimes expresses the utility of some particular object, and sometimes the power of purchasing other goods which the possession of that object conveys. The one may be called 'value in use'; the other 'value in exchange.' " [3]

[3] Book I, Ch. IV.

"The word value," says Mill, "when used without adjunct, always means, in political economy, value in exchange." [4]

The branch of economics known as "economic theory" consists largely in the attempt to explain economic or exchange value as a derivative or mathematical function of value in use. It is an attempt to analyze the specifically economic value, such as price or purchasing power, into non-economic component values such as demands, wants, satisfactions, pleasures and pains. The modern economist would be the first to admit that in this analysis he is handicapped by the lack of a comprehensive and impartial survey of these more primitive or more fundamental categories. He must either borrow from common-sense an ambiguous category such as utility; or he must employ second hand an obsolescent doctrine such as the classic hedonism; or he must formulate a general theory of value for himself. Having in his extremity adopted the third alternative, he has made important contributions toward such a general theory of value, but he is not fitted either by his training or by the focus of his interest to perform such a task adequately.

The more recent developments in economics have emphasized other respects in which this science is virtually dependent on a general theory of value. In formulating a program of economic reform, or in dealing with current economic problems, it proves necessary to employ ethical concepts. Property is in some sense a question of rights; the wage scale, and the distribution of wealth, are in some sense questions of justice. For lack of such a service of liaison as might conceivably be provided by a general theory of value, the economist is again forced to be either dogmatic or naïve in his ethics. Or, if he formulates an ethics for himself it is likely to be an economic-ethics colored by his own bias. Again, the efficacy of any economic remedy depends upon its fitting human nature. It must *induce* labor, or capital, or invention, or management. Its power so to do depends on the human springs of action,—on what men live for, and are willing to do. It is a question of human values in the most inclusive

---

[4] J. S. Mill: *Political Economy*, Book III, Ch. I.

sense, and a question which in its range and complexity exceeds the limits of the economist's technique.

Aesthetics may up to a certain point disregard all considerations save those of beauty and taste. But certain claims made in its behalf inevitably raise more fundamental issues of which connoisseurship and sensibility alone do not qualify one to judge. Consider, for example, the age-long dispute over the relations of art and morals. The protagonist of art for art's sake is not discussing a question of beauty or taste. He is affirming something about the relations of beauty and taste to moral rectitude. Such a boundary dispute usually leads to claims of autonomy by both parties, or to rival claims of annexation in which morality is reduced to beauty or beauty to morality. It is fairly evident that the best solution of such a conflict is arbitration. There would be no conflict unless beauty and morality were both in some sense values; and when this common principle of value is made explicit, it can readily be employed as a method of dividing and co-ordinating their proper spheres.

Similarly, there is the claim, made by humanists, and disputed by humanitarians, that art is the supreme human achievement, or that aesthetic enjoyment is the noblest form of life. This again is not a question of beauty or taste, but a question of the hierarchy of culture. There can be no adequate judgment on such a question without a survey of all types of human activity in the light of some formulated criterion of superiority.

Of all branches of knowledge the *philosophy of religion* is most dependent on a general theory of value, and most confused for the lack of it. In some sense religion deals with the aggregate of all values, as their custodian or champion in the world at large. It deals with the hierarchy of of all values in imputing supreme value to God, and in preferring "salvation" to worldly gain or physical pleasure. It deals with the transmutation of values in its functions of consolation and compensation. It creates new values through its use of symbols. It comprises both the individual value of conversion and the social value of worship. Through the institution of the church its claims rival those of the state, and through the institution of dogma its claims rival those of science. To correlate functions so diverse and so pervasive, to embrace them within an activity that is in some sense one, is possible only in the light of a systematic review of all values. Indeed it is fairly apparent that religion, instead of being a single specific element, is a peculiar grouping or organization from which no value can be wholly excluded.

When thus approached the general theory of value is that branch of knowledge in which such sciences as theory of knowledge, ethics, political science and jurisprudence, economics, aesthetics and philosophy of religion are unified and distinguished. It would be the task of such a theory of value first to bring to light the underlying principle common to these sciences, and then to employ this principle for the purpose of arbitrating between them.

§ 3. **Miscellaneous Values of Every-day Life.** The task of a general theory of value can be further defined as the task of rendering commensurable the diverse and irrelevant critical judgments of every-day life. A general concept of value is indispensable if we are to disengage a generic idea or principle from the overwhelming variety and confusion of our world of praise and disparagement. Consider, for example, some of the various ways in which a single object, such as a book, may be praised or disparaged. First, it may be condemned as *ignorant* by one who is thinking of the author's intellectual incompetence; or second, as *mendacious* by one who is thinking of the author's intent to deceive. Third, it may be deemed *lawful* by one who is thinking of regulations governing the circulation of obscene, revolutionary or libelous publications. Fourth, it may be disparaged as *cheap* by one who is thinking of the little one could get for it; or, fifth, as *crude* or in bad taste by one who is thinking of its binding or style. Sixth, it may be praised as edifying by one who is thinking of its effect on the reader's piety. These various properties 'ignorant,' 'mendacious,' 'lawful,' 'cheap,' 'crude,' and 'edifying,' differ characteristically as a group, from such other properties as the book's color, weight, and size. They are the terms in which the book may be estimated, the predicates of the *critical* judgments that may be pronounced upon it. We need the term 'value' as a term to apply to all the predicates of this group. We may then speak of the book's cognitive value, its moral value, its political value, its economic value, its aesthetic value and its religious value as various species of one genus.

When, furthermore, the concept of value is thus generalized and detached from the special province of any one of these traditional sciences, it is seen to extend even beyond their combined territory. It embraces miscellaneous and homeless values, expressed in such terms as 'nice,' 'terrifying,' 'sublime,' 'ridiculous,' 'amusing,' 'fastidious,' 'hopeful,' 'healthy,' 'dull,' 'heroic,' 'sordid' and a thousand others, —nuances of value whose discrimination lends spice to conversation, color to experience, zest to human intercourse, and vividness to literature. The first effect of the generalization of value is to reveal this rich diversity of everyday values. It becomes evident that the special value sciences have included only such values as have assumed an institutional form, and have therefore acquired a certain prestige or authority. Theory of value in the modern sense is in effect a sort of democratic revolution against a hereditary aristocracy. Though it may arrive at a new constitutional hierarchy, it begins with a promiscuous acknowledgment of the rights of every value, however lowly or disreputable.

This plurality of values appears not only in their difference of kind but in their relative independence. There appears to be no constant relation between them, either in quantity or in sign. The same object may possess positive value in one sense, and negative value in another. Thus a woman may be vicious and beautiful, or grow less virtuous as she grows more beautiful. A drug may increase in price at the same time that it grows more injurious to health. Smith may be at the same time more intelligent and more vicious than Brown. Where this independent variability occurs we may speak of separate types of value, even when a very considerable interaction is possible. Thus if economic commendation implied ethical commendation and in the same proportion, we should be dealing with only one type of value; but inasmuch as what is commended economically *may* be condemned ethically, there are evidently, as we say, two standards; even though in any given case an object may be both wholesome and high-priced, or even high-priced because wholesome.

It cannot, however, be the aim of any branch of knowledge, least of all a branch of philosophy, to create disorder. If theory of value, through the wide and thorough inclusiveness of its initial inventory, aggravates rather than cures the multiplicity of values, this is only from hope of arriving at a system that shall fit the data, in place of a system based on bias or tradition. The very generalization of the concept of value implies that some common character pervades all special values; and it is hoped that when this common character or principle is laid bare, it may be seen to generate the special values as its legitimate progeny. But a general theory of value undertakes to do more than reduce all values to a common descriptive denominator, or attach them to a common family tree. It undertakes also to render them in some sense commensurable. It undertakes to provide a rational ground for judgments of *comparative* value; and in particular for those ultimate judgments in which man estimates his civilization, his progress, or the salvation of his soul.

II. THEORY OF VALUE IN RELATION TO MODERN TENDENCIES

§ 4. **Science Applied to Life.** Theory of value as an attempt to be both empirical and methodical, may be regarded as a part of the modern scientific movement; while as an attempt to be empirical and methodical in the study of *man and his works,* it may be regarded as typical of this movement in its culminating phase. The modern scientific movement first established itself in physical nature, and afterwards annexed human nature. It is true that this operation has been in some sense circular. Certain contemporary philosophers who espouse what they call "humanism," [5] would prefer to say that after having annexed human nature, science shifted its imperial headquarters to its new conquest, and reduced physical nature to the status of a province or self-governing dominion. But in any case, it is characteristic of modern thought to have attacked human nature with weapons first proved in the subjugation of physical nature.

Thus have emerged new sciences such as comparative religion, anthropology, ethnology, sociology and economics. The old science of biology has extended its range so as to include "the descent of man." Old branches of philosophy such as psychology, ethics, politics, and theory of knowledge have adopted a new method, and laid claim to a scientific status. The old Baconian program which promised man power through the conquest of nature, has given place to a new program which promises man power through the conquest of himself. The earlier program having in a large measure fulfilled its promise, nevertheless left man with a sense of weakness. What does it profit a man to have subjugated nature if he cannot govern himself? The very power which man has acquired through the control of the forces of nature has aggravated the evils arising from the maladjustment of man to man. For the moment the great evils seem to be not those which are visited upon man by nature, such as storm, drought, flood, pestilence, famine, darkness, heat and cold, but those which man visits upon himself, such as war and civil discord; or rather, it is realized that man's control of natural forces cannot be beneficently employed, unless that control is itself organized and directed. Through the very power with which physical science has endowed it, the human factor becomes more than ever crucial. Hence the present focussing of attention on what some people like to call "human engineering." It is nothing but the old problem which began in the Garden of Eden, the problem of *living together* with the minimum of friction and the maximum of mutual aid. But that problem is now attacked with a new zest and a new hopefulness owing to the vast increase

[5] F. C. S. Schiller, for example.

of knowledge regarding the materials, the elements, the relations and forces, of which human life is composed.

Theory of value belongs to this general intellectual movement,—shares its aspiration, and participates in its efforts.
Furthermore, as a general science of human life it borrows
both the results and the technique of the special sciences of
human life. It profits by what biology, psychology, and the
new social sciences have learned about man, and it employs
in its own behalf the genetic, comparative, analytical, and
descriptive methods which they have successfully exemplified.

§ 5. **Characteristics of Modern European Civilization.**
Theory of value in the modern and Christian sense undoubtedly reflects something more than this tendency to apply
science to life. It reflects more than the intellectual and
practical demand for a comprehensive and unified system of
values; it reflects also a certain change in the values themselves. There are three characterizations of modern Chris-
tiandom which will probably not be challenged, despite the
doubts which must attach to any sweeping historical comparison. The recognition of these characters will enable us
to understand what is peculiar to a European theory of value
in the twentieth century, as distinguished from a European
theory of value in the thirteenth century or in the fifth century B.C.; or as distinguished from a Chinese or Indian theory
of value in the twentieth century.

In the first place, valuable objects have been vastly *multiplied and diversified by the development of industry and
commerce.* There is a relatively high "standard of living";
which means that the increased production and circulation of
material goods has enabled vast numbers of individuals to
advance beyond the primitive wants of food, shelter and
security, to a demand for luxuries. These luxuries, in turn,
are rapidly converted into needs, and upon this broader base
new luxuries are coveted and provided. A complete inventory
of the commodities in general use in a modern European
society would reveal a volume and diversity of material goods
entirely unparalleled in the history of man.

In the second place, there has been an increased *socialization* of human life. This is in part an outgrowth of the Christian emphasis on compassion, and on the solidarity of mankind. It is more immediately due to the development of new means of communication, publicity and transportation. Whatever the causes, the facts are plain. Modern Europeans are interested in one another to an extent that is unparalleled in earlier or in non-European civilizations. There is an unparalleled volume of human intercourse. The range of love and cooperation, on the one hand, and of hate and conflict, on the other hand, has been extended in all directions. There is an increase both in the radius and in the overlapping of man's social spheres. Loving one's neighbor as oneself has become an altogether different matter now that all the world is one neighborhood.

Thirdly, at the same time that values, material and human, have thus been multiplied, diversified and distributed, there has developed a growing *confidence in their attainability.* There is something in the modern spirit that prevents a man's washing his hands of the whole matter and retiring from the world. Assuming happiness to consist in some sort of harmony between what is and what is desired, between belief and aspiration, there are evidently two ways in which such a harmony may be secured. The most naïve way, represented by appetite, is to adapt the facts to desire,—in short to get what one wants. The rude shock of failure taught man another way, which is to adapt desire to the facts,—in short, to want what one has. The philosophers of antiquity were as a rule disposed to adopt the second way, and to proclaim the gospel of disillusionment. They were impressed by the instability and insecurity of worldly goods. Some were crabbed cynics who proposed to reduce life to the most elementary terms, believing that if man only asked little enough nature might be counted on to grant that little. More often they sought to escape this negation of life by the cult of the intellect. They believed that, though indifferent to man's appetites and worldly interests, nature would in any case conform to his reason. Philosophy in the positive sense, as the love of wisdom and the serene contemplation of truth, was both a safe refuge from misfortune and an exaltation of life.

Christianity continued to proclaim the vanity of the world and the flesh. On the negative side there was little difference, for asceticism comes to much the same thing whether it be practised under pagan or under Christian auspices. At the same time, Christianity introduced a new and positive content, first to replace, and later to supplement, the life of reason. It proclaimed the hope of a life to come where the losses of this life should be compensated; and it proclaimed love,—a love so self-forgetful that man should find all his happiness in the will of God. But Christianity argued from the same fundamental premises as paganism, namely, the disproportion between man's desires and his powers, and the consequent need of renunciation.

It is characteristic of the modern European world, on the other hand, to propose an enlargement of man's powers rather than a reduction of his desires. It would be a serious mistake to press this antithesis too far. The seeds of the modern idea of worldly attainment and progress are to be found both in paganism and in Christianity. It was characteristic of antiquity to delight in the perfection of human nature, and to believe in its attainability through political institutions. It was characteristic of Christianity to undertake the salvation of mankind, and to believe in its attainability through the Church. Both sought to establish kingdoms on earth, the one a kingdom of man and the other a kingdom of God. The program of humanism and the program of humanitarianism alike imply the power of man to work his will by organized effort and by the harnessing of the forces of nature. Indeed the program of modern secular progressivism is in a sense nothing but the combination of these two programs.

But the difference of attitude is none the less striking. The wisdom of antiquity and of early and mediæval Christianity offered a line of retreat. It was pervaded with a sense of doom, of ironic fate, of incurable failure, or of divine intervention. It taught men to believe that worldly attainment could never be more than provisional, and that man should therefore lay up for himself a treasure either in heaven or within the impregnable walls of his own spirit. Men have never abandoned this idea, and will always return to it in their moods of faint-heartedness or disgust. But the triumphs of science have, for better or for worse, resulted in a sort of re-illusionment of the modern European. He proposes to increase production rather than reduce consumption. He has undertaken an aggressive campaign in the open. He believes that all evils are curable, and that he can build permanently, each generation laying its new tier of bricks upon the foundations laid by their predecessors. If he remembers the fate which overtook the Tower of Babel he attributes it to ignorance of modern engineering. If he summons faith to his aid it is not to compensate renunciation, but to invigorate his effort or confirm his illusions.

If we put together these three characteristics of modern European civilization we find that they spell *complexity*. Diversity of interests is multiplied by diversity of individuals. This manyness of kind and number is generally known, and is felt as a claim upon the community; while at the same time it is encouraged and promoted through a sense of limitless resourcefulness. Hence the broad difference between theory of value in the contemporary and European sense, and theory of value in the earlier or in the non-European sense. Once theory of value meant the search for the good, the quest of that good, if any, which is attainable and secure. To-day it springs from a sort of embarrassment of riches. How shall a man choose from what is offered him? How shall conflict be reduced or eliminated? The problem, in other words, is that of establishing a principle of selection and a method of reconciliation by which order and harmony shall be brought out of a bewildering chaos and confusion of values.

III. THE FUNDAMENTAL PROBLEM

§ 6. Theory of Value versus Personal Bias. The fundamental problem of theory of value is to define the *concept* of value. The term 'definition' must not be understood to imply complexity. It may appear that value in the generic sense is unanalyzable. In that case theory of value will identify it and *point it out* as the character common to all species of the genus.

Such an undertaking is to be distinguished, in the first place, from an expression of the author's *personal bias*. In so far, for example, as Nietzsche has indicated his preference for the "strong, brave, domineering and proud" type of manhood, and his contempt for the sick and slavish type which he identifies with Christianity, he is simply manifesting his own personal bias. The pages of his works abound in explosive utterances such as "I find the joy of life in its violent and cruel struggles," "I am fond of the sea, and of all that is of the sea's kin," or "Enough! I can endure it no longer." Such utterances have social importance in proportion as they arouse a like emotion in others, and thus alter the sentiment of a group or of an epoch. Or they may have poetic value in so far as they fitly and permanently embody the emotion which they express. They indicate the existence of values, and may have the power to create values. But with the theory of value they have nothing whatsoever to do. In so far, on the other hand, as Nietzsche affirms that good is a fulfilment of "life" or of the "will to power," and in so far as he affirms that the Christian cult of self-denial is therefore an absolute inversion of good and evil, he is in fact contributing a hypothesis to theory of value.

Theory of value, in other words, is as unemotional as any other theory. The fact that it deals with emotion, or with objects having emotional associations, tends to infect it with emotion. But this tendency does not justify the author in exploiting his emotions; on the contrary, it creates a special obligation to be on his guard. Theory of value is neither reverent nor irreverent, any more than the science of religion is religious or irreligious. Both, according tor their lights, are simply theoretical or scientific.

§ 7. **Theory of Value versus Attribution.** We have distinguished theory of value from the expression of personal bias, that is, from criticism in the impressionistic sense. It is equally important to distinguish theory of value from rational or methodical criticism. By this is meant the application to any given subject-matter of a formulated standard. It consists of judgments of *attribution,* where the attribute itself is already defined, or employed in some ready-made acceptation. Such judgment may be quite independent of the author's personal bias. The fact that the attribute itself happens to connote value does not prevent such a judgment from being as colorless or apathetic as any other judgment. But such critical judgments do not constitute theory of value,—they presuppose it. It is the prior question of the formulation of the standard, or the definition of the attribute, with which theory of value is concerned.

There is a characteristic danger that attends any attempt to reach a new generalization, the danger, namely, of unconsciously assuming and employing the very concept which is under discussion. Ordinarily a concept is used to think *with,* and is not itself thought about. Hence to many persons the problem of value will signify: What is valuable? But this question implies that one already has the predicate 'valuable' in one's possession, and is simply looking for instances to which to apply it. Thus most of the traditional discussions of "the good" have in reality been attempts to discover that particular thing or those particular things that are good, instead of attempts to discover *what it means* for a thing to be good. To use the language of traditional logic, most ethical theory has sought the *denotation* of the term 'good,' instead of its *connotation.* The result has been to leave the fundamental question unanswered, or to adopt some traditional answer unconsciously and uncritically. Thus hedonism, for example, although purporting to examine into fundamentals, has usually sought to prove that pleasure alone is good, in the sense of being the object of desire or the end of action. But this leaves open the prior question whether being an object of desire or end of action makes a thing good. And it is precisely this question with which theory of value is primarily concerned.

The same difference appears within the fields of the other value sciences. The question whether history reveals a progressive improvement of mankind implies a prior question regarding the meaning of improvement. The question whether the art of the Italian Renaissance is or is not superior to that of Greek antiquity implies the prior question of aesthetic theory: What is meant by beauty? When one takes account of stock or appraises property, one employs a standard of monetary value which it is the business of economic theory to define.

There is, conceivably, an art of general criticism in which objects are judged by a universal principle of value, and assigned their places in an all-comprehensive system. Even so the primary task of theory of value would be not the practice of such an art, but the definition of the universal principle, and the framing of the system.

§ 8. Generic Value versus Superlative Value.

There is another confusion against which the reader must be put on his guard. The meaning of value in the generic sense must not be confused with the meaning of value in the comparative or superlative sense. In our review of the modern European attitude to the question of values, we have distinguished between the relatively despairing search for a stable or attainable good, and the relatively confident search for the superior or harmonizing good. Neither of these is, strictly speaking, a search for the *meaning of goodness*. One is again criticising rather than defining, only that in this case one is criticising values. Two principles are virtually employed, the principle by which values are distinguished from non-values, and the principle by which superior values are distinguished from inferior values. If one says "A is good, B is better, C is best," there is one concept of value employed in the predicate of the positive, and some other concept employed in the comparative and superlative. B and C are also good in the same sense as A, but they possess something else that A lacks. It is the first task of theory of value to define good in the common or positive sense.

Theory of value does not ignore the comparison of values. But it attempts to explain such comparisons rather than to make them. That which B and C possess in the above comparison may differ only quantitatively from what A possesses. 'Better' and 'best' may reduce to 'more' and 'most.' In that case theory of value will seek to explain them in terms of the measure of value. Or B and C may possess over and above the generic goodness which they possess in common with A, some specific kind of goodness which A lacks. In this case it will be the task of theory of value to show how species of value arise within the genus, or how the same object may possess value in two or more different senses. When one speaks of a greater value or a more durable value, or of more numerous values, one is evidently implying that value can be measured and counted. When one speaks of true value, or real value, or secure value,—of tainted money, or useful lies, or vicious pleasures, one is evidently implying that value can be compounded. When one speaks of high values, or superior values, or eternal values, or absolute values, one is speaking ambiguously and there can be no certainty as to what is implied. It is the task of theory of value to provide for such implications, and clear up such ambiguities, by an examination of the fundamental concept of value with special reference to its measurability, variability and dimensionality.

Here again it is of first importance to distinguish between theory of value and criticism. Criticism presents the problem, but not the solution. Theory of value is not a critical attitude, or a critical judgment, or a critical comparison, but an attempt to bring to light and set in order the ideas which criticism in these three forms involves.

§ 9. The Question of Terminology. Something should

perhaps be said to justify the use of the term 'value.' The older and more familiar word 'goodness' is disqualified for various reasons. In the first place, we need a term that will refer to negative cases as well as to positive cases, to evil as well as good. We can say that murder has value in a negative sense, but we cannot say that it has goodness. Furthermore, goodness has acquired special meanings which unfit it for purposes of generalization. In common speech the adjective 'good' usually means 'good for,' in the sense of serviceable; or virtuous, in the moral sense. In philosophical literature 'the good' has usually meant the same thing as the highest or greatest good, which, as we have seen, is a very special case.

The principal objection to the term 'value' arises from its use in economics. In that science it has long been used in a narrow sense to distinguish commodities commanding a price from 'free goods' possessing utility. In other words, value in the economic sense is a species of value in the general sense, and we must take pains not to confuse the two. It has been suggested that the term 'worth' (adopted from the German *Wert*) is freer from such exclusively economic associations.[6] But these economic associations do not seriously affect the popular use of the word. Indeed, as a matter of fact in common speech the word 'worth' is more impregnated with economic meaning than the word 'value.' When we speak of a thing as 'worth something,' or of a man as 'worth so and so much' we usually have in mind purchasing power. Where, on the other hand, the word is used in a consciously eulogistic sense, as when we speak of 'a man of worth,' it is too suggestive of a distinctively moral or spiritual quality. On the whole, then, value appears to be the most colorless word that can be borrowed from common speech, and the word that lends itself most readily to a new technical use.

---

[6] It is to be noted that German writers do not escape the difficulty by using the term *Wert*. Ehrenfels, for example, finds it necessary to distinguish between "wirtschaftliche Werttheorie" and "allgemeine Werttheorie" (*System der Werttheorie*, 1897, I, pp. xii, xiii). For a discussion of the question from the standpoint of an economist, cf. H. J. Davenport's *Value and Distribution*, 1908, pp. 296-297, 311, 314-315, 328. The French equivalent of value in the new philosophical sense is *valeur*, and the Italian equivalent is *valore*.

It has the further advantage of being associated with a group of words derived from the same root, and capable of providing a cognate terminology for diverse aspects of the same subject-matter. Thus we have the verbs 'value,' and 'evaluate,' referring to the act; the adjective 'valuable,' referring to the property; and the substantive 'value,' referring to the object.

IV. THE EMPIRICAL METHOD AND ITS DIFFICULTIES

§ 10. **The Data of Value.** In attempting to isolate and exhibit the concept of value we shall employ what may, in the broad sense, be termed the empirical or descriptive method. This does not mean that we shall not distinguish between superior and inferior values, or between valid and false values, but that we shall find these and other such distinctions to depend upon certain given and describable differences. While the best justification of such a method will be its success, there are certain difficulties whose recognition at the outset will throw light upon the nature of the problem.

In the first place, there is a difficulty regarding the delimitation of data. According to the empirical method, we are not to start with a category and then find instances of it, but must proceed in the reverse direction, first collecting instances and then analyzing out their common characteristic.[7] In collecting instances, however, one has to employ a principle of selection; which will turn out, unless one is cautious, to be an assumption of the very concept of which one is supposed to be in search. The difficulty is aggravated by the fact that values cannot even be physically isolated without prejudging their nature.

One can not collect values as one can collect butterflies, and go off into one's laboratory with the assurance that one holds in one's net the whole, and no more than the whole, of that which one seeks. There is no perforation about the edges of values to mark the line at which they may be de-

[7] This is the method recommended and exemplified, for example, in W. H. Sheldon: "An Empirical Definition of Value," *Jour. of Philos.,* Vol. XI (1914).

tached. The great task is to trace the boundaries and detach the entity by an act of discrimination. The Mona Lisa is good, and its theft was evil. But in order to add these to one's collection of values, what must one include? Is all that makes the Mona Lisa good included within its frame? There is at least some ground for asserting that the Mona Lisa is a good only in so far as one includes its enjoyment, or its popularity, or its history. Similarly, there are those who say that its theft as evil must be taken to include the conscience of the thief, or the collective judgment of the times, or the unhappiness of France. If, assuming that the Mona Lisa one had under one's arm was a good, one should forthwith compare it with the money in one's pocket with a view to discovering their common structure, one would have oneself committed too hastily to a limited set of structural possibilities. On the other hand, if one is to leave open the possibility that the Mona Lisa's value includes attitudes and judgments of sentient beings, or demands and opinions of communities, it is evident that one's initial classification must be both broad and flexible.

The fact is that the word 'value' instead of having a clear denotation like the word 'house,' or the word 'Asia,' refers us to a region whose nominal boundaries have yet to be agreed on. It is our task to examine the topography of this region. We shall find various natural lines of cleavage which we may adopt as its frontiers. The area which we ultimately assign to the region will depend on which of these we adopt. Our method is empirical in so far as our frontiers are natural rather than artificial; and provided this is the case, it does not greatly matter where we fix them. The important thing is the accuracy of the topographical survey. This survey must be broad enough to embrace all the claims which have been made in behalf of the term 'value.' We must, in other words, consider whatever is relevant. When once this subject-matter is clearly analyzed, and its principles set forth in their true relations, we shall have a system of concepts whose names are a matter of taste and convenience. One may then, if one so chooses, use the term value to include the tropism of plants, or one may reserve it for the perfection of God. The main thing is to know how they differ and what they have in common.

§ 11. **The Non-Existence of Values.** We are beset by another difficulty which anyone but a philosopher might well regard as insuperable. It lies in the questionable *existence* of the subject-matter. We propose to study 'values.' But *are* there any such things? The scientist waits until facts are thrust upon him, and then attempts to describe or explain them. In the course of his explanation he often introduces new entities of doubtful standing, such as electrons or the ether; but he begins with data whose existence is incontrovertible, and to these his fictitious entities are always anchored. But values, or at any rate some of them, are *ideal*. The whole tragedy of life lies in the fact that some things, like universal peace, are valuable despite their non-existence. We do not wait to be assured of the existence of a thing before we deem it valuable. Immortality, for example, is commonly regarded as good by the same persons who admit doubts as to its existence. Were it not for this duality of value and existence there would be no room for regret.

The most obvious method of meeting this difficulty is to reduce the ideal to the act of idealization, or the object of value to the subject of value. While peace and immortality may be non-existent or questionable, the aspiration and the longing are facts. But though this method may legitimately be employed by certain types of theory, it does not wholly meet the difficulty. For longing and aspiration have objects, and specific longings or aspirations have their specific objects. We seem compelled, then, to provide for non-existent objects, that, is for some supplementary category of being or subsistence. Theory of value can thus be empirical or descriptive only in a sense which is sufficiently elastic to permit of its being extended to this wider realm.

§ 12. **The Subjectivity of Values.** Theory of value is peculiarly exposed to a difficulty with which all philosophy is afflicted, the difficulty of escaping *subjectivism,* with its sceptical implications. *De gustibus non disputandum est,* is a principle that can readily be extended beyond the realm of taste to duty, truth, admiration, law, progress and perfection. In some sense all of these values seem to exist at the pleasure of the individual. If that were all it would be comparatively simple. The matter is complicated by the fact that something more is claimed for them. Some values, at least, seem to be at one and the same time relative to the individual and also binding on him. When one admires beauty one takes an emotional and personal attitude toward it, but at the same time attributes to the object a worthiness to evoke a like atti-tude in others. The point of the maxim about taste is that one *does* dispute about it.

It is this paradox that has given rise in theory of value to the hybrid conception of 'appreciation' or 'valuation,'—the conception of an act that partakes of the nature both of emotion and of judgment. Such an act is supposed to be subjective and personal like emotion, and also objective and universal like judgment. It will be pointed out presently that instead of being a single act in which these contrary natures are paradoxically blended, it is in fact a double act, a com-bination of emotion and judgment, in which each component preserves its own nature intact. Suffice it here to recognize that the existence of this difficulty makes it inevitable that theory of value should for a part of its journey traverse the devious and slippery road of epistemology.

§ 13. **Existence as a Value.** This unhappy conjunction is rendered doubly inevitable by the last of our methodological difficulties. It is urged that the empirical or descriptive method in theory of value inverts the true order of things. It proposes to treat values as facts when facts are really values. This does not mean merely that all facts happen to be valuable; for such an assertion would in no way contradict the supposition that all values are also facts, and may be treated accordingly. What the objection means is that the **very nature of fact must be explained in terms of value.**

It is alleged that there are facts because and only because they satisfy the inner needs of some will or purpose. Value in this fundamental and primordial sense can therefore not be regarded as a fact or existence without a vicious circle.

This difficulty is not likely to trouble any one but the philosopher, and only philosophy can meet it. There are two possible replies. The explanation of fact and existence in terms of value may be disputed, as realism disputes it. It may be contended that existence is more fundamental than value, or at any rate independent of it. Secondly, even if it be admitted that existence is explicable in terms of some cosmic will or purpose, it may still be contended that such a will or purpose must in some sense *be*. If it does not exist then some further category of being must be provided for it. And if it *is*, whatever its special ontological status, then it is capable of being defined or at least exhibited.

The method of theory of value must be capable of dealing with such considerations. It cannot be empirical or descriptive in any narrowly positivistic sense which excludes either epistemology or metaphysics. It may, however, be empirical and descriptive in the sense that it seeks to discover and to report an order of things which is independent of the investigator's bias and preconceived ideas.

CHAPTER II

VALUE AS IRRELEVANT TO INTEREST

I. VALUE AND INTEREST

§ 14. In discussing the definition of value, we shall be dealing constantly with the motor-affective life; that is to say, with instinct, desire, feeling, will and all their family of states, acts and attitudes. It is necessary therefore to have a term which may be used to refer to what is characteristic of this strain in life and mind, which shall be sufficiently comprehensive to embrace all of its varieties, and whose meaning we may refine as we proceed. The term *interest* is the most acceptable, and will henceforth be so employed.[1] But where the context or common usage makes it more convenient to do so, we shall for the present employ such terms as 'desire,' 'will' or 'purpose' in the same comprehensive sense.

There are four possible relations of value to interest. In the first place, value may be, in its essential nature, quite irrelevant to interest. In this case the discussion of interest would not be germane to the definition of value. Interest might as a matter of fact be taken in value, it might be the mode of awareness by which value was immediately apprehended, or it might happen to possess value, but in any case it would not be a necessary constituent of value. In the

---

[1] 'Interest' in this sense is to be distinguished from 'interest' in two cognate, but more limited, senses in which it is often employed. It is sometimes used to mean either curiosity, or the power to arouse curiosity, as imputed to the object when it is spoken of as 'interesting.' On the part of the subject, it is thus opposed to inattention or indifference; on the part of the object, to dulness. Or 'interest' may be used to mean permanent embodiments of motor-affective bias, whether in dispositions of the individual, or in social organizations; or in objects, such as property, tools and other resources, which have a causal relation to such dispositions or organizations. Cf. below, § 49.

second place, value may be held to be that character of an object which qualifies it be an end; in other words, that which implies, evokes or regulates interest. In this case value would be prior to the occurrence of any actual interest, but would prescribe in advance the character which any interest must assume. It is supposed that there is some definable character of desirability or purposiveness, which is the objective complement of interest, as intelligibility is supposed to be the complement of thought; and which may be understood in its own terms, without a psychological examination of the subjective facts of interest. In the third place, value may be assigned to the objects of certain duly qualified interests, such as the final, harmonious, absolute or imperative interest. Finally, there is the simpler and more comprehensive view, that value in the generic sense attaches promiscuously to all objects of all interest. In this case the definition of value will depend upon an analysis of interest itself, not in any qualified or honorific sense, but in the general and psychological sense.

We shall be led to adopt the last of these four alternatives as a result of the successive examination of the other three. According to the first alternative, value is a recognizable character belonging to the world in which we live, and having no necessary relation to interest. It is this notion which we undertake to examine in the present chapter.

II. VALUE AS AN EMPIRICAL QUALITY

§ 15. **Value Immediately Perceived.** The simplest disposition of our problem is to suppose that value neither has nor needs a definition since it can be immediately perceived, as when the poet says,

> "Could I but see before the judgment crash,
> Clean, still perfection in one frozen flash."

Things possess their value as they possess their other qualities, and it is equally evident to any properly sensitized mind.

"There is beauty [says Professor Laird], in sky and cloud and sea, in lilies and in sunsets, in the glow of bracken in autumn and in the enticing greenness of a leafy spring. Nature, indeed, is infinitely beautiful, and she seems to wear her beauty as she wears colour or sound. Why then should her beauty belong to us rather than to her? Human character and human dispositions have value or worth, which belongs to them in the same sense as redness belongs to the cherry." [2]

Good, according to this view, is a quality which needs no definition to one who has perceived it, and permits of no definition to one who has not. "My point," says Professor G. E. Moore, "is that 'good' is a simple notion, just as 'yellow' is a simple notion; that, just as you cannot, by any manner of means, explain to any one who does not already know it, what yellow is, so you cannot explain what good is." [3]

Such a view is, as Professor Laird says, in accord with "Common Sense and the King's English." [4] Things are found good by those who immediately witness them; judgments of goodness often appeal to the evidence of sense; and the term 'good' is employed as a predicative adjective interchangeably with such adjectives as green and yellow. Furthermore, the singleness, brevity and familiarity of the word have begotten a presumption in favor of the simplicity of its meaning. But though the doctrine may find favor with the naïve, it is not to be supposed that its advocates *are* naïve. They represent rather that hyper-sophistication which unexpectedly endorses what plain men would have felt somewhat abashed to confess. Their view may best be understood as an extension of that pan-objectivism, which, having concluded that the so-called 'secondary qualities,' such as color, have as good a title to extra-mental existence as the so-called primary qualities, such as figure, sees no reason why the so-called 'tertiary' qualities, such as good, should not be assigned the same status. [5]

§ 16. **Feeling and the 'Tertiary' Qualities.** There can be only one proof of the existence of a perceptual quality,

---

[2] J. Laird: *A Study in Realism*, 1920, pp. 129, 144.
[3] *Principia Ethica*, 1903, p. 7.
[4] *Op. cit.*, p. 127.
[5] For a fuller discussion of the relation of this question to philosophical realism, cf. below, § 57.

and that is the perception of it. One who upholds this view
of good must be prepared to point to a distinct *quale* which
appears in that region which our value terms roughly indicate,
and which is different from the object's shape and size, from
the interrelation of its parts, from its relation to other objects,
or to a subject; and from all the other factors which belong
to the same context, but are designated by words other than
'good.' The present writer, for one, finds no such residuum.
Mr. Moore's comparison of good with the quality 'yellow'
remains purely hypothetical: good would be like yellow *if it
were* an empirical quality. But then the fact that it does
not possess the self-evidence of yellow argues that it is not
an empirical quality. There is no difficulty over the meaning
of terms connoting empirical qualities, nor is there serious
difference of opinion as to their distribution. Things wear
them in public, and any passer-by may note them. But no
one who has read Mr. Moore's solemn observations concerning what things are or are not good,[6] can for an instant
be deceived into supposing that his perception has lit upon
a quality whose evident presence he reports for our benefit.
He speaks with an air of hesitation and vague conjecture. He
imputes goodness in a miscellaneous way to things that
"appear" or are "commonly held" to be good, and then rounds
it all up with the generalization that "all great goods and
great evils involve both a cognition and an emotion directed
towards its object."[7] This last assertion is plausible because
it sounds so much like the assertion that goodness itself
consists in a cognitive-emotional attitude to an object, but for
our author it purports to be an induction reached after a
direct observation of the divers resting-places of the simple
empirical quality good. That it should have perched exclusively upon the cognitive-emotional attitude, must possess for
him the novelty and indubitableness of sheer fact; but to the
reader, it appears rather as the laborious rediscovery of an
unformulated assumption.

[6] *Op. cit.*, Ch. VI.; *Ethics,* Ch. VII.
[7] With the possible exception of "the consciousness of pain" *(Principia Ethica,* p. 225).

Professor Laird's account of the matter is more explicitly empirical. He appeals to the fact that there is an immediate objectivity in the appreciation of beauty, or in the admiration of conduct. These are not mere subjective states *caused* by an object; they *present* the object, clothed in its quality of charm or moral worth.

That feeling does somehow color its object is an undeniable fact of experience, and a fact recognized by common speech in so far as all of the familiar feelings assume the form of adjectives. We do speak of enticing greenness and delightful melodies. But if we were to trust such evidence of immediacy and accept the language of poetry for the prosaic purposes of science, we should be carried further than even Professor Laird, presumably, would care to go. We should be obliged to reduce feeling to bare sensibility, and to deny that the subject himself was in fact either enticed or delighted. It seems necessary at some point to admit that the qualities of feeling may be "referred" where they do not belong, or that an object may for the summary purposes of poetic suggestion be endowed with characters that accurate judgment will attribute to their effects or to their context. A "coveted book" is evidently qualified by a relation to subjects. A "dull day," a "boresome meeting," a "tiresome place," a "hopeful situation," are less evidently so, but the clarification of the experience brings us in each case to the identification of the quality with a specific reaction of the subject. When, by an act of attention, we endeavor to localize the red of the cherry in the subject we fail. To call the red of the cherry a mode of the activity or process of seeing, or of the sentient organism, remains contrary to appearances no matter how carefully these are scrutinized. With the so-called "tertiary" or affective qualities, however, the reverse is true. The more closely these are examined the more clearly do they appear to be either modes of attitude or impulse, and thus motor; or sensory *qualia* which are localizable in the body. They rapidly lose all semblance of that inherence in the object which becomes increasingly clear and unmistakable in the case of color. In short, the attentive effort at localization, whereas it unites the "secondary" qualities with the object, dissociates the alleged "tertiary" qualities, and tends to unite them with the sentient. It becomes less and less tolerable to speak of a red or yellow organism, as it becomes more and more plausible to speak of one that is covetous, bored, tired, hopeful, enticed or delighted.[8]

The most striking fact in connection with this theory of value is that all of those who profess it, find themselves without exception compelled to associate goodness with agreeable feeling.[9] Good is not only a sort of coating upon objects, it is a sugar coating; it is not only sensible, but palatable as well. In order to avoid *identifying* goodness with feeling they adopt one or both of the following measures. Sometimes they regard feeling as an omnipresent ingredient of all objects which are as a matter of fact good. At other times they regard feeling as the mode of cognition by which good is known. The former is an arbitrary generalization usually supported by an appeal to common-sense, with little or no scrutiny either of the premises or of the meaning of common-sense. The latter affirmation takes from feeling and transfers to its object all of the content which distinguishes affection from bare sensibility. The two alternatives are fundamentally opposed to one another, and neither is convincing by itself. As so often happens, two mutually exclusive and separately indefensible alternatives derive a specious plausibilty from being confused with one another.

Mr. Santayana has viewed the matter more circumspectly. He maintains that value is essentially indefinable, but existentially conditioned. It is true, he says, that goodness is in its essential character indefinable, but its existence as the

[8] This is the same error as that involved in the so-called "pathetic fallacy." Cf. below, § 24. For a further discussion of tertiary qualities, cf. A. Meinong, *Logos*, Vol. III, 1912, p. 12; W. M. Urban, *Valuation,* 1909, p. 21; and below, §§ 51, 117, 118. It is not, I think, an accident that physics concerns itself with color and sound, but not with beauty and goodness; the former having effects outside the sentient organism, in a sense in which the latter do not.

[9] Cf. Laird and Moore, *op. cit.*; H. Rashdall, *Theory of Good and Evil,* 1907, Vol. I, p. 135 (note) and *passim,* and *Proc. Aristotelian Society,* N. S. Vol. V, 1903-05, pp. 1-28; H. Sidgwick, *Methods of Ethics;* B. Russell, "The Elements of Ethics," in his *Philosophical Essays,* 1910.

quality of a real object is dependent on interest. An object is good only relatively to the subject who feels it so. Delight, in other words, is an unanalyzable datum; but the actual delightfulness of music is a synthesis conditioned by the appreciative response of the one who hears it. The delight, furthermore, is "objectified"; that is, transferred from the subject, by virtue of "a tendency originally universal to make every effect of a thing upon us a constituent of its conceived nature." [10] The indefinable *quale* which Mr. Santayana admits, has an existence in the subject which is prior to and more legitimate than its imputed existence in the object. It is therefore pertinent to inquire whether value consists in the pure *quale*, or in the subjective state, or in the response by which the state is imputed to the object. The last alternative would seem most consistent with Mr. Santayana's view as a whole. Beauty, which is a value, is "the transformation of an element of sensation into the quality of a thing." In other words, it is the "transformation" rather than the "element" or the "sensation" in which the value consists. This statement of the matter is consistent, furthermore, with Mr. Santayana's wider generalizations in which beauty is regarded as only one member of the family of values. "No doubt any desire, however capricious, represents some momentary and partial interest, which lends to its object a certain real and inalienable value." And again, "Values spring from the immediate and inexplicable reaction of vital impulse, and from the irrational part of our nature." [11]

Whatever may be said of the "elements" subjectively embodied in feeling, it is certain that desires, interests, and the reaction of vital impulse, are complex processes which deal with objects in a manner that is both analyzable and definable. Indeed, the view that good is a simple quality observably present in objects would scarcely be held at all were its exponents not exclusively preoccupied with the contemplative and aesthetic values. Here there is at least a certain *seeming*

[10] G. Santayana, *Sense of Beauty*, 1899, p. 48, and *Winds of Doctrine*, 1913, p. 141.
[11] *Sense of Beauty*, pp. 19, 44; *Winds of Doctrine*, p. 146.

evidence in its favor. Its inadequacy is too palpable when one passes on to other regions. Are there no values implied in effort, struggle and aspiration? Is there no difference between obligatoriness and charm, or does one propose to deny value of the former while affirming it of the latter? Does anyone suppose that economic value can be explained in terms of delight and enticement, with no regard for appetites and needs? It is, to be sure, permissible to restrict the term value to the objects of aesthetic enjoyment, as it would be permissible to exclude them. But any such delimitation tends to the neglect or subordination of the principle which is common to the several provinces of the field; and it is precisely this principle which a general theory of value should aim to throw into relief. Indeed, the most serious defect of this type of theory is its failure to provide any systematic principle whatsoever. There are as many indefinable values as there are feeling attitudes, and since these are to be regarded as objective qualities rather than as modes of feeling, there is nothing to unite them, not even the principle of feeling. If 'good' is a unique quality, then so are 'pleasant,' 'bad' and 'ought.' There is no way of subsuming pleasant under good, or of defining the opposition of good and bad, or of subsuming both good and ought under a more general category such as value. If, on the other hand, value is defined in terms of interest, then the variability of interest serves to account for both the unity and the diversity of values.

III. VALUE AS A LOGICAL INDEFINABLE

§ 17. **'Good' as Absolutely Indefinable.** The view that good is a simple objective quality is rarely, if ever, affirmed exclusively on empirical grounds. Whatever doubts its advocates may have had regarding the identity of the quality (and these doubts have been plainly apparent), they have adhered to the view none the less, owing to the force of certain logical and epistemological considerations. They have virtually affirmed that good *must* be an indefinable quality, however elusive it be empirically.[12]

In the first place, they have been concerned to point out the difference between the substantive good and the adjective good.[13] One may affirm, for example, that pleasure is *the* good. But this means that a certain state of feeling, which is one thing, possesses preëminently or exclusively a certain quality of goodness, which is another thing. Good as an adjective is not defined in terms of pleasure, but is predicated *of* pleasure. This is an important distinction, and one which we have already found it desirable to emphasize in the formulation of our problem. He who attributes good to a certain object, does not in this act of judgment define good; and in so far as moralists have commonly failed to realize this fact, it can be said that most alleged definitions of good have employed the term in an undefined sense. But the fact that good is undefined does not argue that it is undefinable,—on the contrary, it suggests the desirability of defining it.

It is apparently held by some exponents of the indefinability view that the very fact that an adjective can be *used* without being defined, proves that it is indefinable. Professor G. E. Moore, for example, seems to imply this when he says that "it would be absolutely meaningless to say that oranges were yellow, unless yellow did in the end mean just 'yellow' and nothing else whatever—unless it was absolutely indefinable." [14] But it is not meaningless to say that "the conception of substance is prehistoric," or that "the painting is post-impressionist," or that "the argument is circular"; and yet in these cases the assigned predicates *are* definable. Because concepts are

[12] In other words the emphasis is here placed upon the *indefinability* of value, rather than upon its *qualitative character*. Definition may mean any one of the following things: (1) Definition of a *word*, by restricting its usage, as when one says, "The word 'good' will be used to refer to such and such"; (2) Definition of a particular, by subsuming it under a universal, as when one says "This is a case of good"; (3) Definition of a universal, as when one says, "Goodness consists in such and such." Definition in this last sense may mean either (a) pointing out the universal, if it be simple; or (b) analyzing it into other universals, if it be complex. The view that good is absolutely indefinable means that definition in the sense of 3 (b) is impossible, because goodness is not complex.

[13] Cf. H. Sidgwick, for example, *op. cit.,* p. 110, and *passim.*

[14] *Op. cit.,* p. 14.   Cf. below, § 55.

not defined when used as predicates, those concepts which are
habitually used as predicates tend to assume an elliptical and
specious simplicity. In such cases it is peculiarly dangerous
to appeal to the evidence of usage, as the authors of the
present theory are not disinclined to do. There is rather a
presumption that careful examination of the predicative concept will reveal complexity where the careless use of it has
yielded only simplicity.

But Mr. Moore supports his view with an argument that
is deserving of more serious consideration. His holds that
while the word 'good' can be defined, like any word, in terms
of its connotation, the character connoted cannot in this
case be defined because it cannot be analyzed. To define a
given concept by analysis is to equate it with a set of other
concepts; which is impossible in the case of good, because
there is no set of concepts which, while not containing good,
is in its ensemble the equivalent of good.[15] The argument for
this thesis is that, given any set of concepts not containing
good, it is always pertinent to inquiry whether it is good.
Mr. Moore does not show this for all possible cases, but is
content to show that it is the case with those sets of concepts
which have been commonly offered as a definition of the
good. One may, for example, claim that being-desired-by-
anybody is equivalent to good, or that: War is desired by
some men = War is good. But, he says, even granting that
war is desired by some men, it is still pertinent to inquire
whether war is good; which would not be the case if being
good and being desired meant the same thing. Suppose, however, that for the above equation we substitute the following:
War is desired by some men = War is in some sense good.[16]
Then the further question of its goodness means, Is war,

---

[15] The original author of this view in contemporary philosophy is supposed to be Sidgwick, *op. cit.,* Book I, Ch. IV, §§ 2-3. But for Sidgwick
it is 'ought' rather than 'good' which is held to be indefinable. Since
'ought' is taken even by Sidgwick and by others who follow him to imply
a certain claim upon existence or action, I do not regard it as even *prima
facie* simple. This view is discussed below, Ch. III, Sect. V, Ch. IV,
Sect. V.

[16] Which is, I take it, what Sidgwick means when he says: "I hold
myself that the satisfaction of any desire is *pro tanto* good" (*op. cit.,*
Book I, Ch. IX, § 3).

admittedly good in some sense, also good in some other sense? Or, Is war, admittedly desired some of the time by some men, also desired all of the time by all men? It is absurd to ask whether an object defined as possessing a certain character does in fact possess that character, provided the sense of the definition and the sense of the inquiry are precisely the same. But a character ordinarily possesses a generic form and a variety of specific forms: so that it is entirely pertinent to inquiry whether an object having the generic form has any one of the special forms, or whether an object having one of the special forms has another of the special forms. It is absurd to ask if an object, known to be good in the generic sense, is good in this same generic sense. It is not absurd to ask whether an object known to be good in the generic sense, is obligatory or beautiful, or whether an object known to be beautiful is obligatory.[17]

The reason why the question of goodness is peculiarly recurrent, is that its forms are peculiarly diverse. The reason why the question of goodness may be submitted over again to each individual judge, is because it assumes a new form for each judge. There is, in other words, a sense of good which varies with the individual. If when a given object *a* is already acknowledged to be good the question of its goodness is nevertheless put to a subject *M,* the question is assumed to refer to that special sense of good which is relative to *M.* In entertaining the question, *M* assumes that he is expected to state whether *a* is good to or for *him.* Thus the recurrence of the question, and its fresh significance when submitted to each individual in turn, constitute evidence in favor of the hypothesis that goodness is relative to individuals and their interests.

Such a conclusion, however, is held to be logically or

---

[17] There are two other senses in which this question of double attribution may be raised. To ask whether 'the fact that *A* is good' is good, is logically permissible; the question being empirically significant, provided 'good' is such that it may be applied in different senses to *A* and to the fact. To ask whether 'goodness is good' would, however, appear to be logically excluded by the "theory of logical types" according to which a class may not be a member of itself. Cf. B. Russell and A. N. Whitehead: *Principia Mathematica,* 1910.

epistemologically vicious, because it fails to provide for the "objectivity" of values. The advocates of the view which we have been examining are extremely desirous of escaping a subjectivism which would rob value of universality, or a relativism which would rob it of absoluteness. They are anxious to provide judgments of value with a common object which will determine their truth or falsity. But such considerations lend no support to the view that good is an indefinable quality essentially independent of interest. An interest is as good an object as any other. The fact that M takes an interest in a, consists in a relation of a to M; but this fact itself is not relative to $M's$ judgment about it, or to the judgment of any other subject. The judgments about such facts may be as universal or as absolute, as true or false, as any logic or theory of knowledge can possibly require.[18]

§ 18. **'Better' as Relatively Indefinable.** There is another and quite distinct sense in which value may be held to be indefinable. According to the view which we have just examined, value is absolutely indefinable, in the sense that it is irreducible, or incapable of being analyzed into non-value terms. It may, however, be argued that *one* of the value terms is *relatively* indefinable, that is, incapable of being analyzed into other value terms. This is the view recently formulated by Professor A. P. Brogan.[19] The fundamental value-universal, he argues is 'better.' If we accept 'better' as indefinable, we can then define 'worse' as its logical converse. " 'A is worse than B' means 'B is better than A.' " Similarly, " 'A is good' means 'the existence of A is better than the non-existence of A' "; and " 'A is bad' means 'the non-existence of A is better than the existence of A.' "[20] A similar definition may be obtained for 'indifference,' and, with the addition of specific moral and aesthetic conditions, even for 'right' and 'beauty.' If, on the other hand, one takes 'good' as the fundamental value-universal, one finds it im-

---

[18] Cf. below, Ch. V, Sect. II.
[19] "The Fundamental Value Universal," *Jour. of Philos.*, Vol. XVI, 1919.
[20] *Op. cit.*, pp. 97, 98.

possible or at least relatively difficult, to define the other value concepts in terms of it.

The merit of this original and instructive view lies in its systematic character. It undertakes, as any adequate theory of value must, both to exhibit the fundamental principle of all value, and also to show how the whole family of particular values may be generated by that principle. The fundamental value concept must be both generic, and also fruitful and explanatory. But the adequacy of a theory of value cannot be fully determined until it is applied to the facts. Until such an application is made it can claim to be no more than a self-consistent hypothesis, whose terms are intelligible in terms of one another. To what element in the domain of life does 'betterness' refer? When 'betterness' is thus identified, what will correspond to 'good' and to 'indifference'? Do the terms of the system provide adequately for those elements of life with which a theory of value has to do? These crucial questions cannot be answered so long as nothing is known about 'betterness' except that the other value concepts are to be defined in terms of it. What *is* 'betterness'? Is it a unique and irreducible relation? Is it a unique and irreducible quality? In either of these cases it could be found, though it could not be further analyzed. Or can 'betterness' be defined in non-value terms?

In the article in which Dr. Brogan introduces his theory to the public, he says, that "no attention will be given to the question," which would seem to mean that he reserves all three of the alternatives enumerated above.[21] Professor Dewey, who announces his "adhesion to the theory advanced by Dr. Brogan," holds that "value is constituted by interest, liking, vital bias"; which acts or attitudes must now (on the 'betterness' theory) be interpreted to mean *"preference,* selection-rejection, interest as 'this-rather-than-that.' "[22] Dr. Brogan has not yet announced his adhesion to Professor Dewey's interpretation. If he does adhere, then, '*A* is better

[21] *Op. cit.,* p. 96.
[22] J. Dewey: "Valuation and Experimental Knowledge," *Philos. Review,* Vol. XXXI, 1922, p. 334, note.

than B' means 'A is preferred to B,' and 'A is good' means 'the existence of A is preferred to the non-existence of A.' The meaning of value now hinges on the meaning of preference. It becomes all-important to know whether, as Professor Dewey contends, interest is essentially preferential, or whether preference itself can be analyzed into a rivalry or comparison of interests still more simply conceived. Whatever be the outcome of such an analysis, value is defined as a function of interest.[23]

IV. VALUE AS FORM OR STRUCTURE

§ 19. **Value as Help or Hindrance.** There is no necessary connection between the idea that value is indifferent to interest, and the idea that it is irreducible or indefinable. It is entirely conceivable that value should be definable, that is, reducible to non-value terms, and yet that interest should not be one of those terms. It would then have a status similar to that of circularity, which is analyzable into points and distances. Value would be a type of form or structure, which, though it might be most perfectly exemplified by the living organism or the conscious self, would be definable without reference to these.[24]

The simplest view of this class is the view which defines goodness as the relation of *fitness*. In this sense "to be good means to further something, to be an efficient means." [25] This is the sense expressed in common usage as "good for." 'A is good for B,' means 'A is conducive to the existence or occurrence of B,' as when we say that a sandy soil is good for grapes. To be good means to condition, to facilitate, to promote. This is Plato's meaning when he says: "For that is and ever will be the best of sayings, that the useful (τὸ ὠφέλιμον) is the noble, and the hurtful is the base." [26]

[23] The nature of interest with special reference to preference will be examined below, Ch. XXI, Sect. II.

[24] The clearest presentation of this type of theory is to be found in G. H. Palmer: *The Nature of Goodness*, 1903, Ch. I. II.

[25] Professor Palmer's expression. Cf. *op. cit.*, p. 13.

[26] *Republic*, V, 457 B, Jowett's translation. J. Burnet translates τὸ ὠφέλιμον as "the advantageous." Cf. *Greek Philosophy*, 1914, Part I, p. 243.

Another classic formulation of this view is to be found in Spinoza's *Ethics*, from which the following definitions are quoted: "As for the terms *good* and *bad*, they indicate no positive quality in things regarded in themselves, but are merely modes of thinking, or notions which we form from the comparison of things one with another." "We call a thing good or evil, when it is of service or the reverse in preserving our being, that is when it increases or diminishes, helps or hinders, our power of activity." [27] The same view is formulated by a contemporary writer as follows: "The value of an object consists in its helping to complete or fulfil some tendency already present." [28]

No judgment can be pronounced upon such a view until a fundamental question of interpretation is settled. Does the whole meaning of value consist in the nature of *the relations of help and hindrance*, or does it in part consist in the nature of *what* is helped and hindered. When one says that '*a* is good' means '*a* helps *x*,' and that '*a* is bad' means '*a* hinders *x*,' is *x* undetermined? May *x* be anything, and the definition still hold good? Or must *x* itself be assigned some special meaning which limits the scope of the relation?

It may be answered that the meaning of *x* is limited only to *being*. In that case *a* would have value in so far as it helped or hindered the being of *x*, where *x* may be anything. But we must still ask whether the good lies in the promotion, or in the being. Do we call *a* valuable because it promotes or hinders, or because of what it promotes or hinders? It is clear that our present view must adopt the former alternative. But then value means the same thing as cause or condition, positive or negative. We are not even throwing any light on the meaning of cause or condition. We are simply announcing our intention of using the term 'value' and the terms 'cause' or 'condition,' interchangeably. Then to study values would be to study causes or conditions, and theory of value would lose its subject-matter. Or, if we were to say

---

[27] Part IV, Preface, and Prop. viii. This and the following citations are taken from the translation by R. H. M. Elwes, 1901.
[28] W. H. Sheldon: "An Empirical Definition of Value," *Jour. of Philos.*, Vol. XI, 1914, p. 121.

that theory of value studies a particular type of cause or condition, then we should have to define the type, and we should thus be back at the beginning again.

If, on the other hand, one affirms that a is valuable not simply because it promotes or hinders, but because of *what* it promotes or hinders, then one virtually acknowledges that the view in question defines value only in a secondary and derivative sense.[29]   One affirms in effect that 'a is valuable in a secondary sense' means 'a helps or hinders what is valuable in a primary sense.'   While this primary sense clearly belongs to another view, it is instructive to find that it is usually implied in statements which purport to express the present view.

It is sometimes implied, for example, that being is *ipso facto* good.   What helps or hinders being is therefore good in the secondary sense.   This is a frequent assumption on the part of common sense.   It is expressly formulated by Spinoza, as when he says "Reality and perfection I use as synonymous terms."   Such an assumption may signify simply a proposal to *use terms* synonymously, which would again be equivalent to denying to theory of value any special subject-matter of its own; or, it may signify belief that there is *some* being which is valuable *by virtue of possessing a special feature,* which it is then the business of theory of value to single out for special attention.

Common-sense is relatively clear on this point.   It is not unqualified being which common-sense takes to be good, and whose help or hindrance it therefore accepts as also good, but it is being *in so far as desired.*   When the average man is persuaded to agree that goodness and being are the same thing, he means that his paramount interest is in self-preservation.   The same assumption underlies common verbal usage.   In the strict sense of 'conducive to,' one should say that swamps are good for malaria.   As a matter of fact one does not say that,—one says that *quinine* is good for malaria.   In

[29] A very important sense, no doubt, but not that generic or ultimate sense which we are in search of here.   Value in this secondary or derivative sense is commonly termed 'extrinsic,' 'instrumental' or 'conditioned' value.

other words, 'good for' does not ordinarily mean 'conducive to,' but 'conducive to something recognized as desirable,' such as recovery or health. That which is 'good for nothing,' is fit for no good; it does not lack fitness, but is fit only for the waste-basket or the rubbish-heap.

Spinoza's view derives plausibility from a similar introduction of terms denoting interest. His identification of being and goodness appears admissible because he associates with being an "endeavour wherewith everything endeavours to persist in its own being." [30] He does not seem unmistakably to enter into the field of values until this "endeavour" is "referred to the mind," and "is called will"; or until it is "referred to the mind and body in conjunction," and "is called appetite"; or until there is "consciousness of appetite," and therefore "desire." We then are prepared to accept his famous dictum "that in no case do we strive for, wish for, long for or desire anything because we deem it to be good, but on the other hand we deem a thing to be good, because we strive for it, wish for it, long for it, or desire it." [31]

Such implied definitions of good, in terms of conation, desire or interest, do not belong to the type of theory under examination in the present chapter. But there are other implications which may properly be developed at greater length. In Plato's *Philebus* we are told that the good must possess three qualities: 'τὸ ἱκανόν,' 'τὸ πᾶσιν αἱρετόν,' and 'τὸ τέλεον'.[32] 'τὸ ἱκανόν' means that which is 'sufficient *for*,' in the relative sense of the view which we have just examined. 'τὸ αἱρετόν' means that which is eligible, referring to the act of choice or selection, or to that factor of interest which we shall consider hereafter. There remains 'τὸ τέλεον,' which means that which is *complete in itself*. One may, then, regard that which conduces to being as good, because being possesses, or in so

---

[30] "Conatus, quo unaquaeque res in suo Esse perseverare conatur," *Ethics*, Part III, Prop. vii.

[31] *Op. cit.*, Part III, Prop. ix. I suspect that there is a similar conative implication in Professor Sheldon's conception of 'tendency.' Cf. below, Ch. VI, Sect. II.

[32] Cf. the *Philebus*, 20 C. ff. and 60 C. ff. I have adopted the interpretation of R. G. Bury, given in his *Philebus of Plato*, 1897, pp. 177-178, 211-214.

far as it possesses, this character of self-sufficiency. But self-sufficiency has been interpreted in two senses. It has been taken to mean *self-realization,* that is, the adequate embodiment of a general type; and it has been taken to mean *organic unity,* that is, the reciprocal dependence and mutual support of parts within a whole.[33] Either of these views if clearly and consistently maintained would provide a definition of value without reference to interest. They belong, therefore, to the present chapter and will be considered in turn.

§ 20. **Value as Self-realization and Universality.** Goodness may be taken to mean being, where being is conceived as representing one or more universals. Being is, in some measure, *what* it is; that is to say, it embodies a definable essence or essences. It has a nature logically distinguishable from its existence or occurrence, and it may be regarded as more or less completely expressing that nature. The degree to which this expression is adequate, may be said to constitute the degree of its goodness. This view of goodness is illustrated by the Socratic-Platonic doctrine of "ideas," according to which each individual existence has its prototype or pattern which it may more or less completely resemble; and by the Aristotelian doctrine of "forms," according to which each substance has its own proper function or activity which it may more or less perfectly exercise. The same view is formulated by Spinoza when he defines the good man in terms of "the type of human nature," and says that "men are more perfect, or more imperfect, in proportion as they approach more or less nearly to the said type." [34] A good contemporary presentation of the same view is to be found in Professor Palmer's "good big pumpkin," of which he says, "If you wish

---

[33] This difference corresponds to the distinction which B. Bosanquet makes between "the abstract universal" and "the concrete universal." Cf. his *Principle of Individuality and Value,* 1912, Lecture II. The same difference appears in the common-sense notion of perfection as consisting in wholeness or completeness. In the conception of the broken chair as imperfect, there is, on the one hand, the idea that the notion of a chair implies four legs; and, on the other hand, the idea that the chair is crippled for the lack of its missing member.

[34] *Ethics,* Part IV, Preface.

to find the full pumpkin nature, here you have it. All that a pumpkin can be is set forth here as nowhere else." [35]

The fundamental difficulty with this view was discovered many years ago,—in fact, by Plato himself. When Parmenides, in the dialogue of that name, asks Socrates whether there are ideas for everything, including "such things as hair, mud, dirt or anything else which is vile and paltry," Socrates says:

"Certainly not; visible things like these are such as they appear to us, and I am afraid that there would be an absurdity in assuming any idea of them, although I sometimes get disturbed, and begin to think that there is nothing without an idea; but then again, when I have taken up this position, I run away, because I am afraid that I may fall into a bottomless pit of nonsense and perish; and so I return to the ideas of which I was just now speaking, and occupy myself with them." [36]

The ideas to which Socrates returns as a refuge from his doubts are the "ideas of the just and the beautiful and the good." Platonists have never, succeeded in dispelling these honest Platonic doubts. If there are ideas of everything, then everything is ideal; whereas if we attribute ideas only to "the just and the beautiful and the good," then in this very act of discrimination we have introduced some undefined principle of selection. Similarly, the Aristotelian conception of form works well in Noah's ark, or in a Linnaean world of organic species, but discloses "a bottomless pit of nonsense" when applied to the whole vast complexity and overlapping continuity of natural processes.

The principle is too universally applicable. Goodness in this sense can not be denied of anything. If *a* is a better *m* than *b,* it follows that *b* is a better *n* than *a.* Everything is the most shining example of something. The worst specimen of a man may be the most perfect specimen of inebriety or feeble-mindedness. On such a view theory of value would again lose its subject-matter, for it would be co-extensive with classification and definition. To see what a thing is, *whatever* it be, would mean the same as to see its value.

[35] *Op. cit.,* p. 17.
[36] *Parmenides,* 130 C, Jowett's translation.

There is a seeming escape from this outcome through placing emphasis on degrees of universality. Manhood being more universal than inebriety, the good man would be better than the good inebriate; and as manhood takes precedence of inebriety, so the absolute or maximum universal would take precedence of manhood.

"For we are wont [says Spinoza], to refer all the individual things in nature to one genus, which is called the highest genus, namely to the category of Being, whereto absolutely all individuals in nature belong. Thus, in so far as we refer the individuals in nature to this category, and comparing them one with another, find that some possess more of being or reality than others, we to this extent, say that some are more perfect than others." [37]

But here again the view that goodness consists in the *representation* or *realization* of the universal, is abandoned for the view that it consists in the nature of the universal itself. This may be taken to mean simply that to be and to be good are the same thing, in which case goodness has no specific content of its own. Or it may mean that the world as a whole has a peculiar and distinctive character which may be more or less clearly reflected in its parts. If this cosmic essence is itself affirmed to be the Good, as in the Platonic philosophy, then the definition is circular, and we are as far as ever from the solution of our problem. If, on the other hand, we identify this cosmic essence with the form of the totality, whatever this may turn out to be, we must be prepared to fit our conception of goodness to the facts. In this case, it would be proper to regard the mechanical aspect of human nature as better than its purposive aspect, on the assumption of a materialistic metaphysics; or crime and unmerited suffering as better than justice and happiness, on the assumption that they are more characteristic of the waywardness and caprice of a world of chance; or the abstract factor of bare existence as the best feature of life, on the radically pluralistic ground that there is no other universal feature.

The definition of value as self-realization is saved from

[37] *Op. cit.*, Part IV, Preface.

these extreme and improbable consequences because, like the definition of value as help or hindrance, it is ordinarily interpreted in terms of one or more tacit assumptions. Commonsense does not refer to an object as good of its kind unless the kind is itself already recognized as good. One speaks of a good statesman because it is assumed that a statesman is a good thing to be. If one speaks of a good horse-thief one does so either in a consciously paradoxical sense, or because one is aware that even horse-thieving has its uses for the one who profits by it. Horse-thieving may be regarded as an act to be coveted and perfected for the sake of its results. When one says that "the only good Indian is a dead Indian," one means that since to be Indian is to be bad, the less of him the better. Or if one speaks of a good moron or a good case of tuberculosis, one means that clear and unmistakable examples are useful to medical science. These tacit assumptions of common-sense all play an important rôle in philosophy. They may be briefly summarized as follows:

Good being defined as the fulfilment by an individual existence of its universal nature, in the first place, this universal nature is itself conceived to be good. But then the definition is either *circular*, and hence no definition at all; or it defines good in a derivative sense, in which case it is the implied primary definition which really concerns us. This implied definition cannot be of the same type, that is, the good of the universal cannot consist in its fulfilling *its* still more universal nature, without a vicious and fruitless regress. In either case, the definition of good as fulfilment of a universal falls to the ground.

In the second place, the individual is sometimes conceived as *seeking* to realize its own universal nature, as when a man sets before himself some ideal of character or attainment, and governs his action accordingly. In this case the factor of interest is introduced, and value is virtually defined in terms of it.

Finally, the fulfilment of a universal may be viewed in its relation to knowledge. He who seeks to know seeks to define, classify and explain, and the discovery of the universal in the particular is therefore the goal of his endeavor. It constitutes the success of his effort. But here again the factor of interest is introduced, and is allowed to confer value on its object.

§ 21. **Organic Unity and Reciprocity of Parts.** We have now to examine the second sense of self-sufficiency to which allusion has been made. The value of an object may be thought to lie in the *reciprocal* support of its parts, in its internally *unified* character. The good will stand alone, like the arch, by virtue of the counter-thrust of its own component forces. Comparing this view with the definition of the good as the helpful, Professor Palmer says:

"Extrinsic goodness will then signify the adjustment of an object to something which lies outside itself; intrinsic will say that the many powers of an object are so adjusted to one another that they cooperate to render the object a firm totality. Both will indicate relationship; but in the one case the relations considered are *extra se,* in the other *inter se. . . .* Each part is both means and end, . . . both aids and is aided by all the others." [38]

There are three illustrations of this principle which are commonly cited.[39] The first is the physical organism, whose component functions are both interdependent and also subordinate to the activity of the whole. The second is the work of art, or aesthetic unity viewed as a balanced composition, in which the beauty of the whole springs from the inter-relation of the parts, and at the same time communicates itself to them.[40] The third is systematic thought by which elements are understood in terms of one another, and in terms of the law or idea under which they are all subsumed. In all three cases the value is held to lie in the reciprocal fitness of the parts, and in the fact that in their ensemble the parts compose a unity having a distinctive quality of its own.

As in the view last considered, so here also, there is a

---

[38] *Op. cit.,* pp. 18-19, 24, 51.

[39] For the further analysis of the conception of unity, cf. § 26.

[40] Thus, according to Plato, τό καλόν, is the absolute perfection of the whole derived from τό σύμμετρον, or the relative measure and proportion of the parts. Cf. Bury, *op. cit.,* p. 177.

tendency to identify value with the metaphysical reality. As in the former view the universal whose realization constituted value tended to be the absolutely universal, so here the unity whose internal reciprocity constitutes value, tends to be the all-embracing unity. The tendency arises in both cases from the same motive. In both cases value is held to lie in a sort of self-sufficiency, and self-sufficiency is held to imply completeness, or the absence of restricting and compromising relations. This absolutistic and monistic tendency is well-known to students of the history of philosophy. It is set forth in a famous passage of the *Republic,* which Professor Stewart expounds as follows:

"The Good is that which, in the last resort, makes the existence of parts, and our knowledge of them, possible; it is the Whole Universe over against the Whole Man. As faculties are non-existent without the Man; so the Laws of Nature are insignificant without the Cosmos, or System of the Good." [41]

In Spinoza it appears in the conception of the Infinite Substance or God, which is the necessary form of being, and the only unqualified good.[42] The best contemporary example of the tendency is Bosanquet's definition of the principle of individuality, reality, or value, as the "character of wholeness and non-contradiction": as "that which must stand; that which has nothing without to set against it, and which is pure self-maintenance within." [43]

This view, like that in which good is defined as representative of a universal, falls into a dilemma. If unity is conceived abstractly as a form or relationship, it has no special reference to the subject-matter ordinarily comprised in the science of value. A structural equilibrium, or resultant of component forces, is an organized whole. There is an interaction and reciprocity of parts; there is a distinctive character attaching to the unity itself; and each part both contributes to and is governed by the total situation. Integrity or stability is no more adequately prefigured in the intellectual, sensuous,

[41] J. A. Stewart: *Plato's Doctrine of Ideas,* 1909, p. 52.   Cf. Plato's *Republic,* 509 B.
[42] *Ethics,* Part I, Prop. viii.
[43] B. Bosanquet: *op. cit.,* p. 68.

moral or social unities of life than in the mathematical,
physical, mechanical or chemical unities of inorganic nature.
This form of being is as characteristic of an ellipse, or a
planetary system, or a molecule, as it is of a symphony, or
of a nation,—perhaps more so. Furthermore there is just
as much completeness in an unmitigated tragedy as in the joy
of triumph. A systematic-unity swelled to world proportions
is still a systematic unity and nothing more.[44]

Unity is a feature of the world we live in, no doubt, and
there is nothing to prevent the use of the word 'value' to indicate it. But this conception does not begin to come to grips
with the special problems of the subject-matter of value until
it is supplemented and thickened by the inclusion of another
factor. This factor is interest. The two factors intersect,
since desire, for example, is a sort of insufficiency, and fulfilment a sort of completeness; but that which defines values
and explains their genesis is the concept of interest, and not
the concept of unity.

The present view seems more pertinent to our inquiry
than it really is, because those who expound it commonly
present it in the context of interest.[45] The tendency to employ the expression 'organic unity' suggests a biological context. The systematic unity *of an organism,* is, of course, a
mode of conserving and promoting life. The Platonic conceptions of order and harmony grew out of the Socratic discussion of moral and social problems. The unquestionable
moral value of organization as a means of reconciling interests, and thus of imparting fulness and strength to the person
and to the community, lingers as a sort of afterglow in the
logical and cosmological generalizations of the idea.[46]

[44] It is, of course, sometimes held that a self alone can exhibit the
kind of inwardness and unity-in-variety that this definition requires. Cf.
e.g., J. M. E. McTaggart: *Studies in Hegelian Cosmology,* 1901, pp. 14,
19; M. W. Calkins: *The Persistent Problems of Philosophy,* 1912, pp.
378-379. Although I think this contention contrary to fact, I shall not
argue the question here since it refers not to the definition of goodness,
but to what is or can be good.

[45] For the view that organic unity *presupposes* interest or 'purpose,'
cf. below, Ch. III, Sect. II.

[46] These and kindred notions may have been originally derived from
primitive social experiences, and if so would preserve such associations
in the racial memory. Cf. F. M. Cornford: *From Religion to Philosophy,*

Similarly, it is difficult to free the conception of unity from a reference to the partial and fragmentary condition of man. Man is well aware of the limits that bound him, and has a sense of lack and privation. This is, perhaps, the central fact in his life. As Bosanquet says,

"for a being which is finite, whose life is therefore in time, and its world more or less self-contradictory, the element of purpose and conation cannot be absent. . . . For a purpose or a conation, in general, is nothing more than the operation of a dissatisfaction or a contradiction towards its own removal." [47]

But it would be a mistake to suppose that the parts of wholes are always dissatisfied, and that they always operate towards the removal of their partiality.[48] It so happens that a thirsty man, like the hart, "panteth after the water-brook," and by virtue of that fact he easily accepts the view that wholeness is goodness. It is this instant and unconscious application to the human predicament, and the fact that Bosanquet's thought moves for the most part in this field, that gives his general conception a seeming pertinence to the subject-matter of value.

Finally, there is in the conception of reciprocal unity an evident relation to the intellectual interest. Thought does single out for special attention the general and systematic characters of its object. It may be said that thought seeks to be as all-comprehensive and unified as possible, and that an orderly whole is the goal of its endeavor.[49] This is a characteristic of the intellectual *interest*, which must be taken account of in the study of intellectual or scientific value. It proves that unity is *a* value. But it does not prove that unity is the only value, and still less does it justify a definition of the value-predicate in terms of unity.

1912. It is difficult even for the modern scientist to rid the notions of law and order of all reference to their political meanings.
[47] *Op. cit.*, p. 288. For this reason the Absolute cannot be will, ought or purpose (*ibid.*, pp. 70, 391 ff.).
[48] This assumption is virtually made when it is said of a whole that the parts, in relation to the whole and to one another, are reciprocally means and end. (Cf. G. H. Palmer, *op. cit.*, pp. 24-25.) They are, strictly, neither means nor ends unless they take an interest in one another.
[49] There is, I believe, no absolute maximum of systematic unity. Cf. my *Present Philosophical Tendencies*, Ch. VIII.

CHAPTER III

VALUE AS THE QUALIFIED OBJECT OF INTEREST [1]

I. THE OBJECTIVE 'NORM' OF INTEREST

§ 22. The value of an object is now conceded to lie in its relation to interest. But how shall we conceive this relation? Shall we conceive it after the analogy of the marksman and his target, and say that the interest *directs itself* toward the object? Or shall we conceive it after the analogy of the magnet and the iron-filing, and say that the object draws the interest toward itself? In the former case value would spring from interest, and be conferred on the object; in the second case value would reside in the object as its capacity to command interest. In the one case, being object of an interest means nothing more than being a point defined by the projection of its original bias, as being a target means nothing more than the direction of the marksman's aim. In the other case it is affirmed that objects may be peculiarly entitled to be the goal of interest, as the magnet is peculiarly entitled to be the destination of an iron-filing. In the former case, theory of value would be based upon an analysis of interest, and in the latter case upon an analysis of the alleged title or qualification of its objects.

If certain objects are preëminently qualified to evoke interest, then in any given case interest may be said to be *mis*-directed. The *actual* direction of interest, may or may not be in accord with its "true" direction; that which it *takes* as its object, may or may not be its "proper" object. It is this alleged right of a qualified object to overrule the *de facto*

---

[1] Parts of this chapter, and of Ch. V, VI, are reprinted from an article entitled "Purpose as Systematic Unity," published in the *Monist*, Vol. XXVII, 1917.

preferences of men, that is chiefly emphasized in the view now before us. Theory of value, which deals with the qualified object of interest, is given precedence of biology, psychology and sociology, which merely describe what animals, men and societies as a matter of fact want. It is this which is often meant when it is said that theory of value is a *normative* science. In the present view the norm or regulative principle is conceived as *objective,* as a control operating from beyond the mind; whereas, as we shall see presently, it is also possible to conceive of a norm as subjective, or operative within the mind itself.[2]

Let us consider the analogy of the compass. For ordinary purposes north is the direction indicated by the needle. But this is the case only provided the compass is correct. There is a "true north" by which the compass itself is to be regulated. The compass may properly be subjected to such regulation, because compasses are meant to indicate the north; in so far as they do not indicate it, they are not compasses. The true north, while it has a special reference to compasses as being the norm by which they are standardized, would nevertheless remain the true north even though no compass-needle pointed to it. Similarly, the motor-affective life may be said to have its proper orientation, which may or may not coincide with its actual orientation. The needle of interest should point to the good; when it does not, the motor-affective life is somehow awry, and needs to be trued. The actual direction of interest will usually indicate the good approximately, but there is need of standardization. The 'true good,' while as the norm of interest it must have a special reference to interest in general, would nevertheless remain the true good even though no *actual* interests of animal or man should point to it.

What then is the true north of the motor-affective compass? In what consists that qualification to be desired, that supreme eligibility by which the actual interests of life may be judged? There are four conceptions, all of which have had a long history. There is, first, the conception of *purposiveness,* purporting to define that specific form of being

2 Cf. below, Ch. IV, Sect. I.

which implies an intelligent or interested origin. There is, second, the conception of the *desirable,* as that which evokes desire by a sort of magnetic attraction. There is, third, the conception of the *desirable* as that which is *capable* of being desired, or fit to be willed. Finally, there is the conception of the *ought-to-be,* or that which is conceived to possess a legitimate authority over the creative will. We shall now examine these conceptions in order.

II. THE PURPOSIVE AS THE EFFECT OF PURPOSE

§ 23. **Provisional Definition of Purpose.** According to the first view, there are certain objects which require the category of purpose for their explanation. They are such that we cannot understand their being at all except as the effect of purpose.[3] It will not be possible to examine this view without employing the notion of purpose in some recognized sense. Although this sense must be regarded as provisional, it can be introduced here without offence because it appears to be presupposed by the exponents of the view which we are examining.

According to Kant, "the concept of an object, so far as it contains the ground of the actuality of this object, is the *purpose"*; in other words, we see that a thing is possible only as the product of purpose, when we are forced to attribute it to "a cause whose faculty of action is determined through concepts." An object is purposive when it must be thought to have originated "designedly," "intentionally," that is, through the operation of "intelligence." [4]

An illustration of this alleged mode of explanation is afforded by Socrates's famous allusion to Anaxagoras in Plato's *Phaedo.* Socrates, it will be remembered, distinguishes two ways of explaining his being in prison. On the one hand it may be explained by reference to his bones and muscles. But this, he thinks, would be an inappropriate ex-

---

[3] The classic representation of this view is to be found in Kant's *Kritik der Urtheilskraft.* Cf. the translation by J. H. Bernard, entitled *Kant's Kritik of Judgment,* 1892, especially the Introduction and Second Part.

[4] Cf. Bernard's translation, *cit. sup.,* pp. 18, 272, 302, 320, 331, 341.

planation; not untrue, to be sure, since bones and muscles do supply the necessary "conditions,"—but not the sort of explanation that touches the real cause of a *mind's* acting. The second and preferred explanation is in terms of Socrates's purpose of "enduring any punishment which the law inflicts." [5] A mind, in other words, acts for the best, according to its lights.   To explain its action, therefore, it is necessary to discover what it deems best, and then to construe the particular act as an instance of that best.   In the present case it is supposed that Socrates is actuated by the principle of submission to the law, and that he has judged his remaining in prison to be what, under the existing circumstances, that principle implies.

Let us analyze the situation more carefully, lest we omit any essential factor.   In the first place, there is, as Kant says, a general concept, such as submission to law, of which a particular act, such as remaining in prison, may be regarded as an instance.   In the second place, there is an agent possessed of a stable disposition or tendency to perform acts of a certain class, under varying circumstances.   Then, thirdly, there is some determinate relation between the rule or type of action and the agent's disposition.   But what is this determinate relation?   The simplest alternative is to suppose that the rule of action is identical with the constant or consistent feature of the disposition.   Thus we might suppose that Socrates tended under varying circumstances to submit to the law.   But this will not do.   For if it should happen that his remaining in prison were as a matter of fact *not* what the law required, if it should happen, for example, that there had been some error in transmitting the commands of the authorities, or if it should turn out upon reflection that his escape rather than his passively yielding to tyrannical oppression was more in keeping with his constitutional rights, that would not disprove his purpose to submit to law.   What is necessary is that Socrates should *mean* to submit to law, or that he should *think* his act to be a case of submitting to the law.   The link between the rule and the disposition is

[5] *Phaedo,* 98-99.

an act of interpretation or judgment. In other words, one is said to be governed by a purpose *M*, when *M* is some generalized form of action, and when one is disposed consistently to perform what one *believes* (whether correctly or mistakenly) to be a case of *M*.

When, in the present chapter, we speak of purpose we shall mean this mode of determination; we shall mean that which is, in this sense, "done on purpose" or "meant to be." Our present question thus resolves itself into the following: Is there any general character of objects which compels us to judge that such objects have been produced on purpose, or are the result of being meant to be.

§ 24. **The Pathetic Fallacy.** The commonest notion of this sort arises from the tendency on the part of a purposive being to impute to another purpose that which coincides with his own, but which has not, as a matter of fact, resulted from it. We feel *grateful* for what we like, and we *resent* what we do not like, thus implying friendly or hostile intent on the part of the environment. That which proves beneficent is construed as benevolent, and that which hurts or thwarts or fails is construed as malicious. This natural human tendency is commonly known as the "pathetic fallacy." [6]

Suppose, for example, that in spite of my most painstaking efforts to execute a powerful stroke, the golf ball rolls ingloriously from the tee. I then turn and rend my new driver or call down maledictions upon it. I am angry not with myself but with it. I feel resentment toward it precisely as though it had meant to spite me. I virtually attribute malice to it. Now this, as my less heated partner may remind me, is unreasonable, because the golf-stick really did not mean it, or do it on purpose. It is true that in effect the stick thwarted me, and occasioned my displeasure, but it is an error to impute that displeasure to it as a motive or ground of action.

Or take another example. Basking in its warmth, I praise the sun and feel gratefully disposed to it. If I knew what

[6] This is in principle the same fallacy of false affective reference that arises in the case of the "tertiary qualities." Cf. above, § 16.

the sun liked, I would gladly reciprocate. This is an innocent error, a kind of poetic license, but error it is none the less. For I have responded to the sun as though the pleasure which its rays were about to give me had actuated the sun in shedding them; whereas this effect upon my sensibilities is accidental, and in no way accountable for the radiation of the sun's light and heat.

There is, however, a positive implication in this criticism. My own action in each case *is* purposive. My addressing the ball, or lying in the sun, is to be accounted for by reference to the stroke or the bodily comfort that is to come. My error lies not in employing such a mode of explanation, but in misapplying it. There is a human weakness, doubtless one of the major motives in religion, which prompts one to extend to *all* the agencies involved in any event that purposive type of determination which really holds only of one's *own* participation in it. In the case of one's own agency the prospective sequel does account for the act, but in the case of the other contributory agencies this explanation is out of place; or, some, but not all, antecedent agencies are determined with reference to the sequel. Not to discriminate among them is to commit the inverse of a common fallacy. It would not be inappropriate to term this characteristic teleological error the fallacy of *"ante hoc ergo propter hoc."*

It is not to be supposed that the pathetic fallacy is peculiar to the naïve. There is a form of it which is very common among philosophers. It is often held that nature could not satisfy the scientific or philosophical purpose if it did not mean to,—if there were not a sort of complicity on the part of Nature herself. This notion can usually be found in dualistic philosophies, such as those of Descartes and Kant. Where thought and its object are supposed to have independent characters of their own, their harmonious conjunction in true knowledge becomes a gratuitous piece of good fortune which we attribute to a benevolent intent. Thus, according to Descartes, knowledge implies a sort of honorable veracity on the part of God.[7] According to Kant, the harmony of the

[7] *Meditations on the First Philosophy,* Meditation IV.

data of knowledge with the human faculties of cognition cannot be regarded as resulting from the character of either the one or the other. The data do as a matter of fact submit to law, but since they are under no obligation to do so, we are compelled to explain this happy circumstance ("this conformity of the contingent to law") by a sort of amiable design at the bottom of things.[8]

This grateful judgment would be meaningless if the object were *formed* by thought to suit its purposes, or if thought had no purpose but to accept things as it finds them; it would be meaningless, in other words, on purely idealistic or on purely realistic grounds. But even on dualistic grounds the judgment is not inevitable. It might merely happen [9] that the two independent processes of nature and thought coincided at certain points, as a man with an inborn taste for the sea might find himself born on its shores.

While the pathetic fallacy can be found in the classic philosophical systems, it is there usually supported and in a measure corrected by another argument. Consider, for example, the following statement by Kant:

"The beauty of nature, *i.e.*, its connection with the free play of our cognitive faculties in apprehending and judging of its appearance, can be regarded as a kind of objective purposiveness of nature in its whole content as a system of which man is a member; *if once the teleological judging of the same by means of the natural purposes with which organized beings furnish us, has justified for us the idea of a great system of purposes of nature.* We can regard it as a favour which nature has felt for us, that in addition to what is useful it has so profusely dispensed beauty and charm; and we can therefore love it . . . just as if nature had established and adorned its splendid theatre precisely with this view." [10]

In the italicized portion of this paragraph Kant affirms that the fundamental justification of teleological or purposive judgments is to be found in the peculiar nature of "organized beings." We are thus brought back again to the conception

[8] *Op. cit.*, p. 318 and Part II, Division II, § 77, *passim.*
[9] As to whether the laws of chance would prevent such a happy accident, cf. § 27.
[10] *Op. cit.*, pp. 286-287. Italics mine.

of unity. But whereas formerly this was considered as a definition of good, it is here supposed to constitute an *objective purposiveness,* or form of being implying a purposive origin or determination. Let us examine this supposition.

§ 25. **Types of Unity.** The view which infers purpose from *unity* is distinguished by the fact that as a rule it disregards the time factor, or regards it as accidental. Purpose of this sort may characterize the world *sub specie eternitatis.* It may qualify a static whole, and appear in its mere structure or arrangement, regardless of its origin or history. It follows that the purposiveness of any given reality may be judged by internal evidence, even when it is supposed that the reality in question was produced by conscious design. A purposive object is believed, like Paley's watch, to exhibit its "designedness" in its very form. This formal, static purposiveness is identified with the interrelation of parts in a whole. Let us first consider examples, beginning with an example in which the time factor is clearly eliminated.

An ellipse is more than a mere collection of individual points; it is a curve having a formal unity, which may be expressed by the equation $x + y = c$. Every individual point in the curve is a value of the variables in this equation, and its position is determined according to the law by the position of the other points. Although the position of each point differs from that of every other point, there is at the same time a certain identical character among them all, namely the "$x + y$" character, or the sum of the distances from two fixed points called the "foci." This constant is the law of the parts, prescribes their positions, or, as it is sometimes expressed, "generates" them. In the case of a broken line or a curve having no equation, there is no unity except the mere aggregation of the several segments; but in the case of the ellipse the unity is prior to its elements, that is, it comes first in the order of explanation. The ellipse does not exist except in so far as all the points are in their proper positions, and yet their being so disposed is determined by the nature of the ellipse. Each point is determined by what is required in order that this nature shall be realized. The ellipse is then said to be the "purpose" which regulates the several points.

Let us now turn to examples in which time figures as one of the internal factors of a unity. The unity is not in time, but time is in the unity. First, let us take an example of what is commonly regarded as mechanism. Suppose a body to be moving in a straight line at a uniform velocity, governed by the law of inertia. Although each successive position of the body is new, a certain ratio of its distance-interval and its time-interval measured from any previous position is always the same. Its kinematic history as a whole exhibits a definite character which prescribes what its position must be at each particular moment. It may in its actual behavior be construed as a realization of the principle of uniform velocity. This principle in itself is a universal or ideal entity. It does not exist except in and through the successive positions of a moving body which obeys it. And yet these positions are themselves somehow determined by it.

Let us take one more example, one that is less precise but is drawn from the context of life. Modern civilization may be said to possess a characteristic flavor, which distinguishes is as a form of life. It is conditioned by the co-presence and cooperation of a thousand factors, such as the present phase of geological evolution, temperate climate, fertility of soil, racial blend, cultural tradition and an industrial system. But these many factors *compose* something. There is a unique and simple quality which somehow supervenes when all these factors are aggregated,—a quality which is identical with none of them, and yet somehow takes them all up into itself. In terms of this one quality we can construe all the various conditions as contributing this or that to it. Through it they become, not so many miscellaneous particulars, but various aspects or phases of one thing. This resultant quality is the "purpose" from which they are said to derive their meaning.

These examples serve to give plausibility to the notion

that is now before us. Let us analyze them more carefully.
It will be found that the notion of unity which they illustrate
is divisible into two types, which may be called "analytic"
and "synthetic' unity, or the *system* and the *whole*.[11] The
first is based on the peculiar relation between a universal
and its instances, or a mathematical variable and its values.
A universal is a constant factor revealed by the analysis
of instances. Furthermore, it has a peculiar relation to
any instance of itself: it explains the instance, or serves
as a description of it, and in that sense appears to be prior
to it; but on the other hand it exists, or is exemplified, only
through the instance, and in that sense appears to be posterior
to it. The case which is here stressed is the case in which
all the particulars of a set represent not only the same universal, but the same *system* of universals or function of variables. This system or function is a soluble equation, by means
of which the cases are deducible the one from the other. Such
a unity possesses, therefore, a double reciprocity. On the
one hand, the members are describable in terms of the common formula, which they in turn exemplify. On the other
hand, the members are mutually determined through the
formula.[12]

The second, or synthetic type of unity consists of the
convergence or fusion of many into one. The unity lies not
in the relation of a universal or of a set of universals to the
particulars which may be subsumed under it, but is the
resultant of a conjunction of universals with universals,
or of particulars with particulars. Whereas unity of the first
type is definable or apprehended by discursive thought, unity
of this second type is intuitive. The several parts work together to produce a whole that may be directly felt or perceived. Plurality melts into singularity.

The difference between these two types of unity is further

---

[11] Cf. §§ 172, 174.

[12] It is only in so far as *causal* interdependence is reducible to unity
of this type that it can be in question here. Viewed in the naïve sense
as a reciprocal impact or support it would not exhibit that determination
of part by whole that is essential to the present view. As regards the
special characteristics of the *living* organism, cf. Ch. V, *passim*.

illustrated by the fact that they may both be present in the same object. The *systematic* or *analytic* unity of the ellipse, for example, lies in the fact that the sum of the distances of its points from the foci is a constant. This makes it possible to describe them all by a common formula, which they in turn exemplify; and to deduce the points from one another when their mutual distances are given. The wholeness or synthetic unity of the ellipse, on the other hand, lies in the fact that the points in their *ensemble* present a figure or composite uniqueness that can be immediately apprehended. Similarly, an organism is an analytic unity in so far as its diverse processes may be subsumed under a common law such as the conservation of energy, which renders them deducible from one another; while it is a synthetic unity in so far as the total organism, composed of these processes, exhibits new and unique functions of its own.

What shall be said of the relation of unity, whether of the analytic or of the synthetic type, to the conception of purpose. There is, of course, no logical objection to a simple *identification* of unity and purpose. But to characterize the world as purposive in this general and formal sense, is to say nothing more than all science asserts. It does not differ from saying that nature is determined and intelligible in terms of laws, or that collectivities and complexities are recognizable and describable. Democritus and Spinoza would then be as good teleologists as Plato or Leibnitz. And quite apart from its philosophical barrenness, such a view would be wholly inept for the purpose of a theory of value. It would wholly disregard the peculiar or differential feature of those phenomena which biology, economics, ethics and aesthetics study, and would be of no service whatever in distinguishing and coördinating these sciences.

Let us inquire, therefore, whether unity *implies* purpose, in the specific sense already defined, and borrowed from Kant and Plato.[13]

§ 26. Purpose or Design Implied in Unity. Unity may

[13] § 23.

be thought to imply an *internal* or an *external* purpose. We shall consider each of these views in turn.

The universal may be thought to be the purpose of its instance. A certain given orbit is, let us say, an ellipse. The universal, ellipse, gives the orbit its character, or serves as a description of it; while on the other hand the orbit gives existence or embodiment to the general nature ellipse. There is no paradox here, provided we distinguish the peculiar relation between a universal and its instance, whereby the first qualifies the second and the second realizes the first. But it means nothing to say that the orbit exists *in order to* realize the ellipse. It simply *does* realize the ellipse. The ideal nature of the ellipse explains *what* the orbit is, but it does not explain the fact *that* it exists. Compare the case of Socrates cited above. The purposiveness of Socrates's act lay not in the fact that it was a particular instance of the universal, 'obedience,' but in the fact that its being believed to be such accounted for its occurrence. To construe the orbit similarly, one would be obliged to credit it, in advance of its being an ellipse, with some *reference* to that contingency; which would imply a complexity of determination admissible, perhaps, in astrology, but scarcely in astronomy.

In the case of synthetic unity or wholeness, variety possesses a unitary aspect, but it does not follow that the terms of the manifold exists *for the sake of* that unity. The peculiar cultural quality which supervenes upon an assemblage of historical conditions is not necessarily accountable for them. This would be the case only provided among the determining factors of each condition there were one which referred to the composite sequel; which might, of course, be the case, but could not be argued merely from the fact of the supervening unity.

The situation is not altered if we suppose any degree or any combination of these types of unity. If nature throughout observed the law of gravitation, or that of the conservation of energy, so that every bodily event was an instance of the same set of interrelated universals,—if it were possible to describe everything in nature by one last formula, this would not in the least imply that nature existed for the sake of realizing that formula. If the world as a whole should possess a singularity, to which every existence and every event contributed an indispensable element, this would not in the least imply that such a cosmic *quale* was the aim of its conditions. In short, mere unity as such, whether it be an analytic, logical system, or a synthetic, intuitive whole, does not imply the immanent presence of purpose in our provisional sense. This does not prove that purpose may not involve unity, but only that its differentia must lie in some further and more specific factor.

But it may still be supposed that unity argues an *external agency* of a purposive sort, or that unity is a *product* of purpose. In the first place, unity furnishes an almost irresistible opportunity for the pathetic fallacy. There is a strong human interest in unity: an intellectual and practical interest in system, and an esthetic interest in wholeness. When nature is found to obey relatively simple laws, and so to be predictable and workable, the mind rejoices and praises God. When sky and sea and land compose a pleasing landscape, one feels instinctively grateful. And so strong is the instinct that it creates its own object. But we may dismiss this impulse as an amiable weakness. The fact that a state of things agrees with a present purpose, is no proof that that state of things owes its occurrence to purpose.

A further argument for the purposive origin of unity is the argument from analogy, the argument that Paley employed in the case of the watch. A thing of the type which man makes on purpose is presumably made on purpose,—if not by man, then by God. There is a curious paradox connected with this argument. Man is peculiarly addicted to making machines, or things which work uniformly and automatically. That being the case, those parts of nature which argue a purposive creation ought to be those parts which are most mechanical, such as the periodic motions of the stars, or the conservation of energy. A living organism differs from the typical human artefact just in so far as it is spontaneous and unpredictable; and ought therefore to be the last thing to be attributed to a creative will. As a matter of fact, however, the mechanical parts of nature are the originals of which human artefacts are adaptations and imitations. Machines are made after the analogy of nature, and their machine-like character is due to what they borrow from its independent and self-sufficient forces. Invention does, it is true, correlate these forces in new ways; but there is nothing in the principle of correlation that is new. One could not look for a prettier correlation of forces than that between the centrifugal and centripetal forces of a planet moving in an elliptical orbit. The fact is that man can contrive for his own ends physical systems which resemble those which he finds in nature. The remarkable or unaccountable thing is not that unity should appear in the absence of purpose, but that purpose should have anything to do with it at all. The original mechanisms of nature are relatively intelligible, while the origin of human artefacts is relatively doubtful and obscure.

§ 27. **The Argument from Probability.** There is one further argument from unity which deserves independent consideration, the argument, namely, which employs the notion of *probability*. It is argued that in proportion as a coincidence is *remarkable* it must have been designed. Thus, for example, Professor L. J. Henderson has shown that the physico-chemical constitution of the natural world is uniquely favorable to life. It constitutes a maximum of fitness.

"The fitness of the environment results from characteristics which constitute a series of maxima—unique or nearly unique properties of water, carbonic acid, the compounds of carbon, hydrogen, and oxygen and the ocean—so numerous, so varied, so nearly complete among all things which are concerned in the problem that together they form certainly the greatest possible fitness. No other environment consisting of primary constituents made up of other known elements, or lacking water and carbonic acid, could possess a like number of fit characteristics or such highly fit characteristics, or in any manner such great fitness to promote complexity, durability, and active metabolism in the organic mechanism which we call life."

The author then goes on to argue that "there is not one chance in millions of millions" that all these properties should simultaneously occur "otherwise than through the operation of a natural law which somehow connects them together." That these properties, furthermore, "should be favorable to the organic mechanism, should fit the universe for life," remains a mystery for which "existing knowledge provides no clue." The author is thus led to suggest, with due scientific caution, a "formulative" or "directive" tendency in inorganic nature, yielding results which resemble "those which in human action we recognize as purposeful," and manifesting a bias for life; so that "the biologist may now rightly regard the universe in its very essence as biocentric." [14]

Now, in the first place, this appears to involve a misuse of the principle of probability. It is not proper to infer a law from a single simultaneity, but only from a succession of simultaneities. If the first throw of a pair of dice happens to be a double-six, that does not prove that the dice are loaded, in spite of the fact that the chances were thirty-five to one against that particular combination. There would be ground for suspecting a partiality for double-sixes only provided in the long run this combination turned up more frequently than once in thirty-six times. The general or original physico-chemical composition of the cosmos is like a single throw of dice; the chances are heavily against it, but this proves nothing as to any determining principle over and above chance. It would be possible to make such an inference only provided it were possible to gather in the cosmic elements and throw them again. It makes no difference whatever how heavy the odds are against any particular combination, provided there is only one instance of the combination; for it is entirely in keeping with a combination's unusual or remarkable character that it should occur first. [15]

[14] L. J. Henderson, *The Fitness of the Environment*, 1913, pp. 272, 276, 278, 279, 312.

[15] Bosanquet makes this clear when he says: "We have very small ground for being surprised at the actual occurrence of that alternative which had fewest chances in its favor; and absolutely none for being surprised at the occurrence of a marked or interesting alternative which has against it enormous odds, but only the same as against every alternative which can possibly occur." (*Logic*, second edition, Vol. I, p. 342.)

The same reasoning holds of the "fitness" of the environment for life. A "happy chance" does not differ from an unhappy or indifferent chance as regards the principle of chance. Let us suppose life to be a constant. It will then be comparable to a die having the same number on all of its faces. The environment, on the other hand, has millions of faces only one of which matches the first die. That the two should match in any single instance is highly improbable; the chances are millions to one against it. But the chances would be equally against any other combination that might occur. So long as there is only one trial, its happening to be successful would prove nothing as to there being anything more than chance at work. Professor Henderson insists that the relation of fitness between life and its environment is reciprocal; but he does not sufficiently emphasize this essential fact, that it is the environment which is given once and for all, while the die of life is thrown again and again.[16] It may be argued that life agrees with its environment too often to permit one to suppose that, on the part of life, it is a matter of chance. But nothing of the sort can be inferred on the part of the cosmic environment, because that lies unchanged upon the board.

Suppose that we vary the illustration. It is a remarkable fact that a given individual likes the world just as he finds it. The world agrees with his taste. In view of the vast range of possibilities, the countless worlds that would offend him, this is prodigiously improbable. But it does not follow that the world is determined to please him. That would follow only provided the world came up again and again according to his taste. But, unfortunately for the argument, the world does not come up again and again, but only once. Suppose, on the other hand, that sentient beings come up

[16] Professor Henderson admits that the relation of organism and environment is not "symmetrical" since "each organism fits its particular environment, while the environment *in its most general and universal characteristics* fits the most general and universal characteristics of the organic mechanism" (*ibid.*, p. 271, note. Italics mine). But this, as I see it, is a crucial difference. It is the *variable fitness* of the organism that gives evidence both of a pre-determined physical adaptation, and of a present conscious adaptation.

again and again always liking the given world. This, then, *would* argue that the taste of sentient creatures was somehow determined with reference to their environment, and did not originate independently of it.

But, in the second place, even though we were to admit the force of the argument from probability, what would it prove? That life and the inorganic environment were somehow reciprocally determined. Purpose is not the only alternative to accident. The improbability of accident simply creates a presumption of law or necessary connection. The structural and inborn adaptation of the organism argues its causal dependence on the environment. The reciprocal of this would be the causal dependence of the environment on the structual peculiarities of life. They would be interdependent parts of one causal series. But this would not in the least imply the presence of purpose in the sense which we have provisionally adopted.[17] Suppose all the impressions on a given area of sand to correspond exactly and uniquely to the feet of a certain child that is at play in the neighborhood. This would presumably not be an accident; but would be accepted as evidence that one of the terms of the fitness relation, namely the feet of the child, was the cause of the other, namely the impressions on the sand. It would be necessary, however, to distinguish this case from the relation between the same child's feet and the shoes in his closet. There is fitness in both cases; and in both cases the fitness is determined, not accidental. But in the latter case alone would one say that the fitness was due to purpose. One would not argue the purposiveness from the bare relation of fitness, or from the non-accidental character of the fitness, but from the peculiar way in which the fitness was, in the latter case, determined.

We conclude, then, that purpose in the provisional sense adopted at the outset, cannot be inferred from system, wholeness, coincidence or fitness. In fact we shall find ourselves more and more inclined to affirm that there is nothing pur-

---

[17] I do not mean to assert that Professor Henderson affirms cosmic purpose *in this sense*. What he means by "directive tendency" is not clear. I return to this question, Ch. VI, Sect. II.

posive except purpose itself. So far as formal structure is concerned, there is nothing that might not have arisen from purpose, nor anything that might not have arisen without it.

III. THE DESIRABLE AS POWER TO MOVE DESIRE[18]

§ 28. Such terms as 'desirable,' and 'eligible,' appear frequently in philosophical as well as in popular discourse. To identify their meaning with that of 'desired' or 'chosen' is to lose sight of the distinctive idea that they are meant to convey. For their usefulness lies in the possibility of justifying desire by the desirability of its object, or of regretting that the eligible is not in any given case actually chosen. They are used, in other words, to signify a character which *qualifies* objects to be desired or chosen. The first such qualification to be considered is dynamic, consisting in an alleged power to move or attract desire.

There is a well-known passage in Plato's *Republic* in which he says:

"Let our artists rather be those who are gifted to discern the true nature of the beautiful and graceful; then will our youth dwell in a land of health, amid fair sights and sounds, and receive the good in everything; and beauty, the effluence of fair works, shall flow into the eye and ear, like a health-giving breeze from a purer region, and insensibly draw the soul from earliest years into likeness and sympathy with the beauty of reason." [19]

The good (in the form of beauty) is here conceived as an emanating force which stirs and directs the soul of man. The idea is a common one on all levels of discourse. The Aristotelian God, or Unmoved Mover, "produces motion by being loved," as the object of desire and the object of thought "move without being moved." [20] It is customary to speak of objects or persons as charming, fascinating and attractive, where activity is imputed to the object and passivity to the subject. Plays are said to have 'drawing power,' ugliness is

[18] I shall for purposes of convenience use the term 'desire' here, but it is to be understood as having a broad and flexible meaning equivalent to that of positive interest.
[19] Book III, 401, Jowett's translation.
[20] *Metaphysica,* Book XII, Ch. 7, trans. by W. D. Ross, 1072a.

said to 'repel,' and temptation is said to be 'irresistible.' A' contemporary economist tells us that "value is a *force,* a motivating force. . . . The value is, not in the subject, but in the *object.* The object is an embodiment of the force. It has power over us, over our actions." [21]

In examining this view we recognize that same 'pathetic fallacy' with which we have already become acquainted, that habit of making "every effect of a thing upon us a constituent of its conceived nature." In this case it is the conative factor, the effort, which being occasioned by the object is transferred to it and regarded as its inherent property. The object of my endeavor is credited with the endeavor which it arouses in me. For practical or for poetic purposes there is no harm in this, but for theoretical purposes it is fallacious.

To suppose that the force of desire lies in the object of desire is precisely as misleading as to suppose that the force of the explosion lies in the ignition, or that the force of the steam-engine lies in the throttle. If we were to search there for it, we should not find it. It exists, as we know, in the chemical or physical organization of the "power." Similarly, the force of desire lies in the biological or psychological organization, that is, in the disposition, of the desiring subject. That in temptation which a man finds it difficult to resist is not the strength of the object, but the strength of his own appetites. The object releases this strength but does not supply it. [22]

[21] B. M. Anderson, Jr., *Social Value,* 1911, p. 105.

[22] There are three ways in which the present view may be restated to meet this line of attack. It may be said that the object moves desire as the universal determines the particular, or the whole the part,—a view which has already been anticipated and rejected (§ 27). Or it may be said that the mover of desire is an "entelechy" which directs and presides over the processes of growth and organic regulation. As assuming that the understanding of value is bound up with the understanding of vital and mental processes, this view will be examined later (Ch. VI, Sect. I). Or, finally, it may be said that it is reason which moves desire. If so, it is clearly not as its *object.* There are various senses in which a so-called "rational desire" may be regarded as an *ideal desire,* but this is not the same as to say that reason is the ideal of desire. Indeed the terms 'reason' and 'rational' mean so much and so little that it is futile to use them except very guardedly.

IV. THE DESIRABLE AS CAPABLE OF BEING DESIRED

§ 29. Only Self Can be Desired. We have now to consider those views in which the desirable is regarded as that character in things which *fits* or *enables* them to be desired. Since the object is to find a definition of the good, it will not suffice to say that it is the possession of goodness that qualifies things to be desired; it will be necessary to state their qualification in other terms. According to the present class of views there is a specific *capacity* to be desired, which is complementary to the faculty of desire, and by virtue of the possession of which, things are held to be good. That which is 'edible' possesses certain properties complementary to the processes of nutrition; the 'combustible' has a peculiar fitness to the process of oxidation; similarly, the desirable will be that whose constitution is prescribed in advance by the nature of the process of desiring.

No one would be inclined to accept the bald proposition that only desire can be desired or that only will can be willed. There is evidently a confusion of complementary fitness with identity, or an illegitimate projection into the object of the character of the subject with which it is intimately associated. But this confusion has nevertheless given plausibility to such generalizations as "the will to live" or "the will to power," generalizations which imply that will can be directed only to its own prolongation.

It may be argued that only a future state of the *self* can be desired. Desire is always somebody's desire; and the object of desire, which belongs to the desire, belongs also to the self which owns the desire. But in the sense in which this is true it is only a redundancy, and in the sense in which it is significant it is false.[23] If a man desires peace, peace is his desire; and in desiring it he makes it a part of himself. But such expressions merely conceal the redundancy, that when a man desires peace, it is *his* desire of peace. It is another and quite different matter to say that he desires his

[23] "The fallacy consists in transforming the (truistic) fact of acting *as* a self into the fiction of acting always for self." J. Dewey, *Human Nature and Conduct*, 1922, p. 136.

own peace, or desires that he *himself* should be at peace. The point of this latter statement lies in its asserting that the object of the desire is the self in some sense *other* than its being the subject of that desire. In the former case it is asserted that the desire issues *from* the self, and nothing is specified about its *terminus ad quem;* in the latter case it is asserted that the desire returns to its source, that its *terminus ad quem* and its *terminus a quo* are the same,—in short, that the desire is reflexive. But this may or may not be the case. There is a plain difference between being oneself interested, and being interested in oneself, and there is no justification for reducing the first to the second.

It has been held that the more highly developed cases of desire or interest, in which a certain course is deliberately adopted, or is willed contrary to inclination, are always of the reflexive type. Thus T. H. Green has argued that "all conduct to which moral predicates are applicable" (which embraces all desire above the level of "instinctive impulse") "expresses *a motive consisting in an idea of personal good.*" [24] In other words, all conscious desire is self-regard. If this were true, it would afford ground for arguing that the good, whatever else it is, must possess the form of self, and that the only escape from a vicious relativism would lie in the conception of a universal metaphysical Self. [25]

A similar view has been recently maintained by Professor

---

[24] *Prolegomena to Ethics,* 1890, pp. 115, 118. This statement is sufficiently plain, but concerning Green's view as a whole I find myself in doubt. Sometimes he says that desire must be "consciously directed to objects," and that since consciousness of objects involves self-consciousness, desire is therefore possible only for a self-conscious being (*ibid.,* pp. 125, 118). At other times he speaks of will as the case in which a man "identifies" himself with one of his component tendencies in such wise that the ensuing act expresses him *"on the whole"* (*ibid.,* p. 148). Such an "idea of a satisfaction on the whole," that is, of personal happiness or well-being, involves a reflecting subject "which traverses the series of wants," adopting them all but not identifying itself with any one of them (*ibid.,* pp. 128, 85). In other words, all desire (this being understood in a certain developed sense peculiar to man) implies the capacity of self-consciousness, and self-regard *is* a kind of self-consciousness. But it does not follow that all desire, even of the type in question, is self-regard. Here again, I believe, confusion has invested an extreme and even paradoxical doctrine with a specious plausibility.

[25] Cf. below, Ch. IV, Sect. IV.

William McDougall, who has proposed to define "volition" in terms of the "self-regarding sentiment." The case in which the rivalry of particular impulses is decided by the intervention of the personal will, is explained by the support given to one of these impulses by a sentiment which has been built up around the idea of self.[26]

This view is open to objection on two grounds. In the first place, it is not correct to say that those systems of impulses which distinguish human action on its higher planes are necessarily self-centred. Granting that it is characteristic of human action to be governed by general aims, in which various component impulses are subordinated and coördinated by an idea, it is by no means true that the only idea which is qualified to serve in such a capacity is the idea of self. There is, for example, a genuine psychological difference between the man who aims *to become the pacifier of the world,* and the man who aims *to pacify the world,* even though the results within certain limits may be the same; and love of peace is just as genuine a case of will, or volition, or controlling sentiment, as self-love.

In the second place, this view implies that there are simpler forms of the motor-affective life, such as "instinctive impulse," of which will is compounded. This being the case, will is a special form, or level, or derivative of interest. Since there are other derivatives of interest, such, for example, as those which appear in organized social life, the present view becomes in the highest degree arbitrary. Even if self were peculiarly eligible to will, this would afford no ground for maintaining that the object peculiarly eligible to will is peculiarly eligible to interest in general.[27]

§ 30. **Only Satisfaction Can be Desired.**   A third conception of desirability is derived from the notion of the

[26] "We may define volition as the supporting or reinforcing of a desire or conation by the co-operation of an impulse excited within the system of the self-regarding sentiment." W. McDougall: *Introduction to Social Psychology,* 1908, p. 249.

[27] Unless it be argued that 'will' is somehow the *reality* of which 'instinctive impulse' and other more elementary interests are the *appearances.* Cf. Ch. IV.

satisfaction or *fulfilment* of desire. This view is commonly combined with the view just considered, as when Green says that "self-satisfaction is the form of every object willed." [28] Here also we meet with a concealed redundancy, which lends plausibility to a psychological error. It is self-evidently true that that which is desired is qualified to satisfy desire. But, the self-evidence lies in the fact that it is the *same thing* to say "I desire wealth" and "Wealth satisfies my desire." The desire may be regarded as that which culminates and comes to rest in wealth, or wealth may be regarded as that which crowns and terminates the desire. This analysis, however, yields no results about the object of desire except such redundancies as "I desire what I desire" or "That which I desire is that which I desire." If by satisfaction is meant this peculiar complementary relation of the object to the desire, then it is not only gratuitous but contradictory to say "I desire the *possession* or *enjoyment* of that which I desire." If, on the other hand, one means by satisfaction the *state* of possession or enjoyment, as something which *results* from the complementary relation of the object to desire, then the present view is empirically false. It is *possible* to desire an object for the sake of the possession or enjoyment which it affords, but it is false to say that desire always has this character,—that possession or enjoyment is the only thing which is desired for its own sake.

This critique applies to a considerable variety of conceptions. It applies, for example, to the view that all will is a "will to power," where power is thought of not simply as activity, but as a state of augmented activity, or capacity for further activity, resulting from the success of a primary activity. It applies to the notion that all instincts are forms of a fundamental "instinct of self-preservation." [29] It may or may not be true that "nothing succeeds like success," but in any case it does not follow that nothing is desired but success.

[28] *Op. cit.*, p. 161.
[29] Cf. W. E. Hocking: *Human Nature and its Remaking*, 1918, Ch. X, XI.

The same critique also applies to the view that only "happiness" or "well-being" is desired. Thus Plato, for example, denies that there is "any need to ask why a man desires happiness," since "he who loves, loves the good," and he who loves the good desires "the possession of the good," and he who possesses the good "gains" happiness.[30] Similarly, Aristotle, asking "what is the highest of all practical goods," or the universal and final end of desire, replies: "The masses and the cultured classes agree in calling it happiness, and conceive that 'to live well,' or 'to do well' is the same thing as to be happy." And again: "It seems a truth which is generally admitted, that happiness is the supreme good." [31]

It may seem bold to challenge what is thus held to be unquestionable by Plato and Aristotle, and by so large a portion of mankind, but it not infrequently happens that self-evidence arises from ambiguous redundancy. The redundancy creates an aspect of truth, while the ambiguity creates an aspect of importance.[32] Thus if happiness means the same as what would satisfy if one had it, then it is safe to say that all men desire happiness; for this would then be no more than to say that all men desire that which they desire. Because my desiring a thing such as, let us say, peace, is taken to mean that "I won't be happy till I get it," or that "I would be happy to have it," it is natural and seems plausible to identify peace with happiness. The fact remains, however, that peace and happiness are two different things. If peace is the *condition* of my happiness, that is because peace, and not happiness, is the object of my desire.

[30] *Symposium,* 204-205, Jowett's translation. While the Greek term εὐδαίμων is commonly translated 'happy,' it refers not to felt satisfaction or pleasure (ἡδονή) but rather to the state of *realized* or *fulfilled* desire, the *enviable* condition, which leaves nothing to be desired.

[31] *Nicomachean Ethics,* Book I, Ch. II, VI. J. E. C. Welldon's translation, 1895. Cf. Book I, *passim.* Happiness, here also, is εὐδαιμονία (Cf. note above).

[32] The classic example is the idealistic thesis, that "I know nothing which is not object of consciousness." This affirmation is true in the sense that I know nothing which I do not know, but in this sense it is redundant and trivial. The thesis is saved from seeming trivial because the identity of its subject and predicate is concealed by the use of different words. If being known by me and being object of consciousness are distinguished, the thesis becomes important but loses its self-evidence.

The attempt to define some objective correlate of desire, something specifically capable of being desired, has thus far led only to an illegitimate projection of desire itself into its object. Self and satisfaction, which are characters of desire, are mistaken for characters of its object, because it is evidently and redundantly true that the object of desire is an object *of* a self, and *affords* satisfaction.

§ 31. Only Existence Can be Desired. But it is still possible that the desirable, in the sense of that which is qualified to be desired, may be defined by a closer examination of the objective aspect of desire. Thus it may be argued that desire refers always to the *existence* of its object.[33] Desire may be thought of as a feeling or other attitude, contemplatively directed towards the object's existence or non-existence; or as a motor tendency to bring the object into existence, or to put it out of existence. But assuming this to be characteristic of desire, in what sense shall we impute it to the object? Shall we say that all objects of desire must exist? So far as empirical evidence is concerned, just the reverse is true. Shall we say that all objects of desire must be *capable* of existing? Utopias, chimeras, vain and quixotic desires, constitute unanswerable evidence to the contrary.

Shall we say that the object of desire must be *thought of* as existent or non-existent, or *believed* to be possible? Meinong, for example, has proposed to define the value of an object in terms of the feelings aroused by the judgment or supposition of its existence and non-existence.[34] That such feelings occur, and that they determine or measure values, is not to be denied; but even if it were admitted that all feelings are so aroused, this would not imply any specific objective qualification, since there is *no* object that is not capable of being judged or supposed to exist.

§ 32. Only the Intelligible can be Desired. The last

[33] For a further discussion of this alleged character of desire, cf. §§ 100, 144.

[34] Cf. this author's *Psychologisch-ethische Untersuchungen zur Werttheorie*, 1894, p. 23; *Ueber Annahmen*, 1910, pp. 182-183.

alternative introduces a new suggestion. It may be argued
that capacity to be desired implies *intelligibility*. To be desired, an object must be represented in idea or in judgment,
and it must therefore be in some sense fit for the intellect.
But the concept of intelligibility gives rise to precisely the
same difficulties and ambiguities as the concept of desirability.
The term suggests a specifically *qualified* object of intellect,
but no one has ever succeeded in formulating anything more
significant than the redundant statement, that only objects
of intellect can be objects of intellect; or the false statement,
that intellect itself (its inherent forms or categories) is the
only possible object of intellect.

Let us substitute for the intelligible the *intellectually
apprehended* (analogous to the *desired*). The present view
may then be taken to mean that being intellectually apprehended is a necessary qualification for being desired, or that
only an actual object of intellect is a possible object of desire.
This is doubtless true, but it still fails to qualify objects in
any specific way for being desired. Granting that intellectual
apprehension is a necessary condition of desire, it is not a
peculiar condition. An object which is intellectually apprehended is equally fitted for indifference or aversion. Intellectual apprehension, like being, causation, or unity, therefore
furnishes no differentia for the subject-matter of the value-
sciences, nor any principle for distinguishing positive and
negative values.

V. THE DESIRABLE AS WHAT OUGHT TO BE

§ 33. It is sometimes contended that the desirable or valuable is that which *ought to be*. This means something more
than mere fitness or capacity for existence, whether defined
logically or causally. It is supposed that the ought-to-be possesses some preëminent claim upon the creative will. It is
not merely that which *can* exist, but that which *deserves*
to exist.

Professor W. M. Urban has recently developed the view
that value in the sense of ought-to-be is an ultimate category

under which, in the last analysis, must be subsumed even the categories of existence and truth.[35] It does not attach uniquely to will, as in the case of moral obligation, for one ought to will that which ought to be.

When we know a value, our author tells us, we need know nothing of being, or even of possibility. Thus I may know that "perfect happiness" ought to be, whether or not there is such a thing as perfect happiness, and even though perfect happiness should be impossible. Ideals ought to be, and they possess their regulative value, even when like "complete self-realization" they are essentially unattainable; just as impossible fictions such as "the infinitely little," or "the ether conceived as perfect fluid" may have value in science.[36]

Professor Urban is exceedingly anxious to avoid conceiving value as relative to any actual will, whether human or divine, since the question of value would then become a question of the existence and nature of will. He argues, therefore, that the whole, perfect-happiness-ought-to-be, which, following Meinong,[37] he calls an "objective," has an inner "validity," or character of belonging together, which the value-judging subject directly "acknowledges."

The difficulty, however, is quite palpable, being the same which has always confronted intuitive and formalistic doctrines of value. Acknowledgments of validity unfortunately *conflict*. There are judges of value who acknowledge that perfect happiness ought not to be. If all such acknowledgments are accepted, then value is relative to the fact of ac-

[35] "Value and Existence," and "Knowledge of Value and the Value Judgment," *Jour. of Philos.*, Vol. XIII (1916), pp. 449, 673; "Ontological Problems of Value," *ibid.*, Vol. XIV (1917), p. 309. Although historically this view developed from the type of view considered in the next chapter, it belongs here because of its attempt to free value from necessary relation to any subject, even an "over-individual" subject. For the relation of this view to the similar and antecedent views of Lotze, Münsterberg, Meinong, Rickert, Windelband, etc., the reader may consult Professor Urban's foot-notes, especially *Jour. of Philos.*, Vol. XIII, p. 461. For a similar view, cf. H. Rickert, "Zwei Wege der Erkenntnisstheorie," *Kant-studien*, Vol. XIV (1909); E. Lask, *Lehre vom Urtheil*, 1912, pp. 31, 79, 65; D. Fisher, "The Problem of the Value Judgment," *Philos. Rev.*, Vol. XXII (1913), p. 623.

[36] "Value and Existence," p. 463; "Ontological Problems of Value," pp. 314-315.

[37] Cf. below, § 136.

knowledgment.   The adoption of this alternative leads either
to scepticism (if acknowledgment is treated like a judgment,
as something true or false), or to a relational theory of value
(if acknowledgment is treated as an attitude of interest).
Both consequences being abhorrent to Professor Urban, he
must seek another alternative.   He must provide some criterion by which acknowledgments of validity may themselves
be validated.

This may be sought on the side of the objective itself.
One may say that the objective, 'perfect-happiness-ought-to-
be,' is valid when perfect happiness actually possesses the
quality of oughtness.   But Professor Urban refuses to regard
value as a quality, whether definable or indefinable.   Or one
may say that perfect happiness is implied, while unhappiness is
not, by some system or set of premises, as a circle ought
to be perfectly round.   In this case ought becomes the same
thing as 'must,' in the sense of logical necessity,[38] an outcome which is equally contrary to the author's intent.

The alternatives on the side of the objective being exhausted, there remains the possibility of validating the act
of acknowledgment itself.   This requires the supposition of
some absolute or standard act of acknowledgment, some "met-
empirical will" to which fallible mortals may or may not
conform.   Professor Urban himself refuses to accept even
this alternative.   He agrees, however, that the members of
his school have generally gravitated towards it.   They have
denounced "psychologism," but they have been driven to adopt
a metaphysical "voluntarism" or "imperativism"; which involves what Professor Urban regards as the same error,
namely, the definition of the ought-to-be in terms of the 'is.'

Similarly, Dr. Rashdall tells us that he regards " 'Good,'
'Ought' (when applied to ends), 'Value,' 'the End' . . . as
synonymous terms," and that "it is implied in the idea of
'good' that it ought to be promoted." [39]   But the effect of this
identification of terms is to shift the locus of value from the

---

[38] Cf. § 48.
[39] *Theory of Good and Evil*, 1907, Vol. I, pp. 135 (note), 138. Cf. also
H. Sidgwick, *Methods of Ethics*, Book I, Ch. III, § 3. Cf. also above, § 18.

object to the subject. 'Good' or 'ought-to-be,' although in a secondary sense applied to objects, means primarily that which it is good or obligatory to *will*.[40] Attention is now focussed upon a well-known opposition in human consciousness between the actual inclination and some 'higher' or more imperious demand. Instead of looking for some character of the object which is specifically complementary to purpose or will, from which these may be inferred, or by which these are determined and regulated, one looks for some mode of purpose or will themselves, which is entitled to precedence. Value is held to lie not in a peculiar qualification *for* desire, but in a peculiar qualification *of* desire.

[40] Here is another meaning of "desirable," as that *the desire of which ought to be.*

CHAPTER IV

VALUE AS THE OBJECT OF QUALIFIED INTEREST

I. TYPES OF QUALIFIED INTEREST

§ 34. We turn now to those views which, while admitting that value is relative to interest, insist that the interest in question must be specially qualified. That which is good, or desirable, is that which is the object of a legitimate desire. As a general formulation of this view we may take Brentano's statement that "we call something good when the love relating to it is right." "That which can be loved with a right love," says this author, "that which is worthy of love, is good in the widest sense of the term." [1] In so far as this means merely to substitute 'right' for 'good' as an ultimate indefinable, it would signify no advance over theories already considered. Value in the most ultimate sense must, in the present view, be regarded as a function of will or love. In so far, on the other hand, as a right will or love is only a special case of will or love in general, then its objects may be valuable in a superlative sense, but not in that generic sense of which we are here in search. The present view can satisfy the conditions of a fundamental theory of value only in so far as the right love or will is conceived as the *only* love or will.

The heart of this doctrine will consist of a critique of will. The modes of the motor-affective life, the desires and affections of living creatures, are not to be accepted as they stand, but condemned as partial, blind, apparent or unauthorized as compared with some standard will which is complete,

---

[1] F. Brentano, *The Origin of the Knowledge of Right and Wrong,* trans. by C. Hague, 1902, p. 16. Cf. G. E. Moore, *Inter. Jour. of Ethics,* Vol. XIV (1903), p. 115.

enlightened, real or imperative. In what do the credentials of this standard will consist? We cannot hope to exhaust the varieties of this conception, but must confine ourselves to such as have a major historical importance, and will contribute materially to the progress of our investigation. In the first place, there is the conception of the *final will*, or the love of God as the culminating phase of the natural hierarchy of desires. Closely related to this is the conception of the *harmonious will*, or the desire in accord with nature. Modern idealism has absorbed these and kindred ideas in the conception of an *absolute will*, presupposed in the relativities of human experience. Over and above these essentially metaphysical or epistemological conceptions, there is the moral conception of the *imperative* or *obligatory* will.

II. THE FINAL WILL, OR IMPLICIT LOVE OF GOD

§ 35. Plato is primarily responsible for the prevalence in European philosophy of the view that all purposes belong to one hierarchy culminating in the love of a supreme object, or 'highest good.'

"He who has been instructed thus far in the things of love, and who has learned to see the beautiful in due order and succession, when he comes toward the end will suddenly perceive a nature of wondrous beauty (and this, Socrates, will be the final cause of all our former toils)—a nature . . . not fair in one point of view and foul in another, . . . but beauty absolute, separate, simple, and everlasting, which . . . is imparted to the ever-growing and perishing beauties of all other things. He who from these ascending under the influence of true love, begins to perceive that beauty, is not far from the end. And the true order of going, or being led by another, to the things of love, is to begin from the beauties of earth and mount upwards for the sake of that other beauty, using these as steps only, and from one going on to two, and from two to all fair forms, and from fair forms to fair practices, and from fair practices to fair notions, until from fair notions he arrives at the notion of absolute beauty, and at last knows what the essence of beauty is." [2]

[2] *Symposium,* Jowett's translation, 211 C.

Similarly, according to Plotinus "the soul has naturally a love of God and desires to be united with him with the love which a virgin bears to a noble father." [3]   The inorganic world is an emanation from the One, through the successive stages of Mind and Soul. The soul being in an intermediate position may descend through its sensitive and vegetative capacities towards Matter or Non-Being, or it may ascend through Mind to the One. The flight of the soul, like that of the homing-pigeon, is towards its point of origin; particular souls have a "natural inclination towards the intelligible and turn back to their source." [4]

With important differences that do not concern us here, the same hierarchical conception appears in Aristotle. Nature is an order of substances, in which each is governed by the double principle of actualizing its own distinctive form, and at the same time of supplying the material conditions for the actualization of the form next higher in the scale. Man as the highest being of terrestrial nature is animated by the purpose of realizing the rational life, which in turn culminates in that contemplative activity of the reason which is the goal of the whole, or God.

This view persists in the Scholastic philosophy of the Thirteenth Century, and appears clearly in the view of Thomas Aquinas, as thus expounded by Professor De Wulf:

"Doubtless the man who desires good as such, perfect good, does not at once perceive that it is God alone who can fully satisfy the aspirations of his mind and heart. His reason arrives at this conclusion by the gradual elimination of objects other than God. Until this process of reasoning is performed, man seeks for happiness, unaware that God is his happiness." [5]

It is essential to this view that the ultimate end of the process should be conceived as directing *all* of its stages. Otherwise there would be a succession of desires or purposes,

---

[3] *Enneads*, VI, 9, translated in C. M. Bakewell's *Source Book in Ancient Philosophy*, 1907, p. 389.

[4] *Enneads*, IV, 8, translated in B. A. G. Fuller's *The Problem of Evil in Plotinus*, 1912, p. 315. Cf. *Enneads*, V, 2, *op. cit.*, p. 301.

[5] M. De Wulf, *Mediæval Philosophy*, 1922, pp. 102-103.

instead of one all-pervading desire or purpose. *All* love is love of God:

> "that sustaining Love,
> Which through the web of being blindly wove
> By man and beast and earth and air and sea,
> Burns bright or dim, as each are mirrors of
> The fire for which all thirst." [6]

There is a sublimity in this cosmic spectacle which disarms criticism. But despite its appeal to the religious and speculative imagination it involves several serious psychological errors which we shall do well to bring clearly to light. In the first place, it is affirmed that the development of desires is an orderly series, in which the flower of the old desire is the seed of the new. Or, it is affirmed that desire is cumulative, in the sense that each level of satisfaction becomes in turn the base of a new aspiration which both incorporates and supplements old aspirations. It is not to be denied that interests are vitally connected, in the sense that the efforts and satisfactions which attend them breed new interests. Nor is it to be denied that developed interests *may* incorporate antecedent interests. [7] But the view here considered affirms that such progressive enlargement and incorporation is an invariable law of development. That such is unfortunately not the case, is abundantly proved by the facts of human experience. In disillusionment the satisfaction of a given interest leads to its repudiation and to the search for *other* satisfactions. Furthermore, new interests most commonly arise not through the conversion of ends into means, but through the conversion of means into ends. It may happen that a man having provided for the satisfaction of his biological needs, devotes himself thenceforth to moral or cultural ends in which these biological goods are both conserved and transmuted. This, perhaps, is what should happen. But what more commonly does happen is that, finding certain instrumentalities such as money useful in satisfying his biological needs, a man thenceforth devotes himself to money get-

[6] Shelley's *Adonais.*
[7] Cf. § 261.

ting.[8] In short, interests burgeon from root, stem and branch, and not merely from fruit or flowers.

A further error lies in the affirmation of an absolute desideratum somehow implied in all desire.   The conception of perfection becomes empty and redundant as soon as it is divorced from the *particular* interests of living creatures. The Platonic or Aristotelian good has a recognizable content so long as it is related to the human organism with its specific capacities and conditions, or to human sensibilities, or to the human craving for knowledge.   But when we are invited to contemplate that culminating satisfaction in which all actual desires and all possible desires are brought to port, we are left gazing at an empty canvas framed by formulas;—unless, indeed, we are gifted with a poetic imagination by which we can paint the picture for ourselves.

Finally, there is a third error of attributing to any given desire whatever ulterior desires are causally or logically connected with it.   This is the insidious error connected with such conceptions as *virtuality* or *potentiality*.   It consists in attributing to a limited set of conditions a character that requires the addition of supplementary conditions.   If it is known that $a + b + c$ will produce M, we may say that $a + b$ is such that with the addition of c it would become M. If, for any reason, there is an interest in M, one is apt thus to characterize $a + b$ in terms of it, as "almost," or "virtually" or "potentially" M.   Such expressions are permissible, but they are treacherous, because they tend to obscure the fact that $a + b$ is NOT M; which may be all-important, for practical, as well as for theoretical purposes.   Suppose that we grant that interests have the hierarchical character above attributed to them, and that an aspiring being who has succeeded in becoming a man will thereupon immediately set his heart on God.   One may say that an as yet unsuccessful mortal is virtually loving God, meaning that *when and if* he reaches his human goal he will then set himself a divine goal.   But this is the same as to say that in the absence of such initial

───────

[8] For a fuller discussion of this whole question of the genesis and mutation of interests, cf. Ch. XVIII, XIX.

success, which is the state of many struggling mortals, he does *not* love God. The requisite supplementary conditions of time and achievement may never be provided, and a man will then have lived and died upon his original level of aspiration.

III. THE ALL-HARMONIOUS WILL, OR DESIRE IN ACCORD WITH NATURE

§ 36. All of the errors which we have just considered reappear in the cognate view that the real, as opposed to the seeming desire, is the *all-harmonious* will. This idea is combined with the idea of the final will in the Platonic and Neo-Platonic philosophies, but its most typical form is the Stoic conception of *desire in accord with nature*. Consider, for example, the following passage from the unknown Stoic cited by Cicero:

"In order to have value, a thing must either be itself in harmony with nature or else be the means of procuring something which is so. All objects, then, that are in accordance with nature are relatively choiceworthy on their own account, while their opposites have negative value and call for rejection. . . . Man's earliest attraction is to those things which are comfortable to nature, but as soon as he has laid hold of general ideas or notions and has seen the regular order and harmony of conduct, he then values that harmony far higher than all the objects for which he had felt the earliest affection and he is led to the reasoned conclusion that herein consists the supreme human good." [9]

In so far as this view affirms the value of harmony or order in its formal aspect, it is affiliated with views which we have considered in an earlier chapter.[10] We are here concerned with a specific feature of the view, namely, the affirmation of a single providential will, which both governs the world and also expresses itself in the desires and reason of living creatures. The parts of physical nature and the members of human society "are made for cooperation, like feet, like hands, like eyelids, like the rows of the upper and

---

[9] Cicero: *De Finibus*, III, 20, 21, quoted and translated in R. D. Hicks, *Stoic and Epicurean*, 1910, pp. 80-81.
[10] Cf. § 21, Ch. III, Sect. II.

lower teeth." [11]   Each element in this cosmic harmony is
inclined to pursue what is appropriate to it, that is, to play
its appointed rôle.   Upon the pre-rational level of plant and
animal life this inclination is blind, but in man the reason
discerns the plan of the whole so that it becomes a deliberate
purpose.   Thus both irrational and rational desire are "regulated by Nature."   They do not have to be brought into
conformity with Nature, because Nature herself "produces
the inclination." [12]   Hence,

>   " . . . to thine own self be true;
>   And it must follow, as the night the day,
>   Thou cannot then be false to any man."

—or to God, or to any of his works.

This affirmation that all desires are constitutionally in
accord, as the harmonious parts of one symphonic Will, may,
like the affirmation that all desires are serial phases of the
love of God, be regarded as a claim of faith or poetic fiction.
Or, as we shall see presently, it may be regarded as a necessary
presupposition.[13]   But it is here advanced as an empirical
generalization.   It invites judgment by the evidence of fact,
and when so tested it fails.   Modern evolutionary theory may
be supposed to lend support to the view that the desires of
existing creatures are in harmony with one another and with
the environment, since such harmony is a condition of their
survival.   But the reverse side of the survival of the fit is
the elimination of the unfit.   The theory of natural selection
means nothing unless nature contains discord as well as harmony, and for such natural maladjustments the Stoic view
makes no provision.   Furthermore, the evidence of biological
science indicates that even surviving creatures are only imperfectly adjusted; their endowment enabling them to exist,
but without guaranteeing their perfect functioning.

Upon the level of reason even this incomplete evidence
is lacking.   The intellectual faculties as such are, no doubt,

[11] *Thoughts* of M. Aurelius Antoninus, translated by G. Long, 1890,
p. 96.

[12] Diogenes Laertius, Yonge's translation, p. 290, quoted by Bakewell,
op. cit., p. 273; cf. *ibid.,* pp. 274, 275.

[13] Cf. Sect. IV.

adaptive, since they enable the organism to profit by experience.   But it is a notorious fact that while reason renders possible a more harmonious life than that based on instinct, it also multiplies the possibilities of discord.   Reason is not an insurance, but an opportunity attended by a risk.

IV. THE ABSOLUTE WILL AS A NECESSARY PRESUPPOSITION

§ 37. **The Idealistic or Epistemological Standpoint.**[14] The view which finds a relatively naïve expression in the writings of the Stoics is elaborately developed in modern idealism.   A characteristic statement of it is given by Green, who affirms "a single principle" which manifests itself in all the particular desires of a man, as well as in all his acts of understanding and will.   He goes on to say of this single principle:

"We adopt it in the sense that there is one subject or spirit, which desires in all a man's experiences of desire, understands in all operations of his intelligence, wills in all his acts of willing; and that the essential character of his desires depends on their all being desires of one and the same subject which also understands, the essential character of his intelligence on its being an activity of one and the same subject which also desires, the essential character of his acts of will on their proceeding from one and the same subject which also desires and understands." [15]

One recognizes here the essential thesis of the Stoics, that the motor-affective life of man is, whether blindly or understandingly, one with that life which informs and sustains the universe, so that in so far as one really desires and wills one cannot do so incompatibly with other desires and wills,

[14] I believe that the same criticisms which are here applied to the absolutistic form of idealism will apply in principle to the "personalistic" form, in which a system or hierarchy of wills supersedes the single universal will.   The most systematic presentation of this view is to be found in W. Stern, *Wertphilosophie,* 1924.   In any case, the personalistic view is open to the objection that has been urged against all the views discussed in this chapter, namely, that through ascribing value to one and only one form of interest they confuse the problem of generic value with that of superior or standard value.

[15] T. H. Green: *Prolegomena to Ethics,* 1890, p. 122.

or with the course of physical nature. The difference,—for philosophy, a very great difference—between Stoicism and modern idealism, is to be found in the *argument*. In modern idealism the universal will is advanced not as an empirical generalization, but as a *presupposition* alleged to be *necessary* on *epistemological* grounds. The point of departure is the Kantian critique of knowledge, according to which physical nature, especially in respect of its systematic unity, is the creation of mind. If there is to be one physical nature, as is implied in science, then there must be one mind; which, since it is essentially active and creative, may be regarded as desire or will; and, when so regarded, its immediately controlling principles will be those proper to desire or will, namely, moral principles. This view was foreshadowed in Kant's famous doctrine of "the primacy of the practical reason," [16] and was developed in the system of Fichte, in which the will is conceived as fashioning nature in obedience to the dictates of duty. In such a system nature is a *moral* value. But the essence of active mind may be conceived as thinking or as the artistic impulse, in which case the existent world fashioned by thought would take on the character of truth or beauty. Or these modes of activity may be regarded as different phases of one activity, and reality as the all-comprehensive ideal. In these and cognate conceptions theory of value and metaphysics coincide. The world is what mind in its deepest longings and aspirations would have it. Being is the consummate product of spirit.[17]

It is essential to recognize the specific sense in which this constitutes a general theory of value. It might be taken to mean simply that there is a universal will which *deserves precedence* of particular human inclinations. This would mean that whereas all objects of inclination are *ipso facto* good, and all objects of disinclination *ipso facto* evil, the objects of the universal will are preëminently good or evil. But then the universal will would be invoked not to define

[16] *Critique of Practical Reason,* Book II, Chapter II. Cf. translation by T. K. Abbott, 1889, p. 216.

[17] Cf. the author's *Present Philosophical Tendencies,* 1912, Ch. VIII; *Present Conflict of Ideals,* 1918, Ch. XVII.

value as such, but to define a superlative degree of value.
The discussion of it in this bearing belongs to the later
topic of the gradation and hierarchy of values.[18]   We are
concerned with the attempt to define value in the generic
sense, and the present view is relevant only in so far as it
affirms that there is no value but the supreme value.

Such an affirmation is thought to be justified because the
diverse private inclinations which give rise to conflicting empirical values are all rooted in the absolute will.   As in
the views just presented all particular desires are thought
to consist 'virtually' in the final or harmonious love of God,
so here it is supposed that they all presuppose as their deeper
intent that act of mind that creates and sustains the universe.
There is only one value because in the last analysis there is
only one will.

That which is essentially characteristic of the absolute
will is that it resolves the conflict which is characteristic of
particular wills.   This resolution may be thought of in pessimistic or in optimistic terms.   Schopenhauer, for example,
argued that individual wills, since they are defined by relations of space and time, are products of a deeper universal
will which creates space and time.   The values attaching to
individual wills are determined by local and private conditions
which do not exist for that universal will which creates them;
and they cannot, therefore, find a place in the supreme value
which is the object of the universal will.   The individual will
may make this object its own by renouncing private claims,
—by the cultivation of sympathy and by aesthetic contemplation.   In other words, the supreme value *negates* and
excludes all particular values.   The vanity, the inevitable failure of all human strivings, is due to the fact that their partisanship is essentially contrary to the nature of the impartial
cosmic will.   This is the pessimistic alternative, of which
Schopenhauer is the most notable exponent in European
thought.

The other alternative, which expresses the optimism characteristic of the Occident, is to conceive the universal will as

[18] Cf. Ch. XXII.

somehow embracing all finite wills, and the supreme value as somehow conserving all human values.

There is an evident difficulty in either alternative. The paradox of Schopenhauer lies in the fact that the universal will somehow wills all wills, and is thus called upon to deny its own offspring. The optimistic view, on the other hand, first admits the incompatibility of finite wills as the reason for affirming the absolute will; and then, in conceiving this absolute will as embracing all finite wills, affirms that these are, after all, not incompatible. Between these two extremes lie various compromises according to which the universal will embraces some finite wills, and excludes others; or embraces all finite wills in some abridged or sublimated form. But the difficulty then lies in the very existence of these alternatives. Such limited synthetic wills or moral purposes are undoubtedly possible,[19] and human experience exhibits a wide variety of them. But this very fact stands in the way of adopting any one of them as that absolute and unique will which is here in question.

Let us now examine this view more in detail, and with special reference to its contemporary forms.

§ 38. **The Absolute Will Presupposed in Truth.** The argument is, as we have seen, primarily epistemological. Its force lies in the plausible assumption that contradiction is as fatal to desire, will and feeling as it is to cognition. We say that in so far as perception or judgment contradicts other perception or judgment, their objects cannot be real. Similarly it is argued that in so far as desires conflict, their objects cannot be valuable. Just as we recognize appearance as opposed to real existence in the field of cognition, so in the motor-affective field we must recognize apparent values as opposed to real values. The only real values, in other words, are those "absolute" values or "values-in-themselves" in which the relativities of private inclination are transcended.[20]

[19] Cf. Ch. XXII, Sect. I.

[20] Thus according to Professor Windelband we have to seek a "value-in-itself" just as we have to seek a "thing-in-itself." "We have to seek it in order to get beyond the relativity of actual appreciations; and,

The starting-point of the argument may be summarily stated as follows.[21] Knowledge consists essentially, not in the possession of ideas, but in the affirmation of truth or the rejection of falsity. To know is to judge, and "to judge means not merely to connect ideas with each other, but to affirm this connection as valid and true; or, in negative judgments, to reject it as false."[22] Knowledge, in other words, is an attitude of favor or disfavor on the part of the subject towards a certain content. But this view of knowledge carries with it a corresponding view of truth and objectivity. The real object must no longer be conceived as an external pre-existing thing which the mind's ideas are to reproduce, but as an ideal or goal toward which the mind's activity is directed. Truth must no longer be conceived as agreement between ideas inside the mind and things outside, but as some sort of agreement or accord within the mind itself. On the older theory it was necessary to suppose an independent object, in order to escape a sceptical relativism and give truth some footing beyond the capriciousness and incompatibility of human ideas. So, on the present theory, there is the same necessity for supposing some absolute attitude of assent or dissent by which to escape from the capriciousness and incompatibility of human judgments. Truth is the object of an absolutely right act of acceptance or rejection.

since there is value only in relation to a valuing consciousness, the value-in-itself points to the same normal consciousness which haunts the theory of knowledge as the correlate of the thing-in-itself. In both cases this implication is at the most a postulate, not a thing metaphysically known." It should be added that according to the view of Windelband and his school the thing-in-itself is ultimately reducible to the value-in-itself. W. Windelband, *Introduction to Philosophy*, translation by J. McCabe, 1921, p. 216. Cf. also H. Münsterberg, *The Eternal Values*, 1909, Introduction.

[21] A summary, critique and bibliography of this theory of value will be found in A. Aliotta, *The Idealistic Reaction against Science*, translated by A. McCaskill, 1914, Part I, § II, Ch. III.

[22] W. Windelband, *op. cit.*, p. 170. The author's term for this essential act of knowledge is *Beurtheilung*, sometimes translated "verdict." Cf. *ibid.*, p. 208; and the same writer's *Präludien*, 3d Edition, pp. 52–53. Cf. also the following statement of H. Rickert: "Der eigentliche logische Kern des Urteils, das Bejahen und Verneinen, ein Billigen oder Missbilligen, ein Stellungnehmen zu einem Werte ist." (*Der Gegenstand der Erkenntniss*, 1904, p. 108.)

§ 39. The Parallelism of Truth, Beauty and Goodness.

When knowledge is thus analyzed, it becomes simply a form of 'valuing,' like moral or aesthetic approbation. Consider, for example, the case of the death of Socrates. My knowledge of the event consists in an attitude of assent towards 'Socrates-drank-the-hemlock.' In taking this attitude, furthermore, I assume that it is more than merely *my* attitude, subject to my own caprice. I assume that it is *the* attitude to which others as well as myself are somehow bound to conform. Even if I entertain doubts, I assume that there is at any rate *some* attitude, such as assent towards 'Socrates-died-a-natural-death,' which is authoritative. But exactly the same claim is made in moral valuation. I approve Socrates for refusing to escape from prison, on the assumption that such approbation is more than my personal preference; on the assumption, in other words, that I am delivering a sound moral verdict which is entitled to general confirmation. Similarly, if I deem Socrates beautiful I mean to express more than my private taste in such matters. I claim that my contemplative enjoyment is that of the absolutely qualified aesthetic subject.

In other words, the *parallelism* of these three cases confers on moral and aesthetic values the same universality which I cannot avoid attributing to cognitive values. If I deny that there is such a universally valid affirmation, I claim universal validity for my denial. If I doubt, I virtually appeal to some universally valid affirmation as the potential resolver of my doubt; I am virtually asking whether my particular affirmation is or is not, the universally valid affirmation. If, then, I am compelled to admit a standard affirmation whose object is Absolute Truth, then why not a standard conscience and a standard taste, whose objects are Absolute Good and Absolute Beauty? Or, if I do not accept the intimation of universality in the moral and aesthetic experience, then I should not do so in the parallel case of the cognitive experience; but this would be impossible or self-contradictory. Thus "the act of affirming the true world belongs together with the act of affirming the beautiful world and the moral world;

and we have no right to give any more emphasis to the one act than to the other." [23]   In other words, either no knowledge at all, and no world at all; or, by the same token, a coördinate world of goodness and beauty. The famous trinity of values, the True, the Beautiful and the Good are regarded as values *par excellence,* because they all embody the same claim to objectivity and universality.

Is this argument sound? It turns, evidently, upon the similarity of moral and aesthetic attitudes to cognitive attitudes. Since the latter, in order to escape a sceptical relativism, must presuppose some universally valid act of mind, so, it is argued, must the former. But there are evidently other equally plausible alternatives. Since the moral and aesthetic attitudes differ in *some* respect from the cognitive attitude, then they *may* differ in just that respect which is crucial as regards the implication of universal validity. It is true that in both types of attitude there is the same antithesis of "yea and nay." But over and above this sameness there is a residual difference which distinguishes favor and disfavor from assent and dissent. It is commonly supposed that assent and dissent are dictated by the object, and will therefore tend to be the same in all subjects. In so far as they are not the same, they will not have fulfilled their function, which is to express the common "environment of fact" [24] in which all wills operate. Attitudes of favor and disfavor, on the other hand, may express precisely that subjective factor which is variable among individuals or among the moods of the same individual.

Or, it may be that what is called a moral attitude postulates universality not in any independent sense, but only because it *contains* a cognitive attitude as a component. It may be, as in my approbation of Socrates's virtue, that a sentiment of favor predominates, but is associated with an intellectual

[23] H. Münsterberg, *op. cit.,* p. 81.
[24] *"A judgment is satisfied when its content conforms to the environment of fact, while a desire is satisfied when the environment conforms to it."*   (W. P. Montague, "The True, the Good and the Beautiful from a Pragmatic Standpoint," *Jour. of Philos.,* Vol. VI, 1909, p. 235. Cf. below, Ch. XI.)

judgment regarding Socrates's characteristics; and that my claim of universality, legitimately made in behalf of my judgment, is illegitimately extended to my sentiment.   In precisely the same way an act of judgment, or intellectual assent, may derive a flavor of capriciousness from an associated sentiment.

The present view would seem therefore to have assumed too hastily that because there is a certain resemblance (in respect of the polarity of positive and negative) between cognitive and motor-affective attitudes, therefore, the postulate of universality can be carried over from the first to the second.

§ 40. The Interdependence of Truth, Beauty and Goodness.

The final and most radical step in the argument is to insist that the several standardized acts of spirit must be brought into mutual accord.   Here it is a question of conflict not between individual minds manifesting the same type of interest, but between the several types of interest themselves, whether manifested in different individuals or in the same individual.   It is argued that I cannot affirm as true what I do not virtually approve and enjoy, and demand that others shall approve and enjoy, as good and beautiful.   Thus Münsterberg, having set up his three coördinate worlds of morality, beauty and truth, goes on to contend that "if the world as a whole is not to become contradictory and by that ultimately worthless," . . . "the achievements of morality, the beauties of happiness and the connections of truth" must be "ultimately apperceived as identical." [25]   There is at bottom only one subjective or spiritual bias, which may in a generalized sense be termed "will" (Münsterberg) or "purpose" (Royce), but which these terms in their limited senses, and such other terms as desire, enjoyment, and cognitive assent, only partially convey.   This spiritual bias is indivisible.   It is for or against as a whole.   So long as I am moved to assent intellectually to what I find aesthetically repulsive, or to deny the existence of what ought to be, I have not as yet wholeheartedly expressed myself.   I mean to vote only for that which I can

[25] *Op. cit.*, p. 352.

unqualifiedly endorse. Truth itself, as that which moves to assent, must await such further qualifications as move to approbation and delight. What is not all-valuable, is not valuable at all; nor even existent, since existence itself (as truth) is a value. Or, what I do not approve as good, and enjoy as beautiful, I cannot assent to as existent.

Is there any force in this contention? Although himself a redoubtable champion of the type of philosophy which is here expounded, F. H. Bradley candidly admits that our judgments of existence are not answerable to our moral demands; and points out that if such a principle were to be admitted, morality would with equal logic be compelled to subordinate its claims to those of existence.

"Doubtless," [he says], "a conclusion which fails to content all the sides of my nature leaves me dissatisfied. But I see no direct way of passing from 'this does not satisfy my nature' to 'therefore it is false.' . . . So far as I can see, we must admit that, *if* the intellect is contented, the question is settled." [26]

In other words, cognitive satisfactions are independent of moral or aesthetic satisfactions. The plausibility of the contrary view is due to a vagueness and ambiguity of which Bradley himself is not guiltless, and which betrays him into an almost instant reversal of the opinion just stated. "We cannot argue directly that all sides of our nature must be satisfied, but indirectly we are led to the same result"; [27] the reason being that, while the intellect is autonomous, nevertheless it cannot *itself* tolerate any such "clash" of ideas with sensation as is involved in unfulfilled longings or ideals contrary to fact.

But in thus appealing vaguely to "harmony" as a postulate of intellect, Bradley loses sight of the *particular kind of harmony* which the intellect demands, namely, that its *judgments* shall accord with facts; which, as he has himself shown, in no way implies that *aspiration* shall accord with fact. He tells us with evident sympathy that "to any one who believes in the unity of our nature, a one-sided satisfaction will remain

[26] *Appearance and Reality*, 1893, pp. 154-155.
[27] *Ibid.*, p. 158.

incredible." [28]   But the "unity" of which he here speaks is
the very question at issue.   If with Bradley one can speak
of the intellect as capable of being satisfied "alone," then
one has no business to believe in the "unity of our nature"
in a sense which implies the contrary.   There is a specious
plausibility in saying that I cannot finally assent to what fails
to satisfy me.   But the fact is I can and do, without the slightest
difficulty; since I may favor a thing in one respect and deplore
it in another respect, without ever being required to declare
for or against it on behalf of my total self.   Even should
such a general decision be necessary, it would still be possible,
indeed usual, that while favoring the object "on the whole,"
I should still harbor dislike of it in this or that respect.

§ 41. **The Good as Founded on Truth.**   There is, however, a seeming justification of the view that the satisfactions
of intellect and will are interdependent, in the close interplay
of these faculties in the mental life.   Green, it will be remembered, tells us that the essential character of desire and
will lies in their being the desire and will of a being *who also
understands*.   This means that in so far as desire and will
are fully developed in man, their object is also an object of
cognition.   It is undeniably true that desire and will are
mediated by cognition.   Thus, for example, the League of
Nations is desired in so far as it is judged to be a means
of securing peace.   If this judgment is true, or intellectually
satisfying, my will is said to be "well-founded," [29] or secure.
Were I to be convinced that this judgment about the object
was false, I should cease to desire the object.

But important as it is, this fact does not prove what it
is here intended to prove.   It does not prove that the existence
of the desire depends on the truth of the judgment which
mediates it.   The desire for the League of Nations would
not be in the least affected were the judgment of its peaceful
effects to be mistaken, provided the mistake were not rec-

[28] *Ibid.*, p. 154.
[29] Cf. W. M. Urban, *Valuation*, 1909, p. 405.   This reinforcement of
will by intellect may also be regarded as the essence of obligation.   Cf.
below, § 47.

ognized by the desiring subject. Error, in other words, is just as effective a mediator of desire as truth. When desire is founded on error, one is disposed to speak of it as a false desire, implying that there is no such desire. But this is to exploit a mere play of words. The ill-founded desire may be said to be a precarious desire, and in that sense an inferior desire, but this does not in the least prejudice its reality so long as it lasts; and in so far as value is defined in terms of desire, its objects have every right to be accorded a place somewhere in the scale of values.

We have to note another point brought to light by the same illustration. The object of the desire is not the same as the object of the judgment. One judges that the League of Nations is conducive to peace, and not that it exists; whereas one desires that the League of Nations shall exist, not that it shall be conducive to peace. This case thus affords no evidence that what is affirmed by the will is also affirmed by the intellect.

Sameness of object is, however, present in a second case of the mediation of desire by intellect. When one desires that the League of Nations shall exist one formulates the 'supposition' [30] of its existence, and the desire culminates in a moment at which I can declare triumphantly: "The League of Nations exists." In other words, there is a series of intellectual attitudes, from supposition through doubt and probability to certain conviction, which runs parallel to the successive motor-affective attitudes of wish, aspiration, hope and joy. But, unfortunately for the argument, the two series progress in opposite directions. Affirmation rises and desire declines. One begins with much desire and no affirmation, and ends with much affirmation and no desire. At the moment when I desire that the League of Nations should exist I affirm that it does not exist; and when I am convinced that it exists I cease to desire that it should exist. [31]

Windelband, with a candor which is more admirable than

[30] A. Meinong's conception of *Annahame*.

[31] I do not deny that there *are* motor-affective attitudes directed to the continued existence of what is known to exist, but this is neither the only nor the most characteristic form of will. Cf. below, Ch. IX, Sect. I.

his consistency, recognizes that this duality is an indispensable condition of the will's activity.   The net outcome of his philosophy is to postulate the harmony of a will which is essentially discordant, or the value of that which is essentially "indifferent to or opposed to value." There is indeed, as Windelband acknowledges, "a rent in the fabric of reality." But there is also a rent in the fabric of a philosophical system which converts the undeniable conflict of values, both with one another and with existence, into an "insoluble problem," a "contradiction" and a "sacred mystery." [32]

V. THE AUTHORITATIVE OR OBLIGATORY WILL

§ 42. The 'Ought' as the Ultimate Form of Will. The absolute will is, as we have seen, primarily an epistemological conception.   Certain of its proponents endeavor to adhere strictly to this stand-point, and thus to avoid both the Scylla of psychology and the Charybdis of metaphysics.   It is evident, however, that it is difficult to argue for a principle unless that principle can be exhibited.   If one is to escape verbalism others must know that one is talking *about;* they must be referred to something which they can find and confirm for themselves.   This desire to escape psychology and metaphysics without becoming altogether meaningless, has led members of the neo-Kantian or "neo-critical" school to employ the conception of *ought.*   Windelband, for example, tells us that

---

[32] *Op. cit.,* pp. 356-358.   I am assuming that it is the business of philosophy to dispel mysteries, and not to create them, or to perpetuate them even when they are sacred.   It is the fashion for modern philosophies which affirm the harmony of all values to confess their inability to solve "the problem of evil"; their inability, in other words, to explain the fact that values are not harmonious.   If this confession were read first it would save much labor.

I have not developed all of the difficulties to which this philosophy of harmony gives rise.   I have, for example, ignored the duality of *positive* and *negative* values.   Shall we regard rejection, revulsion, disapprobation, as manifestations of the universal will, and their objects as absolute negative values?   If so, there remain two wills, the will for and the will against.   If not, then it must be supposed that I do not really will unless I will positively, and that all negative values are only apparent.   There is some degree of good, as there is some degree of truth, in everything, and it is this alone which is the proper object of will.   I shall leave it to the reader to pursue this line of reflection as far as he thinks it profitable.

"the only thing we can do is to say that truth is in all cases that which *ought* to be affirmed." [33] When the epistemological 'must' is thus translated, it at once takes on an aspect of familiarity. The 'ought,' as an immediate qualification of the will, is one of the central data of the moral life. It serves at once to *identify* the absolute will. The ought as applied to will or desire, the '*I*-ought,' the 'ought-to-*do*,' as contrasted with that 'ought-to-*be*' which we have already considered,[34] is an indubitable fact of human experience.

The examination of this fact will serve a double purpose. It will indicate one of the things which seems to be meant by the *absolute* will. On the other hand it will serve to define another and independent variety of that type of theory which is under consideration in the present chapter. For that qualified interest which is employed for the definition of value may be the *interest-that-ought-to-be-taken*. Good may thus be defined as the desirable in the sense of what one desires when one desires as one ought to desire; right, as what ought in this sense to be done, or approved; beauty, as what ought to be enjoyed; truth, as what ought to be believed.

If the conception of the authoritative or obligatory will is to be employed for the purpose of a generic definition of value, it must be shown to be in some sense the ultimate form of will. If the ought means the good or otherwise valuable will, then the above definitions are all circular. If ought is an indefinable predicate, then the present view is indistinguishable from several views already considered.[35] If, on the other hand, the ought is a *derived* or *special* form of will, then its object, while possessing value, will not possess value in the generic or inclusive sense. It is this last point upon which attention will be focussed in the analysis which follows.

Treating the matter empirically, we find five varieties of the authoritative or obligatory will: the *imperious* will,—the claim or inner sense of authority; the *personal* will, in its

[33] *Op. cit.*, pp. 173-174. (Italics mine.)
[34] Ch. III, Sect. V.
[35] Cf. §§ 17, 33.

authority over particular impulses; the *awe-inspiring* will, which induces respect for authority; the *collective* will, in its authority over human individuals; and the *rational* will in its precedence of the ignorant or false will.

§ 43. The Imperious Will. A man feels himself, on occasion, to be the instrument or channel of a will greater than his own. This sense of authority may exist in many forms. The most familiar form is *conscience,* in which a man's "higher" self makes certain demands upon his "lower" self. A man's conscience seems to speak to him with an authority that justifies his imposing it on others as well as himself. Besides the moral form of the sense of authority, there are many others. The intellectual form is the sense of infallibility. The artistic form is the sense of inspiration, —the religious form the sense of exaltation. The political forms is the sense of divine right, which expresses itself in such words as, "l'état, c'est moi." The aesthetic form is the sense of absolute taste which prompts the dogmatizing of connoisseurs and critics.

That such attitudes as these exist is not to be denied. Interests may be qualified by a sense of authoritativeness, and in so far as this is the case their objects will possess values of a distinctive sort. But it must be clearly recognized that these are particular attitudes which conflict with other attitudes, both within and without the individual. The conflict between inclination and the sense of duty is a genuine conflict between one interest and another, and there seems to be no good reason for imputing value to the object of the latter while denying it to the object of the other. Furthermore, these attitudes are all indeterminate as regards their object. There seems to be no object to which they cannot be directed. There is little if any subjective difference between the pride of genius and the delusions of grandeur. There is no maxim which one cannot as a matter of fact *will* to be law universal. The most tragic absurdities of fanaticism and bigotry spring from the most perfect assurance of authority, as the most inflexible intolerance springs from the most certain conviction of infallibility. Simmel, who is frequently cited among the prominent exponents of the irreducible sense of ought as the ground of values, has in fact pointed out that its irreducibility, its impressive and categorically authoritative character, is largely an effect of ignorance. Where the reasons for action have dropped out of mind, leaving only a vague, lingering trace of their force, the act takes on an aspect of mysterious imperativeness which the evident calculations of prudence lack.[36]   Indeed it might be said that unreasoning convictions take on a character of inflexibility because, being an expression of will or habit, they cannot be influenced by argument.

Moral experience affords the most familiar examples of the indeterminateness and perversity of the inward sense of authority.   A single example will suffice.   Edmund Gosse has given the following striking description of the state of mind of a religious convert who had committed forgery in order to disinherit his unbelieving son:

"My Father, setting aside by a strong effort of will the repugnance which he felt, visited the prisoner in gaol before this final evidence had been extracted.   When he returned he said that Dormant appeared to be enjoying a perfect confidence of heart, and had expressed a sense of his joy and peace in the Lord; my Father regretted that he had not been able to persuade him to admit any error, even of judgment.   But the prisoner's attitude in the dock, when the facts were proved, and not by him denied, was still more extraordinary.   He could be induced to exhibit no species of remorse, and, to the obvious anger of the judge himself, stated that he had only done his duty as a Christian, in preventing this wealth from coming into the hands of an ungodly man, who would have spent it in the service of the flesh and of the devil.   Sternly reprimanded by the judge, he made the final statement that at that very moment he was conscious of his Lord's presence, in the dock at his side, whispering to him 'Well done, thou good and faithful servant!'   In this frame of conscience, and with a glowing countenance, he was hurried away to penal servitude." [37]

§ 44. The Personal Will. It is in order to avoid the

[36] G. Simmel, *Einleitung in die Moralwissenschaft*, 1904, Vol. I, p. 32.
[37] *Father and Son*, pp. 249-251.

absurdity of attaching value preëminently to the objects of an attitude which may thus be directed to *any* object, even the most repugnant, that moralists have sought to define conscience in terms of the actual structure of will rather than in terms of its subjective form. The authoritative will is now identified not by its specific inward flavor of authority, but by the fact that it represents the individual in whole rather than in part. The authoritative will is the *personal* will. Thus, according to a recent writer " 'Good' is that which is liked on a broader view . . . the broadest an individual 'liking' subject can rise too." "Good is that which satisfies the individual 'character' or his 'abiding tendency.' " [38] "The value of an object," says another writer, "is the relation, whether merely felt or reflected upon, to the activity of the individual as a whole." [39]

We are here invited to consider the actual constitution of the person. It is implied that there are component interests, each directed to its own object. It is further pointed out that these interests subsume themselves under a constant or total disposition, within which they play limited rôles determined by their mutual relations. Finally, it is indicated that this integral or personal will may so far satisfy the component interests that they unite in its support. It then possesses authority by general consent. The personal will is thus in a sense willed in each and every particular or momentary will. In this way the ideal and harmonious self to which Green and others of his school refer, is given a specific content in terms of human nature and history.

But the personal will, so construed, cannot be said to be the only interest. It is, as Mr. Santayana has pointed out, a *resultant* of interests; and, as such, is meaningless unless such constituents are presupposed:

[38] J. Solomon, "Is the Conception of Good Indefinable?", *Proc. Aristotelian Society,* 1905-06, pp. 131, 133, 134.
[39] J. L. McIntyre, "Value-feelings and Judgments of Value," *Proc. Aristotelian Society,* 1904-05, p. 58. For the similar view of Th. Lipps, cf. W. M. Urban, *op. cit.,* p. 50. Cf. also Professor W. E. Hocking's view that "conscience stands outside the instinctive life of man, not as something separate, but as an *awareness of the success or failure of that life in maintaining its status and its growth*" (*Human Nature and its Remaking,* 1918, p. 99).

"If the ideal can confront particular desires and put them to shame, that happens only because the ideal is the object of a more ɪ ofound and voluminous desire and embodies the good which they blindly and perhaps deviously pursue. Demands could not be misdirected, goods sought could not be false, if the standard by which they are to be corrected were not constructed out of them. Otherwise, each demand would render its object a detached, absolute and unimpeachable good. But when each desire in turn has singed its wings and retired before some disillusion, reflection may set in to suggest residual satisfactions that may still be possible, or some shifting of the ground by which much of what was hoped for may yet be attained." [40]

Such an account is evidently a history, in which existent desires struggle, fail and eventually abandon a part of their claims in order to obtain a place in some corporate whole. There are some desires which cannot be accommodated at all, desires which cannot find even a limited satisfaction. Furthermore, even when such an organization is effected it is rarely, if ever, perfected. Particular desires remain rebellious, whether persistently or intermittently, whether openly or covertly.

The personal will, in this sense, is a fact, and if objects of will are valuable, then *its* objects are valuable. But it appears in a context of other dead or mutilated wills, which are equally facts, and whose objects have also a claim to be regarded as valuable. The objects of the personal will are *values of a certain sort*, perhaps of the sort which can most properly be deemed 'moral.' Furthermore, they may well be regarded as values of a superior sort. Because the objects of separate, transient or excluded impulses are *also* valuable, it does not follow that they are *equally* valuable. The personal will does not afford a definition of value, but it may and does constitute one of the criteria by which some values may be regarded as "superior" to other values. It has, in other words, an important bearing on the question of the gradation and hierarchy of value.[41]

[40] G. Santayana, *Life of Reason, Reason in Common Sense,* 1905, pp. 256-258. Cf. below, § 271.
[41] Cf. Ch. XXII, Sect. I.

§ 45. The Awe-Inspiring Will. Exponents of the authoritative will, seeking some anchorage in fact, can be counted upon sooner or later to appeal to *external authority*. It is a notorious and ironical fact that the modern idealistic theory of value, having repudiated the authority of nature, church and state in behalf of the inner authority of spirit, should have completed the circle by finding the criterion of the authoritative spirit in its "objective" institutional embodiments.

The respect for external authority, like the sense of inner authority, can be regarded as a psychological datum, and its varieties are not less numerous. Nature inspires respect by its seeming fatality, and submissive love by its seeming beneficence. Personal authorities, whether kings, priests, judges, heroes, or policemen are invested with authority in the eyes of humbler men. Symbols, whether religious or secular, readily assume the same aspect. Custom, law, the printed word, public opinion, and the judgment of mankind, possess a quality of finality to which the individual yields his assent. The religious imagination creates a cosmic majesty toward which it addresses its characteristic attitudes of abject submission, of awe or reverence, or of self-denying love. The fact is undeniable. Man is by nature fitted to obey as well as to command. It must be granted, furthermore, that men sometimes identify that authority which imposes itself from without, with that authority which they impose upon themselves within. In other words men *acknowledge* external authority as legitimate, and thereby make it internal as well.

With the further analysis or derivation of this state of mind we are not primarily concerned. It may be traced to a specific sense of dependence,—to ancestral or to childish fears. It may be attributed to a specific instinct of self-abasement, or to the magic of prestige. But whatever its specific quality or its natural genesis, it may be and often is regarded as the criterion of that standard will which distinguishes good from evil, or real from specious values. This is the theory of value according to which the essence of all values lies in discipline and loyalty,—a yielding of the private

will to the more august will of Nature, God, or Society, or
to what are taken to be their appointed agents.

The identification of value with the sense of external authority proves unacceptable for precisely the same reason that
discredits the sense of inner authority. External authoritativeness may and has been known to sanction conduct of
every conceivable variety, including the whole calendar of
crime. There is no act which may not be performed in a
spirit of obedience. There are tyrannies and abuses of authority which are no less willingly obeyed than the ordinances
of justice and benevolence.

> "Kings' titles commonly begin by force,
> Which time wears off and mellows into right."

Philosophers from Plato to Nietzsche have remarked that
the essence of true religion is not obedience, but a right conception of that which is worthy of obedience. In like manner
the essence of true patriotism may be held to lie in a right
conception of one's country, rather than in ready surrender
to any claim which is made in its behalf. But it is evident
that the question is now again shifted. We are no longer
content with the trappings of authority, or with the spell
which these exercise upon the individual; we are now ques-
tioning the *title* of authority. We are virtually saying that
an authority is not really such by virtue of the command
which it assumes or the submission which it evokes, but only
by virtue of some inherent nature which it possesses. On
these terms it is quite conceivable that a will should be authoritative even though it spoke in accents of humility, and
even though it was heard with indifference or derision.

§ 46. **The Collective Will.** What sort of authority external to the individual may be said to possess authority
over him? There is a common answer to this question which
invokes the same principle of synthesis that is employed for
defining the personal will. Just as the several component
interests of the person may be subsumed under a resultant
ideal, so, it is maintained, a plurality of persons may be

subsumed under a *collective will.* This may be identified with the unorganized generality of custom, opinion or culture, or with the organized unity of church or state. According to sociologists of the Durkheim school it expresses itself in the "collective representations"; or in that higher social subject which "possesses a moral reality richer and more complex than our own" and therefore evokes our disinterested devotion. According to idealists of the Hegelian tradition it expresses itself more especially in "the laws and the political constitution." [42] In both schools of thought reference is made to a still more comprehensive divine or absolute will, which is conceived as an extension of the social will, and derives its meaning from its social analogue.

Here again, as in the case of the personal will, attention is invited to the presence of a certain complex structure in human life. There is no infallible sign of its existence. A will is not said to be authoritative simply because it claims to be, or is acknowledged to be; but only when and in so far as it does in fact represent, and take up into itself, a plurality of individual wills. It is then said to be authoritative over any given individual by virtue of constituting a will of a higher order, or by virtue of the fact that it incorporates and satisfies that individual. Whether any given custom or sentiment, or ruling power does so embody a plurality of wills, or does embody the particular will whose allegiance is demanded, is in each case a question of empirical fact.

It is by no means certain that it is proper to speak of a collective will. But even granting that such synthetic forms of social will do occur, they are, like personal wills, *products of organization.* They emerge, if they do emerge, in a con-

---

[42] G. Davy, *Émile Durkheim, Choix de Textes,* 1911, pp. 160–161; B. Bosanquet, in *The International Crisis in its Ethical and Psychological Aspects,* 1915, pp. 133–135. Cf. e.g., W. Windelband, *Introduction to Philosophy,* trans. by J. McCabe, 1921, § 15: "This (the evolution of custom into morals and law) shows us that at the base of every existing community there is a psychic collective life, especially a collective will, in a form that is obscure, vague, and unconscious of its own grounds" (p. 266). For a further analysis of these conceptions, cf. the writer's *Present Conflict of Ideals,* 1918, pp. 81–86, and Ch. XVIII; and below, Ch. XIV–XVI, XXII.

text of private wills, which they supersede, or perhaps generate.[43] There is, therefore, no justification for a view which would assert that such a will exists exclusively, or that the values which it determines are the only values. The collective will, like the personal will, should be regarded as one among many forms of the motor-affective life, and its objects as forming one among many classes of values. Such values may perhaps be assigned a superior or the superlative rank in the hierarchy of values,[44] but they do not constitute values in that generic sense which is here in question.

§ 47. The Rational Will.

We have now to consider the doctrine that the authoritative or obligatory will is *the rational will*. According to this view "my ultimate good" is "what I should desire if my desires were in harmony with reason." [45] The authoritative will is that will which the logic of the situation requires, and to which I assent in so far as I am enlightened. The imperative character attaching to such a will consists in the necessity with which conclusions follow from premises. With this view is associated the ethical tradition which identifies conscience with intellect, or rightness with truth; and the religious tradition which identifies the authority of God with his omniscience.

We start with the notion that an act of will like anything else may be deduced from a principle. But there are two quite distinct ways in which this may be done, according as the principle is an explanatory *law*, or a guiding *maxim*. Let us consider, for example, the principle of heredity, as implying that the eldest son of a hereditary ruler shall display the same disinterestedness and sense of responsibility as his father. In the one case, the son's resemblance to his father is adequately explained by the biological *law*, 'like father like son.' The son may or may not be aware of such a law, but in any case this is not a condition of its operation. In the second case, the son's action is guided by the *maxim*

---

[43] Even if, as is sometimes argued, the collective will is genetically prior to the personal will, the antithesis exists none the less.

[44] Cf. Ch. XXII, Sect. II.

[45] H. Sidgwick, *Methods of Ethics*, 1893, p. 112.

of filial piety, 'be like your father.' It is his purpose to emulate his father, and his possession of disinterestedness and sense of responsibility are in this case due to his *judgment* that such sentiments are paternal traits.

Another example is furnished by the principle of self-preservation. This is a *law* of action if and in so far as the agent's conduct is directly implied by it. It is a *maxim* of action in so far as an agent performs what he himself deduces, or believes is implied by it. In both cases the act bears a necessary relation to the principle, and in that sense 'ought' to occur. But in the second case the judgment of necessity is a condition of the occurrence of the act, whereas in the first case it is not. The relation of the two is seen in the fact that when self-preservation is the maxim of conduct, the law of conduct is not self-preservation, but self-*interest*. In the one case, the agent does what *preserves* himself; in the other what he *thinks* will preserve himself.

When one speaks of the rational will one intends the second of these cases rather than the first. It is the conviction of the necessity of an act relatively to a principle, when this conviction is felt by an agent who has adopted the principle as his maxim. Where the agent is thus appropriately disposed, the effect is to transform a logical necessity into an active impulse; or to create at one and the same time a coercion of intellect and a coercion of will.[46]

Owing to the close juxtaposition of these two factors, philosophers are tempted to merge them into something called "practical reason" or the "logic of practise." But this has the unfortunate effect of suggesting that there is something peculiar about the intellectual factor itself, whereas the only peculiarity lies in its context and application. Suppose a man to have adopted the principle of imitating his father. He prefers such acts as he believes to be like his father in their form or in their consequences. Prove to him that any given act, such as charity to the poor, is like his father, and he both sees its necessity as implied by his conception of his

---

[46] When the agent's conviction is true, this is the same as the "well-founded" will, discussed above, § 41.

father, and also feels impelled to perform it, since it is now identified with what is by hypothesis the object of his will. But his inferring of the act from the conception of his father does not differ as such from his other inferences, such as those of mathematical reasoning. It so happens that in this case the inference concerns a general object of his will, and therefore determines the particular direction in which that will shall take effect.

Indeed it is precisely this separability of the purely intellectual factor that gives the act its character of authority. The necessity of the act as implied by the principle is independent of the agent's will. It is this which must be, whether he likes it or not. It is this which is equally evident to others who do not share his will, or to that imaginary "impartial spectator" which moralists like Adam Smith have invoked. It is this which makes his act a fair topic of discussion, and justifies the intervention of critics who may be in possession of evidence that he lacks. It is true that those who remind a man of his duty are ordinarily not disinterested. Here also, as in the case of the personal conviction of duty, there is a blending of cogency and will; or, as Professor Hocking expresses it, "a shade of menace in the attitude with which the 'ought' bears down upon you." [47] This is because a man's maxims are ordinarily *professed,* and thus become promises upon which others base their calculations. Moral maxims, furthermore, are usually adopted jointly by all members of the community. They are engagements which it is every man's interest that every man should keep. It is true none the less that a man can remind me of my *duty* only in so far as he can *deduce* my action from the engagement, as from an accepted premiss. Otherwise he can only exhort or threaten retaliation.

§ 48. **The Categorical versus the Hypothetical Imperative.** Before drawing any final conclusions as to the possibility of defining value in terms of the rational will we must consider a distinction which Kant has made famous, and

[47] *Op. cit.,* p. 92.

which is much emphasized in current thought owing to that philosopher's influence.

"Now all *imperatives* command either *hypothetically* or *categorically*. The former represent the practical necessity of a possible action as means to something else that is willed (or at least which one might possibly will). The categorical imperative would be that which represented an action as necessary without reference to another end, *i.e.*, as objectively necessary. . . . If now the action is good only as a means *to something else,* then the imperative is *hypothetical;* if it is conceived as good *in itself* and consequently as being necessarily the principle of a will which of itself conforms to reason, then it is *categorical."* [48]

It is clear that the imperative which we have just considered is hypothetical in Kant's sense. It owes its force as a motive to the existing disposition of the agent, and loses its force when the agent alters his maxim. Indeed, there is no more effective way of inducing such an alteration than to demonstrate to the agent just what specific duties his maxim implies. One can, it is true, argue the agent's duty to adopt a given principle as his maxim; but only by subsuming this principle under a more general principle which is already the agent's maxim. Thus it may be that a man ought to adopt the principle of emulating his father, because his father is wise. But this will be the agent's duty in the present sense, only provided he is already disposed to emulate the most wise; so that his obligation remains no more and no less categorical than before. The act so sanctioned will, as Kant says, be good as a means, and not good in itself. It cannot, therefore, be good in the fundamental or generic sense.

There is, however, an aspect of rational obligation, which may be thought to justify the use of the term 'categorical.' Let us consider the hypothetical obligation, "If you wish to emulate your father, you ought to be charitable to the poor." This obligation is effective, as we have seen, only provided the agent both harbors the wish to emulate his father, and also is convinced that this implies charity. But there is a force in this conviction which is independent of the wish;

[48] Kant: *Fundamental Principles of the Metaphysics of Morals,* second Section, Abbott's translation, 1889, p. 31.

it depends not upon the agent's sentiment toward his father, but only upon the evidence regarding his father's character. This evidence will not, it is true, induce conviction unless the agent is receptive to evidence, and he must desire the truth if he is to feel any obligation to believe as he does. But this obligation to believe is independent of his filial sentiment, and in that sense is categorical. One may, therefore, construe the categorical imperative to mean *that particular hypothetical imperative which is conditioned only by the subject's cognitive purpose.* This is perhaps what Kant means when he speaks of the categorical imperative as "the principle of a will which of itself conforms to reason." Obligation in this sense is relative to the rational will, conceived as a will to be reasonable.

But while there is such an obligation, it is in its own terms as 'hypothetical' as any other obligation. Its object cannot be said to be valuable in the fundamental sense, because its value is only that of a means to truth. It is, furthermore, an obligation which affects only the act of belief. Such values as it yields can be combined with other values, as in the values of the well-founded will. But they cannot be substituted for other values; nor, as we have seen, can other values be deduced from them.

There remains one further aspect of the situation which may seem to provide for a genuinely categorical imperative. It is a well-known fact that a logical hypothetical may always be converted into a categorical form. This is as true of hypothetical propositions concerning acts, as of any other hypothetical propositions. Thus the hypothetical 'If you wish to emulate your father you ought to be charitable to the poor,' can be converted into the form, 'Emulation of your father implies charity to the poor.' And here, at last, is a "practical necessity of a possible action" that is wholly independent of the agent's will, even of his will to be reasonable. The agent may neglect to adopt it as his maxim; he may even shut his eyes to it; but this does not in the least shake the necessity of the implication. It holds none the less, though no man conforms to it either his heart or his mind.

This is perhaps what Kant means by an action represented as "objectively necessary." We are here brought back to that implication of an act by a principle, with which we started. Obligation is now held to consist not in any bearing which such an implication may have upon the will of the agent, but in the bare element of necessity. The 'ought' of the moral life is identified with the 'must' of logic and mathematics.

It may well be that the peculiar compulsion characteristic of the rational will arises from the lurking presence of just this factor. But in that case we must go further, and acknowledge that the rational will is bound not only by inexorable necessities, but also by the stubborn indifference of brute fact. Indeed the former proves in the last analysis to be only a case of the latter. Objectivity consists essentially in that *independence* of the knowing mind which is possessed by all facts. In so far, therefore, as cognition is a component or condition of any act of volition, there will be this yielding or deference to fact. Thus justice or benevolence is a categorical duty in the sense that whether the agent endorses them or not, whether he recognizes them or ignores them, the interests of his fellows are *there,* and will give to his act a character, additive or privative, that is beyond his control.

But although this independent character of facts may thus be an ingredient of value, and seem to give a peculiarly 'objective' character to certain values, it cannot be used to define value. Even should it be maintained that existence and necessity are values, value must be defined in terms other than those implied by existence and necessity in this naïve and realistic acceptance.[49]

The present chapter has proved the failure of divers attempts to define value in terms of a peculiarly qualified will or interest. But incidently we have learned something about the forms which interest may assume. We have discovered that interests may be final, harmonious, well-

[49] Cf. §§ 39, 41.

grounded, subjectively and objectively authoritative, personally or socially synthetic, and hypothetically or categorically rational. Since all of these forms of interest exist, while none of them exists exclusively, it follows that they define varieties or grades of value, and not value itself. At the same time it has become clear by implication that such a definition of value in the generic sense is afforded by *the generic conception of interest*. To the positive and constructive formulation of such a definition we now turn.

CHAPTER V

VALUE AS ANY OBJECT OF ANY INTEREST [1]

I. PRELIMINARY FORMULATION AND ARGUMENT

§ 49. Exposition and Illustration. It is characteristic of living mind to be *for* some things and *against* others. This polarity is not reducible to that between 'yes' and 'no' in the logical or in the purely cognitive sense, because one can say 'yes' with reluctance or be glad to say 'no.' To be 'for' or 'against' is to view with favor or disfavor; it is a bias of the subject toward or away from. It implies, as we shall see more clearly in the sequel, a tendency to create or conserve, or an opposite tendency to prevent or destroy. This duality appears in many forms, such as liking and disliking, desire and aversion, will and refusal, or seeking and avoiding. It is to this all-pervasive characteristic of the motor-affective life, this *state, act, attitude or disposition of favor or disfavor,* to which we propose to give the name of *'interest.'* [2]

This, then, we take to be the original source and constant feature of all value. That which is an object of interest is *eo ipso* invested with value. [3] Any object, whatever it be,

[1] Parts of the present chapter and of Ch. VII are reprinted from an article entitled "A Behavioristic View of Purpose," published in the *Jour. of Philos.,* Vol. XVIII, 1921.

[2] Cf. § 14. The term 'interest' has been employed for technical purposes by various psychologists, but by none, I think, in the precise sense in which it is employed here. W. Mitchell, in his *Structure and Growth of Mind,* 1907, defines interest as our "feeling towards" an object, or, as how the object "strikes or affects us" (p. 64) ; whereas I propose to use the term to embrace desire and disposition as well. G. F. Stout, in his *Groundwork of Psychology,* 1903, uses the term for organized and permanent forms of the emotional life, such as sentiments [pp. 221 ff.]. More commonly 'interest' is employed by psychology to mean *attention.*

[3] An object is valuable when *qualified* by an act of interest; relation to interest assuming, in the experience or judgment of value, the rôle of adjective.

acquires value when any interest, whatever it be, is taken in it; just as anything whatsoever becomes a target when anyone whosoever aims at it. In other words, Aristotle was fundamentally mistaken when he said, that as a thing's "apparent good" makes it an object of appetite, so its real good makes it the object of "rational desire." [4] By the same token Spinoza was fundamentally correct when he said that

"in no case do we strive for, wish for, long for, or desire anything, because we deem it to be good, but on the other hand we deem a thing to be good, because we strive for it, wish for it, long for it, or desire it." [5]

The view may otherwise be formulated in the equation: x is valuable $=$ interest is taken in x. Value is thus a specific relation into which things possessing any ontological status whatsoever, whether real or imaginary, may enter with interested subjects.

This is value *simpliciter*,—value in the elementary, primordial and generic sense. It follows that any variation of interest or of its object will determine a variety of value; that any derivative of interest or its object will determine value in a derived sense; and that any condition of interest or its object will determine a conditional value. In short, interest being constitutive of value in the basic sense, theory of value will take this as its point of departure and centre of reference; and will classify and systematize values in terms of the different forms which interests and their objects may be found to assume.

This view has rarely found a perfectly clear and consistent expression. It is, however, essentially conveyed in an early work of Mr. George Santayana:

"Apart from ourselves, and our human bias, we can see in such a mechanical world no element of value whatever. In removing consciousness, we have removed the possibility of

---

[4] *Metaphysica*, XII, Ch. 7, trans. by W. D. Ross, 1072a.
[5] *Ethics*, Part III, Prop. IX, Note, trans. by R. H. M. Elwes, 1901. It is, of course, possible to desire a thing because it is good, where its goodness consists in its being desired by other subjects, or by some other interest of the same subject. But *in the last analysis* good springs from desire and not desire from good.

worth. But it is not only in the absence of all consciousness that value would be removed from the world; by a less violent abstraction from the totality of human experience, we might conceive beings of a purely intellectual cast, minds in which the transformations of nature were mirrored without any emotion. . . . No event would be repulsive, no situation terrible. . . . In this case, as completely as if consciousness were absent altogether, all value and excellence would be gone. . . . Values spring from the immediate and inexplicable reaction of vital impulse, and from the irrational part of our nature. . . . The ideal of rationality is itself as arbitrary, as much dependent on the needs of a finite organization, as any other ideal." [6]

A more recent statement, and one more explicitly in accord with the view here proposed, is the following:

"Anything is properly said to have value in case, and only in case, it is the object of the affective motor response which we call being *interested* in, positively or negatively. . . . The being liked, or disliked, of the object is its value. And since the being liked or disliked, is being the object of a motor-affective attitude in a subject, some sort of a subject is always requisite to there being value at all—not necessarily a *judging* subject, but a subject capable of at least motor-affective response. For the cat the cream has value, or better and more simply, the cat values the cream, or the warmth, or having her back scratched, quite regardless of her probable inability to conceive cream or to make judgments concerning warmth." [7]

§ 50. **Approximations and Misconceptions.** It may appear surprising that a doctrine so familiar, if not banal, as that just stated, should have received so little authoritative support. Rarity is the last thing that would have been expected of it, either by its advocates who regard it as sound common-sense, or by its opponents who regard it as vulgar error. It is none the less a fact that this doctrine has rarely

[6] *The Sense of Beauty*, 1899, pp. 17-19. Cf. also William James: *"The essence of good is to satisfy demand"* (*Will to Believe*, etc., 1898, p. 201).

[7] D. W. Prall, *A Study in the Theory of Value*, Univ. of California Publications in Philosophy, Vol. 3, No. 2, 1921, pp. 215, 227. The present writer is in essential agreement with the whole of this admirable monograph.

been explicitly avowed by philosophers. The reasons for this fact are extremely illuminating, and although they have been repeatedly alluded to, a brief recapitulation of them at this point will serve to sharpen the meaning of our definition.

All of these reasons are traceable to an imperfect conception of the problem itself. Theory of value in the contemporary sense has asked a new question, to which none of the traditional philosophical doctrines is precisely relevant. It may, perhaps, be fair to say that this question has been *tacitly* asked and answered; but it is evident that a tacit answer cannot be quoted. This new question, is the question, *In what consists value in the generic sense?* It is because neither philosophy nor common-sense has ordinarily been explicitly and unambiguously concerned with this question that so few explicit and unambiguous answers to it can be found. Most theories of value are intended not as answers to this question, but as answers to some one or more of the following questions: What is uniquely valuable? What is superlatively valuable? What is reflectively or consciously valuable? The history of thought abounds in opinions which identify value with interest, but in nearly all cases these opinions are formulated in terms of one of these questions, and cannot, therefore, be cited as generic definitions of value in the sense here proposed.

Perhaps the most ancient and persistent notion of value is *hedonism,* which construes good in terms of pleasure, and evil in terms of pain. But hedonistic writers cannot be cited in support of the doctrine here proposed, because they have been primarily concerned to show that only pleasure and pain *possess* value. If we turn to the authoritative formulation of this doctrine by Bentham, we read that "nature has placed mankind under the governance of two sovereign masters, *pain* and *pleasure."* [8] John Stuart Mill begins with the assertion that "question about ends are . . . questions what things are desirable"; adds that "the sole evidence it is possible to produce that anything is desirable, is that people do actually desire it"; and presently concludes "that there is in reality

[8] *Principles of Morals and. Legislation,* Ch. I.

nothing desired except happiness." [9] Bentham, in other words, asserts that pleasure and pain are the only governing motives in human action; and Mill, that only happiness is desired. They are both concerned to show that pleasure and pain are the *unique objects* of interest. It is doubtless true that they both assume a more fundamental principle, to the effect that value means motive-power, or object-of-desire-and-avoidance. Without such a major premiss the argument would be palpably incomplete, and would have none of the moral implications which they impute to it. But since this major premiss is only tacitly or dogmatically avowed by the utilitarian school, and since it is the very question at issue in a general theory of value, the members of this school cannot be cited as in clear and explicit agreement with the view here proposed.

Philosophers, like the average man, have been as a rule more interested in the scale of values than in the generic nature of value. As we have already seen, most theory of value that has emanated from "high metaphysics," or from the grand tradition, has been wholly preoccupied with the former of these questions. It has preferred to discuss the Highest Good, rather than low and middling goods; or to deal with value in a eulogistic and edifying manner, rather than simply to describe it. But it is astonishing how persistent, how almost ineradicable, is this tendency even among contemporary and otherwise emancipated philosophers. Thus Professor S. Alexander seems to give us aid and comfort when he says:

"In every value there are two sides, the subject of valuation and the object of value, and the value resides in the relation between the two, and does not exist apart from them. . . . Value is not mere pleasure, or the capacity of giving it, but is the satisfaction of an appetite of the valuer. It satisfies the liking for knowledge, or for doing, or producing. Even the breast is valuable to the infant because it satisfies a need for food. Values arise out of our likings and satisfy them."

[9] *Utilitarianism*, 1863, pp. 51, 52, 56. There is a further ambiguity in Mill, since he does not clearly distinguish between the view that only happiness is desired, and the view that *whatever* is desired yields happiness.

So far, so good. But presently this writer qualifies his statement:

"Value pleases but it pleases after a certain fashion. What this fashion of pleasing is has been shown to be social. . . . . Value has reference to a type, and it relates to the individual only in so far as he represents a type. The individual may like or dislike certain things, but in the proper sense they have value for him if they satisfy him as typical; and his individual liking may be altogether disproportionate, as his liking for alcohol, to the value of what he likes. What is called 'subjective value' (*Werthhaltung*) is not in itself value but is a derivative conception, and so far as it is *value* implies the existence of 'objective,' which is really the only, value."

Thus Professor Alexander betrays the fact that he is really interested in *proper* or *objective* value, in value "in the strictest sense," rather than value in the generic sense. There is not the slightest objection to a study of typical or socialized values; but when after having explicitly shown them to constitute a *special variety* of value, the author states that they are "really the only values," and speaks of the disqualified instinctive or individual values as "quasi-values," we can only conclude regretfully that the author has not *defined* value at all, and must abandon our first hope of his powerful support.[10]

The same difficulty prevents our claiming the support of Mr. J. L. McIntyre, who says that "the value of an object . . . is its relation, whether felt or reflected upon, to the activity of the *individual as a whole*"; or of J. Solomon, who says:

" 'Good' in fact means 'liked' or 'valued' or 'approved,' and yet we may without inconsistency deny that all that is liked is good. . . . For 'good' is that which is liked *on a broad view*, taking in the future as well as the present, others as well as ourselves—not a view however ideally broad, perfectly comprehensive, but the broadest the individual 'liking' subject can rise to." [11]

[10] *Space, Time and Deity,* 1920, Vol. II, pp. 302-303, 304, 307.
[11] J. L. McIntyre, "Value-Feelings and Judgments of Value," *Proc. Aristotelian Society,* 1904-05, p. 58. J. Solomon, "Is the Conception of 'Good' Undefinable?", *ibid.,* 1905-06, p. 131. (Italics mine.)

Even Meinong and Ehrenfels, who explicitly adopt a psychological method, and are relatively free from the metaphysical and ethical tradition, nevertheless manifest this same tendency to limit value to some specially qualified form of the motor-affective life; and in particular to relate value to some *unified* and *constant* interest of the individual. Thus, according to the former, the value of an object lies in the total reaction of the subject, the sum of the feelings and desires evoked by the supposition of the object's existence and non-existence, when conditions are most favorable to bringing these into play.[12]

Professor Ehrenfels, of all the earlier investigators in this field, has most nearly anticipated the views developed in the present study. He has defined value in the following terms:

"Value is a relation between an object and a subject, which expresses the fact that the subject either actually desires the object, or would desire it in case he were not convinced of its existence."[13]

But the author's provision for what the subject *would* desire under suitable conditions, a provision already indicated in this definition and further developed in his later writings, has furnished a certain justification for Mr. McIntyre's contention that he, like Meinong, appeals in the last analysis not simply to "the feeling or willing side of the mental nature," but to "the individual as a whole with his practical interests, his past history, his conviction of a future destiny."[14]

That there is a type of value relative to the individual as a whole, and that such a value may be in some measurable sense greater than that of present feeling or transient impulse, is not to be denied. But the view advanced in the present chapter requires that this value shall be regarded as a value-species, and not as the value-genus.

[12] A. Meinong: "Für die Psychologie und gegen den Psychologismus in der allgemeinen Werttheorie," *Logos*, Vol. III, 1912, p. 7.

[13] *System der Werttheorie*, 1897, Vol. I, p. 65.

[14] J. L. McIntyre, *op. cit.*, p. 65. Mr. McIntyre's argument is, I believe, in the main unfounded, since Ehrenfels's hypothetical desire is an *actual disposition*: but Ehrenfels has undoubtedly exposed himself to the criticism, being betrayed by his desire to obtain a method of *measuring* value.

§ 51. Ambiguity Arising from the Term 'Valuing.' We
have, finally, to note those views which, while they identify
value with interest, propose to limit value to the cases in
which something is *deemed* valuable, or in which value itself
is assigned *by* the subject *to* the object. Some of the writers
already cited, such as Professor Alexander and Meinong, have
aggravated the ambiguity of their position by the partial or
occasional use of this restriction.[15]   A doubtful case is furnished by the view of Kreibig.   This writer declares that

"the value is never an inherent attribute or character of an
object of the outer world, but is of a wholly subjective nature.
We take, therefore, the standpoint of the subjectivity of value,
and disavow the affirmation of 'objective values.' "

But presently it appears that value is "the import which
a content of sense or thought has for a subject owing to the
feeling, actual or potential, united with it either directly or
associatively." [16]   We are thus left in doubt whether the feeling *confers* value on the object, or is a mode of awareness
by which the object's value or 'import' is immediately known.
'Import' in other words, suggests not a relation simply, but
rather a 'tertiary quality' attaching to the object.

The question turns upon a natural but vicious confusion
connected with the term 'valuing.'   In general conformity
with the view offered in the present chapter, value might be
defined as *the relation of an object to a valuing subject*.   But
in what consists the act of valuing?   If it means simply
liking, desiring or being otherwise favorably disposed to the
object, then it yields a definition in essential agreeement with
that which is advanced in the present chapter.   If, on the
other hand, it means finding, deeming or judging valuable, then
it yields a definition which is essentially different, granting that

---

[15] Thus Professor Alexander says that "value in the form of the
tertiary qualities emerges not with consciousness or mind as such, which
the animals also possess, but with reflective consciousness or judgment"
(*op. cit.*, p. 304).   Meinong, who is throughout insistent on the cognitive
and quasi-cognitive character of valuation, says that "Wert ist das durch
Werterlebnisse Präsentirte" (*op. cit.*, p. 12).

[16] J. K. Kreibig, *Psychologische Grundlegung eines Systems der Werttheorie*, 1902, pp. 6, 12.

it can be freed from redundancy.[17] The latter meaning appears to be that adopted by Professor Urban, when he speaks of "sense of worth," "sense of value," and "feeling of value." He appears, in other words, to regard the motor-affective attitude of the subject, which he calls "the worth-moment," not as that which constitutes value, but rather as that which apprehends it.[18]

Professor John Dewey departs fundamentally from the view here advocated in so far as he refers to "the unique, the experienced, but undefinable, quality of value." Neither interest nor judgment can constitute this quality of value, they can only condition a thing's acquiring it. But that which is distinctively characteristic of this writer is his view that "the relation of judgment or reflection to things having value is as direct and integral as that of liking." [19]

This emphasis upon judgment is supported by two arguments. In the first place, objects are valued, and hence acquire value, through being conceived, judged or qualified in a certain manner. There is in valuation a reflective process in the course of which the object is exhibited in this or that light, and prized accordingly. "The purpose of judgment in this case," says Professor Dewey, "is not to state but to enstate a value." [20] Such a judgment is not a judgment *of* value, in the sense of having value for its object; but is a mediating judgment which defines and indicates the object of interest. Value is not conferred by this judgment, but by the supervening interest.[21]

In the second place, Professor Dewey argues that "judg-

---

[17] To say that an object is valuable when it is judged to be valuable, appears to be either viciously or sceptically relative, if *all* judgments are accepted; or merely redundant, if only *true* judgments are accepted. In the latter case one virtually says that an object is valuable when it is in fact valuable. This whole topic of the value-judgment is reconsidered in § 57; and in Chap. XII, Sect. II.

[18] W. M. Urban, *Valuation*, 1909, pp. 38-41. That value is, according to this writer, objective and non-psychological, appears clearly in his later writings. Cf. above, Ch. III, Sect. V.

[19] "Value, Liking and Thought," *Jour. of Philos.*, Vol. XX, 1923, pp. 617, 618. Cf. Santayana's view, cited above, § 16.

[20] *Op. cit.*, p. 326.

[21] The point requires a systematic examination of the rôle of cognition in interest. Cf. Ch. XII, *passim*.

ments of practise," such, for example, as the selection of means, or the adoption of plans, bring their objects to pass. One creates what one judges to be good.[22] But the effect of judgment cannot be said to be its object, since it must have an object in order to be a judgment, and since it occurs as a judgment before its consequences are unfolded. Nor does the object acquire value from being judged or expected as an effect, but only from the fact that this expectation moves one to act.

In neither case, therefore, can it properly be said that value is conferred on an object by the act of judgment; and whatever be the merits of this question, it is evident that Professor Dewey cannot be cited as one who unambiguously affirms interest to be constitutive of value in the basic sense.

§ 52. Summary of the Argument. How is the view here proposed to be proved? What is the evidence upon which it rests?

In the first place, we have reached it by a process of systematic elimination. We have first examined and eliminated those views which affirm value to be indefinable, or to be definable independently of interest. If value cannot be successfully identified or defined without reference to interest, then we must incorporate interest into our definition. We have next examined those views which relate value to interest in some qualified and exclusive sense; first, those views which have proposed to qualify and limit the object of interest; second, those views which have proposed to qualify and limit the act or state of interest itself. The result has been to exhibit a variety of values all having the common generic character of being 'object-of-interest.' We have thus been led to define value as the peculiar relation between any interest and its object; or that special character of an object which consists in the fact that interest is taken in it. We are now justified in framing this hypothesis as a last remaining alternative. There is a certain presumption in favor of this remaining alternative not only because of the elimination of

[22] For a further examination of this argument, cf. § 151.

the others, but also because these have all betrayed a common tendency. They have not only through their failure left the field clear for our definition of value, but they have *pointed* to that definition and incidentally argued in its support.

A certain positive plausibility is given to this hypothesis by the fact that in order to create values where they did not exist before it seems to be sufficient to introduce an interest. The silence of the desert is without value, until some wanderer finds it lonely and terrifying; the cataract, until some human sensibility finds it sublime, or until it is harnessed to satisfy human needs. Natural substances or the by-products of manufacture are without value until a use is found for them, whereupon their value may increase to any degree of preciousness according to the eagerness with which they are coveted. There is no entity that can be named that does not, in the very naming of it, take on a certain value through the fact that it is selected by the cognitive purpose of some interested mind. As interests grow and expand, multiplying in number and extending their radius through experience and imagination, the store of cosmic values is enriched and diversified.

But it may be contended that such proof is redundant or verbal. It proves only that objects of interest appear whenever interest is taken in objects; or, it proves at most that what is added to a given situation when interests are introduced corresponds closely to what it is customary to *call* value. It does not add to our knowledge by demonstrating the existence of value where it was not suspected, or by resolving doubts as to what is *really* valuable.

This objection again brings to light the difference between the general definition of value and the solution of special questions of value. The doubts and perplexities of everyday life, as well as the limited theoretical problems of the several value-sciences, commonly assume a general definition of value, and turn upon some question of fact. Is this distant island worth annexing and defending? The answer depends upon the existence of mineral deposits or a good harbor, assuming that it is worth annexing if the satisfactions and utilities which it affords outweigh the sacrifices which it costs. Ought I to surrender my position for the sake of my scruples, or compromise temporarily in the hope of converting others to my way of thinking? The answer depends on certain probable trains of consequences following from each of the alternatives, assuming that the one or the other ought to be adopted in accordance with the principle of human happiness, broadly applied. Is recent American verse to be ranked as genuine poetry? The answer depends experimentally on the sort of feeling aroused in certain persons, such as the critic himself, by the prolonged and attentive reading of it, on the assumption that such a judgment of taste is decisive. Is the economic worth or the aesthetic superiority of a work of art dependent on its moral wholesomeness? The answer is assumed to depend on the record of market transactions, or the reported sentiments of connoisseurs.

Now the general definition of value does not directly answer any such question, because it does not ascertain the specific facts and probabilities upon which they turn. It concerns itself with the *assumption,* and must therefore always appear to deal with the obvious rather than with the questionable. Its proper task is to make these assumptions explicit and consistent. By so doing it will inevitably affect the solution of such special questions, since it will prescribe the terms or the principle of their solution. But it has to do with the use which is to be made of evidence, rather than with the uncovering of new facts.

It follows that there can be no conclusive proof of a general definition of value, short of its success in facilitating the solution of all special questions of value. Such a definition is *an experiment in generalization.* If we adopt the fact of interest as our centre of reference, and view other facts of the surrounding field *in that relation*—if, in short, we take life *interest-wise,* as it can, in fact, be taken—do the data and the perplexities denoted by 'good' and 'evil,' 'right' and 'wrong,' 'better' and 'worse,' or grouped within the special fields of morality, art, religion and kindred institutions, then fall into place and form a comprehensive system? It is evident that the only proof of which such a hypothesis is capable lies in its complete elaboration. In short the argument for the thesis submitted in the present study is cumulative, and cannot properly claim the assent of the reader until the last chapter is written.

II. REPLY TO THE CHARGE OF RELATIVISM

§ 53. **Relativism as an Epithet.** Although no conclusive proof of the present view is possible until it is completely elaborated, it has been supposed that there is a conclusive *disproof* which can be urged without further ado. To attribute value to any object of any interest is at once to expose oneself to the charge of *relativism,* whatever the psychological details, and however successful such a definition may prove for purposes of systematic generalization.

No one can afford to disregard this charge. Relativism is an epithet which implies disparagement, when, as is often the case, it implies nothing more. Even the respectable scientific authority which has pronounced in its favor has not saved the physical theory of relativity from being regarded as somewhat *risqué,*—as evidence of the corruption of the times or of the malicious influence of the Semitic mind. There is no man who would not rather be absolute than relative, even though he has not the faintest conception of the meaning of either term.

This sentiment is peculiarly strong in the field of values, and preëminently in the province of morals. Nothing could be more scandalous than these lines of Sir Richard Burton:

"There is no good, there is no bad, these be the whims of mortal
    will;
What works me weal that call I good, what harms and hurts
    I hold as ill.
They change with space, they shift with race, and in the veriest
    space of time,
Each vice has worn a virtue's crown, all good been banned as
    sin or crime." [23]

[23] Quoted by L. Dickinson, *Meaning of Good,* 1907, p. 5.

How much nobler and more edifying in tone are such utterances as these of Froude and Carlyle:

"The eternal truths and rights of things exist, fortunately, independent of our thoughts or wishes, fixed as mathematics, inherent in the nature of man and the world. They are no more to be trifled with than gravitation."

"What have men to do with interests? There is a right way and a wrong way. That is all we need think about it." [24]

Yet there can scarcely be more offence in the adjective 'relative' than there is in the substantive 'relation'; and when we investigate the world in which we live, we discover as a rule that what we took to be an absolute does as a matter of fact both stand in relations and comprise relations. In any case we shall be influenced only by such *theoretical* difficulties as may be urged against a relativistic theory of value, and not in the least by practical or sentimental objections.

§ 54. **Epistemological Relativism, or Scepticism.** There is unquestionably one form of relativism which is theoretically objectionable. He who identifies the act of *cognizing* values with that act of the subject which *constitutes* them, or holds that values are both known and created in one and the same act, does imply the impossibility of knowing anything whatsoever about value, and thus belies any statements that he himself may make about it. This objection holds against certain philosophers who have identified value with interest, and it therefore behooves us to discover whether our own view is similarly objectionable.

Professor G. E. Moore distinguishes two forms in which this vicious relativism may be stated. In the first place, "it may be held that whenever any man asserts an action to be right or wrong, what he is asserting is merely that he *himself* has some particular feeling toward the action in question." [25] In this case the act of knowing or judging value, is construed

[24] J. A. Froude, *Inaugural Lecture at St. Andrews*, 1869, p. 41; Letter of Carlyle to Froude, *Longman's Magazine*, 1892, p. 151.
[25] *Ethics*, Home University Library, p. 89.

as simply an expression of the judge's own interest.   The following famous passage from Hobbes is a case in point:

"But whatsoever is the object of any man's appetite or desire, that is it which he for his part calleth 'good'; and the object of his hate and aversion, 'evil'; and of his contempt 'vile' and 'inconsiderable.'   For these words of good, evil, and contemptible, are ever used with relation to the person that useth them: there being nothing simply and absolutely so; nor any common rule of good and evil, to be taken from the nature of the objects themselves." [26]

The *reductio ad absurdum* of such a view, lies, as Professor Moore points out, in the fact that it would lead to the mutual irrelevance of all judgments in which the value-predicates are employed.   If in affirming an act to be right or wrong, good or evil, a judge were always referring to *his own present feeling* about it, then no two judges could ever agree or disagree with one another, nor could the same judge ever reaffirm or correct his own past opinions. [27]   In other words, on questions of value there could not be any such thing as judgment or opinion in the ordinary sense of these terms.   This is not only contrary to fact, but it is inevitably contradicted by the very man who makes the assertion.

A second statement of this vicious relativism is the assertion "that when we judge an action to be right or wrong what we are asserting is merely that somebody or other thinks it to be right or wrong."   Generalized and simplified, this assertion is to the effect that value consists in being thought to be valuable—"There is nothing either good or bad, but thinking makes it so."   Now the fundamental difficulty with this view lies in the fact that one would then have nothing to think about.   If a thing is valuable by virtue of being believed to be valuable, then when one believes a thing to be valuable, one believes that it is believed to be valuable, or one believes that it is believed to be believed to be valuable, and so on *ad infinitum.* [28]   In short, there can be no judgment

[26] *Leviathan,* Part I, Ch. VI.
[27] Cf. G. E. Moore, *op. cit.,* pp. 100-103.
[28] Cf. G. E. Moore, *op. cit.,* pp. 122-124.

about value, or about anything else, unless there is some content or object other than the act of judgment itself,—a judged as well as a judging.

It is this error or confusion which vitiates the work of Westermarck and others who, not content with a history of moral opinion, have attempted to *define* moral values in *terms* of moral opinion.[29] It is the characteristic and besetting error of all anthropological and sociological theories of value, which aim to be scientific or 'positive.'[30] What has been judged with unanimity to be good or evil by members of a social group, is a matter of record; and is thus a fact ascertainable by archaeological or historical methods, and with a precision and indubitableness peculiar to these methods. But such methodological preferences do not alter the fact that these judgments, if judgments at all, must have been *about* something; and in theory of value it is this *object,* and not the acts of judgment themselves, which is primarily in question. There are also recorded opinions about the stars, and anthropologists may and do investigate these opinions; but one does not therefore propose to substitute a history of astronomical opinions for astronomy.

Let us now inquire whether the view here proposed is guilty of a vicious or sceptical relativism in either or both of these two senses. In the first place, although defining value as relative to interest, we have not defined value as exclusively relative to the present interest of the judge. Thus if Caesar was ambitious when he waged war upon Pompey, the definition implies that power was in fact good, as being coveted by Caesar. But this fact may have been affirmed by Mark Antony, or afterwards denied by Caesar himself in his own defence. Value, therefore, lends itself to judgment in the ordinary sense,—to judgments which are true or false, and which may agree or disagree.

In the second place, having defined value as constituted

---

[29] E. Westermarck, *Origin and Development of Moral Ideas,* 1906, Vol. I, *passim.* Westermarck's confusion is largely due to the ambiguity of the term 'approval,' and the absence of any clear notion of judgment.

[30] For a general statement of this position, cf. L. Lévy-Bruhl, *La Morale et la Science des Mœurs,* 1910.

by interests, such judgments have a content or object other than themselves. They may refer to the interest of the judge, or to any other interests, past or present, common or unique; but the interest that creates the value is always other than the judgment that cognizes it. Theory of value is not a history of opinion about values, but deals with that to which such opinion refers.

§ 55. **The Argument from 'Intrinsic' Value.** Professor Moore has further weapons in his arsenal which he believes to be fatal not only to the particular forms of epistemological relativism just rejected, but in general to the view that "by calling a thing 'good' or 'bad' we merely mean that some being or beings have a certain mental attitude towards it"; or that "what we mean by calling a thing 'good' is that it is *desired,* or desired in some particular way." [31] Since we have in effect maintained precisely this view, his objections are relevant and must be met.

He appeals, in the first place, to the fact that we may use the word 'good' without consciously meaning 'object of interest.' Judging by what the speaker has in mind, to say that the object is good is not the same as to say that some one is interested in it.[32] This type of argument would prove altogether too much if it proved anything. No definition has ever been formulated that is perfectly in keeping either with verbal usage or conscious meanings. For words may be mere echoes, and conscious meanings careless and obscure. The absurdity of the argument is especially evident in the case of complex entities, such as the exponents of the present view hold value to be. A complex entity is only summarily denoted in common discourse, and analysis will invariably reveal a structure which is not present to a mind which employs terms in a stereotyped sense. It would, for example, scarcely be urged that circularity is indefinable because one can judge an object to be circular without judging that all

---

[31] *Op. cit.,* pp. 157, 159.
[32] This argument is applied primarily to the term 'right,' but is equally applicable to the term 'good.' Cf. *ibid.,* pp. 111, 163.

points on its perimeter are equi-distant from the centre. In the one case as in the other the nature of the predicate is revealed not in customary usage, but when doubt has arisen as to its applicability. Where the circularity of an object is in question one falls to measuring; and when its goodness is in question one falls to considering its relation to interests.

A much more serious objection is based upon the notion of *intrinsic* value. We judge a thing to be intrinsically good "where we judge, concerning a particular state of things that it would be worth while—would be 'a good thing'—that that state of things should exist, *even if nothing else were to exist besides,* either at the same time or afterwards." [33]   If a thing derives value from its relation to an interest taken in it, it would seem impossible that anything whatsoever should possess value in itself. But in that case value would seem always to be borrowed, and never owned; value would shine by a reflected glory having no original source.

The question turns upon the fact that any predicate may be judged synthetically or analytically. Suppose that 'good' were to be regarded as a simple quality like yellow. It would then be possible to judge either synthetically, that the primrose was fair or yellow; or, analytically, that the fair, yellow primrose was fair or yellow. Only the fair, yellow primrose would be fair and yellow "even if nothing were to exist besides." But the logic of the situation is not in the least altered if a relational predicate is substituted for a simple quality; indeed it is quite possible to regard a quality as a monadic (a single term) relation. Tangential, for example, is a relational predicate; since a line is a tangent only by virtue of the peculiar relation of single-point contact with another line or surface. Let R^t represent this peculiar relation, and A, B, two lines. One can then judge either synthetically, that (A) R^t (B); or, analytically, that (A) R^t (B) is R^t. Similarly, let S represent an interested subject, O an object, and R^i the peculiar relation of interest, taken and received. We can then judge either synthetically, that (O) R^i (S); or, analytically that (O) R^i (S) is R^i. In

[33] *Ibid.,* p. 162.

other words, one can say either that O is desired by S, or that *O-desired-by-S is a case of the general character 'desired.'*

The situation is complicated, but not logically altered, by the fact that either O, or O's-being-desired-by-S^1, may be desired by S^2, and so stand in a second value-relation of the same type. In other words, as we have already seen, the question of value is peculiarly recurrent.[34] But value is intrinsic when it is independent of such ulterior interests. Similarly, the primrose *as enjoyed* is intrinsically good; the primrose *as sought for the sake of* such ulterior enjoyment, is instrumentally, conditionally, or otherwise extrinsically good. In other words, according to the present view an object unrelated to a subject cannot be good in itself, any more than, in Professor Moore's view,[35] an object can be good in itself without possessing the specific superadded quality 'good'; but an *object-desired-for-itself*, that is, any value of the variable function $(O)\ R\ (S)$, can and does possess value in itself.[36]

The special case of the universe as a whole[37] furnishes a further and peculiarly instructive example. It is evident that by definition the universe as a whole cannot stand in relation to any desiring subject outside itself. In what sense, therefore, can it be said to possess value in accord with our definition? In the first place, it might, for certain familiar metaphysical reasons which are not here in question, be conceived as a single all-embracing interest. The total universe would be divided between a universal subject and a universal object, with a relation of will or love (perhaps of self-love) uniting the two. In that case the world in its unity would possess intrinsic value. Or, independently of such metaphysical speculation, the universe may be said to possess value

---

[34] Cf. §§ 17 and 56.
[35] As set forth above, § 15.
[36] Even Professor Moore says (*ibid.*, p. 167): "I think it is true that no whole can be intrinsically good, unless it *contains* some feeling toward *something* as a part of itself." According to this view the 'something' and the 'feeling toward,' taken together, are 'good': there being three factors involved. In my view 'good' *means* the 'feeling toward,' or more precisely, 'the being felt toward.'
[37] Cf. G. E. Moore, *ibid.*, p. 58.

in so far as loved or hated by its own members, taken severally. Or it may be said to *contain* value,[38] in that it embraces interests and their objects. Or it may be said to be an instrument of value, in that it provides the conditions by which interests and their objects may arise and be conserved. There is no cosmic paradox which can be urged against the definition of value in terms of the interest-relation which could not with equal force be urged against any other view of value, including the view that value is an indefinable quality. For if it be urged that the universe so defined as to embrace all interests cannot be synthetically good through any interest taken in it, it can equally well be urged that the universe so defined as to embrace the indefinable quality 'good,' cannot be good through the super-addition of this quality.

We may safely conclude, therefore, that the definition of value herein proposed provides for intrinsic value in such intelligible senses as are provided for in any other theory of value.

§ 56. The Charge of Circularity. In criticising the view that value is a "relational attitude," Professor W. M. Urban argues that it involves "a definition in a circle."

"The value of an object consists, it is said, in its satisfaction of desire, or more broadly, fulfilment of interest. But it is always possible to raise further questions which show conclusively that the value concept is already presupposed. Is the interest itself worthy of being satisfied? Is the object worthy of being of interest? In other words, the fact of intrinsic value requires us to find the essence of value in something other than this type of relation." [39]

This expresses the most popular objection to the present view. The fact of desire is not accepted as final in most judgments of value. Objects of desire are held to be bad despite their being desired, and desires themselves are held to be bad whether or no they are satisfied. Vicious appetites,

[38] And thus to be better than no universe at all, by the principle of 'inclusiveness.' Cf. Ch. XXII, Sect. III.
[39] "Value and Existence," *Jour. of Philos.*, Vol. XIII, 1916, pp. 452, 453.

vulgar taste, o'erweening ambition, are the most notorious of evils.   Indeed the general terms 'desire' and 'interest' have acquired a specific flavor of moral disrepute.   Must we not conclude therefore that value, instead of flowing from interest, is an independent, if not antagonistic, principle by which interests and their objects are judged?   Despite the strong appeal which this argument must make to common-sense, we shall find not only that it rests upon a confusion, but that the very facts to which it refers can be understood only by such a definition of value as is here proposed.

Let us consider, first, the relatively simple case in which *all* desire is condemned.   The argument as presented by Schopenhauer and by other Occidental and Oriental advocates of the cult of apathy, is based upon the generalization that desire is doomed to defeat.   Desire asks what in the very nature of the case it can never obtain.   It asks for private advantage or special privilege in a world which is indifferent to such claims; or it perpetually begets new desires out of its own satisfaction, and is thus in a chronic state of bankruptcy. But why, then, condemn it?   Pessimism is founded on a conception of evil, which in turn must be assumed to be the converse of good.   There would be no reason for condemning the *futility* of desire as evil unless the *success* of desire were supposed to be good.   This implication is more clearly evident in the Stoic cult of resignation.   Thus Epictetus exhorts his followers to "demand not that events should happen as you wish; but wish them to happen as they do happen and you will go on well." [40]   There would be no meaning in such counsel if 'going on well' were not conceived as consisting in some sort of accord between events and what men wish.

Let us now consider those cases which arise not from disaccord between interests and their natural environments, but from disaccord between one interest and another.   The same object may be liked or desired by one man, and disliked or avoided by another.   Our definition requires us to attribute evil to the object as being disliked, *despite* the fact that it

[40] *Ench.* VIII, translated in Bakewell's *Source Book in Ancient Philosophy,* 1907, p. 318.

is liked. It may, then, be argued that liking cannot make an object good. Or it may be objected that our definition requires us to affirm that the same object is at one and the same time both evil and good, which is contradictory. But *is* it contradictory? The fact is, on the contrary, that a relational definition, such as that here proposed, is the only means of *avoiding* contradiction. It is not denied that the same object may be both liked and disliked; this is the very premise of the objection. If, then, good is *defined* as being liked, and evil as being disliked, it follows that the same object may *in this sense* be without contradiction both good and evil. A term may always possess relational attributes in opposite senses, provided such relations are sustained toward different terms. The same physical object may be both 'to the right of' and 'to the left of,' both 'above' and 'below'; the same man may be both friend and enemy, both agent and patient.

A yet more common case is that in which one interest is condemned because of being contrary to another interest. Such condemnation arises from the fact that interests conflict, so that the affirmation of one implies the negation of the other. This occurs in sheer struggle where both interests are upon the same plane. When two appetites require for their satisfaction the exclusive use of the same object, the desired object is *good* in relation to each appetite; while each appetite is *evil* in relation to the other, as tending to prevent its satisfaction.

But the case which has most deeply affected popular habits of thought, and which is mainly responsible for the prejudice against the present theory of value, is the case in which an interest or its object is morally condemned. Interests are deemed 'bad,' and not merely in the sense of being hostile to other rival interests of the same rank; they are deemed 'downright' bad, in a sense in which all judges, including the agent himself, are expected to agree.

The explanation of this case lies, however, in the fact that moral judgments are not concerned with value in the generic sense, but with a specific and complex *aspect* of it. They are concerned with organizations of values, whether in the personal or in the social life.   They do not deal with interests *per se*, but with the relation of interests to the comprehensive purposes in which they are incorporated.   From the moral point of view value *begins* with the bearing of a 'lower' interest upon a 'higher' interest.   To quote Mr. Santayana,

"It is in reference to such constitutional interests that things are 'really' good or bad; interests which may not be fairly represented by any incidental conscious desire.   No doubt any desire, however capricious, represents some momentary and partial interest, which lends to its objects a certain real and inalienable value; yet when we consider, as we do in human society, the interests of men, whom reflection and settled purposes have raised more or less to the ideal dignity of individuals, then passing fancies and passions may indeed have bad objects, and be bad themselves, in that they thwart the more comprehensive interests of the soul that entertains them." [41]

It is in this sense that appetites may be vicious in relation to health, or efficiency; that special inclinations or passions may corrupt character, or hinder a life-purpose; and that personal ambition may imperil the well-being of the nation, or of humanity at large.   But while such values may be absolutes for the moral consciousness, it is the avowed purpose of a general theory of value to analyze and relate them.   Theory of value takes all value for its province, even values which are too evident or ignoble for the judgments of common-sense.   This does not imply any neglect of 'higher' values, but only the method of understanding the special case in terms of the generic type.

§ 57. **Realistic Basis of the Present Definition.** We have reached the general conclusion that while there *is* an epistemological relativism which is vicious and self-defeating, the relativity of values is not only logically innocuous but logically helpful and illuminating.   The genuine logical difficulties that have attended the theory of value have arisen from a persistent unwillingness to accept the palpable fact that values *are* relative in different senses to different subjects.

[41] G. Santayana, *Winds of Doctrine*, 1913, p. 146.

This unwillingness has taken the form of denying that values are relative to interests at all, or the form of affirming their exclusive relation to some one interest, or to some one type or class of interests. The really vicious relativism arises not from the recognition of relations, but from the *insufficient* recognition of relations. The error of the old geo-centric astronomy lay not in its affirmation of the relation of sun, moon and stars to the earth, but in the distorted perspective which under-emphasized or ignored other relations. The same defect has subsequently appeared in the Newtonian mechanics. The error of anthropocentrism lies not in affirming the relation of all things to man, but in an exaggeration of that relation. In all of these cases advancing enlightenment has generalized a relation which was previously thought to be unique.

The analogous case in theory of value is the affirmation in behalf of any subject that its interests constitute the only centre or point of reference for all values. The common and disreputable case is egoism where an agent baldly asserts his own private interests. The more insidious case is that which enjoys among philosophers the highly reputable name of 'idealism.'

This form of relativism arises from the general thesis characteristic of all idealism that the cognitive act creates its objects. According to this thesis, when I know reality, I make it; and since there can be only one reality, what I thus make takes exclusive possession of the field. In making reality myself I must reject the work of others save in so far as it coincides with my own. What holds of objects of knowledge generally, holds of values in particular. Value is held to be relative to the subject's *judgment.* Since one is justified in claiming the assent of others to one's judgment, and must regard other and conflicting judgments as false, one may thus claim priority or exclusiveness for that system of values which centres in oneself. This view is viciously relativistic in that it imputes absoluteness to a limited and partial set of relations. The way of escape lies not in the denial of the relativity of value to interest, but in the *general-*

ization of that relation. Where all interests are viewed as equally constitutive of value, and none is viewed as exclusive or preëminent, then the relativism of values loses those characters of arbitrariness, contradictoriness and asymmetry, which make it morally and logically objectionable.

It has sometimes been supposed that a realistic theory of knowledge, such as is professed in the present study, implies that values shall be conceived as 'objective' in the sense of being independent of *any* relation to a subject. But such an inference is wholly gratuitous. A realistic theory of knowledge is a theory of *knowledge,* to the effect, namely, that *what* is known is independent as regards its existence and essential nature, of the *act* or *state* of knowledge. It is asserted that when the mountain, for example, is perceived by Mahomet, this relation is something super-added to the mountain; in such wise that the mountain can maintain its historic existence and its mountainous nature uninterruptedly, whether in the presence or in the absence of Mahomet's perception. But this thesis does not imply that only mountains or similar inanimate and insensible beings can exist or be perceived. Mahomet, for example, perceived his daughter Fatima and her love for Ali; he was doubtless aware of his own hopes and fears for the future of Islam. Realism contends only that love, hope and fear, like mountains, are independent of the acts of perception or judgment whereby they are known. There is not the slightest ground for imputing to realism the grotesque notion that there are no such things as acts or states of mind, or that such things cannot be known. If a realist entertained this grotesque notion he could not affirm anything about the act of knowledge itself, which is the central topic of his discourse. Because he seeks to avoid a philosophical psycho-mania, there is no reason to accuse him of psycho-phobia.

The view here proposed may properly be termed a bio-centric or psycho-centric theory of value, in the sense that values are held to be functions of certain acts of living mind to which we have given the name of interest. Interests and their objects, or the complex facts, objects-of-interest, can be known like any other facts. But they do not have to obtain from anybody's knowledge of them, permission either to exist or to be what they are. No subject whatsoever, human or divine, has the power to make or unmake them by his own simple affirmation or denial. When value is defined in terms of these facts it possesses the same independence. A value acquires existence when an interest is generated, regardless of any knowledge about it. A value will cease to exist when its own sustaining interest is destroyed or altered; but it does not cease to exist simply because it is cognitively excommunicated. He who knows values, and takes account of them, profits from that knowledge through his better adaptation to the environment in which he lives; and he who ignores them, does so at his peril.

III. PROBLEMS AND METHODS

§ 58. Assuming that value is a function of what may broadly be termed 'interest,' it becomes imperative to examine the fundamental or generic character of this phenomenon. What is that state, or attitude, or act, or process, which is characteristic of living things, which is unmistakably present in the motor-affective consciousness of man, and which shades away through instinct and reflex to the doubtful borderland of tropism? Both the vocabulary and the grammatical structure of common speech provide for the category of interest. There is something in our world to which they serve to call attention. What is it?

The fact that we have found it necessary to paraphrase interest as "the motor-affective life" indicates the complexity of the topic. If value in the generic sense is defined in terms of interest in the generic sense, then it is evident that the varieties of value must be understood in terms of the varieties of interest. These varieties, and the rival claims to which they give rise, have provoked most of the controversies of contemporary psychology. Some interests, called 'instincts,' are held to be innate, and others acquired. Some, called 'reflexes,' are held to be blind and automatic; others are held to be 'intelligent.' The expression, 'motor-affective,' as well as the traditional division of mind into thought, will, and feeling, suggests a duality between active and passive interests; or a duality between interests directed to an imagined or represented future, and those directed to an immediate present. Terms such as 'character' and 'disposition' testify to a type of interest which is latent or unconscious, and which manifests itself in its outward or ulterior effects, rather than in any present subjective state. The antithesis between 'impulse' and 'volition' implies that interest is qualified by the presence, in some degree, of the intellectual process. The difference between desire and aversion, pleasure and pain, or liking and disliking, indicates a peculiar polarity or opposition of interest. Finally, all of these modal differences imply corresponding standards of measurement, such as 'intensity' of feeling, or 'strength' of desire.

In undertaking to refine and amplify the meaning of interest, we are confronted at the outset by a choice of methods. There is a *prima facie* discontinuity between the field of mental states disclosed by introspection, and the field of organic phenomena in which the biologist and other physical scientists conduct their investigations; and if an observer commits himself initially to the former, it would seem that he can never escape its limits. We shall therefore look for interest in the open,—upon the plane and in the context of physical nature.

We cannot determine the rôle of introspective data in interest, unless we first take that view of the matter in which both consciousness and its physical context are taken into account. Behavior or conduct, broadly surveyed in all the dimensions that experience affords, can alone give us the proper perspective. Furthermore, we want if possible to discover what it is to *be* interested, not what it is merely to *feel* interested. What is implied in *being* favorably or unfavorably disposed to anything? It may be that it all comes to nothing more than a peculiar quality or arrangement among the data of introspection, but such a conclusion would be equivalent to an abandonment of the widespread notion that interest is a kind of determination of events. The really important claim made in behalf of interest is the claim that things happen *because* of interest. Are acts performed *on account* of ends? Is it proper to *explain* what takes place in human or animal life, or in the course of nature at large, by the categories of teleology? The most exhaustive introspective analysis of the motor-affective consciousness would leave this question unanswered, and to confine ourselves to the data which such analysis affords would be to prejudge it unfavorably.

For the first time since the moralists and theologians divided the soul from the body, man is beginning to find a place in nature without being stripped of his most distinctive characteristics. He has begun to move about on the surface of the planet while still retaining possession of his faculties. This achievement is due primarily to that general psychological tendency which has acquired the name of 'behaviorism,' from one of its particular and recent manifestations.[42]

Behaviorism, in the general sense, is simply a return to the original Aristotelian view that mind and body are related as activity and organ. The activities of mind, so construed, are observable and describable functions of the physical organism, continuous with those of life, and differing from them in pattern and complexity rather than in constituents. The so-called 'states' of mind, or 'contents of consciousness,' on the other hand, are identified with the environment of behavior, being mental only in so far as behavior selects and combines them. The result is to avoid construing either the subjective or the objective aspect of mind in terms of a unique substance or quality.

It has been objected that this is to leave out 'consciousness.' But what is this 'consciousness' which we are under obligation to include—is it a datum or a theory? It was once said that psychology omitted the soul. And so it did, in so

[42] Summaries of this tendency, with bibliography, will be found in G. C. Dickinson, *Economic Motives,* 1922, Ch. VII; A. A. Roback, *Behaviorism and Psychology,* 1923. The best critical exposition is to be found in K. S. Lashley: "The Behavioristic Interpretation of Consciousness," *Psych. Rev.,* Vol. XXX, 1923.

far as the term 'soul' was the name for a theory formulated in theology or "rational" psychology. But psychology never deliberately neglected any of the facts or problems lying within the field of the mental life of man; and as a result of omitting the older theory of the soul, it reached a very much better understanding of the actual mode of existence in question. No one would now think of conceiving the soul as a simple, indivisible and incorruptible static entity, or as a naked act of pure reason. In every philosophy the soul is now a process; or a flowing, and more or less complexly organized, experience. When, therefore, we say the soul is lost, what we really mean is that a theory is more or less obsolete, as a result of its having been successfully ignored. The soul as an existent fact having a nature and an explanation, is not lost, but found.

Now something of this same outcome may with reasonable safety be predicted in the case of 'consciousness.' If a behaviorist be enlightened he will have no intention of omitting any facts, but only of abandoning a theory which he believes has proved unsatisfactory. He does not abandon *consciousness,* but the introspective *theory* of consciousness; and in so far as the new theory is more successful than the old, consciousness as a group of facts, as something that exists and happens, will have been found and not lost.[43]

The limitations of the introspective theory of consciousness have been most flagrant in the region of the will and the affections; in other words, in that department of human nature with which theory of value is primarily concerned. The

[43] Whether this is or is not a "strict" behaviorism, is a matter of no consequence. I am concerned with the possibilities afforded by a program and a method, broadly conceived. It is too early, even if it were profitable, to discuss questions of orthodoxy and heresy. Most of the current criticisms of behaviorism are irrelevant to the position here taken. Thus Mr. C. D. Broad attacks the behaviorist who says "that all mental processes reduce without residue to the fact that the body is behaving in a certain specific way" (*The Mind and its Place in Nature,* 1925, p. 616). I agree that such a behaviorist (*i.e.,* one who denies or ignores the *content* of consciousness) deserves attack. Mr. Broad also defines the behaviorist as a "reductive materialist" (*ibid.,* p. 612); which fits *some* behaviorists, but not that general tendency of which I make bold to claim Mr. Broad himself as an adherent, in so far as he prefers to view mind as an "emergent characteristic" of the material world (*ibid.,* pp. 610, 650).

failure of introspection to give any satisfactory account of feeling, desire, will, and conation scarcely admits of doubt. The dubious feelings of 'pleasantness' and 'unpleasantness,' which if they *are* a unique species of introspective data ought to be *indubitable,* are held by some to be simple sensations, by others to be fusions of organic sensations, and by others to be acts or 'attitudes' of liking or disliking. Desire, viewed introspectively, can never be anything but a combination of ideas and feelings. Exponents of the introspective method have seen the difficulty of accounting in these terms for actual dynamic differences: such as that between desiring a thing, and liking to think of it; or that between real desire, and the sham-desire characteristic of play and aesthetic detachment.[44] As to will, Münsterberg's reduction of this to such terms as "the perception of an attained effect whose idea has gone before" [45] perfectly illustrates the extent to which the method of introspection endeavors to make up the whole of will by piecing together its cognitive shreds and patches. It is evident that the distinctive feature of will lies in this "attained effect" (*erreichten Effektes*), which is the one element in the situation which cannot be defined in introspective terms.

Similarly, wherever accounts of *conation* preserve anything distinctive, they appear to incorporate something of the action of the physical organism. The basic antithesis of favor and disfavor, which is said to distinguish active feelings, is an echo of the antithesis between positive and negative bodily reactions. Thus Professor G. F. Stout speaks of a "mental striving," which "tends to realize itself," and of which the physiological correlate is "the tendency of a neural system to recover a relatively stable condition." What, one may fairly ask, is the common meaning of "tend-

---

[44] An instructive example of the futility of attempting to reduce desire to introspective terms is afforded by the controversy within the school of Meinong on the relations of desire and feeling. Cf. Ch. Ehrenfels, *System der Werttheorie,* 1897, Vol. I, pp. 41, 248–251; A. Meinong, *Über Annahmen,* 1902, pp. 293–296; W. M. Urban, *Valuation,* 1909, pp. 35–37; and the writer's "Behavioristic View of Purpose," *Jour. of Philos.,* Vol. XVIII, 1921.

[45] H. Münsterberg, *Willenshandlung,* 1888, p. 88.

ency" on the mental and the physiological sides? Or is the
latter, perhaps, the *real* tendency, and the former the feeling
of it?[46] Professor William McDougall says that every instance of instinctive behavior involves "a striving *towards
or away from*" an object; and that in all instinctive behavior
there is "*a persistent striving towards the natural end of the
process,*" which is intensified by obstacles.[47] This account
seems clearly to have been derived in the first instance from
the organism's action on its environment, and irresistibly suggests that the subjective or introspective sense of striving
is the consciousness *of* the stresses and strains incidental to
this action.[48]

Almost every recent advance in the motor-affective field
of the mental life has resulted from the more or less complete abandonment of the introspective method. The most
notable general advance, an advance that has now been accepted by the social sciences as well as by popular opinion,
is the rejection of the once-classic view that conduct is ruled
by the selfish calculation of pleasure and pain. This theory
of human motivation has been superseded by explanations
in terms of reflex, instinct, imitation, the learning process,
habit, or unconscious 'complex.' These and other allied conceptions, characteristic of what is known as "dynamic psychology," have come into vogue as a result of attempts to
describe the behavior of animals, children, men, and social
groups; or the misbehavior of criminals, or crowds, or the
insane. They do not imply the abandonment of introspection,
but they do signify the fruitfulness of a new method in which
mind is conceived as an organic rather than as a purely
subjective entity. The history of psychology, the record both
of its past failures and of its recent successes, thus abundantly
justifies our provisional adoption of the objective method.
In accord with this method we shall begin our study of interest by an examination of certain peculiarities of the biological organism.

[46] *Analytical Psychology,* 1896, Vol. II, pp. 82, 83.
[47] *Social Psychology,* 1910, pp. 26, 27. The italics are mine.
[48] I do not deny the common opinion that the animistic view of nature
results from a projection into external objects of the experience of conation, but I do affirm that what is so projected is mainly if not wholly
the experience of organic action.

CHAPTER VI

THE BIOLOGICAL APPROACH TO INTEREST [1]

I. ORGANIZATION AND INDIVIDUALITY

§ 59. Self-Motion and Spontaneity. The differentia of animal and human behavior which was first remarked, was the power of self-motion.[2] Whereas an inanimate object merely submitted to motion imparted to it from without by impact, a living thing seemed to be an original source of motion. Associated with this phenomenon was the relatively unpredictable character of the action of living organisms. What they did was so far due to internal and unobservable factors, that you could not rely on their yielding in any constant way to the operation of the external forces that you might observe or apply. Living things had a way of moving of themselves, without any apparent cause which might serve to put you on your guard. Hence they were said to exhibit "spontaneity."

It is still customary to characterize living things in this way. Biologists describe the organism as "an active, self-assertive, living creature—to some extent master of its fate." [3] But this spontaneity or self-motion no longer serves to distinguish living from inanimate things, owing to the development of the science of energy. We should now speak of this apparent spontaneity as a release of stored energy. The organism accumulates chemical energy by the process of syn-

[1] Parts of the present chapter are reprinted from an article entitled "Purpose as Tendency and Adaptation," published in the *Philos. Rev.,* Vol. XXVI, 1917.

[2] "For the body which is moved from without is soulless; but that which is moved from within has a soul, such motion being inherent in the soul" (Plato's *Phædrus,* 245 E, Jowett's translation).

[3] J. A. Thompson, *Heredity,* 1908, p. 172. Cf. also H. S. Jennings, *Behavior of the Lower Organisms,* 1906, pp. 261, 283–285, 302–305, 339–342.

thetic or constructive metabolism, and then discharges it when subjected to some kind of stimulation. When the discharge occurs it is out of all proportion to the stimulation. The internal factor is so much more important than the external factor that the latter affords no safe basis for prediction, As organisms become more elaborate the discharge comes to depend more and more upon the quantity and balance of its stored energies, and less and less upon what is done to it from without. But even so, this phenomenon of release or discharge does not differ in principle from what happens in the case of combustion or in the case of the action of high explosives. In the one case as in the other, it is merely a question of the relative preponderance of central over peripheral factors.

Hence we are at present inclined to look elsewhere for the differentia of life, and to find it, not in the sheer spontaneity of action, but in the special forms which this spontaneity, or its underlying structure, assumes. Three such forms have been especially emphasized: internal *organization* and *individuality; tendency* or forward direction; and *adaptation* to environment. The first of these has assumed a commanding prominence in connection with the modern controversy over vitalism, or the issue between 'teleology' and 'mechanism.' Some consideration of this controversy and of its negative results, forms a necessary introduction to the subject.

§ 60. Teleology as the Negation of Mechanism. For
many years biologists have been divided into two camps, those who have insisted that life exhibits a unique and irreducible principle, and those who hold that life can be brought into one homogeneous system with the phenomena of physics and chemistry.[4] Since the former party ordinarily espouses the cause of 'teleology' and the latter that of 'mechanism,' it might be supposed that this principle which vitalists accept and which their opponents reject, was that very principle of interest of which we are in search.

---

[4] For the literature of the vitalistic controversy, cf. *Jour. of Philos.*, Vol. XV, 1918, pp. 550-553.

Unfortunately, however, although there is no doubt of the dispute there is the greatest doubt as to what the dispute is about. As a competent philosophical observer has recently remarked, "the combatants all assume that everyone is agreed as to what is meant by a mechanical explanation, and, presumably in consequence of this assumption, never condescend to inform the reader what *they* in particular mean by it." [5] As a matter of fact, the term 'mechanical' has come to stand not for any specific type of scientific explanation, but rather for scientific explanation in general. Thus the case for teleology is prejudiced by a suggestion of anti-scientific bias, or of unscientific laxity. This is due no doubt mainly to the religious or popular auspices under which it has been advanced. The teleological hypothesis is often invoked to satisfy aspirations, to flatter human nature, or to conceal ignorance. In the present controversy over vitalism the proofs of teleology seem to consist largely in the indictment of rigorous experimental science. Teleology is not recommended on account of its own success, but on account of the failure of something else. When so invoked it tends to mean little more than that unknown fator, *x*, which is needed to *complete* the explanation. It is not surprising that vitalists should be regarded as impatient scientists who cannot wait for a rigorous experimental solution, but must needs invent an agency *ad hoc;* or as irresponsible critics, who remind plodding science of its outstanding difficulties without assisting in the serious work of overcoming them.

Even Professor Driesch, the most eminent of contemporary vitalists, and himself a trained biologist, has earned a certain scientific ill-repute on this account. His arguments for vitalism are essentially negative. He points out the difficulty of explaining what he calls the "equipotentiality" of vital systems.

[5] C. D. Broad, "Mechanical Explanation and its Alternatives," *Proc. Aristotelian Society,* 1918-19, p. 86. This article contains a statement of a half-dozen or more things that 'mechanical explanation' might be taken to mean, and shows how completely the issue is altered when one of these meanings is substituted for another. Cf. the same writer's *Mind and its Place in Nature,* 1925, Ch. II.

"Analytic experimental embryology [he says], has been able to show that there are many kinds of embryonic organs or even animals which, if by an operation deprived of part of their cells, behave in the following way: of whatever material you deprive these organs or animals, the remainder, unless it is very small, will always develop in the normal manner, though, so to speak in miniature." [6]

In other words, the parts of an organism seem to be so charged or impregnated with the nature of the whole, that they can, when occasion requires, develop and exercise all of its functions. This, according to Professor Driesch, is inexplicable in terms of "physico-chemical causality"; since the function of the whole is clearly not dependent on the juxtaposition and interaction of the parts, and may be assumed by any of the parts in isolation. But while the phenomena here cited undoubtedly prove the pervasiveness and elusiveness of the conditions which underlie the functions characteristic of an organic whole, they do not prove that these conditions are not physico-chemical. For they *may* consist in some juxtaposition of elements within the part; and the difference in the behavior of the part before and after it is isolated, may be explicable in terms of the change of environment, or even in terms of the "operation" by which the isolation is effected.[7] It is difficult to see how science could well avoid a persistent search for such an explanation, even though it might be compelled meanwhile, and for an indefinite period, to plead ignorance.[8]

Even a plea of ignorance is better than the alternative proposed by Professor Driesch. The "entelechy" which he invokes for purposes of explanation, is neither an energy nor

[6] H. Driesch, *History and Theory of Vitalism*, 1914, p. 208. (Cf. also the same author's *Science and Philosophy of the Organism*, 1918.)

[7] For a similar criticism of Driesch's argument, as well as an excellent analysis of the whole vitalistic issue, cf. A. O. Lovejoy's review of Driesch, in *Science*, Vol. XXX, 1909, pp. 761-767.

[8] This objection holds with even greater force against Driesch's second argument, to the effect that the past experience of the organism creates only "*a general stock* of *possibilities*" for further acting," and does not account for the later reactions of the organism "quite in detail" (*ibid.*, p. 213). Surely this unexplained residuum of detail is that not-yet-explained, or not-fully-explained, which attends all the efforts of the finite and fallible intellect, and is not an inexplicable-in-principle.

a material substance of any kind; nor, apparently, is it a property or law of energy or of matter. It is a natural agency which can "suspend" physico-chemical processes, and then "allow that to become real which it has itself held in a state of mere possibility." It is an agent whose *modus operandi* is wholly indescribable and unpredictable, if not in clear violation of accepted scientific laws. It is suspiciously like those indefinite potencies which were once in general scientific vogue, and which modern experimental technique has cast out as both futile and irrelevant.[9]

Such procedure is the more unjustifiable in view of the rapid advances which are at present being made in the field of experimental biology.[10] While the origin of life still remains a mystery, and its perfect control an unfulfilled aspiration, its constituent processes in their most simplified forms are rapidly being assimilated to inorganic physico-chemical processes. Growth, in the sense of absorption of water by osmosis, reproduction in the sense of cell-division and fusion, irritability, ingestion and extrusion, selective permeability, metabolism,—both constructive metabolism, in which organic substances are created, and destructive metabolism in which their energy is liberated,—all of these and other like processes, characteristic of plants and animals, can now be simulated in the laboratory. In view of these achievements, and in view of the rapidity with which such achievements are now being multiplied, only the hardiest of obscurantists will venture to assert there is any corner of the organism which such achievements are incapable of penetrating. There may be some virtue in the two-party system in science, with a party in power which is sobered by responsibility, and a party in opposition whose function it is to challenge, censure and imagine vain things. But the conception of teleology has suffered in the past, and will doubtless continue to suffer in the future, from the patronage of this second party. Certainly nothing could be more precarious or more fatuous

[9] Cf. the writer's *Present Philosophical Tendencies*, 1912, Part II.
[10] For an excellent popular review of this field of research, cf. W. J. V. Osterhout's *The Nature of Life*, 1924.

than a theory of value founded on the present limits of experimental science, and insured only by its future failure.

§ 61. The Reconciliation of Mechanism and Teleology.

As a matter of fact it is not at all necessary to suppose
that teleology is the contradictory alternative to some other
hypothesis such as 'mechanism.' The party of teleology insists upon novelty and irreducibility, especially among the
phenomena of life and mind; while the party of mechanism
proclaims the doctrines and the methods of scientific orthodoxy. But there is a growing and justifiable conviction that
the hostile rivalry of these parties is based on a misunderstanding.

It is a well-recognized fact that the *juxtaposition* of certain elements *a, b* and *c* gives rise to unique and novel phenomena; that is, to phenomena peculiar to this specific pattern, and therefore unpredictable from the properties of *a,
b* and *c* taken severally. This is, in fact, the very meaning
of the method of analysis [11]; for the method of analysis in
science, is justifiable only by the assumption of a process
of synthesis in nature. Explanation by analysis is nothing
but the attempt to discover what specific mode of union of
what specific constituents has brought about certain given
properties. Analysis, in other words, is applicable only to
synthetic properties, and its success in explaining natural phenomena is the only reliable proof that there *are* synthetic
properties. Gravitation, for example, and the properties of
chemical compounds, are proved to be synthetic because, and
only because, they are capable of analysis.

There is a special case of synthesis which, under the
name of "emergence," is receiving much attention from contemporary metaphysicians. [12] In this case the synthetic properties are predictable neither from the constituents severally,

[11] For a discussion of this general principle, cf. E. G. Spaulding, *The
New Rationalism*, 1918, pp. 274-283.
[12] Notably from S. Alexander, A. N. Whitehead and C. Lloyd Morgan.
The best summary and critical analysis of the view is to be found in
C. D. Broad, *Mind and its Place in Nature*, 1925, Ch. II, XIV. Cf. also
A. O. Lovejoy, "The Discontinuities of Evolution," *Essays in Meta-
physics*, Univ. of Calif. Publications, 1924.

nor from any prior and more general principle of synthesis. Thus the behavior of living things might be predictable from its constituents, and from the principles of physical and chemical synthesis; or it might contain a new principle of synthesis, and exhibit properties predictable only when this new principle was taken account of. Life might then be said to be emergent in principle, as well as in properties. This could be expressed otherwise by saying that living things obeyed a unique and independent law. There might be a similar emergence of mind from life, and of society or God from mind. Each successive emergent principle would then be *consistent* with preceding principles, although independent of them in the sense of not being implied by, or deducible from them.

On these assumptions 'mechanism' could then be defined in either of two ways. In the first place, it could be taken to mean any or all of those properties (such as mathematical, physical or chemical properties) which preceded that specific property, appearing at some level of vital or mental complexity, which was identified with purpose, Or, in the second place, since this antithesis occurs all along the line, the term 'mechanism' might be used to refer to the analytical properties of any whole, as distinguished from its synthetic properties. In this sense physical properties would constitute the mechanism of chemical phenomena; chemical properties, the mechanism of life; biological properties, the mechanism of mind; and psychological properties, the mechanism of society. or God. In short the mechanism of any system would mean simply its composition and structure. And, *per contra,* teleology would be taken to signify simply the novelty of the synthetic properties; or, the emergent character would be regarded as the purpose of the conditions from which it emerged.

Whichever of these interpretations was accepted, mechanism and teleology would no longer be conflicting hypothesis. Which shall we accept?

§ 62. Emergence as the Criterion of Teleology. Since 'emergence' indubitably occurs, whether one shall or shall

not·call it 'teleology' is a question of terms. The objection
to such a use of the term 'teleology' lies in its excessive
generality. If we were to identify 'interest' with this relationship we should be bound to acknowledge the presence
of interest even in a pair of gravitating bodies, or in the
behavior of a chemical compound, and we should not be aided
in our study of value as something peculiarly characteristic
of the human and social sciences. Furthermore, the teleological vocabulary could scarcely be so employed without
violation of linguistic usage, and without misunderstanding.
If one speaks of the structure and composition of a whole,
as the 'means,' and the peculiar synthetic properties as the
'end,' one naturally supposes that the one 'seeks' the other;
or exists and acts 'for the sake of' it; or that the total
arrangement has been 'designed'; whereas no such thing is
in the least implied.[13]

But it has been argued that this general distinction between analytic and synthetic properties obtains in a *peculiar*
sense at that level of nature where life emerges. A recent
writer has contended that at this level the synthetic properties are *independent* of the analytical properties; and would
propose to define purpose in terms of this independence.
Thus, for example, things having a certain structure and
composition will measure time. But " 'time-pieces' may vary
in composition from a sun-dial to a chronoscope." The function of 'keeping time' as distinguished from all of these
specific structures, he proposes to call a 'purpose.' "If, then,"
he continues, "there is any part of science where peculiar
and specific concepts are defined in terms of purpose, and
place no limit on the variety of mechanism which may be
found to serve this purpose, we might call such sciences
teleological." [14]

But, in the first place, it is evident that there are *some*
mechanical properties that must be possessed by all time-

[13] The view here considered is only a variation of that which identifies
purpose with the formal properties of unity and organization. Cf. §§ 21,
23-27.
[14] E. A. Singer, "The Pulse of Life," *Jour. of Philos.*, Vol. XI, 1914,
pp. 647, 648.

pieces, such as uniform and periodic change; and in the second place, there are *no* sciences in which synthetic properties may not be generalized and correlated with a variety of mechanisms. A 'medium' in physics, and a 'base' or 'catalyzer' in chemistry, are functions which may be differently constituted; 'work' or 'kinetic energy' may be produced by a variety of conditions. Work, for example, is not uniquely related to the chemical composition of coal; the same function may be exercised by water occupying a certain position relatively to the earth. But one does not therefore say that thermodynamics or hydrodynamics is a teleological science. One would not say that coal existed for the purpose of doing work, unless *there were a purpose to do work,* either in the coal or in the God who created it; unless, in other words, one were to suppose, over and above its own physico-chemical properties, certain specific biological or psychological properties attaching to its source or control. We are thus led to the common-sense view that the differentia of purpose is not the embodiment of the same function in diverse structures, but that peculiar embodiment in which the function is pursued as an end.

This view is really the underlying assumption of the analogy between the machine and the organism, when this analogy is employed by the argument for design. This argument denies, on the one hand, that the organism is a *mere* machine; while, on the other hand, it appeals to the fact that the organism closely *resembles* a machine. Confusion arises from the fact that a machine may be viewed in two aspects: as an *organization* having emergent properties, and as an *artefact.* As an organization, the machine is explicable in terms of its composition and structure; that is, the way it behaves as a whole can be accounted for in terms of its parts and their principles of combination. It is a peculiarly perfect type of organization because it is relatively simple, and its elements and arrangement are clearly evident. In this it resembles the situations created by experimental science, which isolates a limited group of elements so that the whole may contain none but recognized and calculable factors.[15]   But when a machine, such as a time-piece, is regarded as an artefact, it is conceived as owing its existence and structure to the will of an inventor who contrives it to satisfy a need or desire of keeping time.   Since an organism resembles a machine internally, it is supposed that analogy justifies the supposition that the organism also has been invented or contrived; if not by man, then by God.

Thus if the argument has any force at all, it rests upon the similarity of the organism to a machine, or to those systems of nature isolated by experimental and exact science; and hence presupposes that as respects the formal properties of organization the living organism marks no radical departure from that which is most typical of the inorganic world.   If there is any novel 'teleological' factor, it must be sought, therefore, in the process of invention and manufacture, rather than in the structure of the product.   It must be sought, in other words, in the behavior of a *second organism.*[16]   This inventing and creating organism, will, like its product, be an organization.   If this, in turn, is attributed to an antecedent maker the issue is only postponed.   So that sooner or later purpose has to be conceived not as organization simply, but as that *special mode of organization* in which occur such specific processes as need, desire, invention and contrivance.   In other words, life is not purposive by virtue of being emergent or organized; but organization is purposive in the particular case of life by virtue of certain special properties which emerge.

§ 63.   **The Principle of Individuality.**   There is a cognate conception of teleology, which can best be considered in the present context.   It is sometimes held that the distinguishing

---

[15] This is also the procedure of 'exact' science, as defined by the 'analytical method' of Descartes. Cf. the *Discourse on Method,* Part I.
[16] We reach a similar conclusion if we think of the behavior of the organism in terms of what it 'advantageous' or 'disadvantageous.' The teleology of it lies primarily not in the behavior of the organism observed, but in the capacity of the observer to conceive of the organism's preservation as desirable, and to judge of its behavior as 'means' to that 'end.' To conceive the organism as itself internally teleological is to impute to it a like capacity.

feature of living things is their individuality; and that if we can find that which constitutes individuality, we shall have obtained a definition of interest or purpose.

Throughout the long history of this subject there have been two great rival doctrines of individuality, which we may term the 'rational' and the 'irrational' doctrines.[17] According to the former, individuality consists in uniqueness. This does not imply that the individual is unanalyzable and inexplicable, but only that it should possess certain properties which are not duplicated elsewhere, or possessed by its parts taken severally. Individuality, in this sense, is a synthetic or emergent property, conditioned upon a structure and composition which, because of its complexity and variety, is unlikely to recur. Such an individuality would be possessed preëminently by the universe, taken as a whole. But so conceived, individuality is only a special case, or perhaps the limiting case, of organization.[18]

According to the second, or 'irrational' doctrine, the essence of individuality lies in its indistinctness and inscrutability. Individuality is the residual discrepancy between nature and abstract concepts, the material imperfection which distinguishes the existent substance from the pure form. The individual cannot be generalized because it cannot be completely analyzed. But individuality so conceived is best exemplified in the brute data of the physical world, and would serve as a negative rather than as a positive criterion of life and mind.

Certain modern writers, desiring both to exalt individuality and at the same time to preserve this aspect of unreason, have proposed to define the individual object in terms of will. "As individual," says Royce, "the object of Will is the object of an exclusive interest, or love, which can permit no other to take its place." [19] In other words, it is here proposed not to define interest in terms of individuality, but individuality in terms of interest. There is a certain flavor

---

[17] For an instructive survey of the history of this topic, cf. J. Royce, *The Conception of God*, 1897, pp. 217-271.
[18] Cf. B. Bosanquet: *Principle of Individuality and Value*, 1912.
[19] J. Royce, *op. cit.*, p. 209.

of the term 'individual' which can only be preserved when this term is limited to beings which assert their preferences, or to the objects which such beings desire and claim.   But it is evident that individuality in this limited sense can only be understood *after* an examination of those specific properties of living beings which are denoted by such terms as 'will' and 'love,' and cannot, therefore, be used to define these properties.

The results of the foregoing analysis may be resumed as follows.   Such general properties of organisms as organization and individuality yield no differentia of life, and still less a definition of interest.   An interested organism is, no doubt, a peculiar kind of organized individual; but that which we seek lies in the peculiarity, rather than in the kind.   This peculiarity lies in some character, not yet clearly ascertained, and occurring at some level in the organic realm, which justifies the use of such terms as 'end,' 'pursuit,' 'desire,' 'love' and 'will.'

Seeking to identify this character, we shall now turn to those aspects of life which are broadly comprised under the conception of self-preservation.   The living organism is not merely an organization and an individual, but it somehow acts so as to bring this organization and individuality into existence, or so as to maintain and conserve them.   We shall examine this character of the organism first in the relatively simple aspect of *tendency,* and then in its more complicated aspect of *adaptation.*

II. TENDENCY AS A DIRECTIONAL OR CULMINATING PROCESS

§ 64. **Causal Futurity.**   When we conceive the organism as growing *towards* maturity, or conceive its activities as tending *towards* certain results, such as its preservation, we seem in some sense to explain the present by the future. Let us, therefore, first examine this notion of causal futurity in general terms.

It may be supposed that explanation by the future can be derived from the time relations of an ordinary causal system, when the *logical* conception of causality is substituted for the older and more naïve view of causality as *impact*. According to this naïve view, causation proceeds from the past toward the future, a cause being an antecedent that exerts force upon something that follows passively after. Causality in this sense is contrasted in the popular mind with purpose, which is supposed to explain what happens now by what is yet to come. But the logical conception of causality appears to destroy this antithesis, because the causality is thought to be exerted not by the particular antecedents of an event, but by the law. Through the law, furthermore, the determination of each event may be said to have a *forward reference in time,* since the law prescribes the future equally with the present. A body which is obeying the law of uniform acceleration is a body that is *going* to move at a prescribed velocity after a certain lapse of time. In terms of the law, it is possible either to predict the future from the present; or to infer the past from the present, that is, from what is future *to the past.* Hence, it may be said, the difference between mechanism and purpose turns out to be nothing more than the difference of direction in the causal relation; the two being complementary aspects of a temporal system determined by law.

Now if by causal determination we mean the relation between the law of the system and any phase of the system, as in the case of the relation between the law $v = gt$, and a particular velocity of the body at any given time, then we have over again that general conception of analytic unity which we have already considered.[20] If there is anything new in the present notion it must lie in the relation among the particular phases themselves. Is it true that in a mechanical system of the ordinary type the temporal relations are symmetrical? Evidently not. In order that a particular physical configuration may be regarded as a phase of the system $v = gt$, its time must be measured *forward* from the

[20] Cf. § 26.

moment of origin. *t* in the formula means time that *has* transpired. When the past is inferred from the present, it is only after the present has already been defined in terms of the past. We virtually say: assuming that the body has moved for a certain time, and has now a certain velocity, its earlier velocities must *have been* such and such. Any particular velocity of the body is completely determined at the moment of its occurrence in terms of the past which that moment terminates; and whether the body continues to move thereafter or not, is indifferent. At the first moment its velocity is zero, however long may be the subsequent period of its motion; at the last moment its velocity is a positive quantity, even though the subsequent period of its motion be zero. Or, in the order of *occurrence,* time, measured from earlier to later, is the independent variable; even though in the order of *inference,* the independent variable may be time measured in the converse direction. Unless this distinction is made, it is impossible to distinguish the case of inferring the past history of a positively accelerated body, from the case of predicting the motion of a negatively accelerated body.

§ 65. **The Tendency and its Crucial Phase.** Although this notion of the temporal convertibility of ordinary mechanical determination has never, in this elementary form, been employed for the definition of teleology, it has been so used in a complex form. It is then spoken of as 'trend' or 'tendency.' But there is in fact no more justification for this use in the one case than in the other.

A determined temporal process is spoken of as a tendency, whenever there is anything remarkable which distinguishes the later from the earlier phases, and may be regarded as that *toward* which the process moves, or that *in* which it culminates. This may happen in one of two ways: either through the appearance of novelty or discontinuity within the process itself; or through the conjunction between the given process and some other process that is external to it.[21]

[21] We may safely ignore that notion of tendency in which it is regarded

Let us first consider the type of 'tendency' in which only a single system is concerned. A moving body obeying the law of negative acceleration is said to 'tend' to a condition of rest. Rest is not a small quantity of motion, but non-motion. A moving body which comes to rest therefore takes on a novel character that is qualitatively discontinuous with its earlier history. The state of rest may thus be singled out from among the phases of the moving body as peculiar and remarkable. There is, however, no reason to credit it with any causal preëminence. The earlier behavior of the body can no more be said to be dominated by the moment of rest, than by any one of the other later moments at which the quantity of its motion only approximates zero. So far as the determination of the process is concerned, the moment of rest is not unique, but is on the same plane with all the others.

Or, let us consider the case of the second law of thermo-dynamics. The total energy of the cosmos is said to tend to resolve itself into heat, and to become so distributed as to be incapable of doing work. This phase is qualitatively peculiar, in respect of its homogeneity; and it is humanly interesting, in that it would make life impossible. But it plays no unique rôle in the determination of the process. There is no sense in which it could be regarded as the goal of the cosmos, that would not hold equally of any inter-mediate phase. Similarly, we speak of two bodies as tend-ing to a common centre of gravity, or cooling water as tending to form ice. But although these states are novel and remarkable, they cannot be said in any sense to control the systems within which they fall, or to have any peculiar potency. They obey the law of the system, and are equally and reciprocally correlated with other phases of the system.

as a loose or relatively undetermined process. Thus bodies were said to tend to the surface of the earth before the law of gravitation was under-stood; and one is said to have a tendency to this or that disease, when exact pathological conditions are unknown. I cannot see that either this notion of tendency, or Royce's *statistical* conception, contribute anything to the understanding or defence of teleology. Cf. Royce, "The Mechan-ical, the Historical and the Statistical," *Science,* Vol. XXXIX, 1914, pp. 551-566.

§ 66. Conjunction and Coincidence of Tendencies.

Let us now consider the type of tendency in which two or more systems are, at least provisionally, assumed. Let us suppose, first, the case of a moving body governed by the law of inertia, and coming into the neighborhood of a second moving body similarly determined. There results a state of equilibrium in which they revolve about a common centre of gravity. This new state differs notably from the earlier states of the two bodies in that it is unified, and in that the motions are circular instead of rectilinear. We now find that we were mistaken in supposing that we had to do with two independent systems which accidentally intersected, and conceive the whole change as successive phases of one system governed by the law of gravitation. The two bodies do not become a system, strictly speaking, but *have been* a system all along by virtue of their mutual attractions. The stable periodicity of their motions is only a phase of this system: a crucial phase, but not on that account in any sense peculiarly accountable for the changes leading up to it.

In the second place, let us suppose that two genuinely independent systems collide, and give rise to resultant states that are not deducible from either system. This, as Professor Palmer has so well pointed out, is the meaning of chance in the positive or 'objective' sense.

"Chance might be defined as planless concurrence; and when it is so defined, we discover it all around us, in great things and in small. It was an accident that the winter was exceptionally severe after the landing on our shore of the Pilgrim Fathers; that the tower of Siloam fell on those particular persons; that the partridge flew past me when I did not have my gun. The liberties of England are largely due to chance in the storm which arose soon after the sailing of the Spanish Armada. For however minutely we might become acquainted with the sequence of conditions which led up to the storm, or with that other sequence which led up to the sailing, we should never discover the wreck among them. That was an accident, the coming together of two independent lines of causation which until that coinciding moment had no reference to one another." [22]

[22] G. H. Palmer, *The Problem of Freedom*, 1911, pp. 138-139. It may be argued that the total cosmos at each moment is a function of similar

If with a complete knowledge of 'mechanical' laws the coincidence remained an accident, this would leave open the possibility that it was *otherwise* determined. In other words, that which is 'mechanically' accidental may afford an instance of something whose only explanation is teleological. But its being mechanically accidental does not *in itself* prove that it is teleologically explicable. Coincidence *may* be the last word in the matter. And this holds quite independently of the extent to which the coincidence is 'remarkable.' If there are to be coincidences at all, some will be remarkable and some not, and that those within our notice should have been of the former variety is, as we have seen,[23] entirely in keeping with the theory of chances. In other words, if a new kind of determination, such as teleology, is to be invoked, it must be because of some further datum connected with the origin of the occurrence which we call a coincidence.

It has sometimes been supposed that the differentia of teleology may be found in the peculiar relation of *concurrence* which may obtain between one tendency and another, or between a tendency and any agency which is external to it. Given a tendency, it is argued that an external agency may either ally itself therewith, or retard it; and that when this is the case, such an agency may be said to be 'for' or 'against' it. This duality of relationship is offered as a definition of utility or disutility.[24] But it seems perfectly clear that the relationships in question are just as characteristic of the inorganic world as of the organic, and that they introduce nothing new in principle. The acceleration of a moving body may be reinforced by impact from without; or a river's flow toward the sea may be 'favored' by the contour of the

cross-sections at previous moments. But this sweeping generalization, even though true, is irrelevant. The special threads of causal connection which science traces cannot be deduced from this generalization, nor is their absence in particular cases contradicted by it. The fact is that there is no single cosmic law, but a considerable variety of laws that are quite independent of one another. In order to deduce a total cosmic phase from an earlier phase, it would be necessary to employ a great many different laws and to make a great many independent deductions. Cf. *ibid.*, p. 148.
    [23] Cf. § 27.
    [24] Cf. W. H. Sheldon, "An Empirical Definition of Value," *Jour. of Philos.*, Vol. XI, 1914, p. 113. Cf. above, § 19.

earth's surface. In such cases we have accidental concurrence of the type already discussed.

Where, on the other hand, the facilitating agency 'conspires' with the tendency, then it is incorrect to regard it as external. It is simply one of the factors of the tendency itself, and its favoring the tendency means nothing more than sharing its determination. In this sense it would be just as reasonable to speak of the mass of the earth as favoring the fall of a body towards its centre. Any partial cause combines with other causes to produce an effect, and may be thought of as auxiliary to these other causes. In so far as we are interested in the effect, we are likely to speak of such an auxiliary cause as 'favorable' to the effect, suggesting that the cause is itself interested in the outcome. But this is the 'pathetic fallacy' again.[25] There is nothing of 'purpose' in an auxiliary cause, that is not present in any cause. It is characteristic of all temporal events that they precede some future event, which they determine according to law, or for which they supply some partial condition. They can be described with reference to this sequel, as leading, conducing, or tending to it. But something more is required in order to make it significant to say that the event occurs for the sake of the sequel: the sequel must, in some sense, play a unique rôle in the determination of the event.

If temporal direction or tendency does not signify teleology in the case of inorganic phenomena, neither of them is more significant in the case of organic phenomena. That life exhibits tendencies cannot be doubted. Growth, for example, may be regarded as a tendency to progressive increase, or to such a crucial phase as maturity. But if this be all there is to growth, then there is no more occasion to invoke teleology than in the case of progressive aging, dissolution and death; or a body's tendency to progressive increase of velocity, or a liquid's tendency to freeze, or energy's tendency to stagnation. Trains and steamships may tend to reach their destinations on schedule time; individual conduct may tend to a state of happiness, power or possession, that we call

[25] Cf. § 24.

the agent's aim or goal; nations may tend to progressive expansion or to a place in the sun; human society in general may tend to a progressively greater complexity and organization, or to a perfect equilibrium of mutually adjusted interests. But if there is any purpose in such changes, or anything to distinguish them from the common characteristics of inorganic changes, it must consist of something over and above that mere aspect of tendency which has already been described.

III. ADAPTATION AS COMPLEMENTARY ADJUSTMENT

§ 67. **The Principle of Adaptation.** Adaptation, in the biological sense, signifies the possession by the organism of a complementary fitness to its environment which enables the organism to survive. This principle is stated by a contemporary biologist as follows:

"In general what we meant by an 'adaptive' feature in an organism is some peculiarity of structural organization or activity that directly aids in preserving the organic equilibrium, *i.e.*, in securing survival. . . . The arrangement of the valves in the heart is adaptive since it ensures the constant flow of blood in one direction. The camera structure of the eye is adaptive in enabling the animal to react effectively to the stimulus of light waves reaching it from different directions of space—these light waves being indicators of the presence and situation of physical objects which are thus discriminated. A countless number of special adaptive structures and habits have reference to the special features of the animal's environment: Arboreal creatures have special clinging devices; parasites are curiously protected; predatory animals are usually swifter, more powerful and more intelligent than their prey; the special instincts of an animal are its congenital adaptive modes of behavior. In brief, unless a character in some way definitely furthers continued existence in an environment it is not classed as an adaptation; its criterion as adaptation is that it favors the persistence of the species. To put the matter concisely, adaptation is a form of equilibration." [26]

[26] R. S. Lillie, "The Place of Life in Nature," *Jour. of Philos.*, Vol. XVII, 1920, pp. 484-485.

That the organism and its environment should be structually complementary to one another, or that their conjunction should yield a remarkable result, argues nothing that is peculiar to life or that promises to throw light on the category of teleology. Such a complementary fitness is reciprocal, and implies no more purpose on the one side than on the other. It is not at all necessary to suppose that such a complementary fitness has a purposive origin; and even if one did suppose such an origin, one would be no nearer than before to an understanding of the precise nature of the purposive process itself. All of this has been abundantly proved.[27]

We must, therefore, confine our attention to that which *distinguishes* the organism from its environment; and which underlies the common view that the organism *adapts itself* to the environment, in some sense in which the environment does not adapt itself to the organism. We must look beyond the bare structural fitness which is true of both terms of the relation, to the functional *fitting* which is peculiar to one of the terms; and regard the structural fitness of the organism, as consisting in the possession of organs which enable it to *act* fitly. We shall in the following analysis, therefore, regard adaptation as *a mode of behavior;* or as a complementary adjustment *enacted by* organisms, *in relation to* their environment. When so conceived adaptation promises to advance our inquiry. For it is at least plausible to say that the organism which, under varying conditions, and in various ways, so acts as constantly to secure its own preservation, is acting 'for the sake of,' or 'in order to' secure, that preservation. Preservation is an *outcome* or ulterior result of action, and at the same time seems to govern or determine it.

§ 68. Compensatory Adjustment. The simplest type of this mode of behavior is equilibration, or what we may term 'compensatory adjustment.' A first system (the organism)

[27] Cf. §§ 26, 27, 61. Professor L. J. Henderson, in his *Fitness of the Environment,* 1913, argues very properly that such structural fitness is *mutual;* but his argument, for that very reason, throws no light on the peculiar character of *organic* behavior.

acts upon a second system or group of systems (the environment) in such wise as to recover and maintain a constant state. We suppose a certain initial or normal state of the first system; and find that when, owing to either internal or external causes, this state is altered, certain compensatory changes arise within the system itself which restore the normal state.

This conception plays an important rôle in the 'biomechanical' philosophy of Avenarius, and in the theory of value which his followers have developed. The *biomechanische Grundgesetz* is expressed as $f(R) + f(S) = 0$, where R is the external stimulus, and S the *Nahrungsstoff*, or the energies and substances of which the organism is composed. The formula then signifies that the changes induced in the organism by the action of the environment, are precisely offset by the *Stoffwechsel* or metabolic processes. In this view, centrally initiated changes by which the organic equilibrium is disturbed, are also construed as the indirect action of the environment. The law prescribes that such compensatory changes shall then be set up within the organism as will restore the equilibrium.[28]

Let us see what this conception implies. In the first place, it is implied that the action of the environment is determined independently of the organism, and imposes from without conditions which the responding organism must meet from within. Whether or not it should turn out to be possible to include the organism and the environment in one larger system, the principle of compensatory adjustment appears only when one thinks in terms of the narrower system of the organism, and regards events in the environment as from that standpoint, at least, accidental. That which an organism adapts itself *to*, must be supposed to vary independently. In the second place, it is implied that the organism contains a reserve of energy, which the action of the environment releases. The action or response of the organism consists of

[28] Cf. F. Carstanjen, *Richard Avenarius' Biomechanische Grundlegung der neuen allgemeinen Erkenntnisstheorie*, v894, p. 24; R. Eisler, *Studien der Werttheorie*, 1902, p. 21.

more or less 'spontaneous' changes, conditioned by the potentialities of the organism itself; and these will bear no constant quantitative relation to the amount of the stimulus. Finally, it is implied that this response of the organism is constant in a certain peculiar respect: namely, it is always such that when its effects are added to those of the stimulus, the net effect is a return to the first state of the organism. The effect of the response is to cancel the effect of the environment. If we symbolize the initial state of the organism by O_1, the action of the environment by E_a, and the response by O_r, we may then express the total operation by the formula, $O_1 + E_a - O_r = O_1$. None of these factors can be omitted without altering the essential character of the operation.

We may speak of this operation as a tendency *to maintain* equilibrium. This is a very different thing from the tendency to equilibrium, simply. This latter would be illustrated, as we have seen, in a moving body's coming to rest, or in the genesis of a planetary system, or in the dissipation of energy. A tendency to *maintain* equilibrium, on the other hand, would be exhibited only provided a body at rest possessed a supplementary mechanism, which so operated as to restore the state of rest, whenever this was disturbed by any adventitious agency. The proof of the possession of such a mechanism would lie in its action's being regularly complementary to varying disturbances. Similarly, a clock tends to equilibrium in so far as it runs down. It would tend to *maintain* equilibrium, only provided there were over and above the tension of its main-spring, an auxiliary mechanism which so acted as to restore that tension whenever it was exhausted. A self-winding clock would in this respect resemble an organism.

Thus, an organism may be said to tend to 'keep' going.' Consider, for example, the following description, borrowed from Hobhouse:

"Mechanically, the organism may be conceived, like any other mechanism, as essentially an arrangement for the transformation of energy. Thus the animal organism takes up energy in the form of food on the one hand and of oxygen on the other.

For each process of absorption it has its appropriate mechanism, the alimentary and the respiratory organs. Next, it has to distribute what it absorbs by means of its circulatory system, and thereby to nourish nerve and muscle tissues wherein the potential energy of the foodstuffs is converted into energy of motion, so directed through the nervous control as to secure fresh supplies of energy and at the same time maintain at the right point, neither too high nor too low, the temperature at which this persistent activity of change or metabolism can go on." [29]

To construe this as a case of compensatory adjustment, means that when the organism is below par, when the scales are tipped, when the vitality is depressed, energies are liberated which so combine with the environment as to bring the organism back to par.

Let us take another description which emphasizes the central rather than the peripheral source of the disturbance.

"In all animals we find that when the supply of food is decreased below the normal the activity of the search for food increases correspondingly; there is increased reactivity to food materials; this is the physiological correlate of 'hunger'; the chances of securing what is needed to maintain the equilibrium are thus increased." [30]

In this case, a certain degree of exhaustion on the part of the organism sets up those complementary acts which are to revive the organism. But the process of nutrition is by no means the only physiological process which exhibits this principle. It is equally well illustrated by the simple reflexes, such as the coughing reflex, by which a foreign particle is removed from the mucous membrane of the larynx; or by the acceleration of breathing when an excessive amount of carbon dioxide is given off by the muscles, or the healing and regenerative process, or the formation of callus on the skin; or by the activity of the anti-bodies in resisting the invading micro-organisms of disease. In all of these cases there is. a mechanism of recovery, which is released whenever the system rises above or falls below a certain zero point; and the effects

[29] L. T. Hobhouse, *Development and Purpose*, 1913, p. 303.
[30] R. S. Lillie, "What is Purposive and Intelligent Behavior from the Physiological Point of View?" *Jour. of Philos.*, Vol. XII, 1915, p. 592.

of which are equal in quantity, and opposite in sign, to those of the disturbing agency.

The principle [31] is equally well illustrated by the operation of certain inorganic mechanisms. Some instances which have frequently been cited in this connection evidently will not serve. The candle-flame exhibits a certain constancy of form despite the change of its materials; and if its form is altered, as by a gust of wind, it will return again to the same form. But this means only that when the disturbing cause is removed, the original causes will operate as before. It means only that the effect of the disturbing cause is temporary: the system itself does nothing to counteract it. The same analysis holds in the case of the whirlpool or cataract. There is here nothing more than is to be found in the simplest mechanical phenomena. Suppose a body to be obeying the law of inertia and to be moving with a uniform velocity. A second body may be introduced and the motion will be accelerated. Then when the second body is withdrawn, the law of inertia resumes its sway, and the first body returns to a condition of uniform velocity. Meanwhile the first body has done nothing to offset the disturbance, or to maintain its first state against the intruding force.

But a genuine case of compensatory adjustment is afforded by the governor of a steam-engine, and by the thermostat. A house equipped with a furnace and a thermostat does tend to maintain a constant temperature. When the temperature rises or falls above the point at which the thermostat is set, whether owing to changes in the environment or to changes within, a mechanism of recovery is released, and is so determined in its operation as to neutralize the disturbing agency. Provided the heating-plant is able to cope with fluctuations of temperature which are usual in its environment, the building so equipped may be said in respect of temperature to 'adapt' itself to that invironment.

[31] Its widest generalization is to be found in the so-called "principle of Le Chatelier-Braun," which attributes to all bodies or systems a tendency by internal changes to maintain the existing state against attack from without, this "faculty of accommodation" being extended to inorganic nature. Cf. O. D. Chwolson, *Traité de Physique,* French trans. by E. Davaux, 1910, Vol. III, pp. 476-483 [bibliog., p. 547].

§ 69. **Progressive Adjustment.** Let us now consider what appears to be a different type of complementary adjustment, which may be termed 'progressive adjustment.' A growing organism evidently does not merely tend to maintain itself; it increases to or toward a certain maximum, which thereafter it tends to maintain. It is as though the equilibrium were unbalanced at the outset. The growing organism tends to arrive at an equilibrium which it has never as yet possessed. Such an operation can be represented as follows: $O_1 + E_1 + R_1 = O_2$; $O_2 + E_2 + R_2 = O_3$; $O_3 + E_3 + R_3 = O_4$, etc., where R_1, R_2, R_3, represent the successive responses, and O_1, O_2, $O_3 \cdots O_n$ successive states of the organism approaching O_n. When the organism reaches the state O_n, the operation comes to an end, or takes the form of simple compensatory adjustment described above. The successive responses of the organism are complementary to an independently varying environment, but the sum of environment and response, instead of being zero, is some intermediate term of an orderly series which has a last term. This last term, which in the case of the growing organism is the state of maturity, may be said to be what the organism is tending to do or accomplish. It is not merely a tendency to become something, exhibited by an isolated system, but a dealing with external and contingent events so as to promote the tendency. This implies an independent variability on the part of circumstance or environment, and a complementary variability on the part of the organism. The responses of the organism are not simple functions either of the existing state of the organism, or of the confronting environment; but they are such as, when combined with the confronting environment, produce a state of the organism which belongs next to its existing state in an orderly progression.

Growth is far from being the only instance of this process which life affords. Such a process is illustrated by all reflexes that are not of the simple protective type. Consider, for example, the instance of hunger already cited. The decrease of the food supply below par excites the organism to compensatory adjustment. But in its dealings with the environment the hungry organism exhibits adjustment of the progressive type. It does not act so as to neutralize the environment, but so as to combine with it in producing an orderly increase of satisfaction. In other words, equilibrium is achieved or restored progressively.

Needless to say it is quite possible that when a first progressive adjustment is completed, it may be succeeded not by a compensatory process, but by a second progressive adjustment, or by a series of progressive adjustments. In so far as instinctive action, such as the begetting and rearing of offspring, can be reduced to a series of reflexes it is evidently of this type.

§ 70. **Preparatory Adjustment.** But what is ordinarily regarded as instinctive action involves a new principle, which we may now introduce under the name of 'preparatory adjustment.' Consider the following account of instinct offered by Professor R. S. Lillie:

"Many animals in temperate zones make in autumn or throughout the year special provision for passing the winter. Frogs hibernate, many birds fly south, squirrels collect stores of food, various insects such as bees do the same, others construct cocoons, cysts, or burrows in which they or their larvae lie dormant during the cold period. . . . How are these various reactions to be regarded from the physiological standpoint? It is first to be noted that all show one evident characteristic. They may be regarded as *protective* reactions having reference to a certain definite and regularly recurring situation in the external world, namely, the coming of a prolonged period in which temperature is low and food is scarce. Now what is to be especially noted is that in every one of the above cases the characteristic behavior, which has reference to the *whole* situation, is called forth or initiated by only a *part* of the same, and often a quite inconspicuous part." [32]

Although, as our author says, this performance is one of maintaining equilibrium, as a matter of fact the equilibrium is not disturbed. Its disturbance is not offset or neutralized,

[32] *Op. cit.,* pp. 603-604.

but is *averted*. If we wish in this case to view the responses of the organism as complementary to the action of the environment, we must correlate a series of the former with a series of the latter. A cycle of organic responses is complementary to a cycle of environmental changes. Or, in order that a certain environmental change may be met so as to maintain the organism's equilibrium, it is necessary that the organism's response should be begun at a certain time in advance. The adjustment to it takes time, and must be started before the environmental change has been completed. The early stages of the response will, in that case, fail to exhibit the compensatory relation to those changes of the environment which call them forth.

This type of response can be represented as follows: Let R_1 represent the initial response of an organism to E_1 which marks the beginning at t' of a cycle of changes in the environment. E_1, for example, is the autumnal temperature, and R_1 the first movement of a migratory bird toward the south. E_2, E_3, etc., would then represent the further seasonal changes, and R_2, R_3, etc., the birds continued southerly flight. Then, although R_1 does not exhibit the complementary relation to E_1, nor R_2 to E_2, etc., the cycle of responses $R_1 \cdots R_n$ is complementary to the cycle of environmental changes $E_1 \cdots E_n$; that is, the removal to a warmer climate is complementary to the coming of winter, in that it prevents a disturbance of equilibrium which would otherwise have taken place. We can say that $(E_1 \cdots E_n) - (R_1 \cdots R_n) = 0$; but must bear in mind that since the two cycles develop simultaneously, the disequilibrium $O_1 + E_n$, or the bird's presence in the north in winter, does not occur. When at t^n the environmental change is completed which would have disturbed the balance had the organism remained as at t', or had its responses been tardy, these responses have reached a point which nullifies the environmental change.

But it is not necessary to look for examples among serial responses of so complicated a nature. The animal which endeavors to escape its enemy illustrates the same principle of preparatory adjustment. The commencement of the movements of escape is not complementary to the appearance of the enemy at a distance, but these movements as a whole are complementary to the pursuit as a whole. In some measure this principle is obeyed by all protective reflexes that are stimulated by telesthesia or distance sensation, such as vision, hearing and smell.

This principle may be combined not only with simple compensatory adjustment, but with progressive adjustment as well. The animal which pursues its prey engages in a series of responses which exhibit their progressively complementary character only when they terminate in the capture of the prey. The pursuit as a whole, taken as a response to the flight as a whole, produces a result which constitutes a phase in the progressive satisfaction of hunger. Or, this last series of responses may be said to be continued in the internal secretion of gastric juice, given off in anticipation of the entrance of food into the stomach. Similarly, the complex series of responses involved in the perpetuation of the species, is progressive, and not compensatory merely; but only in so far as these responses are subdivided into unit-cycles, such as procreation, nest-building and food-getting, where the earlier phases of each unit-cycle are complementary only in respect of what they prepare or make ready.

§ 71. **Complementary Adjustment as Automatic.** Shall we, then, regard behavior of this complementary sort as teleological or interested? Shall we say that the organism *seeks* to avoid death or loss of vitality? Shall we say that the organism procures food *for the sake* of completing its growth? Shall we say that the organism stores food or builds nests, *in order to* perpetuate the species?

That complementary adjustment is important, and distinctive in principle, is not to be denied. It would appear that in its more complicated 'progressive' and 'preparatory' forms it is peculiar to living organisms. There is no absolute ground for rejecting this as an interpretation of teleology. The important thing is to distinguish principles, and not to label them. It certainly would not be nonsense to speak of the interior temperature for which the thermostat is set as 'good,' since the heating-plant tends to maintain it; or to speak of a cold wind or open window as 'bad,' since it needs to be offset by a restorative mechanism. Still less would it be nonsense to speak of the maturity of a plant as good, since the organism's responses tend to bring the organism to that form; or to speak of food as good since the organism's responses utilize them. The propriety of such a use of terms will depend on whether or not there is a more restricted use which is more convenient for purposes of the theory of value. That there is such a more restricted use is evident. These terms can be reserved for *modifiable* or *inventive* adjustment, as distinguished from adjustment of the *automatic* type.

Complementary adjustment of the types so far considered can be summarily expressed by the formula, $E + R = C$. The responses of the adaptive system vary with the action of the environment according to some constant rule. The sum of the stimulus and the response may be zero, as in the case of simple compensatory adjustment; or the sum may be some value of an orderly series, as in the case of progressive adjustment; or, as in the case of preparatory adjustment, a series of responses may so combine with a series of stimuli as to give rise to a sum, which is either zero, or some value of an orderly series. In all of these cases, whether simple or complex, the independent variable is the environmental action, the dependent variable is the organic response, while the outcome or resultant is constant. Hence we may say that the organism *behaves in a variety of situations in such wise as to produce a constant result.* The organism may be said to be constitutionally adapted to the environment in respect of that constant result.

Professor Lillie argues that the elaborate preparatory responses characteristic of animal instinct, are in this respect of the same type as the simpler reflexes which are ordinarily supposed to exemplify automatism.

"On closer examination such an instinctive action, though complex, is seen to have all the characteristics of a simple protective or food-securing reflex, as regards both the conditions under which it is aroused and its ultimate effect on the life of the animal itself or of its species.   In every case of a purposive instinct we find the organism reacting *in a constant manner* to a condition *that recurs with constancy*.   The case differs from the direct reaction to the presence of food-material only in its complexity, and in the fact that the total situation to which adjustment is made *takes time to develop*, and, hence, an essential part of the reaction involving adjustment is made in advance." [33]

The cycle of the seasons is a constant feature of any given environment.   An organism adapted to any given environment will possess not only specific responsive propensities, but a more complex propensity to a temporal series of responses which form a cycle complementary to that of the seasons.   If natural selection can account for the more simple case it can equally well account for the more complex case.

Reduced to its lowest terms, the law of natural selection means simply that systems of the above type, in which *C* constitutes or causes survival,—will survive.   It means that out of the plenitude of nature there emerge systems whose characteristic action obeys the law of self-maintenance and self-perpetuation.[34]   Such systems are said to exhibit automatism in so far as it is supposed that their action, when combined with the environmental conditions which provoke it, is immediately and inherently self-preservative.   The constitution of such a system provides for a class of acts which in variable combination, are complementary in respect of survival to a class of environmental conditions.   Their action is adaptive, in other words, in relation to specific circumstances and a specific result.

Such systems might be said to constitute the limit of strictly biological achievement.   But nature has evidently transcended this achievement, in producing organisms which are adaptive in an undetermined variety of situations to an undetermined variety of results.   This occurs in what

[33] *Op. cit.*, pp. 604-605.
[34] James sums up the whole story of natural evolution (Spencerian) by saying that arrangements "of which one part helps to keep the other parts in existence . . . will tend to accumulate." *Memories and Studies,* 1911, p. 136.

appears, on reflection, to be the only possible way. Systems cannot be *constitutionally adapted to nothing in particular*, but they may conceivably possess a constitutional capacity to *adapt themselves as contingencies arise.*

Nature here rises to that level which we recognize as characteristic of mind or intelligence. A result not directly attainable is attained by indirection. Unfamiliar conditions are met by the use of tools, or by new combinations of familiar conditions. Complementary responses not already possessed are learned from experience. Through all this more or less protracted phase of problem-solving,[35] a certain outcome is in control, or is enabled to direct the present course of action through being in some sense presently anticipated. These controlling eventualities become diverse in nature, mere survival being only one among the rest. *Anything,* provided the present anticipation of it regulates the system's activities, may now play the rôle of that end-result in respect of which the system is adaptive.

The crucial difference which marks this advance, and which is the contribution of mind, is *control by anticipation;* which constitutes the essential meaning of what is variously known as prescience, prospicience or foresight. Since biology and psychology evidently overlap, or since it is as impossible for biologists to ignore the fact that bodies have minds as it is for psychologists to ignore the fact that minds have bodies, some brief consideration of this function is in order here.[36]

---

[35] The view that intelligence is essentially connected with *problem-solving* is implied, as we shall see presently, in recent studies of animal behavior. But this important doctrine has long been proclaimed by Professors John Dewey, G. H. Mead and A. W. Moore, and I wish here to testify to my agreement and indebtedness. Cf. Dewey, *Essays on Experimental Logic,* 1916; and papers by Mead and Moore in the University of Chicago *Decennial Publications,* and *Contributions to Philosophy.*

[36] The view presented here and in the following chapter closely resembles those of Bergson and of Lloyd Morgan, in spite of underlying philosophical differences. Cf. Bergson, *Creative Evolution,* trans. by A. Mitchell, 1911, p. 144; *Mind-Energy,* trans. by H. W. Carr, 1920, pp. 17, 57–58. Cf. Lloyd Morgan's conception of "conscious anticipation"; . . . "physical in so far as it provides for 'proleptic' action in behaviorist interpretation; psychical, in that it provides for 'prospective' reference." For Lloyd Morgan, as for the present writer, this function marks a "turning-point" in natural evolution ["A Philosophy of Evolution," in J. H. Muirhead's *Contemporary British Philosophy,* 1924, pp. 301-302].

§ 72. **Prospicient Adjustment.** It is characteristic of animals, if not of plants, or of some animals, if not of all animals, that they not only *possess* adaptation but *acquire* it. They exhibit not only organization and adaptation, but re-organization, and re-adaptation. They not only act in a manner that is adaptive; but select an adaptive course of action in consequence of their past experience of its consequences, and perform it in the expectation of these consequences. Owing to the capacity of memory, life is circumspect and prophetic. Forewarned is forearmed. This is what we mean when we speak of living things as exhibiting 'intelligence.' We do not credit all living things with intelligence; but we have no hesitation in imputing it to the higher forms of animal life, and the phenomena of instinct and tropism have led to our imputing at least a quasi-intelligence to the lower animals and even to plants.

In so far as we impute intelligence to living things, we feel the need of explaining their action in a peculiar way. The explosion is satisfactorily accounted for as a resultant of two physically existing factors, the internal organization of stored energies and the external spark or trigger. The organization and individuality of the animal's action may be accounted for in terms of its present composition. Tendency and adaptation refer both to present factors, internal and external, and also to certain later phases of the process. But in the case of intelligence it seems necessary, or at least appropriate, to refer to the sequel as being somehow in prospect at the moment when the action occurs.

Thus a dog moves rapidly away, or gets behind some intervening obstacle, when his master takes down the whip. In so far as this implies intelligence, we think of it not in terms merely of the organized, complementary and serial relations of its terms; we take account also of what is expected to happen, namely, the painful beating. We say that this also explains why the animal is acting as he does. Or, we say that the animal is acting with a view to avoiding the beating. Since the beating which is avoided does not as a matter of fact occur, we are thus appealing to a sequel which is in some sense merely possible or hypothetical. There must be some additional factor which refers to this mere possibility, and which decisively determines the direction which the discharge takes. However he may have come by it, the animal is supposed at the moment of action to possess a capacity for *prospiciently* determined action. He acts not because of what is or has been, merely, but because of what he anticipates. He acts, we say, from fear of a painful whipping, or from hope of escaping it. There is no way of describing either the fear or the hope, without admitting it to be the fear or the hope *of something,* which something is not upon the plane of past or present physical existence as ordinarily conceived.

Professor Jennings has termed this characteristic of behavior, "reaction to representative stimuli."

"The sea-urchin responds to a sudden shadow falling upon it by pointing its spines in the direction from which the shadow comes. This action is defensive, serving to protect it from enemies that in approaching may have cast the shadow. The reaction is produced by the shadow, but it *refers,* in its biological value, to something behind the shadow.

"In all these cases the reaction to the change cannot be considered due to any direct injurious or beneficial effect of the actual change itself. The actual change merely *represents* a possible change behind it, which *is* injurious or beneficial. The organism reacts as if to something else than the change actually occurring. The change has the function of a *sign.* We may appropriately call stimuli of this sort *representative* stimuli." [37]

If we construe this statement strictly we must provide for a type of adjustment which is easily confused with mere preparatory adjustment, but which is profoundly different. Preparatory adjustment means simply that a present adjustment is complementary only with respect to the relation between its effects and future states of the environment. But a "reaction to representative stimuli," means a reaction to stimuli *as representative;* or, in other words, a reaction to what the stimulus represents. Such a response is prospicient

[37] H. S. Jennings, *op. cit.,* p. 297. Cf. M. F Washburn, *The Animal Mind,* 1908, p. 256: "It seems probable that anticipation rather than retrospection is the primitive function of ideas"; and pp. 273 ff.

or *anticipatory* in that there is a present excitation of a response *to* a future situation. The response anticipates its own proper object. The dog who anticipates a beating is not merely behaving in a way that averts a beating, but is in some measure presently enacting the behavior appropriate to the possible future beating which the whip represents to him. He cries *before* he is hurt, but his cry is none the less his response to hurt.[38]

If, now, we combine this analysis with that of the more developed intelligence exhibited by Socrates in his prison,[39] we shall have a provisional view of interested or purposive action in the new and stricter sense. In both cases there is an organism with certain accumulated energies and certain organized propensities adapted to their environment. In both cases there is a specific external situation which acts upon the organism and liberates these energies and propensities. But in both cases there is an additional and differential factor which will hereinafter be said to constitute their purposive aspect. *The situation is construed by the agent in terms of something ulterior.* Socrates judges his act to be of the general type of submission to law; to the dog, the whip is a sign of beating or pain-to-come, and his flight is a response "as to" pain. In both cases the agent views the situation, whether by association, inference, or spontaneous insight, in the light of some aspect or relation that transcends given fact; and he acts *accordingly,* that is, his acting as he does is determined by his viewing the situation as he does. We are here clearly upon psychological ground.

[38] It is, of course, possible, or even probable, that the sea-urchin's behavior should be interpreted as mere preparatory adjustment; or that the migiation of birds should be interpreted in terms of representative stimuli. I do not presume to settle such special questions of animal behavior, but only to distinguish *in principle* the case in which a present anticipation of the future is an actual and determining feature of the situation. I should add that I am by no means sure that Professor Jennings has this in mind, or that he would not accept preparatory adjustment as covering the facts. In that case I must beg leave to borrow his words while rejecting his meaning.

[39] Cf. above, § 23.

CHAPTER VII

THE PSYCHOLOGICAL DEFINITION OF INTEREST [1]

I. PRELIMINARY STATEMENT

§ 73. The living organism provides the context of interest, but until mind appears we do not recognize that specific type of organic complexity which is peculiarly characteristic of human behavior, and whose diverse modes furnish the data of the sciences of value. Although spontaneity, organization, individuality and adaptation may serve to distinguish life in the broad sense, they do not adequately provide for its moral, economic, and cultural developments. That which is lacking in the strictly biological picture has been provisionally termed 'prospicience,' and consists in the capacity to act in the light of expectation. While this capacity may doubtless be traced far back along the line of biological evolution, it is *notably* characteristic of man; and is that one among the primitive factors of life which constitutes the seed of the characteristic human developments.

Spontaneity is an unmistakable feature of human life; and the depth of a man's inscrutability is due not merely to the fact that his organism contains internally stored energies that are released by stimuli from the environment, but to the fact that their release depends in some sense upon what he *thinks*. Because it has commonly been supposed that nobody but the agent himself knows what he thinks, it has been supposed that nobody but the agent himself knows what he is going to do. The organization of a human life consists not

---

[1] Parts of the present chapter and of Ch. XIII are reprinted from an article entitled, "The Appeal to Reason," published in the *Philos. Rev.*, Vol. XXX, 1921; and from an article entitled, "Docility and Purposiveness," published in the *Psych. Rev.*, Vol. XXV, 1918.

merely in the interdependence of parts within a whole, but in the subsumption of activities under an *idea*. The individuality of a man implies something more than his uniqueness; it implies that he has in some sense *elected* to be what he is, or that he *aspires* to be that which he is not. The course of a man's life cannot be adequately described as a tendency towards some ulterior or culminating phase. The goal and the outcome of his action may or may not coincide. He may follow the thoroughfares of nature, and arrive on schedule in some existing port; but he may also cross the Atlantic in search of India, or chase rainbows for a pot of gold.

The inadequacy of the stricter biological categories is most clearly apparent in the case of adaptation. It is impossible to interpret the characteristic human prerogatives in terms of *mere* adaptation. There are unicellular organisms which are much more snugly fixed than is man. The vegetating peasant, the hibernating Eskimo and the naked tropical islander, are all in better equilibrium with nature than those whose distinctively human faculties have been more completely developed. Civilization is delicate and fragile, rather than secure. Man is characterized not by the perfect balance of his account with nature, but rather by his over-drafts. He is speculative and prodigal; he is a spend-thrift whose demands are forever outrunning his supplies, and who counts upon making good the deficiency. If he adapts himself to his environment it is only as a means of adapting the environment to himself.

With man the basic need of organic preservation is quickly overlaid with a great variety of special desires. While these are no doubt conditioned by organic preservation, that need is often lost to view; or a man may feel that life is not *worth* preserving unless his special desires can be satisfied. It is evident that any picture of life which represents the organism as trimming sail, stopping leaks and storing supplies in order to ride the sea, must fail to convey the physiognomy of man. It is characteristic of him to be primarily concerned with the freight which he carries; and to set sail for distant parts, rather than merely to keep afloat. It is this creative and adventurous aspect of life for which the narrower biological categories fail to provide, and which indicate the presence of a capacity to direct action by hope, fear and expectation.

That aspect of life which is progressively characteristic of animal organisms and preëminently characteristic of man is not adaptation, but *adaptability*. It consists not in an equilibrium between the existing organization of the species and the constant features of its environment, but rather in a capacity to form projects, deal with novel situations, overcome difficulties, and *plan ahead*. This capacity is the source at once of human strength and of human weakness. For it enables man to contrive new and far-reaching adjustments; but at the same time overstrains, impairs or confuses those more basic adjustments with which in the economy of nature he has been already equipped.

If intelligence is needed to complete the biological conception of interest, and make it adequate to man, this is still more evidently the case with those avowedly psychological conceptions with which we have met in our earlier chapters. 'Higher' or qualified forms of interest, such as design, self-realization, the love of God, the all-harmonious desire, the absolute, authoritative, personal, collective or rational will, evidently imply something more than spontaneity, organization, tendency and adaptation. While we have refused to limit interest and value to these specially qualified cases, we must nevertheless provide for them. They clearly imply the capacity to form ideas, or to see the meaning of things and events, or to pass judgment, or to imagine ideals; that capacity, in other words, which distinguishes man as a cognitive being. Especially significant is the fact that in all of these more advanced forms interest proves to be *fallible*. It is more or less *enlightened*. We shall not, therefore, have provided for these more advanced forms of interest unless our generic conception includes some intellectual factor which can be expanded and complicated.

It might be supposed that since we concede the necessity of recognizing intellect as a factor of interest, we must therefore abandon biological ground altogether,[2] and adopt the distinctively psychological method of introspection. But we have already noted that the method of introspection is especially inept in respect of that motor-affective aspect of mind with which we are primarily concerned. Its results are questionable and obscure, and it creates a breach between mind and that organism which is both its seat and its means of contact with the physical environment. While, therefore, we shall neither level man down to those capacities which he possesses in common with the most rudimentary organism, nor level these organisms up to man by imputing to them, in some 'virtual' form, capacities which they do not evidently possess, we shall nevertheless continue to regard man as a organism. We shall view him in that objective and dynamic aspect in which he is homogeneous both with his biological antecedents and with his encircling physical environment. Indeed it would not be too much to say that it is the central task of a scientific psychology to close the gap between man and nature, a gap created by man's pride in himself and widened by the misguided indulgence of metaphysics and religion.

The definition of interest which will be elaborated and illustrated in this and the following chapters may be briefly stated thus: *An act is interested in so far as its occurrence is due to the agreement between its accompanying expectation and the unfulfilled phases of a governing propensity.* This definition involves, in the first place, a *governing propensity,* or determining tendency, or general 'set,' which is at any given time in control of the organism as a whole.[3] It further

---

[2] Thus, for example, Professor W. McDougall believes that the persistence, variability and intelligence (that is, determination by 'meaning') of instinctive action place it beyond the limits of the 'behavioristic' method. Cf. his *Body and Mind,* 1911, Ch. XIX; and "The Use and Abuse of Instinct in Social Psychology," *Jour. of Abnormal Psych. and Social Psych.,* Vol. XVI, 1921-22, pp. 304-305.

[3] Professor E. C. Tolman ("Instinct and Purpose," *Jour. of Philos.,* Vol. XXVII, 1920, p. 222) prefers to use the expression "determining *adjustment.*" I use the term 'propensity' which suggests expenditure of energy, rather than adjustment, which suggests a sluicing or distributing of energies otherwise provided, because I wish to regard the governing propensity as including whatever may be necessary to initiate effort. This

involves *subordinate* or auxiliary responses by which this propensity is executed. Finally, these subordinate responses are *tentative*, in the sense that they are selected owing to their promised results, and are on a sort of perpetual probation in the light of experience.

This definition of interest both continues the biological account of life, and paves the way for the philosophical account. As prospicient adaptation, interest may be regarded as 'teleological' without implying any breach with 'mechanism.' On the other hand, the presence of intelligence, in the simpler forms of perception, memory, meaning and expectation, paves the way for ideation and judgment, and for the more developed forms of will and personality in which these occur.

In order to preserve and emphasize this aspect of continuity between man and lower forms of life, we shall illustrate our definition first from the field of animal behavior, and then from the field of human behavior.

II. INTERESTED RESPONSE IN ANIMAL BEHAVIOR

§ 74. **The Governing Propensity.** It is customary among comparative psychologists to measure animal intelligence by docility, or by the rapidity with which an animal learns to adjust itself to a novel situation designed by the experimenter. It is characteristic of the earlier experiments, described by Professor Yerkes and Professor Thorndike, that the animal is acting under some major impulsion such as

will doubtless involve originating stimuli; but I should not like to use an expression which suggested that the determining set plays a waiting game. Otherwise Professor Tolman's is the best account I know of the agency which I have here in mind.

I find much to applaud in an article by Professor L. L. Thurston, entitled "The Anticipatory Aspect of Consciousness" (*Jour. of Philos.*, Vol. XVI., 1919, pp. 561-569). I believe that this writer makes the mistake of defining behavior in terms of consciousness instead of consciousness in terms of behavior. But he makes skilful use of the serial arrangement of the response, and the function of the "unfinished act." His account of intelligence in terms of the degree of remoteness of "consciousness" from the overt act, and his application of this view to instinct (563) are admirable. Although I did not read this article until I had formulated my own views, I am glad to find in it at least a partial corroboration of them.

hunger, pain or fear, and that it acquires by 'trial and error' a new means of executing the impulsion. In other words, the situation involves *two levels of response:* the controlling or inciting propensity, on the one hand; and, on the other hand, the subordinate responses or 'trials,' among which occur both the errors which are eliminated, and the success which survives. Let us illustrate these from a case of animal learning described by Professor Thorndike.

We take a box twenty by fifteen by twelve inches, replace its cover and front side by bars an inch apart, and make in this front side a door arranged so as to fall open when a wooden button inside is turned from a vertical to a horizontal position. . . . A kitten, three to six months old, if put in this box when hungry, a bit of fish being left outside, reacts as follows: It tries to squeeze through between the bars, claws at the bars and at loose things in and out of the box, stretches its paws out between the bars, and bites at its confining walls. Some one of all these promiscuous clawings, squeezings and bitings turns round the wooden button, and the kitten gains freedom and food. By repeating the experience again and again, the animal comes gradually to omit all the useless clawings and the like, and to manifest only the particular impulse (*e.g.,* to claw hard at the top of the button with the paw, or to push against one side of it with the nose) which has resulted successfully. It turns the button around without delay whenever put in the box.[4]

The subordinate responses or 'random' movements comprise one which proves 'successful,' such as clawing hard at the top of the button with the paw. This eligible response is complementary to the environment in that it so combines with the environment, and with ulterior responses such as seizing, chewing and swallowing, as to restore the vitality of the hungry organism to par. But in the course of acquiring this response the kitten cannot as yet be determined by it. We need therefore to recognize another or higher propensity to account for the kitten's 'trying.' This higher or selective propensity controls the whole process. It excites the animal to efforts that continue *until* a certain subordinate act occurs; and it determines what specific character that subordinate

---

[4] E. L. Thorndike, *Educational Psychology,* 1913-1914, Vol. II, *The Psychology of Learning,* p. 9.

act shall possess in order to become recurrent. In the maxim 'if at first you don't succeed, try, try again,' the higher propensity both accounts for the repeated trials and defines what shall constitute success. Or, in the saying 'he won't be happy till he gets it,' the governing propensity accounts for the unhappiness, and for that specific thing which alone will remove it.

Although its peculiar importance has not, I think, been recognized, this governing or selective propensity is familiar enough to psychologists. Professor Thorndike calls it "the learner's *set* or *attitude* or *adjustment* or *determination*." [5] Professor Woodworth describes it as follows:

> We must assume in the animal an adjustment or determination of the psycho-physical mechanism toward a certain end. . . . His behavior shows that he is, as an organism, set in that direction. This adjustment persists till the motor reaction is consummated; it is the driving force in the unremitting efforts of the animal to attain the desired end.[6]

The same conception appears, again, in descriptions of instinctive behavior, as when Professor McDougall says:

> The process, unlike any merely mechanical process, is not to be arrested by any sufficient mechanical obstacle, but is rather intensified by any such obstacle and only comes to an end either when its appropriate goal is achieved, or when some stronger incompatible tendency is excited, or when the creature is exhausted by its persistent efforts.[7]

§ 75. **Learning and Problem-Solving.** Assuming that the animal learns under the impulsion of a governing propensity, we have next to ask how this learning takes place? How does the animal solve his problem, or discover and adopt the "right way"? "Apparently we have to do with a selective agency which preserves or repeats certain activities and rejects others on the basis of their results." [8] How does this selection

---

[5] *Op. cit.*, p. 13.
[6] G. T. Ladd and R. S. Woodworth, *Elements of Physiological Psychology*, 1911, p. 551.
[7] W. McDougall, *Social Psychology*, 1910, p. 27.
[8] S. J. Holmes, "Pleasure and Pain and Intelligence," *Comp. Jour. of Neurol.*, Vol. XX, 1910, p. 147.

take place? There is a general disposition among comparative psychologists to abandon the traditional explanation in terms of the pleasurableness and painfulness of the results. Such an explanation commits the fallacy of *obscurum per obscurius*, since feeling still remains the most unsettled province of psychology. The student of animal behavior hopes to be able to throw light on the nature of pleasure and pain, rather than to receive light from the very inconclusive theories on that subject which have already been proposed.[9] But there is an equally marked disposition to reject the excessively simplified explanation of Dr. J. B. Watson, in terms of habit-formation.[10] According to this view the selected act is the act which being the last of each series of trials, becomes fixed through occurring most frequently, recently and intensely. But the act which is thus uniquely qualified to become habitual is already selectively determined, as that act *short of which the effort persists, and upon the occurrence of which the effort desists.* We seem, in other words, forced to recognize some relation of congruence between the selected act and a governing propensity which is in control of the performance as a whole. Without the introduction of such a relation, it is impossible to explain learning, or even to give any meaning to the terms 'success' and 'failure.' [11]

A recognition of this type of relationship is to be found in Professor Hobhouse's *Mind in Evolution*.[12] When the

[9] Cf. J. Peterson, "Completeness of Response," *Psychol. Rev.,* Vol. XXIII, 1916, p. 157-158. "The pleasurable tone which accompanies certain of our acts is of course only a subjective indication that the response is along the line of least resistance . . . We are coming to the point now in psychology at which we cannot look upon states of feeling as *causes* of action." Cf. also S. J. Holmes, *op. cit., passim;* and below, Ch. XI.

[10] *Behaviorism,* 1914, p. 351, and *passim;* H. A. Carr, "Principles of Selection in Animal Learning," *Psychol. Rev.,* Vol. XXI, 1914; M. Meyer, *Fundamental Laws of Human Behavior,* 1911.

[11] Why, on Dr. Watson's grounds does a certain act always terminate the series? Furthermore, as has been pointed out by B. Russell (*Analysis of Mind,* 1921, p. 53), the factor of frequency cannot account for the fact that the animal shows improvement on the second attempt, when the successful act has occurred only once. The successful act is from the beginning in some sense a 'favored' act. For Watson's later recognition of the part played by "the general setting of the situation as a whole," "emotional tensions," etc., cf. his *Psychology from the Standpoint of a Behaviorist,* 1919, p. 3.

[12] Second edition, 1915.

chick pecks at the yolk of egg or at green caterpillars, "the 'result'—the tasting or swallowing—is such as to *confirm* the original mode of reaction"; whereas when the chick pecks at orange peel or cinnibar larvae, the effect is to *inhibit* the original reaction. For the future the chick is more likely to peck at objects of the first sort, because the excitement which they would arouse independently is now enhanced by the "assimilation" of the excitement characteristic of the confirmatory sequel. Similarly, objects of the second sort will have lost their former power to excite, through being neutralized or overbalanced by the associated inhibitory excitement.[13]

But this is evidently an imperfect account of the matter. The reaction of rejection is no more inhibitory to that of pecking than is the reaction of swallowing. Why, then, should the chick not learn to pick up and reject orange peel, rather than to pick up and swallow yolk of egg? Or why should it acquire either of these habits to the exclusion of the other? To explain the prepotence of one of these sequences over the other, it is evident that what we need is some original connection uniting the pecking reaction with the swallowing reaction, but not with the rejecting reaction. The connection cannot be one of simultaneous campatibility or incompatibility between the reactions as such. It must be a connection between successive movements. We must conceive the pecking reaction as part of a total response of which the swallowing is the complementary *after*-part. Swallowing must be regarded as a prolongation or completion of the pecking response, in the direction of first intent, whereas rejection is an interruption or reversal of it. We must say that a pecking chick is an eating chick; and that it is this total eating response which selects the objects habitually to be pecked at. In other words, in this case *eligible* means *edible*.

If pecking is a part of eating, then it will be accompanied by the partial excitement of the swallowing reaction,—by a 'getting ready' to swallow. This anticipatory reaction will be brought to completion by certain stimuli such as the yolk

[13] L.T. Hobhouse, *op. cit.*, 1915, pp. 118, 121.

of egg, inhibited by others, such as the orange peel. In the future the former will awaken these anticipatory reactions more strongly, and so reinforce the pecking reaction; whereas the latter will partially excite the rejecting reflex, which will diminish the force of the pecking reaction by inhibiting the anticipatory swallowing with which that reaction is normally correlated. This would not be the case unless swallowing were in some sense the natural sequel to pecking, or unless the two were parts of one total act. This view of the matter finds expression in some of Professor Hobhouse's statements, as when he speaks of "confirmatory movement tending to prolong the reaction, or *carry it out* strenuously *to its final development.*" Similarly, he speaks of the result of the first reaction as following "closely enough to impinge upon and so confirm or inhibit *the conational impulse by which that reaction is initiated and sustained.*" [14]

A more explicit statement of the view is to be found in Professor Peterson's formulation of what he calls "the *principle of completeness of response.*" Learning processes "involve more or less complex *attitudes.*"

"The total reaction is in a degree incomplete, tentative. It is conditioned by various muscular 'sets,' or tensions, partial responses to immediately distracting stimuli, which cannot relax wholly until relief is obtained from confinement, or food is reached."

In other words, there is a "general" or "main" response, marked by tension and nascent activity. This tension is relieved only when "the act as a whole is complete."

"There is . . . a continuous overlapping of responses, some of which are in opposition while others are mutually helpful and *serve to the main response as additional stimuli, the latter leading to a more easy and complete expression.*" [15]

[14] *Op. cit.,* pp. 120, 123. The italics are mine. Cf. also, S. J. Holmes, *op. cit.,* pp. 135-136; and *Studies in Animal Behavior,* 1915, pp. 148-149. This writer follows Hobhouse in the main, and recognizes a relation of reinforcement or inhibition between a response and a "proclivity."

[15] *Op. cit.,* pp. 158, 156, 159. The writer goes on to say: "In our observation of animal behavior we have been too much interested in the princi-

Support for the present view may also be found in the latest of all psychological movements. The so-called *"Gestalt-school"* [16] has developed as a protest against sensationalism, associationism, automatism and other tendencies accused of treating the mind as a mere aggregate or complication of elementary processes. The new school emphasizes the unities rather than the composite multiplicity of mind, finding both in the field of conscious experience and in the functioning of the experient organism, what the authors call "configurations" (*Gestalten*). A "configuration" is a system of the type in which the change of any part induces such compensatory changes in other parts as shall be required for the maintenance of some optimum or maximum character of the whole. As the field of experience contains objects, forms and structures of this integral and solidary type, so the experient organism responds *as a whole,*—in unified deeds that suggest an equilibrium of energy or field of force, rather than a congeries of independently operative neuro-muscular elements.

In the case of the animal confronted with a problem, such as the procuring of food, it is supposed that there is a tension created by an imperfect equilibrium or "open configuration." Behavior, in this case, will take the form of perfecting the equilibrium or "closing" the configuration. [17] Professor Köhler's observation of chimpanzees discloses the fact that these animals often solve the problem, not by a series of random movements terminating in a chance success which thereafter becomes habitual, but by what appears to be a sudden flash of "insight." [18] Thus bananas are placed *beyond* Tschego's

pal response of the animal and have neglected to note sufficiently all the subordinate attitudes and responses." I should say rather that there had been too much neglect of the principle of subordination itself, whether through attention to the constituent reflexes or to the total performance. Cf. also, S. Smith, *Jour. Comp. Neur. and Psychol.*, Vol. XVIII, 1908.

[16] The most convenient general statement of the position of this.school, with bibliography, and available in English, is K. Koffka, *The Growth of the Mind*, 1924. Cf. also W. Köhler, "Gestaltprobleme und Anfänge einer Gestalttheorie," *Jahresbericht über die gesamte Physiologie*, 1922. For the application to animal intelligence, cf. W. Köhler, *The Mentality of Apes*, 1925; summarized in Koffka, *op. cit.*, pp. 179-230.

[17] Koffka, *op. cit.*, pp. 103, 205.

[18] *Ibid.*, p. 179.

reach, and sticks are placed *within* her reach. She does not act aimlessly, but having failed to grasp the banana by extending her arm, she becomes quiescent for a time, until stirred by the approach of other animals to the coveted food, she suddenly "leaps to her feet, seizes a stick and quite adroitly pulls the bananas till they are within reach." [19] In other words, the problem is solved then and there, and all at once, by what appears to be a *seeing of the connection* between the stick and the goal.

Often the solution is preceded by a more or less protracted interval during which the animal "gazes about" (or, as it were, "casts about") for some clue, until his eye lights upon a suitable tool or indirect route to his ulterior objective.[20] Sometimes the animal stumbles upon the solution by chance, but even in that case it appears to be suddenly *recognized as a solution*. In order that solutions of this intelligent type shall be possible it is necessary that the situation shall contain visible (or very recently observed) intermediaries,—objects whose meaning, whether through familiarity or similarity, suggest the use to which they are now put. The gap is closed through some factor which, under the pressure exerted by the open configuration of behavior, assumes an appropriate meaning. The stick (or the limb as "stick-like") suggests "something-to-reach-with." [21]

Animal behavior as thus described by Professor Köhler presents the same general features as those already emphasized. There are two levels of response, a governing propensity and a tentative act, recognized in Professor Köhler's distinction between the "major objective" and the "mid-objective" [22]; the governing propensity through being thwarted

---

[19] Köhler, *op. cit.*, p. 32. R. M. Yerkes observed similar behavior in the orang-utan; cf. his *Mental Life in Monkeys and Apes*, 1916.

[20] Köhler, *op. cit.*, p. 180. "Sultan slowly scratched his head and moved nothing but his eyes and his head gently, while he most carefully eyed the whole situation," *ibid.*, p. 200.

[21] Köhler, *op. cit.*, p. 110. There is a configuration of the *field* which conditions the closing of the configuration of *behavior*, Koffka, *op. cit.*, p. 203. It would not, I think, be inconsistent with this statement to suppose that the meaning "something-to-reach-with" consisted in incipient movements of reaching.

[22] *Op. cit.*, p. 186.

excites the animal to activity of a type which, while not infallible, is calculated to bring a solution (there is a tendency to "good errors" rather than "bad errors") ; [23] whatever presents itself is viewed so far as possible in relation to an ultimate consummation or goal; there is an unmistakable future reference, the bearing of the animals displaying "eager anticipation, directed, in short, and beyond any doubt, upon what was to come next." [24]

§ 76. **Variability, Futurity and Fallibility.** It has not been thought necessary for present purposes to discuss the extent to which such behavior as has been described is dependent on hereditary factors.[25]   That hereditary structure defines the range of possibilties from which the learning or solution arises is doubtless true; but, nevertheless, a selection is *now made* in terms of the animal's *own and actual* experience.   It is this margin of modifiability, be it great or small, to which we must look for the factor of interest.

Once the lesson is learned or the problem solved, the force of habit begins to operate; but behind the habit lies the higher propensity which has selected it, and which still exercises a certain control upon it.   The subordinate response is always on trial or sufferance, so to speak; the acts which it determines occur only so long as they agree with the higher propensity. An organism in so far as acting interestedly is *always* docile and experimental; the controlling propensity is always capable of inciting to new and untried efforts, and of exercising a selective function with reference to the tentative acts which it instigates.   In other words, it is essential to behavior of this type that the higher propensity should be *alive,* or actually at work in the organism.   At the moment when the habit becomes independent of this higher control, it can no longer be said to operate *owing to its success.*   Its success may account for its genesis; but the habit has now been weaned, and is no longer answerable to the conditions with which it had to comply at birth and during its period of dependence.

[23] *Ibid.,* p. 31.
[24] *Ibid.,* pp. 181, 282-283.
[25] Cf. Ch. VIII, Sect. I.

Herein lies the essential difference between intelligence and natural selection. According to the latter principle the character of hereditary structure is accounted for by its having been adaptive in ancestral organisms. But in so far as natural selection alone is predicated, the action of the organism cannot be said to be presently governed by this condition. In so far as its hereditary structure ceases to be adaptive through a change in the environment, the organism tends to weakness or death, and is not likely to transmit its traits; but it goes on with its maladjustment none the less. There is nothing in its constitution to forbid, or to prompt to new and more successful modes of adjustment. Intelligent behavior thus lies mid-way between inheritance and habit. It might be described as the exercise, under contingencies imposed by the environment, of a hereditary capacity to form habits.

How far and in what precise sense this capacity is conditioned by memory and repetition, it is for the observers of animal behavior to determine. That which is indispensable to intelligence is not that behavior should reflect the past, but that it should anticipate the future. Its adaptive character will lie in the agreement between this anticipation and objective causal connections. It is important that the chimpanzee should expect of the stick that relation to movable objects which its rigidity and length actually determine. Whether the chimpanzee derives this expectation from associative memory, or from spontaneous insight, is less important than that it should be a well-grounded expectation. The virtue of the explanation in terms of associative memory lies in its providing a genetic explanation that shall at the same time afford some guarantee of truth. Expectations that reflect the order of past sensory experience and are constantly subject to modification from this source, will from the outset correspond in some measure with the order of external events, and will be perpetually verified or corrected.[26]

Insistence upon expectation, meaning, and other modes of

[26] Criticisms of *associationism* have failed, I think, to attach proper weight to its *empiricism*, or to its offering an account of the genesis of ideas that shall at the same time provide for their cognitive function as reproducing the order of objective existence.

future .reference does not require us to substitute introspective categories for the biological objectivity to which we have thus far adhered. Whatever excites endeavor inaugurates the very state in which that endeavor is to terminate. As Professor Warren has pointed out, although "the dog certainly does not eat the rabbit before he catches it . . . nevertheless, the act of eating is begun before the appropriate food stimulus appears." [27] As even Professor Warren appears not sufficiently to recognize, the process of eating is actually inaugurated in so far as the dog is trying to eat the rabbit, in the form of such preliminary adjustments as the secretion of gastric juices, or the incipient muscular contractions required for seizing and tearing the prey. In this sense what the animal is trying to do may be said to be anticipated, or we may say that the animal expects it momentarily. Where this is the case we may say that the appearance of the prey is a *sign* of the eating, or awakens the expectation of it.

All intelligence, even in the elementary forms already considered, is fallible. It is of the essential nature of an expectation that it may be disappointed. In defining interested response as conditioned by expectation we have therefore provided for its fallibility. Error arises from the fact that events are responded to in a manner that is adaptive only provided the sequel is of a certain sort. To respond to a part *as to* a whole is always to incur the risk that the ulterior facts should be such as to render the act inappropriate, as when the bird flies south at the first signs of a winter that through some climatic change never eventuates. Behavior may even be deceived by apparent success. In animals, as well as in men, endeavor is often terminated by a belief which may, as it happens, be mistaken. In such cases, we must say that the present object of endeavor is a situation which in turn creates certain new expectations. These expectations may in any given case be *doomed* to disappointment. Thus the animal may store away against the winter's famine what he takes to be food; whereas the objects collected may as a matter of

[27] H. C. Warren, "A Study of Purpose," *Jour. of Philos., Psychol.*, etc., Vol. XXIII, 1916.

fact not be edible, being made to deceive by their resemblance to familar forms of food. We must then say that the endeavor of the animal was to reach a condition in which there is an anticipation of eating; the anticipation being excited, the endeavor comes to rest. The successful means employed to collect the spurious food is learned just as if it were really edible. We must therefore predicate a propensity that is satisfied independently of the actual edibility of the objects in question. And this satisfaction must be held to consist again in expectations. Upon this model we may construct our account of the higher purposive processes of man, in which the purpose is none the less present even when misled and founded on error.[28]

A survey of the learning process in animals thus yields an account of behavior to which the term 'interest' is properly and significantly applicable, but without implying any factor out of keeping with the most rigorous scientific method. The important feature of learning and problem-solving is not adaptation to the environment, but the *acquiring* of specific modes of adaptation; or performance determined by expectation founded on experience. It appears to be necessary to predicate two springs of action in the intelligent organism: (1) the more deep-seated, sustained and general propensity, which accounts for the increased reactivity called 'trying,' and which prescribes when this shall be brought to rest; (2) the more superficial, transitory, and specific responses, which are rendered hyper-excitable by the former, but are ordinarily released by sense-stimuli. The former we may call the selective or governing propensity, and the latter the tentative or subordinate responses. That one among the tentative responses which is selected, and which we may term the eligible response, is one which confirms, facilitates and amplifies the selective propensity. When a general propensity is moving the organism, or is dominant, the tentative response in question has a prepotence over others because of the greater compatibility between the expectation which it arouses and the

[28] Cf. below, Ch. XII.

general direction or set of the propensity. Action so performed may fairly be said to be performed *owing* to its promise, or the eligible response may be said to be performed 'on purpose.' [29]

III. INTERESTED RESPONSE IN HUMAN BEHAVIOR

§ 77. The Governing Propensity in Instinct, Complex and Emotion.

The history of psychology during the last quarter-century has been marked not only by the study of animal behavior but by a renewed interest in human nature itself, and by the tendency to extend to man the methods of observation that have proved fruitful in their application to animals. The social or human sciences, such as education, medicine, politics, economics and sociology, have always been nominally dependent upon the results of psychology, but this dependence has come in recent years to be more clearly recognized, and a conscious effort has been made to revise the social sciences in the light of the latest results of psychology. There has, in fact, been something like a new rendering of the Baconian maxim that "knowledge is power." Whereas this was once taken to signify the power of man over his environment through the knowledge of physics, it is now taken to mean the power of man over man through the knowl-

[29] Professor E. C. Tolman (*op. cit.,* p. 227) says, speaking of a cat's efforts to get out of a cage, "The mere fact that on each single trial it hits about *until* it gets out, seems to me to be sufficient to characterize its activity as purposive. The cat hits about *in order to* get out, *for the sake* of getting out . . .," etc. While the article as a whole is an admirable statement of a view that I hold to be fundamentally sound both in method and in doctrine, I can not believe that the author is correct in this claim. What the exponents of purposiveness are looking for is an act of which it can be said that its occurrence is due to its *promise* or *forecast.* No act, even though it be aroused by a governing propensity, can be of the sort required unless it has *meaning,* that is, arouses anticipatory reactions to its sequel; and unless it is *selected* because of such anticipation. Such anticipations are ordinarily the result of experience. But when an act is called 'random' it is implied that it is of the nature of a pure reflex, that is, unguided by experience. Professor Tolman makes the important point that random activities of the sort aroused in connection with a determining tendency "vary within a class" which persists as a whole, and so are in type determined in advance. But even so we do not get the means selected because of its future or implicit relation to the end, until the factor of meaning becomes effective.

edge of psychology. It is now customary, especially in English-speaking countries, to speak of "human engineering"; meaning that one may now hope to control the forces of human nature, as one can already control the forces of inorganic nature.

This interest in the control of man through a better understanding of the dynamics of motivation, has encouraged the substitution of naturalistic for eulogistic methods. The first step was to get rid not only of the flattering superstition that man is a throughly rational being, acting always for the good as he sees it, but also of the cynical reproach that he is governed only by a prudent calculation of pleasurable and painful consequences to himself.[30]

This latter key, which was once supposed to unlock the mysteries of human nature, has now been exchanged for a whole set of keys of a new pattern. The most important and widely used of these new keys are the *instinct* and the *complex*. The view that man, instead of being distinguished from the animal by the substitution of reason for instinct, does in fact even exceed the animal in the range of his instinctive endowments, obtained wide acceptance among psychologists owing to the influence of William James.[31] The enumeration and classification of human instincts has since become one of the principal tasks of the science of human behavior.[32] The popularization of this view, and in particular its adoption by the social sciences, is due largely to Professor William McDougall's widely read and widely quoted *Social Psychology*. This book defines an instinct as

"an inherited or innate psycho-physical disposition which determines its possessor to perceive, and to pay attention to, objects of a certain class, to experience an emotional excitement of a particular quality upon perceiving such an object, and to act in

[30] Cf. G. Wallas, *Human Nature and Politics,* 1909, Introduction; W. McDougall, *Social Psychology,* Introduction, the first edition of which appeared in 1908. That this repudiation of reason has led to the equal, if not greater, error of the opposite extreme, will appear below.

[31] *Principles of Psychology,* 1890, Vol. II, Ch. XXIV.

[32] The present reaction against this view turns upon the question of inheritance, rather than upon the question of 'reason.' Cf. Ch. VIII, Sect. I.

regard to it in a particular manner, or, at least, to experience an impulse to such action." [33]

Meanwhile, the influence of Freud, first upon psychiatry, and indirectly upon psychology, has given wide vogue to the conception of complex, in which the Freudian 'libido' is generalized, and freed from an exclusively sexual meaning. [34] The complex has this advantage over the instinct, that it is not necessarily a genetic conception, and thus avoids the vexatious question of inheritance.   It is true that orthodox Freudians trace all complexes to infantile eroticism.   But in its generalized form the complex is essentially a present dynamic agency; in Dr. Hart's words, "a system of connected ideas, with a strong emotional tone, and a tendency to produce actions of a certain definite character." [35]   A complex in this sense may be appealed to for explanatory purposes without identifying that most doubtful and elusive line that divides what is original from what is acquired.

What have these two conceptions in common?   Why may the instinct and the complex be said to be keys of the same pattern?   In the first place, because both are essentially *dispositions.*   They exist whether they are exercised or not. And when they are exercised they are activities, like circulation and respiration, describable in terms of characteristic organic and environmental changes; and not describable except in a most incomplete and misleading way, in terms of introspective data.   There are three possible ways of assigning a status to dispositions.   Assuming that the mental is non-physical, and that dispositions are mental, they may be construed as belonging to an 'unconscious' mental life. What this mental life is which is neither physical nor introspective no one has yet succeeded in making clear.   And since every indication points to a physiological interpretation of dispositions, the conception of the unconscious is · as gratuitous as it is unintelligible.   Seeing the force of this, one may conclude that since dispositions are physiological

[33] Edition of 1910, p. 29.
[34] Cf. *e.g.,* B. Hart, *Psychology of Insanity,* 1912.
[35] *Op. cit.,* p. 61.

they are therefore not mental. Or, thirdly, accepting the behavioristic version of mind, one may regard dispositions as both physical and mental: physical because consisting in certain physiological structures, mental because of the peculiar type of function or activity in which these structures are engaged. Instincts as a rule have been so interpreted largely because the conception was derived from the observation of animals, where mind has always in practice meant behavior. That complexes have not as a rule been so interpreted seems to be due to the fact that the Freudians have been primarily interested in the pathological activities of the complex rather than in its structure and place in nature.[36] Of one thing they have been sure, namely, that this fundamental mode of mind is not a datum of introspection. Their interpretation in physiological terms would not contradict any observed properties which they possess; while it would have the great advantage of removing them from an obscure and doubtful region where they may be the victims of loose speculation and popular superstition, to a well-defined and open region where they may be further illuminated by the observations of the associated sciences.

The instinct and the complex are, then, first of all organic dispositions, or systematic arrangements in the physical organism which condition specific modes of performance. There are further common characteristics. In each case there are stored energies, and specific conditions external to the system, which release its stored energies and determine their course. In each case the system tends to find expression in co-ordinated muscular changes, usually involving the skeletal muscles, and some change in external objects or in the relation of the organism to them. But this responsive behavior, while prescribed within broad limits by the disposition, is always concretely adaptable to changing conditions. The generic nature of the instinct or complex leaves a margin of plasticity, or a *way to be found,* by which contingent facts may be taken account of. Finally, in each case the system comes tem-

[36] For a physiological interpretation of complexes, cf. E. G. Holt, *The Freudian Wish,* 1915, pp. 3-99.

porarily into possession of the organism as a whole, competing with other systems for the control of the common parts in which they overlap. It is evident that the instinct and the complex indicate in the case of man a mode of behavior similar to that which we have already observed in the case of animals, and to which we have given the name of 'governing propensity.'

A further example is provided by emotional "seizures"; the situation in which "any strong emotional state whatever is upon us," or "the fever fit is on us." [37]   Studies of the major emotions, such, for example, as anger, have concerned themselves primarily with the stimuli to anger, or with its characteristic patterns. We have heard comparatively little of the *state of being angry,* as a mode of control. Professor Cannon's experiments have shown, however, that in anger the whole organism is virtually commandeered for war purposes:

Thus are the body's reserves—the stored adrenin and the accumulated sugar—called forth for instant service; thus is the blood shifted to nerves and muscles that may have to bear the brunt of struggle; thus is the heart set rapidly beating to speed the circulation; and thus, also, are the activities of the digestive organs for the time abolished. Just as in war between nations the arts and industries which have brought wealth and contentment must suffer serious neglect or be wholly set aside both by the attacker and the attacked, and all the supplies and energies developed in the period of peace must be devoted to the present conflict; so, likewise, the functions which in quiet times establish and support the bodily reserves are, in times of stress, instantly checked or completely stopped, and these reserves lavishly drawn upon to increase power in the attack and in the defense or flight.[38]

What is true of the bodily functions regulated by the autonomic nervous system is also true of the functions regulated by the central nervous system. In an angry organism bodily movements and postures, speech, imagery and ideation, attention, and even receptivity to sensory stimulation, are all

[37] James, *Principles of Psychology,* 1890, Vol. II, p. 563.
[38] W. B. Cannon, *Bodily Changes in Pain, Hunger, Fear and Rage,* 1915, p. 269.

drawn into one comprehensive response. Only stimuli whose meanings are congruent with this general cast of mind are responded to. Other responses involving different uses of the same parts and organs are temporarily inhibited. The organism literally lives and moves and has his being in anger.

§ 78. The Determining Tendency. While the major emotions exemplify the extent to which a governing propensity may master the total organism, and select its own auxiliary and constituent activities, they are in several respects peculiar. There is usually no specific end-response in which the course of action culminates. It is rather a series of acts of a similar type, such as abuse or blows, in the case of anger. It is not highly articulated and subordinated, but moves from point to point upon the same level. Such action is usually too precipitate to be nicely discriminating. And, finally, such action is unique in the extent to which it interferes with the internal economy of the organism. Too much emphasis on the major emotions tends, therefore, to obscure the essential characteristics of the governing propensity.

Recent studies of the thought-process have given vogue to another set of cognate conceptions, such as 'attitude' (*Bewusstseinslage*), 'problem' (*Aufgabe*) and 'determining tendency' (*determinierende Tendenz*). Ignoring the shadings of difference among these terms, and postponing for the present their bearing upon the specific problems of meaning and judgment, we have here to note the general principle which they serve to emphasize.[39] It is characteristic of the mental life of man that it is for limited periods *set* in a certain *direction*, or towards a certain *object;* very much as a mechanical musical instrument may be set by the insertion of a record or perforated roll which, so long as it is in place, distributes the tension-energy of the spring in specific simultaneous and successive patterns. This regulative control may

[39] The literature of this movement is extensive and difficult. Students of philosophy and psychology owe a great debt to Professor E. B. Titchener for the bibliography, summary and criticism contained in his *Experimental Psychology of the Thought-Process*, 1909. The topics of meaning and judgment are examined below, Ch. XI.

arise from "instructions" given to the psychological subject as to the course his thoughts are to follow, or from a question or command given in ordinary human intercourse, or through the free adoption of a project or problem by the agent himself. In any case once the mind is "set," its subsequent activities are predetermined, or selected to the exclusion of alternative activities of which the same mind would be capable if otherwise controlled.

It is significant that this principle, also, cannot be adequately interpreted in purely introspective terms. In so far as thinking is held to consist in a *posture* of the mind, it cannot be identified with any peculiar imagery or even train of imagery. There will be such imagery, no doubt; but it is highly variable and idiosyncratic, and does not itself constitute the factor of control which is in question. Those who have adhered to the traditional introspective method have been driven to conceive of conscious attitude or "imageless thought," which possesses an ambiguous and elusive status similar to that of the 'unconscious'; but it proves impossible to avoid the use of terms which already refer to the state of the physical organism, and which imply that the attitude or determining tendency is in fact a physiological disposition.

There is another respect in which the determining tendency transcends the introspective field. Determining tendencies are "dispositions, unconscious in their operation, which take their origin from the meaning of the idea of the end and look towards the coming perception of object." [40] The determining tendency, in other words, cannot be described without alluding to its predetermined end-result or *object of reference*. This aspect of mind is sometimes termed its "intentional inexistence," since the object to which it points is not only outside the field of introspection but even outside the field of physical fact. [41] In short, an adequate account of mind carries us not only into all the biological dimensions

---

[40] Quoted from N. Ach, *Ueber die Willenstätigkeit und das Denken,* 1905, p. 228, by Titchener, *op. cit.,* pp. 127-128.
[41] Cf. Titchener, *op. cit.,* pp. 43 ff.

of the organism, but even into the philosophical dimension of definable possibility or hypothetical being.[42]

The 'determining tendency,' while it resembles the instinct, the complex and the emotion, and embodies the same general principle, is free from the primitive, pathological or catastrophic implications which limit the rôle of these conceptions. The determining tendency is characteristic of human life in its normal activities, and its higher and more specialized developments. A determining tendency may culminate in a skilful and delicate adjustment like the spelling of a word or the picking of a lock. It may be highly organized, and convergent in long-delayed achievement, like the realization of a political ambition.

Instincts, complexes, emotions and determining tendencies illustrate the presence in man of governing propensities.[43]

[42] Cf. § 136.

[43] Another cognate conception, having considerable vogue among recent psychologists, is that of "sentiment." (Cf. A. F. Shand, *Foundations of Character*, 1914.) One hesitates to group sentiments with instincts, complexes, emotions and determining tendencies, because in the former the unity is said to lie in the object, whereas the latter emphasize a dominant activity. It does appear to be possible to divide a man either into his 'A-system' of responses, his B-system, etc., where A and B represent single objects; or into ambitions, enterprises, problems, *etc.*, each of which involves many objects. I believe, however, that the more these things are analyzed the more indistinguishable they become. In so far as my A-responses have unity, as for example in my sentiment of love for my friend, some particular instinct, complex, emotion or determining tendency has come to dominate my dealings with A, and prescribes what my reactions shall be. An instinct, complex, emotion, or determining tendency, on the other hand, has a unique reference to certain objects, perhaps to one object, which is the object of its culminating and 'satisfying' activity.

Over and above the question of the formation and structure of a governing propensity there is also the profoundly important question of its being called into play, or of its onset. What is it that puts any given governing propensity in the ascendancy at any given time and causes it to be successively superseded by others? Why am I now angry, now running to catch a train and now thinking out a problem? We may surmise what some of the causes are, such as routine, the intrusion of new stimuli, the completion of the previous course of action, health, fatigue, or the requirements of some long range program of action. It is with no intention of slighting this question that it is omitted here. (For some light on these causes, cf. Ch. XVIII, XIX.) Whatever be the facts they will not invalidate anything that we may learn about the structure and working of a governing propensity when once it is in control. If we assume the physiological hypothesis of "synaptic resistance," then we must suppose that this resistance is lowered or heightened not merely as a result of the past history of the nervous system, but as the

As in the case of animals, so also in the case of man, we shall discover the factor of interest or purpose in the *modus operandi* of these governing propensities; and, more specifically, in their future reference, and in their tentative selection of subordinate responses.

§ 79. Future Reference and Anticipatory Adjustment.

Let us consider first that state of a man in which he is said to be prepared for future action, or to have his plans made so far as concerns what he is himself to do. A good example is afforded by the chess player who has a series of moves ready in advance, or the foresighted housewife who has made up her mind what to cook for each successive meal of the coming week. Future responses are at least partially organized, and are held in reserve in the order of their appropriate stimuli. As each in turn is called into play the next in order moves into its place, just as in baseball the "batter-up" moves toward the batter's box, selects his bat and makes a few preliminary swings. While the serial order of prepared responses is not always as clear as this, something of the kind is a constant feature of human conduct. Immediately behind what I am doing now there is what I am going to do next, and behind that, successive lines of reserves which advance toward the front as my action unfolds.[44]

A similar situation must be supposed to exist when a result of some present systematic readjustment. The passing of impulses through certain channels must be conceived not simply as the result of erosion, but as the result of a correlated raising and lowering of gates.

[44] Cf. E. L. Thorndike: "When a child sees an attractive object at a distance, his neurones may be said to prophetically prepare for the whole series of fixating it with the eyes, running towards it, seeing it within reach, grasping, feeling it in his hand, and curiously manipulating it." (*Educational Psychology*, 1913-14, Vol. I, p. 126.)

The nearest approximation with which I am familiar to the view here presented is to be found in B. H. Bode's "Consciousness and Psychology," in *Creative Intelligence*, 1917, by J. Dewey and others:

"Purposive control . . . consists in giving direction to behavior with reference to results that are still in the future. The basis for this anticipation of the future is furnished by the nascent responses which foreshadow further activity. . . . These suppressed activities furnish a sort of diagram or sketch of further possible behavior." (p. 240). The article abounds in illuminating examples and should be read entire.

response is only partially executed. A football player about to catch and run back a punt has the whole action outlined in advance. At the same time that he is watching the ball in its course through the air, he is ready with neuro-muscular coördinations of the arms and legs to grasp the ball, ward off tacklers and run down the field. At any given instant in the course of this action some part of it is being carried out, while other parts are carried as far forward as is possible without interference. So far are these anticipations carried that the organism is at the time incapable of doing anything else, and will if "overanxious" carry the anticipation too far, as when the running-response crowds the catching-response and causes the player to fumble the ball. Or the anticipatory set may have so much momentum that it is impossible to readjust quickly to a change in the situation; as in the case of the psychological subject, who being prepared to lift a heavy weight, is given a light one instead, with the result that it is flung high above the head with a wholly disproportionate expenditure of energy.[45]

Or, suppose that I am awaiting a visitor with whom I have made an appointment for the discussion of some matter of business. My preoccupation with the affair takes the form of various preliminary adjustments. I arrange my furniture, books and papers to accord with activities that are about to occur. I also adjust my nervous system. I prepare certain modes of sensory accommodation which will facilitate my recognition of the visitor; in other words I 'look for' him, or 'listen for' him. I make ready even my words and gestures of salutation. Furthermore, I reflect in advance upon the stages of the discussion, anticipating both questions and answers. My anticipation is organized to follow a temporal succession. I not only prepare my *adieux*, but assign them their place at the end of the discussion. The elements of my organized preparation are correlated with the stages of the development of the external situation. The extraordinary functional complexity of the nervous system renders me

---

[45] Cited from G. E. Müller by James, *Principles of Psychology*, 1890, Vol. II, p. 502, note.

capable of thus forming and holding simultaneously in reserve, modes of response corresponding to so great a variety
of temporal, spacial and qualitative contingencies in the environment. Thus most human action, instead of being born *de novo*
at the moment of the performance, merely passes over from
an implicit or partial state to an explicit or complete state.
The human organism is ordinarily in a state of being committed in advance of performance. It is loaded and aimed
before it is fired. It is not only provided with the necessary
munitions, but is prepared for hostilities in a certain quarter;
and like an alarm-clock or a time-fuse its action is determined
for a certain hour. These reserve responses must be supposed
to possess an unqualified physiological existence, even though
they are not in action and even though they should never be
called into action. It is unnecessary to dwell upon the various
forms which they may assume. They may be so related that
the action of each provides the stimulus for the action of the
next, in which case they are in some sense parts of one plan;
or they may be correlated with successive stimuli externally
and independently supplied, as when one is prepared for a
sequence of probable contingencies.

§ 80. Tentative Selection of Subordinate Response.
Let us now consider the manner in which such a set and
commitment of the organism selects the particular acts that
shall occur. While I am waiting for my expected visitor,
external events and objects impinge upon my senses, and
ideas are aroused within through the associative processes.
Each nascently initiates appropriate reactions. The reactions
which are irrelevant to my project, or which would interfere
with it, are inhibited as incompatible with my general adjustment; others, which are germane and auxiliary, are assimilated
to the adjustment, or are executed as overt modes of preparation. If one is hunting for a pin, the 'problem' is clearly
in command of the situation from beginning to end. Sundry
responses, such as walking about, probing corners, or lifting
objects, are *sub*ordinate, and not *co*ördinate reflexes. They

are due to the increased reactivity to which the problem gives rise; they possess a liability to occurrence according as they do or do not facilitate the finding; interruptions are repelled; and eventually there is built up the integrated response of finding a pin. There would be a specific difference between hunting a pin for the sake of exercise, and moving about for the sake of finding a pin; and this difference would appear in the inclusion and exclusion of minor acts, and in their persistence and fixation.

Or, let us suppose such an organized course of action to be checked midway, through the non-appearance of the complementary stimulus or through some impediment. Either one of two things will happen. If there are other prepared responses for which the appropriate stimuli are present, the organism may go over to another course of action. If, however, the first course of action possesses a temporary monopoly of the energies of the organism, responses will occur which have the character of being tentative. They *may* assume the form of 'random' activities, or of habits and inherited reflexes for which suitable stimuli are presented. These will continue until some one of them provides the complementary stimulus or removes the impediment, and so permits the original response to complete itself. But in proportion as an organism is 'experienced' in the matter, such tentative activities are not random. Certain of the present stimuli possess 'meaning.' The immediate response which they excite is again, as in the case of the major course of action, the first of a train of anticipations. But in some cases these ulterior anticipations will coincide, and in some cases they will conflict, with the suspended course of action. Where the former is the case the tentative act will be performed, and where the latter occurs the act will be abandoned after having been 'considered.'

Suppose, for example, that my project is to obtain a book from my study. I approach the door and turn `the knob, having in readiness and in serial order the neuro-muscular coördinations involved in pushing open the door, walking across the room and grasping the book, The door, however, resists my push. This act being checked, the ulterior acts are also checked and crowd it from the rear. I do not desist, responding irrelevantly to some other stimulus that happens to engage my attention, as a baffled kitten may turn to playing with its tail, but I "try," or engage in auxiliary responses. Being a person of intelligence, however, instead of kicking, pounding, shouting or running back and forth, I look around, that is, I increase the number and range of stimuli that affect me. Finally I see a key hanging on a nail. This key means something to me. It has its immediate meaning as something to be grasped, and an ulterior meaning in terms of a series of anticipatory sets arranged in depth. In other words, when I grasp keys I also get ready to perform certain further acts in orderly succession. Near the head of this tentative line of action is that same anticipatory set (for pushing open the door) which now stands at the head of the original line, pressing for release. The implicit phase of the auxiliary course of action coincides with the suspended portion of the dominating tendency, and the auxiliary course of action is adopted.[46]

The central feature of this conception of human behavior is that general state of the organism which has been termed a governing propensity, and which we have seen to regulate the learning process in animals. The organism as a whole is for a time preoccupied with a certain task which absorbs its energy and appropriates its mechanisms. As in the case of animal behavior, so also in the case of man, the essence of intelligent and interested action lies in the fact that acts are selected by such a governing propensity according to their 'promise'; that is, according to the agreement between their expected sequel and the as yet unexecuted but predisposed phases of the governing propensity.

§ 81. Summary and Definition. We have thus reached

[46] In this case the suspended course of action is resumed at the same point at which it was interrupted. I might have adopted a course of action whose reserve phases coincided with those of the dominating tendency further on. In other words I might have gone around and climbed in a window, or borrowed my neighbor's book.

the following provisional definition: *Interested or purposive action is action adopted because the anticipatory responses which it arouses coincide with the unfulfilled or implicit phase of a governing propensity.* In conclusion let us consider how far this account of interested action satisfies the requirements of the traditional conception, as these requirements are embodied in philosophical and psychological literature, and in common-sense. To satisfy these requirements interested or purposive action must be *actively \selective, tentative, instrumental, prospective* and *fallible.* It will be useful to resume our results under these heads.

The central contention in William James's epoch-making *Principles of Psychology* is that *selection* is the essential and distinguishing feature of mind. "Consciousness is at all times primarily a selective agency." [47] Our senses themselves are organs of selection. Attention, perception, thought, taste, and the moral will are all modes of choice by which a man's personality and his world are finally individuated and stabilized. In one of his early essays, an essay that has been too little read, James distinguishes between real teleology in which the agent asserts his own end, and "hypothetical" teleology, or the case in which an external observer, finding the results of an action to be useful, imputes them to the agent as an end:

"We can describe the latter only in teleological terms, hypothetically, or else by the addition of a supposed contemplating mind which measures what it sees going on by its private teleological standard, and judges it intelligent. But consciousness itself is not merely intelligent in this sense. It is *intelligent intelligence.* It seems to supply both the means and the standard by which they are measured. It not only *serves* a final purpose, but *brings* a final purpose—posits, declares it." [48]

[47] Vol. I, p. 139. The best statement (too long to quote) is to be found in Vol. I, pp. 289-90. Cf. also I, pp. 8, 11, 402, 583-84, 594; II, pp. 558-59, 584. In the account in I, pp. 583-84, of voluntary association James speaks of "some general interest which for the time has seized upon the mind"; and gives an admirable account of pressure exerted by an obstructed response.

[48] From "Spencer's Definition of Mind as Correspondence," *Collected Essays and Reviews,* 1920, p. 64.

No one would now be disposed to dispute the essential soundness of this position. The human individual does not merely do things that are useful as judged by an external observer, but by its own activity adopts and seeks that result in relation to which its deeds are useful. And as James has so persuasively shown, the individual's experience is not dictated to him by external events, so that his mind merely echoes what goes on around him; but his experience is always in some sense what he makes it, what he is himself disposed to look for. This does not, however, drive us to a dualistic sundering of mind and body.[49] Endowed with governing propensities, the organism itself assumes just that selective character which James insists upon as the fundamental prerogative of mind. Its movements are governed by its own internal organization. Through these movements the organism not only acts on the environment, but introduces, terminates and varies those relations which enable the environment to act on *it*, and so determines even its own experiences and fortunes.

James has also emphasized the fact that it is characteristic of mind to *solve problems*, or *try* until some end-result is attained. Cover the poles of a magnet with a card, he tells us, and the iron-filings "will press forever against its surface," as bubbles will remain lodged beneath the bottom of an inverted jar of water. The movement of the iron-filings towards the magnet, or of the bubbles towards the outer air, is a mere simulation of that love or attraction that moves living things:

"Romeo wants Juliet as the filings want the magnet; and if no obstacles intervene he moves towards her by as straight a line as they. But Romeo and Juliet, if a wall be built between them, do not remain idiotically pressing their faces against its opposite sides like the magnet and the filings with the card. Romeo soon finds a circuitous way, by scaling the wall or otherwise, of touching Juliet's lips directly. With the filings the path is fixed; whether it reaches the end depends on accidents. With the lover it is the end which is fixed, the path may be modified indefinitely.

[49] As James here argues, *ibid.*, pp. 64-65.

"Suppose a frog in the position in which we placed our bubbles of air, namely at the bottom of a jar of water. The want of breath will soon make him also long to rejoin the mother-atmosphere, and he will take the shortest path to his end by swimming straight upwards. But if a jar full of water be inverted over him, he will not, like the bubbles, perpetually press his nose against its unyielding roof, but will restlessly explore the neighborhood until by re-descending again he has discovered a path round its brim to the goal of his desires. Again the fixed end, the varying means." [50]

This conative, experimental or *tentative* character of mind, is amply provided for in our account and without invoking any agency which is alien to the physical organism. The same is true of that *instrumentalism,* or subordination of means to ends, which James's examples also emphasize, and which he affirms to be a mark and criterion of mentality.[51] Interested or intelligent action involves two levels, or two factors, of which one rules and the other serves. Just this duality and subordination is provided in the relation between the governing propensity and the tentative or auxiliary response. This conception employs the wider cognate conceptions of whole and part, and of cause and effect, but it retains a peculiar and distinguishing character of its own.

That a *prospect* or reference to the future, as in some sense governing the act, is an essential feature of the traditional conception of purpose, appears in the commonest terms of the teleological vocabulary, such as 'for the sake of,' 'in order to,' 'with a view to,' 'in fear of,' 'in hope of,' or 'lest.' It is evident that no account of human conduct which fails to set apart some special feature as the connotation of these expressions will, either in or out of scientific laboratories, seem to cover the facts. It is not sufficient to conceive the organism as making random efforts instigated by a determining tendency, nor it is sufficient that these efforts should cease when one of these efforts 'succeeds.' For there is as yet no act of which it can be said that it is done *with a view to* or *for the sake of* a future act. 'Random,' 'hit-or-miss' action is essentially unguided action, which so far as its own

50 W. James, *Principles of Psychology,* 1890, Vol. I, pp. 6-7.
51 *Ibid.,* p. 8.

immediate determination is concerned, is as disposed to miss as to hit. The solution would seem to lie in the action of present dispositions which are correlated with future contingencies. A calendar of engagements filled out for the next month exists and acts in the present, while being correlated serially and progressively with the future. Similarly, the responses organized and serially adjusted so as to be executed in sequence, exist now among the determining conditions of present events; and nevertheless are functionally correlated with a sequence of events in the historical future,—in their own future. A series of dated anticipatory responses is thus a projection of the future upon the present spacial field, and provides a means by which the contingent may be causally related to physical existence.

Finally, we have provided for that element of *fallibility* which accounts for the unfortunate fact that the result of interested action does not always coincide with the end or aim. The key to a man's bias is not to be found in the results of his action, but in what he expects of it. There will be a discrepancy between what he seeks and what he gets just in so far as there is room for error in his expectation. Even if it were not inherently paradoxical, it would not be in accord with the facts to say that in interested action a cause occurs because of its effects. It occurs because of its *expected* effects. But at the same time our account provides for the close relation between end and effect. Both possess the same character of futurity in relation to the means; and in so far as the expectation is correct and the action succeeds, the two coincide.

Through this recognition of the fallibility of interested action provision is made for the whole apparatus of cognition, and for those higher rational performances on which man prides himself. To the very intimate, confusing and compromising relations which interest bears to intellect we shall presently turn. But first we must discuss certain variations and extensions of our definition, which will serve both to amplify its meaning and to fortify it against the charge of inadequacy.

CHAPTER VIII

MODES OF INTEREST

I. REFLEX, HABIT AND INSTINCT

§ 82. **Interests and their Objects.** Having set forth the nature of interest in the broad sense, we must now examine its varieties. Value has been ascribed to objects in respect of the interest taken in them. We must discover, therefore, just what is meant by being *object-of-interest*. But this question can be clearly and adequately answered only by considering the different modes of interest with a view to detaching some common character of objective reference. Interests are directed to past, present and future; to the near and the remote; to the existent and the non-existent; to internal states of the organism itself and to the external environment; and in all these senses interests are directed towards and away from, for and against. The orientation of interests, in other words, is multi-dimensional and highly variable; and if we are to obtain any single principle of value we must be able, amidst all this variability, to assign some constant rôle to that which we call the object of interest. Interests also have their genesis and history, which should enable us to see under what conditions anything *becomes* an object of interest and *acquires* value.

An examination of the variable orientation and modality of interest not only will bring into relief the common status of all objects of interest, and therefore the generic nature of value; but will also indicate the most fundamental differences among values,—those differences which spring from the essential nature of our defining principle.

Finally, we shall thus further illustrate, clarify and test the general definition of interest that has already been offered.

It will possess adequacy neither as an account of mind nor as the basic principle of value, unless it fits the complexity and diversity of the motor-affective life of man. The objective, dynamic view of interest so far adhered to is still on trial, and must now be judged in the light of those data, such as feeling, desire, emotion, instinct, appetite and will, which are commonly approached by the method of introspection, on the assumption that they are 'subjective' and therefore discontinuous with the physical organism.

In keeping with the method thus far employed, we shall begin with those modes of interest which would by general consent be regarded as the most primitive, and which raise the question of inheritance.

§ 83. The Ambiguous Question of Instincts. Never before in the history of human thought has the world so eagerly awaited the verdict of psychology, and never before has the psychologist been so uncertain of his verdict. This attitude on the part of the psychologist is due, no doubt, to his having lately acquired the cautious and self-critical temper of science; and, as such, it is a sign of hopeful augury. But meanwhile those branches of knowledge which require the results of psychology must either close up shop, or manufacture these results provisionally for themselves.

This hesitation and disagreement among psychological experts is, by a strange irony of fate, proportional to the urgency of the problem. That which philosophy and the social sciences most need is a workable theory of human motivation, and it is precisely this which psychology is least able to provide. The case of instinct furnishes a striking illustration. Thirty-five years ago William James stated that the existence of instincts "on an enormous scale in the animal kingdom needs no proof"; and went on to say that man is distinguished from other animals not by the absence of instincts but by their comparative multiplicity.[1] To-day the psychologists speak of "giving up instincts" altogether,[2] although the laity, having

---

[1] *Principles of Psychology*, 1890, Vol. II, pp. 383, 393.
[2] Cf., "Giving up Instincts in Psychology," Z. Y. Kuo, *Psych. Rev.*,

been converted to the view of James, are moving *en masse* in the opposite direction. It is evident, therefore, that we cannot cite authorities. We must draw what lessons we can from this abrupt reversal of scientific doctrine, and estimate the probabilities as best we can. Fortunately the question of instinct is not a central one for our purposes, since we are primarily concerned with the structure of interest and not with its origin.

The doubts of psychology regarding instinct arise in part from the difficulty of ascertaining the facts, but in part, also, from the ambiguity of the conception. Let us first see if we can accomplish something towards its clarification. The meaning of instinct turns upon the meaning of the closely related conceptions, 'reflex,' and 'habit.' If these terms are to be of any service in psychological discourse they must have specific and limited meanings. The desire to introduce mechanistic principles into psychology, has led some psychologists to reduce all behavior to trains and integrations of reflexes; the desire to emphasize the effect of its past history upon the present action of the organism, has led others to reduce all behavior to habit; while the desire to emphasize the originative and impulsive activity of the organism, or its dependence on the inherited capacities of the species, has led still others to generalize behavior in terms of instinct. The result is that all three terms have become so excessively elastic that it is difficult to determine exactly what their proponents are affirming or their opponents denying.

§ 84. **The Character and Limits of the Reflex.** The conception of reflex is derived from the fact that the individual organism is equipped with certain ready-made units of behavior, or adaptive responses, which require only a specific stimulus in order to be executed. Since they possess

Vol. XVIII, 1921. The literature of the subject is so extensive that a bibliography is unnecessary. No one who consults current psychological publications can escape it. A convenient summary of, and defence against, recent attacks on instinct will be found in W. McDougall's article on "The Use and Abuse of Instinct in Social Psychology," *Jour. of Abnormal Psych. and Social Psych.*, Vol. XVI, 1921-1922.

survival-value, their existence is accounted for by natural selection. The examples ordinarily cited fall into two groups: the internal reflexes, such as those involved in respiration, circulation, digestion, secretion and excretion; and the external or peripheral reflexes, such as equilibration, coughing, winking, sneezing and weeping. To these are ordinarily added a more doubtful group, including hand-withdrawal, grasping, sucking and locomotion.

If we take the most unmistakable cases of reflex, such as winking, coughing and sneezing, we find a clue to its nature in the fact that these reactions take place with *relative independence of their context or setting,* provided only a specific stimulus be presented. A sudden motion in close proximity to the eye causes the closing of the eye-lid, and the irritation of the mucous membrane by the presence of a foreign body produces coughing or sneezing, *regardless of circumstances.* It is a fact of human behavior that the same stimulus may be variously combined with other stimuli, and that the results may differ accordingly. It is also a fact that the same bodily mechanisms may be used in different responses, their use in one precluding their use in another; and that the same response may be variously combined with other responses on the part of the organism, so as to vary the resultant effect. In so far as a response is a function of its stimulus, and is unaffected by these ulterior factors, whether in the environment, or in the organism itself, we may say that it is 'reflexive.'

But if the reflex is to be distinguished from habit it must be thought of as independent in yet another respect. It must be conceived as independent of the previous exercise of the mechanisms which it employs, being sufficiently conditioned by structural arrangements which emerge in the course of the organism's growth. In so far as these can be accounted for by the principles of natural selection, the reflex will form part of that general native endowment which the individual possesses in common with others of the same species. It cannot therefore take account of the peculiar incidents and circumstances characteristic of the individual's history.

Summarizing these characteristics we can obtain some idea of the limits of reflex action. Given a certain stimulus *s* and an individual organism *O*, a response *r* is reflex in so far as it occurs invariably regardless of the environmental setting of *s*, the organic setting of *r*, and the previous behavior of *O*. Such action will be adaptive in proportion as *s* recurs in the environment of all members of the species; in proportion as *r* does not interfere with other responses on the part of *O;* and in proportion as there is some one constant effect of *s* which is relevant to *O*. *Per contra, r* will lack the reflex character, and will be something else, such as habit, instinct or intelligence, in proportion as *r* is a function of the special circumstances under which *s* appears, of other responses on the part of *O*, and of *O's* past history.

§ 85. The Nature of Habit. Let us turn now to the case of *habit*. Once a habit is formed, it is evidently indistinguishable from a reflex save in that it usually varies from individual to individual. The distinguishing mark of habit, lies, therefore, in the fact that it *is formed,* or is an effect of the individual's previous activity.

The most important general principles of habit-formation are those of recurrence and of transference. The principle of recurrence means that a reaction tends to occur in proportion to the frequency of its previous occurrence. This principle operating by itself would not induce new reactive dispositions, but would tend only to strengthen and fixate those already existing. It would, for example, so modify the coughing reflex as to make it more and more susceptible to stimulation. A given degree of irritation would acquire a greater power, both to induce the coughing reaction, and to exclude other stimuli that might be jointly presented. At the same time the coughing reflex would acquire a prepotency over other reflexes. The result would be a peculiar liability to cough, or a coughing "on the slightest provocation." In order to account for the acquisition of new responses it is necessary to introduce the principle of transference. This means that when two responses occur together as parts of one response their stimuli may be interchanged. This principle is seen most clearly in the case of the so-called "conditioned reflex." [3] A bear placed on a hot floor will reflexly withdraw its feet in rapid alternation. When an auditory stimulus (music or spoken command) is presented simultaneously with the heat stimulus, a cross-relation is established between the two reponses. The conjunction of stimuli being repeated this connection is deepened until eventually the auditory stimulus will induce the foot-withdrawal in the absence of the heat stimulus. We then say that the bear has been trained to dance to music or at command. In other words a new response has now been established, which is a function of the individual's life history.

It is important to note that the establishment of a new habit implies reduction or simplification. The cross-connection operates as a short-circuit. The heat stimulus, the relief afforded by withdrawal of the feet, and the ulterior phases of the original response to the auditory stimulus (such, for example, as exploration or alert posture) are now eliminated. The habit like the reflex exhibits an independence of context, whether environmental or organic. James cites the case of the old soldier who while carrying home his dinner heard the command of "Attention!", and thereupon promptly brought his hands down, losing his mutton and potatoes in the gutter.[4] The character of habit is here exhibited not only in the fact that the reaction is a consequence of the soldier's past history, but in the fact that it occurs regardless of his errand and of accompanying circumstances. Habit formation, in other words, passes from an original dissociation of reflexes, through association, to new dissociations.

[3] The experimental proof of this principle is credited to the Russian psychologists, von Bechterew and Pawlow. The best general statement is to be found in C. L. Evans, *Recent Advances in Physiology*, 1926, Ch. XIV. Convenient summaries and extensions of the principle by American psychologists may be found in E. B. Watson, "The Place of the Conditioned-Reflex in Psychology," *Psych. Rev.*, XXIII, 1916; and *Psychology from the Standpoint of a Behaviorist*, 1919, pp. 57-65; F. L. Wells, "Von Bechterew and Uebertragung," *Jour. of Philos.*, XIII, 1916, pp. 354-356.
[4] *Principles of Psychology*, 1890, Vol. I, p. 120.

Originally independent units of behavior are first united and then redivided.

The rôle of reflexes and habits in life may now be briefly summarized. They serve as the mode of response characteristic of relatively simple organisms, adapted to the comparatively few environmental stimuli which are constant features of the habitat of the species, group or individual, and adapted to these in comparatively few ways. Or they will find a place in more complex behavior in so far as various responses contain identical components, and in so far as responses are dissociated. An agent whose behavior on the whole is highly variable may be automatic as regards certain elementary constituents, or as regards certain detached accompaniments and interruptions. Thus reflexive and habitual movements of the hands or modes of sensory accommodation may be automatically repeated as parts of different complex performances such as musical instrumentation, while breathing may occur simultaneously, and coughing or sneezing may irrelevantly intervene.

§ 86. Instinct Conceived as Automatic and Reflexive.

Let us now consider the highly ambiguous conception of instinct. In the first place, we may discard the view that behavior is instinctive simply in so far as it is a function of inherited connections. For in this case instinct would mean nothing more than reflex, and the introduction of the conception would be both gratuitous and confusing. Nor can instincts be regarded simply as *complex* reflexes. All reflexes are complex. Even the opening of the hand involves the relaxation of the antagonistic group of muscles by which it is closed, and the dog who scratches himself with his right hind-leg has to shift his weight to his other three legs.

A closely related view would define instincts as *chains* of reflexes. Here, to be sure, a new idea appears to be introduced, for each successive reflex is conceived as stimulated by the effect of the last, and the sequence is adaptive as a whole, or in its ultimate outcome, rather than in respect of its component units. Thus the nest-building performance of the bird may be described as follows:

"The bird picks up a straw, flies to a limb, deposits it, and returns for another. This is repeated until several straws are accumulated, whereupon arrival at the nest causes the bird to execute certain turning movements by means of which the nest is shaped. The completion of the nest stimulates the egg-laying mechanism. The presence of eggs leads to brooding." [5]

Another illustration is provided by the food-taking perform-. ance, in which seizing of the food, conveying it to the mouth, mastication, salivary secretion, swallowing and digestion follow in sequence, each unit being aroused in succession by the previous unit, and the biological utility of the process lying in the whole, or in the culminating phase, rather than in the separate units.

That such chains or sequences of performance are inherited cannot be doubted, because they are embodied in anatomical structures and physiological functions. Teeth imply the presence in the mouth of materials that must have been conveyed thither from outside the organism, as the functions of the stomach imply the reception of salivated materials entering through the esophagus. The laying of eggs implies a place to lay them, and brooding implies the presence of eggs. Organs and mechanisms, which are clearly inherited if anything is inherited, are dependent for their functional exercise upon their relations in time as well as upon their relations in space. We have already considered and recognized this preparatory or cyclical type of complementary adjustment.

But it does not follow that the units of a serially correlated performance are reflexive. Theoretically the presumption should be against it, for the more complicated a performance the less likely is it that all the necessary factors can be counted upon to appear when they are necessary.

Let us suppose that a reflex r requires a stimulus s, which results from the previous reflex r' to s', which results in turn

[5] W. S. Hunter, *General Psychology*, 1919, p. 164.
[6] Cf. § 70.

from the reflex r'' to s''. Then the occurrence of s will depend upon the appearance of the particular stimuli s' and s'' in a particular spacial and temporal juxtaposition. As a matter of fact r will rarely, if ever, be sufficiently conditioned by s, but will require the concurrence of other environmental factors, as the carrying of the straw to a limb requires not only the presence of a straw but also the presence of a limb. New external stimuli constantly intervene in all overt performances. The likelihood of such a specific pattern of stimuli will be inversely proportional to its complexity, to the number of individual organisms concerned, and to their change of environment. That a highly complex pattern of stimuli should recur for all members of a species of scattered and mobile animals is so unlikely, that if the terminal reflex r were a vital reflex such as digestion or egg-laying, the individual would ordinarily starve or the species become extinct. Such a train of performances would be rendered more adaptive in proportion as the responses r' and r'' could somehow control the conditions of their own occurrence. How this is possible we have already discovered from our examination of learning and problem-solving. Supposing r'' to be partially awakened and to be prepotent, such responses as are attended by the expectation of s'', or of other conditions of the execution of r'', will be congruent with this dominant set, and will be more likely themselves to be executed.

§ 87. **The Variability of Instinct.** Returning now to those modes of behavior that are commonly referred to in discussions of instinct, we find that the most recent observations emphasize their variability rather than their automatism.[7] Birds of a given species do build nests of a certain general pattern at certain seasons of the year, but they build individual nests in individual ways that are accommodated to the special circumstances in which the individual bird finds

---

[7] For reference to the work of E. P. Swindel, W. Craig, C. O. Whitman, G. V. Hamilton and others, cf. the notes to E. C. Tolman's "Can Instincts be Given up in Psychology?", *Jour. of Abnormal Psych. and Social Psych.*, Vol. XVII, 1922-23. Cf. also W. M. Wheeler, "On Instincts," *ibid.*, Vol. XV, 1921-22.

himself. Nest-building is not a series of stereotyped acts, evoked by the same stimuli and having a stereotyped result, but is a flexible and experimental process in which trials are made, failures abandoned and successes conserved. All that remains of the original picture of the chain reflex is that this tentative procedure is *internal* to successive units. The chain remains, but its links are no longer reflexes. Although it is the whole series r'', r', r which is adaptive, at any given time the animal is evidently trying to obtain s' rather than s. Thus the male is trying to carry a straw to the limb of a tree, rather than to accumulate enough straws to shape into a nest, or prepare a situation which will awaken the egg-laying and brooding responses of the female. So far as these ulterior performances are concerned, the initial acts of the series are 'teleological' only from the standpoint of the observer; they are not actively interested beyond the limits of expectation.

There is always question of the range of these expectations, or the remoteness of the anticipated result which exercises a selective control over antecedent activities. It is this which appears to distinguish the bird from a human house-builder. In the case of the former, the completed nest and subsequent reproductive activities are apparently not anticipated, whereas in the case of the latter the domestic complex is guiding the action throughout. Everything which the human agent does from the first consultation with his architect is in some measure qualified by this meaning, and selected on this account. As a result there is not merely variability within each component, but variability of components. The human builder has subordinated his auxiliary acts to his governing propensity to a greater depth; and in order that this should be possible, he must be capable of a much more complicated and far-flung play of meaning.

That which distinguishes the nest-building 'instinct' of the bird from a reflex is its variability relative to a result. The same is evidently the case with the alleged human instincts such as pugnacity and flight. These performances are highly variable in different situations and among different individuals. In order to find their generic and distinguishing characteristics we have to look to some type of result, such as injury and escape, or to some emotional attitude. The former may be arrived at by indirection and guile, and may utilize any means which lies ready at hand; while the latter may variously *express* itself. In other words, pugnacity and flight have to be described as motor-affective dispositions to injury and to escape, under variable circumstances.

We may now understand the characteristic difficulty that besets the conception of instinct. In so far as its hereditary aspect is insisted upon, it tends to reduce to reflex action and so to become a superfluous conception. In so far as its variability is insisted upon, it tends to merge into either habit or intelligence, and again to become a superfluous conception. Regarded as an inherited mode of intelligent performance, it seems to be a self-contradictory conception since intelligent performance implies learning and profiting by experience. In other words, the psychologist seems to be discussing the question of the inheritance of non-inherited modes of performance.

§ 88. **Instinct as Inherited Propensity.** There is only one remaining alternative by which the conception of instinct can be preserved and usefully employed. It may be taken to mean not an inherited mode of intelligent performance, but an inherited mode of intelli*gence*. It is self-contradictory to speak of a response as both inherited and learned, but it it is not self-contradictory to speak of the inheritance of a specific disposition to learn. This would mean the inheritance of such determining sets, or dispositions to try until a specific result is attained, as we have already discussed under the name of the 'governing propensity.'

This conception of instinct has recently been expounded with clearness and convincing force by Professor Tolman, who employs the expression "driving adjustment" in place of governing propensity. This writer summarizes his view as follows:

"(1) Whereas there are no innate connections of external response to original stimulating conditions, there are innate connections of specific driving adjustments to original external or internal stimulating conditions. (2) These driving adjustments tend to release particular sets of random acts. (3) They also set a particular goal for the random acts in that these acts tend to continue until some one occurs which provides a stimulating condition which *innately* relaxes the driving adjustment itself. (4) These driving adjustments are definable in terms of the purely abstract types of success which they predicate. (5) As so defined they necessarily involve a teleological use of language. (6) The theory predicates no mysterious degree of pre-established harmony between the nature of the environment and the nature of the organism." [8]

There is one factor needed to complete this account. The recurrence of the "success" is due to its meaning. The instinct, as compared with the reflex or habit, is a response to what the stimulus *represents*. Suppose r to be the activity which would complete and relax the driving adjustment, and s to be the complementary stimulating condition which would enable this to occur. Suppose $s' - r'$ (stimulation s' of response, r') to mean s, that is, to have the effect of partially arousing the response to s, namely r. Then $s' - r'$ will, relatively to this driving adjustment, have a prepotence over such other antagonistic or irrelevant responses as may be initiated.

§ 89. **The Question of Inheritance.** The question of the existence of instincts is thus, in the first place, a question of the inheritance of driving adjustments or governing propensities, with their peculiar power to take possession of the organism, incite effort and select acts according to their results. This question cannot in the present state of the subject be answered with any assurance. There is strong evidence for such a view in the prepotence of certain responses, such

[8] E. C. Tolman, *op. cit.*, p. 147. The article contains an interesting speculation as to the physiology of the "driving adjustment," as well as much psychological evidence in its support. For an earlier presentation of a similar view, cf. R. S. Woodworth, *Psychology, a Study of Mental Life,* 1921. Cf. also the view of L. L. Thurstone that "an instinct is an innate tendency to assume a motor attitude which requires conscious particularization before it becomes an overt response." ("The Anticipatory Aspect of Consciousness," *Jour. of Philos.,* Vol. XVI, 1919.)

as food-taking, pain-avoidance, sex and parentage, all of which seem under certain conditions to exercise a "right of way" that is difficult to explain by the circumstances of the individual's history; in the fact that the trials by which such performances are perfected are not wholly random, but form a limited class definable only as approximations to success; and in the fact that general dispositions, such as savageness and wildness, seem to be traceable to heredity.[9]

The present reaction against the theory of instincts is undoubtedly a wholesome scientific symptom. In so far as this theory rested upon negative evidence it tended to suspend the effort to explain. Like the theory of innate ideas or the Aristotelian theory of forms, it indicated too great a readiness to accept classification in place of analysis. A hesitation to accept instincts implies a more patient and careful attention to the learning process, to the influence of the environment, and to the continuity of individual development. It stimulates inquiry into hitherto unsuspected modifying influences, such as infantile or even pre-natal experience.[10] The question can be settled in one way or the other only by *positive* evidence. The absence of instincts in infancy does not disprove them, since hereditary traits, such as sexuality or walking, may require the growth and maturing of the structures involved. Instincts can be definitely rejected only when the performances which they denote are otherwise explained. On the other hand, instincts are not definitely proved by the present failure of such explanations, especially in view of the fact that such explanations are gaining ground. The theory of instincts can be conclusively established only when the performances which it denotes are positively explained in terms of a Mendelian or other experimentally authentic theory of heredity.

There is another aspect of the question. The type of

[9] Cf. R. M. Yerkes, "The Heredity of Savageness and Wildness in Rats," *Jour. of Animal Behavior*, Vol. III, 1913.

[10] A notable example is provided by J. B. Watson's careful observations of infant behavior. Cf. his *Psychology from the Standpoint of a Behaviorist*, 1919. The more speculative theory of pre-natal behavior is illustrated by R. C. Givler's "The Intellectual Significance of the Grasping Reflex," *Jour. of Philos.*, Vol. XVIII, 1921.

learning or solving process which we have identified with interest involves the play of meaning. It is generally assumed that meanings are lessons of experience. In so far as instinct is identified with meaning, it is natural, therefore, to ask whether the lessons of experience may not be inherited. This supposition, known as the theory of racial memory or "lapsed intelligence," [11] is at present out of favor because it implies the inheritance of acquired characters, for which, in general, there is little empirical or physiological support. There remains, however, another possibility. If the meaning of a given stimulus consists in its power to awaken expectations of a second and impending stimulus, there is no *a priori* reason why this should not occur without any previous experience of the second stimulus. In other words, meaning is essentially prospective, and only accidentally retrospective. It might, therefore, be innate without having been *acquired* in ancestral experience. Something like this is strongly suggested in telaesthesia. It seems to be the immediate effect and biological function of visual and auditory stimuli to put the organism in a condition of readiness for contact, or for contact spacially and temporally correlated with a train of subsequent bodily movements. In this way it would be possible to elaborate a "nativistic" theory of space-perception, which should at the same time provide for the interplay of visual and kinaesthetic factors. Similarly, fear is evoked by visual stimuli which in and of themselves are innocuous. It is an anticipation of injurious or painful bodily contacts. If fear in this sense is to be regarded as an hereditary trait of the species, it seems necessary to adopt the same view of the anticipation, or meaning.

Although the question of the inheritance of interests must be left open, it does not follow that the conception of primitive interests must be abandoned. For even though it should prove possible to explain all intelligent performances in terms of the previous experience of the individual, there would still be a difference between such performances as result from the

[11] Cf. W. Wundt, *Outlines of Psychology*, trans. by C. H. Judd, 1902, p. 314.

common habitat and structure of the species, and those which result from individual histories. An interest of the former type would be relatively universal, inalienable and fundamental. For purposes of education or social control it might well be regarded as an irreducible element.

On the other hand, even though the theory of instincts should be definitively established, the instinct is in its very nature so general and so highly modifiable, that it would not stand in the way of any transformation of character or social reconstruction that would be conceivable on the contrary hypothesis. Thus, for example, the idea that war and property follow inevitably from 'pugnacity' and 'acquisitiveness,' is now generally abandoned, because even if such instincts exist they can be so redirected or "sublimated" as to be consistent with profound alterations of concrete behavior.

§ 90. **Interest and Habit.** We have come to the conclusion that interest and instinct are the same thing, save in that instinct implies a further theory of inheritance, which must at present be regarded as at best a probable hypothesis. Let us now briefly consider the relation of interest and *habit.* We have seen that the essential characteristic of interested action is the presence of a certain intermediate link, and also that it is characteristic of habit that intermediate links which were essential to its formation should afterwards drop out. It follows that interested action becomes habitual in so far as its characteristic mediating factor disappears. The response, r' to s', is an interested act in so far as s' means s, and in so far as this meaning determines the occurrence of r'. The hungry kitten's pawing at the button which fastens the door of the box in which it is confined, is interested in so far as the sight of the button arouses expectations which cause the pawing owing to their congruence with hunger. According to the law of habit the response $r' - s'$ acquires a certain tendency to recur owing to its repetition, and independently of the ulterior occurrence of s. In other words, s, having served as a condition of the recurrence of $r' - s'$, may thereafter cease to operate as a factor of control. The proof that the anticipated result had ceased to operate would lie in the fact that changes in the result were not reflected in changes of behavior. There would then be a specific loss of docility. In other words, the kitten, having learned to turn the button as a means of executing its hunger-impulse, would thereafter turn the button whether hungry or not; or continue to turn the button when hungry, even though, owing to a change in the situation, the results were contrary to the requirements to the food-taking propensity.

The turning of the button is adaptive with reference to hunger so long as this event is causally connected with conditions which enable this propensity to be executed, and is intelligent in so far as this connection is represented within the organism by the meaning of the button. The turning of the button ceases to be adaptive with reference to hunger when the causal connections are altered, and is unintelligent in so far as this alteration fails to give a new meaning to the button. The dancing of the bear was adaptive with reference to pain-avoidance so long as the music was associated with the proximity of a hot body. The bear who goes on dancing after these factors are disassociated is non-adaptive and unintelligent because its behavior is no longer linked, either by sensation or meaning, with a stimulus appropriate to pain avoidance. It may, however, become adaptive and intelligent in a new sense, if we suppose the rhythmic movements of foot withdrawal to become themselves a governing propensity which in turn gives rise to new associated and selected activities. In this case the bear would have acquired an impulse to dance, similar to its original impulse to avoid pain. The behavior of the old soldier is likewise unadaptive and unintelligent in so far as it has ceased to be controlled by those circumstances, such as punishment or the ulterior train of military performances, that originally gave it its meaning. But in this case also we may suppose the soldier to acquire an interest in precise mechanical execution for its own sake, —in other words, to become a martinet.[12]

The paradox of habit arises from the fact that it tends

[12] For the genesis of new interests by this method, cf. § 221.

to the elimination of the very conditions which gave rise to it. Interest or intelligence consists in the capacity to learn, while habit gives stability to what is learned and renders it a permanent acquisition. A performance once learned possesses an inertia which tends to detach it from the relations which originally made it useful, and therefore less susceptible of being altered to meet a change in these relations. In other words, having habits tends to prevent forming habits; or, old habits stand in the way of new ones. "Our failure" is not, as Walter Pater would have it, "to form habits"; it is this formativeness or modifiability which is the mark of intelligence, and the condition of consecutive and coherent performances. Our failure is rather to *have* habits, or to be *governed* by them. Or, more accurately, our failure is to allow habit to control actions whose utility depends on results that change with concomitant circumstances, either within or without the organism. Automatism, whether habit or reflex, is adaptive in the case of actions whose utility is not thus subject to change: namely, in the case of elements, like the component parts of manual skill, that may enter identically into a great variety of complex performances; or, in the case of total performances, like dressing and undressing, walking, sitting, coughing and breathing, which may be parallel to other activities or interpolated among them without affecting them either positively or negatively. Intelligence implies a susceptibility to change in respect of whatever is relevant to any given interest or system of interests. For a highly developed organism such as man there is a profounder truth than is ordinarily supposed in the aphorism, "To live is to learn."

We are now in a position to indicate provisionally that factor which plays the part of the *object* of interest. It is precisely that factor which mediates between a governing propensity and a subordinate act, and whose elimination signifies the degeneration of interest into habit. Suppose $r' — s'$ to owe its occurrence or recurrence to its resulting in s, because of the organism's being governed by a propensity which can be executed only in a response $r — s$. In so far as this is the case, that is, in so far as s plays this multiple rôle, as the condition by which the propensity is completed and brought to rest, and at the same time as the expectation which accompanies *r'*, or the meaning which qualifies *s'*, — *s* is the object of an interest, which is ordinarily named for it.

II. POSITIVE AND NEGATIVE INTERESTS

§ 91. The Presence and Absence of Response. In our discussion of interest up to this point, attention has been called to its selective, prospicient, conative, tentative, instrumental and fallible characteristics; but there is one of its characteristics which is of central importance for a theory of value, and which has hitherto been neglected. This characteristic, to which we must now turn, is its *polarity,* or that duality of *for* and *against,* which is repeated throughout the whole range of interests in such pairs as desire and aversion, liking and disliking, favor and disfavor. Thus Royce says:

"By the evil which we experience we mean precisely whatever we regard as something to be gotten rid of, shrunken from, put out of sight, of hearing, or of memory, eschewed, expelled, assailed or otherwise directly or indirectly resisted. By good we mean whatever we regard as something to be welcomed, pursued, won, grasped, held, persisted in, preserved. And we show all this in our acts in presence of any grade of good or evil, sensuous, aesthetic, ideal, moral." [13]

In the first place, we have to eliminate that conception of positive and negative response in which the one denotes the presence, and the other the absence of response. Chemical tests are said to yield a 'positive' or 'negative' reaction, according as a specific reaction either occurs or fails to occur. Similarly a blind man's response to a visual stimulus is in this sense negative. But this is evidently not the duality of which we are in search, because it fails to provide for an actual response having a negative character.

Nor, secondly, shall we say that a response is negative when, although it occurs, it lacks the character of interest. In this case a negative response would be an apathetic or neutral response, as when the stimulus is 'noticed' or 'viewed,'

[13] *Studies of Good and Evil,* 1898, p. 18.

without either favor or disfavor. Although this question requires and will receive further examination,[14] curiosity or bare attention seems clearly to furnish a case of such a response. There is also evidently a difference between the passionate and the apathetic types, each being capable of exaggeration to a degree that is pathological. But this difference, although of great importance to the understanding of the rôle of cognition, throws no light on the difference between positivity and negativity as modalities of interest. Positive and negative response in the sense of the presence or absence of interested response to any given object, have significance as denoting the object's possession or lack of value; they do not define the polarity of good and bad, which arises only upon the level of interest.

Nor, thirdly, is such a definition provided by the distinction between potentiality and actuality. Interest may exist in a dispositional form, or it may be effectively realized. It may be repressed, or expressed; dissociated or integrated; latent or active. The difference of latency or activity is not, however, that polarity of which we are in search, since attitudes of favor may be latent, and attitudes of disfavor, active. It does not affect the sign of value, or good as opposed to bad, but the place of values, whether good or bad, in the organized personality.

§ 92. **Approach and Withdrawal.** It is evident that the difference of which we are in search must be one of sense or direction attaching to the process of interested response. The simplest possible view is that which identifies this difference of direction with that of the movement of the responding organism, positive response being construed as approach to the object, and negative response as withdrawal. The classic exponent of this view is Hobbes. Having defined "endeavour" as "small beginnings of motion, within the body of man," he goes on to say:

"This endeavour, when it is toward something that causes it, is called 'appetite' or 'desire.' . . . And when the endeavour is

14 Cf. below, Ch. XI, and above, §§ 39-41.

fromward something, it is generally called 'aversion.' These words, 'appetite' and 'aversion,' we have from the Latins; and they both of them signify the motions, one of approaching, the other of retiring." [15]

This account possesses a certain plausibility because it fits the superficial aspect of such behavior as flight and hand-withdrawal; but it breaks down when the attempt is made to carry it further. Flight may take the form of hiding as well as of running away. Withdrawal does not even describe facts of simple sensory repugnance. The reaction to a blinding light, a loud or discordant sound, a nauseous smell or taste, may take the form of the closing of the eye-lids, the stopping of the ears and nostrils, or the spewing of a substance from the mouth. These are evidently reactions of the same type as the withdrawal of the organism or one of its members from an offensive stimulus, but it is quite impossible to describe them in the same simple terms. Such a description is even more inadequate when we turn from these reactions to the aggressive reactions of riddance, destruction or prevention. These are equally manifestations of disfavor, and their objects are none the less bad. Escape reactions undoubtedly have their own specific character in that they take effect in the organism itself rather than in the environment, and they undoubtedly define a significant class of values; [16] but we must first provide for that broader principle which reactions of escape and reactions of attack have in common. While the former may in certain cases take the form of withdrawal, the latter characteristically take the form of approach, so that direction of motion cannot be definitive of their common principle.

That which escape and attack have in common is some negative result, which may be accomplished by the removal or destruction of the external body, or by a change of position or posture on the part of the organism itself. The conception of approach and withdrawal is evidently designed to fit the single case in which this negative result consists in

[15] *Leviathan,* Part I, Ch. VI.
[16] Cf. Ch. IX, Sect. III.

the termination or prevention of *contact*. It may well be that contact with the environment is the most primitive concern of the organism. But for an organism endowed with telaesthetic capacities, such as vision, hearing, imagination and thought, this factor tends to assume less and less importance; and, in any case, the *making* of contact may afford as good a case of negative response as the breaking of contact.

There is still another, and for our purposes, fundamental, respect in which approach and withdrawal fail adequately to describe positive and negative response. They fail to provide for that variability and tentativeness of response which we have seen to be essential to its interested character. Even in the simplest cases of escape, from which the conception of withdrawal is originally derived, there is no uniformity in the direction of motion. It is not a mere matter of electrical or magnetic repulsion, or of increase of distance between the object and the responding organism, but involves the use of ways and means in which the direction of motion may be reversed or varied without limit. Escape is the consummation of an endeavor, which may or may not be realized, and whose subordinate and component acts may follow no kinematic rule whatsoever. We shall be led to a similar conclusion if we approach the question from another angle.

§ 93. **Positive and Negative Results of Response.** The conception of approach and withdrawal is derived from the superficial aspect of certain relatively simple cases of disgust or escape. The examination of this conception has suggested that the generic feature of negative response is not a direction of motion, but a negative result. This account of negative response would have been immediately suggested had we started with attack rather than with escape. Attack is marked by its destructive effects upon the object, and is thus distinguished from creative or protective action, which is constructive in its effects. But if we confine attention to the object it is evident that this account will be as inadequate as the account in terms of approach and withdrawal. As **the latter** account fails to provide for attack, so the **former** fails to provide for escape; for this, evidently, does not destroy the object.

Suppose, then, that we think of the result of action in terms of a relation between the object and the organism, and conceive positive and negative response in terms of their positive and negative effect upon this relation. Attack would then be interpreted not simply in terms of the destruction of the object, but in terms of the interruption or prevention of its interaction with the organism. This account would cover the case of escape as well as the case of attack.

There remains, however, a further difficulty. All change can be described equally well as either destructive or constructive: eating both destroys the food, and constructs new organic conditions. A response is a change from an initial situation to a resulting situation. The resulting situation can be described as the presence of something which was absent in the initial situation, or as the absence of something that was present in the initial situation. Every action will in point of fact be both a doing and an undoing. If we are to avoid this difficulty, and describe any given response as uniquely positive or negative, it is evident that either the positive or the negative aspect of the situation must *play some rôle which the other does not play*.

As regards the initial situation this further determining factor may be the function of stimulation. A given situation may serve as a stimulus by virtue of what is absent rather than by virtue of what is present. Otherwise there would be no accounting for the undeniable psychological fact of missing or losing. There is no insuperable logical difficulty in supposing that a stimulus is describable only in negative terms. This would mean simply that the only common character among the different operative sensory stimuli lay in what they lacked rather than in what they possessed.[17] As the purely sensory stimulus was superseded by perception and judgment these would assume the form of negative propositions. The

[17] The stimulus would be describable only *ambiguously*, by use of the relation of opposition or contrariety. Cf. R. Demos, "A Discussion of a Certain Type of Negative Proposition," *Mind*, N. S., Vol. XXVI, 1917.

man who missed his hat, would react in a characteristic way to objects whose only class-characteristic was their 'not-being-his-hat'; and in so far as his reaction was mediated by more developed cognitive acts, these would assume the form of perceptions and judgments that this or that was not his hat.[18]

Similarly the end-result of the response may be expected or anticipated as regards what it is, or as regards what it is not. In the latter case, that which is expected is describable only in terms of the absence of some object, as the absence of the beloved one tinges the whole future of the bereaved. In so far as such expectation assumes an explicit cognitive form it will then find expression in negative propositions regarding the future.

We may thus speak of a negative stimulus, meaning not the absence of a stimulus, but a present stimulus which is negatively qualified by the absence of a certain specified element. And similarly we may speak of a negative expectation of an object, where there is an expectation describable only in terms of the absence of that object. Thus the negative expectation of *A* does not denote the non-expectation of *A*, but the expectation of *non-A*.

§ 94. **Positive and Negative Responses Defined and Illustrated.** We are now in a position to undertake a definition of positive and negative interested response. We understand by interested response in the general sense, performance for the sake of its consequences, or performance determined by what the agent expects as a result of it. Positive interest will then be a response determined by a positive expectation; and negative interest a response determined by a negative expectation. Just as in our previous analysis it is the object of the expectation which is the object of interest, so here it will be the sign of the expectation rather than that of the original or stimulating situation that defines the sign of the interest.

[18] For a brief examination of these cognitive aspects of negative responses, cf. the writer's article, "The Truth-Problem," *Jour. of Philos.*, Vol. XIII, 1916, pp. 506-510.

A comparatively simple illustration is afforded by the behavior of doves as described by Professor Wallace Craig. The positive response is illustrated by what this writer terms "appetence," and which he defines as follows:

"An appetite (or appetence, if this term may be used with purely behavoristic meaning), so far as externally observable, is a state of agitation which continues so long as a certain stimulus, which may be called the appeted stimulus is absent. When the appeted stimulus is at length received it stimulates a consummatory reaction, after which the appetitive behavior ceases and is succeeded by a state of relative rest." [19]

The writer then goes on to show that this "state of agitation" assumes the form of "varied effort," and that it is accompanied by a certain "readiness to act" or "incipient consummatory action"; an analysis which clearly recognizes the distinction which we have made between subordinate tentative responses and the governing propensity. It would be wholly consistent with this analysis to suppose that in so far as such appetitive performance is learned, or intelligent, the "varied effort" will be less varied, and more largely confined to stimuli which *mean* that absent stimulus which is the condition of the consummatory reaction.[20] This selection is explicable, as we have seen, by the fact that the incipient action which constitutes the meaning, and that which constitutes the unexecuted phase of the consummatory response, are coincident or congruent. In so far as this is the case, we can say that the stimulus in question is the object of a positive interested response, in the sense that another stimulus which means or promises this stimulus, or arouses the expectation of it, is reacted to on that account. In short, that, the expectation of which is the cause of its existence, is the object of positive interest, and hence is, by definition, good.

[19] "Appetites and Aversions as Constituents of Instincts," *Biological Bulletin*, Vol. XXXIV, 1918, p. 91.
[20] "In later experience with the same situation, the modes of behavior which were followed immediately by the appeted stimulus and consummatory reaction are repeated; those which were not so followed tend to drop out." (W. Craig, *op. cit.*, p. 94.)

Professor Craig also gives us an account of "aversion," as follows:

"An aversion is a state of agitation which continues so long as a certain stimulus, referred to as the disturbing stimulus, is present; but which ceases, being replaced by a state of relative rest, when that stimulus has ceased to act on the sense-organs." [21]

The "disturbing stimulus," in other words, excites a response which is its own undoing. But this type of response, like that described as "appetence," can be learned. Professor Craig cites the case of the male dove who, being "annoyed" by the presence of another male near his mate, learns under different circumstances either to drive away the intruder or to drive away his mate. In this case the response is selected which "promises relief," or which means the absence of the disturbing stimulus. We must suppose that in this case the selected response is accompanied by incipient relief; or coincides in its ulterior phases with the unrealized consummatory response, which is a response to the non-propinquity of other males. In other words, when the expectation of the object's undoing is the cause of its undoing, we may speak of it as object of negative interested response, or as bad.

§ 95. **Interest as Uniquely Positive or Negative.** In both positive and negative interest an expectation is the cause of its own fulfilment, or an act is performed because of its anticipated results; and in both cases the sign of the interest is the sign of the expectation. Where the expectation is constant in respect of the absence of some element, it is said to be negative; and when it is constant in respect of the presence of some element, it is said to be positive. We have now to consider whether all interested responses, by virtue of being selective, are not both positive and negative; whether a response that is negative in respect of *a*, is not necessarily positive in respect of some other element such as *b*. Suppose, for example, that we watch a father and son as they walk down the street during a January thaw. The father, who is middle-

[21] *Ibid.*, p. 91.

aged, apprehensive and lightly shod, selects his footing in one way; while the son, who is youthful, adventurous and equipped with a new pair of rubber boots, selects his footing in another way. In describing the two performances we say that the son steps in all the puddles, while the father steps *anywhere but* in a puddle. That which is constant in the performance of the father is the negative of that which is constant in the performance of the son. The one performance is constant in respect of what is selected, the other in respect of what is rejected. The one is a case of seeking, and the other of avoidance.

But can these performances not be equally well described as the father's seeking and the son's avoidance of a dry footing? Superficial observation might doubtless fail to reveal any difference between the two cases. But the question is whether the two cases are *necessarily identical*. Is seeking a dry footing essentially the same thing as avoiding puddles, and seeking puddles essentially the same thing as avoiding a dry footing? Is aversion to suffering the same as benevolence? Is misanthropy the same as love of solitude? Is gregariousness the same as the inability to endure loneliness? Or to put the question more roundly, does it mean nothing to say of a given individual that his *general* cast of mind is positive or negative? Must we say that any given interest or series of interests is always *equally* positive or negative?

The answer to this question lies in the fact that while positive interest will have its negative, and negative interest its positive, implications, it does not follow that these implications are themselves interested. It is possible, in other words, that the only *determining expectation* should be either a positive expectation or a negative expectation. The complementary aspect of the performance may not be expected at all, or its expectation may not govern the performance. Thus in so far as the father's action is determined by the negative expectation of wet feet, this implies as its complementary positive aspect the securing of a dry footing; but there may be no expectation of a dry footing, or, if there is such an expectation, it may not account for his action.

Similarly the son's exclusion of dry footing from his performance may be merely incidental to the control of his action by the positive expectation of puddles. Similarly, a man's isolation from his fellows may be due to his positive predisposition to a situation such as primitive nature, or unbroken silence, which implies the absence of his kind; or it may be due to the fact that he finds the presence of his fellows unendurable. There is, in other words, a genuine psychological difference between misanthropy and love of solitude, though their results may largely coincide. Goldsmith tells us that "Olivia was often affected, from too great a desire to please. Sophia even repressed excellence, from her fear to offend." [22] While the results might in any given case be the same, Olivia, whose expectations referred to the observer's *pleasure,* is a very different kind of person from Sophia whose conduct was governed by anticipations of its absence. This is only another way of saying that the same results may be either positively or negatively motivated.

This must not be taken to imply that positive and negative interests cannot be associated together. As a matter of fact they are ordinarily so associated as to supplement and reinforce one another. But this characteristic association cannot be clearly understood unless the associated elements are first distinguished. The most familiar case of such association is presented by desire, where this contains both the positive component of seeking the satisfying object, and the negative component of avoiding the present state of deficiency.

§ 96. **Outstanding Problems.** Our conclusions regarding positive and negative interest may be briefly resumed as follows. Their difference lies not in any character possessed by the response itself, viewed as movements of the organism, nor in the character of the actual results of such performance either within or without the organism, but in the *expected results so far as such expectation determines the performance.* The general form of interested action is the same, whether positive or negative; the difference lies in the positive or

[22] *Vicar of Wakefield,* Ch. I.

negative sign of the governing expectation. In both cases one is trying to do something; but that which one is trying to do is describable in the one case in positive and in the other case in negative terms. Unless negative interest is to mean non-interest, a negative interest in *a* must be the same thing as a positive interest in *not-a;* negative interest in the sense of the polar opposite of positive interest, being defined by transposing the negation from the act to the object of interest.[23] Having thus defined positive and negative interest, we have by implication defined the antithesis of good and evil: *a* being good in so far as interest is taken in it, and evil in so far as interest is taken in *not-a.*

Our analysis of positive and negative response has brought to light further distinctions, to which we must presently turn. We have described positive responses which occur in the absence, and negative responses which occur in the presence, of a given stimulus. But it is also possible that a present stimulus should be responded to positively, and an absent stimulus negatively. One may in other words like, or seek to perpetuate, that which is already given; and one may dread and prevent that which has not yet occurred. These possibilities are distinguishable not simply by the sign of the determining expectation, but by the varying relations between the determining expectation and the given situation.

[23] Just as denial in the cognitive sense is the assertion of a negative proposition, since otherwise it would be mere non-assertion. It follows from the view here taken that a negative interest in *not-a* is the same as a positive interest in *a.* This is apparently contradicted by Meinong's view that the value of an object may be represented by the formula $V = C \ I + C' \ I'$, where I is the intensity of the feeling excited by the judgment of the object's existence, and I' that of the opposite feeling excited by the judgment of its non-existence, and C and C' are constants. ("Wert-haltung u. Wert," *Arch. f. Syst. Philos.,* Vol. I, 1895. Cf. also his article in *Logos,* Vol. III, 1912, p. 7; *Ueber Annahmen,* 1910, pp. 329-327; and *Grundlegung der allgemeinen Werttheorie,* 1923, pp. 82-99.) The plausibility of this formula rests on too hasty an assumption that what is described in negative terms is really a negative object. Thus, for example, in so far as death means not-life and nothing more, then the fear of death and the love of life are the same thing. But in so far as death means pain, bereavement, violence, or any other positive quality, then it is obvious that the fear of it constitutes it a distinct evil; in which case, however, since the object is now different, it cannot be regarded as a component of the positive value of life.

This distinction is of special importance in its bearing on the question of existence, and will be examined in the following chapter.

We have also found it necessary to distinguish between those responses in which the result is sought by an alteration of the environmental object, and those in which the result is sought by the introduction or withdrawal of the responding organism itself. There is, in other words, a fundamental and far-reaching difference between aggressive responses and submissive responses, depending on the factor of control. Furthermore, in our discussion of uniquely positive or negative responses we have recognized the fact that positive and negative responses may supplement one another. This supplementary relation assumes a special importance in those cases of appetite and desire, in which there is at the same time the positive attainment of a coveted object and the negative escape from a state of lack or deficiency. But these cases, in turn, involve a further distinction which has not as yet been explicitly recognized, the distinction, namely, between those cases in which the stimulus is received from the environment and those cases in which it is received from within the organism itself. This distinction will afford a clue to the rôle of appetite and feeling.

CHAPTER IX

MODES OF INTEREST *(continued)*

I. RECURRENT AND PROGRESSIVE INTEREST

§ 97. **Liking versus Desire.** In our analysis of interested response we have emphazied its aspect of futurity, or its determination by expectation. While this analysis evidently fits the case of desire, where the object of interest does not yet exist, it may be supposed by the same token to be inapplicable to the case of liking, where the object of interest already exists. We meet here with one of the fundamental paradoxes in the theory of value. It would be manifestly absurd to contrive a theory which implied that existence is a disqualification for value. It would be a fantastic departure from common-sense to exclude from the category of value all cases of felt satisfaction and enjoyment, while including only cases of unfulfilled longing and deferred hope. But it would be equally fantastic to exclude that forward reference in time, that transcendence of present existence, which distinguishes purposes and ideals. Indeed, there is no more fundamental notion in our whole field of discourse than that which assigns a greater value to objects of aspiration than to objects already achieved.

The difficulty is, however, by no means insuperable. It is created by the false supposition that liking or enjoyment is directed to the present instant of time, and thus disappears when it is remarked that enjoyment is directed to the immediate future. If enjoyment were directed to the present instant of time then the passage of time would dispel it, instead of fulfilling it, as is actually the case. Suppose a situation *a* at time t^1. The enjoyment of this situation does not imply any disposition to hold the instant t^1 and suspend the flow of time, but a disposition to hold *a* through time. It is an interest not in *a*'s occurrence at t^1, but in the prolongation or recurrence of *a*; an interest, therefore, which will be satisfied by *a*'s occurrence at t^2, t^3 etc. When such enjoyment is interrupted there is a baffled expectation of 'more-*a*-to-come.'

That which distinguishes enjoyment from desire is not the prospective reference, which is equally essential to both processes, but the relation between the given and the prospective situations. In the case of enjoyment the given and prospective situations possess a common element which is both that "in view of which" and that "for the sake of which" the response occurs. In other words, the stimulus and the governing expectation are, except as respects time, the same. One responds to *a* at time t^1, for the sake of *a* at time t^2. In the case of desire, on the other hand, one responds to *a* at time t^1 for the sake of *b* at t^2.

It is evident, however, that such terms as 'desire' and 'enjoyment' do not clearly indicate this distinction. Desire is often used to denote all action governed by the future, and is then virtually equivalent to interest in the broad sense. Such usage would compel us to say that all enjoyment, since it tends to prolong the given situation into the future, is desiderative. On the other hand, such terms as 'liking' and 'enjoyment' while they do usually denote interest in what is already given, lead to confusion because they are commonly correlated with 'disliking' or 'displeasure.' Dislike is an impulse to terminate the given situation, and to pass to another situation which shall be "anything but" that which is present. The prospective aspect of such interest is *different* from its present aspect, and in this respect resembles desire rather than liking. Therefore, reluctant though one may be to coin new terms, it seems in the present case to be unavoidable if we are to keep clearly in view the relation of identity or difference between the present and prospective phases of interest. We shall therefore employ the terms 'recurrent' or 'circular' for those interests, whether positive or negative, in which the *terminus ad quem* and the *terminus a quo* are the *same;* and the terms 'progressive' or 'linear' for those

interests in which they are *different*. It follows that in positive recurrent interest the transition is from *a* to *a;* and in
negative recurrent interest, from *not-a* to *not-a*. Similarly,
in positive progressive interest the transition is from *not-a*
to *a*, or from *a* to *b*, or from *not-a* to *b*; while in negative
progressive interest the transition is from *a* to *not-a*, or from
not-a to *not-b*, or from *a* to *not-b*.

The distinction between recurrent and progressive interest
does not contradict our fundamental analysis of interest in
terms of governing propensity and tentative act. In enjoyment as well as in desire, the present act is on trial; that is
to say, its occurrence is determined by the accompanying
expectation. But in order to provide for the case of recurrent
or circular interest it must be clearly understood that a governing propensity or general system of response may be either
tentatively advancing towards a culminating success, or tentatively renewing itself.

§ 98. **Illustration and Analysis of Recurrent Interest.**
The illustration and analysis of interest which have heretofore
been offered more obviously fit the case of progressive or
linear interest. In order to emphasize the teleological structure of interest, that is to say, its essentially tentative and
prospective character, it has been deemed best first to present
those types of interested performance in which the futurity
of the object of interest and the pastness of the guiding experience are marked by a clear time-interval, and in which
the subordination of the tentative acts is marked by their
external and instrumental relation to the governing propensity.
But once the analysis is made, we can transfer it to those
cases in which the temporal relations are abridged, and in
which the subordinate acts are parts of the governing propensity.

The progressive type of interest is illustrated by the case
of the hungry animal which is seeking access to food. The
process as a whole is a tendency to substitute a new and more
auspicious situation for the stimulating situation. The consummatory activity is definitively postponed to a future which

is indeterminate but separated from the present. The auxiliary movements by which access to the food is gained are
related to the food-taking response only as regards their ulterior sequel. When, however, the food is obtained, a new
and recurrent type of activity is inaugurated. A part of the
animal's response takes the form of sensory adaptation and
attention by which the stimulus is prolonged. Other parts
of the response, such as seizing the food, mastication, swallowing and gastric secretion, occur continuously or in cycles.
All phases of the response are both waning and waxing.
Memory passes over at once into expectation. The immediate
past fills the immediate future. There is a continuous anticipation of "more to come," more, that is to say, of that which
has just been lived through.[1] The same description fits the
case of what is ordinarily called aesthetic enjoyment. If we
consider the relatively simple case of sensory enjoyment, we
find that its distinguishing feature is prolonged receptivity
to a given stimulus. The eye "dwells fondly" on the given
visual field, or "caresses" it by bringing the same elements
again and again into the focus of attention. It is this continuous or periodic reinstatement of the stimulus that distinguishes the aesthetic response from curiosity, which, starting
with the same elements, looks for new stimuli from the adjoining field. To this type of response may be assimilated
all forms of consumptive as distinguished from productive
responses. The former is self-renewing, the latter self-
transcending. In both cases there is a forward movement
guided by the projection of meaning; but in the one case the
movement is circular or repetitive, whereas in the other the
movement is rectilinear or innovating.

The specific character of recurrent response may also be
expressed teleologically in terms of means and ends. In the
case of progressive response, as we have seen, the means and
the end are distinct. The means is adopted for the sake of
something other than itself, as when the button is turned for
the sake of gaining access to the food. But when the process

[1] Interest of this recurrent type, when the object is given in sensory
cognition (cf. § 133) may be termed *immediate* interest.'

of food-taking is in the act of being successfully performed, its several phases are both means and ends. There is no contradiction in this description, because of the different temporal aspects of the several phases of response. The given situation at any moment both satisfies the governing propensity and promises ulterior satisfaction by its persistence or reappearance; a at t^2 is end in relation to a at t^1, and means in relation to a at t^3. The swallowing of the masticated food is both the consummation of a cycle of antecedent activities, and also a point of departure for a cycle of imminent activities which are consummated in its subsequent recurrence. The act of sensory accommodation at any moment is both that *for* which the same act was performed at a previous moment, and that *by* which the same act is repeated at a later moment.

A similar description will fit the case of negative recurrent response. The common term which most nearly fits the case is 'avoidance,' as the term which most nearly fits the case of negative progressive response is 'aversion.' These terms are satisfactory in so far as one thinks of avoidance as manifested in the absence, and aversion in the presence, of its object. Negative recurrent response consists in purposely prolonging a negative situation. It differs from negative progressive response as prevention differs from cure. This type of performance is illustrated by the example, cited above, of the jealousy of the male dove, and by a wide range of human conduct such as timidity, apprehensiveness, keeping at a distance or "holding at arm's length."

§ 99. Relations of Recurrent and Progressive Interest.
Although it is necessary, for the sake of clearness, to distinguish between the recurrent and the progressive types of interest, it must not be assumed that they are unrelated, or that any given performance must be exclusively the one or the other. As a matter of fact they are usually, perhaps invariably, associated. There are two forms of such association that deserve special mention.

In the first place, recurrent and progressive interests may reinforce one another as dominant and subordinate phases of

one performance. Thus a response such as that of aesthetic
enjoyment or delight in bodily activity, which is on the whole
recurrent, may contain progressive segments or accompaniments in which there is an advance to novel situations. Some
such blend of progression with recurrence, or seasoning of
sameness with novelty, seems to be one of the distinguishing
characteristics of the aesthetic experience. Music, for example, contains both a unity and persistence of form, and
also its preliminary and its culminating phases. On the
other hand, an activity which is primarily constructive, in
which present means are clearly subordinated to a future end,
may be, as we say, "enjoyable in itself." The builder may
dwell with fond attention on the growing structure, or prolong and repeat the movements and manipulations by which
it is brought into being. Virtuosity and the joy of creation
may thus attend skill, and augment, or even eventually supersede, its primary motivation. There is also, in the second
place, a natural relation of succession which links recurrent
and progressive response. This relation may be expressed by
saying that recurrent response, when thwarted, normally gives
rise to progressive response, and that progressive response,
when consummated, ordinarily gives rise to recurrent response.
Thus if the food-taking activity is interrupted it is superseded
by an effort to recover the lost food, while the successful
effort to obtain food is commonly followed by the activity of
consuming it.

It cannot be affirmed, however, that either of these sequences is invariable or necessary. Because the possession
of a certain object begets an impulse to keep it, one cannot
argue that the same object will be coveted in its absence.
There are people who are disposed to be content with what
they have rather than to seek what they have not, like the
man who loves his friends when he is with them but never
misses them when they are removed. The keenest aesthetic
enjoyment is quite consistent with indolence. Indeed a lack
of ambition and effort, a quiescent preoccupation with whatever may happen to be present, is very commonly associated
with highly developed aesthetic sensibility.

Similarly, the consummation of a progressive interest is not necessarily followed by a recurrent interest. Games and sports consist ordinarily in activities which terminate in success, but the coveted situation becomes a matter of indifference when it is attained. Effort is often succeeded not by the prolongation of the result, but by another effort. The foot-ball player who carries the ball across the goal-line does not try to keep it there, nor does the successful wrestler hold down his fallen adversary and gloat over his prostrate form. The huntsman or fisherman may throw away the game which he has expended enormous effort to obtain, as the artist may lose all interest in his work as soon as it is completed. It would not be correct to say that in these cases the interest is in the activity rather than in the result. The sportsman and the artist are not simply enjoying the exercise,—they are striving earnestly to gain their ends. But the interest does not carry beyond the point of success.

It is proverbial that the expectation of an event is both better and worse than its occurrence. "All things that are," says Shakespeare, "are with more spirit chased than enjoyed"; and, according to Quintilian, "suffering itself does less afflict the senses than the anticipation of suffering." In other words, that whose prospect is a strong inducement to action, may in its occurrence be a matter of relative indifference. It is a trite and ironic fact that a man will seek that which he does not enjoy, and avoid that for which he has no aversion.

§ 100. **Value and Existence.** The distinction between recurrent and progressive response has an important bearing upon the fundamental question of the relation of value and existence,[2] and will serve at once to remove an ambiguity with which this question is attended. On the one hand, there is evidently a sense in which existence is a variable factor, which distinguishes some values from others. That which is valued may or may not exist. It may have existed in the past, it may exist in the present, it may come into existence as a consequence of being valued; it may be non-existent, in

_____
[2] For a further discussion of this question, cf. §§ 31, 141, 144.

any or all of these temporal aspects. These variable existential phases of the valued object distinguish such familiar attitudes as regretful and agreeable retrospect, living in the present, or realized desire. The case of recurrent response is the case in which one values that which *already* exists; progressive response is the case in which one values that which *does not yet exist.* If, then, we are speaking of *that which possesses value at any given moment,* we can say that in some cases it does exist, and in some cases it does not exist. Peace, for example, may possess value in time of peace, when it is enjoyed, or in time of war when, in its absence, it is longed for.

But, on the other hand, there are senses in which existence is an invariable factor of all values. In the first place, it is evident that the value itself in some sense exists whether the object valued does or does not exist. Thus peace may be said to *acquire* value in time of war, that is to say, its value may come into existence when the object passes out of existence.[3] In this case it is the interest which comes into existence, and which is by definition the existential constant in all value.

But there is another and less obvious sense in which existence is an invariable factor in value. Interest itself, as we have seen, always has reference to future existence. It is a motor impulse or disposition, a doing or undoing, an activity which takes effect in the existence or non-existence of its object. This has sometimes been thought to mean that the object of interest is always existentially qualified, or that it is the object's existence or non-existence to which interest is directed. But this statement of the case depends upon the assumption that interest itself is an unanalyzable attitude, having no existential implications. If, as has been proposed in the present study, interest itself is a cause of the existence or non-existence of its object, and if this existential determination is a constituent of the interest, then we must avoid imputing it to the object as well. If to be interested in peace means a disposition-to-bring-about peace, then we must

---

[3] This is the commonest of all phenomena in the economic field, where lack or rarity creates demand and induces value.

not say that it is the bringing about of peace *in* which one is interested. If, generally speaking, to be positively interested in *a* means that the expectation of *a* is a cause of *a*'s existence, then this does not imply interest in *a*'s existence. For an interest in *a*'s existence would then mean by definition that the expectation of *a*'s existence was a cause of the existence of *a*'s existence; which is a logical impossibility, as well as palpable absurdity.

There remains one further aspect of the question. The emphasis placed on the 'realization' or 'satisfaction' of interest, suggests a fundamental paradox to which allusion has already been made.[4] All interest has a forward reference in time; it is a striving after the not-yet-attained. The object attained is no longer desired; or, if enjoyed, its *present* existence does not suffice. This view is unavoidable once it is granted that interest is essentially active and teleological. On the other hand it seems equally evident that this situation of non-fulfilment is evil; and that therefore the only escape from evil is afforded by a suppression of interest, that is, by a destruction of all values. This paradox may lead either to pessimism of the Schopenhauerian or Oriental type,[5] or to an abandonment of the category of value as inherently self-contradictory. The difficulty is instructive, but not insuperable. It brings to light two general principles. In the first place, the value of an object is not a function of its existence. Peace, for example, does not become more valuable when it exists; it may, as we have seen, even lose its value. Money is not worth more when you have it than it is when you lack it. An ideal does not become better by being realized. If God be conceived as an ideal, then it is fallacious to argue that his perfection implies his existence. He is not any the less perfect for being non-existent. If this seems a hard saying, it is because of a natural confusion. When peace is achieved, it is not peace, but the world, which is better; or when a man makes money it is not the money, but the man, who is worth more. In short, when existence takes on value or value takes

---

[4] Cf. § 97.
[5] Cf. § 111.

on existence, it is the existence whose value is enhanced, through the utility or immediate satisfaction which it now affords.

In the second place, the situation of non-fulfilment of interest may or may not be evil. Carelessness has begotten the habit of supposing that desire is necessarily attended by a painful sense of deficiency. Sometimes it is, and this special case has been allowed to color the general conception. But there may be desire which is attended by no aversion whatsoever. To suppose the contrary would be to suppose that one cannot go abroad without running away from home. As a matter of fact those periods of life in which bliss is unalloyed are those in which one is having what one likes, or getting what one wants; periods in which satisfaction is a continuous achievement, rather than a completed fulfilment. Success, in other words, is a process, and not a state. Interest is always alive and looking forward. Philosophers have recognized this fact even when they have conceived intellectual contemplation as the supreme interest. For contemplation, even the contemplation attributed to an Aristotelian God, is a speculative *activity*,—a continuity of thinking, rather than a frozen stare. But philosophers have not fully recognized what this implies as regards the inseparable relation between value and time. They have been disposed to emphasize the negative aspect of time as robbing existence of value, or as postponing fulfilment; and have tended to neglect its positive aspect as providing opportunity, as defining the locus of every hope and aspiration, and as constituting the essential medium of activity.

II. REAL AND PLAYFUL INTEREST

§ 101. **Play as Partial Activity.** While all interest has an existential reference, or is definable in terms of some existential change in which it would, if completed, take effect, it is not always completed, and does not always take effect. Moreover, interest may occur without being intended to take effect. Interested performance of any of the types so far considered, inherited or acquired, positive or negative, recurrent or progressive, may occur seriously or playfully, wholeheartedly or half-heartedly. The psychological and physiological interpretation of this difference is obscure and doubtful; but the difference indubitably exists, and is of first importance in the theory of value. It is evidently indispensable to any account of aesthetic "detachment" or the religious imagination; and evidently resembles the difference between belief, and supposition or speculative conjecture.

In all cases of playful interest, from the play of animals to the play of the human imagination, there appears to be one common principle. An action-system having a certain normal result, is only partially executed; not because it is externally thwarted, but because it is only partially consistent with some predominant action-system. The most evident characteristic of playful activity is self-imposed restraint. The cat that plays with the mouse *almost* kills its prey, but stops just short of the consummation of the performance. The dog at play bites, but bites gently; runs away, but does not run far away. The spectator at the melodrama feels moved to rescue the heroine, and may even warn her of her danger, but he remains in his seat. The man who playfully imagines that he is a millionaire does some of the things that a millionaire would do, but not all. In these cases restraint is evidently a very different thing from failure, the interest being checked not by external circumstances but by some internal and interested control. In no case is the agent carrying the activity as far as he *could*. The dog could bite harder, but he does not want to; the imaginary millionaire could be more extravagant, but he is deterred by his own recognition of the facts. Playful activity is also commonly characterized by make-believe or pretence. But except in so far as it is confused with imitation,[6] this turns out to be also a form of restraint. The child who pretends to be a soldier or a mother is executing some but not all of the characteristic combative

─────

[6] It is evident that "serious" performance may be imitated, as well as playful performance; and that pretence may be original and creative, as well as imitative.

or parental activities. Indeed the examples cited above to illustrate restraint could equally well be cited as illustrations of pretence. The playful dog is pretending to fight or to run away, and the imaginary millionaire is pretending to possess wealth.

How shall we interpret this limitation of interested activity that is characteristic of play? The limitation does not relate to the type of performance, for one may play at anything. Play is not limited out of regard for other interests, for it is not the same thing as prudence, moderation or self-sacrifice. The boy who plays at being a soldier or pirate, is not controlling his warlike or piratical propensities out of regard for his own or another's well-being. There is some sense in which he is not a soldier or pirate at all,—some sort of flat difference between reality and pretence.

In order to understand this difference, it is necessary first to conceive of an interested activity as taking effect in certain changes which have both conditions and consequences beyond the activity itself. It unites with a given situation so as to produce a subsequent situation which, in turn, will inaugurate an ulterior train of effects. Such activity is characterized by a recognition of the existing situation, a search for means, and a regard for the future; and is commonly named for that normal ulterior consequence whose expectation is its governing motive. Now the phenomenon of play seems to consist, first, in the fact that part of such an interested performance occurs without the expectation for which it is named. Some care is needed in the statement of this principle, if make-believe is not to be confused with error. An expectation may occur and may inaugurate action, in the absence of the external conditions which render its fulfilment possible. In this case the interest is 'real' or 'earnest,' but is founded on error and "doomed to defeat." The case of make-believe, on the other hand, is the case in which the requisite external conditions are not only absent, but known to be absent; so that the action is checked from within, short of that point at which their absence is fatal.

Let us consider, for example, the case of the dog romping

with his master. The dog is said to be playing in so far as certain of its activities are organized parts of other activities, dissociated from the normal expectations for which they are named. Thus, for example, the dog springs upon its master, seizes his hand, bites at it, and growls. These activities are primarily associated with a train of other consequences, such as injury, retaliation on the part of the object attacked, death or devouring of prey. These ulterior consequences do not, however, occur, nor are they expected or sought. The dog is not mistaking his master for his enemy or prey, or deceived into misapplied effort, as he might be by a dummy cunningly contrived to simulate the proper object of ferocity. He recognizes his master throughout, and deals with him as such. But though differently motivated the dog's performance coincides in part with that which he would execute in the presence of a rival, an intruder, or his natural prey. The performance is called playful in so far as there is this partial coincidence, and is the playful form of that activity which in its entirety is called the real, earnest or serious activity.

In the second place, however, the dog who is playfully fighting, or pretending to be ferocious, is 'really' romping with his master. In other words, although the normal expectation for which the fictitious activity is named is lacking, there is an expectation which *is* governing the performance. Although divorced from the circumstances with which it is nominally associated, the activity is related to the circumstances which actually exist. It is transposed to unnatural circumstances, and so abridged or modified as to be consistent with these circumstances. There is a change of control which sets limits to it. In the case of the playful dog this control or actually dominating motive is an interest of the recurrent type, which is substituted for the progressive interest of attacking and slaying. There is, in other words, a tendency to prolong the existing situation, and the development of the activity is arrested at a point which will guarantee its repetition. This is commonly described as interest in the activity itself rather than in its result.

§ 102. **Theories of Play.** Such an analysis serves to correct two standard theories of play which are ordinarily thought to be inconsistent. Thus Professor William Mc-Dougall, following Schiller and Spencer, holds that play is "a purposeless activity, striving toward no goal," and explicable as an overflow of surplus energy. He bases this opinion on the evident fact that playful activity is not the same either in its effects or in its accompanying emotion, as the real activity for which it is named; and on the association of play with the abundant vitality which characterizes youth, health and freshness.[7] Such a view, while emphasizing the absence of the motivation commonly governing the activity, does not sufficiently emphasize that resemblance between earnest and playful activity owing to which the one is named for the other. The opposing view, maintained by Groos, Schneider and James, takes this resemblance as its point of departure, and interprets play as the partial exercise of instinctive activities.[8] But this view tends to neglect the fact that these instinctive activities do not really occur. Both views neglect the actual motivation of play, the former by viewing play as aimless, and the latter by identifying its motivation with that of the instincts which it resembles.

All writers on the subject are influenced by the unnecessary supposition that if play is to be governed by any motive at all, it must be either the same as that of the several instincts, or a new and unique motive invented *ad hoc,*—an "instinct to play." The former alternative is excluded because of the absolute difference between doing a thing in fun and in earnest, and the latter by the fact that play reproduces all of the performances of real life without having any specific form of its own. To avoid this *impasse* it is only necessary to suppose that all partial activities are capable, whether by inheritance, or by experience, of possessing a motive power of their own. According to James, "all simple active games are attempts to gain the excitement yielded by certain primitive instincts, through feigning that the occasions for their

[7] *Outline of Psychology*, 1923, pp. 170-172.
[8] Cf. *e.g.*, W. James, *Principles of Psychology*, Vol. II, p. 427.

exercise are there." [9]   But this statement fails to explain what
is meant by "feigning," and implies that the excitement is
the same in the playful and real exercise of the instinct.   We
may now understand the feigning to consist in the fact that
an instinctive activity, suitable to a certain situation, is executed only so far as is consistent with the recognition of a
contrary situation.   The playful dog is treating his master
like an enemy so far as this is compatible with treating him
as a friend.   The accompanying excitement will not be that
of ferocity but that of love, tinged with ferocity.   The component of fighting which is embodied in romping will carry
with it some portion of the fighting impulse.

§ 103.   Rôle of Play in Human Life.   We are now in
a position to understand something of the place of play in
life.   The playful form of any activity is an abridgment of
the activity under the control of inopportune or inauspicious
circumstance.   It is such transformation of an activity as
may enable it to fit into an action-system which is based on
the recognized absence of the conditions suitable to the activity's full performance.

Play, so construed, provides, in the first place a means
of circumventing the rule that "you cannot both eat your
cake and have it."   It is a means of reconciling consumption
and possession.   It is the cat-and-mouse manner of life.   It
expresses the fact that you can both eat your cake and have
it, *if you do not carry the eating too far.*   There is a crucial
point at which the rule takes effect, but by stopping just
short of that point one can escape its application.   One cannot swallow one's cake and have it, but one can handle it,
look at it, gloat over it or even mouth it,—and still have it.
The dog can bite his master's hand and still have it to bite
again, provided he bites gently; or he can run away from his
master and still have his master to run away from, provided
he remains within range and tempts pursuit.   In play, activity
is changed from a rectilinear to an asymptotic or elliptical
form, stopping just short of consummation for the sake of

[9] *Loc. cit.*

prolongation or recurrence. Play thus provides a means by which an activity may be saved from its own natural *dénouement*.

This aspect of play may be generalized as immunity from consequences. One can dance without paying the piper. In "real life" consequences are taken account of; as events in the environment, and having their own train of effects, they require a general readjustment to the future, or a systematic correction of expectations. The playful activity is somehow dissociated and insulated from this causal field. In the case of the child, eventualities are looked out for by others. The child, like the lilies of the field, is delivered by parental care from the necessity of toiling and spinning. The adult who takes a holiday or an hour of recreation, has made provision for it by "arranging his affairs," that is by securing his future. The holiday-activities themselves are characterized by their discontinuity with that series of means and ends that constitutes his main current of endeavor. A man's sports and recreation are so organized as to have the minimum of consequences, being conducted on a plane that does not intersect with that of his imperative needs or his vocational purpose. They are artificially contrived so that they may be performed spontaneously, that is, without calculation of consequences. This mood of spontaneity is further induced by a change of scene in which the habitual to-morrow may for a time be forgotten. The adult at play is thus said to be relieved from his "cares," or from that watchfulness and persistent effort with which his ordinary occupations are attended. Like the horse at pasture he may be healed from the fatigue and friction of harness. Recreation may therefore be playful in a double sense, as being divorced from the context of work, and as consisting in activities which simulate those of real performance.

Activity is deemed frivolous or excessively playful when, like Nero's fiddling, it disregards facts or consequences that press for consideration. From the standpoint of the devout all worldly living is frivolous, because it ignores reality, both present and future. A serious life, on the other hand, is a life wholly permeated by the conviction of reality, and closely applied to the main purpose. If "life is real! life is earnest!" this means "to act that each to-morrow find us farther than to-day." The grim spirit of Puritanism expresses itself in the resolve:

"Never to lose one moment of time, but to improve it in the most profitable way I can."

"Never to allow any pleasure or grief, joy or sorrow, nor any affection at all, nor any degree of affection, nor any circumstance relating to it, but what helps religion." [10]

If play denotes an activity delivered from consequences, it also denotes an activity delivered from circumstances. It is not only a means of eating one's cake without ceasing to have it, but also a means of eating one's cake without having it at all. It provides a way of making bricks without straw. Here lies the great compensatory value of play, or the so-called "pleasures of the imagination." The principle is the same, consisting in the fact that a complete performance which requires the support of external conditions may be partially executed in the absence of these conditions. One cannot wholly be a millionaire without the effective possession of wealth, but there is no man so poor that he cannot assume some of the postures of the millionaire. 'Wishing' in the limited sense, as something less than earnest desire, is interest attended by the recognized absence of auspicious conditions. That which distinguishes the 'idle' wish from the genuine interest is the absence of endeavor. The object of mere wishing does not operate as a governing expectation.[11] One *does nothing about it:* that is to say, one does not react to the given situation with a view to fulfilling the wish, because there is nothing in the given situation that *promises* this fulfilment. A wish is a governing propensity without trial or effort; or a longing without hope, though not without satisfaction. The modern who wishes he had been born an ancient

---

[10] From the *Resolutions* of Jonathan Edwards, 1722-1723.
[11] Being 'glad' or 'sorry' bears the same relation to present as wishing bears to prospective existence. Circumstances agree with my disposition, but I do not act so as to preserve them, for lack of means so to do. The object of interest lies beyond my causal range.

Greek, or the self-confessed failure who wishes for power and leadership, does not fit the object of his dreams into his living environment, present or future. Nevertheless he indulges in some of the activities appropriate to that other environment; and conducts himself implicitly, if not overtly, as one whose "game is empires," or as one who dwells "where burning Sappho loved and sung."

The enjoyment of art may be playful in all of the above senses. It forms an interlude detached from the major series of means and ends, and thus provides the value of recreation. At the same time it may simulate the instincts and purposes of real life, enabling these to obtain a partial compensatory expression in the absence of the conditions necessary for their complete expression, and without precipitating the consequences which would normally bring them to an end.

III. AGGRESSIVE AND SUBMISSIVE INTEREST

§ 104. **Purely Aggressive Interest.** In the course of the analysis of positive and negative response a difference was noted between attack and escape,[12] which, while it failed to provide the principle for which we were then in search, suggested another principle which must now be recognized on its own account. Attack and escape do not afford a clue to the distinction between positive and negative interest, since both are forms of negative interest; but they do indicate another and independent distinction, that, namely between aggressive and submissive interest.

Performance is interested in so far as it is governed by expectation. An act is a manifestation of interest in a given outcome b, in so far as its performance is due to the fact that b is expected of it by the agent himself; and b will then occur, provided the expectation is true. As a matter of fact, however, the interested act is never a sufficient condition of b's occurrence, but must combine with external supplementary conditions. These may or may not be recognized by the agent. Normally they are recognized in part, as when, reacting

[12] Cf. §§ 100, 101.

to *a* in a manner that promises *b,* the agent expects *b* both
of *a* and of his act as their joint consequence.   But the agent
may ignore the supplementary conditions of successful performance, and thus enjoy a sense of absolute control; or he
may ignore the causal efficacy of his act, and suffer from a
sense of comparative impotence.   We may say, therefore, that
judged by the observer, all interested action is both submissive and aggressive: submissive, in that it takes things as it
finds them; aggressive, in that it enters itself into the causal
nexus and determines the outcome, perhaps decisively.   But,
on the other hand, conceived in terms of the agent's own
meanings and expectations, interested performance may be
characterized as purely aggressive, as purely submissive, or
as both aggressive and submissive.

Purely aggressive interest is a conceit begotten by ignorance or forgetfulness.   The external conditions necessary
to successful performance may be ignored because they are
uniformly supplied, the agent taking for granted that which
he has never lacked.   We may suppose that there is always
in some measure a preëstablished harmony between interests
and their environment, attributable to natural selection.   Air-
breathing animals do not as a rule live in the water, and
they tend to be unaware of what they owe to their native
element.   Privileged classes and spoilt children are unaware
of the extent to which their satisfactions depend on conditions
beyond their control.   They enjoy a sense of mastery and
easy triumph.   Where success has resulted from an accumulation of past efforts, there is a tendency to ignore the fact
that from its very complexity the situation has passed beyond
personal control.   Success, in other words, breeds over-confidence, and conquerors fall owing in part to the easy assurance with which they disregard the objective conditions of
their power.

§ 105. **The Stoic's Ruling Faculty.**   Philosophical reflection has begotten another type of purely aggressive interest, in which a sense of perfect mastery is obtained by
a limitation of the sphere of action.   The classic example is

afforded by the Stoic conception of "the ruling faculty." According to Epictetus, Zeus has left free and unhampered not our property or even our bodies, but only "a small part of us," namely, "a certain disposition of the will with respect to appearances." [13]

"Can any man hinder you from assenting to the truth? No man can. Can any man compel you to receive what is false? No man can. You see that in this matter you have the faculty of will free from hindrance, free from compulsion, unimpeded. Well then, in the matter of desire and pursuit of an object, is it otherwise? . . . And what can overcome desire and aversion except another desire and aversion? But, you object, 'If you place before me the fear of death, you do compel me.' No, it is not what is placed before you that compels, but your opinion that it is better to do so and so than to die. In this matter it is your opinion that compelled you, that is, will compelled will." [14]

In other words, that which lies wholly within the agent's control is his *judgment of good and evil,*—whether he shall view with favor or disfavor that which is given to him. God has given us faculties "by which we shall be able to bear everything that happens without being depressed or broken by it." A man cannot escape sickness, but can govern his attitude to it, and "bear a fever well." He cannot escape death, but he can die "as becomes a god." [15]

Notwithstanding its proud spirit of self-reliance, such freedom is in large measure an acknowledgment of impotence. It is begotten by failure and disillusionment. That which is free is only a "small portion of us,"—the greater part of expectation is imputed to circumstance and is passively awaited. As respects this greater part, the attitude is one of submission rather than of creative will. Thus the sense of power is intensified by being narrowed. Even the Stoic's power, furthermore, is in large measure an escape rather than an achievement. Having discounted human failure once and for all, the Stoic was delivered from those sudden reverses and pangs of disappointment that arouse complaint. The

---

[13] *Discourses,* trans. by G. Long, London, 1891, Vol. I, pp. 5, 38.
[14] *Op. cit.,* Vol. I, pp. 70-71. Cf. Vol. II, pp. 81-82.
[15] *Op. cit.,* Vol. I, pp. 29, 159; Vol. II, p. 42.

philosopher who knows the firmness of his prison walls, learns, once the discovery is made, to live within them; whereas the vulgar, like the caged animal, repeatedly flings and bruises himself against them.

The philosopher escapes not only the bitterness of repeated failure, but also the humiliations of tyranny. This is a negative value which was peculiarly heightened by the social system in which the Stoics lived, and by the exposure of wise men to the arrogance of fools. "If a man is going to be overpowered by a man," says Epictetus, "he must long before be overpowered by things." One man is in the power of another through his desire for that thing which the other can promise or threaten, give or take away. If I cease to desire that thing which lies in the control of others, "who then has any power over me? Philip or Alexander, or Perdiccas or the great king?" [16] Through renunciation the philosopher, if he does not gain that which he first coveted, at least avoids the ignominy of ministering to the vanity of others. There is, furthermore, in the Stoic cult that motive of self-respect which prompts a man to appraise highly that which he has, and to belittle that which he has not. The man who has only wisdom praises wisdom, and despises worldly power; while the fool in his turn reciprocates, and despises wisdom.

For wisdom is in fact as much beyond the reach of some men as health, life, riches or political power are beyond the reach of others. It is not uncommon for a man to seek by his more facile control of material things to compensate for his inability to control himself. Self-indulgence and aggrandizement thus appear as a confession of intellectual and moral weakness. This fact brings to light a further respect in which the Stoic's freedom is conditioned by circumstance. He must adapt his conduct not only to his external physical and social environment, and to the state of his body, but also to the state of his mind. It is childish to cry for the moon, but it is equally childish to cry for wisdom, as though it were to be had for the asking. A man cannot by taking thought add

[16] *Op. cit.*, Vol. II, p. 115.

a cubit to his stature, but neither can a man merely by taking thought add new powers to his soul.

This form of dependence is unlikely to be remarked by wise men, as is dependence on external conditions to be remarked by the favorites of fortune. The philosophies of freedom are written by the wise men, rather than by the ignorant or the insane. Epictetus, who was a slave, understood human dependence on external conditions; and, being lame and perhaps sickly, he understood the extent to which bodily vigor and perfection lay beyond the will to control. It was natural that he should have affirmed a man's control over his own judgment and desire as his peculiar prerogative. It would not have been strange if he had ignored altogether the conditions of its exercise. This, however, he did not do. He affirmed that the beginning of philosophy lay in "a man's perception of the state of his ruling faculty; for when a man knows that it is weak, he will not employ it on things of the greatest difficulty." Beginning with "a consciousness of his own weakness and inability," a man must overcome ignorance by learning, and he must "add study and practice." [17] He who would be a philosopher must exercise himself like the athlete. He must consider his own nature, "what it is able to bear," like the wrestler who examines his shoulders, thighs and loins; for different men are naturally formed for different things. There is, furthermore, a degree of folly which is "untractable," and a madness or sickliness of soul which cannot be overcome by argument but must be treated with "ellebore." [18]

Thus the Stoic freedom from hindrance is in the end only relative and not absolute. Even within the confines of his own mind he must meet and take account of conditions as he finds them. All men have a capacity for virtue, but this capacity can be realized only under favorable conditions, and after a prolonged struggle in which there is for the average man a high probability of failure. It is also true that men have a capacity for riches and worldly power, in that they possess some of the necessary conditions, and a chance by

[17] *Op. cit.*, Vol. I, pp. 101-102, 161-162, 169.
[18] *Op. cit* Vol. I, pp. 190-191, 213; Vol. II, p. 58.

discipline and effort of gaining the rest. Knowledge of the given properties of nature, submission to the natural consequences of things, is as much a condition of success in the one case as in the other. A man who would be Marcus Aurelius is as much dependent on the laws of mental hygiene for his disposition, as he is on the laws of physics and politics for his worldly eminence. There is then no purely aggressive interest, no sheer creativity of will, save such as appears subjectively owing to the conscious or deliberate ignoring of the conditions of activity. Let us now examine the other alternative, and ask what can be meant by a purely submissive interest.

§ 106. **The Purely Submissive Attitude.** As a matter of definition it should be clear that a purely submissive interest is self-contradictory. The submissive attitude is one of passive expectation, in which the object of expectation is awaited without being achieved. By interest, however, is meant dynamic expectation, in which expectation qualifies the act and determines its performance. It is as absurd to speak of a purely submissive interest, as to speak of a dispassionate passion or an apathetic feeling.

Although there can, strictly speaking, be no such thing as a purely submissive interest, this does not preclude the possibility of a purely submissive *attitude*. There may be said to be two varieties of this attitude, the unsophisticated and the sophisticated. The unsophisticated variety is the fatalism bred by failure and disillusionment. The repeated experience of futile effort may lead to that sense of helplessness, in which one waits for the blow to fall without seeking to avert it, or accepts what life brings with no effort to alter or augment it. The sophisticated variety of adaptation is based upon a philosophy of impotence. There are many such philosophies, ranging from a materialistic theory of the causal inefficacy of spirit to a spiritualistic theory of the causal inefficacy of matter. In other words, man may be deemed impotent in the realm of nature by virtue of his superiority, or impotent in the realm of spirit by virtue of his inferiority.

Both views rest upon the false premise of dualism, by which the living man is divided into a corruptible and an incorruptible part, each powerless to swerve the other from its appointed course. Such philosophical fatalism may take the form either of the scientific sense of dependence on physical nature, or of the religious sense of dependence on God. In either case this attitude of submission signifies passive expectation, or the inference of the future from some law or set of conditions in which one takes no part oneself. In so far as such an attitude is achieved in its purity it implies the total absence of interest.

Such an attitude of pure submission may, however, be an *object* of interest. The wise man may hope to escape the greater evil of desire unfulfilled, by attaining the lesser evil of freedom from desire. Or the scientist may seek in the interest of truth to cultivate disinterestedness. This is that interest in the having of expectations or the possession of ideas which constitutes the root of the cognitive impulse, whether in its methodical, speculative or contemplative forms.[19] Epictetus tells us that "God has introduced man to be a spectator of God and of his works."[20] One may strive interestedly to play this rôle; one may seek passionately to become a passionless sage, or feel favorably disposed towards the state of apathy. Submission, in other words, may be the object of an aggressive interest.

§ 107. **Acquiescent Interest.** But there is also another attitude, which Epictetus has in mind when he exhorts his pupils "to learn to wish that everything may happen as it does"; "so that nothing may happen which you do not choose, and nothing shall fail to happen which you do choose."[21] This means that one shall form one's expectations in accordance with nature, as though one's own will had nothing to do with their realization, and then bring one's interests into accord. Expecting an event owing to circumstances beyond

---

[19] Cf. Ch. XI.
[20] *Op. cit.*, Vol. I, p. 26.
[21] *Op. cit.*, Vol. I, pp. 55, 206.

one's control, one is then voluntarily to endorse it. One is to swim with, and not merely float with, the current. In this case there is interest in a double sense. There is not merely an interest in cultivating the attitude, but the attitude itself,— the disposition of the perfect sage, is to be a state of willing acquiescence, and not one of apathy. Interest of this type, like all interest, implies an activity conducive to the existence of its object; but in this case the activity is not a necessary condition of the object's existence. Like Margaret Fuller's "I accept the Universe," it is favorable but not indispensable.

If one is to speak of an individual's attitude as being on the whole submissive rather than aggressive, the description will best fit this case of acquiescent interest, or willingness that the inevitable should happen. Such an attitude is psychologically conceivable, and it plays an important rôle in the religious experience. It is based, ordinarily, on an *a priori* judgment regarding the unitary source of natural and historical events. These are interpreted as the several acts of a being with whose fundamental purpose man has allied himself once and for all. So great are the vicissitudes of human fortune that it would be impossible to be glad of each and every event as it occurs, without such an interpretation. There is no interest of man which is uniformly satisfied by the course of cosmic and historical events. He can take no interest, not even in his own state of mind, without giving hostages to fortune and exposing himself to disappointment, as judged by appearances. But he can believe all fortune, be it *prima facie* good or evil, to originate in an ultimately beneficent will. So believing he can be glad of everything that happens to him, not for what it is but as a sign of this will. Such an attitude is one of the characteristic achievements of religion.

A variation of this attitude is to be found in the aesthetic enjoyment of the cosmic order.

"Let us build altars to the Beautiful Necessity. If we thought men were free in the sense that in a single exception one fantastical will could prevail over the law of things, it were all one as if a child's hand could pull down the sun. If in the least particular one could derange the order of nature, . . . who would accept the gift of life?" [22]

This attitude, also, is one of acquiescence based on the recognition of human impotence. Like the loving acceptance of God's will it is also an attitude of interest; what happens whether one wills or no, is confirmed by the will. And like the acceptance of Providence this attitude, also, is mediated by an interpretation of nature as forming one indivisible system, "which secures that all is made of one piece" and "compels every atom to serve a universal end."

§ 108. The Interrelations of Submission and Aggression.
Aggressive and submissive interest are abstractions, or signify a difference of emphasis. The notion of purely aggressive interest, of sheer achievement without reference to given conditions, is an extravagance of human folly. The proverbial ostrich who thinks to annihilate impending danger by ceasing to look at it, is unknown in the animal kingdom; like the serpent of the Garden of Eden, he is a symbol and scapegoat of human frailty. The purely submissive attitude of research or contemplation, on the other hand, is a specialized human attainment which emerges and maintains itself only in a context of interest. The acquiescent interest of religious faith is an occasional mood, which has to be achieved by effort, which no man has achieved consistently, and which few men have achieved at all. The normal course of human action is one in which aggression and submission are the interdependent and complementary parts of one whole.

Relatively to any given object an interest may be said to be either submissive or aggressive, according as that object is sought or merely awaited. When it is said that escape is submissive and attack aggressive, it is meant that the future state of the enemy is expected in the one case without effort, and in the other case as a result of effort. The interest is then aggressive or submissive *in respect of the enemy*. In this sense the maxim "discretion is the better part of valor," or the jealous dove's withdrawal of its mate from the proximity

22 Emerson, *Conduct of Life*, 1886, p. 51.

of the rival male, or Napoleon's retreat from Moscow, signify a transition from aggression to submission. But performance which is thus submissive relative to an object lying beyond a certain radius, is aggressive relative to what lies within that radius. Discretion signifies a control of the organism, marital jealousy a control of the mate, and retreat a control of all the vast and intricate mechanism of an army. Within these interior lines interest is aggressive.

Whether Mahomet goes to the mountain or the mountain is brought to Mahomet, the interest is *both* aggressive and submissive. The former is generally regarded as submissive and the latter as aggressive, because it is assumed that it is easier for the organism to move itself than to move mountains, and that the latter therefore signifies a greater range and sum of aggression. It is commonly supposed that the organism is endowed with the capacity of self-motion, and hence this sphere of control is taken for granted and neglected, the interest being deemed aggressive or submissive according to the extent with which it intervenes in the course of events outside the organism. But when, as did the Stoics, one focuses attention upon organic control, one becomes acutely aware of the fact that here, too, concessions must be made to an external causal nexus. As a man retreats into himself the circle of his control narrows, but within that narrower circle there remains the same necessity of taking account of the given facts. He now recognizes as he did not recognize before, the organic, moral and intellectual conditions which set limits to his achievement.

The interrelation of the factors of aggression and submission throws light on the nature of man's interested control of the circumstances of his life. It is a well-known fact that the increase of knowledge has enabled man to work his will. Despite the fact that the advance of science has resulted from the cultivation of a submissive attitude it has not conduced to fatalism and quietism, but rather to that innovating and constructive temper of mind that distinguishes modern European civilization. The explanation of this seeming paradox received its classic formulation from Bacon:

"Knowledge and human power are synonymous, since the ignorance of the cause frustrates the effect; for nature is only subdued by submission, and that which in contemplative philosophy corresponds with the cause in practical science becomes the rule. Man while operating can only apply or withdraw natural bodies; nature internally performs the rest." [23]

Natural causes ignored operate none the less, and the ignorance of them can give man nothing better than an illusory sense of power. But the knowledge of natural causes, that is, the knowledge of what is to be expected of given conditions in and of themselves, defines a locus of intervention. The immediate and direct effect of the will is little, but this little, if it be applied at a certain point where natural causes balance and conjoin, may indirectly move mountains. The development of knowledge multiplies these fulcra for the leverage of the will. Products of the will become in turn its instruments, and provide a broader base for man's attack upon the unsubjugated territory that remains. Thus his interested control over his present act, which means the nervous control of his musculature, becomes to an increasing extent the crucial or decisive factor, and the surface of the planet is refashioned and domesticated. Man rules over nature by virtue of holding and exploiting a balance of power.

[23] *Novum Organum,* Book I, Aphorisms III, IV.

CHAPTER X

MODES OF INTEREST *(concluded)*

I. HUNGER AND APPETITE

§ 109. Proprioceptive and Interoceptive Sensations. The opinion has been expressed that the motor-affective life of man can best be oriented and grasped in its general contour, if approached objectively or dynamically. It was at the same time recognized that such an account could not be deemed satisfactory unless it provided for those data with which the introspective account is primarily concerned. Otherwise the new psychology would be as abstract and one-sided as the old. The description of interest which has been elaborated in the last four chapters, must be acknowledged to be seriously defective unless such palpable facts as pleasure, pain and emotion can somehow be fitted into the picture.

The method by which this is to be accomplished may first be stated in general terms. We have hitherto neglected the fact that the stimuli which evoke interested response may arise within as well as without the organism. It is a fact well known to psychologists and physiologists that in addition to the 'exteroceptive' organs located on the surface of the body and sensitive to external conditions, there are also 'proprioceptive' and 'interoceptive' organs embedded in the tissues of the body itself, and sensitive to internal conditions.[1] Such internal or central stimuli, like peripheral stimuli, may be responded to either positively or negatively. These intra-organic responses may arise independently or in the course of the demands made upon the organism by some primary extra-organic response. In the latter case they serve either to

[1] These expressions have been widely adopted from C. S. Sherrington's *Integrative Action of the Nervous System*, 1906. Cf. below, § 113.

augment or to check the primary response, according as they are positive or negative. Feeling and emotion may, then, be interpreted in terms of this internal sphere of behavior. Due allowance may be made for the constancy of their presence, and for their importance in motivation, without prejudice to that objective and dynamic method which has hitherto been followed.

That feeling and emotion should be inaccessible to general observation presents on this view no difficulty of principle. The internal conditions of any given organism are uniquely related to that organism's nervous system by virtue of its interoceptors and proprioceptors. Organism A can see organism B, and both can see a third object C. But organism A cannot 'feel' the muscular tensions of organism B, nor can either be sensorially aware in this particular way of anything outside of itself. Organic sensations are thus data for one and only one observer.[2]

§ 110. Hunger versus Appetite.

Interested response to internal stimulation is most clearly exemplified in hunger, as distinguished from appetite. An excellent summary of this distinction from the angle of experimental physiology is given by Professor W. B. Cannon:

"Careful observation indicates that appetite is related to previous sensations of taste and smell of food. Delightful or disgusting tastes and odors, associated with this or that edible substance, determine the appetite. . . . Among prosperous people, supplied with abundance of food, the appetite seems sufficient to ensure for bodily needs a proper supply of nutriment. We eat because dinner is announced, because by eating we avoid unpleasant consequences, and because food is placed before us in delectable form with tempting tastes and odors. Under less easy circumstances, however, the body needs are supplied through the much stronger and more insistent demands of hunger. The sensation of hunger is difficult to describe, but almost everyone from childhood has felt at times that dull ache or gnawing pain

---

[2] Introspection in this sense of unique awareness of organic sensations is a very different thing from introspection in the sense of heightened attention to visual or auditory stimuli which may be shared with other organisms. Cf. the author's *Present Philosophical Tendencies*, Ch. XII.

referred to the lower mid-chest region and the epigastrium, which may take imperious control of human actions. As Sternberg has pointed out, hunger may be sufficiently insistent to force the taking of food which is so distasteful that it not only fails to rouse appetite, but may even produce nausea. . . . Hunger may be satisfied while the appetite still calls. . . . On the other hand, appetite may be in abeyance while hunger is goading. . . . Although the two sensations may thus exist separately, they nevertheless have the same function of leading to the intake of food, and they usually appear together." [3]

The hunger-pang, "a sensation so peremptory, so disagreeable, so tormenting," as to induce suicide or crime, is traced by Professor Cannon to periodic or spasmodic "muscular contractions of the stomach and other parts of the alimentary canal." [4] It is unmistakably an organic sensation. The sensory factor in appetite, on the other hand, is olfactory or gustatory. [5] This difference is further accentuated by the fact that hunger is negative, while appetite is positive. Both are interests in a sense conformable to the definition already adopted; but while the organism is 'goaded' by hunger, and seeks *relief*, it is 'tempted' by appetite and seeks *satisfaction*. Viewed in their motor aspects, hunger is an activity determined by a negative expectation, namely, the absence of the inciting stimulus; whereas appetite is an activity determined by a positive expectation, which embraces the prolongation or renewal of the inciting stimulus. Where the two are united there is a summation of interest, the same end-state serving both to appease the hunger and gratify the appetite.

Hunger has, then, three important characteristics: (1) it is a negative interest; (2) it is initiated by a somatic sensation; (3) it is associated with a specific appetite which supersedes it and converts it into a positive interest. Hunger being so conceived, it can be extended to other functions

[3] W. B. Cannon: *Bodily Changes in Pain, Hunger, Fear and Rage,* 1915, pp. 233-235.
[4] *Op. cit.,* pp. 232, 251.
[5] Appetite may, of course, be excited by ideas or images, and be in this sense of central origin. But the ideas or images are in the case of appetite representations of peripheral sensations.

than food-taking. Thirst is a negative interest stimulated by a dryness of the mouth and pharynx; asphyxiation, by a lack of oxygen. Employing the conception in this sense, there may be said to be a 'sex-hunger,' in so far as there is an impulse to be rid of a sensation occasioned by an excess of seminal fluid; or, perhaps, a hunger for exercise stimulated by a sluggish circulation. In these, as well as in such doubtful cases as 'war-hunger' or 'hunger for companionship,' the stimulating physiological state is so closely associated with an appetite, that it borrows the name of the appetite, and is ordinarily accompanied by ideas which induce a mild incitement of it. The appetite, on the other hand, is a positive interest, initiated by an extra-organic stimulus, and giving rise, when 'starved,' to certain physiological changes which induce a correlative hunger.

§ 111. **Thwarted Appetite and Bodily Distress.** Having defined a meaning for hunger and appetite in the strict sense, we may now without confusion introduce two closely allied conceptions. In the first place, there is the case of thwarted appetite. This may occur in the absence of hunger. Food-hunger is physiologically possible only when the stomach is empty, whereas appetite may continue beyond the point of repletion. Where there is appetite without hunger, the thwarting of the appetite none the less induces a negative form of interest, which may, as in annoyance and anger, be stimulated peripherally by the intervening obstacle, or centrally by vague and imperfectly localized sensations known as 'uneasiness' or 'craving.' The latter commonly occur when the appetite is aroused by the imagination in the absence of the appropriate object, and where its satisfaction is prevented by the general situation rather than by any specific obstacle.

It is equally important to observe that appetite *may* be attended by craving, and that it *need not* be. Any interest if checked or retarded beyond a certain point may develop a vexation which seeks the removal of the present state. There is no constant rule which governs the emergence of this negative interest. It is the measure of the greed, impatience or persistence of the particular agent or of his particular mood. The term 'desire' has no specific meaning, except so far as it refers to that state of interest in which it is doubly motivated, being both attracted by what lies ahead and goaded or pricked from the rear. Its realization then implies both gratification and relief, both a getting of what is wanted and an escape from the intolerable state of deficiency. But this mixture of positive and negative interest, while it is psychologically characteristic, is not psychologically necessary. Life brings intervals of wholly prosperous activity in which there is progressive achievement without undue retardation, or prolonged enjoyment without interruption.

Schopenhauer's philosophical pessimism [6] rests upon a false psychology of desire. He is correct in supposing that all desire is forward looking, and that to desire is to seek for more than one has. For, as we have seen, even the love of what one has is directed to its continued and therefore future possession. Schopenhauer's error lies in supposing that interest in this sense is negative. The present state of the desiring subject is negative in the sense that it is not that future state represented in the moving expectation. But there is no *negative component of desire* unless there is, over and above the desire for the future, a discontent with the present. This may or may not occur. When it does not occur there is gratification, but without any element whatsoever of relief or deliverance. Even the more moderate view that there can be no positive satisfaction without antecedent craving is psychologically false. So much the more false is Schopenhauer's extreme contention that there is no positive satisfaction whatsoever, but that "all satisfaction . . . is always really and essentially only negative." [7]

The foregoing analysis throws light on the well-known fact that desire is strengthened when it is blocked.[8] This is not the only means of strengthening desire. The effect may be produced by a greater intensity of stimulation, or a greater clearness in the governing expectation, or by divers other

[6] Cf. his *World as Will and Idea*, Book IV, §§ 57 ff. (trans. by Haldane and Kemp, 1883).
[7] *Ibid.*, § 58.
[8] Cf. below, §§ 236, 237.

conditions which will receive attention later. But the specific effect of obstacles in redoubling effort is well known. We may now understand this augmented effect as due in part to the occurrence of central stimuli, the removal of which serves as a further incentive to the achievement. Where the interruption is sufficiently prolonged these central stimuli may be deepened and intensified to the point of genuine hunger. The initial positive interest is reinforced by a negative interest which, although of opposite sign, realizes itself in the same end-state. A is sought not only for its own sake but as a case of *not-B*.[9]

Hunger is a negative interest initiated by somatic sensations, and associated with a specific appetite. We have found in craving the case of a negative organic interest which is induced by the interruption of a primary appetite. We have now to consider a second allied conception in which a negative interest is initiated by somatic sensations, but without being associated with any specific appetite. There is evidently a difference between hunger and a stomach-ache, although both are internal and although both seek relief. The difference lies in the fact that while hunger seeks and finds relief through the satisfaction of a positive appetite, so that negative is blended with positive value, the stomach-ache seeks relief through random efforts of which nothing is required save their removal of the inciting stimulus. The remedy for hunger is the activity and satisfaction of food-taking, the remedy for the stomach-ache is anaesthesia. In other words, while hunger and craving imply the presence of a positive interest, and may even be used to measure the strength of that interest, there are forms of bodily distress attended by no interest whatever save that in their own removal. The former, in other words, define positive as well as negative values, the latter only negative values. It is, of course, true that bodily distress may be regarded as symptomatic of organic disorder, and that a cure may be sought for the disorder rather than

---

[9] The further reinforcement of blocked impulse in which the obstacle serves as a challenge, and evokes a militant or emotional response, will be considered in Sect. III.

for the symptom. But this interpretation and methodical purpose is a secondary product of experience, and does not belie the fact that the initial impulse of bodily distress is purely negative. It is an impulse to be rid of the stimulus, whatever the means and whatever, otherwise, the result. In this sheer dislike of organic sensations in which the mode of relief is undetermined, we have an important clue to the understanding of feeling. To this topic we shall now turn.

II. FEELING, PLEASURE AND PAIN

§ 112. **The Problem of Feeling.** It would be in the highest degree presumptuous in the present state of the subject to claim finality for any theory of feeling. Neither the introspective nor the behavioristic method has yielded results which are generally accepted among psychologists. For this very reason, however, there may be some virtue in an attempt to carry through consistently a hypothesis which promises to unify the mental life by avoiding the introduction of a new and irreducible element.[10]

There is no term whose common usage is less reliable than the term 'feeling.' We have first to note the most extended meaning, authorized by James, in which it signifies "mental states at large, irrespective of their kind." [11] Thus to lack feeling in this sense is to be numb or insensible. With feeling in this most inclusive sense we are not here concerned. When one speaks of feelings of drowsiness, languor or alertness, one refers to diffused, blended or imperfectly localized organic sensations. When one speaks of feelings of surprise, familiarity, or contrast one refers to data of consciousness

[10] The view that feeling is a unique and irreducible element or attribute is represented in psychological literature by W. Wundt, O. Külpe, H. Ebbinghaus and E. B. Titchener, as opposed to C. Stumpf, who regards it as a mode of sensation. In connection with the discussion that follows, it may be noted here that Professor Titchener both insists on the essential duality of feelings ("pleasantness" vs. "unpleasantness") and remarks that "they show a strong introspective resemblance to organic sensations." (*Text Book of Psychology*, Part I, 1909, pp. 228, 230.) For a good introduction to the whole subject of feeling and emotion, cf. Th. Ribot, *La Psychologie des Sentiments*, 1896; Eng. trans., *Psychology of the Emotions*, 1897.

[11] *Principles of Psychology*, 1890, Vol. I, pp. 186-187.

that are non-focal or relational ("transitive" or "marginal" states, in James's sense). We shall find that both of these uses of the term are significant for our purposes, though neither affords a useful point of departure. There remains a further sense of the term, in which feeling is contrasted with apathy. To be 'unfeeling' in this sense, is to lack interest, or to be unresponsive in the sense of being either for or against. Whatever its other characteristics feeling must be either identified or closely associated with those opposed attitudes of favor and disfavor with which we are already familiar.

Over and above this aspect, however, feeling possesses its sensory aspect. The term denotes not only an attitude for or against, but also a state, with an introspective content so familiar and easily recognizable that most pleasure-pain philosophies have not thought it necessary to define it at all. The plain man is supposed to know what it is to 'feel' pleasure and pain, as unambiguously as he knows what it is to see blue or taste bitter.

Still a different case is presented when pleasure and pain appear as qualities of other contents, as when one "takes pleasure in" the landscape or finds it painful. It is customary to refer to such cases as 'feeling-tone,' and to affirm that in some degree it accompanies and qualifies all states of consciousness. Feeling-tone is often said to consist of pleasantness and unpleasantness, or agreeableness and disagreeableness as distinguished from pleasure and pain sensations.[12]

The essential difficulty of the topic lies in the fact that feeling thus means three things, *attitude,* *state* and *attribute.* It does not suffice simply to distinguish the three, or to insist on one to the exclusion of the others. There is no virtue in any account of the matter that does not provide for all three aspects and explain their relations. Let us begin with what appears to be the clearest and most authentic conception,—that, namely, of affective sensibility, or substantive feeling.

---

[12] The distinction between unpleasantness and pain-sensation is recognized in the German terms *Unlust* and *Schmerz.* But with this exception there is no exact usage in any language, since the distinction is a theoretical one on which the theorists are not agreed.

§ 113. The Sensory or Substantive Aspect of Feeling.

There is a general consensus of opinion among psychologists and physiologists that pain should be regarded as a sensation. According to Professor Herrick,

"an essential condition for the appearance in consciousness of a definite sensation like touch or vision is the differentiation in the nervous system of a system of localized tracts and centers related to this function, and in the human body such localized tracts and centers seem to be present for pain. Pain, therefore, considered psychologically and neurologically, is a sensation." [13]

These "localized tracts and centers" are held to consist, first, in certain specific sense-organs or 'nociceptors,' usually identified with the free nerve endings found among the cells of the epidermis. The support for this view lies in the fact that these endings alone are found in certain parts of the body, such as the dentine and pulp of the teeth, the cornea of the eye, the tympanic membrane of the ear, and the so-called 'pain-spots' of the outer skin, the stimulation of which yields a 'pure' pain sensation.[14]   But this specialization of receptors is by no means clear. The excessive stimulation of other receptors such, for example, as those of touch and heat, is also painful; and physiologists are not agreed as to whether in such cases the stimulus is spread to the adjacent nociceptors, or the touch and heat nerves themselves function as pain nerves. There is the same ambiguity regarding visceral pains, which seem to be stimulated by a stretching or tension of the mesentery and thus to be an aggravated form of muscular sensation.[15]   But even the broad categories of cutaneous and muscular sensibility do not cover the facts. Excessive stimulation of the eye by light and of the ear by sound, and certain stimuli applied to the organs of taste and smell, may also be felt as painful.

The ascending pathway of the "painful impulse" has recently been traced with increasing exactness, though it ap-

---

[13] C. J. Herrick, *Introduction to Neurology*, 1918, p. 285.
[14] *Ibid.*, pp. 90-91, 277.
[15] *Ibid.*, pp. 270, 277, 280-281; W. S. Hunter, *General Psychology*, 1919, p. 233.

pears to be marked by a diffuseness of conduction, or by the
readiness with which, through collaterals, it receives the overflow from other sensory processes.

Finally, the pain tract is peculiarly associated with the
optic thalamus. While for other sensory processes the
thalamus is only a station which is passed on the way to the
cerebral cortex, for painful impulses of the more elementary
forms the thalamus is the terminal, where these impulses are
associated through adjacent motor centres with quick avoiding
reflexes. But this terminal rôle of the thalamus is not confined to pain. It extends to vague discomfort, to pleasure,
and to a wide range of "affective stimuli." [16]

There are two further facts regarding the rôle of the
thalamus that deserve to be noted. In the first place, the
thalamus contains centres of integration and discharge for
afferent nerves from the viscera, and conditions that consciousness of general well-being or malaise which reflects the
functioning of the organs of respiration, circulation and digestion.[17] In the second place, the thalamus belongs to that
archaic portion of the brain which antedates the development
of the cerebral hemispheres. It is the seat of the more
primitive integrations and instinctive reactions, which in man
are ordinarily subordinated to the great cortical system of
projection and correlation that forms the physiological aspect of discrimination and associative memory.[18] This fact
may account for the difficulty of both *having* feelings and
at the same time attentively observing and describing them.[19]

Taking into account both the facts and the difficulties
which these physiological studies have brought to light, it is
not unreasonable to adopt the following hypothesis regarding
the *substantive* state, or sensation, of pain and pleasure.

The organism is sensitive to its own activities or changes
of condition. This is possible owing to the existence of several

<hr/>

[16] H. Head and G. Holmes, "Sensory Disturbances from Cerebral
Lesions," *Brain*, Vol. XXXIV, 1911, p. 177.
[17] C. J. Herrick, *op. cit.*, p. 288.
[18] Cf. C. J. Herrick, *op. cit.*, Ch. XX; H. Head and G. Holmes, *op. cit.*,
Ch. V. §§ 2, 3.
[19] Cf. E. B.Titchener, *op. cit.*, p. 231.

groups of sense-organs, which can be roughly, though not precisely, distinguished. In the first place, there are the so-called interoceptors; on the internal or recessed surfaces of the body, which are sensitive to chemical stimulation in the tongue and pharynx (taste); or to mechanical or chemical stimulation in the alimentary, respiratory, circulatory and sexual organs (commonly through contraction or stretching of the smooth, unstriated, or involuntary muscles located in the coatings of these organs). In the second place, there are proprioceptors which are sensitive to equilibration, to the contraction of the striated or voluntary muscles (ordinarily skeletal), to the flexion of the joints and the stretching of tendons.[20]   In the third place, when the stimulation of the exteroceptors (visual, auditory, cutaneous) is sufficiently intense or is spread to adjacent areas, the organism is sensitive to the condition of the affected organ, rather than to the external conditions which affect it. The organs of smell and taste afford an interesting case, because they may serve as a means of sensing either the environment or the organism itself.[21]

The sensations derived from these stimuli, and having their centres in the thalamus, may, then, be taken to constitute substantive feeling, or feeling in so far as this is content of experience to the subject having the feeling. This sensory experience has certain peculiarities which correspond closely to the notions of feeling that obtain in common sense. It is relatively undiscriminated, it is internal rather than 'projicient,' and it is highly impulsive in two opposed directions, for and against. Let us now briefly consider each of these peculiarities in turn.

§ 114. **Substantive Feeling as Non-Discriminatory.** We have first to note a difference among organic sensations that emerges clearly from the experimental clinical studies of Doctors Head and Holmes. These studies deal with sensory disturbances due to cortical and thalamic lesions re-

20 Cf. C. J. Herrick, *op. cit.*, pp. 92-98.
21 *Ibid.*, pp. 96-98.

spectively, the stimuli being cutaneous (both superficial and deep sensibility) and proprioceptive. The results show that where the lesion is cortical there is loss of capacity to recognize bodily posture, to compare weights, to discriminate differences of texture or of temperature, to localize accurately, or to appreciate size and shape. There is a loss of the faculty of comparison or correlation, by which new stimuli are fitted into a preëxisting schema. Sensations are, in other words, vague and incoherent; and the answers of the subject are relatively "untrustworthy."

When the lesion is in the lateral part of the thalamus, which is the seat of the control of thalamic by cortical activities, the sensory disturbances are of a different order, which the authors describe as "an excessive response to affective stimuli," or an "overloading of sensation with feeling-tone." [22] This is interpreted as a freer play of the essentially thalamic activities, due to the removal of cortical inhibition. There may or may not be a diminution of sensory discrimination of the types described above. In any case, the notable fact is not the loss of discrimination where this normally exists, but the increase of sensitivity of a type which is always relatively undiscriminating; such as that produced by visceral changes, or by tickling or scraping, or by pricking or pressure or thermal stimuli, where the stimulus is intense, and where it spreads, reverberates and persists. This condition of abnormal thalamic activity possesses two unmistakable characteristics. On the one hand, there is an added body of organic sensation which the subjects describe variously as "aching pains," "soreness," "stinging," "unpleasant," "delightful," "soothing," "tingling," "pins and needles," "numbness," "something crawling under the skin," "a curious tickling," "a tight feeling in the face," "as if rats were always gnawing at my side," "cold, stinging feeling," "a crawling feeling which affects me all up the side." On the other hand, there is a sharp duality of attitude, which is described both by the observers and the subjects: there is "a strong vigorous reaction and rapid withdrawal of the limb," or "an apparently uncontroll-

[22] *Op. cit.*, p. 177.

able tendency to withdraw the part"; "her general response denotes intolerable discomfort"; "he always wears a glove on this hand"; "he states that this gives him not merely local pleasure, but 'makes him feel happy all over,' and this is indicated by his general reaction and expression"; "I can't stand it so well on the left side"; "his face lights up with a definite expression of pleasure"; "she cannot lie on the left side as it is so tender, and cannot bear anything cold to touch it"; "favorite tunes now wake me up till I can't bear them." [23]

In short, there is, on the one hand, a mass of organic sensory content, not readily describable, widely diffused, resonant, and only roughly localized.[24] This sensory content is further qualified, on the other hand, not by organized relations and expectations, but by an instant impulse either to terminate or prolong it. The factor of interest, positive or negative, intervenes and short-circuits the discriminatory and reflective processes.

§ 115. Substantive Feeling as Non-Projicient. In Professor Sherrington's account of affective processes the emphasis is placed not on the difference between discriminated and undiscriminated organic sensations, but rather on that between organic sensations and projicient or distance sensations.

"The receptor-organs adapted to odors, light and sound, though stimulated by the external matter in direct contact with them,—as the vibrating ether, the vibrating water or air, or odorous particles,—yet generate reactions which show 'adaptation' . . . to the environmental *objects* at a distance, the sources of those changes impinging on and acting as stimuli at the organism's surface." [25]

[23] Head and Holmes: *op. cit.,* pp. 213-252.
[24] Thus Professor Herrick says that "pleasurable and unpleasant experiences are not true sensations" because they are "diffuse" and "unlocalized," and antedate "anything so clearly analyzed as a sensation with specific external references" (*op. cit.,* p. 285). Pain, however, eventually becomes a "true sensation," when it is "distinct and localizable" (287), and when on the neurological side it is correlated with a specific "system of localized tracts and centres" (285).
[25] C. S. Sherrington, *op. cit.,* p. 324.

These so-called distance-receptors initiate "anticipatory, *i.e.*, precurrent reactions"; which are characterized by a tendency "to work or control the musculature of the animal as a whole," and are integrated in the cerebrum where they acquire a general "ascendency . . . in the organization of neural functions." [26] Through the development and the elaboration of this projicient function, "as the individual ascends the scale of being the more reactive does it become as an individual to the circumambient universe outside itself." [27] On the other hand, "none of the sensations initiated in the proprioceptive or interoceptive fields possess this property of projicience." They are "referred to the body itself." The reflexes which they initiate are as a rule "consummatory" rather than "anticipatory." They tend "to excite motor centres directly and imperatively." [28]

When Professor Sherrington discusses feeling, he points out that it is characteristically associated with non-projicient rather than with projicient sensations.

"A salient character of most of the reactions of the non-projicient receptors taken as sense-organs is *'affective tone,' i.e.,* physical pain or physical pleasure." "All sensations referred *to the body itself rather than interpreted as qualities of objects in the external world,* tend to be tinged with 'feeling.' " "To consummatory reactions affective tone seems adjunct much more than to the anticipatory, especially the remotely anticipatory of the projicient sense-organs. . . . The affective tone of the reactions of the projicient receptors is less marked: physical pleasure or pain can hardly be said to accompany them." "Affective tone inheres more intensely in senses which refer to the body than in those which refer to the environment, that is, it is strongest in the non-projicient senses. It is, therefore, strong in the cutaneous senses, and in them is inversely as their projicience, therefore least in touch spots, more in thermal spots, most in the so-called pain spots." [29]

§ 116. The Immediately Impulsive Character of Feeling.

The accounts of feeling offered by Dr. Head and Pro-

[26] *Ibid.,* pp. 326, 327, 333.
[27] *Ibid.,* p. 352.
[28] *Ibid.,* pp. 266, 324, 329.
[29] *Ibid.,* pp. 266, 327, 330, 331; Shafer's Physiology, 1900, Vol. II, p. 1000.

fessor Sherrington are complementary rather than opposed. The first emphasizes its non-discriminatory character, the latter its non-projicient character, while both emphasize its *immediately impulsive character.* Combining the two accounts, feeling may be regarded as a sensory experience referred vaguely and diffusely to the body itself, and immediately initiating responses of prolongation or rejection.[30] Feeling in the broadest sense is any organic sensory complex in proportion as it is immediate and non-discriminatory. Feeling in a narrower sense, in which it is associated with the duality of pleasure and pain, is any such sensory complex together with the interest taken in it for its own sake. Pleasures are non-discriminatory organic sensations which are immediately liked; pains, non-discriminatory organic sensations which are immediately disliked. The first is a recurrent positive interest in a bodily state; the second, a progressive negative interest in a bodily state.

Viewing the matter from the biological angle, we may say that the organism is endowed with a strong interest in its own internal conditions. The correlation of this interest with the thalamus and other centres belonging to the archaic portion of the brain, and the functional subordination of these centres to the cerebral cortex, indicate that this interest is peculiarly primitive, and that in highly developed organisms such as man it is controlled by more objective and far-reaching interests. On the other hand, this interest, especially in its negative form, has a certain force of appeal which is not inconsistent with its primitive character, and which is biologically intelligible. The body is the instrument of all interests, and its well-being is therefore a primary concern. Pleasures and pains are in a quite literal sense, *vital* interests. Hence the presence in the organism of the so-called 'nociceptors.' These sense organs are excited by a wide range of stimuli, mechanical, thermal, chemical, electrical, whenever these stimuli "are of such intensity as *threatens damage to the*

[30] The symbol of agony," said Leslie Stephen, is the "writhing worm." "Pain represents tension, a state of feeling, that is, from which there is a tendency to change; pleasure represents so far equilibrium, or a state in which there is a tendency to persist" (*Science of Ethics,* 1882, p. 51).

skin." The same type of stimulus is capable of stimulating free and unspecialized nerve-endings, such as are widely distributed in the epidermis, and exist alone in the pain-spots, cornea and other surfaces sensitive only to pain. There thus attaches to the skin "a so-to-say *specific sense of its own injuries."* Such reflexes are *prepotent, protective* and *imperative.*[31]

It is the prepotence of nociceptive sensation that accounts for the tendency of pain to prevail over pleasures in cases of thalamic disease or in hyper-sensitive individuals. Dr. Head's patients both suffer and enjoy with exceptional intensity. They pass rapidly from the one state to the other, and are often in a mixed state which cannot be unambiguously described as exclusively agreeable or as exclusively disagreeable. But the negative reaction tends on the whole to prevail. This may be expressed by saying that the organism's well-being is safeguarded by alarms and warnings rather than by favorable reports. The organic sensation exercises a veto-power rather than a directive guidance. Undiscriminated organic sensation puts the organism on its guard and arouses defence-reactions. This same prepotence of negative over positive interest appears in the excessively sensitive condition which is characteristic of "over-wrought" nerves, or of the "artistic temperament." Speaking of his health in one of his letters, Shelley writes:

"Mine is far better than it has been; and the *relapse* which I now suffer into a state of ease from one of pain, is attended with such an excessive susceptibility of nature, that I suffer equally from pleasure and from pain. You will ask me naturally enough *where I* find any pleasure? The wind, the light, the air, the smell of a flower affects me with violent emotions. There needs no catalogue of the causes of pain." [32]

This *immediacy* of response distingishes sensation in its affective rôle from sensation in its distinctively cognitive rôles, as in perception and in introspective analysis. In so

---

[31] C. S. Sherrington: *The Integrative Action of the Nervous System,* 1906, pp. 231, 227-228, 319. Cf. below, § 252.
[32] *The Letters of Percy Bysshe Shelley,* edited by R. Ingpen, 1909, Vol. II, p. 843.

far as feeling is interested, there is, it is true, some degree of expectancy, and therefore a germ of cognition. But that which is expected of the sensory experience is in this case nothing more than its own presence or absence in the immediate future. In affective sensibility objective meaning is reduced to a minimum, in that there is no reference to anything other than itself, whether external or internal. The sensory content is neither interpreted nor analyzed, but is responded to *as itself,* whether positively or negatively.[33]

§ 117. **Attributive Feeling.** Having considered pleasures and pains as substantive states enjoyed or suffered for themselves, we may now turn to the case in which pleasure and pain appear as the 'attribute' or 'feeling-tone' of other states. The latter rôle of feeling is recognized in such popular phrases as 'taking pleasure in' or 'finding painful,' or in the adjectives 'pleasant' and 'painful' used to qualify any activity.

Bodily states and activities are a constant factor in life. The functioning of the bodily organs is the background of all of the individual's experience, and all of the individual's interests call the organism into play and induce internal changes. These organic functions and changes, even when subordinated to the individual's objective interests, will at the same time commonly be attended by their own interests of the type just considered. They will assume the forms of pleasures and pains, but they will be secondary and non-focal. It will be convenient to divide pleasures and pains of this subordinate or attributive type, into two groups, the *co-existent* and the *induced.*

It is a well-known fact that when one "feels well," or is in "high spirits," one's positive reactions are so strongly reinforced that one is sometimes said to be capable of enjoy-

[33] Cf. Grace A. de Laguna: "In so far as the stimulus calls into play an attentive postponement of response, it arouses cognitive awareness and possesses perceptual quality . . . The distinctive characteristic of the stimulus perceived, as contrasted with the stimulus emotionally felt, is the complexity and indirectness of its relation to response" ("Emotion and Perception from the Behaviorist Standpoint," *Psych. Rev.,* Vol. XXVI, 1919, pp. 426, 422, 421). Cf. below, § 134.

ing *anything.* Malaise, pain or fatigue, on the other hand, may rob any activity of its satisfactions. Health is probably, all things considered, the most important single factor in human happiness. In other words, the quickening impulse attending the activities of the body itself, the relish of life, allies itself concurrently with all coexistent interests, and reinforces their motive power; while a condition of bodily distress or lowered tone interrupts or diminishes them.

The induced pleasures and pains are those which are incidental to the activities constituting the major interest. Responses directed outward to the environment and forward in time commonly engage the organism as a whole. They involve "the assumption of some total posture," or muscular coördination, in which some elements are called into play and others inhibited;[34] and they involve appropriate adjustments of the vital functions, such as circulation and respiration. These induced internal changes stimulate proprioceptive and interoceptive sensations in the parts affected; and these, in turn, are qualified by positive or negative interest. In this way the initial impulse is either accelerated or retarded by the effects of its own discharge. Where the induced organic changes themselves generate positive reactions the impulse gathers force as it goes, or is confirmed and augmented in the direction of first intent. It may be said to be self-sustaining, in the sense of drawing new supplies of energy from within itself. Where, on the other hand, the incidental reactions are negative, these act as a drag or brake upon the primary impulse. They may have the effect of checking it all together, or of reducing its energy by a sort of internal friction.

This view of the auxiliary or obstructive rôle of attributive feeling agrees broadly with the trend of speculation among psychologists. Thus, according to Professor Max Meyer,

"While the correlate of sensation is the nervous current itself, the correlate of pleasantness and unpleasantness is the increase or decrease of the intensity of a previously constant current, if

[34] C. S. Sherrington, *op. cit.,* p. 327.

the increase or decrease is caused by a force acting at a point other than the point of sensory stimulation." [35]

This statement need not be taken to imply that the change of intensity of the nervous current is not caused by sensory stimulation at all, but only that it is not caused by the sensory stimulation that initiates the primary response. It may be supposed to be caused by incidental or induced sensory stimuli. According to Professor Herrick,

"the normal discharge . . . of definitely elaborated nervous circuits resulting in free unrestrained activity is pleasurable"; whereas, "the unrelieved summation of stimuli in the nerve centers, involving stasis, tension and interference with free discharge of nervous energy, gives a feeling of unpleasantness." [36]

"Free unrestrained activity" may be interpreted to mean activity reinforced by its own incidental stimuli, as opposed to activity which is obstructed by induced or coexistent systems of response.[37].

§ 118. 'Objective' Feeling. We have thus far considered two forms of pleasure and pain, the substantive and the attributive. The former consists of relatively undiscriminated organic sensations attended by immediate positive or negative interest. They are liked or disliked bodily states. Attributive pleasures and pains differ from substantive only in their subordination to some other major interest with which they are coexistent, or by which they are induced. So defined, it is natural and correct to speak of states of pleasure and pain as "bodily." So defined, it is easy to explain why they should by general consent have been rated low in the scale of values. They denote an interest on the part of the individual in his own body, in contrast with interests directed to other organ-

[35] "The Nervous Correlates of Pleasantness and Unpleasantness," *Psych. Rev.*, Vol. XV, 1908, p. 307.
    [36] C. J. Herrick: *Introduction to Neurology*, 1918, p. 286.
    [37] A more recent theory proposed by L. T. Troland illustrates the same general mode of interpretation. According to this writer the organism is innately endowed with checks and accelerators which regulate its activities to accord with its well-being, pleasure denoting rising, and pain falling, conductance in the synapses ("A System for Explaining Affective Phenomena," *Jour. of Abnormal Psych.*, Vol. XIV, 1919-20).

isms, or to the remoter spacial and temporal environment.
Pleasures and pains are now in a perfectly intelligible sense
subjective rather than objective. They appertain to the narrower bodily self, and their content (as organic sensation)
is immediately accessible only to one subject. Phylogenetically
they are associated with what is primitive and characteristic
of the animal stage of existence, in contrast with the evolutionary phase represented by man.[38] Functionally they involve
the exercise of the lower rather than the higher centres of the
nervous system. There now remains the important question of
those "nobler" feelings which, like Spinoza's intellectual love
of God, or the refined forms of aesthetic appreciation, seem
free from any admixture of bodily content.

In our analysis of bodily pleasures and pains we have
distinguished between the sensory content, and the seeking or
avoiding reaction with which it is attended. The former is
the feeling *of* the body, the latter the attitude of interest
toward the bodily state thus felt. If this distinction be war-
ranted, it follows that similar likings and aversions may be
aroused by extra-organic sensory content. As one may like
or dislike the feel of the body, so one may like or dislike
the look of the sky, the sound of the brook, the taste of the
wine, or the smell of the rose. In the one case as in the
other, one means that the sensory stimulation has the effect
of opening the organism to more of the given stimulation, or
of closing the organism against it. The interest is of the
positive, recurrent type or of the negative progressive type,[39]
manifesting itself in the prolongation or interruption of the
sensory process itself. Similarly, one may find ideas or intellectual systems agreeable or repugnant in the sense that the
cognitive processes return to and reinstate their object, or turn
away from it. In the case of projicient sensation or thought,
the total content may be referred beyond the body, without,
however, implying the absence of interest. There is a question, then, of the propriety of describing such a case in terms

[38] The Freudian theory of motivation (infantile eroticism) might be
regarded as an ontogenic application.
[39] Cf. Ch. IX, Sect. I.

of 'feeling.' If this term is to be reserved for those cases in which the content of the experience is supplied by organic sensation, then it is evident that it will be inappropriate here. In the present state of the subject there is no mode of description that will not, if consistently adhered to, in some measure violate popular usage. Let us say, then, that there may be interest, and even immediate, sensuous interest, without feeling; that is, without bodily pleasures and pains.

Let us consider several modes of interest related to the same visible object, such as one's own home. A wholly objective interest would signify a disposition to act causally in such wise as to prevent or avert change. One could express this interest by saying, "I like my home as it is." The wholly subjective interest, on the other hand, would express itself in the words, "I like the way my home makes me feel," or, "I enjoy myself at home"; which would imply a disposition to prolong organic sensations associated with, or induced by, the visible presence or home. Between these two modes of interest there lies a third, which would express itself in the words, "I like to look at my home"; and which would signify a dwelling fondly on one's home, caressing it with the eye, tracing its familiar features and outlines. In the last case, which is a form of aesthetic or cognitive interest, the content of the experience is the visual aspect of the home itself, which might be free from any admixture of organic sensation, that is to say, of feeling in the strict sense. This would not mean, however, that one was apathetic or unfeeling in the sense of indifference; but only that one's interest was directed outward, through the accommodation of one's faculty of perception, to the home itself, rather than to the states and changes of one's own body.

This distinction between feeling and interest enables us to adopt James's account of "the subtle emotions," and at the same time to rid it of its inherent ambiguity. Having adopted the general view that affective or emotional [40] content consists in the feeling of bodily changes following directly from

---

[40] We are reserving the term "emotion" for the cases of emotional *excitement* considered in Sect. III.

the perception of the exciting fact, this writer then undertakes
to account for "the moral, intellectual and aesthetic feelings,"
which seem "to borrow nothing from any reverberation surg-
ing up from the parts below the brain."

"In reply to this we must immediately insist that aesthetic
emotion, *pure and simple,* the pleasure given us by certain lines
and masses, the combinations of colors and sounds, is an absolutely sensational experience, an optical or auricular feeling that
is primary, and not due to the repercussion backwards of other
sensations elsewhere consecutively aroused. To this simple
primary and immediate pleasure in certain pure sensations and
harmonious combinations of them, there may, it is true, be *added*
secondary pleasures. . . . These secondary emotions, themselves
are assuredly for the most part constituted of other incoming
sensations aroused by the diffusive wave of reflex effects which
the beautiful object sets up. A glow, a pang in the breast, a fulness of the breathing, a flutter of the heart, a shiver down the
back, a moistening of the eyes, a stirring in the hypogastrium,
and a thousand unnamable symptoms besides, may be felt the
moment the beauty *excites* us." [41]

While contending that "the bodily sounding-board is at
work . . . far more than we usually suppose," James nevertheless concedes that in the more refined forms of appreciation
this sounding-board is "mute." His difficulty lies in providing
any sense in which this "simpler primary and immediate
pleasure," or this "subtler emotion," is pleasure or emotion
at all. It tends to reduce altogether to a cognitive or judicial
state of indifference.[42] This difficulty may be avoided and
the fundamental position maintained, by a distinction between
interest and feeling such as has here been proposed. We
should then say with James that in the more refined forms of
aesthetic, moral and intellectual appreciation the total content
is provided by extra-organic objects perceived or thought, but
that this is accompanied by the interested impulse to perceive
or think them. Such states are interested, but not, strictly
speaking, pleasurable or affective. They become so only when
the bodily sounding-board "vibrates," and when to the primary

[41] W. James, *Principles of Psychology,* 1890, Vol. II, pp. 449, 468-470.
[42] *Ibid.,* p. 471.

projicient interest there is added the interest in the prolongation of these attendant and secondary organic states.[43]

§ 119. Happiness versus Pleasure.

The distinction between happiness and pleasure is one of great ambiguity and of wide popular acceptance, despite the fact that the terms are often used interchangeably. There appear to be two differences for which this distinction is intended to provide, and which we are now prepared to understand.

In the first place, the term 'pleasure' when used in contradistinction to the term 'happiness,' has possessed a relatively ignoble connotation as being primarily associated with the body. There is a certain impropriety in speaking of the "pleasures of Heaven," as a certain ignominy attaches even in this world to the so-called "life of pleasure"; while happiness, bliss or felicity is not accounted unworthy of saints, of angels, or of deity. This difference of dignity may now be provided for if the term pleasure is taken to mean the satisfactions of the body, or the positive value attaching to organic sensations. The term happiness may then be used in the broader and more objective sense to signify all satisfactions of interest; or differentially to signify those satisfactions, practical, aesthetic, moral or intellectual, which are derived from objects beyond the body, and which call into play the so-called "higher faculties." If this distinction is made, one can properly say with Aristotle that happiness is good by definition; one can discuss the place of pleasure in happiness; and one can legitimately say, as is so often said, that pleasure is inadequate, inasmuch as man is more than a creature of feeling.

In the second place, pleasure in contradistinction to happiness is limited and transient. A man may enjoy pleasure without being happy, in the sense that the former appertains to the moment, whereas the latter appertains to his life as a

---

[43] Similarly, in his account of the "coarser" emotions James's consistently introspective account neglects their impulsive aspect, unless taken in close conjunction with his account of instincts. Had he made it clear that all feeling contains a motor factor of interest along with its purely sensory aspect he would have disarmed many of his critics. Cf. § 121.

whole. A man might even enjoy pleasure continuously, and
without any admixture of pain, and yet be unhappy; meaning
that this continuity and purity of pleasure was obtained by
a narrow concentration upon bodily sensations. Happiness
would then signify that life was auspicious in all its aspects,
or that one could look widely in all directions without regret
and without fear. The happy man has nothing to hide from
himself; all of his interests are prosperous; and he finds satisfaction in a life that is at the same time well-rounded and
well-developed. More specifically, happiness will imply that
a man can enjoy the universe, that is to say, the widest world
which is brought into view by the exercise of self-consciousness, memory, imagination and foresight.

Although happiness means more than pleasure, in that it
embraces the whole system of personal satisfactions,[44] including those derived from the objects of projicient consciousness, certain pleasures will nevertheless play an important part in it. Those arising from the moderate satisfaction of
the inalienable bodily appetites will be both necessary, and also
compensatory,—as filling the gaps, and relieving the tedium
and fatigue incidental to patient waiting or prolonged effort.
Most important of all is the pleasure of health or of abundant
vitality which may give a glow of satisfaction to any activity.
It is this general organic interest, this appetite for work, or
relish of exercise, that enables the organism to face any prospect with eagerness. It is this more than any other single
factor that conditions that sense of adequacy which is so
essential to human happiness. It enables a man to carry his
load lightly and to rejoice in it. In its absence all problems
seem insoluble, all efforts hopeless, and life itself insufferably
complicated.

III. THE EMOTIONS

§ 120. **Correlation of Emotion and Instinct.** The term
emotion' is often used interchangeably with the terms 'feeling' or 'passion' to denote the affective division of the mental

[44] Cf. § 180.

life generally, as distinguished from cognition and will. With this extended meaning of the term we are not here specifically concerned, since it may be said to be the theme of the entire chapter, or even, in a sense, of the entire book.

But there is another and more limited sense in which the term is used to denote certain complex affective states which are sufficiently stereotyped to possess common names in all languages. These are commonly called '*the* emotions,' and are most familiarly illustrated by the so-called 'major,' 'coarse' or 'primary' emotions, such as anger and fear. Emotions in this sense are patterns or complex configurations whose components may vary, so that, like syndromes in clinical psychiatry, they are recognizable by a certain rough similarity of physiognomy rather than by any absolute mark.

In the recent history of the subject there has been a steadily growing tendency to identify an emotion by its correlative instinct. Anger is evidently correlated with fighting, and fear with escape. The bodily "expressions" of emotions and the correlated instinctive reactions "shade imperceptibly into each other," the difference being that the former "usually terminates in the subject's own body," while the latter "is apt to go further and enter into practical relations with the exciting object." [45]   But even when the emotional expression does not take effect in the outer world, it can usually be recognized as an obsolete or abridged form of such overt action, as in the case of the clenched fist or bared teeth; or as an organic readjustment, such as quickened respiration or circulation, which is necessitated by the overt action.

Hence, according to James, "every object that excites an instinct excites an emotion as well"; and according to Professor McDougall, the "primary emotion" is an indicator or criterion of the excitement of an instinctive impulse.[46]

This view has recently been summarized in explicitly "behavioristic terms," by Professor E. C. Tolman. According to this writer, a particular emotion can be recognized and

[45] W. James, *op. cit.*, Vol. II, p. 442.
[46] W. James, *loc. cit.*; W. McDougall, *Outline of Psychology*, 1923, p. 325, and *Social Psychology*.

identified only as a "response" taken "as affecting or calculated to affect the stimulus situation" in a specific way. While emotion has its presentative side that can be reported in introspection, *an* emotion is essentially impulse, and is definable "as a *drive* or *tendency* toward a particular type of behavior-result, of *response-as-affecting* stimulus; e.g., in the case of fear, protection from stimulus, in the case of anger, destruction of stimulus, and in the case of love, encouragement or enticement of stimulus." [47]

§ 121. **The James-Lange Theory and its Critics.** While James explicitly affirmed this correlation of emotion with instinct, his name is more particularly associated with the so-called "James-Lange Theory." According to this theory the 'feel' of the emotion, the aspect presented in introspection, consists of organic sensations. Certain bodily changes, proprioceptive and interoceptive, "follow directly the perception of the exciting fact," and *"our feeling of the same changes as they occur is the emotion."*

"What kind of an emotion of fear would be left," says this writer, "if the feeling neither of quickened heart-beats nor of shallow breathing, neither of trembling lips nor of weakened limbs, neither of goose-flesh nor of visceral stirrings, were present, it is quite impossible for me to think. Can one fancy the state of rage and picture no ebullition in the chest, no flushing of the face, no dilatation of the nostrils, no clenching of the teeth, no impulse to vigorous action, but in their stead limp muscles, calm breathing and a placid face? The present writer, for one, certainly cannot." [48]

The history of this famous doctrine is not unlike that of Darwin's theory of natural selection. It is so strongly fortified by proof and so repeatedly confirmed by experience that it cannot be denied substantial truth. In spite of elaborate refutations it shows no signs of obsolescence. Nevertheless, like most daring and innovating theories, it requires both refinement and supplementation. The objections which have been raised against it build upon it and extend it, but do

[47] "A Behavioristic Account of the Emotions," *Psych. Rev.,* Vol. **XXX,** 1923, pp. 222-223, 227.
[48] W. James, *op. cit.,* Vol. II, pp. 449, 452.

not undermine it. These objections will now be briefly considered.

§ 122. The Rôle of Thought and Imagery. In the first place, James has neglected the part commonly played by thought in the excitement of the emotions. He has not said, but he has created the impression, that in his view emotions are excited only by external sensory stimuli, whereas as a matter of fact they are often excited by the meanings of such stimuli, or the judgments pronounced upon them. The object may be interpreted as dangerous or fearful before the emotional onset is aroused, and *in that sense* the emotion may be said to exist in a cognitive form before the organic sensations are aroused. There is, however, no reason whatever to suppose that James would have denied this fact. He was primarily concerned with the emotional onset itself, and not with the cognitive form in which its object is presented.

He has also neglected the rôle of imagery, both in the initiation of the emotion, and in its content. Organic sensations, like other sensations, are reproduced in the imagination, and in any given case it is quite possible that such organic imagery should provide an emotional content even though there should be no sensory organic reverberations whatsoever. It is inconceivable that James should have denied this possibility, even though he makes no explicit avowal of it.[49]

§ 123. The Impulsive Aspect of Emotion. Through his preoccupation with the organic-sensory aspect of emotion, James at times lost sight of that impulsive aspect which has been noted above, and which he himself has elsewhere so flatly affirmed. To be sure in the passage already cited he speaks of an "impulse to vigorous action" as an essential element of anger, but in his anxiety to call attention to the commonly neglected visceral sensations he allowed this element to fall into the background. This is the objection urged most emphatically by Professor McDougall, who insists upon conation as the most indispensable feature of emotion.

[49] Cf. W. McDougall, *Outline of Psychology*, 1923, pp. 326-328.

"He [James] ignores the fact that an impulsive striving toward a goal is the essence of every emotional reaction. When we say 'I feel angry,' or explain our striking at an offender by saying 'I struck because I was angry,' we do not mean that the emotional quality of our experience was the active agent that caused the striking; rather, we mean quite properly that the being angry does, as a matter of empirical fact and experience, involve an impulsive tendency to strike; and our explanation is true and valid; we implicitly use the emotional quality that we recognize as the indicator of the instinctive tendency that has been aroused in us. Hence the ordinary statement, 'I struck because I was angry,' is essentially truer, gives a truer explanation of my action, than James's inverted statement, 'I am angry because I struck.' " [50]

In other words the state of *being* angry denotes the arousal of a specific motor response or tendency of which the bodily changes, together with the feeling of them, is the sequel. Even were these changes to be prevented, or not felt, it would still be true that in a sense the subject was in a state of anger. His state would not be, as James says "merely cognitive or intellectual." [51] He would be, in our sense of the term, interested and not apathetic.

James would, perhaps, have insisted that though such a corporeally anaesthetic subject might *be* angry, he would not *feel* angry; and that he, James, had assumed that in the case of emotions to be was to be felt. Professor McDougall's view contradicts that of James in so far, and only in so far, as the former affirms that there is a feeling of impulsive striving which is not a sensory experience of organic changes. Denying this more extreme contention, while accepting Professor McDougall's objection in its more limited form, as applying to impulse in the sense of a phase of behavior, James's view may readily be stated so as to meet it. Emotion would then be a complex response with a strong impulsive character, presumably instinctive in origin, and attended by a proprioceptive and interoceptive awareness of its organic manifestations.

[50] W. McDougall, *op. cit.*, p. 328.
[51] *Op. cit.*, Vol. II, p. 453.

§ 124. **Physiological Objections.** There is a body of physiological evidence which indicates that certain emotional expressions in animals persist after the removal of the cerebral hemispheres.[52] Goltz's decerebrate dogs and Sherrington's decerebrate cat gave evidence of anger but not of other emotions. This would seem to indicate that the absent emotions, such as fear, commonly require some projicient sensory stimulus, or perceptual elaboration, which the cerebral cortext conditions. As regards anger, since the afferent nerves from the viscera to sub-cortical centres are presumably intact, two interpretations remain open. We may suppose that the animal does not feel anger, though he manifests it; or we may suppose that the undisturbed subcortical centres suffice for such undiscriminated organic sensations and reflexes as constitute the strictly affective life. While neither interpretation would be in conflict with the James-Lange Theory, the latter would confirm Professor Head's view of the function of the thalamus.

More decisive physiological evidence against the James-Lange Theory is apparently afforded by Professor Sherrington's observations upon dogs in whom "appropriate spinal and vagal transection removes completely and immediately the sensation of the viscera and of all the skin and muscles behind the shoulder." Selecting for special observation an animal of "markedly emotional temperament," he finds that "her anger, her joy, her disgust, and when provocation arose, her fear, remained as evident as ever." [53]

Waiving the fact that organic sensations from the facial portion of emotional expression, as well as images aroused from the centres of memory and association, were not eliminated, it is evident that Professor Sherrington's conclusions beg the question at issue. The expressive and behavioristic aspect of emotion remained intact, showing that their innervation was not affected;[54] but whether in the absence of any sensory experience of these changes the emotion is *felt*,

[52] Summarized in C. S. Sherrington's *Integrative Action of the Nervous System,* 1906, pp. 262-268.
[53] C. S. Sherrington, *op. cit.,* pp. 260, 261.
[54] Though how this is to be reconciled with the absence of fear and joy in the decerebrate animals, is not clear.

remains as much in the dark as ever. Professor Sherrington
replies:

"Had their expression been unaccompanied by, and had they
not led on to, trains of acts logically consonant with their expressed emotion, that objection would have weight. Where the
facies of anger is followed by actions of advance and attack with
all appearances of set purpose I find it difficult to think that the
perception initiating the wrathful expression should bring in
sequel angry conduct and yet have been impotent to produce
'angry feeling.' " [55]

But that is exactly what would be supposed in the James-
Lange Theory, and Professor Sherrington's evidence does
not argue in the least either for or against it. It proves only
that the *expressive* and *behavior* aspects of emotion are closely
united, as is presupposed both by James and by all psychologists of the biological school.

Furthermore, if the external manifestation of the emotion
is to be taken as proof of the occurrence of its internal aspect,
and if the former is possible without any nervous connection
with the cerebrum, what becomes of Professor Sherrington's
view that "emotion is primarily a cerebral reaction," or that
its visceral and reflex aspects are secondary and derived?
We seem, in other words, to be led to one or the other of
two conclusions regarding the abnormal conditions created
by surgical transection or ablation.   Either the organic response occurs without any awareness of it on the part of the
mutilated animal, constituting a sort of emotional anaesthesia;
or the sensory function is restituted, being vicariously assumed
by the lower centres which remain intact.

§ 125. The Uniformity of Emotional Excitement. A
final objection to the James-Lange Theory is that urged by
Professor W. B. Cannon on the basis of his study of visceral
and, in particular, glandular changes induced by emotionally
exciting stimuli. His results, in so far as they emphasize
and report in much detail the profound and pervasive character of these disturbances, and their biological connection

[55] *Op. cit.*, p. 263.

with the circumstances under which emotions arise, may be said to corroborate and clarify the James-Lange Theory. But, on the other hand, he finds that "in terror and rage and intense elation, for example, the responses in the viscera seem too uniform to offer a satisfactory means of distinguishing states which, in man at least, are very different in subjective quality." He concludes, therefore, "that the visceral changes merely contribute to an emotional complex more or less indefinite, but still pertinent, feelings of disturbance in organs of which we are not usually conscious." [56]

In other words, it appears that the visceral changes contribute primarily a state of vague excitement which is common to all the intense emotions. The same visceral changes may be induced chemically by the introduction of adrenin into the blood stream, and subjects who have received such injections report that they feel "a general nervousness" or "all worked up and on edge," or that they feel *as though they were* experiencing a deep emotion.[57]

This objection is not, however, fatal to the James-Lange Theory. In the first place, James himself took pains to insist that the emotions are not distinct substantive entities, but permutations and combinations of the endlessly various organic sensations. It is in entire accord with this view that the major emotions should have many elements in common, and that excitement *per se* should be such a common factor among the intenser emotions. In the second place, the emotion is primarily an impulse, and Professor Cannon's findings in no way invalidate the supposition that the main difference between rage and fear may lie in their proprioceptive rather than in their interoceptive patterns; that is to say, in the motor set rather than in the visceral reverberation. Granting this, and assuming some visceral differences, the qualitative uniqueness of rage or fear may readily be accounted for in terms of the James-Lange Theory, especially if one supposes

[56] W. B. Cannon: *Bodily Changes in Pain, Hunger, Fear and Rage,* 1915, p. 280.
[57] W. B. Cannon, "New Evidence for Sympathetic Control of some Internal Secretions," *Amer. Jour. of Psychiatry,* Vol. II, 1922, p. 29.

that in each case the motor-visceral integration is inherited and stereotyped.[58]

As thus amended and fortified against attack,[59] we retain, therefore, the James-Lange Theory that the emotion in its internal or felt aspect, is a relatively diffused and undiscriminated sensory complex comprising those organic sensations which are incidental to the arousal of some major (and probably instinctive) response.

§ 126. The Function of Emotional Excitement. We have already found that the function of feeling generally is to reinforce or check some primary response. In emotion this function is emphasized in a manner appropriate to the exceptional circumstances in which the emotion occurs. The work of Professor Cannon and other physiologists upon the glands of internal secretion has thrown great light upon this function, and marks a step toward the understanding of the emotions which ranks in theoretical importance with the James-Lange Theory, and is supported by decisive experimental evidence.

The sympathetic nervous system controls the viscera, and as an auxiliary to the central nervous system it regulates such visceral adjustments as may be necessitated by the organism's overt behavior. In times of emotional stress it not only brings about these compensating adjustments, but also liberates from the adrenal medulla a substance which, when absorbed from

---

[58] Professor Cannon himself suggests that we may find "these differential characters in the nervous *pattern* that lies ingrained in the archaic portion of the neurone system." "And when the nerve impulses flash through these ready but unworn pathways, the effects may be quite as strange and as startling and as rich in feeling tone as if the impulses arose from the altered viscera or the tensions of facial and skeletal muscles." (*Op. cit.*, p. 29.) This view evidently assumes "feelings of innervation." To reconcile it with the James-Lange Theory it would only be necessary to suppose that the visceral and muscular changes do occur, at least partially, and that these changes are sensorially reported and integrated in the same "archaic portion" of the neurone system, such, for example, as the thalamus.

[59] For the objections anticipated and answered by James himself, cf. his *Principles of Psychology*, Vol. II, pp. 454-467. For his later reply to objections, cf. "The Physical Basis of Emotion," in his *Collected Essays and Reviews*, 1920.

the blood-stream, produces the same adjustments. Thus Professor Cannon finds that this substance (adrenin)

"can accelerate the heart beat, increase arterial pressure, shift the blood from the abdomen to the limbs, stop the motions of the gastro-intestinal canal, check the secretions of the digestive glands, dilate the bronchioles, augment the sugar content of the blood, and besides these effects, can speed up the rate of metabolism, hasten the clotting of blood and quickly abolish some of the effects of muscular fatigue." [60]

All of these changes have the character of facilitating supreme exertion, by concentrating and augmenting available energies, and by protecting the organism against the effects of strain and injury. These changes taken as a group, together with their nervous control in the sympathetic system, constitute a specialized mechanism of emotional excitation through which the organism is enabled to meet great crises. It is the physiological aspect of that *reserve for emergencies* which James had already so well described in the general terms of human experience. [61]

Through this reinvigoration of the organism, emotional excitement gives a positive feeling-tone to responses that are primarily negative. If the enemy is to be overcome he must be faced and dealt with; if he is to be escaped, it must be by prolonged activity. Emotional excitement gives a zest both to attack and to flight, so that they may come to be liked for themselves. In terms of the view of feeling already proposed, this means that the bodily changes and states induced by emotional excitement arouse impulses directed to their own prolongation and renewal. In desire a primary positive response may be supplemented by a negative response, namely, by an impulse to escape the state of lack or deficiency. In emotional excitement a primary negative response, an impulse to destroy, remove or avert, is supplemented by a secondary positive response; namely, by an impulse to continue and elaborate those bodily movements which are incidental

[60] *Op. cit.*, p. 17. Cf. the same writer's *Bodily Changes in Pain, Hunger, Rage and Fear*, 1915, *passim*.
[61] Cf. his "Energies of Men," reprinted in *Memories and Studies*, 1911.

to the primary response. Emotional excitement makes it not only physically possible to achieve unusual feats, but psychically agreeable to deal with initially disagreeable situations. Emotional excitement even has the effect of blocking the nervous impulses underlying pain.[62] A threat or a danger becomes a challenge in which one exults owing to the plenitude of one's augmented power.

Passion is deliberately invoked to bring not only the power, but the will, to face emergencies. This has always been recognized in the case of anger. The last extremity brings with it a kind of saving desperation.

"Purpose shall be sterner, heart the bolder, courage the more, as our strength littleth."

"When pain smote him sore, up he pulled his heart, and was himself again." [63]

The goading of anger is a well-known expedient for arousing courage. It is practised deliberately by drill sergeants who teach their men to simulate ferocity in the bayonet drill. A recent writer tells us that the Buddoo or Bedouin Arab

"would salute you with a salvo at 3000 yards or more, as the Chinaman is said to beat his gong, or the orang-outang his breast, to intimidate the foe or put heart into himself. . . . Before starting they danced on the sand-hills to give themselves heart, then mounting, they galloped around in little circles, calling upon Allah and firing off their rifles in the air." [64]

The far-reaching importance of this motivating effect arises from the fact that anger may be aroused in behalf of others of the species, and so reinforce the social impulses; and from the fact that it may be aroused by any obstacle encountered by a primary activity.[65] Anger may, in other words, put "heart" into any performance, and in both its cruder and sublimated forms is one of the chief motivating elements in human life.

[62] W. S. Hunter, *General Psychology*, 1919, p. 234.
[63] Quoted by J. L. Lowes, *Convention and Revolt in Poetry*, 1919, pp. 341, 342.
[64] E. Candler, *The Long Road to Bagdad*, 1919, Vol. I, pp. 113, 246.
[65] Cf. below, Ch. XIX, Sect. I; and W. McDougall, *op. cit.*, pp. 139-142.

IV. RECAPITULATION

§ **127.** The last three chapters have explicated and forti-fied our definition of interest in terms of the behaving organ-ism. They have also enabled us to provide explicitly for those modalities of interest which must serve as the basis of any classification of the varieties of value. Borrowing their status from the interests which determine them, values themselves may be spoken of as inherited or acquired, positive or nega-tive, recurrent or progressive, real or playful, aggressive or submissive, subjective or objective.

At the same time, although our general outline of interest is organic rather than introspective, we have found a place for those data which the introspective account of the motor-affective life has emphasized. 'Feelings' of which the in-dividual subject is uniquely aware do not drop out, but take their place in the picture. The introspective cross-section is defined as part of the larger solid field which embraces the organism and its environment.

In the course of this analysis it has become increasingly clear that feeling cannot be taken as the basic factor in theory of value. If it be taken substantively to denote certain quali-tatively recognizable contents, these are indistinguishable from sense-data, save in their reference to the organism rather than the environment, or in the relative absence of discrimination. As sense-data they are objects of value, and not acts of valuing. In pleasure and pain they are closely associated with an instant liking or dislike, which means an impulse to pro-long or get rid of them. That pleasures and pains may be regarded as valuable objects, sought or avoided on their own account, has always been recognized, and can only be accounted for when there is added to their qualitative character an ac-tive attitude toward them. And it is this active attitude, rather than their quality, that invests them with value, positive or negative.

On the other hand, the attributive rôle of feeling, which is notably characteristic of the great emotions, can be under-stood only in terms of some major desire which is directed

to an external object, and which incidentally arouses organic
sensations similar to those which are focally present in substantive pleasures and pains. One may like or dislike organic
sensations for themselves, and thus enjoy pleasures or suffer
pains; or one may in the course of liking or disliking some
other object, also like or dislike the attendant and subordinated
organic sensations.

Organic sensations may be incorrectly 'referred' within
the organism or beyond the organism, and when so referred
they carry their attendant impulses with them. The so-called
tertiary qualities, or objectified 'pleasures' and pains, are the
appearance constituted by such mistaken reference.[66] But
whether the tertiary quality be so construed, or regarded as
"really" objective, in any case its value lies in the favor or
disfavor with which the subject responds to it, and not in the
bare quality itself.

The inadequacy of feeling as the constitutive principle of
value, appears, furthermore, in its failure to provide for those
objects which derive value from being sought by effort and
indirection. It is necessary to recognize the rôle of desire,
and to construe desire in terms that do not admit of its being
reduced to feeling. Desire is not a pleasure taken in the
idea or judgment of an object, together with a displeasure
felt in its absence. It is a tendency to realize the one, or
to escape the other. It is commonly a performance which
is at one and the same time positive and negative, and
in which these two impulsive components reinforce one another.

In an analysis of interest we have thus been obliged constantly to introduce motor or dynamic terms. There has
also been a perpetual and unavoidable reference to the cognitive faculties. Objects of interest are somehow presented
or represented. Interests may be founded on truth and error.
Means are adopted owing to what is expected of them.
Knowledge is or may be in itself a form of interest. To
these and other questions centering in the relation of cognition to interest, we must now turn our attention.

[66] Cf. § 16.

CHAPTER XI

ANALYSIS OF COGNITION [1]

I. THE RELATIONS OF INTEREST AND COGNITION

§ 128. **Interdependence of Interest and Cognition.**[2] The broad fact of the dependence of interest on cognition has been amply illustrated by the impossibility of discussing the one without allusion to the other. It is historically illustrated by the extent to which in modern life purposes and emotional responses are altered by the advancement of knowledge. A striking example is afforded by the change of attitude toward defective human beings. Certain types of abnormal behavior were once attributed to malicious magic or demoniacal possession, and were an object of fear and anger. The modern science of psychiatry having construed the same behavior in terms of disease, the unfortunate defective is now regarded with pity and solicitude. The witch with the "devil's claw" was loaded with chains or burnt at the stake, whereas the "anaesthetic hysteric" is attended with indulgent care. This change of sentiment towards the same crude phenomena is due to a change in the judgment pronounced upon them.

The rapid advance and dissemination of scientific knowledge is the most conspicuous feature of modern life. Never before in the world's history have human beliefs been so diverse and so mutable. But this variability of belief is attended by a variability of sentiment. As we conceive things

[1] Parts of the present chapter are reprinted from an article entitled, "The Independent Variability of Purpose and Belief," published in the *Jour. of Philos.*, Vol. XVIII, 1921.

[2] "Modes of thinking, such as love, desire, or any other of the passions, do not take place, unless there be in the same individual an idea of the thing loved, desired, etc. But the idea can exist without the presence of any other mode of thinking." (Spinoza's *Ethics*, Part II, Axiom III.)

so do we feel towards them; and as in modern life we readily change our minds, so do we readily change our hearts. The agencies by which new ideas are disseminated, and by which for a brief time members of a social group are brought to think alike, can be safely counted upon to induce a temporary uniformity of feeling. He who can determine how men shall conceive a certain object, governs their passions and their actions towards it.[3]

It is also true, on the other hand, that men's opinions are affected by their interests. As men will what they think, so in some sense and in some measure do they think what they will. Stereotyped ideas conduce to uniformity of feeling, and emotional contagion is one of the chief sources of collective opinion.

That interest and cognition are intimately interdependent may, then, be taken for granted. Shall we therefore slur the difference by using the terms interchangeably, or by introducing ambiguous terms, such as 'appreciation,' 'assent' or 'approbation'?[4] On the contrary, where there is intimate complexity the sound method is that which analyzes and distinguishes. One can not expect to follow two closely interwoven strands until one has first clearly identified each of them, and in that preliminary stage it is necessary to dwell upon their differences. This is quite consistent with a full recognition of their intimacy. It presupposes that intimacy,— there is a problem only because of such intimacy.. Interest affects cognition in countless ways, by directing it to a certain context, by accompanying and impregnating it with attitudes of favor or disfavor, and by weighting the evidence on which it is based. Cognition, on the other hand, affects interest, by exciting or depressing it, by knowing it, by illuminating it, or by determining the forms in which it expresses itself. But how can we say these things without implying that cognition is one thing and interest another? And how can we under-

---

[3] Hence the importance of those "stereotyped" conceptions of men, institutions and events which arise in default of accurate and trustworthy organs of publicity (cf. W. Lippman, *Public Opinion*); and hence the importance, for better or for worse, of propaganda and advertising.
[4] Cf. § 39.

stand these complexities, relations and interactions without some preliminary understanding of the terms themselves?

§ 129. **Division and Circumscription of Topic.** Where complexity of relations is a source of confusion the only hope of escaping confusion lies in some initial division of the topic. If such a division be artificial then that fact will disclose itself and require correction as we proceed. Assuming that to *know* any object, and to be positively or negatively *interested* in it, are two distinguishable things, then it is at least schematically possible that an act of interest should be an object of cognition, and that an act of cognition should be an object of interest. Value being defined in terms of interest, the former is the case of the cognition of value. The case in which the acts or achievements of cognition are objects of interest, is, by definition, the case in which cognition has value.

There remain two further relations of cognition and interest arising from the fact that cognition and interest are interpenetrating, or that each may condition and partially constitute the other. That which is essentially an act of cognition, may be generated or affected by interest. It is often supposed that this intrusion of interest is prejudicial to knowledge and negates or diminishes its value. Since the question is thus traditionally associated with that of the special values peculiar to knowledge, it is not central to our present task.

The conditioning and penetration of interests by cognition, on the other hand, is a topic of primary importance for a general theory of value. Whatever is essential to the structure of interest is essential to the understanding of all value. It is this topic of the internal qualification or 'mediation' of interest by cognition with which we are especially concerned in the present and following chapters.

§ 130. **The Ambiguity of Verbal Expression.** The topic being so divided and circumscribed, we may now undertake to specify the difference between interest and cognition with a view to distinguishing them when they are conjoined or associated.

We have first to note the unreliability of *verbal expression* as evidence of the existence of either cognition or interest. In our analysis of interest we have found that the essence of the matter lies in a disposition or motor tendency. When an expectation begets its own realization or when the anticipation of an object brings that object to pass, this cycle of events or mode of determination is called interest. Thus hate, for example, is constituted by a disposition to destroy or thwart its object, together with the organic sensations or feelings induced by this motor attitude. This is the core of hate which is necessary and sufficient to give it being. At the same time hate will ordinarily manifest itself overtly in characteristic postures, gestures or words. In so far as these are *manifestations* of hate they are parts of it, and may serve to identify it. They do not, however, constitute unmistakable evidence of its existence, and for two reasons. In the first place, they are variable and uncertain according as the individual in question is relatively histrionic or unexpressive; in the second place, as being signs and means of communication they may be assumed or suppressed in accordance with the impression which the subject desires to produce upon others. The verbal expression of emotion is preëminently unreliable for these reasons. In taciturn persons it may be absent altogether, while in voluble persons it is disproportionate to the intensity of the emotion. It is a recognized instrument of communication, readily controlled and habitually employed to serve a social purpose. The words "I hate you" may express hate and constitute a part of it; or they may over-express and exaggerate it; or they may indicate a desire to persuade the object that he is hated, whether in fact he is or is not; or they may be employed as a means of inducing hate in other subjects.

What is true of interest is true also of cognition.[5] This, like interest, consists in a disposition to behave in certain specified ways in relation to certain specified objects. The

[5] For a discussion of judgment as *expressing* the belief of the subject, as distinguished from *meaning* its "objective," cf. G. E. Moore, *Ethics,* Home University Library, p. 125.

overt and grossly observable expressions of cognition are unreliable signs of its existence, subject to individual differences,
and governed by the purposes of communication. The words,
"the King is dead, long live the King!" are ordinarily taken
to indicate both a knowledge of fact and a sentiment of
loyalty; but just as one may be animated by loyalty without
acclaiming its object, so one may be cognizant of a fact
without declaring it. One may say that the King is dead
without believing it, for the sake of inducing the belief in
others. Or, believing that the King is dead, one may dis-
semble the belief. Or, desiring to communicate the belief
to others one may do so in a hundred different ways, by
gesture or by a wide range of verbal forms. While the
rôle of language in cognition is of the highest importance, and
deserves greater rather than less attention from philosophers,
it has been customary to dwell too much upon its grammatical
structure and to neglect its psychological and social functions;
with the result that the analysis of cognition has often
amounted to little more than an analysis of the indicative
sentence. To understand cognition and speech itself it is
necessary to go behind those stereotyped forms which constitute grammar, to the acts of mind which they express or
subserve.

If one too hastily assumes that the declaratory sentence
constitutes an act of cognition, one will be betrayed by the
fact that this grammatical form is often employed as an expression of emotion. The poetic drama, in which the spoken
word is elaborated for the purpose of intensive expression,
provides abundant examples of this fact. The scene in Shakespeare's *Richard III,* in which Anne, accompanying the corpse
of King Henry, is confronted and woo'd by Gloucester,
obviously intends to present a conflict of passions, and not
an exchange of opinions, although both persons express themselves largely in declaratory sentences. Thus Anne:

> "Avaunt, thou dreadful minister of hell!
> Thou hadst but power over his mortal body,
> His soul thou canst not have; therefore be gone.
> .   .   .   .

Foul devil, for God's sake, hence, and trouble us not:
For thou hast made the happy earth thy hell,
Filled it with cursing cries and deep exclaims.

.   .   .   .

O, gentlemen, see, see! dead Henry's wounds
Open their congeal'd mouths and bleed afresh!
Blush, blush, thou lump of foul deformity;
For 'tis thy presence that exhales this blood
From cold and empty veins, where no blood dwells;
Thy deed, inhuman and unnatural,
Provokes this deluge most unnatural." [6]

It is the function of Anne's words not to formulate and announce a set of historical, metaphysical and physiological convictions, but to express hate, to wound her enemy, and to communicate a like attitude to her partisans. Her words are angry gestures, poisoned darts, and signals of alarm, rather than descriptions of fact.

Lovers' descriptions of their mistresses are notoriously unreliable, judged by standards of portraiture, and they tend to a uniformity that accords ill with the variety of their objects. The reason is that they are not in fact descriptions at all but expressions of sentiment, and the sentiment being the same its expression tends to assume the same verbal forms.

Likewise in religion. Man characterizes God in negative and superlative terms, such as 'infinite,' 'eternal,' 'most high,' 'most great,' 'just,' 'holy,' 'creator.' He uses these terms of God, says Hobbes,

"in such sense as if he meant not to declare what He is (for that were to circumscribe Him within the limits of our fancy), but how much we admire Him, and how ready we would be to obey Him; which is a sign of humility and of a will to honour Him as much as we can." [7]

But while the use of epithets does obscure, it does not remove, the difference between cognition and interest.[8] If

[6] Act I, Scene II.
[7] *Leviathan*, Ch. XXXI.
[9] For the view that all judgments of value are epithets, cf. *e.g.*, J. L. McIntire's assertion that "the judgment of value merely expresses in

the declaratory sentence be the expression of an emotional attitude, this attitude itself is a fact to be cognized, whether by the same or by another subject. To be aware that one hates, or to recognize hatred from its manifestations, is evidently something other than hating; and this would be none the less true even though it should have to be conceded that the one is psychologically impossible without the other. It may be argued that one cannot hate without feeling it, or that one cannot hate a given object without being cognizant of that object, or that one cannot recognize hatred in others unless one has hated; but all of these arguments presuppose that cognition and hate, being specifically different, may be conjoined and interwoven in act and in object. When Anne calls Gloucester a "dreadful minister of hell," this phrase expresses and partially constitutes her hatred of Gloucester. Supposing that she is cognizant of her hatred, this cognizance is evidently different from her hatred, in that it has a different object, namely, herself rather than Gloucester. Supposing that she is aware of Gloucester and knows something about him, this also is different from her hatred in that it imputes different predicates to the same object. She hates him in terms of the epithet, but she identifies him and qualifies him in other terms, as her cousin and as the murderer of her husband.

We may, of course, suppose a case in which this same epithet was employed in a strict theological sense, and in which Gloucester might significantly deny that he was a diplomatic representative of the Prince of Darkness. All epithets are doubtless reminiscent of such primitive cognitive reference. But this alternative usage only emphasizes the need of distinguishing the case in which a phrase is an expression of interest from the case in which the same phrase is an act of cognition. "The rose is sweet," or "my lady is an angel," may indicate that the one is enjoyed and the other loved; or they may indicate a belief that the one possesses a specific

language what is already implied in the emotional attitude towards the situation." ("Value-Feelings and Judgments of Value," *Proc. Aristotelian Soc.,* 1904-05, p. 59.)

olfactory quality, and that the other possesses a specific status in the heavenly hierarchy. The difference lies not in the grammatical form, which is the same, but must be sought in the underlying disposition of the subject with reference to the object, and in the diverse functions which this grammatical form therefore serves.

II. THE DIFFERENCE BETWEEN INTEREST AND COGNITION

§ 131. **Expectation versus Interest.** In recognizing a cognitive component in interest we have hitherto employed the term 'expectation,' and have accounted for the fallibility of interests by the fact that this component expectation may be true or false.[9] Since we are already to some extent familiar with this mode of cognition, and since it presents the characteristics of cognition most clearly and most unmistakably, it will serve best as the starting-point of analysis.

To expect an object or event is to be prepared for it, that is, to have ready the appropriate response. That the organism has its performances scheduled in advance, or set for an orderly sequence of occasions, has already been shown. In order to make room for the superadded element of belief or conviction which is also present in expectation, we shall employ the term 'supposition' to indicate this bare anticipatory set, or implicit course of action correlated with a specific object.[10] If, for example I suppose or "entertain the idea" that the barn is on fire, I in some measure set my fire-response in readiness. I talk to myself in terms taken from my fire-vocabulary, and I am peculiarly receptive to such visual or other sensory stimuli as fire presents. Other trains of anticipatory responses such as fire itself is most apt to excite, are now partially excited in its absence. In short, a reaction-system of which fire is the complementary environmental factor, is in momentary possession of my mind. This may be the end of the matter, so far as this particular system is

[9] Cf. §§ 87-89.
[10] This is approximately the same as the *Annahme* of A. Meinong, who deserves credit for having brought this process to light. Cf. his *Ueber Annahmen*, second edition, 1910.

concerned. In the course of the implicit elaboration of this response some other system may have been started into action, and I may wander from supposition to supposition through a more or less protracted sequence of "idle" conjecture. It is essential to a supposition that it should be set *for* a specific occasion or class of occasions. Supposing my barn to *be* on fire, is a readiness for fire-stimuli when I *now* at this moment look out of the *east* window, rather than when *to-morrow* I look out of the *west* window. The supposition determines not only what my response shall be, but when and where it shall be applied. Having a supposition that my barn is on fire, there is a specific situation which will find me, by virtue of that supposition, on the look-out for fire and ready to deal with it. By virtue of my supposition I shall be more or less ready to act according as fire is or is not presented on *that* occasion. If fire is presented, I shall be able to respond to it without preliminary adjustment, and shall be in advance of another to whom, as we say, no such possibility has "occurred." *Per contra,* if fire is not presented, I am taken by surprise, and have, perhaps, a more difficult readjustment to make than another who has not thought at all.

Truth and error are said to be relative to the intent of a judgment.[11] This is readily describable in the terms here proposed. Truth and error qualify an expectation as regards its fitness to meet a specific occasion, or as regards the occurrence of the appropriate object *when and where* it is looked for. There can be no determination of its truth or error so long as the locus of its application remains ambiguous. A charge of error can always be effectively met if one can show that *that* was not what one was talking about; that is, if there is disagreement as to where the evidence is to be sought. The questionable *fitness* of the expectation means that the anticipatory set does or does not there find the complementary object by which it can move to completion. This complementary object may be a single actual stimulus, or a group

_____

[11] A distinction and comparison of the different senses of the term 'truth,' will be found in the author's essay on "The Truth-Problem," *Jour. of Philos.*, Vol. XIII, 1916.

of stimuli, or a group of physical properties, by which a response is enabled to execute itself. Fire as an object consists of the way it looks, sounds or feels; and also of the other things that can be done with it, such as burning things with it, or quenching it. In fact, since my response to it may consist in part of a further extension of plans, the object must include even its capacity to mean or to act as a sign.

A bare supposition, then, has in itself the functional relations that are necessary in order to determine truth or error. But in the case of expectation a supposition is further qualified so as to assume the form of conviction or belief.[12] A belief is a supposition to which one has committed oneself. This is evidently a matter of degree. Doubt is feebleness or vacillation of belief; and disbelief is contrary or antagonistic belief. There is some belief in all supposition because all supposition is action, and action which precludes other action. When one is following up, exploring, or elaborating a certain supposition, other suppositions are cut off, and for the time being one is committed. But for practical purposes it is easy to distinguish such momentary and innocuous committal from irretrievable committal, in which one's bridges are burnt behind one. Irretrievable committal is the case in which the supposition has gone so far as to exclude all other suppositions in the same quarter. There are no mental reservations, no anchors to windward. The non-occurrence of the complementary objects finds one utterly maladjusted.

This condition may develop in various ways. If upon supposing my barn to be on fire, I cry "Fire!" telephone for the police, and rush out of the house in the direction of the barn, I am engaging in activities which for the time inhibit the alternative supposition that the barn is in a state of normal well-being. I am also creating a rapidly shifting series of new situations to which I must react as they arise, and which prevent vacillation, that is, the alternation of the two major

[12] A supposition may also assume the form of a question or a command. For an examination of the imperative form of supposition, cf. the author's essay, *cit. supra*, pp. 564-566.

suppositions. Or I may have carried my supposition so far
as to make it impossible to reverse, because of the momentum
of the response. Even though the complementary stimulus
should not appear, the organism would be caught off its balance and unable to bring another response into play. Or a
supposition may have been carried so far as to lead to amend-
ments in other systems of response. Supposing my barn
to be on fire, I give up my trip to the city and suspend household activities, so that the contrary supposition is impeded
through requiring a general rearrangement of plans. Or the
supposition may come in the shape of a suggestion, which,
finding an unresourceful and unresisting mind, may obtain
exclusive possession by default.[13]

An expectation, then, is an implicit response unreservedly
set for a specific occasion; as when, believing that my train
leaves the station at three o'clock, I correlate my readiness
to depart, or my train-taking activities, with a place and time
in my field of action. If when I reach the appointed place
at the appointed hour there is no train to see or to enter,
my belief is proved erroneous. Truth and error, in other
words, depend on the presence or absence of the complementary object on the occasion at which the belief prepares me
for it. But this is quite *independent of any attitudes of favor
or disfavor with which I may view the presence of such an
object.* It is wholly a question of whether I have my attitude
of favor or disfavor (whichever it be) in readiness when
its complementary object appears. It is a question of whether

[13] The phenomena of suggestibility, and the question of "ideomotor"
action, present no special difficulties for the present view. For the view
that all ideas are *per se* qualified to induce action, cf. W. James, *Principles of Psychology,* 1890, Vol. II, pp. 522-528. For a critique of this
view, cf. E. L. Thorndike, *Educational Psychology, Briefer Course,* pp.
75-83. According to the view here presented ideas *are* actions, more or
less completely executed. Suggestibility or the impulse to leap from the
precipice (cf. Ch. V, Ehrenfels, *Einleitung in der Werttheorie,* Vol. I,
pp. 241-242) mean that through dissociation or attentive preoccupation
with the given stimulus, the more remote and modifying stimuli are inoperative.

There are undoubtedly other factors in belief, such as the immediate
"sense of reality," which can be interpreted as the receptive attitude to
external stimuli; and the factor of earnestness or zeal, which is a blend
of belief with resolution or will.

my plans (be they inspired by hope or by despair) are scheduled in accordance with the facts.

The specific character of expectation as distinguished from
interest, is further indicated by the existence of a group of
disinterested "feelings" [14] which are characteristically associated with it, such as surprise, familiarity, recognition, certainty and doubt. These feelings may be interpreted as the
sensory incidence of the peculiar shocks, conjunctions and
transitions which enter into the history of the cognitive process. It would not be illegitimate to define expectation as a
liability to such feelings, or as the disposition which is the
organic factor necessary for their occurrence. To be surprised, for example, at the occurrence of a certain event,
would imply a specific expectation in that quarter. While
these cognitive feelings may occur independently, they are
commonly combined with interest to form such hybrid states
as hope, chagrin, or disappointment.

§ 132. **The Independent Variability of Interest and
Cognition.** Cognition and interest being specifically different, there is no mystery in the fact that they may under
certain circumstances vary independently.

Their separability and independent variability is assumed
by common-sense, as is indicated by such expressions as the
following: "I am compelled to believe" (by implication
"against my will"); "I have reluctantly concluded"; "I was
agreeably disappointed"; "I am sorry to find"; "I wish it were
so." The child who sees his mother enter at one door with a
bottle, and his father at the other with a slipper, doubtless does
so with feeling; but he none the less entertains expectations
with reference to both stimuli similar to those of the unfeeling
psychologist who stands by to observe the phenomenon. A
belief may remain unaffected through the whole repertory
and cycle of the passions, including the point of indifference.
Similarly, an interest may remain fixed while belief varies.
Let us now seek more fully to interpret and illustrate this
independent variability.

[14] In the broader sense of the term. Cf. § 120.

Expectation is an anticipatory response correlated with a contingent object. It implies no disposition to bring its object into being, but only a readiness to deal with it when and if it occurs. Interest, on the other hand, promotes its object. To expect an event signifies only a disposition to act *on* it; while to be interested in an event signifies a disposition to act *for* it, or to provide an occasion for acting on it. This supplementary dynamic factor which distinguishes interest, lies in the governing propensity which renders the anticipatory set prepotent, and which gives a peculiar eligibility to any antecedent performance which affords promise of it. An expectation becomes an interest when the anticipatory response in which it consists, is *in demand*. The expectation sets the anticipatory response for a specific occasion; the interest provides subjective conditions which help to create the occasion, and so to facilitate the execution of the response.

To say that I expect a visit from X to-morrow at four o'clock means that my X-responses are scheduled for that place and hour. X's appearance at that hour will find me as ready to deal with him as my experience with him, or with others like him, enables me to be. Any responses of which X is the appropriate object are drawn from my-arsenal, tuned up and placed where they can be promptly brought to bear on the appointed occasion. This preparation on my part does not affect in the slightest degree the probability of X's arrival. If, however, I desire X's arrival, then one or another of these X-responses is required for the fulfilment of some propensity which governs me. I am alone and my sociability is starved for lack of an object. Among the anticipated X-responses is that of communication with X, and any act of mine which confirms or strengthens this expectation will, other things being equal, have priority. Sending X a fresh horse, or going to meet him and showing him the way, would arouse expectations congruent with my governing sociability, and these actions are therefore likely to occur. In so far, in short, as my performance enters causally into the situation at all, it tends to *expedite* X's arrival, and so to enable me to execute the anticipatory response. I am, in other words, as an agent favorably disposed to his arrival.

In the case just described, we have illustrated the fact that the expectation of a certain event such as X's arrival, may exist with or without an interest in that event. Let us now consider the case in which the same expectation is associated with varying modes of interest. I expect and desire a visit from X to-morrow at four o'clock. My initial attitude to X being one of enmity, I schedule my combative response for that hour, and am disposed to expedite his arrival as affording an occasion for the realization of my hostile designs. Meanwhile I experience a change of heart about X, and come to regard him as a friend in disguise.[15] What is then changed is the character of the X-response. My expectation of his arrival is unchanged; that is, my X-response, which is now a grateful response, is still scheduled for to-morrow at four o'clock. My surprise at his non-appearance will be in no way affected by the change in the greeting which I have prepared for him. Amidst all this emotional change there is a cognitive invariant.

Similarly, there may be identity of belief with variety of interest in different individuals. The rumored signing of the armistice on November 8, 1918, was greeted by some with delirious joy, by others with rage. The defeat of Germany was already linked with different reaction-systems in the minds of these two groups. The one group struggled to bring it about, the other to avert it. The identity of belief lay in the fact that both took the same occasion to discharge these different reaction-systems; and both were equally in error, in that in both cases the response was equally premature.

Or, there may be stability of interest associated with variability of belief. A mother loves her son with steadfastness. This means that she is disposed to rejoice at his success and to grieve at his failure. She will then rejoice or grieve in

[15] This is a change of belief about X's attitude, but there is no change in the belief whose stability is here in question, namely, the belief in his projected arrival.

accordance with her beliefs. She hears a report of his success and believes it. This means that she responds to the situation with the response that constitutes her way of greeting her son's success. The father, being more sceptical, suspends his rejoicing, though he is no less disposed to rejoice at his son's success when once he believes it. Additional evidence then leads to the mother's abandonment of her belief, that is to the abandonment of her rejoicing,—which turns out to be ill-timed. The situation is one to which her grief rather than her rejoicing is appropriate. Meanwhile she has not in the least changed her sentiment, that is, her system of reactions in relation to the fortunes of her son. She has revised only the schedule, the timing, the application of these reactions. Similarly the sentiment of humanity may beget in one man a chronic melancholy, in another a spirit of joyful service. The difference between the pessimist and the optimist is not a difference in what they love and hate, but a difference in what they think, that is a difference in the occasions on which they bring their love and hate to bear.

There is also a converse relation between belief and purpose. In hopeless longing there is a positive response which is never applied. The man who longs to see his dead sweetheart, but without belief in any such possibility, is perpetually rehearsing loving greetings which he never assigns a place in his plan. There is no occasion in his life when he enacts these greetings, nor any occasion which he is prepared to meet thus and thus alone. Or consider the opposite case of dread, —the positive expectation of that which is contrary to one's will. This means that one's fixed response to a certain situation, such as the loss of money, is one of grief. To dread the loss of money means, then, that this grief is set for the reading of the financial news in the evening paper. It is *now* set, and in some degree partially excited, which distinguishes this situation from the situation that might be described in the words "I expect to be sorry to-morrow." In the latter case I am now implicitly enacting, not the sorrow, but that response with which I am accustomed to deal with my sorrow, which may be to read a detective story.

There is one further case of the conversity of interest and expectation, which occurs at the moment when the belief is tested. One may then be "pleasantly surprised," or have one's "worst fears realized." To be pleasantly surprised, as, for example, at one's election to office, means that the response prepared for the occasion of the reception of the news was one of regret, of fortitude, of redirection of activity to other objects. In spite of efforts in the past to obtain election one had subsequently arranged to deal with failure rather than with success. But although the news of one's election finds one unready, the response which one awkwardly and tardily brings into play is a positive and joyful response. The news is grateful to the ear and releases constructive activities subordinate to the political purpose which is now renewed. When one's worst fears are realized, on the other hand, one has prepared for the worst and finds that preparation suitable to the event. One's expectation is verified, though one's desire is thwarted.

This conversity of interest and belief implies that the two may be in conflict. The expectation based on experience may be contrary to a governing propensity; or the implicit part of a governing propensity, pressing for realization, may resist the suggestions of experience. The planes of cognition and interest intersect in the expectation and may there interfere with one another, with the result that cognition succumbs to interest (one believes what one wants) or interest succumbs to cognition (one wants what one believes). And *per contra* interest may reinforce belief, or belief, interest. When the interest *in* cognition develops, this conflict or union becomes one of interests, or a relation between the cognitive interest and all other interests. But such a relation would not occur did not the cognitive process itself move in the same causal field as interest, and so become liable to modification from this context.[16]

[16] That cognition acts as a compelling force which may contend with interest, is recognized in all studies of the genesis of opinion. Cf. *e.g.*, A. L. Lowell, *Public Opinion in War and Peace*, 1923, p. 39: "A man often finds himself compelled to reach a conclusion upon the evidence which grieves him profoundly, although other honest and rational people with no stronger desire than he hold a different opinion."

III. MODES OF COGNITION

§ 133. **Sensory Cognition.** In the course of distinguishing between cognition and interest, it has proved necessary
to set forth the characteristic nature of cognition under the
name of 'expectation.' A brief examination of the familar
modes of cognition, such as *sensation, meaning, judgment*
and *memory,* will serve to render this exposition more precise,
and at the same time to introduce certain complexities which
are necessary for the understanding of the rôle of cognition
in interest.

Ordinarily sensation is part of a mental state whose object
transcends the stimulus. The dog who "knows his master's
voice" is not merely sensing its peculiar quality, pitch or
intensity, but is prepared for a train of ulterior stimuli, such,
for example, as his master's visual appearance. The sensation,
in other words, *means* something, the cognition which it serves
being a cognition of what is meant rather than of what is
given. Sensation is commonly the *terminus a quo* of cognition, rather than its *terminus ad quem;* or is centrifugal
rather than centripetal. For this reason pure sensation
is said to exist but rarely, if at all. Can we, however, distinguish a sense in which sensation is cognitive in its own right;
or in which what is sensed may be said to be known?

The answer is evidently to be found in the circular aspect
of sensory adjustment, where the sensory process returns
to its point of origin and renews its source. When we say
that a sensory stimulation such as a sound, "attracts attention
to itself," we mean that it evokes from the sensitive organism
a specific reaction which attunes the organism to the sound,
and prolongs or perfects its receptivity thereto. In so far
as all sensation implies attention to the stimulus, there may
be said to be some degree of sensory cognition whenever
sensation occurs at all, but the state would be one of pure
sensory cognition only when the response was wholly directed
to the stimulus. Whether pure sensory cognition in this sense
ever occurs, it is unprofitable to argue. There is no reason
why it should not occur. While most sensory stimuli acquire

ulterior meanings which are aroused when these stimuli recur, there may be novel stimuli which have as yet acquired no ulterior meanings; there are sudden stimuli, which require a period of attentive prolongation before their meanings are evoked; there are levels of sub-human or primitive experience, in which a sensory alertness or watchfulness seems to be the only characteristic response; and there are phases of human experience in which whether through the recrudescence of primitive mentality, or the development of the aesthetic interest, all reactions appear to be suspended save the play of sensory adjustment.

Sensory cognition may then be defined as the case in which a sensory stimulus means itself. The object cognized is that to which the organism is sensorially accommodated. This will include not only the specific character and intensity of the stimulus, or the so-called sense *quale,* but also its more or less finely localized *out-thereness,* its temporal *imminence,* and its *objectivity* or 'givenness.' These make up what is commonly spoken of as the 'sense of reality' or 'vividness,' which characterizes sensation as distinguished from imagination.

When sensory cognition is so construed it is possible to understand its alleged freedom from error. It is not infallible in the sense that it is constitutionally incompatible with error, but only in the sense that liability to error is reduced to a minimum. It is the threshold of error, or the limiting case in the order of certainty. In sensory cognition there is a reference to contingency, an anticipation of stimulus-to-come, of more-of-the-same, of stimulus-out-there. There is, in short, expectation; and expectation is always at the mercy of events. But in the case of sensory cognition the verdict of events is continuously pronounced, without interval of suspense. Verification immediately precedes and follows hypothesis. There is room for doubt, but this room is indivisible; being like the point and the instant, a locus without extension. The improbability of a slip approaches infinity as the interval between the cup and the lip approaches zero.

The case of sensation exhibits the characteristic physiognomy of cognition in such close quarters that its features are distinguishable only with difficulty. Even so, one may trace the *tetradic structure* which becomes more and more evident as cognition is developed and schematized. There is what is immediately sensed, and there is the sensing of it; there is what is about to be sensed, and there is the preparatory sensing of it. In the case of sensory cognition these differences appear in the minimum degree, because the ulterior object differs from the present object, and the ulterior act from the present act, only in respect of time; and because the present object and the present act stand in that peculiarly intimate relation, presently to be examined, in which the former is a datum.

This tetradic structure of cognition appears more explicitly in the analysis of *meaning* and accounts for the peculiar ambiguities which obscure this topic.

§ 134. **Meaning.** We have first to eliminate a purely logical or metaphysical sense of the term 'meaning,' which is not here in question. If we suppose an irreducible objective difference between universals and particulars, as, for example, between human nature and Marshal Foch, it is necessary to suppose a relation, equally objective, between the two. The first may be called the essence, connotation or intension of the second; and the second may be called the existence, denotation or extension of the first. Taken in one direction this relation constitutes definition, and in the other direction, exemplification or realization. The term 'meaning' is sometimes employed for this relation; and either of the terms taken in this relation may be called the meaning of the other.

But this relation does not at present interest us. Meaning in the sense germane to the present discussion occurs only when an act or state of mind intervenes. The question whether meaning in the logical or metaphysical sense may eventually be explained in terms of meaning in the psychological sense is not here prejudged. In any case, there remains a difference between the specific relation which characterizes the pair universal-particular, and that which characterizes the pair mind-object. Suppose that one thinks of human nature, and at the same time of a particular man, such as Marshal Foch. We have in this case a relational triangle whose three sides are: *a*, which relates the thinker to Marshal Foch; *b*, which relates the thinker to human nature; and *c*, which relates Marshal Foch to human nature. Then *a* and *b* are relations of the same type, while *c* is problematic. If *c* is a unique relation, we are not concerned with it at all; if it can be defined in terms of relations *a* and *b*, then these deserve prior consideration.

Even when so limited the nature of meaning is obscured by its existence in elliptical and incomplete forms, and by careless habits of speech. Let us take an example in which all relevant aspects of the situation are unmistakably present, and introduce such terms as may be necessary to identify these aspects unambiguously. The word 'Fire' (*A*) shouted in my presence, attracts my auditory attention to itself (*B*), and at the same time arouses in me the anticipatory response of extinguishing (*D*), whose complementary object is the event, fire (*C*).[17] Let us now note the several senses in which the term 'meaning' is applied to this situation. As in the case of the terms 'painting' and 'carving,' the form of the active participle is used for the product, or *relatum*, as well as for the activity itself; in other words, the term 'meaning' is used in place of the term 'meant.' There is a further verbal difficulty in the fact that there is no term in common usage to indicate *that which* means, the term 'sign' having, as we shall see, a more limited application.

(1) In the first place, *A* and *C* are said to mean *B* and *D* respectively, or *B* and *D* to be the meanings of *A* and *C*. The word 'Fire!' means something listened to, and the event fire, something to be put out. Meaning in this sense is the response to any object (together with the accompanying organic sensations, if any) taken as qualifying that object.

(2) But this relation may be taken in the reverse sense,

[17] The depth or reach of meaning in the case of the human mind may go far beyond these four terms, even to some "far-off divine event towards which the whole creation moves." But beyond these four terms the process involves no new *kind* of term.

and then B and D are said to mean A and C respectively. The listening means the object listened to, the extinguishing the object to be extinguished. It is important 'to distinguish the case in which D means C to an onlooker, from the case in which D means C without the intervention of any second mind. In the former case, D is a 'sign,' in a sense yet to be defined. It is the latter case which is here intended. It would commonly be described in such terms as, "I mean 'Fire!' "; or my fetching and application of water (D) define, point to, or refer to the occurrence of fire (C) as their complementary object. D may be said to be the "idea of" C, in the simplest sense. It may be carried to the point of the imagination of C, or it may be attended by organic sensations. Provided both of these factors are absent, as appears to be possible, then there occurs what is sometimes referred to as "imageless thought."

(3) A may be said to mean C, that is, the word 'Fire!' may be said to mean that event, fire, for which it puts me in readiness. In this case A is said to be a 'sign' of C.[18] The word 'Fire!' will thus be a pure sign, or signal of alarm, in proportion as B is immediately superseded by D, or in so far as A functions vicariously for C.[19] This does not mean that C may be eliminated, for D is by definition a response to C, and it would cease to be this if it were simply transposed to A. In the case in which the word 'Fire!' arouses alarm entirely without reference to the occurrence

[18] The case in which I "understand" what another person means, is the case in which the response of another subject is a sign to me of the same object to which that response refers [in sense (2)], and in which my own response to the object takes the form of supposition rather than belief (cf. § 131).

[19] Cf. Mr. B. Russell's statement that meaning attaches to "signs," which are "sensible (or imaginal) phenomena which cause actions appropriate, not to themselves, but to something else with which they are associated." (*Mind*, Vol. XXIX, 1920, pp. 398, 402.) Cf. also James's account of meaning in terms of "experiences to be expected," in the article "Pragmatism," in J. M. Baldwin's *Dictionary of Philosophy and Psychology*; and C. K. Ogden and I. A. Richards, *The Meaning of Meaning*, 1923. An acute criticism of this last work is to be found in W. C. Swabey's "The Phenomenology of Experience and Psychologism," *Philos. Rev.*, Vol. XXXIII, 1924. This writer properly objects to the reduction of meaning to the function of signs, but his general attack on psychologism seems to me to under-rate the possibilities of psychology.

of fire, this alarm becomes a part of the immediate meaning of the word, in the first sense distinguished above.[20]

(4) Finally B may be said to mean D, or the listening to mean extinguishing. This meaning would ordinarily be imputed to the agent rather than to one of his acts, and one would say *he* means to extinguish. In so far as this is a case of pure cognition there would be no implication of a desire to extinguish, but only of an expectation so to act.[21] The agent at the moment of completing act B, would be inaugurating and shaping act D.

Reviewing the four modes of meaning which our analysis has revealed,[22] we discover an important difference between the first and fourth, on the one hand, and the second and third, on the other hand. When A means B, C means D, and B means D, the *meant* in each case is a state or act of the responding subject; when B means A, D means C and A means C, the meant is the object of response. It will be appropriate and convenient to speak of these two species of meaning as 'subjective' and 'objective' respectively. A subjective meaning always exists. Thus A could not be actually meaning B, or C, D, or B, D, unless the responses B and D were occurring in some form, whether partial or complete. Objective meaning, on the other hand, betrays its cognitive character in presenting a familiar difficulty. A

[20] "In order to maintain the strength of conditioned reflexes constant, they must be regularly and repeatedly *'reinforced'* by the unconditioned (original) stimulus" (C. L. Evans, *Recent Advances in Physiology*, 1926, p. 338). This suggests that the conditioned or associated stimulus may owe its effectiveness to its *meaning* the original stimulus.

[21] Or what is sometimes referred to as the 'intention' rather than the motive.

[22] The uses of the term 'meaning' have not been exhausted. Thus A may be said to mean C, and B, D. In fact it might not be wide of the mark to say that the only comprehensive definition of meaning is that which would extend it to all the relations internal to the cognitive tetrad. The term being so extended, one might then say that the mental is that which *means*, such as A, B, C and D in this analysis, A and C being mental content, and B and D mental activity.

Mention should perhaps also be made of the view which would identify meaning with the intimation of the whole by the part. My only objection to this view is that it is not sufficiently specific. In the foregoing analysis A–B, C–D, A–C, B–D, A–B–C–D, etc., constitute wholes of certain specific types, and one may always say that the meaning is the sequel, the complement, or the completion of that which means.

and *D* could mean *C,* even if there were no *C;* while in the case of *B* and *A* it is clear that one cannot strictly be said to be listening to a shout of "Fire!", if there is no such shout. Objective meanings, in other words, may or may not exist.

Here, then, are further distinctions and difficulties which will be brought into clearer light by the examination of the cognitive tetrad in its most explicit form, namely in judgment.

§ 135. **Judgment, Index, Predicate and Truth.** The present topic introduces no novel principle. Judgment is marked by the fact that it is, or may be, verbally expressed. This is both advantageous and disadvantageous: advantageous, in that the parts and varieties of the act of cognition are rendered more articulate and explicit; disadvantageous, in that the situation is complicated by the presence of the additional factors of expression, communication and language.[23] It seems quite evident that a judgment cannot be identified with any combination of words, since the same judgment may assume diverse verbal forms. The words "President Harding is dead" and "Death has numbered President Harding among its victims" *may* express the same judgment, the difference being due to habits of speech or the rhetorical conditions of effective communication. The subject-predicate form of sentence-structure, does, however, appear to express something constant and significant in the act of cognition itself, and the topic of judgment will therefore serve as a suitable occasion for the closer examination of this form, and of the cognitive variations to which it gives rise.

In judgment there is that *of* which something is judged, and there is that which is judged *about* it. The former is called the subject, and the latter the predicate. This distinction we may now interpret in terms of that tetradic structure which has been revealed by the analysis of expectation, sensation and meaning. We have seen that a complete cognitive act contains two component acts, one defining the *locus* or

[23] Cf. § 130.

occasion of verification [fulfilment or surprise], the other being that act which *is* fulfilled or surprised. Both of these acts have their objects, which constitute the subject and predicate of the judgment. As being both a less ambiguous and a more descriptive designation, the subject will hereinafter be termed the 'index,' while the two acts will be termed the acts of 'indication' and of 'predication' respectively. The act of indication serves to apply the act of predication to a specific context, and to transform it from a latent to an active form. It also serves the purpose of communication and 'instruction' by directing the attention of several subjects to a common locus, so that their findings are relevant, or so that they either agree or disagree. In other words, a state of judgment is an organization of mind, or dispositional system, such that when a first response, called the indicating response, occurs, there is a second response, called the predicative response, whose execution or non-execution begets fulfilment or surprise. This means that the indicating response inaugurates the predicative response; and that either fulfilment or surprise will occur according as the conditions which enable the indicative response to occur, either are or are not objectively associated with conditions permitting the occurrence of the predicative response.[24]

The moment of verification is the moment at which the indicative response occurs and the predicative response is launched. In order to provide for the possibility of *either* fulfilment or surprise at this moment, it must be possible that the predicative response should exist in an anticipatory form independently of those conditions which permit of its being consummated. This distinction between the anticipatory and consummatory phases of response is therefore essential to the understanding of judgment even in its simplest forms.

Let us suppose a total process, such as walking, swimming, or hearing a sound, to involve two factors, an environmental factor o, and a neuro-muscular response, r, so that the total

[24] Two responses may be reciprocally related as indication and predication. The conception of a *thing*, for example, is a system of responses such that any one may indicate any other.

process cannot occur without both factors in a mutual and complementary relation, which we may represent as *ro*. One cannot walk without ground to run on, or swim except in water, or hear a sound unless there be a sound to hear; that is, *r* cannot be consummated without *o*. But there are certain internal, organic phases of these responses which can occur in the absence of the appropriate external conditions. One can "start to" walk, swim, or hear, without ground, water or sound. Such incipient activity leaves so much the less to be done when the conditions requisite for execution appear. It may consist of certain preliminary innervations and accumulations of energy in the parts of the organism engaged in *r*, and in the inhibition or de-energizing of other parts. Anticipatory response, then, is this tributory process up to the point of confluence with the complementary object, *o*. It may be said to constitute a readiness to perform *r*, or an anticipation of *o*. To possess such an anticipatory response in the shape of neuro-muscular organization is to *know how* to walk, swim or hear; or is to know something, or possess some idea, of ground, water or sound. To *rehearse* this anticipatory response, or activate the preliminary phases of *r*, is to be thinking about *o*.

Let us now suppose that the anticipatory response is not only organized, but scheduled or timed. This means that it is suspended, checked, or inhibited, *until* released. This factor of release is itself a response, which we have distinguished as the indicative response. When the indicative response occurs the predicative response is launched, and there results either the harmony of fulfilment or the shock of surprise, according as its environmental complement, or the predicate, does or does not occur. In the one case the predicative response occurs instantly and easily, all the conditions of its occurrence being mobilized save the predicate. In the other case there occurs either a conflict of responses as a result of the appearance of something other than the predicate, or a malequilibrium owing to the momentum of the discharge in the absence of environmental resistance. In the one case the judgment proves true, and in the other case it proves erroneous; precisely as wood proves combustible or asbestos non-combustible when fire, the indicated condition of these properties, is supplied. A judgment is verifiable in *advance* of the moment of verification, in the same sense in which an object is combustible or non-combustible in the absence of fire.

§ 136. Forms of Objectivity.

The conception of response involves two factors, the responding act, and that to which the response is directed. We shall employ the term 'object' to refer to this second factor in the most inclusive sense, and we have now to consider several characteristic forms of objectivity.

When a response is consummated the object and the response are in some sense united. They form parts of a whole which can be designated either from the standpoint of the response, or from that of the object; as 'walking-on-ground' or 'ground-walked-on,' 'swimming-in-water' or 'water-swum-in,' 'hearing-sound' or 'sound-heard.' Strictly speaking, 'walking,' 'swimming' and 'hearing' are adequate designations, as implying all that is explicitly designated in these more awkward verbal forms; but the latter serve to stress the complexity, as the former serve to stress the unity, of the event. Where the relation of o and r is of this interactive type, such that each involves and is involved in the other, they must possess the same ontological status; so that whatever variety of being r possesses must be possessed by o also. Thus, if ro be the event of psycho-physical sensory stimulation, then o must possess physical existence; or, if ro be the event of introspection, then o must possess whatever mode of mental existence is possessed by the act of introspecting.[25]

When o is so related to r as to form part of a whole, ro, o is said to be a '*datum.*' This term has significance only relatively (that is, whatever is given must be given *to* or *for*), and conveys two implications, namely, immediacy and certainty. In ro, o is immediate to r in the sense of conjunction

[25] It must not be inferred that because o possesses physical existence it cannot possess mental existence, or *vice versa*. o may be on a line in which the physical and mental planes, or the planes of the self and not-self, etc., intersect.

or fusion; and o is certain relatively to r in the double sense, that whatever certainty attaches to r must attach also to o, and that r is acting on o and not doubting it.

But the conception of an objective datum owes its importance in philosophical discourse to the conception of an objective *non-datum*. This latter conception needs no further elucidation. It has been shown that certain activities of the organism can properly be described as parts of a total response which is incomplete for lack of its complementary object. The partial activity or anticipatory response is then said to *have* this object as *its* object, although the object clearly lacks that ontological status which would permit the response to be executed, and which it would have were it a datum. The object may then be termed a questionable, dubitable, or *problematic* object. This aspect of the cognitive situation may be crudely represented as follows:

$$(r') - ro - (o')$$

Whereas r is a completed response and o its complementary object or datum, (r') is the incomplete phase of that response r', whose complementary object is o'. We may then say that o' is the object of the actually existent (r'), whether o' exists or not. o' as so *related* to existence, independently of its *own* existence, is represented by (o').[26]

The verification of a judgment requires the introduction of one more mode of objectivity. Though the problematic object as such does not exist (that is, does not *necessarily* exist), that which is problematic *may* exist. The response may start when the complementary object is absent, but, fortunately, this object may, and usually does, arrive "in time." When the anticipatory response occurs the conditions then exist which *will* produce the object *when* it is needed for

[26] Students of philosophy will perhaps be reluctant to recognize another member of the growing family of quasi-entities, such as 'intentional inexistence,' 'objective,' 'subsistent,' 'possibility,' etc.; but I prefer the expression "problematic object" for present purposes because I wish to be just as non-committal as possible regarding metaphysical questions, and this expression does not take one beyond the context of the cognitive situation.

consumption. This can be represented by an adaptation of the schema already used: [27]

$$v$$
$$(r') \longrightarrow r \mid o \longleftarrow (o')$$

The vertical line v between r and o represents the locus of verification, at which r is consummated in o, or meets with the shock of surprise. The arrows indicate the moving of the series of responses and of the series of objects toward this locus; so that when (r') reaches v, it will there be met by o', and thus be enabled to enter into $r'o'$. The symbol (o') may now be taken to represent a present objective situation, simultaneous with (r'), but which determines the future occurrence of o' at v. Let us call this the *transcendent object,* assuming it to exist, and to be existing independently of that response whose verification it nevertheless guarantees.[28] We may then say that (r') is true, owing to (o'), in advance of v.

[27] The same situation could be represented by the figure in the Virginia reel in which the divided files of ladies and gentlemen converge to a point at which partners are "resumed." A gentleman approaching this point is prepared and scheduled to find a partner's hand to grasp when he gets there. If there is a lady in the corresponding place of the other file, then he is at present properly disposed and will be justified when the time comes. What happens to the unhappy gentleman who finds no partner or two partners just as the junction is about to be effected, exemplifies what is meant by a 'mistake.'

Employing another figure, cognition may be thought of as the progressive coalescence of two solids, the plane surface contact representing sensation, and the depths representing meaning and expectation. The two solids might be regarded as intersected by vertical planes which meet successively at the point of contact, as they take their places at the front. There will be a correlation between these two series, by which each objective plane is determined to be that which fulfils or surprises a certain specific subjective plane.

[28] Employing this schematism and terminology, the problem of perception hinges on the question of the precise sort of whole constituted by $r'o'$ (immediate sensory experience); and the extent, if any, to which (r') and (o') are transformed when they enter into it. Or, it is a question of how much of $r'o'$ is lost when it is analyzed into these two constituents.

Because r' and o' do form a whole it does not follow that they are not more or less completely preserved in it. They may effect a contact or conjunction rather than a fusion, and that which they are jointly, may embody proportionally more of the one than of the other. In other words, the familiar alternatives of realism and idealism, primary and secondary qualities, etc., remain open.

In brief, the ground walked on, the water swum in and the sound heard, are data; the ground one is about to set foot on, the water one is going to swim in, and the sound one is listening for, are problematic objects; the ground, water and sound that are *there to be* walked on, swum in and heard, are transcendent objects.

It will be convenient to use the term 'objective' for the object-side of a total judgment. It will contain both the index and the predicate. The objective of a judgment is always problematic. This is because at the moment of judgment the act of predication is as yet an anticipatory response, whose object is problematic, and which contributes at least this element of doubt to the objective of which it is a constituent. When this element of doubt is entirely removed at the moment of verification, the judgment ceases to exist as such. There has been a judgment, and it may be superseded by new judgments, but that particular judgment is terminated.

When the judgment is true the index and predicate must both be either data or transcendent objects. They must not only be existent on the same plane with the responding organism, but they must be so related to one another as to constitute what is commonly called a *fact*. It is not necessary to suppose that there is any unique objective relation that constitutes the inner bond of a fact. The kind of relation will depend on the kind of object. Thus the relation of 'sky' and 'blue' in the fact designated as the 'sky's being blue,' is different from the relation of 'John' and 'brother of James,' in the fact, 'John's being brother of James.' From the standpoint of judgment, a fact is such a connection of the objects of two responses, as shall justify the response to the one on the occasion presented by the other; or such a union of objects, as shall be complementary to a union of their respective responses. The fact constituted of *o* and *o'* is the objective condition of the execution of a response compounded of *r* and *r'*, the response which is said to *"treat o as o'."*

The fact that index and predicate may be either data or

problematic objects accounts for a difference of simplicity and complexity to which we now turn.

§ 137. **Simple and Complex Judgments.** The simple judgment will be that in which *at the moment of verification* both the act of indication and the act of predication are consummatory acts. There is then no propriety in describing either the act of indication or the act of predication as true or false. This limiting case is exemplified by such judgments as "that [to which I am pointing] looks blue," or "this [which I am masticating] tastes sweet." In such cases the index is a datum, and the predicate becomes a datum at the moment of verification provided the judgment is true.

But the function of indication may be exercised by an anticipatory response as well as by a consummatory response; that is, the act of indication may be the act of predication released by an anterior act of indication. Thus in the judgment "American Beauty roses are sweet," the act of indication is the judgment, "there are American Beauty roses," for it is the occurrence of this constituent judgment which releases the expectation of sweet savor. This indicative judgment is not verified, that is, one does not prove the system of anticipatory responses which define its predicate; but these anticipatory responses, occurring as 'meaning,' exercise the function of indication. Whatever arouses them, they occasion my fulfilment or surprise at the occurrence or non-occurrence of the sweet savor.[29]

Similarly, a judgment may be proved by an anticipatory response as well as by a consummatory response; that is, the act of predication may be the indication of an ulterior predicate. In the judgment, "The man whom you will find in the next room is your father," the predicate is the judgment "this is my father," which consists in a certain system of anticipatory responses to a visual appearance. These anticipatory responses

[29] When the predicative response of the major judgment is one of the system of responses which defines the predicate of the indicative judgment, the major judgment is called, in the Kantian sense, "analytic"; otherwise, it is called "synthetic."

may verify the major judgment without themselves being verified. The major judgment is proved, or there occurs a moment of fulfilled expectation, when I recognize someone *as* my father.

Complexity of judgment thus consists in the fact that either the index or the predicate or both may be a problematic objective rather than a datum. This complexity is psychologically possible, and is compatible with the swift movement of thought, by virtue of the fact that these component judgments are not themselves verified. They are none the less true or false inasmuch as they provide occasions for fulfilment or surprise, according as the objects do or do not exist.

It is owing to the fact that objectives may serve both to indicate and to verify judgments that the cognitive life of man is so inscrutable. It may be carried on without any data whatsoever, and in this case its object is not revealed to an external observer of the physical environment. Or even when the judgment is indicated by a datum, this may indicate indirectly through being the index of an indicating judgment; in which case the datum is ambiguous as regards the major judgment. Thus the sound of the noon whistle may indicate the arrival of a train or the hour for dinner, and these judgments, functioning as indices of complex judgments, may be predicated very differently.

Furthermore, since the judgment may terminate in an objective rather than in a datum, its object cannot be identified by observing the conclusion of the judgment. The complex judgments cited may be verified by the judgments "this is the dinner table," or "my friend has arrived." In short, the course of thought cannot in this case be traced, nor its objects identified, by the observation of overt behavior in which the organism interacts with its physical environment.

§ 138. **Attributive, Existential and Ideal Judgments.** A further classification of judgments which will prove useful for the understanding of the rôle of cognition in interest, is that which turns upon the relation between the act of indication and the act of predication. In the judgments "some horses are white," "it is raining to-day," or "this is my father," the act of indication and the act of predication are qualitatively different responses. Each is independently determined, and the two are integrated in the state of judgment, in which the one is attributed to the other. Judgments of this type may be termed 'attributive.'

In the judgment, "the white horse exists" the act of predication expressed by the word 'exists' consists only in the reiteration or prolongation of the act of indication itself. It will be convenient to term this mode of judgment 'existential.' Such a judgment is verified by the recurrence or non-recurrence of the act of indication. The contingency which determines fulfilment or surprise is the persistence of the conditions which enable the act of indication to occur, or their persistence long enough to enable this act to be repeated. Judgments of this type, which may be either simple or complex, may be termed judgments of identity, because they predicate nothing new of the subject; or, because they predicate the subject of itself; or, because there is no difference between the subject and predicate save the temporal difference which distinguishes the acts of indication and of predication. Special importance attaches to simple judgments of identity in which the act of indication is a consummatory response and the index is a datum.[30] Such is the judgment "this white (at which I am looking) exists," where the act of predication is a reiteration of the act of looking by which the index is identified, and where the act of looking involves the existence of its object. These may be termed judgments of existence in the strictest sense. The index must occur, and the predicate, which differs only temporally from the index, must have occurred, and be about to occur. The object of such a judgment is the unit of known existence, or the least existence with reference to which there yet remains the possibility of error.

In the judgment "there is such a thing as a white horse," or "somewhere there is a white horse," or "something is a white horse," the act of predication is ambiguously indicated. The predicative response is prepared at large. Its occurrence on

[30] Cf. sensory cognition, § 143.

any occasion will fulfil it, and only its occurrence on *no* occasion will disprove it. Surprise is the cumulative effect of its non-occurrence, rather than the crucial effect of a single non-occurrence. This type of judgment may be said to be freely creative in the sense that it is conditioned only internally. In the attributive judgment the predicative response is conditioned by the occurrence of a specific indicative response other than itself. In the existential judgment the predicative response is conditioned by its own prior occurrence, and in the stricter case it is existentially or "empirically" conditioned. But in the type of judgment here considered the predicative response is determined by nothing outside of itself. In order to emphasize this peculiar rôle of the predicate, and its freedom from external conditions, we shall term this type of judgment speculative or *ideal* judgment.

There is no limit to the formation of ideal judgments save the requirement that they shall be "significant," or that they shall mean "something"; by the requirement, in other words, that they shall have an objective. Anticipatory responses may be combined to any extent provided only they constitute a genuine anticipatory response when they are combined. The rules which govern the formation of ideal judgments or hypotheses, are the rules of discourse or of grammar. The terms 'blue' and 'horse' being determinate expectations severally, the phrase 'a blue horse,' being grammatically correct, expresses an integral expectation, which is significant despite its empirical falsity. The phrase 'round square' is significant despite its contradictoriness. This contradictoriness is brought to light only when for the ideal judgment "there are round squares" there is substituted an attributive judgment such as "squares are round." [31]

[31] I do not, of course, mean to deny that the falsity of the judgments 'some squares are round' and 'the round square exists' precludes the truth of the judgment 'there are round squares'; but only to affirm that this last judgment can be enacted without being indicated either by the datum 'this square,' or by the judgments 'this is a square,' 'the square is round,' etc. I am, in other words, attempting to provide for the peculiar unconditionality that finds expression in the terms 'there are' or 'there is.' The wide range of significant possibilities is due to the fact that responses may be combined in their incipient stages although they prove incompatible as they approach their object.

§ 139. **Knowledge of the Past.** In our analysis of cognition we have heretofore made use of expressions such as expectation, persistence and anticipatory response, which imply that the moment of verification lies ahead of the moment of belief. An act of cognition is fallible by virtue of the fact that it is *not yet* proved; or by virtue of the fact that some determined event which is *yet to come* will, according as it does or does not occur, either fulfil or surprise the knowing subject. There appears to be no escape from the fact that cognition is thus an appeal to the future. How, then, can cognition have a past event as its object? This and kindred difficulties have led many philosophers to abandon altogether the notion that the subject of cognition sustains a temporal relation to its objects, and is one of the standing objections to a naturalistic account of cognition such as is here proposed.

Those who, like James, have been disposed to regard the cognitive subject as a part of physical nature, operating in the same temporal field as its objects, have proposed to define knowledge of the past in terms of the still impending results of the past.[32] It is argued that an archaeologist's hypothesis is verified by the finding of certain records or remains which the hypothesis leads him to expect. Thus believing that Tutankhamen *was* buried in a certain hillside, one looks there for certain marks of royalty, and the belief is true according as it prepares one for what the excavation discloses. Similarly, hearing noises in the night which I take to be rain on the roof, I arise in the morning with conviction that it *has rained*, and am surprised when I look out of the window and find no "evidences" of it. My morning expectation fails to fit the antecedent facts of the night by virtue of being maladapted to certain of their results which still await me. Or the announcement at the breakfast-table by some other member of the family, that "it rained last night," results in my putting on rubbers before I go out; in other words, begets in me a protective, anticipatory response to the results of

[32] Cf. W. James, *The Problem of Truth,* 1909, pp. 221-224.

rain. This forward looking attitude to the past is sometimes expressed by saying "I expect that it rained last night."

This account undoubtedly satisfies many cases of cognition which are verbally expressed by the past tense. That it does not cover all of the facts is, however, easily proved. If this were all, then in the case last cited there would be nothing but a verbal difference between the judgments "It rained last night," and "The grass is wet." They would both express the same disposition of mind, and the latter would express it more accurately than the former. In order that the first judgment shall express something which the second does not, the past tense must be significant of something inherent in the disposition itself. The words 'last night' must mean something to somebody as establishing the locus of the supposed occurrence of the rain, as distinguished from that of the supposed occurrence of the wet grass. The subject of cognition must, in other words, be capable of a direct reference or pointing to the past.[33] There must be responses of which the past can be said to be the object. Unless this capacity is assumed, it is not only impossible to remove the ambiguity attaching to such judgments as have been cited, but it is also impossible to account for those cases of memory-judgment, such as, "I heard it rain last night," in which the past reference is unmistakable.

Contrary to a widespread belief there is no logical difficulty in supposing that a present act of cognition may refer to a past event as its object. That I should now think of last night does not imply that last night occurs now, but only that the thinking occurs now.[34] There is no reason whatever why the two terms related as meaner and meant should not, like effect and cause, be *also* related as later and earlier, or

---

[33] Cf. B. Russell, "On the Experience of Time," *Monist*, Vol. XXV, 1915. According to this writer the possibility of "immediate memory" must be assumed in order to account for the meaning attaching to 'past' as distinguished from 'earlier than.' In immediate memory the recent past is an object of 'knowledge by acquaintance' (p. 225). Cf. this same writer's *Analysis of Mind*, 1921, Lect. IX, pp. 174-175, and *passim*.

[34] For a discussion of this alleged difficulty, and for a fuller analysis of the whole question, cf. my "Knowledge of Past Events," *Jour. of Philos.*, Vol. III, 1906.

present and past. It remains only to indicate this reference to the past more clearly and more concretely.

It appears to consist in the act of recollection, that is to say, in the reëxcitation of responses uniquely correlated with certain events in the past history of the organism. We have already seen that the organism's preparatory responses are arranged in an order of depth which is correlated with the march of coming events. It is equally true that the traces of past responses are deposited and stored in the order of their original occurrence. The order of projected responses at any given period may or may not coincide with the order of their acquisition; it will not always coincide, because it is continuously readapted to unfolding events and modified by the shifting control of governing propensities. This coincidence is closest when the organism is functioning under the control of attentive recall, that is, when one is "trying to remember." When one remembers that it *rained* last night, the index of the judgment is "last night"; that is to say, one revives any response to an event of that time. This revival then defines the locus for which the rain-response is set. If when so set the rain-response also occurs in the order of revival, one's memory judgment is verified, and it may be confirmed by a similar coincidence of recall on the part of another organism which is set for the same period.

In such "searching" of the memory, one may literally be said to *expect*. The predicative revival whose occurrence verifies the judgment of memory, occurs after the judgment itself. The past may be either a datum or an objective, and judgments of the past may be either simple or complex. In the former case, the act of indication and the verifying act of predication are revivals of past consummatory responses, and these acts are themselves consummatory in the sense that their occurrence depends causally on the past occurrence of their objects. The only factor of contingency is the consummation of the act of predication *on the occasion of* the act of indication. In complex judgments of the past the act of indication, or the act of predication, or both, are anticipatory responses. The judgment that "it rained last night," may signify "remembering to have thought last night that it rained," and its confirmation by other witnesses may signify that they also remember to have thought that it was raining. There is thus in complex memory a double chance of error. One may now be mistaken as to what one thought last night, that is, one's memory may be false; and one may have then thought incorrectly. It may be that it was not last night, but the night before, when one had the impression of falling rain; and it may be that it was wind, and not rain, which produced the impression. It is peculiar to a complex judgment of the past that it can never be wholly reduced to simple judgments. A past anticipatory response may be revived and its conjunction with other past responses may be verified, but it cannot be consummated. If its object was an objective, it must always remain an objective. This is due to the fact that in knowledge of the past a specific time is a constituent of the object. If an object so constituted were to change from an objective to a datum, or to become a datum at a later time, it would have lost its identity.

The chance of error in knowledge of the past is reduced to a minimum when the original sequence of responses is so recent as to leave no gaps between it and the present. Memory therefore approximates infallibility in so far as it takes the form of the recall of the immediate sensory past, as in the judgment "I have just heard a noise." I may easily be mistaken in judging that it rained last night because it may not have been rain that I heard, and it may have been night before last that I heard it. But I am unlikely to be mistaken in judging that "I have just heard a noise,—the sound of it is still ringing in my ears." In the latter case the original response was instantly and continuously verified, and its recall is a reverberation of the original occurrence, which maintains a qualitative constancy as it recedes and dies away.

Memory is an inadequate instrument of historical knowledge because of the shortness of its span, because it is limited to what has been already known, and because the earlier knowledge which is recalled cannot now be verified. The only way of acquiring knowledge beyond the range of memory, or of acquiring *new* knowledge of the past, is to frame judgments regarding its persistent causal results that may be verified by future experience. But the fact remains that in order to refer such knowledge to the past the individual must relate it to his memories. The prehistoric world lies beyond the horizon of memory, but it is oriented by that horizon. The imagination of the past is an imagination of the *past,* only so far as the station of the hypothetical observer is fixed by the direction of memory. To imagine what Athens looked like in the age of Pericles is to set a determinate visual expectation for an occasion which lies more or less remotely upon a projection of my own past. Similarly, what I learn of the nearer past is interpolated among my memories, and usually ends by becoming indistinguishable from them.

In the judgment of the past both the act of indication and the act of predication must be acts of memory, the past being predicated of the past, and the connection between index and predicate whose occurrence makes the judgment true being a connection *in* the past. To judge that my hair is black, where the act of indication is the revival of a past visual response, and the act of predication the expectation of a prospective visual response, is not a judgment of the past, because it is verified not by what I remember, but by what I see. Similarly, a judgment of the past may be the index of a judgment which is not a judgment of the past, as when I judge that my hair which was once black is now gray. This may be said to be a judgment *about* the past, but not a judgment *of* the past, since the contingent event which proves it true embraces both past and present.

CHAPTER XII

THE RÔLE OF COGNITION IN INTEREST

1. THE MEDIATION OF INTEREST BY COGNITION

§ 140. The Interest-Judgment. Having distinguished cognition and interest, and having analyzed cognition in its own terms, we are now prepared to follow the interweaving and functional interdependence of these two factors without losing sight of their difference.

It has often been remarked, and in particular by Meinong,[1] that the structure of desire is similar to that of judgment. As I judge "that rain will fall to-morrow," so I may desire "that rain shall fall to-morrow"; both cases being marked by a clause beginning with the conjunction 'that,' and denoting what we have termed an 'objective.' We have found that in the case of judgment the objective is divisible into index and predicate, the former being that which is judged *about*, and the latter that which is judged about it. Similarly in desire there is that of which I desire something, and that which I desire of it. The former may be termed the index, and the latter the predicate of interest.

Before elaborating the varieties of interest which follow from this structural analogy between interest and judgment, let us first restate that which distinguishes interest from judgment. This differential factor may now be described in terms of the reciprocal determination of the act of indication and the act of predication. In judgment the act of indication releases the act of predication, and induces fulfilment or surprise according as the act of predication is or is not executed. In interest the fact that the act of indication and the act of

[1] *Ueber Annahmen*, 1910, §§ 24, 25.

344

predication are so connected is a condition of the occurrence of the act of indication. *The act of indication occurs owing to the prospective occurrence of the act of predication.* This implies that the agent is predisposed to the act of predication independently of the act of indication, as is the case when the act of predication coincides or is congruent with a governing propensity. The act of predication is such that it advances or consummates a response which at the moment has right of way, or priority in the disposal of the organism's energies. The act of predication fulfils or surprises in so far as it does or does not occur as indicated. It induces *satisfaction* or *disappointment* in so far as, over and above its opportuneness or inopportuneness relatively to the act of indication, it is also congruent or incongruent with the governing propensity. Interest is thus functionally more complex than cognition.

To judge that there is money in my purse, signifies that the act of dealing with money (seeing it or handling it) is so connected with the act of opening the purse that the former is released by the latter. If when I open the purse my anticipatory dealing with money is thereupon executed, my judgment is fulfilled or proved true. To desire that there shall be money in my purse signifies that the act of dealing with money is in agreement with a governing propensity such as avarice or need, which predisposes me to its performance independently of my response to the purse. The opening of the purse, possessing the function of releasing the money-response, may then occur because of this fact, or because of what is expected of it. If when I open the purse I see or handle money, my judgment is fulfilled because what I expected has happened; and my interest is satisfied, because what has happened also harmonizes with my governing propensity. While I can judge that there is money in my purse without desiring it, I cannot desire it without judging it. I cannot open the purse because of what I expect of it, unless I expect something of it. The money in the purse can fulfil without satisfying, or its absence can surprise without disappointing; but I cannot be satisfied without fulfilment of expectation, or be disappointed without being surprised. This cognitive factor which is essential to the interest as such, or which *mediates* the interest as a whole, may be termed the *interest-judgment;* and its object is the object of the interest as a whole, or the end. It is the fallibility of this judgment which renders all interest fallible. As all judgment is liable to error, so all interest is by virtue of the interest-judgment liable to failure or disappointment.

To act interestedly argues both an interest-judgment, and a governing propensity so correlated therewith as to make it possible to infer the one when the other is known. If the agent is asked to explain his action in terms of his governing propensity, he will state his interest-judgment; if he is asked to explain it in terms of his interest-judgment, he will state his governing propensity. Thus a politician who consents to be interviewed for the press, will refer to his desire for office, if he supposes you to be familiar with the effects of publicity; and will argue that it pays to advertise, if he supposes you to be acquainted with his ambitions. That he should perform an act attended with such an expectation, is accounted for by his governing propensity; that with such a governing propensity he should act when and as he does, is to be accounted for in terms of his expectation.

The act of predication is open to pressure from two sides: on the one hand, through its connection with the act of indication; and, on the other hand, through its connection with the governing propensity. This fact may result in the occurrence of the act of predication when it is not indicated, or to its strong occurrence when it is only faintly indicated. The contamination of judgment by interest, or the inopportune predication of that which one is disposed to predicate, is a prolific source of error and a besetting weakness of the intellect.

§ 141. The Causal Efficacy of the Interest-Judgment.

The judgment that there is money in my purse does not of itself tend to create the conditions of its own fulfilment. It signifies a disposition to deal with money *when* I open my purse, but not a disposition to open it.   The desire that there shall be money in my purse, on the other hand, signifies that I am disposed to do that of which dealing with money is expected; and, therefore, that in so far as the expectation is true, the dealing with money will occur.   In other words, interest has the effect, so far as the interest-judgment is true, of transforming the object of that judgment from a problematic into an existent object; while mere judgment unattended by interest, has no such effect.   This is what is meant by the impotence of the purely intellectual act.

Interest does, therefore, have a certain existential purport, in the sense that it tends to bring its object into existence. This has given rise to the confused notion that existence or creation is an invariable constituent of the object of interest.[2] This view possesses plausibility only in so far as the essentially motor character of interest is obscured.   To be interested in an object is so to act as to bring that object into existence, that is, into the same domain as the act itself.   In this sense interest is existential.   But when the existential factor is thus conceived as belonging to the nature of the *act* of interest, it becomes manifestly absurd to conceive it as the predicate, as that *in* which the interest is taken.   For then we should have to say that to be interested in *a* is to bring into existence the existence of *a*.   "To desire peace" is not an elliptical expression for "to desire the existence of peace"; but "to desire the existence of peace" is a redundant expression for "to desire peace," because the factor of prospective existence is already contained in the nature of the act of desire.

The same is true of the act of production or achievement. One may argue that "desiring peace" is an elliptical expression for "desiring to *make* peace," or "desiring wealth," an elliptical expression for "desiring to obtain wealth."   But this is true only in the sense that the making or obtaining, the bring-

---

[2] It would be more exact to say that interest conduces to the existence of its object so far as circumstances permit.   Interest may as a matter of fact not be a necessary condition of the existence of its object, nor even an effective condition, and yet be said to confirm its existence through presupposing it, or through being prepared to promote its existence in hypothetical contingencies.   Cf. "acquiescent interest," § 107, and "interest in the past," § 145.

ing to pass, is a part of what is meant by desire. Similarly, the view that such a causal factor is a universal predicate of interest,[3] is a confusion arising from the fact that desiring is a kind of causing. It is virtually redundant to say that one is interested in the causing, because this amounts to saying that "to be interested in *a*," means "to cause the causing of *a*." Such redundancy may be used for rhetorical effect, as when the apostle praises running a good race and fighting a good fight; but, strictly speaking, producing, achieving, or other causal activity is a *universal* feature of interest only as a constituent of being interested, and not as a constituent of that in which one is interested. This does not preclude the possibility that a causal activity should *in any given case* be the object of interest. This possibility is realized when, and only when, there is a second causal activity which conduces to the first; as when, desiring to paint a picture, one so acts as to obtain the skill or bring to pass the circumstances which condition the act of painting.

In short, the object of interest, or the end, is whatever objective tends by virtue of being judged, and so far as judged truly, to become an existent object. Or it is the object of judgment when the judge by virtue of judging it, is a condition favorable to its existence. Anything which can be judged is thus qualified to be an object of interest.[4]

It has been objected that the causal efficacy of the interest-judgment is a "paradox" because its object is its own effect.[5] Such a paradox exists, however, only in the absence of the distinction between the problematic and the transcendent objects. It is the former which is a constituent of the

---

[3] Cf. § 29.

[4] To be qualified to be the object of *specific modes* of interest, such, for example, as the aesthetic interest, the object may require to be judged in terms of specific predicates, which thus determine the relevance of disputes concerning matters of taste. Cf. § 255. There is no other criterion of *desirability* than the capacity to be judged. Cf. Ch. III, Sect. III.

[5] Thus Professor Dewey says that "the object of a practical judgment is some change, some alteration to be brought about in the given, the nature of which change depends upon the judgment itself and yet constitutes the subject-matter of judgment" ("The Logic of Judgments of Practice," *Jour. of Philos.*, Vol. XII, 1915, pp. 521-522). Cf. the present writer's "Dewey and Urban on Value Judgments," *ibid.*, Vol. XIV, 1917.

interest-judgment, and which, *as such,* is a cause of the latter. The effect of the interest-judgment is the *realization* of its own object, implying that what *becomes* real as a *result* of the interest-judgment was not real when the interest-judgment itself occurred. Nor is there any paradox in supposing that the event whose future occurrence makes the judgment true now, and which when it occurs will verify the judgment, should be an effect of this judgment. Indeed, *all* interest appears to exemplify James's notion that a belief may make itself come true.[6]

§ 142. **The Mediated Index of Interest.** We have found that complex judgments arise from the fact that the indication of a judgment, or its predication, or both, may themselves be judgments. We have now to note that a judgment may serve as the index or as the predicate of an interest. All interests are mediated by an interest-judgment, and when this is the only cognitive factor in judgment the interest may be said to be simply mediated. When the index or predicate or both are judgments it may be said to be complexly mediated.

In the case of a simply mediated interest the act of indication, and the act of predication at the moment of verification, are consummatory acts. The interest is indicated and satisfied by data; or is indicated by a datum, and disappointed by the non-occurrence of a datum. In the complexly mediated interest, on the other hand, an objective, rather than a datum, serves in one or both of these capacities.

Let us consider, first, the case of the interest with a mediated index, in contrast with the simply mediated interest. The cry of "Fire!" arouses the anticipatory visual response to red flames, which according as it is consummated or not proves a true or false judgment of the simple type, In the case of the small boy who is eager to see a fire, or who is looking for a fire to see, the consummatory indicative act of hearing the alarm, or the auditory datum, is in some measure *due* to its being conjoined with this expectation. He is listening

[6] *Will to Believe,* 1897, p. 59.

for what promises the spectacle of a fire, is peculiarly attentive to such stimuli, or places himself in a situation where they are likely to occur; and is correspondingly unreceptive to other stimuli. This is a simply mediated interest. The mediated index, on the other hand, is illustrated by the case in which the cry of "Fire!" arouses the fear of fire. One is not afraid of the cry of "Fire!", but of the 'red-flames-there,' that is, of the objective of a judgment of which the cry of "Fire!", or auditory datum, is the index. This judgment is not verified. One is afraid, simply, of what one takes the auditory datum to *mean*. The fear may be occasioned or indicated even if the red flames are fictitious, for these exercise their function of indicating the interest, in a problematic and not in an existential capacity.

Most human interests are indicated by what one judges of data rather than by the data themselves. Thus I love him whom I "take to be" my friend, and grieve at "the news of" his death; or I admire what I "suppose" others to admire; or hate that which I "think to be" a lie; or otherwise react interestedly to things *as I conceive them.* In all such cases the fallibility of interest is doubled. There is not only an interest-judgment but also an indicative judgment which is liable to error. My interest may not only be misguided as regards its determining expectation, but be based upon a misconception.[7]

§ 143. **The Mediated Predicate of Interest.** The predicate of interest is, as we have seen, defined by an anticipatory response of which it is the *object,* as anticipatory eating, for example, constitutes an anticipation *of food.* Anticipatory eating is not the anticipation of eating. In order that this should occur it would be necessary to suppose another anticipatory response, or the partial execution of a response whose consummation would require *eating.* To say that the act of eating is required for the consummation of the act of eating

[7] Cf. § 44. For further examples, the reader may consult Ch. V, Ehrenfel's discussion of *"vermittelten Wertungen,* in his *System der Werttheorie,* 1897, Vol. I, pp. 75, 103.

is a meaningless redundancy. It is psychologically possible to anticipate the act of eating, as when one prepares one's after-dinner speech or one's post-prandial siesta. But in no case does the anticipatory response anticipate itself.

Unless we adhere strictly to this definition of the predicate in terms of *the object* of the anticipatory response, rather than the response itself, we shall be hopelessly confused by the ambiguities of popular verbal usage. But this distinction being carefully observed, we are prepared to deal with those verbal expressions of interest in which the anticipatory response is employed as the grammatical predicate. One may say, for example, that one desires "to eat his dinner," or "to smell a rose" or "to hold the baby" or "to possess wealth." Or, it may be argued that all expressions of interest are elliptical in so far as they do not contain a verb denoting the response; in other words, that to desire *a,* is to desire to do something with, to, or about, *a.* Thus "desiring wealth" is said to be an ellipsis for "desiring [to expend] wealth," or "desiring [to exhibit] wealth," or "desiring [to control] wealth." We now understand that this argument has force only in so far as it emphasizes the existence and modal varieties of the anticipatory *response,* and its rôle as linking the object with the motor disposition of the subject. It proves the importance of providing for the *act* of predication over and above the predicate itself.

There is, however, the special case in which a response is itself the predicate, as when it is the *expenditure* of wealth which I desire, or which attracts me because of some ulterior governing propensity, such as pride. In this case the act of expending wealth is the complementary object of a self-congratulatory or boastful response; the former being anticipated, the latter being the anticipatory response. Similarly, we may distinguish between the case in which one "desires to see one's *friend,*" where it is the friend who is desired, and the seeing which is the anticipatory response; and the case in which the blind man "desires to *see* his friend," where it is the seeing which is desired, and the whole prospective sequel of restored vision which is the anticipatory response. In all cases to anticipate *a* is to execute the earlier stages of a response which requires *a* for its consummation.   It follows that where *a* is itself a response, it must be anticipated in terms of *ulterior* responses of which the *a*-response itself is the object.

Whatever can be anticipated can be the predicate of interest.   In the case of simply mediated interest the interest is satisfied by the consummation of the act of predication, and the predicate becomes a datum, as in the case of the gratification of the senses and appetites.   But as a judgment may be verified, so an interest may be satisfied, by an act which is itself a judgment.   The desire to see my friend may be satisfied by the judgment "this is my friend," maternal love may be satisfied by "the news of" the child's well-being, or avarice by the belief that one's possessions are augmented. In such cases the predicative act of judgment satisfies by virtue of what is judged, in the absence of verification; it satisfies, in other words, by an objective rather than by a datum.   The interest is then fallible, or liable to error, in respect of its predicate.

All interests are fallible in respect of the interest-judgment.   Over and above this universal fallibility, an interest may also be fallible in respect of its index, its predicate or both.   The man who consults the physician does so for the sake of the recovery which he expects of it.   Recovery may or may not follow from consulting physicians, that is, the interest-judgment may be true or false.   But he may be in error in supposing that he is consulting a physician; and he may also be in error, at the moment of satisfaction, in supposing that he has recovered.

§ **144. Attributive, Existential and Ideal Interests.** Interests may be classified according as the interest-judgment is *attributive, existential or ideal.*[8]

In attributive interest the act of indication and the act of predication, or what one is interested *in,* and one's interest in it, are qualitatively different.   The interest takes things as

[8] Cf. § 138.

they are, and modifies them. There is an adaptive factor and an aggressive factor, and the proportion between them may vary.[9] This type of interest is exemplified by the desire "that the rainfall should be heavy," or that "the stranger should be kind," or that "Europe should be at peace." The interest makes one thing of another. Such interests may be simply or complexly mediated. I may desire the rainfall to be heavy, when the rainfall is a datum, or when the rainfall is an objective. I may desire the stranger to be kind when at the moment of verification kindness is the object of a consummatory act, or the objective of a judgment. Or I may desire that what I take to be peace should occur in what I take to be Europe, both the index and the predicate being objectives.

In existential interest the act of predication is a prolongation of the act of indication. The indicative act occurs because it forecasts its own object. One looks at the color for the sake of the color to look at. Interest of this type does not alter its object, but on the contrary conserves it as it is. It is the case of wanting what one has. It is called existential because it asks nothing of the environment save that it shall continue to be what it is; or because it takes the form of preserving the *status quo*.[10]

The ideal interest, like the ideal judgment, is ambiguously indicated, or unconditional. One occasion is as apt as another for its release. The object of the ideal judgment is not expected specifically of any particular situation, and its absence in any particular situation will therefore not be decisive. Such a judgment is never empirically disproved, but through the cumulative effect of the repeated absence of its object it may become increasingly doubtful. Similarly, the object of ideal interest being expected of the universe at large, will satisfy whenever and wherever it occurs; while absence on any given occasion will not defeat the interest, though its perpetual absence will beget discouragement of the interest.

[9] Cf. Ch. IX, Sect. III.
[10] In other words, it is 'recurrent,' rather than 'progressive.' Cf. Ch. IX, Sect. I.

In the existential interest the index is all important, as in the act of approbation, "Let this peace continue forever!", the predicate being only a repetition of the index. In the ideal interest the predicate is all-important, as in the resolve, "Let there be peace, no matter how, or where or when!" Existential interest is relatively submissive,[11] endorsing things as they are; ideal interest is relatively aggressive, or revolutionary, since its object is always problematic and therefore independent of existence.

The attributive interest is characteristic of the practical man, who is attentive to means and works with the materials at hand; the existential interest is characteristic of aesthetic enjoyment or of contemplation; the ideal interest is characteristic of the visionary, or, the idle wisher, or the devotee of ends so universal and remote that every situation is an occasion for them.

§ 145. Interest in the Past. It is unnecessary to carry out in detail the application of these distinctions to the case in which the objective of the interest-judgment is qualified as past. We have already dealt with the difficulty arising from the fact that whereas the object of knowledge is past, the act of knowledge is present and the moment of verification future. We have seen that the past may be expected because the act of memory has a past object, and the time of the act rather than of the object is the time of the judgment and of the verification. To judge the past is to set one act of memory for another. The predicative act of memory may be prospective, and may fulfil or surprise according as it does or does not occur, even though its object is retrospective.

Whatever can be judged can be an object of interest. If I can judge that "I saw my friend at the theatre yesterday," I can be *glad* or *sorry* that I did so. And there may be as many varieties of interest in the past, simple and complex, attributive, existential and ideal, as there are varieties of judgment of the past.

It is important to note that interest in the past, like judg-

[11] Cf. Ch. IX, Sect. III.

ment of the past, requires that both the act of indication and the act of predication shall be acts of memory. I am not interested in the past simply because the act of indication is an act of memory. To be interested in what I am familiar with is not to be interested in the past, though it does argue a certain stagnation of interest, since my interest is excited only by what has happened to me already, and not by new events or imagined possibilities. Still less correct is it to say that I am interested in the past when *that which* is the index or object of my interest happens to have existed in the past. The effect of such an interest is to reproduce the past, but the past is not in any sense its object.

Similarly, judgment of the past may be the index of an interest whose integral object is not past. The desire to revive the past, or to bring to pass again that which one believes to have once existed, may be said to be an interest about the past; but it is not, strictly speaking, an interest in the past. Despite the verbal ambiguities that beset any attempt to express it, there is a difference between an interest *in a thing's having been,* and an interest in the prospective being of that which one judges already to have been. Similarly, there may be an interest in the previous occurrence of the present, where the index is present or prospective, and the predicate past. Here again the objective is not the past but an event including the past as one of its components.

The differentia of interest lies, as we have seen, in the control exercised upon the act of indication by the congruence of the act of predication with a governing propensity. Interest in the past is the case in which an indicative act of memory occurs because of the predicative act of memory which it releases. But how can interest of this type be said to be essentially creative or disposed to bring its object to pass? The act of interest, in the case of interest in the past, occurs later in time than its object; how, then, can it be said to be a condition of the occurrence of its object?

The answer, of course, is that it cannot. But while this implies a qualification of the creativity of interest, it does not contradict it. The interest tends to bring its object into existence, but is subject to limiting conditions. Where the object is already in existence the attitude can only be that which we describe as being "glad that it has occurred," or being disposed to "do it again if one had it to do over again." The only effect of interest on the past is to bring it into a new affirmative relation. Whatever course of action promises such a relation is adopted. The past is *irrevocable* in the sense that the only responses to it that are possible are (like memory) such as presuppose it.[12]

It does not follow that interest in the past is interest in *remembering* the past. The interest is taken in the object and not in the act of memory, for it is the former and not the latter which is past. The act of memory is the act which mediates the object of interest, or which makes it object. In the case of interest *in* the act of memory, the interest is directed to the future rather than the past, and the act of memory must itself be the object of another mediating act.

Among the various derived senses of interest in the past which are to be distinguished from this its strict sense, is the painful sense of the past as no-longer-existing. In this sense all past objectives have a negative value. A good example is furnished by the following description of the feelings of a man who has received news of the death of his wife:

"The happy miles to Weyanoke, the smell of the sassafras in its woods, the house all lit and trimmed. The fire kindled, the wine upon the table . . . her hand in mine, her head upon my breast—
The vision faded. Never, never, never for me a homecoming such as that, so deep, so dear, so sweet. The men who were my friends, the woman whom I loved, had gone into a far country. This world was not their home. They had crossed the threshold while I lagged behind. The door was shut, and without were night and I."[13]

This furnishes a good example of the transition from positive interest in the past, to the negation of interest in the present. The events of the past satisfy the hero's

12 Cf. § 141, note.
13 Mary Johnston: *To Have and to Hold*, 1900, p. 389.

interest so long as he is *living in the past;* but their pastness, or their non-presence, thwarts and disappoints his present love. In such cases the character of being past signifies the non-occurrence of the object of a present interest which has survived from the past, and which evokes responses which were once consummated. The subject rejoices in the past, but finds the present intolerable by virtue of the non-existence now of objects that once existed.

II. INTEREST AS OBJECT OF COGNITION

§ 146. The Cognition of Interest. In examining the rôle of cognition in interest we have thus far examined the case in which cognition mediates interest. We have found that this cognitive mediation is inherent in all interests to the extent of the interest-judgment, and that it may and commonly does characterize the index and predicate of interest as well. Interest may thus be said to be a product, derivative or *function* of cognition, in the sense that its satisfaction varies with the truth of the cognition which mediates it. This is very different from saying that the act of interest is the *same* as the act of judgment, or that to be object of judgment and to be object of interest are the same thing. The nerve of judgment is the connection between the index and the predicate; whereas the nerve of interest is the connection between the predicate and a governing propensity. This is illustrated by the fact that the one connection may be strong when the other is weak. One may faintly expect, or half-heartedly believe, that to which one is strongly disposed; that is, the act of indication may release the act of predication only tentatively, or without complete committal, even when this act of predication is in urgent demand from the side of the governing propensity. Thus one may eagerly desire what one only half expects. On the other hand, the act of indication may find one fully committed to the act of predication, even though the governing propensity is weak. One may confidently expect what one scarcely desires.

The object of interest, or what one desires, is the same as the object of the interest-judgment. In the case of complexly mediated interests, the object of the indicative judgment is index of the interest, or that *of which* one desires; and the object of the predicative judgment is the predicate of the interest, or *what* one desires of the index. In no case is the interest which is mediated the object of the mediating cognition. In order that the interest itself shall be cognized it is necessary to introduce a new act of cognition, with a new occasion for fulfilment or surprise. Interest having a determinate nature of its own, and capable of occurring or not occurring, may be an index or a predicate or an object of any of the modes of judgment which we have distinguished.

It follows that although interest cannot exist without cognition, it can and does exist without cognition of itself. It would mean nothing to speak of knowing an interest, unless there were the same contingent relation between the act of interest and the act of knowing it, as between any other existent object and the act of knowing it. Being known is something that may or may not happen to an act of interest. This independence of interest on the knowing of it, is indisputable in the case in which the knowing and the interested subjects are different. It is a part of the tragedy of life that the longings of a lonely soul may be hidden from the rest of mankind, or that the interests of an individual may be ignored by his fellows. It is also an indisputable fact that an individual may neglect his own interests, and need to be reminded of them by another. It remains only to insist that an individual may be unaware of his interest at the moment when he is interested. It is true that he must be aware of the *object* of his interest in order that he shall *be* interested, but it is not necessary, either logically or psychologically, that he should be aware that he is interested. In other words, it is possible that there should be an interest without there being any liability to error as to its existence, either on the part of other subjects or on the part of the agent himself.

The case in which the agent is both interested and aware that he is interested, is sometimes distinguished as the case of "conscious interest," or "conscious purpose" or "conscious desire." [14] But in employing such expressions it is important to note that they signify not *any* associated consciousness, but consciousness *of* interest, purpose or desire.

In this distinction between interest and the knowledge of it, there is no intention of slighting the importance of the latter. The knowledge of interest, whether of one's own or another's, plays an important rôle, both in the integration of interests and in their strengthening, conservation and satisfaction.

§ 147. **Self-Knowledge and Other-Knowledge.** The knowledge of interest may be knowledge by any given subject of his own interests, or the interests of other subjects. It may be argued that in either case it is impossible to know interests without *having* them, or that all knowledge of interest must in the last analysis be self-knowledge. This argument implies the close association in the same subject of cognition and interest, but it does not imply that they are the same thing. Loving is not the same thing as knowing that one loves, even if one cannot know what it is to love without having been in love oneself.

We must not too hastily conclude that in the case of interest self-knowledge is more infallible than social knowledge. Interest consists, as we have seen, in the control of action by what is expected of it. The evidence of interest lies in a consistency of performance in respect of what is judged of it by the agent, or a constancy of anticipatory response amidst a variability of present response. This factor of consistency or constancy may be more correctly observed by a second subject, who is in a position to review the agent's performance, or obtain a synopsis and perspective in which the unities are thrown into bolder relief. Those whose business it is to control the action of others by appealing to their interests learn what promises or threats are in the long run efficacious, or learn the characteristic terms in which an act must be represented to any given agent in order to induce

[14] Cf. *e.g.*, B. Russell, *Analysis of Mind*, 1921, p. 72.

his performance of it. Such masters of the art of persuasion often know an agent's governing propensities, in the sense of permanent disposition and character, better than he knows them himself.

There is, however, an unmistakable advantage enjoyed by the agent, in respect of his object at any given time. It cannot, strictly speaking, be contended that the object of interest is a datum to the agent. For the object of interest is *never* a datum during the life of the interest, but is always the objective of the interest-judgment, or the object of an anticipatory rather than of a consummatory response. But the object of interest at any given moment is primarily the objective of the *agent's* interest-judgment. The agent, in other words, knows it whether anyone else knows it or not; and a second subject knows it only in so far as his judgment has the same object as that of the agent's judgment. This can be expressed by saying that if the agent does not know the object of his interest, no one does. No one can know the object of the agent's interest better than he does himself, for the object of the agent's interest *is what he judges,* whether he judges truly or falsely. If the judgment be erroneous a second subject can know its object only by duplicating it, and not substituting another. It is a well-recognized fact that persons of superior intelligence have difficulty in understanding the performance of persons of inferior intelligence, because they judge indices differently or think different objectives.

What is true of the interest-judgment is true also of the index and the predicate of judgment, where these are mediated. In complexly mediated interest the agent is interested in and satisfied by, what he *believes* to be the case, and the external observer may therefore be misled rather than illuminated by being in possession of the facts. His interpretation of the agent's conduct depends on his knowing what these facts (including stimuli which he deliberately presents) mean to the agent. And such knowledge presupposes that they *do* mean something to the agent, or that the agent is in prior possession of their meaning.

In the case of simply mediated interest the index of the interest-judgment and the predicate at the moment of verification, may be data both to the agent and to the observer, as in the case in which the observer presents his own sensory stimulus to the agent. But there are important cases in which the index is a datum to the agent, and an objective to the observer; or in which there is room for error as regards the index on the part of the observer, but not on the part of the agent. The same difference holds of the predicate at the moment of fulfilment or satisfaction. Among these cases the most important case is that in which the index is a datum of proprioceptive or interoceptive sensation. Organic sense-data are data for only one subject, the stimulus and response belonging to the same organism. It follows that in affection and emotion, in which the object of interest is the prolongation or interruption of organic sensations, the agent himself enjoys a relative freedom from error as compared with the external observer. Whether a given child does or does not like olives may perhaps best be judged by the watchful parent in the light of the child's total behavior. Whether the child does or does not like the *taste of olives* will be more evident to the child or to the parent according as the question turns on the taste, or its extra-organic object. But of the fact that he likes *this taste* (assuming it to be of olives or waiving the question of its external origin) the child is the best judge. It is this interest in data exclusively possessed by the agent himself, which provides the case in which the agent's own report is accepted as indisputable.

The act of response may comprise data for both the agent and the external observer. There are elements which can be data for the observer and not for the agent, and elements which can be data for the agent and not for the observer. The former are ordinarily visual data, such as the physiologist or by-stander observes; the latter are the kinaesthetic data felt by the active organism. In overt action the agent and the external observer enjoy complementary advantages. But in the case of anticipatory response it may often happen that the only data are those felt by the agent himself. In every-day life this is commonly the case, though the use of delicate instruments such as the plethysmograph, or the shrewd observation of posture and facial expression, enable the external observer to bring anticipatory response as well as overt response into the field of his data. The facts cited above justify the following generalization. As regards the existence of a governing propensity, or the stable nature of the interest which governs the agent, the cognitive advantage lies with the external observer; but as regards the present object of the agent's interest, whether its index, its predicate, or its total objective, the advantage lies with the agent himself. As regards *what* the agent at any moment expects, or as regards the data of interest when these are internal to the organism, the agent himself is less liable to error; but as regards the fact that he *has* such and such an interest, or the fact that a certain expectation is consistently prepotent in his action, the external observer is better qualified to judge.

§ 148. Judgments of Value. Assuming, as heretofore argued, that to be valuable means to be object of interest, it follows that a judgment of value will be that which assigns this rôle to any subject-matter. Much confusion has arisen from the failure to observe the distinction between the interest-judgment or other mediating judgment, and the *judgment of value*. This confusion is embodied in the expression 'value-judgment,' which may signify either a judgment which mediates interest, and is therefore a constituent of the act which creates value, or a judgment of which value is the object. The same ambiguity attaches to the verb 'to value,' which may mean either the motor-affective act, which is qualified by judgment and which confers value, or the cognitive act which assigns value as a predicate.[15]

The confusion is doubtless in large measure due to a complexity which has not yet been considered. We have noted that interests may be complexly mediated, or that they may

---

[15] This ambiguity and the doubts to which it gives rise, have already been discussed above, §§ 51, 54.

comprise indicative and predicative judgments, as well as the interest-judgment proper. We have now to note that either the indicative or the predicative judgment of an interest may be a judgment of value. This possibility and the confusion arising from a failure to observe it clearly, is admirably illustrated by the view of Westermarck, which is typical of the anthropo-sociological school. This writer states that "moral disapproval is a sub-species of resentment, and . . . resentment is, in its essence, an aggressive attitude of mind towards an assumed cause of pain." [16] In the case of moral, as distinguished from other forms of resentment, the pain in question is assumed to be inflicted upon others or upon society at large. In other words, the resentment felt toward the act is *mediated* by a judgment which predicates painful consequences of it. But it is possible also to form judgments to the effect that the act is or has been resented. Thus the author tells us that "the moral concepts are essentially generalizations of tendencies in certain phenomena to call forth moral emotions," and that "a moral judgment is true or false according as its subject has or has not that tendency which the predicate attributes to it." [17] In other words, disapproval (an act of interest) both contains a mediating judgment of which interest is an object, and is also itself the object of a second judgment. This being the case there is no justification whatever for the author's rejection of the "presumed objectivity of moral judgments" on the ground that "the contents of an emotion fall entirely outside the category of truth"; or for his argument that "the predicate of a moral judgment may thus in every case be traced back to an emotion *in him who pronounces the judgment"*; or for his conclusion that "this objectivity ascribed to judgments having a merely subjective origin springs in the first place from a similarity in the mental constitution of men." [18] Both judgments have objectivity of the ordinary sort in that they appeal to contingent facts, independent of the act of judgment, for their

[16] E. Westermarck: *Origin and Development of Moral Ideas*, 1906, Vol. I, p. 73. Cf. above, § 54.
[17] *Ibid.*, pp. 13, 17-18.
[18] *Ibid.*, pp. 17, 6, 9. (Italics mine.)

verification. That these facts happen to be tendencies to arouse feeling or sentiment does not distinguish them formally from any other object of judgment. The epistemological relativism or subjectivism which the author believes himself to have demonstrated, is only the effect of carelessness and confusion, and is belied by his own analysis.

Westermarck proposes to limit value (or, at any rate, moral value) to objects of approval or disapproval, but there can be no objection to extending the category to include also that which is found pleasurable or painful. Adopting this wider conception of value, Westermarck's analysis reveals the fact that some sentiments (such as approval and disapproval) are mediated as regards their index by judgments of value. Another instance of this type of complexity is afforded by the case in which approval is mediated by a recognition of the approval of others, or in which approval is accompanied by a sense of participation. Indeed such terms are 'approval,' 'admiration,' 'aspiration,' 'acknowledgment' and 'appreciation' are ordinarily intended to refer to the fact that the object of interest is thus antecedently qualified in terms of interest. In such cases interest is taken in what is *deemed* good; or, there is a value found, as well as a value conferred. One and the same act of sentiment both judges a value which is independent of itself, and creates a value which is dependent on itself, and which may be the object of a second judgment. There is no difficulty, either logical or psychological, so long as these distinctions are strictly observed; whereas their confusion, or the ascribing to one factor of the characters which belong properly to another, has led to characteristic absurdities and contradictions with which the literature of the subject is infested.[19]

Interests taken in that to which value is ascribed, have a peculiarly "objective" character, in that their objects are already objects of interest; or their correlative values may

[19] While Westermarck affords the *clearest* illustration of this confusion, his very clearness has exposed the error and rendered it comparatively innocuous. The more insidious forms of the error occur in the literature of philosophical idealism, where it is obscured by metaphysics. Cf. above, Ch. IV, Sect. IV, *passim.*

be said to be peculiarly objective, in that what is made valuable is already valuable. But the value which is ascribed, or which is already *there*, is not the same as the value which is introduced. Nor can there be any reason other than that of verbal convenience for limiting the term value to such cases of double or multiple interest. In these special cases value is created by an interest which is mediated by a judgment of value. But it would be incorrect to say that a judgment of value creates that value which it judges. The mediating judgment of value judges one value and creates a second, not directly by judging it, but indirectly by conditioning the formation of the sentiment which creates it. The sentiment being formed, the second value occurs, *whether or not* this becomes in turn the object of a second judgment of value.

The occurrence of this second judgment of value cannot, as we have seen, be necessarily inferred from the fact that the subject issues a declaratory verbal statement.[20] For such a statement may, in any given case, be only an expression of the sentiment. The sentiment itself, or the subject's knowledge of his sentiment, may employ identical verbal expressions. The words "I love you" may express my love, or they may express my judgment about my love. There is a genuine psychological difference even when there is no verbal difference. A verbal statement which employs epithets, or purely eulogistic and dyslogistic terms, expresses not a cognition but an interest. The writer who said that " 'Virtuous' and 'Vicious,' 'Good' and 'Bad' are in fact eulogistic and dyslogistic epithets" should have said that they *may* be.[21] But when they are, then those interested attitudes which they express are facts which may be judged not in terms of epithets, but in terms of descriptive predicates.[22]

[20] Cf. § 130.

[21] J. Solomons, "Is the Conception of 'Good' Undefinable?", *Proc. Aristotelian Soc.*, 1905-06, p. 130.

[22] Similarly when Mr. J. L. McIntyre tells us that "the judgment of value merely expresses in language what is already implied in the emotional attitude towards the situation," he contradicts his own later procedure where he asserts that "value is never a character or quality of an object, but always a relation between an object and a subject." ("Value-Feelings and Judgments of Value," *Proc. Aristotelian Soc.*, 1904-05, pp.

§ 149. The Index, Predicate and Object in Judgments of Value.

Judgments of value do not differ formally from other judgments, and it follows that the structure and modes of judgment as already analyzed hold of them. They have their indices, their predicates and their objects; they are true or false, according as the predicative act does or does not occur upon the occasion defined by the act of indication; they may be examined as regards their simplicity and complexity; and as regards their attributive, existential or ideal form. It would be gratuitous to repeat and illustrate all of these distinctions. It is, however, desirable to distinguish clearly the index, predicate and object of such judgments in order to clarify verbal usage.

To be valuable is to be object of interest.[23] To be judged valuable, as in the case of the judgment of value, is to be judged to be object of interest. The judgment of value is the judgment about anything to the effect that interest is taken in it. It follows that in the judgment of value *the object of interest is the index,* and the *act of interest is the predicate.* We may thus speak of "the index of the judgment of value," when we mean *that which* possesses value; and thus avoid the ambiguity contained in the expression "object of value," which may mean the object qualified as valuable, or in the expression "subject of value," which may mean the interested agent. Thus peace possesses value, or is the index of the judgment of value, "peace is good."

We have already observed that the object of interest is an objective, mediated by an interest-judgment. This gives rise to a peculiar ambiguity in the verbal expression of judgments of value, or of psychological judgments generally. The

---

59, 63.) For if value is an emotional relation between an object and a subject, then the judgment of value is the judgment of this relation, and the relation does not imply the judgment of it. A similar contradiction appears in Ch. Ehrenfels's virtual statement that to desire is to be aware of value, and to be valuable means to be desired. If to be valuable is to be desired, then to be aware of value is to be *aware of desire.* Cf. "Werttheorie und Ethik," *Vierteljahrschrift für wissenschaftliche Philos.,* Vol. XVII, 1893, p. 89.

[23] This is the fundamental, synthetic judgment of value. Value, like other adjectives, may be predicated indirectly, analytically, inclusively, etc. Cf. § 55.

object of interest must be believed by the interested agent; but when this object becomes the index of a judgment of value, it may be merely *supposed*.[24] Thus, if the object of interest be "peace by negotiation," peace must be expected of negotiation by the interested agent. But the observer's judgment that such is the expectation of the interested agent may or may not mean that this second judge shares the expectation. The second judge *may* share the expectation, in which case his interest may be in agreement or in opposition; or, he may share the expectation without any interest in the matter; or, his expectation may be opposed to that of the first party. The second judge may expect peace of negotiation, and either hope for it or dread it; or, he may expect it with indifference; or, he may disbelieve in it, and thus correct the interest-judgment of the first party at the same time that he recognizes what it is. In order that all of these alternatives may be compatible with a judgment which *assigns* a certain objective to the interested agent, it must be possible for the second judge to indicate the objective not only with indifference, but without conviction. Both confirmation and correction imply the bare supposition as to *what* the first party judges.

The predicate of the judgment of value is the act or state of interest, the analysis of which is the central theme of the psychology of value. The object of a judgment of value is the objective composed of its index and its predicate. Like all objects of judgment, it is problematic. When the judgment of value is true, that which is its objective is also a transcendent object. This statement requires, however, a certain qualification. The only existent object in the case of true judgments of value is the *interest qualified by its objective*. In other words, the judgment "peace is good" is true when there is an interest such that peace is its objective. It is not necessary that peace should exist, or that the question of its existence should be raised.

---

[24] Cf. § 131. The logical equivalent of the objective which is not believed is the "unasserted" proposition. Cf. Whitehead and Russell, *Principia Mathematica*, 1910, Vol. I, pp. 8-9.

It will be convenient to employ the term 'value' in the
substantive sense, as when one speaks of "this or that value,"
for the object of the judgment of value, when this judgment
is true.   It will be a longing, hope, desire, fear, love, or other
case of interested act, state or attitude, referred to a specific
objective; as 'peace longed for,' 'immortal life hoped for,'
'riches desired,' 'death feared,' and 'God loved.'

In the foregoing analysis of the judgment of value we
have limited ourselves to the case in which value is predicated
in the primary and original sense, or the case in which interest
is directly predicated of an index.   It is, however, possible
to predicate value indirectly, or to assign value in a derivative
sense to that which is the cause of an object of interest, or
to that which contains an object of interest, or to that which
is qualified to be an object of interest.   These more extended
senses of the category of value, and more complicated forms
of the judgment of value involve no new theoretical difficulties, and rest upon the fundamental analysis offered in the
present chapter.[25]

[25] If, for any logical reason, or reason of general philosophical consistency, it should be deemed desirable to restrict the subject of a judgment to existent particulars, it would be necessary to revise the position
taken in the present chapter so that value should be predicated as follows:
first, of a presently existing object which, in recurrent interest, serves as
the intermediary of its own prolongation into the future; second, of a
presently existing instrument which, in progressive interest, is employed
for the purpose of bringing into existence an object other than itself.
This would be consistent with the position taken in the present book,
that value is bestowed on objects by the interest taken in them, but it
would be extremely awkward to have to deny value to that *toward which,*
as its consummation, interest is directed.   The need of predicating value
of that which does not exist, seems in other words, to afford a good
reason for rejecting the view that only existent particulars can be subjects
of judgments.

CHAPTER XIII

COMPLEXES AND INTEGRATIONS OF INTEREST

I. INTEGRATION OF INTERESTS BY THEIR MEDIATING JUDGMENTS

§ 150. Complexes of Interest. We have now distinguished and discussed the mediation of interest by cognition, and the cognition of interest. Every unit-interest embraces an interest-judgment, and may, if complexly mediated, embrace an indicative and a predicative judgment as well; and every interest is the possible object of a cognition, which, when the act of interest assumes the rôle of the predicate, constitutes a judgment of value. We have now to recognize and elaborate the fact that in and through this cognitive factor interests overlap and interpenetrate. The phrase "complexes of interest" is not meant simply to convey the idea that interests are complex. This has already been abundantly attested. Nor is it meant to convey the obvious idea that interests are multiple. It means that interests are so interrelated through possessing common constituents, or through being constituents one of another, that the satisfaction of one is a function of the satisfaction of another. Complexity of interest in this sense implies that interests are in some sense conjoined or linked together, so that in analyzing modes of complexity we shall at the same time be describing modes of integration.

The simplest case is that *community* of interest in which two or more interests are connected by a common mediating cognition. A second case is *intermediation* or *subordination* of interest, in which one interest mediates another through constituting its act of indication or of predication. Finally, there is the case of *mutuality,* in which the mediating cognition is a judgment of value. The first is the case in which two or more interests have the same index, predicate or object; the second, the case in which the object of one interest is the index or predicate of another; the third, the case in which one interest is the index, predicate or object of another.

§ 151. **Interests with a Common Object.** Two or more interests may intersect in their object, whether this be the object indicated, the object predicated, or both. Where both index and predicate are the same, the object of the interest, or the end, is the same. These cases will be referred to as exemplifying *community* of interest.

That two or more judgments should have the same index is possible by virtue of the difference between the act of response and its object. Two or more organisms may respond to the same object, or the same organism may respond at different times to the same object. Furthermore, different organisms, or the same organism at different times, may respond to the same object *in different ways*. Thus two organisms may indicate the same object when one points to it with the index finger and the other names it. This diversity in the mode of indication is brought out clearly when there is difficulty of communication and one subject seeks to establish an index in common with another. If I am seeking to express to another what I am judging about, I try different modes of indication until I find one that will serve as a sign of the same object to the other subject. If I am indicating food, and the other subject does not understand English, I substitute for the word 'food,' the word '*Speise*' or the word '*nourriture.*' If the other subject is deaf, I point to the food with my finger, or if he is both deaf and blind I bring the food into contact with his hand.

The same community of object with diversity of response is possible in the case of the predicate. Two or more organisms may predicate the same object, or the same organism may predicate the same object at different times, or the same or different organisms may predicate the same object in different ways. In other words, one may expect the same object in terms of different anticipatory responses. The qualitative diversity of anticipatory response is clearly demonstrated in the effort to communicate expectation. If two judgments can have the same predicate, it follows that two interests have the same predicate when their interest-judgments have the same predicate.

Judgments may thus be distinguished in two ways: by their objective difference, or by their subjective difference. And, similarly, they may be integrated by way of their objects in two ways: through combining different objects (indices or predicates) with the same object (predicate or index), or through combining different acts with the same object (index, predicate or objective). The same holds, *pari passu,* for the interests which the judgments in question mediate.

Two judgments may have different indices with different predicates, or the same index with different predicates, or different indices with the same predicate, or the same index with the same predicate. Where both their indices and their predicates are different, they may be said to be both *irrelevant* and *dissimilar.* Where their indices are the same and their predicates different, two judgments are relevant but dissimilar. In this case there are two further possibilities. If the predicate which fulfils one judgment surprises the other, the two judgments *disagree,* their objectives being *contradictory.* If that which fulfils one judgment neither fulfils nor surprises the other, the two judgments and their objectives are *consistent.* When the indices are different and the predicates the same, two judgments are similar, but irrelevant. When both their indices and their predicates are the same they are said to *agree.*

The relations of interests follow the relations of their interest-judgments. By virtue of their community or difference of index and predicate, interests may be relevant or similar, irrelevant or dissimilar. When they are relevant but dissimilar they may be consistent, or, where the two objectives are contradictories, they may disagree. When interests in this sense disagree, it will be convenient to speak of them as *opposed,* since the one tends to bring into existence that which the other tends to negate. When two interests have both index and predicate in common, they agree. Interests which agree may be said to be *allied,* since they both tend to bring the same to pass, or function as supplementary and reinforcing causes having the same effect.

Two judgments which agree may be said to judge the same, but they are not the same judgment. Their objective is the same, but their acts are different. The same environmental conditions will surprise or fulfil both, and prove them true or erroneous; but there are two surprises or fulfilments, two truths or errors, and not one. As two judgments may have the same objective without prejudice to their numerical diversity, so two interests whose interest-judgments have the same objective may have the same object or end and remain none the less two. They desire the same of the same, but they are not the same desires.

> "Two souls with but a single thought,
> Two hearts that beat as one,———"

are two, none the less. Thus two citizens may both desire that President Coolidge be reëlected in 1928, and yet they may indicate or deal with him by different acts, anticipate his reëlection in different terms, find their satisfaction or disappointment in different states, and be governed by different propensities.

Those who have failed to distinguish between the act and the object of response, and to provide for both of them, have been led to one or the other of two opposite extremes. Those who reduce the object of judgment to the act find themselves forced to the extreme view known as relativism, according to which there are as many objects as there are acts of judgments, as many worlds as there are judges, and as many ends as there are interests. Those, on the other hand, who reduce the act of judgment to the object, are led to conclude that two or more judgments of the same object are the same judgment; that as there is only one world, there can be only one judgment; and that singleness of end implies singleness of will.

There are various schematic possibilities which follow when community of object is combined with complexity of mediation. Thus, for example, the community of object which connects two interests may consist in their being indicated and predicated by judgments having common objectives. Thus two or more subjects may be interested in putting out what they *judge* to be a fire, and they may be satisfied by what they *judge* to be its extinction. Their interests have the same index and predicate, their end may be said to be the same. Or, the synthetic objects of systems of judgments, such for example, as physical things, or other persons, may be the synthetic objects of systems of interest.[1] Just as my cognition of wealth may consist in an intricately interrelated system of acts of indication, predication and judgment, so my love of wealth may denote the fact that I desire many things of money, and that I desire money of many things, and that I deal with money in many ways. The objects of interrelated judgments are themselves objects or complexes of a higher order. This is equally the case when judgments mediate interests, so that integrated interests imply complex ends. When one judges that 'I' am interested in 'wealth,' 'I' signifies a complex interest, and 'wealth' a complex object. When one judges that "I love wealth" one asserts that all the interest constituents of the complex interests are favorable interests, and that all the modes of activity are congruent with governing propensities. Similarly, when I love a person, the person's name signifies a system of judgments any or all of which may be false. Thus Shelley, after being disillusioned, says of his sister Elizabeth

"I loved a being, an idea in my own mind, which had no real existence. I concreted this abstract of perfection, I annexed this fictitious quality to the idea presented by a *name;* the being, whom that name signified, was by no means worthy of this."[2]

[1] Such systems are sometimes called 'sentiments.' Cf. § 78, note.
[2] *Letters,* edited by R. Ingpen, 1909, Vol. I, p. 88.

II. INTERESTS MEDIATED BY INTEREST

§ 152. When the Act of Indication is an Interest.
Interests may also be connected through mediating one another, or through what may be called 'intermediation,' involving an interrelation of subordination and dependence. The schematic possibilities are evident, though it does not follow that all of these possibilities are either humanly important or empirically possible. In a complexly mediated interest either the act of indication, or the act of predication, or both, are judgments; and it follows that, theoretically at least, they may be interest-judgments. Thus an interest may constitute the act of indication or the act of predication in what is, as a whole, an interest. In other words, either the index, or the predicate of an interest, or both, may be objects of interest or ends.

Let us consider, first, the case in which an interest is indicated by an interest, or in which the index is an end. It is characteristic of an interest that the indicative act occurs because the predicative act with which it is associated is congruent with a governing propensity. When the indicative act is an interest, then this act of interest, implying its own governing propensity, must occur because it begets an expectation congruent with a more deep-seated governing propensity. The full complexity of such behavior can best be understood if it is expounded progressively.

In the first place, a complex *judgment* may, as we have seen, be indicated by a judgment, as when I predicate *c* of *a*-judged-to-be-*b*. There are in this case two chances of fulfilment or surprise, according as *b* does or does not occur on the occasion of *a,* and according as *c* does or does not occur on the occasion of the judgment '*a* is *b*.'

In the second place, a complexly mediated *interest* may be indicated by a judgment, as when I desire *c* of *a*-judged-to-be-*b*. That this is an interest rather than a mere judgment, implies that I judge *a* to be *b* because I predicate *c* of this objective. I judge of *a* that which, namely *b,* affords promise of *c*. At the same time the fact that I *do* judge *b* of *a,* implies that b is one among the predicates that a indicates. My interest consists in the fact that my governing propensity predisposes me to one rather than another of the predicates which are cognitively available. There are in this case two chances of fulfilment or surprise; and one chance of satisfaction or disappointment, according as c does or does not occur.

In the third place, a complexly mediated interest may be indicated by an interest, as when I desire c of that, namely a, of which I desire b. In this case I not only desire b of a because I predicate c of this desire, but I indicate a because I predicate b of it. Such performance is doubly selective, and implies two governing propensities, a subordinate propensity which renders a eligible because of b, and that which renders 'b of a' eligible because of c. There are two chances of fulfilment or surprise, and two chances of satisfaction or disappointment.

These three stages of complication may be illustrated by the different attitudes that may be directed to the same objective, such as "money is power." First, "This which I take to mean money, means power" is a complex judgment, in which the index is the judgment "this is money"; as when grasping the gold, and anticipating purchase, I anticipate my ascendency over him who has something to sell. Second, if I interpret what I hold in my hand as money, that is, anticipate the *expenditure* of it, because this promises my ascendency over my neighbor, I am governed by the love of power and the index of my interest is the judgment "this is money." Third, if I grasp the gold because it promises purchase, and if I am thus interested in expending it because of the ascendency which I anticipate, I am doubly interested, in money and in power; but my ambition is a more deep-seated propensity than my avarice.

This analysis brings to light an important feature of the present view. All interest, even the simplest and most rudimentary, involves a subordination of means to end. There is no object of interest which is not an end, and there is no end which does not contain a means as one of its constituents. Interest is, in other words, essentially teleological. But a means in this basic sense is not an object of interest, since it lacks the necessary complexity. The case which we have just been considering is, then, the special case in which a means *is* an object of interest, or an end; requiring its own subordinate means, and itself subordinate to an ulterior end. There are thus two kinds of means, those which are only means, and those which are also ends. The latter alone are valuable objects in the primary and original sense of the phrase.

§ 153. When the Act of Predication is an Interest.
A complex judgment may also contain a judgment as its act of predication, as when judging that this which I hold in my hand is money, my judgment is verified by the disclosure of that (namely gold) of which I judge that it has purchasing power. Similarly, an interest may be complexly mediated as regards its predicate, as when I grasp the gold because this promises the judgment of purchasing power. In this case my avarice is satisfied by the judgment, "I can buy with this," without its verification. The index of the predicative act satisfies by virtue of what it promises, or by virtue of what is predicated of it. Finally, an interest may be *satisfied by an interest,* even when that interest is not satisfied; as when, desiring money by which to obtain power, this desire is satisfied by the possession of that from which I *hope* to derive power.

A complex interest may be thus satisfied by a recurrent or by a progressive interest. The man who desires to *become* President, is satisfied by the judgment, "I am President." His interest (complexly mediated as regards its predicate) terminates in a judgment of fact, or a *mere* judgment. The man who desires to *be* President is satisfied by the occurrence of the interest in being President, that is, by the impulse to prolong the situation once it is indicated. This recurrent interest may be thwarted, that is, the successful candidate may be cut off at the moment of achieving his goal; but he has succeeded none the less if he has had time enough to like or enjoy the situation which he has achieved. If a candidate described as desiring to be President does not like the office when he obtains it, then we should not say that his interest in being President has been defeated, but that his interest has been improperly described. The fact that he does not like the office proves that he desired not to hold it, but to obtain it. Progressive interests may or may not culminate in interests of the recurrent type, this sequel furnishing evidence of the nature of the original interest.

A progressive interest may be satisfied by the emergence of a new progressive interest. Such interests are of common occurrence, and are described as desiring "something to live for," "some one to love," "a cause to fight for." In order to avoid confusion it is necessary to insist that the object of such complex interests is the *object* of the predicative interest, and not the act. The complex interest is satisfied when this object assumes the rôle of being 'lived for,' 'loved' or 'fought for'; when, in other words, it becomes an end. Just as I may desire of democracy in a sense that is satisfied by its being judged "safe," so may I desire of democracy in a sense that is satisfied by the desire that it shall be safe, or when its safety has become my cause.[3]

The mediation of interest by interest may be summarily stated as the case in which the indication of one interest is the predication of another. In the case of an interest indicated by an interest, the predication of the indicating interest is the indication of the total interest; in the case of an interest predicated by an interest, the indication of the predicative interest is the predication of the total interest. The absence of this relation of *subordination* is the relation of *independence*.

The relation of the mediating interest to the total interest, or the relation of subordination, is a relation which holds only within a single organism, as it is internal to the structure of the interest, or is conditioned by the functional relation

---

[3] In this case one does really struggle to bring about democracy. It has to be distinguished from the case in which the activity of pursuit is itself the object of interest, as when the dominant propensity is *ennui* or a general longing for activity. In this case one would pursue democracy but without, fundamentally, wishing to achieve it. This case would resemble that of play. Cf. Ch. IX, Sect. II.

of the acts of indication and of predication. *Your* interest cannot indicate or predicate *my* interest any more than your lungs can oxidize my blood or your stomach nourish my tissues. It follows that the interests of different organisms are always independent.[4] If this seems to be a startling and paradoxical conclusion, it is because of a failure to distinguish an interest mediated by another interest from an interest mediated by the *object* of another interest, and an interest mediated by the *judgment* of another interest. The second is the case, already considered, of two interests having a common object. The third is the case to which we now turn.

III. INTERESTS MEDIATED BY JUDGMENTS OF INTEREST

§ 154. Interests may also be connected through standing in the subject-object relation to one another, or through the fact that interests may be mediated by judgments of interest. This may be referred to as '*mutuality* of interest,' though this expression is commonly restricted to the case in which the relation is reciprocal.

The simplest case is that in which the *interest-judgment* is a *judgment of interest*. The crucial importance for the moral and social life of the special case in which these two types of judgment coincide, proves the necessity of avoiding the confusion of them. The interest-judgment is the judgment whose act of predication determines its act of indication. The judgment of interest is the judgment whose index or predicate is an interest. The occurrence of the case here in question implies the existence of governing propensities, such as mother-love, or self-interest, whose consummation requires the presentation or representation of an interest.

The mother who ministers to her child may react aggressively to a stranger for the sake of quieting the child's fears; in which case the predicate is an interest, while the index is not. Or she may appease the child's appetite for the sake of obtaining quiet; in which case the index is an interest,

---

[4] This has very important implications. Cf. Ch. XV, XXII.

while the predicate is not. Or, finally, she may appease the child's appetite for the sake of silencing the complaint of the neighbors, or for the sake of insuring the child's future happiness, in which case both the index and the predicate are interests. In all three cases the object of the mother's interest contains another interest as a constituent, and two or more interests, that of the mother together with that of the child or of the neighbors, are interconnected as subject and object.

It has thus far been assumed that interests may be simply indicated or predicated; that they may, in other words, be data. This possibility need not concern us here. Nor need we consider the differences in this respect between the case in which the indicative or predicative acts and their objects belong to the same, and that in which they belong to different, organisms.[5] If or when interest-objects are not data they are objectives. Certainly the more common and indisputable case is that in which an interest in interest is complexly mediated. For interests may be mediated by judgments of interest as regards their index, as regards their predicate, or as regards both. We have already cited examples in the course of our analysis of such attitudes as appreciation and approbation, which are favorable interests in objects judged to be good; that is, objects of which favorable interest in some form or relation is predicated. Appreciation, for example, may signify the liking of that which is judged to be liked, where a datum indicates a recurrent interest by virtue of meaning a like recurrent interest on the part of another subject; or, it may signify the liking of that which is judged to be judged good by another subject. The idiosyncrasy sometimes known as 'negativism' signifies the liking of what is judged to be disliked or judged bad by another subject, or by other subjects generally. In other words, the predicate of other-interest may serve to qualify an object for being the index either of a favorable or of an unfavorable interest.

In the case of benevolence the interest-predicate is a judgment of interest. The indicative act is performed for the sake of what is *judged to be* the satisfaction of an other-

[5] Cf. §§ 148, 149.

interest. Similarly, in malice the indicative act is performed because it promises what is taken to be the disappointment of an other-interest. Both benevolence and malice are satisfied by judgments which may be true or false; that is, their satisfactions may occur whether the satisfactions or disappointments which are judged in their predicative acts occur or do not occur.

Cases in which both the index and the predicate of interest are judgments of interest are equally common. Appreciation and approbation, for example, may be predicated as well as indicated by the favorable interest of others. Thus an act of appreciation becomes an act of snobbery when one likes what one judges to be liked by others, because of what one judges to be the favor of others. An act of approbation becomes an act of prudence when one favors an act deemed agreeable to others, because of the applause which one expects; that is, because of certain data which one construes as signs of a favorable attitude. Negativism becomes malicious when one persists in it because of its contrariety to the attitude of the group. Or malice may take the form of perpetrating what one takes to be an injury to the child, for the sake of the wound which one hopes thereby to inflict upon the mother. In this case, one may be mistaken in both judgments. One may in point of fact hurt neither the child nor the mother. But one's interest is none the less malicious, and is satisfied when what one believes to be contrary to one interest results in what one believes to be contrary to the other.

Interest in interest is itself a mode of integration. Its mere absence is a form of non-integration, for which the term 'indifference' may be employed, provided 'indifference to interest' is understood. Interest in interest itself gives rise both to a mode of integration and to a mode of non-integration,—benevolence being a form of harmony, and malice of conflict.

IV. COMPATIBLE AND INCOMPATIBLE INTERESTS

§ 155. We have shown that interests are connected by virtue of their mediation, whether this assume the form of mere judgments, or of interest-judgments, or of judgments of interest. We have, in other words, distinguished various modes of union that are definable in terms of the objects with which interests are provided by their constituent judgments. Interests may have common indices or predicates; the index of one may be the predicate of another, and *vice versa;* or one interest may be the index or predicate of another. Such relations may be referred to as *'inter-objective.'* We have still to consider a type of union and disunion which depends not on the object but on the act of interest, and which may be referred to as *'inter-active.'* Since there may be different acts of response to the same or to different objects, it is evident that these responses may or may not interfere with one another. Where they do interfere we shall speak of the interests as rival, competing or *incompatible* interests, and where they do not we shall speak of them as *compatible* interests.[6] There is a third case in which two compatible interests whether with or without community of intent, *reinforce* one another.

Two responses are incompatible when they inhibit one another in the same organism, or when because of employing the same nerves, muscles or energy they cannot occur simultaneously. They may be rendered compatible through taking their turn. Eating and speech-making are incompatible responses when upon being simultaneously innervated the one prevents the other, but they are rendered compatible through assigning speech-making a time *after* dinner. Similarly, two responses enacted by different organisms may inhibit one another through colliding, or through employing the same phys-

[6] While the terms 'competing' and 'incompatible' will sometimes be used interchangeably, it is well to observe that 'competition' is sometimes used to refer to *complementary* activities, as, for example, in a game. Strictly speaking, there are also compatible and incompatible judgments according as the acts of indication or predication interfere or do not interfere. One of the objects of scientific technique is to avoid such interference.

ical instruments, as when the interests of two individuals in the same spectacle take the form of looking at it simultaneously from the same vantage-point. This rivalry may also be resolved by "taking turns."

But such a simple solution is not always possible. Some responses are more radically incompatible in that they have the effect of exhausting or destroying the object, so that a later response to the same object is precluded. The parade may have marched by, or the food may be gone, before the second interest has its turn. In such cases a more radical solution is necessary which involves an alteration of the second interest as regards its object, or its response, or both. Incompatiblity of this second type is characteristic of consummatory responses, but it is not characteristic of all consummatory responses. Two cats can look at the same king.

It is important to note that the interactive relations of interests are independent of their inter-objective relations. Interests may compete even though they be irrelevant and dissimilar. Objectively unrelated interests seated in the same organism may compete for its mechanisms and store of energy, as when a man's passion for drink competes with his love of truth; or objectively unrelated interests in different organisms may compete for the same external conditions, as when the child's play interferes with his father's meditations. Especially noteworthy is the case in which competitive interests have the same end, as when two hungry men desire the same food. They have the same end in the sense that they both react to the same index (or adopt the same means), because of expecting the same predicate. Their behavior is convergent so far as its object is concerned, and they may even reinforce one another in bringing that object (the food) into existence, as when a pack of wolves hunts the same prey. But their interests are none the less so related that the consummatory activities in which the object *satisfies* their several interests are mutually inhibitory. It is a familiar fact in human as well as brute life that concord in the period of struggle is often followed by discord at the moment of success. The convergence of interests in a common end is in fact one of the most prolific sources of rivalry, since it brings interests into close proximity and increases the likelihood of interference.

Although the incompatibility of interests is independent of their objective relations, it need scarcely be said that it breeds opposition and antagonism. One competing interest becomes an object of enmity to the other through intervening judgments of interest. Two individuals who desire the same bread are merely rivals, but when each seeks to deprive the other, they have become enemies.

V. THE RATIONALIZATION OR JUSTIFICATION OF INTEREST

§ 156. **The Problem of Integration.**[7] The non-integration or disunion of interests may thus mean several quite different things. It may mean that they are independent, irrelevant, dissimilar, opposed, indifferent, antagonistic or incompatible. The problem of integration is the problem of removing any of these conditions, and of achieving dependence, relevance, similarity, consistency, alliance, interest (in interest), friendliness, compatibility or reinforcement. With the single exception of compatibility all of these modes of integration exist by virtue of the mediation of the related interests, or by virtue of being somehow objectively connected. Compatibility may be due to irrelevance, dissimilarity and isolation. But all modes of integration are *achieved* or *created* in the personal and social life, by acts of mediation. For even compatibility can be voluntarily brought about only by making the competing interests objects of interest, or by introducing some other form of mediated integration among them.

It is clear, however, that the introduction of one type of integration renders possible a new type of non-integration. When two interests become relevant, they become capable of opposition; when they become allies, or when one is subordinated to another, they tend to become rivals; when one interest becomes the object of another, there arises the possibility of hostility and malice; when interests are rendered

[7] For this topic, cf. also §§ 235-238, and Ch. XXII.

compatible, this often leads to their becoming irrelevant and dissimilar. Social integration may be obtained at the cost of personal disintegration, and personal at the cost of social integration; as international unity may imply the relaxation of the bonds of nationality, and patriotism may be an obstacle to humanity. It is evident, then, that the problem of integration is not merely the problem of connecting interests in all possible ways. Indeed the most acute difficulties of modern life have arisen from the very fact that interests have become so diversely and so widely connected. It is this fact that furnishes the motive of anarchy and of extreme individualism, which is the cry of interests to be saved from one another,—from their friends as well as from their enemies. It is this fact that moves a pioneer to seek a new wilderness, a modern to long for the solitary state of nature, or a nation to adopt a policy of isolation. The difficulty is inescapable, because interests by their own internal development become relevant and similar, and so must be rendered consistent or allied if they are not to be opposed; because ends cannot be attained, without the interested effort to attain their means;. because the biological conditions of human life force one interest upon the attention of another, so that they must be friendly if they are not to be hostile; and because the existence of many interests in the same organism, or upon the same planet, renders them incompatible unless by the introduction of some other mode of integration they are rendered compatible.

The problem of integration is thus an inevitable problem, despite its attendant risks and the incidental evils to which it gives rise. Taking account of these hazards and penalties, the problem of integration becomes that of achieving each mode of integration without those modes of non-integration which it conditions. It is the problem of introducing relevance, similarity and subordination without opposition; or of introducing alliance without rivalry; or of arousing human interest without hostility; or of achieving compatibility without irrelevance and dissimilarity. Interests that are either compatible, consistent, friendly, reinforcing or allied may be termed 'harmonious'; and interests that are incompatible, hostile, or opposed may be referred to as 'conflicting'; so that the central problem of integration is to achieve *harmony* in place of *conflict*.[8]

§ 157. The Function of Rationalization.

The reason of an interested act is its mediating judgment. Every interested act has a reason, for every interested act has at least one mediating judgment, namely the interest-judgment. Complexly mediated interests will have additional reasons attaching to the index or the predicate. This does not imply that an interested act is limited to three reasons, for either the act of indication or the act of predication may be a system of judgments. If an interested agent is asked for his reason he may express the interest-judgment, or an indicative judgment, or a predicative judgment, according to what information he supposes his interlocutor already to possess.

The recognition of this fact that every agent has a *bona fide* reason for his action, whether true or not, and whether he profess it honestly or dishonestly, is the beginning of all historical and social wisdom. No interested act is understood until one has for a moment shared the judgment that mediated it, or until it has been made to *seem* reasonable in terms of those expectations with which it was associated in the agent. Such understanding, where it is mutual, is the beginning of reconciliation.

Thus rationalists or intellectualists are correct in insisting that one or more judgments are constituents of every interest; and that it is, therefore, pertinent to apply the terms 'true' and 'false' to an interest; and that argument, calculated to affect the agent's judgment, is therefore calculated to affect his interest. But the voluntarist or anti-intellectualist is also correct in insisting that an interest is not *mere* judgment. There is, as we have seen, a residual factor peculiar to interest, which is the prepotence of the predicate of the interest-judgment by virtue of the congruence of the act of predication with a governing propensity. There is a bias or spring of

---

[8] *Cooperation* and *concord* of interests are special cases which must be examined later. Cf. Ch. XVII, Sect. V; and Ch. XXII, Sect. II.

action in the agent which renders acts eligible according to their promise, and which determines what arguments will or will not "appeal" to him.

Whether the term 'motive' be employed for the predicate of interest, or for the act of predication, or for the governing propensity, is unimportant provided both the difference and the intimate relation of these three factors are carefully observed. The motive of which the agent is conscious at the moment of interest is the predicate, and the predicate is therefore most readily communicated. It is only necessary that the act of predication should be *expressed* in order to communicate its object, namely the predicate. The agent does not make an *object* of his act of predication or of his governing propensity, without becoming self-conscious. It does not, however, follow that in stating the predicate as his motive the agent would deny or falsify his governing propensity. When he says his motive is money, it is because his attention is already directed to money, and not because he is disposed to deny that he is avaricious.

Rationalization is not a mere stating of his reasons by the agent. It is a finding of new reasons, or the introduction of new mediating judgments. These have the effect of linking interests in new ways, or of introducing integration where it did not exist before. These acts of mediation may deal with the index, predicate or end of the given interest, or with the interest itself. In any case, they bring interests into new relations through common objects, or through making one the object of another. Rationalization is the introduction of such acts of mediation for the sake of the integration which it effects. Its purpose is to attract to any interest or to its object, the favor and support of other interests. It may therefore be termed 'justification' or 'apologetic reasoning.'

The result of rationalization is often to create a new end which is distinguished by its integrative character, or by the fact that it is confluent with many interests, drawing them together, embodying them, satisfying them, and engaging them jointly. Such ends, or constructive ideals, are both synthetic and creative. They are commonly represented by symbols, the art of symbolization being elaborated to offset the abstractness and remoteness that would otherwise result from their highly mediated character.   The importance of constructive ideals in both the personal and the social life, will receive proper recognition in the appropriate context;[9] but a further consideration, at this point, of the general function of rationalization will serve both to illustrate it, and to free it of a certain odium which it has recently acquired.

§ 158. Reason Held to be Inefficacious.

The term 'rationalization' has recently been appropriated by psychiatry and by a cynical psychology for the purpose of belittling or discrediting the practical use of reason.   In this pathological or disparaging sense, rationalization means that the practical reason is *ineffectual, self-deceiving* and *mendacious*. Those who formulate or imply them are not ordinarily aware of the extent to which these charges are mutually inconsistent. If reason were ineffectual it would at least be innocuous.   If a man can deceive himself or others as to the reasons for his action, this is because he does ordinarily *have* reasons. The question "Why do you do so?" whether answered truly or falsely, mendaciously or veraciously, implies that a true and honest answer is possible; in other words, that the act *was* actually performed for reasons.   Finally, if rationalization were essentially self-deceptive, then it could not be mendacious, for mendacity implies that the liar himself is free from the deception which he practises on others.

This caricature of rationalization arises primarily from the false notion that the *reasons* for action are not *causes* of action.   Dr. Bernard Hart tells us that men are governed by "an overwhelming need to *believe* that we are acting rationally."[10]   We rationalize our action because we have an "ideal of rationality."   This statement suggests that rationalization is something gratuitously added to action to satisfy a special taste, a sort of ornamental façade, having no structural significance.

[9] Cf. Ch. XXII.
[10] *Psychology of Insanity*, 1919, pp. 65-67, 135.   (Italics mine.)

Similarly, Mr. A. G. Tansley, writes that

"the acts resulting from a complex which is not in harmony with the mind as a whole, and of which one is ashamed, are generally rationalised, that is to say, some reason is given for the acts which has nothing to do with their true cause, but which is intended to satisfy the mind, or some outside enquirer, that the acts are justified."

The same writer tells us later that it is also "perfectly possible to have valid reasons for a course of conduct entirely distinct from the psychical *causes* of the conduct." [11]

But this view of the matter is clearly untenable. The causal operation of complexes involves cognition or judgment as one of its indispensable factors. The complex is causally linked with the particular act through the expectation which the act begets, and this expectation is its reason,—none the less so because reasons are sometimes "far-fetched," or falsely imputed. The reason for an action is essentially and primarily a mediating condition of its performance. It is not only a determining condition, but is that proximate, crucial and controllable condition for which the term 'cause' is peculiarly appropriate.

The tendency to elaborate reasons, by which the agent is betrayed into self-deception or mendacity, signifies not the excessive indulgence of an appetite for rationality, but, as Mr. Tansley himself states, an unconscious effort "to put an end to conflict," or to conciliate "some other important complex which is felt to have a prior claim in determining conduct." [12]   Reasons could not "put an end to conflict," or remove the inhibiting effect of an antagonistic complex, if they were not psychical causes.

According to Dr. Hart [13] the politician adopts a course of action dictated by his partisan interest, and then invents fictitious reasons for it to satisfy his "ideal of rationality," or his "overwhelming need to believe" that he is acting ration-

---

[11] *The New Psychology*, 1920, pp. 104, 168. Notwithstanding the misleading character of these statements, the book as a whole contains the admirable presentation of the practical rôle of reason.

[12] *Op. cit.*, pp. 169, 160.

[13] *Op. cit.*, pp. 64-65.

ally. He ends by falsely "persuading" himself that the action is the result of these reasons. The correct analysis is as follows. His action is initially or primarily rationalized in terms of his partisan interest, and his reasons of public policy are invoked to quiet his scruples or conciliate his other interests. If these, or other reasons, were *not* invoked the action would not take place. They are genuine, but auxiliary causes of his action; though not, perhaps, indispensable, since others might have been substituted for them.[14]

§ 159. **Rationalization as Self-deceptive and Mendacious.** In the cases just cited the agent may be *self-deceived*. The politician may be mistaken in thinking that his policy will benefit the public, and the flirt may be mistaken in believing that her conduct will make her lover happy. Or, either may be mistaken in the reflective judgments (if any) which they pronounce upon their own motives. They may, for example, ignore or underestimate the rôle of the more ignoble motive. But the fact remains that the true source of this self-deception lies in the motivating power of the rationalization. It is because the original instigating interest *needs* the support, or at least the consent, of the ulterior interest or nobler motive, that the latter tends illegitimately to influence the agent's judgment. It is because this ulterior interest is really potent that it can exercise the rôle of "censor," and force acts to assume at least a disguise which is agreeable to it.

Mendacious professions imply that the agent both has a real reason for his action, and knows it truly. They imply, furthermore, that a certain judgment of his action which he implants in the minds of others will induce in them a favorable or unfavorable attitude either toward his act or toward himself. Thus a mendacious profession implies that one judgment determines the agent's interest, and that another

[14] Mr. Tansley's example of the woman who encourages the attentions of a lover whom she does not want to marry, may and should be similarly described. The conduct dictated by her vanity or sex-instinct, is in conflict with her pity or with her "principles"; meaning not merely formulas which she recites, but moral dispositions or scruples which govern her conduct. By rationalizing the act as one of kindness to the lover, she removes this conflict, or even converts it into positive support.

judgment will determine his neighbor's interest. Just as the success of a simple lie depends on true knowledge, so the success of mendacious professions depends on sound rationalization. Rationalization is not, therefore, inherently self-deceptive or mendacious. Suppose, for example, that an author is writing a book for profit. His determining tendency is money-getting, and his belief that money will accrue is the interest-judgment or effective reason that conditions his performance. But suppose that other interests (such as a desire to help his fellows) solicit his time and attention, and that he finds it impossible to do his work with an undivided mind. He may then reflect and believe that his book will do good. This new reason disarms the hostility of his humanitarian impulse, and of any other interests that may already have been subordinated to this impulse. He thus puts his activity on broader ground and obtains augmented support for it. This supplementary belief is then as genuinely a condition of his work as was the initial belief in its remunerativeness. In any given case he might have obtained the necessary support by putting it on other ground, and in that case it would mean something to say that the *specific* ulterior motive which he generated was not indispensable. It may be true that the justifying reason has brought no new ally, but has only conciliated and neutralized a possible opponent. It may also be true that the sordid motive was the initial and immediate motive. The fact remains, none the less, that the agent *did* perform the act because (among other things) of its anticipated beneficence. This ulterior reason is neither ineffectual, nor self-deceiving, nor mendacoius; though it may properly be regarded as apologetic, that is, as a reason summoned to the support of an act already selected for another reason.

It is evident that this type of behavior will be characteristic of personalities which are already highly integrated. A personality such as Professor McDougall describes in terms of 'self-regarding sentiment,' [15] in which all determining tendencies are subordinated to the tendency to promote an ideal

[15] *Social Psychology,* 1910, pp. 193 ff.

self, will be a personality in which action will to a relatively large extent be attended and conditioned by a supposition of its effect upon that self. It will be relatively necessary for such a person to have ulterior reasons if he is to act at all.

Now let us turn to the social aspects of this same apologetic reason. Men want for their action reasons which will appeal also to their fellows. They need help or fear interference, or they may merely be sensitive to social approval and disapproval. Such being the case, a man hesitates to act unless he possesses a belief about his action which when professed will dispose others favorably towards the action. This does not imply that the agent makes false or mendacious statements either about his act or about his motives, but that he makes *such* statements as are calculated to conciliate or attract the interest of others. A manufacturer produces a commodity and sells it for money, or pays money to a laborer and secures his services. He may sell for the profit, and hire for the services. These would be sufficient reasons if he were in no degree affected by the attitude of others. But being so affected he requires other reasons. He sells for the reason that his commodity is useful, and he hires for the reason that he gives the laborer the means of livelihood,— and such are his professions. He does not advertise for customers by urging them to come and make him rich, nor for laborers by urging them to come and be useful to him. In his statements about his business he explains it by reasons which others, in terms of their own interests, may also find convincing. These reasons are not the agent's only reasons, or his initial reasons, and they may be reasons for which substitutes could be found; but they may be *real* reasons, and they need not be less sound and truthful because of being socially efficacious.

The sound and valid use of rationalization is thus prior to its corruption and abuse. Because it involves judgments, it is liable to error, and in so far as it involves communication it permits of mendacity. The circumstances under which rationalization occurs do, furthermore, increase the likelihood of error, and the temptation to lie. The cure lies not in avoiding rationalization, which would put an end to any attempt to integrate interests; but in developing it, while at the same time purging it of untruth and dishonesty. Like all human instruments it should be used and not abused.

The Freudian or psycho-analytic view of human conduct is often taken to be pessimistic and cynical, and it is no doubt intended to be. It might be summarily stated as the view that the real motives of conduct are those which we are ashamed to admit either to ourselves or to others. But to regard this view of conduct as pessimistic and cynical is to neglect the meaning of shame. If man is unable to perform an act until he can see it in some relatively honorable light, this implies both that scruples are efficacious and that man is highly scrupulous. To affirm that man censors all of his acts before he performs them, is to attribute to him a degree of conscientiousness for which his best friends have hesitated to give him credit. If the modern American business man finds it impossible to devote himself to money-getting without joining a Rotary Club and proclaiming his public-spirit, it follows that public-spirit is an important factor in his motivation. It does not follow that he *is* public-spirited, for he may misjudge himself and his acts; but it does follow that he has a moral bias, and that a little more truth will perhaps make him public-spirited. If a man finds himself compelled to act in the *name* of the common good, then it is only necessary to see to it that his conduct deserves the name. He has at any rate admitted an important premise, and has exposed himself to persuasion.

That among the reasons of action we should *communicate* to others those which *appeal* to others, is only natural. That the reasons which we keep to ourselves should be the relatively un-social or anti-social reasons, is the other side of the same thing. Where social intercourse is highly developed and human performance highly organized, there is, no doubt, a danger that the professed reasons should be unduly emphasized, or that the reserved reasons should be neglected altogether, in such judgments as a man pronounces on himself. But it does not follow that a professed reason is not a real reason, or that a reserved reason is bad reason. Indeed a professed reason may acquire greater reality or efficacy by virtue of being professed, and men become in fact better by virtue of the social necessity of showing their best to the world. By casting themselves in a rôle favorably regarded by others they identify themselves more closely with it, and sometimes *become* that which at first they merely sought to appear.

§ 160. **Ex Post Facto Reasoning.** We have now to consider a case in which the charges of inefficacy, self-deception and mendacity seem to be better grounded,—the case, namely, in which the rationalizing process invokes reasons after the act.

Ex post facto reasons are clearly ineffectual as regards the original performance, but not as regards its subsequent repetition. Furthermore, although it is customary to speak of them as "invented," they are not arbitrary, since they are judgments, and as such are accountable to their objects. It is not implied that judgments are false simply because they are offered as *ex post facto* reasons.

But in offering them as his *reasons,* does not the agent deceive himself and mislead others? This evidently depends on the sense of the question which is put to him, or which he puts to himself. As a matter of fact the question, "Why did you sell me this land at twice its real value?" is commonly understood to mean, "What reasons can you *now find* for doing it?" It is a question of the defensibility of the act, and refers not to its original performance but to present culpability, to possible retraction, or to future repetition. If a man now finds and states reasons for his act which did not condition its performance, he is mendacious only provided he is understood to be accounting for the past, which is usually *not* what is understood by either party.

It is absurd to suppose that when challenged to 'explain' one's action one is supposed to give an historical account of its conditions. The point of the question is to render the action susceptible to the influence of opinion and discussion. The agent is called upon to give reasons for his action, because these are the conditions of performance by which it is subject to control by persuasion. It is a well-known fact that we describe as *the* cause of an event that particular condition by which we hope to control it. The chemist will explain human action in terms of drugs, the eugenicist in terms of heredity, and the psychiatrist in terms of complexes. In ordinary human relations one man is not permitted to control another except by persuasion. To seek out other conditions of action would be an invasion of privacy. He will therefore seek for an explanation of another man's action in terms of that other man's creed, which is the point at which he may legitimately influence it. An *ex post facto* reason given in response to such a demand, and understood as the introduction of a new condition by which one's present or subsequent action is subjected to persuasion, may, again, be effectual, truthful and sound.

§ 161. **Group Professions.** As illustrating rationalization which is essentially apologetic and may also be *ex post facto,* let us now consider the more complicated case of group professions, such as party-platforms, or statements of national policy. In order to avoid confusion we have first to distinguish between a pledge and a creed. A party-platform may conceivably contain in it no common beliefs whatsoever. A group of men may pledge themselves as a group that if elected to office they will abolish the tariff and introduce universal military service. There may not be a man in the party who believes that either policy is right or expedient. To find a discrepancy between the party-professions and the convictions of individuals is under this interpretation entirely meaningless, since the profession is not a matter of conviction at all— unless it be the conviction that by making promises of a certain sort the party's success will be assured. It would appear that this is as a rule the correct interpretation of political platforms. A party is an organized will, and not a unanimous opinion. It is united by a common resolve, which makes it possible for public opinion to choose it for the sake of its prospective deeds.

But it is clear that group-professions do have another function, the function namely of basing united action on common fundamental convictions. When a modern nation goes to war it needs something more than a common resolve. It needs to have that resolve sustained by a creed. It needs to justify its resolve to itself and to the world, Burke spoke of the Napoleonic menace as an "armed doctrine." Arms need to be indoctrinated, as doctrines need to be armed. We have here again a case of the apologetic function of reason.

The case is comparable, though not wholly similar, to the case of the integrated personality. In both cases action must be put on fundamental ground so as to avoid internal conflict. But while in the case of personal life a subordinate tendency may inaugurate, and even complete, the act before the dominant tendency is invoked, in the case of the nation at war there must be united action from the outset. The "higher reason" has to be proclaimed in order that there shall be any war. All are, it is true, moved by fear and anger; but as instinctive and emotional reactions, these are aroused only in the presence of the enemy. They may unite combatants in action, but they cannot unite a nation in preparation, support and prolonged perseverance. There must be some interpretation of the war, some meaning or belief, that will render it acceptable to the entire nation in its moment of deliberate action. This interpretation must recommend it to all men not only in their moments of passion, as when goaded to fury by reports of atrocities, but in their more reflective moods. It must represent the war in an aspect that makes it congruent with those higher determining tendencies by which each man's personality is integrated. Even if a war is waged defensively in one's own territory, where instinctive and emotional reactions are constantly aroused even among the civilian population, a man needs to conceive his action as the protection of his country and his home, in order that he may reconcile his violence with his ideal self and avoid internal conflict and remorse. Where the enemy is distant and the danger remote, where the war is offensive rather than defensive, he must represent the enemy as evil

and transform anger into righteous indignation. In so far
as the war inflicts suffering upon enemies who are personally
innocent, it is necessary for a conscientious man to conceive
it as a war for a cause, or for that end which he acknowledges as supreme.

There is, of course, another aspect of the matter. With
nations as with individuals there is need of agreement and
confirmation. In waging war a nation solicits the support
of neutral opinion and the approving judgment of posterity.
It will therefore endeavor to find reasons for its action which
will also weigh as reasons in the minds of others not sharing
the narrower national interest. It will translate its cause
into general principles, such as self-determination, or peace,
or the security of small nations. But here, as in the cases
already cited, the motive which instigates the *finding* of such
reasons does not in the least prevent their *being* reasons when
they are found.

It is not an accident that these creeds which sustain united
effort are moral creeds. For this is precisely what a moral
creed is. What all men in their sober moments agree to
serve, is *ipso facto* a moral cause. It is a moral cause because
it has fortified itself against external protest by including all
interests, and against internal conflict by reconciling all interests.[16] The national morale is insecure in so far as the
nation develops a bad conscience, either through the violated
ideals of its own members, or through a sense of guilt in
the accusing presence of mankind. It is to avoid the weakness arising from such a lack of moral integrity that nations
profess the best that is in them when they go to war.[17]

Enough has been said to make it clear that such professions are real and effective causes of action. What of
their honesty? That is as it may be. A statesman's lie
is not different from any other lie. If a nation's policy is
officially misrepresented in order to deceive another nation

---

[16] Cf. Ch. XXII.
[17] Under the circumstances it is not strange that the professions of
warring nations should be similar, nor does this in itself suggest that
such a profession is, as LeBon maintains, a "paroxysm of collective
madness" (*Psychology of the Great War*, English trans., 1916, p. 268).

or its own members, then such a profession is mendacious. But to suppose that this is a usual or even a common course of procedure is to lose sight altogether of the real bearing of political action. A national profession of faith is not primarily intended as a means of deceit, but as a means of solidifying the nation itself on grounds that are at the same time acceptable to the deliberate judgment of mankind. The effect which it is primarily intended to secure is an effect which a lie cannot secure.

That there will remain a wide discrepancy between such a national profession and the convictions of individuals, is to be taken for granted. The national profession includes only that element of individual conviction by which individuals are united. This element may have relatively great or relatively little weight with any given individual. The man who would fight anyway, from hope of gain or from love of fighting, does not need this higher moral motivation. With him the effect of the war upon the security of his country, or upon the cause of international peace, is an unobjectionable but superfluous consideration. For the man of pacific disposition, or the man who fears pecuniary loss, on the other hand, be no inducement to war save such an ulterior end. The result is that the man who would fight anway for more immediate or sordid reasons, is credited with the same high motivation that is necessary to induce the services of the scrupulous man. Since the services of the entire nation are required, the national profession of faith does not describe the grouping or balancing of motives in any individual, but expresses the moral inducement which is necessary to bring the services of all to market. It is levelled at the marginal man, and the warlike man enjoys a sort of producer's surplus. He acquires a moral status which is no fair measure of the actual cost to him. The same thing is true of the partisan who hopes for office. The expectation of personal gain might have been a sufficient inducement for him, but he is credited with loyalty to the principles of the party.

If the national profession is not to be identified with the

whole complex of an individual citizen's beliefs, still less is it to be identified with the personal convictions of the statesman. It is the statesman's function to formulate a creed to which all within the nation will assent, which will give to all a reason for prosecuting the war, and which will afford neutral observers a reason for favoring the nation's victory. He will not simply formulate his own creed. It may be that the creed which is effective for the purpose is one which he invents, but to which he himself never gives more than a half-hearted assent. He is not speaking for himself, but for the nation. Whether, incidentally, he misrepresents himself is a matter of little account. But if he misrepresents the nation, if his statements do not express the common conviction, they will be empty and wasted words.

The beliefs which divide men are in their turn not less important than the beliefs which unite them. During the recent war human action was interpreted in terms of the national professions, even though these were in many individuals factors of minor importance. Every man was conceived, and was encouraged to conceive himself, in the rôle of a patriot and crusader. The emergency having passed, and this common purpose being eliminated, the residual motives are again disclosed in their variety and comparative selfishness. We see men once more as individuals, classes, groups, and factions. When men act as a nation their common convictions are emphasized; when they cease to act as a nation the emphasis shifts to those convictions which divide them. Had this been remembered and discounted, much painful disillusionment might have been avoided.

The national creed, like that of the individual, may be *ex post facto*. It is possible, in the one case as in the other, that one should find reasons for what one *has* done, which will now serve to reinforce it against attack, or sustain it through prolonged effort, even though they did not condition its original performance. And there is neither deceit nor intent to deceive unless one is understood to be writing history.

Apologetic reasoning, whether personal or social, is too fundamental and significant a thing to be dismissed either as gratuitous, or as self-deceptive and mendacious. The root of this thing is not to be discovered in "an overwhelming need to believe that we are acting rationally," or in any other queer human idiosyncrasy. The function of apologetic reasoning is to enable a man or a nation or mankind, despite the wide variety of opinions and interests that must divide them, to find some common ground for harmonious and united action. If apologetic reasoning when so interpreted is to be called by the name of 'rationalization,' then that name must acquire new associations and come to mean the use rather than the abuse. For the thing itself is a normal and effective condition of all personal and social life, and in the exercise of its true function is as much bound to honesty and truth as is any other mode of reasoning.

CHAPTER XIV

THE UNITY OF SOCIETY [1]

I. THE NATURE OF THE PROBLEM

§ 162. Recent Emphasis on Society. That some, if not all value is in some sense a function of society, or of social relations, is an undisputed fact. The social aspect of value has been repeatedly alluded to or implied. We are now prepared to face it directly.

First, what *is* society? In what sense, if any, is it proper to speak of society as an entity, existing and acting in its own right? Is there such a *thing* as society; and, if so, what kind of thing is it? This question has of late been forced into prominence by several causes.

There has been a swing of psychological doctrine away from an excessive emphasis on the individual. We are still in a stage of reaction against the errors of the eighteenth century. It was then thought that man was naturally self-centred, and that he acted solely from a calculation of self-interest. To offset this error it has been necessary to exaggerate the extent of his regard for others; in other words, to put the emphasis on sympathy, imitation, gregariousness, and the parental instinct. Again, it was once thought that man was self-sufficient, and that for his happiness and perfection he needed only to be removed from the intrusion and tyranny of his fellows. To offset this error it has been necessary to insist upon the value of organization and institutional control. Furthermore, the old psychology, which was excessively rationalistic, neglected the unconscious and elusive, but wide-

---

[1] Parts of the present chapter are reprinted from articles entitled, "Is there a Social Mind?", published in *Amer. Jour. of Sociology,* Vol. XXVII, 1922.

spread and unceasing, play of mind on mind. Thus the new movement has been a wholesome corrective and supplement to the old psychology. It has required its catchwords for driving home the truth—such catchwords as "the crowd," "the group-mind," "the social consciousness," and "the collective will."

At the same time that there has been a swing of psychological doctrine toward the social aspects of human nature, these aspects have themselves been greatly increased in number and variety. Thus Maitland, in his Introduction to Gierke's *Political Theories of the Middle Age,* remarks that "in the second half of the nineteenth century corporate groups of the most various sorts have been multiplying all the world over at a rate that far outstrips the increase of 'natural persons.' " [2] This is true not only of corporations in the legal sense, but of national states having a vivid sense of corporate unity, and of innumerable associations within the state. Organization has become a habit, if not a disease. There is no individual who does not belong to something, and the average individual belongs to a great variety of intersecting groups, in each of which he has a different status and plays a different part. The activities incident to this multiple membership make up the larger part of a man's life, and the whole of his obituary. Unorganized social groups have also shown a tendency to increase in number, variety, volume, and importance. There have always been crowds; but whereas close physical proximity was once their necessary condition, modern facilities for communication, publicity, and transportation, together with the wide diffusion of literacy, have made it possible for crowd influences to overcome distance and to act upon the individual almost continuously.

§ 163. **The Importance of the Problem.** In view of these facts, it is not strange that the last three-quarters of a century should have witnessed an enormous and diversified growth of social science; or that fe should find ourselves equipped with an extensive and vivid social vocabulary. Nor would it be surprising if this vocabulary should require some overhauling,

[2] Edition of 1913, p. xii.

lest terms and phrases which have served a useful purpose in dislodging old prejudices and exciting the speculative imagination, should in their turn conduce to incoherence, credulity, sentimentality, or even fanaticism.

We shall be particularly concerned to examine the propriety of conferring on society the attributes of man, as did Durkheim, when he referred to society as a "collective personality" and "a subject *sui generis*"; or as did Espinas, when he referred to it as "a living being like the individual." [3]

The importance of the question for the theory of value, and in particular for a theory such as that here advocated, is clearly evident. It is not merely a question of the value to be ascribed *to* society, which will be affected by any prerogatives or perfections which may be imputed to it; but it is also a question of the value conferred *by* society. If society is in fact a "subject *sui generis*," then over and above those values which arise from the interests of men or of animals, we must also provide for those arising from the interests of societies. The purposes of societies may then be distinguished from those of men, and may with some justification be preferred to them or superimposed upon them.

II. THE SOCIAL-SUBSTANCE THEORY

§ 164. **The Conception of Substance.** The problem of the nature of society has very deep roots, and one's solution of it will inevitably reflect one's logic and fundamental philosophy. There is danger, therefore, of begging the question. If we were to proceed forthwith to *analyze* society, we should in effect be assuming that it was complex; we should virtually be committed in advance to the conclusion that it is composed of individuals, and constituted by their relations. An opponent might then object that our very method of procedure had eliminated the true view, namely, that society is an indivisible and substantial unity. This view may be

[3] E. Durkheim, *Bulletin de la Soc. Française de Philos.*, Vol. VI, 1906, p. 128; A. Espinas, *Des Sociétés Animales*, 1877, p. 10.

termed the doctrine of "social-substance," and must be examined first.[4]

The conception of substance is a habit of mind which is innocent for practical purposes, but vicious for scientific or theoretical purposes. It is the habit of imputing to unitary complexes an entity (their substance) over and above their qualities, properties and relations. The correction of this habit does not imply the rejection of "things," physical or spiritual, if by "things" is meant unitary complex. That which is rejected is the notion that the unity of the thing *substands*, underlies, transcends, or is otherwise concealed beyond or within, its manifestations. The corrective of this habit of thought is the notion that the unity of the thing consists in the *systematic* character of its manifestations. According to this view a thing is a complex with some sort of unifying relation.

To think substantially, rather than analytically and relationally, is undoubtedly a primitive and inveterate habit. The explanation of this habit is of first importance for the understanding of the history of the human mind. Two of its sources are readily recognizable.

The notion of substance arises, in the first place, from imputing to things themselves the structure which belongs to the knowledge of them. Knowledge, as we have seen, consists essentially in expectation. It is concerned with data not for themselves simply, but for what they mean, or for what is anticipated of them. Cognitively speaking, the data of experience are signs. When a cognitive expectation is fulfilled there is some implied relation between the index and the predicate, which renders the former a suitable occasion for expecting the latter. This objective environmental relation is not itself one of forward or future reference, as is the cognitive relation itself. The geometrical curvature of the shield justifies the expectation of its convex surface when its concave surface is given, and the expectation of its concave sur-

---

[4] Cf. M. R. Cohen's "Communal Ghosts and other Perils in Social Philosophy," *Jour. of Philos.,* Vol. XVI, 1919. I find myself in almost entire agreement with this admirable article.

face when its convex surface is given. In the shield as an objective reality these aspects are reciprocal, or constitute a system of relations in which neither is the sign or promise of the other. But when the cognitive relation is imputed to this system, whichever aspect serves as the index of the judgment takes on the character of a sign, while the other, serving as predicate, takes on the character of its promise or potentiality. But since the index and predicate are interchangeable *both* may assume this character of potentiality. In judgments whose index is 'this,' the datum is only a locus in experience, all other characters assuming this character of potentiality. In ideal judgments, such as "there is a so and so," the index reduces to the undifferentiated environment, and the entire object becomes an unlocalized potentiality. In one way or another the index of judgment may thus reduce to a bare 'that which,' distinguishable only by what is expected of it; while all the specific characters of experience take on the character of the expected, that is of a latency or virtuality. Names, such as 'Caesar,' 'gold,' 'I,' 'you,' whether proper names, common names, whether nouns or pronouns, are symbols for systems of expectations. In so far as these expectations are not verified the object is simply a focus of expectancy, an environmental imminence,—a promise or threat of something to come.[5]

There is, in other words, a 'cognitive fallacy' similar to the familiar 'pathetic fallacy,'[6] and even more fundamental. The latter consists in assuming that an interesting effect must have an interested cause, or that in so far as nature is good or bad, nature must be benevolent or malicious. The cognitive fallacy is the assumption that an expected effect must

[5] For an examination of the conception of substance in the development of modern materialism, cf. the author's *Present Philosophical Tendencies,* 1912, pp. 65-75. The close relation between the theory of judgment and the notion of substance has been forcibly expounded by B. Russell in his *Critical Exposition of the Philosophy of Leibnitz,* 1900. Leibnitz's view that the predicate of judgment is contained in the subject, combined with the fact that all other parts of the universe may in some sense be predicated of any indicated part, leads to his paradoxical monadism, according to which each element of the universe is potentially the whole universe.

[6] Cf. §24.

have an expectant cause, or that in so far as nature is fulfilling or surprising it must be anticipatory. The effect of
both fallacies is to impute to all natural elements and causes
in so far as they are objects for the mind, that character
of forward reference, or determination by the future, which is
in fact peculiar to the mind itself, that is, to the specific functions which in nature are uniquely characteristic of an organism endowed with a nervous system.

A second factor in the development of this notion of
substance is the psychology of self-knowledge. To others
I am a characteristic set of responses which, being functionally
associated in my body, are conjointly and summarily expected.
In self-knowledge these responses are attended by organic
sensations, and in particular by a sense of alertness, tension
or effort, which fills the interval of delayed response. I am
sensible, in other words, of *the act of anticipation,* of being
about to do this or that. Such sensations may, then, be imputed to any index of expectation. When I anticipate *b* of *a,*
I may impute to *a* not only this anticipatory relation to *b,*
but a sense of activity and power, which is regarded as its
present actuality and secret inwardness.

Whether or no this analysis of the notion of substance
is adequate,—and it would be presumptuous to claim more for
it than its broad agreement with the trend of critical opinion,
in any case it is obvious that the notion of substance is readily
applicable to the case of society. A man deals with the fellow-
members of his group *en masse.* He perceives them in the
aggregate, he is helped or injured by their combined force,
he engages with them in divers forms of collective and organized activity. In countless intricate and intimate ways
they are associated in his experience both with one another
and with himself.[7] They form a highly solidified system of
expectations and ends. Being so unified and segregated, the
group tends to assume the aspect of a substance, to which
he may conceive himself to belong, or to which he may conceive himself to be opposed. Viewed substantially the group
becomes a soul or spirit, manifesting itself in individuals, but

[7] Ch. XVI, *passim.*

having an ulterior reality of its own. It becomes a disembodied potency, a mere threat or promise; or it may be charged with a sense of activity, and become a "power." In other words, society is an object peculiarly apt for the cognitive and pathetic fallacies, and for a misguided anthropomorphism.

§ 165. **Primitive Society and Primitive Sociology.** The modern French school of sociologists founded by Durkheim has emphasized the disposition of the primitive mind to substantialize society, and has construed this disposition as evidence of the *real* substantiality both of primitive society and of society in general.[8]

If the notion of substance is a primitive notion, or a pre-scientific habit of mind, then it is reasonable to expect primitive man to be peculiarly addicted to it. The history of science amply supports the thesis that the progress of modern science has been due mainly to a substitution of the category of relation for the category of substance. This does not mean that the scientist himself has ceased to employ the notion of substance, but that his technique consists in methods of observing and verifying relations; that he admits substantive terms only when they stand for relational systems of manifest properties; and that he states his results in terms of laws, which are summary formulations of exact quantitative relations.

It is evident that the notion of substance tends to beget a naïve and premature intellectual satisfaction. To ascribe manifestations to a substance is an easy way of shirking intellectual responsibility. The precise nature of a substance being undefined, it is deemed capable of anything and everything. An indeterminate potentiality, a something whose manifestations are known, but which, for all one knows, might equally well manifest itself otherwise, is the most seductive and infantile of all intellectual conveniences. If by primitive mind we mean the comparatively immature and un-

---

[8] E. Durkheim, *Elementary Forms of the Religious Life,* trans. by J. W. Swain, 1915; L. Lévy-Bruhl, *Les Fonctions Mentales dans les Sociétés Inférierures,* 1910, and *La. Mentalité Primitive,* 1922 (trans. by L. A. Clare, 1923). Cf. §§ 185, 186.

trained mind, or the mind which is easily satisfied, then it is evident that the primitive mind would find the notion of substance peculiarly congenial, and would apply this notion to an object at once so familiar and so perplexing as society.

We may agree, furthermore, that, according to the ordinary view, the character of primitive society is peculiarly apt to evoke this substantializing tendency of thought. Primitive society is comparatively undifferentiated, the division of labor is comparatively undeveloped, and custom is comparatively inflexible. Religious ceremonies, war, and other collective activities are comparatively frequent and impressive. A comparatively large fraction of the individual's life is a matter of public concern. The individual lives under the watchful and censorious scrutiny of his fellows, and what he does is largely prescribed for him. Comparatively little scope is allowed to personal liberty, and to that which is unique and private in the individual. Assuming this to be the case, the primitive mind naturally thinks of his group as a mysterious and unlocalized power-behind-the-scenes, and of his priest, chief or other leader as its instrument or embodiment. So much may be granted.

The argument becomes significant for our purposes, however, only when it purports to deal, not with primitive man's primitive ideas about primitive society, but with *the nature of primitive society,* and hence by implication with society in general. The besetting danger of the historical and comparative method in sociology is the confusion between the social processes or structures of any given time, and the ideas contemporaneously held about them. Sociology, in the broad sense, is concerned with both, and with their interaction; but this only renders it more imperative that their confusion should be avoided. There was or is a society that we call primitive, and a primitive idea about it held by its members. It is the task of the sociologist to discover the nature of this primitive society, and of this primitive idea. It is his task, furthermore, to show how the nature of primitive society is affected by the primitive idea its members have of it, and how the idea which primitive men have of society is affected by the primitive nature of the society in which they live. But in so doing the sociologist forms his own, namely a modern and corrected, idea of the nature of primitive society; and while he aims to discover the primitive idea of society, he does not credit it or accept it. Otherwise the standard sociology would be the primitive sociology, or sociology would be sound in proportion as it was atavistic. And just as the modern sociologist aims to obtain new and modern ideas about primitive ideas of society, so he aims to obtain new and modern ideas about their object, namely, the constitution of primitive society. He obtains these results by employing a reflective, analytic and technical procedure which primitive man in his relatively naïve and untutored condition of mind has not yet acquired.

By employing such a method he discovers, for example, that in the religious thought of primitive man the sacred object is not the visible object with its empirical properties, but something which this object "brings to mind and symbolizes." Since its "virtues" are "not intrinsic in it," or since it plays only the "rôle of reminder," it can be as sacred in any of its parts as it is on the whole; so far as sacredness is concerned, "the part is equal to the whole." [9] This is equivalent to saying that the objects of primitive religious thought are substances in the sense just analyzed.

Or, the modern sociologist finds that the primitive mind is addicted to the idea of "mana," describable as follows:

"It is a power or influence, not physical and in a way supernatural; but it shows itself in physical force, or in any kind of power or excellence which a man possesses. This mana is not fixed in anything, and can be conveyed in almost anything." [10]

He discovers, furthermore, that primitive man conceives society itself as a sort of mana or "diffused force." To grasp this idea it may be desirable that the sociologist should achieve a sympathetic insight into primitive ways of thinking, by reviving, let us say, certain primitive elements of his own intellectual inheritance.

[9] Durkheim, op. cit., p. 229.
[10] Quoted by Durkheim, op. cit., p. 194.

But the sociologist does not therefore permanently alienate his critical consciousness, and fall to thinking of society as mana. He asks himself what sort of society it really is that the primitive mind conceives as mana, and why the primitive mind so conceives it. He understands the belief, and he understands its object, but *he does not adopt the belief as his own belief about the object.* Or if he does, he falls into confusion, and forfeits the advantage of belonging to a scientific rather than to a primitive stage of culture.

Observers living in the early years of the twentieth century observed the growth of a sort of Teutonic Totemism, which answers closely the description which Durkheim gives of primitive religion. Those who were not subject to its spell, or those who have exorcised it, understand something of the structure and genesis of the cult, but do not credit it. In the light of the facts they call it a dangerous superstition, and not a sociology.

Similarly, contemporary Americans have witnessed the growth of the Ku Klux Klan. They have observed that by mask, hood, secrecy and darkness, by names and symbols, by ceremonies of initiation and by deeds of violence, this organization has succeeded in creating among its more naïve members and victims the idea of a mysterious and menacing Thing, a "diffused force," "a power or influence, not physical and in a way supernatural," a "mana" that "is not fixed in anything, and can be conveyed in almost anything." Shall we then say that the Ku Klux Klan *is* all these things? Shall we believe that the Ku Klux Klan is a "subject *sui generis*"? Shall we speak literally as well as methaphorically of "the spirit of the Ku Klux Klan"? Evidently not, because to do so would be to yield ourselves to its spell, shut our eyes to the facts, and reduce ourselves to the intellectual level of those upon whom its tricks are practised. As critical observers, as judges of social phenomena, or as scientific sociologists, we note the mechanism of the impostor, exchange winks with the augurs, and analyze the method by which the illusion is created. We know that the Ku Klux Klan is a group of human beings brought into certain relations, invested with certain trappings, subject to certain ideas and emotions, and enabled thereby to create certain ideas and emotions in the minds of others. The same critical and analytical method would lead to a similar result in the case of the primitive totem, or the "soul of the nation," or the "collective will," or the "state-personality," in so far as substantively conceived; not that these ideas imply any deliberate or malicious deception, but only that they are errors if accepted literally either by the naïve or by the speculative mind, and errors which can be pathologically explained in terms of complex and analyzable processes.

III. THE SOCIAL FORCE THEORY

§ **166. Meanings of 'Social Force.'** The conception of 'force,' like that of substance, has given initial plausibility to the view that society is an entity distinct from human individuals. The employment of the expression, 'social force' in any of three senses tends to discourage analysis, and to provide a facile and superficial explanation of social phenomena.

In the first of these three senses, 'social force' is only the dynamic aspect of social substance, and arises from the same naïve habit of thought. A social substance is, as we have seen, a potency or virtuality, a being characterized wholly in terms of what may be expected of it. Whether one thinks of it statically as a social soul, or thinks of it dynamically as a social energy, or combines both ideas in that of a sort of social juice, an active substance, or a substantial activity,— does not greatly matter. The being in question is too protean and mysterious for any nice and scrupulous definition.

In a second sense social force signifies an inter-individual socializing agency: a power that operates in a kind of no-man's land between individuals, like Tarde's "current of imitation"; or which lurks in the individual, ready to spring into action when other individuals enter the field.[11] Those who

---

[11] G. Tarde, *Les Lois de l'Imitation,* 1895, p. xiii. Cf. also, below, § 191. Tarde has been accused by the followers of Durkheim of explaining

hold this view regard society as generated by the relations of individuals; and they are open to attack rather because of their manner of conceiving these relations, than because they invoke them. It will be convenient to postpone the consideration of this notion of social force [12] until after we have disposed of those views which hypostasize society itself, and neglect or disparage the individual components.

There remains a third sense of the expression 'social force,' arising from what Le Bon has called "the principle of fatality." [13] Thus, for example, T. E. Cliffe Leslie contends that it is not this or that particular individual that governs the course of history, but "the more lasting forces of society decide."

"Napoleon I," he continues, "carried the boundaries of France to the Elbe, but they are now what they would have been had no Corsican adventurer ever found his way to Paris. And not the will of Napoleon III, but the will of France upon the one hand, and of the rest of Europe on the other, and the balance of European power, will determine whether the French flag shall float over Antwerp, Coblentz, Genoa, and Alexandria at the end of the present century." [14]

What holds of the Napoleons will hold *a fortiori* of all humbler men. By taking one individual after another and demonstrating his impotence, one arrives at the conclusion that no individual counts for anything, but that history is governed entirely by "lasting forces" such as "the will of France" or of Europe.

This view is not naïve, like that of social substance, but arises from the wide perspective of the historical imagination. It is an erroneous inference from an indisputable fact. It is an indisputable fact that great historical events are re-

phenomena by "the occult virtue of substances" as one once explained "the flame by phlogiston and the fall of bodies by gravity" (P. Fauconnet and M. Mauss, article on "Sociologie" in *La Grande Encyclopédie*, Vol. XXX, p. 166). It is a question, I think, whether these writers have not transferred this occultism from the part to the whole, instead of removing it altogether.

[12] The topic is resumed below, Ch. XVI, Sect. I.

[13] G. Le Bon, *Psychology of Revolution*, trans. by B. Miall, 1913, pp. 126-130.

[14] *Essays in Political and Moral Philosophy*, 1879, pp. 30, 33.

sultants or summations of many causes, and that no individual is solely responsible for them, but it is erroneous to infer that no individual is responsible for them at all. The individual *participates* in their causation, *shares* responsibility for them, and may properly be *held* responsible for them, provided such a judgment on the part of public opinion or legal authority will serve as an effective means of controlling them. The fiction of a 'social force' which overrides individuals as alien fatality, arises from three facts, each of which is quite simple in itself: individuals are always only partial and insufficient causes of historical events; individuals are sometimes superfluous; individual efforts are sometimes, if not always, deflected from their course by other causes.

§ 167. **The Individual Cause Insufficient.** Neither a purposive human agency nor a mechanical agency operates *in vacuo,* but supplements given conditions. We may agree entirely with Cliffe Leslie, when he says:

"The dominant ideas and associations of the time and place, the help or hindrance which individual genius meets from other minds, the appliances at hand, the things already done, the reward and countenance, or the condemnation or organized resistance of the world around, are inevitable guides or masters. There could be no Demosthenes or Socrates without an Athens; no Cicero without a Roman forum, a senate, and the aid of Greek philosophy.[15]

In other words Demosthenes, Socrates and Cicero were both products and joint agents. They could not have been the agents they were without antecedent causes, and they could not have brought to pass what they did without auxiliary causes. It does not follow, however, that Demosthenes, Socrates and Cicero did not act as causes and were not responsible for the events of their epoch; but only that they were not exclusively responsible. The events of their epoch are not to be attributed to causes *other* than their personal agency, to diffuse impersonal causes operating independently of them, but to these persons *together with* other and supple-

[15] *Op. cit.,* p. 33.

mentary causes. To eliminate their activities and the activities of other participating agencies, simply because no one of them is sufficient by itself, would result in leaving no cause at all.

Grant that the agency of the human person is a partial cause, and it follows that in any given case it may be the decisive cause. There is no historical event so momentous that the difference between its occurrence and its non-occurrence might not have been made by the intervention of such an agency at a crucial point. Le Bon tells us that "events so great and awe-inspiring can not have been dependent upon the will of any one man, but are due to deep-seated, remote and varied causes which had been slowly piling up until the day when their effects swam suddenly into our ken."[16]

The author can scarcely mean to argue anything so obvious as that a single man cannot produce a great historic event unaided. A man cannot produce *anything* unaided, not even his own thoughts. One must suppose, therefore, that Le Bon is temporarily lapsing into the fatalism which he himself so emphatically disavows; and that he is temporarily oblivious of the fact that the greatest and most awe-inspiring events may be due to the slightest causal increment, provided this is applied at the right place and at the right time. If a human will can be a cause at all, it can be such a final increment. When we say that the historical event is due to it, we do not mean "due to it exclusively," but that the event would not have happened if *it* had not happened. The fall of the avalanche may be due to the slight push that starts it even though its mass has been "slowly piling up" as a result of "deep-seated, remote and varied causes." It will not do to say that the avalanche would have fallen without the push that started it, because, for all one knows, it might otherwise have evaporated.

Human relations define strategic points, such as a position of authority and influence, or a balance of power, or a mo-

---

[16] *Op. cit.*, p. 18. The same author tells us elsewhere (pp. 32, 33) that "a collective opinion is usually derived from an individual opinion," and that a crowd is incapable of action without a leader to direct it.

ment of transition, when the addition or subtraction of an individual's act may precipitate a revolution or create an epoch. The complex organization of modern society multiplies these strategic points, though their very multiplication tends to narrow their radius of efficacy. The "organic" character of society does not reduce the power of the individual, but increases it. If, as Professor Seignobos has pointed out, a spermatazoon can create a man, and a bacillus destroy him, it is no more incredible to suppose that a Napoleon or Bismarck can overturn states, an Augustus or a Peter the Great found empires, or the death of Henry IV upset the equilibrium of Europe.[17]

§ 168. The Individual Cause Superfluous. A further misunderstanding arises from the fact that a given personal agent may be not only insufficient but superfluous. It may be a fact that the event would have taken place without him. A man may die as a result of several diseases, any one of which would have been fatal; and we may then belittle the causal efficacy of any one of the diseases, by saying that "the man would have died without it." Similarly, when President Harding was elected by a majority of 7,000,000, there were several million more votes than were necessary. A man might have excused a purely partisan vote cast for purposes of political record, or a failure to vote at all, by saying that Harding would be elected "anyway." But it does not follow that the sick man did not die of particular diseases, or that Harding was not elected by individual votes. The explanation and control of both events lies not in the denial of component causes but in the recognition of their excessive number.

A personal agency may also be said to be superfluous in the sense that while it was as a matter of fact necessary, some substitute for it would have eventually appeared, so that the event would have occurred *"sooner or later* anyway." Thus according to Cliffe Leslie "the discovery of America

<hr>

[17] Cf. Ch. Seignobos, "La Méthode Psychol. en Sociologie," *Jour. de Psychol.*, Vol. XVII, 1920, p. 509.

was the inevitable result of its actual existence at one side
of the Atlantic and the spirit which at the other side animated Europe toward the end of the fifteenth century." [18]
In other words, there existed at the time in question many
potential Columbuses, one or another of whom *would have*
discovered America if the famous individual of that name
had not done so. Nevertheless Columbus did discover America and introduced a new epoch in human history. America
was not discovered by a "spirit" which "animates Europe."
Nor would it be especially illuminating to say that this was
the deeper cause both of Columbus and of his discovery,
unless one was prepared to go further and reduce this spirit
to terms of the interaction of individuals.

While it has to be admitted that the agency of the individual *may* be superfluous in one or both of these senses,
it by no means follows that such is universally the case. It
may or may not be true that Europe of the seventeenth century was full of potential Cromwells, or that if Pasteur had
never been born another would have taken his place. If there
are some cases such as that of Columbus in which the assumption
is probable, there are others in which it is highly improbable.
Some historical events are the work of typical men, others
of atypical men, distinguished by their rare and exceptional
traits. It is the essential characteristic of a genius that his
occurrence is improbable and unpredictable, and therefore that
history would have been different without him.[19]

§ 169. The Individual Cause Modified and Deflected.

It is also a fact, finally, that things do not always turn out
as the individual intended. The action of the individual is
not only augmented, but is modified or deflected by external
agencies beyond his control, so that the results are often wide
of the mark.

"There are then innumerable forces thwarting one another,
an endless group of parallelograms of forces, from which one

[18] *Op. cit.*, p. 29.
[19] For an admirable discussion of this question, cf. W. James, "Great
Men and their Environment," and "The Importance of Individuals," in
his *Will to Believe*, 1898.

resultant—the historical event—is produced which itself can again be looked upon as the product of a power working as a whole without consciousness or will. For what every single man wills is hindered by every other man, and the result of the struggle is something which no man had intended." [20]

But even though the outcome be something "which no man had intended," it may nevertheless be due to the fact that men intended what they did. A resultant of several forces is none the less due to these forces because it differs from the result of each of the forces operating singly. The principle of the parallelogram of forces implies the operation of component forces, rather than a "power working as a whole." In the case of historical events these component forces are in large measure interested activities of human individuals, and the method of analysis would recognize this fact and examine their conjunction and reciprocal modification.

The fact that the agency of the human person operates in a field of forces in which it is effect as well as cause, and in which it is compounded with other causes, does not argue that it is *not* a cause; but, on the contrary, gives it a generic resemblance to all causes. It signifies nothing more than that historical causation, like natural causation, is highly complex. The resultants of complex causes have to be explained *as such*, that is, by bringing to light the elements and their combining relations. To attribute such resultants to integral causes, in which the fusion of the result is imputed to a special cause named after it, is as though one were to impute the pull of two horses to a team-power rather to a summation of horse-power. It implies a preference for the antique "power of gravity," rather than the Galilean analysis and formulation of the behavior of falling bodies.

It often happens that a complexly caused effect recurs with uniform frequency. This fact is brought to light in statistical laws, such as actuarial averages or records of suicide. Such laws make it possible to predict the numerical

<hr/>

[20] Friedrich Engels, quoted by E. Bernstein, *Evolutionary Socialism,* trans. by E. C. Harvey, 1909, p. 11.

occurrence and distribution of the effect, and serve a useful purpose in locating the operative causes or in determining their gross fluctuations. But in order to *control* the effect it is necessary to discover its elementary causes. One does not reduce suicide by imputing it to a sort of suicidal force which operates at large. Even a suicidal mania, if there be such a thing, can be checked only by tracing the act of the individual suicide first to its motives, and then to the ulterior psychological, physiological or biological conditions which produce these. The theatre in which the causes are focalized and consummated is the behaving human being.

IV. SOCIETY AS A COLLECTIVE UNIT

§ 170. **Forms of Collective Unity.** Our question regarding the general nature of society has thus far received no explicit answer, save in negative terms. We have learned that it is neither profitable nor illuminating to regard society as a substance or as a force, if by these terms are meant something behind, above, below, or within its human components. Whatever else it may be, society is a collection of men. women and children; and nothing which we may later attribute to it should be allowed to contradict or obscure this essential fact.

But to reject 'social substances' and 'social forces' in the senses in which these expressions have been employed in the present chapter, does not imply the rejection of social reality, or of social unity, or even of social personality. The rejected conceptions are rejected on *general* grounds, and are held to have *no* valid application. If all things are complexes, then the complexity of society evidently does not prevent its being as good a "thing" as anything else. If unity is consistent with complexity, then no argument has as yet been adduced against the unity of society. As for the personality of society, the most formidable advocates of this view disavow any intention of separating society from human individuals. They explicitly accept the view that individuals constitute society, or that society is an organization of individuals. They simply add the further thesis, that when so organized, individuals compose and constitute a new individual of a higher order. The force of their contention lies in their asserting that human persons are themselves organizations of interests, and that societies, being organizations of human persons, are therefore more complicated persons. The exponents of this view do not, in other words, reject the principles of analysis and integration, but carry them to what they believe to be their logical conclusion.

It is thus granted by all parties at this stage of the argument, that society is an organization or collective unity of men. The next step is to examine certain relatively abstract forms of collective unity. It will be useful to consider them more or less independently of social aggregation, because the ideas are much more simple than the application. They are, in fact, very common, workaday ideas. It is customary to apply them with awe and reverence to society when, as a matter of fact, they can equally well be applied to the alphabet or to a five-foot shelf of books. There are five abstract features of grouping which will be examined in turn: (1) *class*, (2) *whole*, (3) *individual*, (4) *system*, and (5) *compound*.

§ 171. **Society a Class.** By a class we mean an aggregate of individuals, of which the same thing is true.[21] Thus all the men of whom it is true that they were born on August 2, form a class. The extreme lower limit of a class would be an aggregate of individuals of all of whom it was true only that they existed, or that they were mentioned, as, for example, Lewis Carroll's class of "shoes and ships and sealing-wax, and cabbages and kings"; or Stevenson's "the world is full of a number of things." Ordinarily, however, we think of a class as an aggregate of individuals having much in common; or where that which is true of all is the most definitive and explanatory truth about each, as in the case of an animal or plant species. When this is the case the class-name is the common noun used for designating the in-

21 C. I. Lewis, *Survey of Symbolic Logic*, 1918, p. 261.

dividual. Now it is plain that there are innumerable classes of human individuals, from the definitive biological class 'man,' to such comparatively accidental classes as those who have just now eaten dinner, or the men whose names begin with 'T.' Since it is an implied property of a man that he has or is a mind, then we can say that these are all classes of minds; and if by 'a social mind' we mean only 'a class of minds,' then there is unquestionably such a thing.

But one may properly object that this misses the real point at issue. All it means is that instead of there being only one of the kind, as in the case of the Tower of London or Vesuvius, there are, in the case of man, many of the kind. In this sense 'collectivism' and 'individualism' would not mean two alternative and mutually exclusive doctrines or ideals, but two sides of the same fact. As Bosanquet has remarked, "so far from an antithesis these terms rather suggest an identity. A collection means a collection of individuals." [22] There is this man, and there are these men, and you may study the member or the collection, as you please. The real question is whether the collection is not more than a collection, as is suggested by expressions such as the "Great Being" of Comte or the "Leviathan" of Hobbes. Bosanquet objects to both collectivism and individualism for failing to recognize the fact of social *fusion*. In his view there are, over and above such human individuals as are enumerated in a census or city directory, human individuals of a higher order, as distinct from the former as water is distinct from hydrogen and oxygen.

It is evident that in order to illuminate this question we need something more than the conception of a class, something less formal and more dynamic. But meanwhile it is worth remarking that *sometimes* when we speak of a human society, 'class of men' is all we mean. This is commonly the case with the terms 'mankind' and 'humanity'; which, if their symbolic and sentimental values are disregarded, signify

---

[22] B. Bosanquet, Review of Vaughan's "Political Writings of Rousseau," *Mind*, N. S., Vol. XXV, 1916, pp. 403-404.

no more of unity or transcendence than do the terms 'catkind' and 'felinity.'

§ 172. **Society as a Whole.** Our next conception is the conception of a 'whole.' The term is here used to signify an aggregation of individuals such that something is true of the aggregation which is not true of the individuals. We might speak of this as collective novelty. The traditional logic has recognized it in the so-called fallacies of 'composition' and 'division,' commonly illustrated by the old riddle, "Why do white sheep eat more than black?" The answer, as will doubtless be seen, is, "Because there are more of them." The point is that when individuals are aggregated some things are true of the individuals that are not true of the aggregation, and some things are true of the aggregation that are not true of the individuals; and it is desirable not to mix them up. If one undertakes to say the same things of each of the angles of a triangle that one says of all, one falls into the error of 'division'; if one undertakes to say the same things of an army that one says of a soldier, one falls into the error of 'composition.' [23]

Now there is no doubt whatsoever of the existence of wholes composed of human beings, that is, of aggregations of human beings which possess properties which are other than those of their constituents.[24] Human beings are brought together in a great variety of relations in which they compose something new. A population, an audience, a family, a crowd, an army, a labor-union—each of these does things and has

[23] Cf. J. N. Keynes, *Formal Logic*, 1906, p. 16, note.
[24] Strictly speaking, every class is a whole, and every whole a class. The extreme lower limit of a whole would be the case in which its only collective novelty was its plurality or number; and the extreme lower limit of a class would be the case in which the only thing true of all its members was their belonging to the same whole. Wholeness does not begin to be important until the collective novelties consist of dynamic properties, arising from the joint or reciprocal action of the members, and requiring temporal and spacial proximity. It is in this sense that a society is thought of as a whole, and a "social fact" defined as "a thing which resides in no one individual and which yet has no existence apart from individuals" (W. M. Davis, *Psychological Interpretations of Society*, Columbia Studies in History, etc., Vol. XXXIII, 1905-09, p. 65).

properties which it would be fallacious to attribute to its members.

Before we leave this conception there is a further distinction that it is desirable to make. Although we have considered wholeness as a dynamic conception in the sense that novelty emerges, wholeness must not be identified with *effect*. We are thinking not of the case in which a small boy and a match produce a fire; but of the case in which one small boy and another small boy *compose* a riot; or of the case in which "two is company, three's a crowd." Or, take the case of ten men pulling on a rope attached to a balloon. The force of the pull is a whole composed of the forces exerted by the individual men, while at the same time having a magnitude and a causal efficacy that are peculiarly its own. But the effect, the position or motion of the balloon, if a whole at all, is of a totally different composition.

Now, while this is obvious, it has social applications that are not so obvious. While, for example, we may speak of the combined aspirations and efforts of men as creating a total force which realizes itself in certain works of civilization, these works are not themselves wholes composed of aspirations and efforts. If we say that aspirations and efforts have "gone into" them, we must mean rather that they have "gone" than that they are "in" them. A calf may go into the making of an anaconda, but it would not be correct to say that the calf composed the anaconda. Similarly, if it should appear that society devours and assimilates men, it would be correct to say of society that its sources or conditions were human, but it would not be correct to describe it as a whole composed of men. There is a moral to this, which may appear later.

§ 173. **Society an Individual.** In the third place, a whole may be said to have *individuality*. This term, like many terms in this field of discourse, is badly overworked. It appears to mean at least three independent things, two of which are not only independent but opposite. Thus (*a*), a whole is said to be an individual when it is itself a member

of a class. Just as we speak of individual men in relation
to the class of mankind, so we may speak of individual
societies in relation to the class of societies, or of individual
nations in relation to a league of nations. Individuality in
this sense implies the possession of a class-characteristic *in
common* with other individuals. But sometimes, (*b*), we use
the term 'individuality' to signify uniqueness. A society with
a "well-marked" individuality would be comparatively lacking
in common characteristics, and the *individual* part of it would
be the *distinctive* part of it. Another meaning of individuality
is (*c*) identity. This is disclosed, if not constituted, by
persistence through change. In this sense a highly individual
society will be one whose characters as a whole remain constant, while its external relations and its component members vary. Its constant character may consist in its territorial
location, its racial inheritance, its peculiar mentality, or its
form of organization.

In all three of these aspects, class-membership, uniqueness, and persistence, it is clear that a society may be said to
be an individual; or, in some cases, to be possessed of a high
degree of individuality. It does not follow, however, that
a society is a person, because 'personality' implies certain specific psychological characteristics which many individuals
such, for example, as an individual mountain, do not possess.[25]

If we are to use the term 'individual' for societies, we
must first free it altogether of its distinctively human associations. Individuals may compose individuals; in other
words, there are hierarchies of individuals. But if we are
not to be lost in hopeless confusion we must employ *some*
term to indicate the *place* of an individual in the hierarchy.
Otherwise, composite individuals cannot be distinguished from

---

[25] There is another and somewhat more technical sense of individuality,
cited by Royce, in his *Conception of God*, 1897, p. 239. An individual is
logically indivisible, that is, it cannot belong to both of two mutually
exclusive classes. Thus Americans in the collective sense can be both
white and black (including negroid), while America, as an individual,
cannot. A society may be so conceived, in other words, as to imply its
belonging either wholly to one or wholly to the other of all mutually
exclusive classes to which it belongs at all. Pp. 217-271 of this book
provide an admirable introduction to the whole subject of individuality.

component individuals. In current discussions it is customary to employ the expression '*the* individual' to signify a man, with the result that when society is proved to be an individual, it at once assumes in the imagination the semblance of a man. Whenever this ambiguity is likely to arise it is desirable to employ the phrase 'individual man,' to signify the unit of which a society is composed. It will then be false by definition to speak of a society as an individual man.

But unfortunately there is a similar difficulty attaching to the term 'society.' This term is not used so abstractly as the term 'individual,' for one does not as yet speak of a society of atoms. But there is a growing practice among biologists of speaking of an animal or plant organism as a society of cells, so that 'society' as well as 'individual' must be freed from its distinctively *human* associations. Wherever doubt is likely to arise we should therefore speak of a 'society of men' or 'society of cells,' or a 'colony of ants,' rather than of a 'society' simply. It may be proper to speak of a man as a society of cells, but it would be false by definition to speak of him as a society of men.

The ambiguities attaching to the terms 'individual' and 'society' are further aggravated by the use of the expression 'social individual,' which might mean an individual society, or an individual with social qualifications, or an individual composed of societies.

It is necessary, therefore, to employ such terms as 'cell,' or 'man,' or 'nation,' in an absolute, rather than a relative sense; or, in such wise as to indicate unique places in the hierarchy of individuals. A man may then properly be spoken of as both a society and an individual, meaning that he both comprises cells and composes societies. But it would be nonsense to say that a man is either a cell or a nation; or that a cell is either a man or a nation, or that a nation is either a cell or man.

§ 174. **Society a System.** Fourthly, we speak of a whole as a *system*, when we refer to the connecting relations rather than to the members so related; as when we conceive a waterfall in terms of its pattern, rather than in terms of its drops. In common speech this distinction is conveyed by the term 'relationship.' The family, for example, is a complex relationship, or system, in so far as we think of the particular members as negligible, provided only a specific set of relations is maintained. There must be a marital relation, a parental relation, a filial relation, and a fraternal relation; and these relations are arranged in a fixed pattern. Thus, for example, if A stands in the marital relation to B and if C stands in the filial relation to A, then B stands in the parental (or step-parental) relation to C. In a system the terms appear only as defined by the relations, or as enabling the relations to obtain. When a concrete object enters into a system it is called by a special name to indicate that it has assumed a specific set of relations. Thus a man is called a 'father' or 'husband,' where these names mean only having such-and-such relations. Sometimes we speak of the concrete object as having assumed this or that rôle, or as having acquired this or that status or capacity. It is the same thing as the familiar distinction between the office and the man.

Now societies of men may be systems,—there can be no doubt about that. When members of an army die in battle, other men take their places and assume their rôles, leaving the relationship intact. At least in one of its aspects, an army is a mechanism of inter-changeable parts. During the mediæval period when collective entities like Church and State were favorite topics of speculation, this systematic aspect of relations was clearly recognized and distinguished. The Church, as Gierke tells us, was conceived both *"genossen-schaftlich"* as the congregation of the faithful, and *"anstaltlich"* as a hierarchy of ecclesiastical offices.[26] The offices, like, for example, the papacy, were thought of as having a higher being than their temporary incumbents. Similarly, we may think of almost any society either as a collection of concrete human beings; or as an institution, that is, an abstract system of relations.

[26] Gierke, *Political Theories of the Middle Age,* Maitland's translation, 1913, pp. 58, 161.

In this discussion of *class, whole, individual,* and *system,* we have first dissociated them from the social context, and then illustrated their social applications. The purpose is two-fold: on the one hand, to present them as simply as possible; and, on the other hand, to rob them of any honorific associations which they may have acquired. They are all terms which need deflating, and the best way to deflate them is to use them in other contexts where one's idolatrous proclivities are less likely to be aroused. Take a row of books, for example. (1) They constitute a class in that they are all books; and (2) they constitute a whole, in that there are things which are true of the row, such as its five-foot length, which are not true of the members. (3) They constitute an individual whole in all three senses: (*a*) this is but one of many rows; (*b*) it is more or less unique; and (*c*) it maintains its identity though all the books should be gradually replaced. Finally (4), they constitute a system in that the complex of relative positions can be abstracted from the concrete members. Shakespeare's *Merchant of Venice,* for example, assumes the rôle of "the fourth from the left"; and as such it must be next to the left of "number five from the left." But there is nothing in all this which exalts a row of books, or impels us to spell it with a capital letter and worship it.

Similarly, then, while a society is a class, and a whole, and an individual, and a system, these are not prerogatives which dignify it, but very humble characteristics which it shares with most collections. Nor are they *doubtful* attributes, which require any peculiar ingenuity for their discovery or proof. The great question of social philosophy must, then, be a material rather than a formal one. The novelty or value of society must lie not in its being an individual and systematic whole, but rather in its being a particular kind of individual and systematic whole. The point is, one may say, that it is a whole of the living, mental, moral, human, or superhuman kind. But there is a further formal conception involved in this view. The suggestion is that these characters which attach to the *members* of the social whole, attach also in some sense to the whole itself. Let us employ the term 'compound' for a whole made up of members like itself, and sharpen the definition as we proceed.

§ 175. **Society a Compound.** We have first to note that there is no *a priori* reason why a collection which is a class, a whole, an individual or a system, or which is all four, should be a compound. There are undeniable facts to the contrary. It does not occur to us to call an alphabet a compound or collective letter, or the row a collective book, or the army a collective soldier. Similarly, the pictures in an exhibition may compose a thousand square yards of canvas, but without composing a picture. Or two thousand Harvard students may be so arranged in position and costume as to compose a letter "H," though the unity of the student himself is neither literate nor aspirate.

During the Middle Ages it was customary to conceive of the aggregate of men as composing a unity, an order, a harmony, or corporation, which was a partial whole within the greater whole of the world itself. This was called the universal community, or realm, or church, or the "Commonwealth of the Human Race." [27] This commonwealth was composed of men, but its unity was conceived in formal terms and not in the distinctive terms that give unity to a man. It is true that each constituent man was also conceived as a unity, order or harmony; but the point is that it was not this that made him a man. The objection which some modern writers urge against the mediaeval conceptions of society is just this, that they did not apply to social wholes those properties, such as mind, personality, and will, that distinguished the individual man.

It is, therefore, not necessary on the face of it, that a whole composed of men should be a man; or a whole of wills, a will; or that an individual composed of minds, should be a mind; or a system of interests, an interest. Indeed,

---

[27] Gierke's *Political Theories of the Middle Age,* Maitland's translation, 1913, pp. 9, 10.

judging by the foregoing analogies the presumption would seem to be against it.

There are, furthermore, certain formal or logical difficulties in the way of such a supposition. It is impossible, as has already been observed, that a whole should possess the same character as its elements, when the characters in question depend on relative simplicity. A society of men cannot be a man, because a man is by definition *one* unit of a type of which society requires at least *two*. 'Man' and 'society of men' signify different levels in an ascending order of complexity.

It is impossible, *a fortiori*, that a society should be one of its own component men. This is the so-called 'vicious-circle' principle.[28] Mankind cannot be a man in the sense of a member of the species. The American nation cannot be an American of whom the census would take account. The American mind cannot be one of those "best minds" that make up the Republican Party. The mind of the President's cabinet cannot, like the Secretary of State, attend as a member at the conference table. In conceiving society as a compound we must, therefore, be careful to avoid these offences against logic.

Nor, on the other hand, must we fall into mere redundancy or ambiguity. A forest, being composed of trees, may be said to be arboreal; a pack of dogs is canine; a nation of men, human. This means absolutely nothing more than that a nation of men is a nation of *men*. As a collection may be described in terms of its members, so the members may be described in terms of the collection. As we may speak of an arboreal forest, so we may speak of a forestal tree; and mean nothing more than a tree that grows in a forest. As we may speak of a mental society, so we may speak of a social mind, meaning nothing more than a mind that grows in a society. We may mean to emphasize the *kind* of mind exhibited by members of a society, and speak

[28] It is formulated by Whitehead and Russell as follows: "Whatever involves *all* of a collection must not be one of the collection," *Principia Mathematica*, 1910, p. 40.

of its as 'social mentality,' or, more simply, but more ambiguously, as 'social mind.' This last mode of expression
is possible owing to the fact that the word 'mind' is used
both as an ordinary common noun to which the indefinite
particle is prefixed, or in the plural, as when one says, "two
minds are better than one"; and also as a *"substantive
term,"* [29] like 'water,' 'salt,' or 'oxygen,' as when one speaks
of mind as the correlative of matter.[30] The ambiguity is
rendered even more subtle and elusive by the fact that it is
possible to use the indefinite article with such a substantive
term. Thus one may speak of 'a salt' or 'an acid' when one
means to refer to a variety of the kind. So, similarly, one
may speak of 'a mind,' meaning a variety of the mental kind;
and the expression 'a social mind' would be perfectly correct
in this sense, as referring to one of the varieties of social
mentality.[31] But it is more common in such cases to use
the definite article, as when one speaks of 'the scientific mind,'
or 'the infant mind.' Social mind in this sense there undoubtedly is. The fact is important, and well worth study-
ing; but the proof of the fact is not important because, once
its meaning is clear, there cannot be the slightest doubt about
it. It is obvious, or even, in the last analysis, redundant.

But there is unquestionably something more that lurks
in the background and furnishes the real bone of contention.
There is a sense in which the question "Is a society of minds
a mind?", is neither illogical nor redundant. If compounds
are conceivable at all, it is proper to raise the question in
the case of society. A machine can be composed of machines;
and, if we are to believe the biologists, an organism can be
composed of organisms. A group of men may be composed
of groups of men, and an organization, of organizations.
This is possible because these terms 'machine,' 'organism,'
'group,' and 'organization,' signify general modes of unity
that may be duplicated on ascending levels of complexity.
Thus society is certainly a compound in so far as both society

---

[29] Cf. Keynes, *op. cit.,* p. 12.
[30] The same ambiguity attaches to 'life,' 'soul,' and other words.
[31] Or a man could be said to be or have 'a social mind' when his mind
was of the socialized type. ·

and its component men are conceived as machines, organisms, groups or organizations. In so far, on the other hand, as they are conceived in terms of their biological classification, society is certainly *not* a compound.

If, then, we ask whether society is a 'mind,' a 'person' or a 'subject of interest,' what we mean to ask is whether these are *special* characteristics of man, identified with his unique position in the hierarchy of living things, or generic characteristic that can be transposed from one level to another.

Men lie somewhere in the scale of complexity between protozoa and nations. They comprise cells and they compose societies. Certain of their properties, such as laughing and climbing trees, are functions of this intermediate phase of complexity. Cells are too simple and societies too complex to laugh or to climb trees. Are the properties in question, namely, thought, will, or interest, of this distinctively human type, belonging to man by virtue of his intermediate position? Are cells too simple and societies too complex to be persons? Or is personality something like mechanism, organism, collectivity and organization, that can exist both in the parts which a man comprises and in a whole which men compose?

A component of a whole is determined by that relation. This is true both positively and negatively. Certain functions are possible and others are impossible by virtue of its membership. A cell which is a member of an animal body acquires activities and loses activities thereby. We may assume that it may be organic in some basic sense, but it does not follow that it can be an animal. It may be a condition of its being part of an animal that it should not be the whole of an animal; it may, in other words, be true that the nature of animal life does not permit of animality on the part of its components. Similarly, it may be that a person does not permit of personality on the part of its members, or that personality cannot be compounded. In that case it would require components that were not persons, and one person could never in conjunction with other persons compose a person.[32]

[32] Espinas is quite mistaken in arguing that if we deny consciousness

In order to settle this question we shall have to decide what we mean by persons, and discover both what they do to their parts and what the wholes into which they enter do to them.

of society, we must deny it also of the individual animal because the latter also is "un tout de coalition, une unité multiple dont la vie des éléments histologiques et des organs forme le contenu." (A. Espinas, *Des Sociétés Animales*, 1879, p. 371.) There are unquestionably some properties which attach uniquely to the stage of complexity represented by the individual animal, and which are possessed neither by what it comprises nor by what it composes. Consciousness may be one of these properties. It does not follow that the straight line and the square are both right-angle triangles, because right-angle triangles contain straight lines and compose squares.

CHAPTER XV

IS SOCIETY A PERSON?[1]

I. PERSONALITY AS A TYPE OF INTEGRATION

§ 176. Restatement of the Question. According to Durkheim, "if there is to be any morality, or system of duties and obligations, *society must be a moral person qualitatively distinct from the individual persons which it comprises.*"

He does not mean that society must be so imagined, or personified, but that it must be so conceived *literatim et verbatim;* for he tells us that it is not only a necessary moral postulate, but a postulate *verified* by *experience.*[2] Nor does he in this statement permit any doubt as to the immanent and composite character of the social personality which he affirms. His contention is that the human persons who compose a society at the same time compose a person of a higher order. The italicized passage expresses succinctly and unambiguously the thesis which we have now to examine.

Although we should now be clear as to the nature of the problem, it does not follow that it admits of easy or even of definitive solution. For it is not, strictly speaking, a question of fact, but rather one of interpretation. It is not as

---

[1] Parts of the present chapter are reprinted from an article entitled, "Is Society a Person?", published in the *Jour. of Philos.*, Vol. XXI, 1924.

[2] *Bulletin de la Société Française de Philos.*, 1906, pp. 128, 129. Cf. J. Royce: "For me, at present, a genuinely and loyally united community which lives a coherent life, is, in a perfect literal sense, a person" (letter to Professor Mary W. Calkins, *Philos. Rev.*, Vol. XXV, 1916, p. 205).

The view defended in the present chapter, on the other hand, resembles the Thomist view, as thus formulated by Professor M. De Wulf: "The collectivity . . . is not a substance as such, . . . and the very notion of 'a collective person' is contradictory. Its unity is not the internal unity which belongs to a natural substance, and which ensures coherence within it, but rather an external unity" (*Mediaeval Philosophy*, 1922, p. 118; ref. to Aquinas, *Summa Theol.*, X. 1).

though all parties knew precisely what they meant by a 'personality,' and were concerned only to establish the fact of its existence. This would be comparatively easy. But in the present question the issue lies mainly if not wholly in the meaning of the conception. The attempt to apply the conception of personality to society is found to involve a re-examination and re-definition of the conception itself. There are two conceptions of personality which would answer our question summarily and unmistakably. If a person is a collection of states, an aggregate of "mind-stuff," or a "stream of consciousness," then it is evident that persons can be compounded by the simple process of addition. A social person would be the sum of the states or mind-stuff, or a confluence of the conscious streams of its members. James, who originated the expression "stream of consciousness," has, in fact, himself suggested that an individual mind is only a sort of trickle from a wider "sea" of consciousness which finds an outlet through the body.[3]

On the other hand, if persons be defined in terms of their exclusiveness, then they can*not* be said to be compounded, or included in one another, without contradiction. This view is maintained by those who insist upon the essential privacy of the mind, or the peculiar internality which renders it accessible only to introspection. On such a theory a social person which was excluded from the privacy of human minds, would not contain them; while if it did invade their privacy both it and they, having lost their privacy, would cease to be persons.

These two views may be dismissed: the first, because it so evidently fails to provide for the unity of personality; the second, because even if it were acceptable as a view of personality, it would in any case serve only to confirm the conclusion which will presently be formulated.

There remain two further views which seem to leave our question open. Both of these views would define personality

---

[3] "We need only suppose the continuity of our consciousness with a mother sea, to allow for exceptional waves occasionally pouring over the dam" (*Human Immortality*, 1898, p. 27).

in terms of organization, and suggest the possibility that, as a human person is organized out of simpler constituents, so a social person may be organized out of constituent personalities—more complexly, but after the same fashion.

According to the first of these views, personality is the systematic unity of experience, or the organization of objects into a world. This view may be dismissed because it appears to eliminate our question altogether. The scientific and logical motives which impel us to affirm that there is only one organized world of objects, would on this view impel us to affirm that there is only one Person, who is *neither* man nor society.

There remains the view that a person is an organization not among the objects of mind, but among its *acts*,—of cognition or of interest. Our thesis may then be briefly stated as follows: There are two ways in which acts of mind are integrated. They are integrated *directly* as acts of one agent, or *indirectly* through their objects. The former is the type of integration that is characteristic of personality and allied forms of mind; the latter is characteristic of society. In other words, society is an integration of mind, and a genuinely psychological unity, but it is not that specific mode of integration or unity which constitutes a person.

§ 177. **Personality as Intermediation of Interests.** So far, at least, as observable, the first or personal type of integration is limited to such acts as are embodied in the same physical organism, and so connected by one continuous and concentric nervous system; while the second or social type of organization obtains among acts embodied in two or more organisms which are neurally discontinuous and eccentric. We may speak of these respectively as 'intra-organic' and 'inter-organic' integration.

Intra-organic integration is most simply represented by habit and memory. One organism does not acquire habits as a result of the actions of another, nor does it recollect another's past. Similarly, one organism does not learn by the trials and errors of another organism, but profits in this

sense only by its own experience.   Although the underlying
mechanisms are more obscure, it will, I think, be admitted
that the several acts of one cognitive process must likewise
be embodied in the same organism.   A judgment is a synthesis, but one organism can not enact the subject and another the predicate.   Nor can a process of inference be constituted by a division of the premises and conclusion among
three organisms.   In the verification or correction of hypothesis the evidence and the expectation must meet in one
organism, otherwise they neither collide nor concur.

The same is true of interest or purpose.   An act is interested, as we have seen, when it is performed because of
what is expected of it.   The term 'because' here signifies
an internal and not an external nexus.   *I* can not in this
sense act because of what *you* expect of my act, unless indirectly through duplicating your expectation or making it
the object of an expectation of my own.

The final case of intra-organic integration, which is here
of central importance, is that in which one interested activity
is subordinated to another, so as to generate a hierarchy of
purposes.   If I want this because I want that, if I seek money
because I covet power, or aspire to virtue for the love of
God, the subject of both interests must be the same organism,
and the control exerted by the one over the other is of the
type which a single nervous system subserves.   This relation,
which we have described as the mediation of one interest by
another, or the *intermediation* of interests,[4] constitutes that
which best deserves the name of personality, and can be
shown to underlie the traditional prerogatives of personality,
such as rationality, freedom, responsibility, and happiness.

Of inter-organic, as distinguished from intra-organic, integration there are at least two types, namely, *community* and
mutuality of interest.[5]   The former is the case of two interests with a common object, the latter the case of two
interests which are stimuli or objects to one another.   These
modes of integration are present also in personality, where
they are combined with the principle of intermediation.   But

[4] Ch. XIII, Sect. II.   [5] Cf. §§ 161, 164.

in their purity, or independence of this mediating relation, they are peculiarly characteristic of what are called social relations.

Let us suppose a benevolent father to be indulging his son's propensity to play, and let us suppose the child to be sophisticated enough to realize the ulterior benefits of exercise. The son's play-interest mediates his ambition, which is a personal integration. The father's parsimony is overruled by his parental love, which is also a personal integration. But the play-interest and parental love do not in this case compose a person. There is no playing for the sake of love, or loving for the sake of play. The play-interest of the son is, however, the object of the father's parental love, and the two, therefore, constitute a social relation of persons, though they do not constitute a person.

Our conclusion can be stated in two ways. If one prefers to use the term 'personality' in a sense broad enough to include all integrations of interest, or all organizations of which both the terms and the combining relations are acts of mind, then societies may be regarded as persons. But in that case there would still remain an absolute difference of principle between the kind of personality in which acts of interest directly mediate one another, and the kind in which they intersect in their objects. It is in closer accord with verbal usage and with the traditional meaning of the concept of personality to reserve it for the first of these forms, in which the integration is effected in the act or at the source.

We conclude, therefore, that personality and its prerogatives are peculiar to organic individuals of the human species, or to units of life having the peculiar structural and functional organization characteristic of organisms endowed with a highly developed central nervous system. Personality consists in a type of integration or interdependence of interests such as occurs when the interests in question are dispositions or activities of one concentric and integumented organism. It is a peculiar autonomous system, or field of control, such as in the physical man is conditioned by one continuous nervous tract having a continuous history.

§ 178. **The Development of Personality.** When several interests are so situated, or are structually so related, that they are capable of assuming personality, they may be said to compose a subject of interest, or an interested subject, or a self. Personality is thus capable of attaining different degrees. Interests may mediate one another only intermittently, as when *a* (the play-interest) sometimes does and sometimes does not mediate *b* (professional ambition); or only blindly, as when the interest-judgment or foresight which subordinates *a* to *b* is untrue or partial; or only incompletely, as when *a* mediates *b* and *c* (family affection), but *b* does not mediate *c,* or *c, d.* When two or more non-mediating or independent systems of inter-mediating interests belong to the same subject of interest, there exists a multiple personality.

The process of developing personality within a subject of interest, or of increasing the degree of a personality already formed, is a *process* of integration; and interests are integrated, as we have seen, by the process of rationalization, that is, by an extension and amplification of their cognitive components.[6] This is sometimes described as thinking over one interest in terms of another, which means projecting them to a common point, or projecting them upon one another. Where such a convergence or intersection occurs, interests are integrated; but integration does not assume the form of *personality* unless as a result of the foregoing process one interest comes to mediate another, or yield to its control.

Suppose, for example, a wife and mother to be divided between indulgent love for her child and loyalty to her husband. She is disposed to indulge her child's whims, and to promote her husband's ambition. Let us suppose that at the outset these two interests are unintegrated (although they belong to one subject), and make incompatible claims upon her time, energy and physiological mechanisms. The play-interest of the child and the ambition of the father are also competitive, in that they involve incompatible uses of the same limited domestic conveniences.

---

[6] Cf. above, Ch. XIII, Sect. V; and below, Ch. XIX, Sect. II, and Ch. XXII, Sect. I.

Now let us suppose that the mother thinks these interests over in terms of one another. She becomes more fully aware of what it means that the child should play, and that the father should work; with the result that she discovers that the child's play implies the interruption of the father's work, and *vice versa.* Her two interests, being prolonged, have met and intersected in their objects: she wants the same room, at the same time, to be a play-room for her child and a work-room for her husband. And the one interest has appeared among the objects of the other: her indulgence is directed to an object which is qualified in terms of her loyalty, that is, she wants *for* her child a room which she recognizes as a room which she also wants *for* her husband; and *vice versa.* At this stage her interests may be said to be integrated both in the sense of having common objects (community), and in the sense of being objects for one another (mutuality).

But the integration of her interests has not yet assumed the form of personality. Up to this point the integration might have occurred inter-subjectively as well as intra-subjectively. It might, for example, have occurred between the child and the father. Both might have developed their interests to the point of desiring the same room, and of feeling hostility to one another through recognizing the conflict.

But now let us suppose that the wife and mother finds a way of reconciling her two interests. She provides a play-room for the child and a work-room for the father, or divides the use of the same room between them, or teaches the child how to play without disturbing his father. Her maternal indulgence is then mediated by her conjugal loyalty, and her conjugal loyalty by her maternal indulgence. Each is controlled by the other. Her maternal indulgence has in some measure assumed the form of a means to her conjugal loyalty, even though it be only in the negative sense of permitting it. In other words, she now indulges her child because she foresees the realization of her husband's ambition. We may suppose the same thing to be true in the reciprocal sense. Or, we may suppose that both maternal indulgence and conjugal loyalty are now means to a new end of family cooperation, and that to foresee this outcome has become a condition of her enacting either the one or the other. The form of unity here achieved is personality, and is internal to a single organism which is both wife and mother. The child may achieve a similar personal integration of his playfulness and his filial affection, and the father a similar personal integration of his ambition and his paternal affection. As a result of the development of these three personalities the playfulness of the child and the ambition of the father are reconciled, and in some sense, integrated. But they do not compose a person. Playfulness is not mediated by ambition or ambition by playfulness. There are, in other words, three cases of personal integration: maternal indulgence and conjugal loyalty, playfulness and filial affection, ambition and paternal affection; and there is one case of non-personal or purely social integration, namely that of playfulness and ambition.

§ 179. **Individuality, Personality and the Organism.**
It has sometimes been contended that whereas human individuality is a function of the body, personality is derived from above or abroad; individuality being a limitation of personality by its embodiment. The body is regarded as a confining organ which narrows the range of personality, or as a prison which hampers its action and darkens its view.

That the body serves as an organ of selection which defines unique perspectives and gives concentric unity to a partial experience, is unquestionably true. But while the body does exercise a private function, and may therefore properly be regarded as a symbol of human finitude, it is none the less true that it exercises a creative function and serves as the instrument of human prerogatives. While it is true that the body frames *in* that fragmentary and unique glimpse which each man has of the world, it is none the less true that the body accounts for the fact that there is any glimpse at all.

The position and visual capacity of the eye determines that a man shall see just this and no more, but it also enables him to see. To contrast the little that man sees with the infinity of visible things is not to disparage the eye. Similarly, if we disparage the body because it does not know all the things there are to know, that is because we have confused the objects of knowledge with the knowing of them, or have imagined a knowledge proportionate to the totality of the world. The bodily functions extract only a mean fragment of reality, but that is not to their discredit, since it is due to them that anything is extracted at all. An organ both conditions its appropriate function and determines the limits of its exercise. That it should exercise its function within limits, should not be allowed to obscure the fact that it does exercise its function.

And so with the question of personality. The body is no doubt accountable for the fact that a man's knowledge is dim and incoherent, and that his interests are few, blind and ill-ordered; but it is also accountable for the fact that he knows or has interests at all. That the body imposes limits on personality should not be allowed to obscure the fact that it is the organ of personality and of its distinguishing prerogatives.

§ 180. **The Prerogatives of Personality.** The elementary processes of interest and cognition are both, as we have seen, complex processes which consist essentially in a linking of the present act with memory of the past and with anticipation of the future. This essential linkage is internal to one organism, with its threads of nervous connection and its physical continuity. Personality is a more complex development of the same process, in which multiple interests and acts of cognition are similarly interrelated. The prerogatives commonly imputed to personality arise from this same essential mode of unity, or are only diverse aspects of it.[7]

[7] Although I do not employ the same arguments, because of my emphasis on the function of the central nervous system, and although I do not make the same inferences in the field of ethics, I nevertheless find myself largely in accord with the view of Professor W. Fite. According to this writer the practical reason is essentially a subordination of acts to consequences, which only the individual is capable of effecting; so that social action, at least on the reflective level, is "action by mutual agreement." Cf. his *Individualism*, 1911, pp. 100, 117, and *passim*.

Thus, being a subject of interests or *self*, is, as we have seen, to be composed of interests which are structurally so conjoined as to permit of the development of personality. Each interest may be taken to represent the rest, inasmuch as it is subject to their control. The personal pronoun, or proper name, symbolizing the identity of the self, may be applied to any of the component interests which happens at the time to be active, because all have a voice in each.

Self-consciousness consists in the fact that interests which are members of the same self, and are therefore capable of mediating one another, may also be objects for one another. Expressed in more general terms, applicable to cognition as well as to interest, self-consciousness consists in the fact that two responses which modify one another as acts of the same organism, may have one another as objects. The commonest case of this sort, by which the occurrence of self-consciousness is most readily verified, is the case of speech, internal or overt, in which a man "hears himself talk"; where the act of articulation and the act of listening are parts of one physiological system, and thus affect one another directly, while at the same time the one is the object of the other.[8]

Will or *volition* is distinguishable from interest in the simpler sense, only in so far as it implies a serial subordination of interests in which a dominant interest exercises a selection among interests, and designates one as its mediating interest. Or, in a still narrower sense, the term *volition* may be reserved for the special case in which such a dominant interest is interest in self.[9]

The degree to which a man is *free* is the degree in which his action is positively interested; the degree, in other words, in which he does what he wants or chooses.[10]   Man is en-

---

[8] W. McDougall, in his *Group Mind*, 1920, pp. 215-17, appears to regard group self-consciousness as occurring when " the idea of the people or nation as a whole is present to the consciousness of individuals." But unless one commit the fallacy of composition and attribute to the whole what is true only of the members, there is no *self*-consciousness here. The individual is not conscious of *him*self, nor the group of *it*self, but the individual (one self) is conscious of the group (another object).

[9] Cf. above, § 29, and below, Ch. XXII, Sect. I.

[10] An excellent presentation of this view which identifies freedom with

slaved by automatism, by passion or by circumstance. To be enslaved by automatism is to behave reflexly or habitually, rather than interestedly.[11] To be enslaved by passion implies that one of his interests is uncontrolled by the rest, and usurps their share of the common resources of the organism. To be enslaved by circumstance means that the range of choice is restricted, or that interest is mediated either by indifferent judgments, or by negative interests. One does what one wants, but under circumstances not of one's own choosing.

Enslavement of the first type is escaped by the *development* of interest. Enslavement of the second and third types is escaped by *intermediation* of interests, that is, by subjecting interests to mutual control. The free agent in the second sense is the agent all of whose interests confirm and promote one another. The free agent in the third sense is the agent who is not only acting interestedly in a given situation, but who has chosen the situation. His present interest is not merely an interested reaction to circumstances imposed by nature or other men, but is a means adopted for some ulterior end of his own. Freedom in this sense is proportional to the depth of the agent's ulterior motivity, or the extent to which he is actuated by reasons of his own. The animal or child may be wholly content with his lot without being conscious of it; a dependent may be conscious of his lot, and make the best of it without willing it. The free man is he who knows and desires his lot, and in whom, therefore, the circumstance has lost its alien character. It is evident that freedom in the second and third senses is a form or aspect of that same type of internal integration which defines personality.

Responsibility means that the agent of the present moment is in some sense the agent of the past and of the future. Responsibility has its retroactive or retributive aspect; and its prospective aspect, or aspect of control. Retribution signifies that the past agent is preserved in the memory or disposition of the present agent, or that the present agent was

choice, will be found in G. E. Moore's *Ethics* (Home Univ. Library), Ch. VI.

[11] Cf. §§ 84-86.

anticipated in the past agent. Control through reward or punishment implies that expectations of the future, threats or punishments, are effective; or that judgments now pronounced upon the agent's action may be adopted by him, and may regulate his future performances. Responsibility thus implies that a temporal sequence of interests may be so linked as to mediate one another, or that the present interest is causally projected both into the past and into the future in that manner which is characteristic of personal integration.

Finally, if *happiness* be thought of as a prerogative, it is evidently a function of personality. Happiness in this sense is not satisfaction, or a mere uninterrupted sequence of satisfactions, but that state of an individual in which he can review all of his interests without regret and without fear. It is a present satisfaction qualified by remembered and anticipated satisfactions,—the imaginative exploration of the whole system of one's interests, where every report is favorable. Satisfaction which requires repression or forgetfulness is not happiness, one of the most familiar forms of unhappiness being that in which a present interest is extravagantly indulged as a means of rendering oneself insensible to the rest. Happiness is a general auspiciousness, in which each satisfaction is enhanced by the promise of ulterior satisfactions. It is the peculiar satisfaction which attaches to a well-ordered personality.

§ 181. **The Genetic Priority of Society and the Individual.** We have been led to the conclusion that personality, together with its prerogatives, is a property of an individual of the human species; and that a society of such individuals, despite its undoubted possession of unity of the several types considered in the last chapter, appears to be incapable of possessing this particular kind of unity for lack of the necessary functional connections. This question of the seat or locus of personality is commonly confused with another question, regarding the social origin or social dependence of personality. To avoid the confusion it is necessary to state this alternative question and recognize its irrelevance.

According to Dr. J. M. Baldwin,[12] the individual person first distinguishes other persons by their behavior, then imitates this behavior and experiences it inwardly, after which he imputes to the original model a like inward experience. The conception of a person thus passes through its "projective," "subjective" and "ejective" phases. Assuming this or some similar analysis to be correct, what does it prove?

In the first place, it does not prove that individuals arise from society, but at most that their *ideas of* individuality have a social origin, or that any given individual distinguishes other individuals before he distinguishes himself. If other individuals were not already there to be noticed and distinguished, the process would not be initiated at all.

If, in the second place, it be argued that personality is definable only in terms of self-consciousness, or that one does not become a person until one knows it, then the analysis shows that personality is derived from a response to other *individuals*, and not from a response to other *persons*. Personality would begin at home with the synthesis of its inward and outward aspects, being afterwards projected to other individuals.

Thirdly, even if it were granted that we become self-conscious only in the presence of other persons, or that in order that there shall be any persons there must be at least two, this would create no presumption whatever that society is a person. Personality would be a multiple and mutual affair, social in its context and determining relations, but not social in its seat or locus. There is no reason to suppose that a pair or group of interdependent persons would compose a person, even if they were reciprocally dependent for their possession of the attribute of personality.

All such arguments for the genetic priority of society tend to confusion on one or both of two points. In the first place, they tend to confuse the development of ideas with the development of their objects. It may be true, as Royce argues,

[12] *Social and Ethical Interpretations in Mental Development,* 1897, pp. 334 ff. Cf. also J. Royce, "Self-consciousness, Social Consciousness and Nature," in his *Studies of Good and Evil,* 1898; and C. H. Cooley, *Human Nature and the Social Order,* 1898, pp. 135, 147.

that the *idea* of physical nature arises from a "community of interpretation"; and that physical nature first assumes to human cognition the aspect "illustrated by the way in which two men who row in the same boat regard the boat and the oars which they see and touch, and the water over which they fly." [13] But it does not follow that the boat, oars and water, or physical nature as a whole, are *themselves* products of a social consciousness.   Similarly, when Durkheim says that "the soul is nothing other than the totemic principle incarnate in each individual," [14] he bases his argument largely on the contention that the *idea* of 'soul' is first applied to society and afterwards to the individual.   But, supposing this to be true, it does not imply that society's *soul* antedates the soul of the individual, or that either society or the individual has a 'soul' at all.   It is entirely true that the individual man develops in intercourse with his fellows, and that his ideas both of nature and of himself are impregnated with a social flavor; but it does not follow that the objects of his ideas have the same social causes as his ideas about them, or that his ideas may not be falsified by their social coloring.

Arguments for the genetic priority of society tend also, in the second place, to confuse the properties which the individual derives from his social relations, and the supervening properties of society itself.   One might assume the extremest dependence of the individual on his social origin and environment,—or suppose that personality and all of its prerogatives sprang from the intercourse of individuals, and could therefore exist only *within* society; but this would not imply that any tinge or flavor of personality whatever attached to society as a unit.

§ 182. **Personality and Society.**   While persons do not compose a person, it is still possible that human individuals should be integrated into groups or societies possessing wholeness, individuality and systematic unity, and compounded in

---

[13] *Problem of Christianity,* 1913, Vol. II, p. 240. Cf. also the same author's *World and the Individual,* Second Series, 1901, Lecture IV.
[14] *Op. cit.,* p. 248.

respects other than that of personality. What happens to personality in such cases? There are three theoretical possibilities.

In the first place, *impersonal groups may be constituted of impersonal members.* Even when men are selves in the sense of possessing the structural organization that renders personality possible, personality may be as yet unachieved; or personality may be momentarily dissolved; or different personalities may interpenetrate upon their sub-personal levels. In all these cases the *elements* of personalities may enter into social or objective relations, into which the personalities as such do not enter. There is then, in the case of any given element, a rivalry of control between the associated elements of the same personality, and the elements of other personalities which form the social environment.

This type of social integration is illustrated by a wide variety of phenomena, in which it is recognized that the impersonal elements of personality, such as bodily movements, or simple acts, or elementary impulses, are added and multiplied to form impersonal units. This recognition appears in the use of descriptive terms or figures of speech of a class ordinarily applied to infra-organic or infra-human phenomena. Thus one speaks of the "cake" of custom, or the "sea" of humanity, or the "tide" of immigration, or the "seething" masses, or one likens the mob to a "brute" or "monster." It is implied that such social unities tend to decompose and supersede the personal unities into which the same elements are qualified to enter; [15] so that the individual's behavior is a function of the behavior of other individuals, rather than of his own experience, judgment and rational purpose. This type of social integration evidently tends to eliminate personality. There remain a second and a third possibility in which personality is preserved.

The second possibility is *uni-personal* society, or a personal whole composed of non-persons. If we are to accept the conclusion that the seat of personality is the neurally cen-

[15] Cf. G. Le Bon, *Psychology of Revolution*, trans. by B. Miall, 1913, pp. 102-103.

tralized organism, it follows that a society can be personal
only in so far as one of its members assumes the rôle of
personality for all, the others being reduced to the status of
its objects or instrumentalities.

The third possibility is a *multi-personal* society, or an
impersonal whole composed of persons. Such a whole may
be loosely aggregated or highly consolidated, but in any case
its *personal* control will be divided among its members. It
may be a collection, a conflict, or a federation of persons,
but in any case it will not be a person.

The second and third possibilities taken together yield the
general principle that *the personality of the whole is inversely
proportional to the personality of the members.* The development of personality in the group implies the prevention or
loss of personality in all members but one, while the development of personality in the members implies its prevention
or loss in the whole.

II. THE PERSONAL SOCIETY OF NON-PERSONS

§ 183. **The Organismic Theory.** The analogy between
the social group and the animal organism has often been
employed figuratively, and has not infrequently been soberly
accepted and elaborated in great detail. This view has recently derived a certain biological confirmation from the discovery that plants and animals may be conceived as colonies
or "societies" of cells. If cells can compose organisms, why
should not these in turn become the cells of greater organisms? If plants and animals are compounds of organisms,
why should not these compounds be again compounded in
the second or third degree?

In accepting this principle it is important, however, to
note that the achievement of plant or animal individuality
by the whole implies its loss on the part of the component
elements. Plants and animals may be formed *out of* plants
and animals, but in such cases the components do not remain
plants and animals. To become part of a plant or animal
implies the transfer to the whole or to some one of its parts,
of the plant and animal prerogatives.

Thus the botanists describe an Alpine aquatic plant known as the *Hydrurus foetidus,* which is made up of a colony of unicellular algae which have lost their independence and assumed specialized functions relative to the life of the plant as a whole. When the Hydrurus organism is fully formed the component unicellular algae have as a group become more heterogeneous, but at the same time each in itself has become more homogeneous and primitive. It has proved possible in the case of another alga, Cladophora, to reverse this process of assimilation. The compound organism has a definite plant form with an attached base and a growing apex, and the component cells are subordinated in structure and function to the life of the whole. When, however, the plant is put in a strong salt solution it is transformed into a mere aggregate of unicellular algae, each cell proceeding to set up in business for itself with its own base and its own apex.[16]

Or, we may express the plant as a sum of relations to diverse aspects of its environment, such as gravity, soil, moisture and light. In the plant organism as a whole all of these different relations are functionally represented and coördinated. But the specialized part of the plant is limited to some one of these relations, and is a comparatively primitive unit of life.[17] Similarly an animal organism can both see and hear; but the ear is blind, and the eye is deaf.

John of Salisbury, in the twelfth century, and Nicholas of Cusa, in the fifteenth, made especially notable attempts to correlate the parts of the "body natural" and the "body politic." According to the former writer, "the prince is the head, the senate the heart, the court the sides, officers and judges are the eyes, ears and tongue, the executive officials are the unarmed and the army is the armed hand, the financial department is belly and intestines, landfolk, handicraftsmen and the like are the feet." [18] When these feet are in distress, as is so often the case, the state has gout. The ecclesiastics, using the same method, argued against the claims of the state,

---

[16] Cf. J. B. Farmer, *Plant Life,* 1913, Ch. iv.
[17] Cf. J. M. Coulter, *Plant Relations,* 1900, Introduction, Ch. VIII, and *passim.*
[18] As summarized by Maitland, in Gierke, *op. cit.,* pp. 131-132.

that if the emperor as well as the pope were a head, the organism of mankind would be a "two-headed monster, an *animal biceps.*" [19] The state, owing to the number of its feet, turned out to be a centipede; and the growing strength of the imperial party forced the conviction that mankind did in fact have two heads. Thus the outcome of an effort to enhance the dignity of men was to conceive them as members or organs of a bicephalous centipede.[20]

The fact is, as will scarcely need to be argued, that whatever of truth there is in this view is analogical or figurative. A society has certain abstract characteristics which it is convenient to represent by that embodiment of them, namely man, which is most familiar and striking. But it is clear that if the analogy between human society and the cellular composition of the organism is adopted, in so far as an aggregation of men are organized in the image of a man, it must be at the expense of their manhood. If men assume the rôle of cells or organs they must forfeit personal autonomy or delegate it to one of their members.

§ 184. **The Centralized and Autocratic Society.** That which appears in the crude and figurative analogies of the "organismic" theory, appears more realistically in certain special modes of social organization. In so far, for example, as a modern industry approaches the solidarity of the physical organism, the workers are absorbed and debased, precisely as unicellular plants surrender their autonomy when they are incorporated into multicellular plants. They are reduced to specialized and repetitive functions like the machines which they operate. They are parts of an industry rather than the whole of a man. Similarly, the perfectly oranized army, the consummation of military discipline, implies a head that is infinitely wise; and members that are wholly conformed to

[19] Gierke, *op. cit.,* p. 22.
[20] In more recent times this mode of thought has been revived by Spencer and others, with greater plausibility, but with no greater eventual success. Cf. F. W. Coker, *Organismic Theories of the State,* 1910. Ch. IV; J. S. Mackenzie, *Introduction to Social Philosophy,* 1890, Ch. III; Paul von Lilienfeld, *Gedanken über die Socialwissenschaft der Zukunft,* Vol. I, 1873.

their several rôles, and unhesitatingly obedient to command. The distinguishing mark of organic and personal unity is centralization of control, represented by the function of the brain. The development of life is marked by the progressive elaboration of this integrating and directing organ. The same is true of the development of personality. Diseases of personality consist mainly in the dissociation of centres of cerebral control. A normal mind is a mind all of whose manifestations are governed by a single will, or by a single system of inter-mediated interests. The same principle of unified control defines the difference between the child and the adult, the primitive and the civilized, the ignorant and the educated, the man of serious purpose and the idler or drone. The lower type is in each case marked by a relative dispersion of its constituent elements, and is characterized in such terms as 'impulsiveness,' 'dissipation,' 'disintegration,' or 'demoralization'; the higher type is distinguished by self-mastery and unified control, in which one purpose and one judgment direct all acts from one centre.

In so far, then, as the aim of social organization is to imitate the highly developed personality, it follows that such a society will be centralized and autocratic. Since this function of centralized control can be literally realized only in the integrating will and reason of a single organic individual, it follows that a society can be unipersonal only in so far as such a single individual assumes the role of head.[21]

Where the control is divided, society will resemble a multiple and therefore abnormal personality. Divided control does not preclude organization, but the fact remains that *judged by standards of personality,* such a society will exhibit the pathological characteristics similar to those which in a

[21] Lester F. Ward uses the term "telesis" to designate the conscious pursuit of ends, or action guided by intellect. There is "social telesis," he thinks, as well as "individual telesis"; but he confesses that the former "is as yet so rare as to be almost theoretical" (!) It is realized in so far as a society is "cunning, shrewd, strategic, diplomatic," etc. But this social telesis, so far as there is any, "must be located in the governing body of society." It remains only to add that the only governing body capable of these attitudes is a single head. Cf. *Outlines of Sociology,* 1899, pp. 181-182, 186-187.

human individual are attributed to dissociation. To correct this dissociation and secure for the group that normality or health of personality which we esteem in the individual, will require that all of its activities be subordinated to the judgment of one man, and that all others become his objects and instrumentalities. Such a society must be ruled throughout by one decision, embraced within one self-consciousness, and directed by one purpose, which implies that these functions shall be assumed by one individual for all. The consummation of such a type of integration is represented by a centralized and autocratic society in which one individual is literally justified in saying, "l'état c'est moi"; or unites in his own person the prerogatives which Cardinal Manning assigned to the Pope, as the head, the heart, the mind, and the tongue of the Catholic Church.

In short, the several members of a society can be embraced within one person only in so far as all members save one are subordinated to the purpose which that one has *for* them. Their interests will then be integrated not by their own direct inter-mediation and inter-dependence, but indirectly or vicariously, through the judgments which the ruler passes upon them, or the interests he takes in them. They will enter into the personally integrated society not as interests but as objects.

III. THE IMPERSONAL SOCIETY OF PERSONS

§ 185. **The Colonial Organism as Inferior to its Members.** As the personalization of society has the effect of de-personalizing its members, or all of its members save one, so the persistence or development of personality in the members has the effect of preventing the personalization of the whole. Here also, light is to be obtained from biological phenomena of a lower order.

In the case of the *Hydrurus foetidus,* the component algae have lost their autonomy. In order to become parts of a plant they have ceased to be plants. The whole outranks its members by usurping their prerogatives. Animal colonies, on the other hand, represent the opposite case; in which the autonomy of the members resists the organization of the whole, with the result that this total organization fails to attain the rank possessed by its members.

An admirable example is to be found in a study by Professor W. M. Wheeler, called *The Ant-Colony as an Organism.*[22] Having defined organism to mean a coördinated system of activities directed to its own nourishment, reproduction, and protection, the author shows that the ant-colony taken as a unit exhibits not only these fundamental characteristics common to all organisms, but also many of the more specialized characteristics found in plants and animals. The colony maintains its identity and resists dissolution or fusion with other colonies. In its nest it has a shell like a mollusk. This nest is built toward the sun, or is heliotropic. In the division between the mother queen and the virgin males and females, who are devoted to working and fighting, the colony manifests the duality between the germ plasm and the soma. Similarly, the ant-colony manifests many of the specific characteristics of growth, restitution of lost parts, recapitulation, and other distinctive organic phenomena.

But the most significant feature of this illuminating analysis is one which the author himself has not emphasized. In so far as we regard the ant-colony as an individual organism, *we find it to be of a lower variety than its components.* An ant-colony, in other words, is a less developed animal than an ant. "Undoubtedly," says our author, "if we could see it acting in its entirety, the ant-colony would resemble a gigantic foraminiferous Rhizopod, in which the nest would represent the shell, the queen the nucleus, the mass of ants the plasmodium and the files of workers, which are continually going in and out of the nest, the pseudopodia." [23] Now without inquiring too curiously into the precise characteristics of

[22] *The Journal of Morphology,* Vol. XXII, 1911, pp. 307-325.
[23] *Op. cit.,* p. 312. Professor Wheeler refers to the more comprehensive colonial individuals as more "efficient" (p. 324). But apparently simpler (such as unicellular) forms of life are just as efficient as the higher forms, if we mean capacity to survive. Perhaps it is the very primitiveness of the colony that constitutes its strength. Cf. J. B. Farmer, *op. cit.,* pp. 55-56.

the foraminiferous Rhizopod, it may be observed that it is classified among the protozoa, which presumably is sufficient to establish its inferiority in the scale of animal life to the proverbial ant. We have here a clue of first-rate importance for the clarification of our question. It should rid our minds wholly of the assumption, which is both natural and habitual, that a more inclusive whole must be a whole of a higher order. It is clear that just the opposite may be the case. If a colony of ants may compose a big but rather rickety Rhizopod, so an organization of men may conceivably compose nothing better. When elements compose a whole there is no implication whatever that this whole shall possess the same type of unity as that possessed by its members, and when it does possess the same type of unity (such as that which Professor Wheeler defines as characteristic of the organism) there is no implication whatever that this type of unity shall be exhibited by the whole in so high a degree as by its members. Indeed, where the type of unity in question involves that character of unified control which distinguishes an individual animal, there is good reason to suppose its possession by the members will preclude its possession by the whole.

A whole is sometimes more highly integrated than its members, as in the relation of the plant to its component cells; and sometimes less integrated, as in the relation of the colony to its component ants. Combining these two types of relationship, we get the case in which an individual whole is both higher than its own constituent members, and also higher than the whole of which it is itself a member. The progression from cell to colony is not a steadily ascending progression, as is readily and mistakenly supposed, but an ascent and a descent in which the highest point is reached half-way. This intermediate and highest point, is the animal or man.

§ 186. **The Pluralistic and Federated Society.** As the organicity of its members detracts from the organicity of an animal colony, so the personality of its members detracts from the personality of a human society. Where the personality of the whole is magnified, the personality of all members but one is sacrificed; where the personality of all members is cultivated or safeguarded, it is necessary to sacrifice the personality of the whole. In the former case, a society is consolidated, and control is exercised autocratically; in the latter case, a society is plural and loosely-knit, control being divided or exercised in partnership.

A human group in which the personality of its members is respected, does not possess its members exclusively, but borrows them and shares them with other groups. In the history of human society this tends to be the case to an increasing degree. The number of social groups to which any given human individual belongs tends to diversify and multiply; with the result that a man is not wholly assimilated by any one of them, but possesses an independence proportional to the number of other groups in which he might continue to function were he to be excluded from the first. Economic interdependence is not diminished,—it is doubtless increased. But in the highly developed communities the economic group is only one of many to which a man belongs. It is doubtless true also that one among these groups, namely the political, is designed to exercise supreme control in case there is a rivalry of allegiance, but the fact remains that the citizen is only partially political. He conducts the greater part of his life in other spheres and under other forms of control.[24] If a cell were to belong to several natural bodies, passing freely from one to another, and thus having a career of its own independent of that of any one of these bodies, it would be analogous to the case of the member of a modern society, who may be an American, a Republican, a Hoosier, a Klansman, a farmer, a father, and many other things beside.

Not only does the individual belong to several groups, but within each group he shares control of the group with

[24] In other words, while admitting *social* pluralism, I should not concede what I understand to be the contention of Laski and others that the conception of the state implies no priority of authority. Cf. H. J. Laski, *Studies in the Problems of Sovereignty*, 1917; *Authority in the Modern State*, 1919.

other members. In so far as social organization is dictated by a respect for the personality of its members, it aims to secure control by agreement or consent. Where this mode of control is realized the action of each individual is governed in the last analysis by his own judgment. He submits to law which his reason approves or to a force which he imposes on himself.[25] Such a mode of organization exhibits personality in the parts, but not in the whole. The collective behavior is describable as an association or federation of persons, but not as a person.[26]

Hesitation or reluctance to accept this conclusion may be ascribed to two causes. In the first place, there is a tendency to suppose that a whole composed of men must exhibit the same advance in respect of personality that a man exhibits in comparison with his members. This is, however, neither necessary nor, as it now appears, in accordance with fact. It is not necessary, because if persons can be composed *of* non-persons, they can equally well *compose* non-persons. As a matter of fact, personality characterizes preeminently that intermediate stage of organization which lies half-way between a human interest and a human society. Personality, like organicity, ascends as we pass from the part to the whole of a man, and declines as we pass from a man to the more inclusive whole of society.

In the second place, there is a disposition to credit any whole with the qualities and prerogatives of its members, or to overlook the difference between its integral properties and those which it includes. This is to commit the elementary logical fallacy of composition. An army includes the soldiers, but it does not possess in its own right the characters which

---

[25] Cf. Ch. XXII, Sect. II.

[26] Precisely the same dilemma holds in the case of the metaphysical hypothesis known as the "Absolute." If the Absolute is to be indeed a person, preëminently qualified as such, then it can be so only at the expense of the personality of men. The Absolute must be the *only* person. If, on the other hand, the personality of individual men is to be conserved, then the Absolute *judged by the standard of personality*, must be of a relatively low, if not pathological variety. Cf. F. C. S. Schiller, "Idealism and the Dissociation of Personality," *Jour. of Philos.*, Vol. III, 1906, and "The Madness of the Absolute," *ibid.*, Vol. IV, 1907; and James, "The Mad Absolute," in *Collected Essays and Reviews*, 1920.

its members possess. It includes soldiers who write letters to their mothers, but *it* does not write letters to *its* mother. Similarly a society of persons is to be credited with personality by inclusion or distributively, but not integrally.

One is readily confused by the spell of such expressions as "the national life" or "humanity." How infinitely richer, it may be objected, is the national life than that of any of its members? But one who voices such an objection betrays the fact that he is thinking of the American nation, for example, in terms of everything that is American instead of just those things which are national. Only a very small fraction of the things which the American nation includes can be said to be done by the nation as such. The nation does, perhaps, own the public domain, or claim cable-rights on the island of Yap, or return to a state of normalcy; in any case, the nation does not seek office, or beat its wife, or study Einstein, though these are all things that are done by members of the American nation.

If then we deny of a society as a whole the quality and prerogatives of personality, or anything else that is worthy and admirable, this does not in the least imply that they do not belong to its members, or that as the aggregate of its members it does not contain more that is worthy and admirable than does any one of them individually.

§ 187. **Corporate Personality.** The present issue is pointedly raised in recent discussions of the personality of corporations.[27] A corporation is an organization of persons for a common end by means of the consolidation of their private resources. The legal recognition of the corporation arises from the fact that such organized activity needs to be both protected on its own account and restrained in behalf of the other interests which it affects. A corporation cannot function without guarantees, nor is it safe that it should function unless society as a whole be secured against the abuse of its power. It is therefore taken account of by the

[27] Cf. *e.g.*, H. J. Laski, "The Personality of Associations," *Harvard Law Review*, Vol. XXIX, 1916.

law, and allotted a limited sphere of activity. It has legally
defined rights and legally defined obligations. In these respects it is treated *like* a person; or is a "fictitious," "quasi,"
or "legal" person.

But this does not mean that it is a "natural" person, or
"mens rea." It is not treated as having a mind and will of
its own, distinct from those of its members. The meaning
of corporation law is not addressed to a corporate mind, or
its penalties to a corporate will. The law addresses itself
to the directors or stockholders, as exercising control in their
several persons. The principle of "limited liability" means
that the pecuniary liability *of the stockholders* is limited to
their several contributions to the common fund. The responsibility attaches to the stockholders and not to the fund,
and its limitation is due to the expediency of encouraging
participation in corporate activity by the reduction of its
hazards.

Those who argue for the personality of associations
would wish to restrict them more closely because of a realization
of their large and varied powers. The range of the activities
of a corporation is as wide as the range of the activities of
persons. In other words, men can by concerted action, or
through the instrumentalities which such concerted action
creates, produce on a larger scale any of the effects which
they can produce severally. The way to secure society against
the abuses of corporate action is not, however, to conceive
a new and corporate centre of responsibility, but, on the contrary, to insist more rigorously upon the responsibility of the
individual members. The tradition of the English law, with
its insistence that the corporate agent shall either be held
directly accountable or viewed as standing in the relation of
servant and master to those who employ him, signifies a sound
impulse to fix responsibility upon some real person; upon one
who is psychologically qualified to act responsibly and to be
held responsible, and through whom corporate action can be *controlled* in the interest of society. The conception of corporate
personality, like that of state personality, can tend only to
a vague and equivocal diffusion of responsibility, in the course

of which it disappears altogether either through sub-division, or through being transferred from the component souls to the soul-less whole.

The corporation further illustrates the fact that persons may engage in joint activities without being absorbed by them. A person may invest so much and no more, and it may be thought expedient that the amount of his investment should determine the extent of his liability. But it is the investor and not the investment that is responsible. If his share of the common fund is assessed or appropriated, it is he and not his investment that is punished. In other words, it is the whole of a man, or that peculiar unity which is called a person which is responsible, even though only a fraction of this whole enters as a constituent into the corporate entity.

§ 188. **Social Personification and Social Idolatry.** The recognition of facts is not incompatible with the use of symbols, and the recognition that society is in fact impersonal is not incompatible with its personification.

To personify is intentionally to apply personal epithets, or forms of personal representation, to an object that is known not to be a person, for the purpose of evoking a sentiment toward the object, or for the purpose of bringing it within the scope of certain rules of action. To describe the church as the 'Bride of Christ,' or one's college as one's 'alma mater,' or to represent America as a goddess of liberty, is legitimate personification in so far as it has the effect of securing devotion to an object that is entitled to it. Or a corporation may be called a fictitious person for the purpose of indicating that its legal status and liability is in certain respects identical with those of real or natural persons. The danger of personification lies in the fact that terms employed symbolically tend through constant usage or through a lack of nice discrimination on the part of vulgar minds, to be construed literally. The effect in the present case is to secure devotion to an object that is unworthy of it, or the practice of treating as altogether personal an object that resembles personality only in certain limited respects. Religious or political allegiance may by this means be prolonged when it should have been forfeited, and the venerated object invested by superstitious belief with properties which it does not actually possess,—so that the will is misled and effort misdirected.

It is essential that the symbol should not be confused with that which it symbolizes. A good symbol will not attract attention to itself but to its object. It will illuminate, but not dazzle or blind. Or it will serve, like a transparent lens, to focus the light and to reveal nature. The danger which attends the use of all symbols is the intrusion of their own intrinsic characters. They may then either become objects in their own right, and borrow, besides, the characters of the objects which they symbolize; or they may lend their own characters to their objects. Thus the evil of verbalism lies in imputing to words the substance and power which belong to their objects, or in imputing to their objects the grammatical structure and function which belong to words. The evil of idolatry lies in imputing divinity to the graven image, or in imputing the nature of wood and stone to God.

There is a similar idolatry which arises from the misuse of personal symbols. In the case of the centralized or autocratic society the person of the head is taken as the symbol of the whole. So long as such personification has only the effect of emphasizing the unity of society or of vivifying the loyalty of the members to the whole, it serves as an auxiliary to reason. It brings the fact of human interdependence to the attention of those who are likely to lose sight of it, and thus illuminates action by revealing its premises. In so far, however, as the ruler is *identified* with the society which he rules, there arises a two-fold superstition: the person of the ruler is invested with a dignity which it does not really possess, and society is invested with a personality which it does not really possess. In the first case, one renders to the ruler the homage and obedience which are appropriate to society, and thus fails to pay honor where it is due. The symbol instead of directing sentiment towards its object draws it towards itself. The person of the ruler being thus invested with the attributes of society, all distinction is lost between the office and the man; with the result that the opinion of one man is mistaken for authority, and his will for law. The error consists not in supposing that Louis XIV is the state, for, assuming his control to be absolute, this may be the fact; but in supposing that because he is the state he is something more than Louis, and in thus showing him a deference which enables him to *make* his control absolute. Personal symbolism thus affords a specious justification of personal aggrandizement, and becomes a source of blind and slavish submission.

The second and converse error, in which the object is construed in terms of the symbol, leads to a neglect of the plural and diverse composition of society. Construed in terms of the personal symbol society, assumes a false aspect of unity and simplicity. It is supposed like the symbol to have one judgment and one will. The many judgments and wills of its members are thus ignored or subordinated because their very plurality contradicts this supposition. The claims and values which represent the *actual* interests of men are disparaged in the name of the *fictitious* claim and value of an imaginary interest.

CHAPTER XVI

MODES OF SOCIAL INTEGRATION

I. SOCIETY AS A COMPOSITION AND INTERACTION

§ 189. **Summary of Results.** The two preceding chapters have paved the way for a restatement of social facts in terms of the integration of interests. The rejection of the conception of social *substance* implies the acceptance of the conception of social structure. Viewed in its static aspect, society is not a simple transcendent entity distinguished from men, but is a *composition* or interrelation of men. The rejection of the conception of social *force* implies the acceptance of the conception of social *interaction*. Viewed in its dynamic aspect society is not a simple transcendent power which overrules or supersedes the activities of men, but is their resultant or field of force. Society in short is analyzable into men, both in its static and in its dynamic aspects; and in the case of society, as in the case of any other phenomenon, the way of analysis is the way of explanation.

This conclusion in no way invalidates the view that the social man differs from the non-social man, or that society differs from man. It is not a *reduction* of society to men, in the sense of denying that society has peculiarities of its own, any more than the analysis of a liquid such as water into gases such as hydrogen and oxygen, is a denial of the peculiar physical properties of a liquid. On the contrary, the composite and interactive view of society implies that its members compose something, and that they act upon, and thus modify, one another.

They compose that which may properly be termed a *whole*, possessing properties *as* a whole, which cannot be attributed to the members severally. They compose that which may properly be termed a *system,* possessing an orderly structure that persists when its members change. A social whole or system possesses, furthermore, an *individuality* of its own, which renders it unique within the class of such wholes or systems.

Finally, society is also a *compound* in the sense that some of the characters which attach to it as a whole, duplicate on a larger scale the characters which attach to its members. This is true, for example, of the characters just enumerated. The men who compose a society are wholes, systems and individuals, which are in turn composed of cells or of interests; so that a society may properly be said to be a whole of wholes, a system of systems, or an individual of individuals. But a society does not duplicate *all* of the characters of its members, and among those characters which attach exclusively to the members, is the character of personality, together with its associated prerogatives and modes of determination. Although a society is a whole, system and individual composed of interested, willing, thinking, self-conscious, free, responsible and happy men, a society does not have or take an interest of its own, does not will or think, is not self-conscious, free or responsible, and does not enjoy happiness.

The members of society are conditioned, governed and modified by their interaction. A man's behavior in a group or in a crowd differs altogether from the same man's behavior when alone. There is nothing remarkable in this fact. A man's behavior on dry land differs from his behavior in water, —he acts differently indoors and out, in summer and in winter. His behavior is always a function of his environment, that being one of the things we mean by behavior. Most of what is interesting about the individual consists of what he will do under such and such circumstances. But a man's reactions to his physical environment, and the modifications he acquires from them, are commonly regarded as his own; and similarly, it would seem clear that a man's reactions to another man should be regarded as his—or the other man's. There is no more reason in the one case than in the other

why we should attribute the properties arising from the interaction of a man and his environment, to a third subject,
unless the new properties which thus arise contradict those
of the man. If a man and a woman marry, the interrelation
generates qualities in each; and these qualities should be predi-
'cated of each, as the marital qualities of the man or of the
woman. There are also, in the second place, certain characteristics, such as being an even number, or walking down
the street arm in arm, that can only be attributed to the
couple, and cannot be attributed either to the man or the
woman without contradicting his or her numerical or anatomical properties. But most of the interesting and significant
facts of married life are of the first rather than of the second
variety; and even for the understanding of the second it is
more fruitful to study the history of the man and the woman,
each in the environment of the other, than to study the history
of the couple as such.

It is possible, of course, to use the expression 'social
mind' to describe the properties of the individual human mind
in so far as these are genetically, causally or otherwise relative to others of the species, as one may speak of a man's
spring mind or autumn mind, his before-breakfast mind or
his after-dinner mind, his domestic mind, and his company
mind. But it is one of the unfortunate accidents of language
that this is possible for its has added illegitimately to the
population of an already over-crowded world.

The rejection of society as a subject *sui generis,* having
interests and claims of its own over and above those of its
members, is a conclusion of first importance for the theory
of value. It implies, so far as concerns this mundane sphere,
or such parts of it as lie at present within the range of
observation, that there is only one original source of value,
namely the interests of men.[1] If society had interests of
its own it would generate values of its own. These values
would have to be taken into account, and they might prove
in some sense intrinsically superior to those generated by the

---

[1] Since it does not affect the present argument, I waive here the question of the interests of animals. Cf. § 278, note.

desires, hopes and fears of men. It might even be concluded that their superiority gave warrant to the denial of all human interests. If, on the other hand, there be no interests save those of men, the claims of society must be interpreted in terms of the claims of its members.

The rejection of society as a subject of interest, and hence as an original source of value, implies, furthermore, that attention should be directed to the principles by which the interests of one man are qualified by or united with the interests of another. We have already examined the general principles governing the integration of interests. We have now to consider more particularly the *modus operandi* of these principles when the interests integrated are those of different subjects. We shall thus bring to light the values which are conditioned by the interrelations of two or more valuing subjects, and which may in this sense properly be termed "social values." In adopting this method of procedure we shall hope to avoid both the errors arising from an excessive emphasis on the individual, and those arising from an excessive emphasis on social environment and solidarity.

§ 190. **Recent Sociological Controversy.** The difference of method and fundamental doctrine that divides contemporary sociologists is due to an antithesis that loses its meaning when society is conceived in terms of composition and interaction. This dispute arises from pitting one fiction against another. These two fictions are in part the product of careless thinking, and in part the product of polemics.

The first of these fictions is that of an individual man independent of the society to which he belongs, and the second is that of a social being independent of the individual men who belong to it. Each of these fictions derives plausibility from the absurdity of the other. Instead of being construed as contraries, both of which may be false, they are construed as contradictories of which one must be true and the other false; and the falsity of one is thus argued in support of the truth of the other.

Among American sociologists the relatively individualistic

position is represented by the late Professor Lester F. Ward and by Professor Edward A. Ross. According to the former the fundamental "dynamic agent" in human life is feeling, or "wants seeking satisfaction through effort," or "whatever interests prompt to action." These latter he speaks of as "social forces." He classifies them as "Ontogenetic," "Phylogenetic" and "Sociogenetic" (the last being divided into "Moral," "Esthetic" and "Ethical"), and appeals to them as ultimate potencies in a manner not unlike that of pre-Galilean physics.[2] Professor Ross's view is similar:

"When a phenomenon such as a falling off in births . . . or a shrinkage in crimes against the person is followed back link by link along the causal chain until we arrive at some impulse, appetite, propensity, passion, desire, or purpose of human beings in a specific situation, then, and not till then is it *explained* from the point of view of the sociologist."[3]

To which Professor E. C. Hayes replies that such propensities as the individualist invokes are either congenital, in which case they are universal and do not account for differences and changes of human behavior; or they are acquired, and then have themselves to be accounted for in terms of the modifying influences of environment.

"I maintain that instead of talking of feeling as a cosmic force and *the* social cause, we ought rather to say that the living psychophysical organism, the consummate biological product, is the last complex resultant of the cosmic process to be added to the conditioning phenomena before the final and most complex phenomena of all can emerge, namely, those studied by sociology; that the psychophysical organisms of men with their inherited and acquired tendencies to react upon stimuli are the physiological conditions of social activities; and that the 'impinging environment' is made up of geographic conditions, . . .; of technic conditions, such as roads, tools and houses, the products of the past invention and labor of mankind; and of the present social activities which lap us round and appeal to our imitativeness."[4]

As a counter-blast to an individualism which seems to neglect the determination of one individual's action by that

---

[2] *Pure Sociology*, 1903, pp. 99, 256, 261; *Outlines of Sociology*, 1899, p. 148.
[3] *American Journal of Sociology*, Vol. XVI, 1910-1911, p. 641. Cf. also A. W. Small, *op. cit.*, pp. 639-641.
[4] *Ibid.*, p. 620. (Cf. also, p. 642.)

of others, or the joint products, patterns and resultants of collective activity, such an argument is cogent. But in speaking of "social activities," as though they *supervened* upon those of individuals, or "lapped them round," Professor Hayes gives his opponent an excuse for returning to the attack with the obvious remark that these social activities themselves, in so far as describable at all, are describable only in terms of the activities of two or more individuals.

The quarrel between individualists and environmentalists in a confusing as well as a fruitless quarrel, because the opponents represent two parts of the same complex fact. If individuals interact, one may take each individual in turn and call attention to the fact he is determined by the rest, both severally and in the aggregate, and in terms of this distinction "the rest" may be spoken of summarily as the "social environment"; or one may examine this social environment, and show that it is composed of interacting and jointly acting individuals. That which is true in both the individual and environmental views is preserved without contradiction and without confusion if society is regarded as "a group of individuals carrying on a common life-process through interstimulation and response." [5]

§ 191. **Durkheim versus Tarde.** The controversies among American psychologists are echoes of the mightier conflict that has raged for many years in France between the school of Tarde and the school of Durkheim, or between the party of individualism, and the party of "solidarisme." [6]

Tarde was primarily concerned to *analyze* social phenom-

[5] C. A. Ellwood, *Sociology in its Psychological Aspects,* 1915, p. 131. "This is equivalent," he further adds, "to saying that there is a collective mental life, but no such thing as a social mind in the same sense in which there is an individual mind" (p. 330). The author is not, however, wholly free from the confusions which statements such as these are intended to correct. "From the sociological point of view mind belongs quite as much to the group as to the individual," because, apparently, "the individual mind . . . has been *created* largely through the process of interaction with other minds," and despite the fact that "the individual alone thinks, feels and wills" (*Ibid.,* pp. 281, 329, 330, italics mine).

[6] For an account of a certain historic occasion on which these two champions "soutinrent avec beaucoup de chaleur leurs thèses respectives," cf. *Revue Internationale de Sociologie,* Vol. XII, 1904 .

ena, or to obtain for sociology an explanatory theory that should correspond to the cellular theory in biology.[7] He employed for this method such expressions as "inter-cerebral psychology," "inter-mental psychology," and "inter-psychology."[8] This action of one individual mind upon another he conceived as *imitation*, and exposed himself to criticism, in the first place, because he placed too much emphasis on this conception; and, in the second place, because he did not adequately analyze it. Through the use of figurative expressions such as "photographic reproduction," "current of imitation," "vibratory movement" and "generation at a distance" he gave his opponents cause for reproaching him with the same "pure ontology" of which he accused them.[9] Above all, by his zeal for abstraction, he was misled into affirming, or seeming to affirm, that society can be reduced to the diffused or radiant action of one individual upon another; thus neglecting the fact that both individuals are products of multiple forces which converge upon them from all quarters, and that these forces in their sum determine both how the one individual shall act and how the other individual shall react.[10]

The school of Durkheim presses the considerations which Tarde neglected. Thus Durkheim himself tells us that there is a "type of mentality" or "ensemble of beliefs and sentiments" which is common to the members of the same society, independently of their particular condition or station, and persisting from generation to generation. This "collective consciousness," although it is "realized only in the individuals,"

---

[7] *Ibid.*, pp. 85, 86.
[8] Cf. L *'Opposition Universelle*, 1897, pp. 165, 336; *La Logique Social*, 1895, p. 87; "La Psychologie Intermentale," *Revue Internationale de Sociologie*, Vol. IX, 1901 (trans. in *International Quarterly*, 1903).
[9] Cf. his *Lois de l'Imitation*, second edition, 1905, pp. viii, xiii, 15, 16.
[10] That the view of Tarde can be so corrected or qualified as to avoid this objection appears clearly in its more recent formulation by Professors Ch. Seignebos and G. Dumas, *Journal de Psychologie*, Vol. XVII, 1920. Cf. especially pp. 498-592, 517, 532-533. This "numéro spécial," devoted to the subject of "Psychologie Social et Sociologie," offers the best general statement of the present issue. The position of the Durkheim school is acutely defended by Professor G. Davy. Cf. also an excellent article written from the point of view of Durkheim, by C. Bouglé, "Sociologie et Psychologie," *Revue de l'Enseignement Français*, Vol. XVIII, 1923, No. 34.

is nevertheless held to be "a distinct reality" which is "an entirely different thing from particular consciousness." [11] The "collective consciousness'" seems here to be the typical or characteristic consciousness, the sum of the elements in respect of which the consciousness of one member of a collection resembles the consciousness of the others. It would, on this interpretation, be equally appropriate, or inappropriate, to speak of the Nordic skull as a collective skull, and to say that it was a reality distinct from the skulls of particular Nordics.

But there is a deeper meaning in Durkheim's view which this passage very imperfectly represents, and which contains the real distinction between this view and the view of Tarde. The latter would be equally insistent upon the likemindedness of the members of society, but while *he* would explain it in terms of imitation, Durkheim and his followers would explain it in terms of the organization or structure of society as a whole. Tarde assumes a state of mind to exist in one individual and traces its diffusion through the group, while Durkheim assumes a group to have a general form, and traces its effects upon the individual. Thus, for example, a follower of Tarde is concerned to show that the mentality of any given Frenchman tends to infect other Frenchmen, and thus to beget a likemindedness among all Frenchmen; while a follower of Durkheim is concerned to show that the mentality of Frenchmen individually reflects the characteristics of the French system of life. According to the one, a Frenchman is what he is because he lives among his neighbors; according to the other, because he lives in France.

§ 192. Reconciliation of Opposing Views.

Now there is not the slightest reason why these views should be regarded as conflicting. On the contrary they present aspects of the same truth. Tarde undoubtedly misunderstood imitation and exaggerated its rôle. But that is not the essential feature

[11] *De la Division du Travail Social,* 1902, p. 46. The author speaks of the beliefs and sentiments which constitute the "type psychique" as "communs à la *moyenne* des membres d'une même société." Just what distinguishes this "moyenne" unless it be the "type psychique," is not clear; but I do not press the difficulty.

of his view, and his followers have outgrown it. He was interested in the discovery of the elementary forces by which men influence one another, while the school of Durkheim, on the other hand, directs attention to the systems or fields in which they operate.

The issue can be simplified by taking the example of the family group. Tarde deals with the processes and mechanisms by which father, mother and child act and react upon one another. Durkheim deals with the fact that father, mother and child compose a peculiar triadic structure, which remains the same despite changes of personnel, in which each member has his peculiar station, and in which each member is determined by that station. For Tarde a father is an individual interacting with other individuals; for Durkheim he is a 'father,' related in a peculiar way to a 'wife' and 'child.' For Tarde the father is a function of other individuals, for Durkheim he is a function of the family. The two views are complementary and not conflicting because the family, while possessing its division of labor, and its stereotyped form, is *composed* of interacting individuals.

The method of Tarde should bring to light the elementary modes of inter-individual influence, and the method of Durkheim should bring to light the resultant effects dependent upon the diverse arrangement of individuals. The motion of any body is governed by the force of gravitation, and may be said to be a function of the mass and distance of any other body; but it is equally true, and wholly consistent wtih this truth, that the motion of the Earth is a function of the Solar System, in which the operations of gravitation are determined by the number and arrangement of the individual bodies which obey it.[12]

---

[12] It has been proposed that the experimental or laboratory method should be employed in social psychology (Cf. F. H. Allport, "Behavior and Experiment in Social Psychology," *Jour. of Abnormal Psychology*, Vol. XIV, 1919). It is undoubtedly possible that the social conditions of behavior should be in some measure "controlled." Thus one can compare the reactions of the individual when isolated, with his reactions in the presence of one or more other individuals. But a follower of Durkheim might reasonably object that a socius is always something more than a numerical unit of the species. He is a father, a teacher, a friend, an

The followers of Durkheim are justified in insisting that there are to be found in every group facts which "manifest the nature of the group as group," and "are what they are because the group is what it is." They are justified in insisting that the members of any given group "would have neither the same tendencies, nor the same habits, nor the same prejudices had they lived in other human groups"; and that the members of a crowd "neither think nor act as would isolated individuals." [13] This is precisely as true, and true in precisely the same sense, as if one were to affirm that the motion of the earth is different from what it would be if it belonged to another planetary system or to no planetary system at all. But this does not imply, in the first case, that the group or crowd itself has tendencies, habits, prejudices, or that it thinks or acts; any more than it implies, in the second case, that the planetary system itself moves.

Durkheim and his followers are justified in affirming the existence of "modes of action and thought" which are "capable of exercising an external constraint upon the individual," which are "general over the whole extent of a given society," which "the individual finds pre-established," which are "ordinarily transmitted by education" and which are accompanied by a sense of obligation. There is no objection, other than that of ambiguity, to designating such modes of action and thought as "collective representations," and to insisting that they constitute the inward aspect and meaning of all "institutions." [14] But it is meaningless to say that such collective

enemy, etc. If he is another laboratory subject he is judged and reacted to accordingly. In other words, social reactions are always functions of a complex or organized "situation." It does not follow that laboratory methods may not be fruitful so far as they go, but only that the laboratory situation, having its own peculiarities, cannot duplicate the domestic or political situation. There is much to be expected of the "case" method now employed by social workers whose ministrations enable them to compare the reactions of an individual in his home, with the reactions of the same individual abroad, in his club, his office, etc. Cf. the volumes of the Social Work Series, edited by Mary E. Richmond, and published by the Russell Sage Foundation.

[13] P. Fauconnet and M. Mauss, *op. cit.*, p. 166. Cf. C. Bouglé, *Qu'est la Sociologie?*, 1907, pp. 6, 7.

[14] Durkheim, *Les Régles de la Méthode Sociologique*, 1904, p. 19; Fauconnet and Mauss, *op. cit.*, pp. 168, 171. For the more precise meaning of 'collective representation,' cf. below, § 197.

representations "have an existence in themselves, independently of their individual manifestations," since they clearly owe their independence of *some* individuals to the fact that they are manifested in other individuals, and their survival to the fact that they are transmitted to new generations of individuals. Since they are transmitted by education, and constrain or oblige by virtue of a sort of "double sentiment," or tension between love and fear,[15]—since, in other words, they are discoverable only as incidents in the history of individual minds,—it is surely unprofitable to ascribe to them "an entirely different nature" from that of individual representations, or to treat them as "psychical phenomena of a new *genre,* capable of evolving by themselves" and possessing their own peculiar mode of determination.[16]

Professor Davy has given us a vivid account of certain "seasonal societies," which lead their characteristic social life only during a part of the year. In the summer they live dispersed and without "cohesion," but in the winter, being "concentrated and organized," "the general mentality is completely transformed." A new "sentiment of solidarity" appears; each individual assumes "his rank and function"; and all are "plunged into a sort of mystic delirium and sacred fury."[17] The existence and the significance of such facts is not to be denied, and the sociologist may properly concern himself with them. But nothing is gained by regarding them as "irreducible," or by declaring that "the collective life is a datum and not a product." Such a method discourages analysis and explanation without serving any positive purpose. The very description of the facts contradicts their alleged irreducibility. For Professor Davy has himself indicated that they are somehow conditioned by concentration and organization, by ritual and initiation, by leadership and tradition.

This author is mistaken in supposing that there is any-

---

[15] Durkheim, remarks reported in *Bulletin de la Société Française de Philosophie,* Vol. VI, 1906, p. 125.
[16] Fauconnet and Mauss, *loc. cit.*
[17] G. Davy, "L'Explication Sociologique en Psychologie," *Journal de Psychologie,* Vol. XVII, 1920, pp. 549-550.

thing in such facts to which an "inter-mental psychology" might not properly be applied. Indeed it would be difficult to conceive a more suitable and auspicious occasion for the use of this method. The thought and feeling of any given member of such a group is profoundly altered by changes in the distance, the behavior and the arrangement of his fellows. The part played by changes of climate or of physical environment would not be denied, nor would it be emphasized, by either school. Both would find the social process in the sphere of mind, and would agree that a society is formed by "a plurality of individual consciousnesses, acting and reacting on one another." [18] But whereas a follower of Tarde would attempt to analyze society into these actions and reactions, and explain it by them, the follower of Durkheim refuses. Since the attempt to analyze and explain in no way implies the denial of the facts, such a refusal can only be accounted for on the theory that the school of Durkheim is willing for explanatory purposes to fall back upon the category of substance; [19] or on the theory that it prefers history to psychology, and is prepared to renounce explanation altogether. Such a preference would be unobjectionable if it were accompanied by a recognition of its limits and a tolerance of other preferences.

§ 193. **Limitation of Society to the Category of Interest.** Accepting as a principle of method the view that "the mechanism of social facts can be accurately ascertained only in the manifestations of individuals," [20] we are concerned only with society in so far as it is a composition of subjects who interact *interestedly,* or are integrated in and through their *interests.* There are two broad principles of social integration which may now briefly be considered under this limitation.

Plants may be grouped in terms of their common *external*

---

[18] This is the statement of Fauconnet and Mauss (*op. cit.,* p. 166) but might have been written by any orthodox Tardeian. For the school of Durkheim society is apparently neither constituted nor explained by that *of* which it is formed.

[19] Cf. § 177.

[20] Ch. Seignobos, *op. cit.,* p. 509.

relations or in terms of their *inter*relations. The first principle defines what are called "ecological" societies, that is, societies which are functions of the same physical environment conceived in terms of heat, moisture, wind, or chemical conditions. Any given region of the earth's surface will be distinguished by a peculiar combination of these factors, and will give a certain unity to the local vegetation, thus creating a rock-society, a swamp-society or a desert-society.[21] It is evident that there are human societies in the same sense,— such as insular societies, sea-faring societies, mountain societies, tropical societies, and perhaps planetary societies. The human individuals occupying the same territory compose a society which is a function of space, contiguity, and physiographic conditions.

According to a second principle, plant societies are constituted when one plant serves as the environment of the other, providing a wind-break or shade, conserving the water-supply, or serving as a host for parasites. It is needless to point out that human beings are interrelated in like manner. Each is a part of the environment of the other, and provides him with protection or with the requisite conditions of life.

This distinction between the common external relations and the mutual internal relations of a group, defines two fundamental principles of integration in society, but upon the plane of interest these principles must be translated into other terms.

Common external relations must be translated into terms of common objects. That the members of a society of interested subjects should occupy the same territory, or the same planet, and that they should be causally dependent on a common environment, is a condition of their community of interest, but does not of itself constitute such a community. It is necessary that they should respond to it interestedly, that it should become their common object, in the sense in which this can be predicated only of interested subjects. Community

---

[21] Cf. J. M. Coulter, *Plant Relations,* 1900, pp. 178-179. For an introduction to the study of societal forms in plant life, cf. this work, *passim.* and J. B. Farmer, *Plant Life,* 1913.

of interest means interest *in* the same, although this may be conditioned by proximity and causal dependence. Even the "common past," which is first a temporal and causal relation, becomes a community of interest only when the same past is reacted to as memory or tradition.

Similarly, in order that internal relations shall create a society of interests, the connecting relation must be a relation of interest. The members of such a society must be *mutually* interested. In this case also, the relations of physical and causal dependence pave the way for relations of interest. Thus the relations of paternity and maternity by which the offspring is causally linked with the parents by the physiological process of reproduction, constitutes in the basic biological sense that social group which is called the family; but the family constitutes a society of interests only in so far as the parental interest in the child, and the filial interest in the parent, supervene. Plant relations, such as symbiosis or parasitism, whether advantageous or disadvantageous to the related organisms, are paralleled in the life of man. In innumerable ways human beings profit or suffer from their mutual contacts and intimacies. A man may be dwarfed and stunted by his neighbor's hardier growth, just as he may find him a refuge, or bask in the light of his presence. There is scarcely any known type of physical interdependence which is not exemplified in the relations of human organisms. These relations condition the interest of one living organism in another, and his peculiar interest in another of the same species, but they do not, in and of themselves, constitute this interest.

The principles of similarity or likemindedness, and of social structure or pattern, are reducible in like manner to community of interest and to mutuality of interest respectively. The members of the human species constitute a class by virtue of their possession of common characters, such as a highly developed nervous system, or a capacity of language, or a stock of innate reflexes; and the same is true of the more limited human groups that possess peculiar characters, such color of skin, stature, shape of skull, temperament or degree of intelligence. The possession of such common characters by two or more human individuals does in a certain proper sense constitute a social fact, to be taken account of by ethnologists. But in so far as similarity or likemindedness constitutes a principle of unity among interests, it means that interested reactions are directed to the same objects, communicate common meanings, and converge in a common past. Similarly, the structure or pattern of a group, the order of arrangement of its members, their inter-adjustment of function and distinctive "division of labor," gives to the group a characteristic physiognomy, which is a quality attaching to the whole, and a unified system which is capable of persisting through changes of personnel. A type of inter-human organization may, in a proper sense, be regarded as a society. But we are concerned with social organization only in so far as it is an object of interest to its members, or to an external subject; or in so far as it determines the manner in which its members are interested in one another.

Construed in these terms we accept the view of those sociologists who define society as a *psychological* rather than a physical, chemical, mechanical or merely biological unity.

The principles by which subjects of interest are so integrated as to compose a society in the limited sense appropriate to the theory of value, are thus reducible to two: the principle of community of interest, according to which interests have common objects; and the principle of interrelation or mutuality of interest, according to which they have one another as objects. But while these are the ultimate principles of social integration, that which is most distinctive of human societies is the union of the two. We shall therefore recognize two derived principles, the mediation of community by interrelation of interest, and the mediation of interrelation by community of interest; or convergence mediated by mutuality, and mutuality by convergence. These derivative principles determine the peculiar character of cooperation in which the common end is valued by each as the object of the other, and in which each is valued by the other as his partner in a common enterprise.

II. COMMUNITY OF INTEREST

§ 194. **Social Integration through Community of Object.** Society has now been reduced, for purposes of a theory of value, to those general principles of the integration of interests, which have already been formulated.[22] Interests may be integrated in three ways; through their common objects (community), through being objects for one another (mutuality), and through mediating one another (inter-mediation). *Subjects* of interest, in turn, are integrated through the cross-integration of their component interests. In this case, however, the third alternative is eliminated. The integration of interests by their inter-mediation can occur only when the interests belong to the same organic individual. It is the distinctive form of personal integration, and does not apply to social relations except indirectly, through the first and second principles.[23] In other words, subjects of interest can be integrated only objectively, or through the objective intersection of their interests. We consider, first, the case in which two or more subjects of interests are integrated through what are called "common interests," but which may be more precisely described as component interests having common objects.

What is meant by "interests having common objects" has already been stated.[24] A brief *résumé* will throw light upon certain social applications and illustrations which are suitable to the present context.

Different interests may have the same objects in two senses. On the one hand, two interests may have the same object (index or predicate) by virtue of the difference between the physiological or subjective *acts* of indication or predication, and *that which* is indicated or predicated (the object). The social application is obvious. The same conditions which permit of sameness of objective reference on the part of different words, gestures or other responses oc-

---

[22] Cf. Ch. XIII.
[23] Cf. Ch. XV, Sect. I.
[24] § 151.

curring at different times and places in the history of one organism, will permit of a like identity of reference in the case of two or more organisms. Two or more organisms can point at the same thing precisely as one organism can point repeatedly, or by different acts, at the same thing.

On the other hand, two or more objects of interest, such as the reëlection of President Coolidge and his defeat, may have a common objective constituent, which may be the index, as in the case just cited, or which may be the predicate. Community of *both* index and predicate implies identity in the object of interest. Combining these two principles, the interests of two different subjects may be integrated through having the same total object, or through having different objects which are identical in respect of either their index or their predicate.

Similarly, two interests of different subjects, like two interests of the same subject, may be in conflict, through the incompatibility of their acts, or through the contradictoriness of their objects; or they may be in harmony through the compatibility of their acts, or through the consistency or alliance of their objects.

The integration of two or more subjects of interest through their common objects defines at one and the same time a society of interests and a social value. We may represent this situation as a triadic system, in which A and B are two different subjects, and O their common object. The relation of O to both A and B, as distinguished from its relation to either A or B singly, gives it social value. The relation of A to B through O their common object constitutes a type of society, composed of two subjects integrated by the object of interest.

§ 195. **Common Existent Objects.** There is, as we have seen, always a hazard of failure in interest, and a hazard of error in its mediating interest-judgment. The object of interest is always, during the life of the interest, a possibility rather than an actuality. To indicate this status which an object of interest shares with an object of judgment, we have termed it an 'objective,' as distinguished from an existent object.[25] Existent objects may, however, play a part in the history and context of interest in two senses, as transcendent object or as datum.

The transcendent object renders judgments true or false in advance of verification, and thus determines whether human hopes and fears are or are not well-founded. It is permissible, therefore, to speak of several subjects of interest as socially integrated by their actual environment, even when they construe it in different or even in conflicting terms. They are in some sense referring to the same facts, otherwise their judgments could never prove inconsistent, and the one would never correct the other.

But though the actual constitution of their common environment may be said to give a certain unity to interests, as conditioning their verification, this unity remains conditional, and conditional only, until the verification occurs. A society is psychologically integrated by a common existential environment only so far as the judgments of its members are corrected or confirmed by experiment. While man has from earliest times inhabited the same planet and the same stellar universe, human society is to-day, thanks to the advance of science, much more completely a function of these natural conditions than ever before in its history. Not that man is either more or less *causally* dependent on his physical environment, but that in his interested activities he responds to this environment more nearly as it is. The judgments which mediate his interests being truer, his several interests are in closer accord with the facts, and their integration is more largely definable in terms of these facts. Nor is it implied that there is any diminution of the rôle played in human and social life by meanings, ideals and other objectives, but only that these, in turn, being more completely verified, may be said more perfectly to reflect the common facts. Common existent objects brings about a psychological meeting of minds, rather than a more logical unity of reference, when and in so far as they assume the form of data, or when the consummatory

25 Cf. § 136.

responses of two or more subjects of interest directly engage them.

Without attempting any exhaustive enumeration or systematic survey of the varieties of social integration that may arise from the varieties of common data, we shall consider such examples as serve to introduce certain further modifying principles.

Two or more subjects of interest living in the presence of a "common scene," are convergent in respect of their aesthetic activities. Their eyes dwell familiarly and fondly upon the same landscape,—the same plain or mountain or sea-coast; their ears are gratified by the same sound of waters, or of forest winds; their nostrils by the same odor of flowers, or of ocean brine. The same community of aesthetic data is provided by the common monuments and outward sensible aspects of the common culture. In this case the common data unite and do not divide. Interests so integrated are harmonious both subjectively and objectively. They have the same object, which is the persistence and recurrence of the same datum; and the activities with which the same datum is engaged by several subjects are free from mutual interference.

Common resources or instruments, on the other hand, may divide as well as unite. A group of men interested in the same water-system, may quarrel as to the *use* which is to be made of it. This conflict of use may be either subjective or objective. In the one case this conflict consists in an interference between two activities whose end is the same, as when two men seek the same water to drink, or the one to drink and the other to swim, or the one to swim and the other to fish. These interested activities are all, if taken singly, satisfied by the same datum. The incompatibility arises from their spacial and temporal juxtaposition, or from the fact that the one spoils the object for the other. The test of incompatibility is the fact that it can always be removed by rotation, division or extension; by taking turns with the object, by taking different parts of it, or by duplicating it.

The case of *opposition* is the case in which the same datum serves as the index of two contradictory objectives. The man who enjoys the waterfall as scenery and the man who wishes to use it as power are both interested in a future state of the waterfall. But whereas the one wishes to preserve it as it is, the other wishes to reduce its flow or alter its channel. The situation which would satisfy one interest contradicts the situation which would satisfy the other. Such conflict can be escaped only by a change of object on the part of the one interest or the other.

It is important to note that communities of interest consist in rivalries and struggles as truly as in agreements and partnerships. A nation is, among other things, a group of persons competing for the use of the same natural resources or instruments of production. A family is, among other things, a group of persons competing for the same food, shelter, protection or domestic conveniences. In both of these groups there is an intersection of interests in immediately surrounding objects, a proximity of space and time, a crossing of causal paths, and a meeting of minds, of which conflict is the most immediate and inevitable effect.

Out of this conflict spring those readjustments and constructive solutions of which it is customary to think when social unity is in question. There are always, no doubt, conflicts as well as harmonies; and social reconstruction may be motivated by the more positive hope of enhancing harmonies and of converting them into a mutual reinforcement and enrichment. But the most potent spur to social reconstruction is the fact or the threat of conflict, and it is only because society is already a unity in this tragic and ominous sense that it becomes a unity in the more auspicious sense. There is a basic truth in Hobbes's view that the whole system of law and order is an escape from war and an insurance against its recurrence. But even Hobbes did not sufficiently stress the fact that war arises from intimacy and not from remoteness.[26] The quarrels of lovers, brothers and neighbors, the

---

[26] "And therefore if any two men desire the same thing, which nevertheless they cannot both enjoy, they become enemies." *Leviathan*, Ch. XIII.

bickerings of husband and wife, the bitterness of internal dissension and of civil war are not paradoxical or accidental. They signify the recrudescence of those conflicts which forced the adoption of institutional forms of life, and they testify to the fact that every contact is an occasion of difference.

Common data may be divided according as they are parts of man's primitive environment or are the products of his own activity. In the environment as well as in man himself there is an "original nature" and a "second nature." Artefacts, like natural resources, may be the common objects of present interests, whether conflicting or harmonious.

But artefacts are social phenomena in a second sense, which may or may not be combined with the first. They are relics or fossil remains of extinct interests, or high-water marks of a tide that has receded. As data for the archaeologist or palaeontologist, they enable us to reconstruct the interests of the dead past. It is worthy of remark that social products may thus record the success of the interests which created them, and bear no other relation to interest whatever. Like foot-prints left behind in an abandoned desert, they may crown effort or fulfil aspiration without thereafter being put to use or contemplated with admiration. It is important to acknowledge this fact in order to understand that monuments and artificial utilities are more commonly social phenomena in a double sense. They possess both a retrospective and a prospective component, being at one and the same time the consummation of old enterprise and the index or starting-point of new.

§ 196. Social Function of Symbols.

There is another class of data, usually but not necessarily artefacts, which serve as the connecting link between the community of data and the community of objectives. These data are symbols.

Any datum may be a symbol if it means something, or operates as a sign.[27] Conspicuous features of nature, monuments, spoken or written words, images, small and familiar objects easily duplicated and distributed, any of these is a

[27] Cf. § 134.

symbol, provided it directs expectation or interest to something other than itself. A symbol may be itself judged, as when

"the rocket's red glare,—the bombs bursting in air
Gave proof through the night that our flag was still there."

But the virtue of the flag as a symbol lies in the fact that its "broad stripes and bright stars," are more palpable than "the land of the free and the home of the brave." The latter is an objective, mediated by a complex system of judgments and expectations, while the latter is, or may readily be, a datum.

The power as well as the utility of the symbol lies in the fact that it may evoke the beliefs and passions which are proper to the objective for which it is substituted. It has been said that the Comte de Chambord's failure to attain the throne of France in 1873 was due to his insistence upon employing the white flag instead of the tri-color as his emblem. He thus directed upon himself the accumulated hatred of the *ancien régime,* whereas if he had adopted the tri-color powdered with *fleurs-de-lys* he might have rallied both the reactionaries and the revolutionaries in his support.[28] The potency thus exercised by a colored piece of cloth is conditioned upon the fact that the judgments and interests of many individuals converge upon the common meaning or end which it represents. The colored piece of cloth is a common datum, and defines a community of interest of the type already considered; the meaning or end which it represents is an objective, and defines community of interest of a new type.

The secret of understanding the rôle of symbols, whether individual or social, lies in holding fast to the distinction between the symbol and what it symbolizes. The simplest example is afforded by the case of language. The possession of a common language implies, in the first place, the use by several individuals of the same set of symbols. The members

[28] Cf. St. George Mivart, *Essays and Criticisms,* 1892, Vol. I, p. 148.

of a certain group located in Central Europe all employ the visible or auditory pattern *Sonnenuntergang* when they wish to direct attention to a certain familiar natural event. This common word signifies a sameness of visual and auditory data, and also a sameness of use. Since the word arouses in all members of the group the expectation of the same natural event, it may be used by any member of the group for the purpose of inducing this expectation in any other member. In other words, it renders communication possible. There are, then, three common objects, the common word (in the visible and audible sense), the common natural event, and the common habit by which the one begets the expectation of the other. But the members of another group, located on an island off the northwestern coast of Europe, employ another visual and auditory pattern, *sunset,* to refer to the same natural event. This group differs from the other group in the word and verbal habit, but not in the objective. It is easy to suppose that two groups should employ two entirely different languages while agreeing entirely in what was talked or written about. In this case both societies would react cognitively and interestedly to the same environment except for the difference of verbal stimuli and verbal behavior. The difference of their literature and discourse would consist entirely in a difference of linguistic form. It would always be capable of exact translation, although the sensory qualities of the spoken and written word could not be duplicated.

This possibility is insisted upon only for the sake of emphasizing the fact that it is never realized, since there is as a matter of fact always another difference added to the difference of signs. This second factor which unites the members of a cultural group, but which divides one such group from another, is the sameness of objectives. The objects of thought and imagination, of fear and of hope, are in large measure identical. Means of signifying and communicating these characteristic objects will then also be characteristic, and will be symptomatic of the community of objects.

§ 197. **Collective Representations.** The difference and connection between a community of symbols and a community of objects is relatively clear in the case of language. The same analysis will serve to clarify the notion of "collective representations," which in its current acceptance seems at once to emphasize and to obscure an important fact. This notion, as employed by Durkheim and his followers, seems to mean at least three distinct things, as well as several indistinct things.

In the first place, a collective representation is a representation of collectivity. According to Durkheim, society is the preëminent object of interest to man, and was in the beginning almost his only object. At any rate society is the object from which man has originally abstracted his fundamental categories.

"It is not surprising," he says, "that social time, social space, social classes and causality should be the basis of the corresponding categories, since it is under their social forms that these different relations were first grasped with a certain clarity by the human intellect." [29]

Proof of this is to be found in the fact that primitive divisions of time and space "correspond to the periodical recurrence of rites, feasts and public ceremonies," and to the shape and quarters of the tribal encampment.[30] Whether or not it be true that social structures and activities are the most primitive objects, in any case they *are* objects. We have already noted that they furnish an occasion for certain characteristic misconceptions, such as substance,[31] and there is no reason to deny that they also furnish an occasion for certain fundamental and valid conceptions, such as space, time and causality. Social representations in this sense, as representations having

[29] *Op. cit.,* p. 444. Cf. p. 440.
[30] *Op. cit.,* pp. 10, 11. How these temporal and spacial arrangements are themselves fixed is not explained. It is difficult to escape the suggestion that the periodic changes of nature or the configuration of the earth's surface may have had something to do with it.
[31] Cf. § 164.

society as their object, belong to a later division of our subject.[32]

In the second place, a collective representation is a representation which arises in the course of the interaction of two or more minds.

"Collective representations are the result of an immense cooperation, which stretches out not only into space, but into time as well; to make them, a multitude of minds have associated, united and combined their ideas and sentiments; for them, long generations have accumulated their experience and their knowledge. A special intellectual activity is therefore concentrated in them which is infinitely richer and complexer than that of the individual.[33]

This "special intellectual activity" despite Durkheim's habit of imputing it to "a unique intelligence," a "collective consciousness" or "consciousness of consciousnesses," [34] evidently consists in communication. To such relatively meagre ideas as he derives from his own private experience, an individual may add the ideas of other individuals. Ideas may be transmitted and exchanged so that each indirectly profits by the experience of all. This compounding and accumulation of ideas takes place within the individual mind, since it is always a human organism that is the recipient and depository, as well as the agent, of communication.[35]

The sociality of collective representations in this sense consists not in the social character of their object, as in the case above, but in the social character of the process which generates them.[36] This process, however, resembles the case

---

[32] Cf. Ch. XVII, Sect. II.

[33] Durkheim, *op. cit.,* p. 16.

[34] *Ibid.,* pp. 434, 444.

[35] I am assuming that a museum or written record does not constitute a storage of ideas, but only a storage of symbols, which conserve and transmit ideas only in so far as there exist organisms in which they evoke responses to determined objectives. As regards the distinction insisted upon above, between the symbol and the thing symbolized, I am giving Durkheim the benefit of the doubt. I am assuming that he means by representation *that which is represented,* and not the sign or image by which it is represented.

[36] This is the sense of sociality emphasized in Wundt's extensive study of *Völkerpsychologie,* 1900. Cf. *e.g.,* p. 6.

previously discussed in that it is a case of mutuality, rather than community of interest, and so belongs to a later division of our topic.

In the third place, the social process of communication results in a situation that is social in the sense with which we are here concerned, in the sense, namely, of community of object.[37] In so far as two individuals adopt one another's ideas and add them to their own, individuals cease to be distinguishable as regards their ideas, and the ideas cease to appertain exclusively to either individual. Concepts thus assume a "common" and "impersonal" character. They are stable and independent of any individual mind because they are sustained by many minds. For the same reason they wear an aspect of authority.[38] Ideas which the individual borrows from the common fund, are *a priori*. He does not derive them from his private experience but interprets his private experience in terms of them.[39] Such concepts are usually "general," but they need not be so. Their universality lies not in wide distribution in the environment, but in the fact that many minds converge upon them.[40]

The totality of the concepts or representations thus common to the members of a group constitute a system, or "kingdom of ends and impersonal truths," and this common environment of ideals and meanings becomes in turn a condition of further cooperation and mutual interest.[41]

[37] Communication doubtless begins as well as ends in this situation. There is, so far as I can see, no satisfactory account of the genesis of language or other means of communication, that does not presuppose common data at the outset.

[38] Durkheim, *op. cit.*, pp. 14, 17, 434-435.

[39] That one should be able to do this successfully, or apply to nature categories that he has derived from society, argues, thinks Durkheim, that "society is a part of nature, and indeed its highest representation" (p. 18). He must be credited with recognizing the difficulty, but I leave it to others to reconcile this statement with what appear to be opposite views expressed in pp. 441-442 of the same work.

[40] Durkheim, *op. cit.*, pp. 14, 17, 434-435.

[41] *Ibid.*, p. 446. The system of collective representations may thus be said to be the 'correlate,' not of any single mind, but of the collectivity of minds, and in two senses: in the first place, as the product of their interaction; and, in the second place, as their common object. Cf. Durkheim's "Représentations individuelles et représentations collectives," *Révue de Métaphysique et de Morale*, Vol. VI, 1898.

§ 198. Common Objectives.

Thus collective representations in this third sense, signify common objectives, as distinguished from common existent objects or common data. Their possibility lies in the fact that two or more individuals may mean the same, judge the same, desire the same, or pursue the same, without the consummation or verification of their convergent activities. They may be so constituted that the same events or existences *would* fulfil or surprise their expectations, *would* satisfy or disappoint their interests. There is community of reference and interest, with or without community of experience and achievement.

It is in these terms that we are to understand that which sociologists, ethnologists and historians embrace under such notions as myths, moral sentiments, tradition, social purposes, and culture. Myths are common imaginative constructions, which may be the objectives of belief, or of mere supposition. Moral sentiments are common demands made by all of the group upon each, manifestations of favor or disfavor implying an ultimate resort to coercion, describable in terms of a mode of conduct which would satisfy them, but which need not in point of fact be realized. Tradition does not consist in a common past, nor even in common memories, but in a common interpretation of the past which strongly resists historical criticism. Social purposes are common goals of achievement to which individuals subordinate their private interests. Culture is a name for the whole set of common objectives in its characteristic differences from other sets, or in its characteristic internal relations.

It is in these terms that we may accept Professor Giddings' notion of "like-mindedness," or cultural homogeneity, or "concert of thought, emotion and will." It is not, strictly speaking, a question of "like response to the same given stimulus," for there may be no same given stimulus. Like-mindedness consists essentially not in a relation to the same data, but in a relation to the same objectives.[42]

---

[42] F. H. Giddings' *Elements of Sociology*, 1898, pp. 77, 120; *Descriptive and Historical Sociology*, 1908, p. 185; *American Jour. of Sociology*, Vol. X, 1904-05, p. 164.

This is also the meaning of Le Bon's "national soul," which he describes as "a manner of seeing, feeling, and willing common to the majority of the individuals of the same people"; which acts as a constraint upon the natural impulses which manifest themselves in the behavior of a crowd, and accounts for the recovery of equilibrium after the excesses of revolution.[43]

In these terms, also, we may understand Tarde's contention that desire and thought have a power to unify society, while sensation tends rather to divide and individuate.[44] The community of objectives has a breadth and a stability that a community of data can never possess. Community or convergence of interest may be represented as a triangle in which the breadth of the base is proportional to the altitude. Data are conditioned by temporal and spacial proximity. Only a few individuals can share the objects of consummatory activities. But as the object recedes into the past or future, or into the remote distance, it may be the focus of an indefinite number of anticipatory responses. The eye-witnesses of the same event form a small and transient group, but there is no reason why a whole nation, or even the totality of mankind throughout a prolonged period of time, should not share the same tradition, or direct their aspiration and effort to the same ideal.

[43] G. Le Bon, *Psychology of Revolution*, trans. by B. Miall, 1913, pp. 61, 77, 103, 106.
[44] *Essais et Mélanges Sociologiques*, 1895, pp. 235-368.

CHAPTER XVII

MODES OF SOCIAL INTEGRATION *(continued)*

I. MUTUALITY OF INTEREST

§ 199. **Other Subject as Object.** Two or more subjects of interest are united by their convergent reference to the same object. This relationship constitutes a social fact because it embraces two or more individuals of the human species; and it would constitute a social fact if no other relationship supervened, as in the case of two or more witnesses of the same scene who were unaware of one another. The abstraction of this relationship does not, however, imply the existence of historical societies in which it is the sole bond of union. It is commonly associated with a second principle, that of interrelation, inter-interest or mutuality, to which we now turn. The full complexity of the actual social integrations which are characteristic of human life can be appreciated only when these two principles are both distinguished and united.

By interrelation of interest is meant the interest of one subject of interest in another.[1] The simplest case of such a relation is the interest of *a* in *b,* where *a* and *b* are both subjects of interest. In other words, while community or coincidence of interest is essentially a triadic relation, involving at least three terms, interrelation of interest is in its simplest form a dyadic relation, involving only two terms. More complex relations of the same type are represented by the reciprocal interest of *a* and *b,* or their interest in one another; and by the interest of *a* in *b-and-c.* As in the case

---

[1] Where an interest is the object of the mediating judgment of another. **Cf.** § 154. I am employing the term 'mutuality' to include both the case in which interest is reciprocal, and that in which it is non-reciprocal.

of community of interest, so here also, we are conceiving society to exist only upon the level of mind. As two or more human individuals may be brought into one physico-chemical system through their causal relations with the same environment, so may they also through their causal *inter*relation. We are here concerned only with interrelations of the type characteristic of mind in which one individual is the object of another.[2]

The fundamental fact underlying these relations is the fact that among the data of any given human individual's environment are to be found the tactual, visual, auditory, olfactory and other sensory appearances of other human individuals. These data constitute stimuli of a notably arresting and potent character. Whether the peculiar force of such stimuli is congenital or is a result of familiarity and interdependence does not primarily concern us. In any case it is undeniably the case that the presence and behavior of another individual of the same species attracts attention and evokes response. It is specifically and uniquely "interesting." This fact underlies all of the more complicated interactions of mind, and constitutes gregariousness or sociality in the most fundamental sense in which it can be predicated of the psychological constitution of men.

Manifestations or expressions of another subject may as data be themselves objects of interest, as when a mother delights in the laughter of her child or a stranger is annoyed by its cry; or they may serve as signs, and in either of two ways. On the one hand, they serve as signs of the object to which the response of the other subject is directed, as when a cry of alarm begets the expectation of something to be feared. In this sense another interest serves to mediate

[2] This conception is employed by some sociologists as the *definition* of society. "The only criterion by which we may decide whether any group constitutes a society or not is its possession or non-possession of the essential mark of a society, namely, the *functional interdependence of its members on the psychical side.*" (C. A. Ellwood, *Sociology in its Psychological Aspects,* 1915, p. 14.) For other examples of the same view, this author cites J. H. W. Stuckenberg, *Science of Human Society,* 1904, Vol. I, pp. 80-102; G. Simmel, *Sociale Differenzierung,* 1890, pp. 12-20; A. W. Small, *General Sociology,* 1905, Ch. I; E. A. Ross, *Foundations of Sociology,* 1905, p. 9.

response to a common object,—a mode of social complexity which will be reserved for later consideration.[3] On the other hand, the appearance of another subject serves as a sign of ulterior aspects of this subject himself, as when the cry of alarm draws attention to the organism from which it emanates, or generates the expectation of further manifestations of fear. This is the case with which we are here concerned.

Another subject may be an object without being conceived as a subject, as when the other subject is regarded only in his bodily aspect. Men, like gregarious animals, seek refuge in the midst of their kind, where they enjoy both a sense of familiarity and a sense of security. The delight taken in the beauty of the human form, or the sculptor's regard for his model, may have no reference to the mind or interested behavior which manifests itself in this form. The other organism is conceived as mind only when viewed as a system of responses, which I describe in terms of their objects and control through these objects. In order to make an object of another mind I must, therefore, in some measure make his objects my objects. I need not believe or seek his objects, but I must at least share them in the sense of supposing or understanding them.[4] There will still be a difference, however, between the case in which the response of the other mind serves as a sign of his object, and the case in which it serves as a sign of his beliefs or interests. In the one case, my expectations will be directed to ulterior phases of the object, and the other mind having exercised his function as sign, will retire from the field; in the other case, my expectation will be directed to the ulterior behavior of the subject himself.

It is evident that a second individual may present himself in the aspect of mind without presenting himself in the aspect of interest. This possibility arises from the independent variability of interest and cognition. I may view a fellow-mind as one who supposes or believes, and I may understand what he means or observe his convictions, without knowing or car-

[3] Cf. Sect. II.
[4] Cf. § 149.

ing what he wants. Similarly, the other mind may be the object of cognition without being the object of interest. This possibility underlies the science of psychology, or the observation of human nature. It is possible, in other words, to form expectations regarding the behavior of others, which, when verified, beget fulfilment without satisfaction, or surprise without disappointment. A special case of this is the judgment on the part of one individual that he is himself the object of the cognition or interest of a second individual. He may be aware of this fact without either seeking or avoiding it.

In other words, all that is indispensable for a mental or psychological rapport between two individuals is that one should function as mind with the other as object. Beyond this minimum there lie the various possibilities which have just been indicated. The case with which we are primarily concerned, and which marks the culmination of this type of social integration, is the case of interest in interest, or the case in which two interests are linked by the fact that each is an object of interest to the other. Upon this basis develop those "higher" human interrelations which are functions of interest, such as friendship and love, in which each of two subjects of interest is in his totality an object of interest to the other. The relation between human individuals of opposite sexes may be traced through all these ascending levels, from the interest of one in the body of the other to the reciprocal love of two persons.[5]

§ 200. **Interest as Object of Interest.** We turn now to the several forms of interrelation of interest, or social integrations in which a relation of interest directly unites two or more interests.

The first distinction which we have to note, is that between interest in the act of interest, and interest in its satisfaction.

[5] H. N. Wieman calls a relationship of this sort a "personal group," meaning not that the group is a person but that its members engage one another as persons ("Personal and Impersonal Groups," *Inter. Jour. of Ethics,* Vol. XXXI, 1921). This author as well as J. E. Boodin, whom he cites ("The Unit of Civilization," *ibid.,* Vol. XXX, 1920), recognizes that human interrelations may lie on different levels, as here indicated.

One who deals in a certain commodity seeks to create a *demand* for it. He desires that the value of the commodity shall be enhanced through the multiplication of the subjects who covet it, and through the intensification of their effort to obtain it. This interest is quite distinct from his interest in satisfying the demand. In the case of one who has no intention of parting with his property, the desire to have it coveted by others, the desire, for example, to live in a "desirable location," may exist without any interest whatever in satisfying the other-interests which his property evokes. Similarly a flirtatious woman seeks to be desired, or enjoys being loved, without herself being moved by either tenderness or pity. If she makes concessions it is only in order to tempt or excite an appetite to whose gratification she is entirely indifferent. A parent or teacher may endeavor to cultivate the interests of a child, or direct them to this or that object, without any effort to provide the object, or to satisfy the interest implanted.

Benevolence, pity, love, tenderness are not, therefore, adequately described as interest in interest. They signify interest in the *satisfaction* of interest. According to Adam Smith,

"how selfish soever man may be supposed, there are evidently some principles in his nature, which interest him *in the fortune of others,* and render their *happiness* necessary to him, though he derives nothing from it, except the pleasure of seeing it. Of this kind is pity or compassion, the emotion which we feel for the misery of others, when we either see it, or are made to conceive it in a very lively manner." [6]

The maternal interest is aroused by a sign of distress on the part of the young, and is satisfied only by signs of its removal. She is interested in the child's getting what he wants, or having what he likes. The hungry child is satisfied by food, the mother's solicitude by the evidence of the child's

---

[6] *Theory of the Moral Sentiments,* 1808, Vol. I, pp. 1-2. For a contemporary account of this principle, cf. W. McDougall's conception of "the parental instinct and the tender emotion," *Social Psychology,* 1910, pp. 66-81. Whether this principle of action be instinctive or acquired (and if there be instincts at all it would be difficult to deny at least a maternal instinct), its actual manifestation in animal and human life is unquestionable.

satisfaction. The objects of interest in the two cases are different, but it is clear that the mother's interest in obtaining food as a means to the satisfaction of the child will be allied with the child's effort to obtain the food as an end in itself.

The use of the term 'sympathy' for the designation of this principle brings to light the distinction between a genuine or objective interest *in interest,* and a subjective interest in the substantive feelings which the symptoms of this interest arouse.[7] Let us consider the case of the suburban business man who explains his habit of reading his newspaper in public conveyances by saying that he "can not bear to see ladies standing." It is evident that his interest is not in ministering to the comfort of the ladies, but in avoiding a species of discomfort induced in himself by the simulation of the posture of others. The effect of the strap-hanger acting as stimulus is to evoke a responsive strap-hanging which, although only implicit, is nevertheless attended by a certain bodily strain and tension. The interest of the business man is in relieving this tension, and the simplest method of putting himself at ease is to withdraw attention from the stimulus. Were this impossible he might find it necessary to alter the stimulus by giving her his seat. But even this would not imply that he wished to save her from fatigue. Similarly an adult irritated by a hungry child may feed the child, as, in the circumstances, a more effective means of relieving the irritation than stopping his own ears or removing himself to a distance. Or, the rich man who dislikes the evidences of poverty in others and who for that reason avoids the slums, may find himself so cornered by them that he is compelled to buy them and "clean them up." All of these are cases of a negative, subjective interest, in that the removal of a state of the subject himself is all that is necessary to satisfy his interest. The positive form of this subjective interest in the symptoms of other-interest, is the disposition to frequent the society of cheerful people; or that form of sen-

---

[7] Cf. Ch. X, Sect. II. The distinction which I am here making is similar to that which W. McDougall makes between "passive" and "active" sympathy. Cf. his *Social Psychology,* 1910, pp. 95, 168.

sitiveness so characteristic of tired husbands, and which artful wives know how to indulge by the simulation of gayety.

Since the term 'sympathy' is commonly used in a sense so broad as to include this case, it is desirable to use the term 'benevolence' when this case is excluded. The mother's attitude to her crying child differs from that of an unloving bystander in that the mother is positively interested in the satisfaction of the child's interest. She is benevolent in the sense that she is satisfied when and only when she is convinced that the child has what it wants. Her concern is not with the symptom of the child's distress, still less with the reverberations of it in her own breast, but with the desire which underlies it; and in order that this desire may be fulfilled, she exposes herself mercilessly to the assaults of the stimulus.

The negative form of interest in interest is malice, which is satisfied by the *disappointment* of another interest. Malice, in other words, is as objective and self-forgetful as benevolence. It is a highly developed social relation in which one individual employs his knowledge of the interests of another in order to circumvent and defeat them.

There is one further distinction which is needed in order to clarify the nature of interest in interest. Such an interest may be either dominant or subordinate. In accordance with the principle of the mediation of interest by interest, this relation of subordination is internal to a person.[8] It means nothing to say that *A* subordinates his interest to *B*'s; but *A* may subordinate some other of his interests to his interest in *B*'s interest. Such is the case when a father labors for money in order that his son may be educated. His benevolent interest here dominates his property interest. Similarly, one individual cannot subordinate another individual's interest to his own, but men can and do commonly subordinate their interest in the interest of others, to another of their own interests. A slave-holder who is interested in the physical efficiency of his slaves is not interested in their interest at all, since they may have no such interest. They are in this case no more than the tools which he sharpens, or the draught-

8 Cf. Ch. XIII, Sect. II; and § 177.

horses which he seeks to make healthy and powerful. In the same sense an employer may desire that his laborers shall be skilful and efficient in order to reduce the cost of production, or a military officer may desire that his men shall be well-equipped and well-drilled. But the slave-holder may desire the *contentment* of his slaves in order to secure their good-will and loyalty. In this case he has a positive interest in the satisfaction of their interests, but only because of his dominant interest in the fruits of their labor. Similarly, the emphasis in recent years on *morale,* both in industry and in war, implies a desire for the satisfaction of interest with a view to the more zealous and whole-hearted service which such satisfaction will yield. Paternalism of this type implies benevolence, but a benevolence subordinated to an ulterior motive.

§ 201. **Reciprocal Interest.** The interest of one individual in another may be asymmetrical or unrequited. Such one-way inter-interest does constitute a genuine social bond, and it may in certain cases be the only bond, as in hero-worship or the mother's love of her new-born child. We have next to note the special case in which interest in interest is symmetrical or reciprocal.

This type of relationship begins upon the cognitive level, where the cognitive response of each of two individuals is the object of the cognitive response of the other. Such a relationship is verified to each of the two participating individuals by his control of the attention of the other. He discovers that he is himself creating the stimuli to which the other responds. He finds that his movements, his gestures, his words, even his slightest changes of facial expression are followed by the other. This relation underlies all the more complicated forms of reciprocal intercourse. In reciprocal communication, or conversation, the response of each in turn may serve only as a sign of its object, so that the effect is to direct the attention of both individuals to a common series of events or objectives. This relation is best exemplified in an exchange of signals according to a pre-arranged code, where each acknowledges the signals of the other, but only in order to verify the fact of its receipt. In such a case the residual aspects of each subject may be entirely ignored. Each attends to the other only in so far as may be necessary in order that both may attend continuously to the same objects. Keeping "in touch" with one another is only a means of creating or maintaining community of experience or expectation.

But inter-communication ordinarily means more than this. The reference to a common object may be accompanied by or subordinated to the anticipation by each of the other's ulterior responses. Each is "watching" the other, and adjusting his own prospective action to the promise of the other's behavior. This relation, on the purely cognitive level, is illustrated in every form of mutual adjustment; most vividly, perhaps, by the protracted effort which two individuals sometimes make to pass one another on the street.

As in the simpler case of asymmetrical relations already described, so here also, the response of one party may be interested while that of the other remains upon the purely cognitive level. An individual may know himself to be the object of another's interest and be quite unmoved thereby. He may be so accustomed to the favor of others that he takes it as a matter of course. Like Aristotle's "highminded man," he may recognize, but remain quite indifferent to, the praise and the censure of "ordinary" men. Conversely, there is an interest in the attention of others regardless of any interest on their part. The scrutiny or curiosity of others may be intrusive and annoying. The phenomenon of shyness seems to indicate that the avoidance of the attention of others is a primitive, if not instinctive, impulse [9] which finds its developed expression in the love of solitude. But the "attentions" of others are more commonly found gratifying. One would rather be disliked than ignored altogether. The small boy and his elder brother as well, will find many things

[9] "We must, therefore, admit a certain amount of purely instinctive perturbation or constraint, due to the consciousness that we have become objects for other people's eyes." James, *Principles of Psychology*, 1890, Vol. II, p. 432.

worth doing when watched, which he would never dream of doing unobserved.

If there is an interest in being the object of the bare attention of a fellow-man, there is a more powerful interest in being the object of his interest. His interest is a virtual threat or promise of help, and such is the dependence of man on his fellows that such intimations of favor or disfavor will commonly take precedence of every other consideration. Either or both of two reciprocal interests may be either dominant or subordinate. Where both are subordinate interests the relation is that which Aristotle described as a "friendship of utility." [10] Each seeks and enjoys the support of the other in the pursuit of some ulterior interest, as in business partnerships or political alliances. The reciprocal interest may be dominant on one side and subordinate on the other, as when an indulgent parent craving the favor of his child is forced to buy it by catering to the child's appetites; or when a politician exploits the personal affection and loyalty of his followers.

Reciprocal interest may also vary in the degree to which it engages either party. It may be casual and intermittent, and be confined to some single interest, in either party or in both, as in the case of the impulse to succor another in bodily distress, when this awakens a momentary gratitude. Or, on the other hand, reciprocal interest may express the total self of the subject, and be directed to the total self of the object. This represents the consummation of reciprocal interest, and it is seen to be a bond woven of many strands. The mutual hate or the mutual love of two persons is compounded of their inter-communication, of their attention to interest and interest in attention, of the subordinate interests growing out of their interdependence, and of all the particular exchanges of interest which express the variety of their activities. This personal bond of mutual love or hate has, furthermore, a character of circularity which leads to its progressive intensification. Each person in proving his interest in the other becomes a more exciting stimulus to the other's interest. Thus

[10] *Nicomachean Ethics,* Bk. VIII, Ch. III.

hate is embittered by the resentment which it provokes, and love nourishes itself on love.

II. THE MUTUAL INTEREST OF ONE AND MANY

§ 202. Having examined the principles of community and mutuality of interest each in its own terms, we are now prepared to understand the social relations in which the two principles are combined. The simplest and most obvious case is that in which an interest or subject of interest is a common object of interest. Each member of society is in turn both a focus and an originating centre of lines of interest connecting him with his fellow-members. Such a relationship is both convergent and divergent, many-one and one-many, according to the point of view which one adopts.

Viewing this relation first in its convergent or many-one aspect, we have the social group cemented by common hate or common love. The strength of a common antipathy as a bond between two individuals is well recognized. The cultivation of hate of "the Kaiser," as a means of securing unity among the Allies during the recent war, is a tribute to the strength of this bond even when extended to national and international relations. Similarly a family may be united by devotion to the common mother, or a nation by love of the person of the ruler, or a religious sect by the worship of its tutelary deity, or mankind by the love of one God.

The converse aspect of this relationship presents certain facts which it is important to deal with more specifically. Each individual finds himself surrounded by his fellows, and he may take them collectively as the object of his attention or of its interest. A society, in other words, may be an object for each of its members. But this relationship has often been mistakenly described.

In the first place, it is customary to speak of certain interests which have a social *effect,* as though they were interests *in* society. The most notable case is the sexual instinct. This has the effect of preserving the race, and that effect being known, the sexual interest may be subordinated to it.

But it is palpably false to say that sexual desire *is* an interest in race-preservation, since it is an unmistakable fact that the one may occur without the other. The wide use of methods of birth-control is an endeavor to satisfy sexual desire, without the natural consequence of reproduction; while the paternal desire for an heir, or the maternal desire for children, may occur with little or no desire for sexual relations.

In the second place, there may be an interest whose object is society, but without reference to the actual interests of its members. Just as a parent may desire *for* his child what the child itself does not desire, so a ruler or patriot may desire for his country what none of his countrymen desire for themselves. It is characteristic of the paternalistic statesman to impute to a nation a destiny, rôle or mission which is of his own conceiving. This is a common source of confusion. One speaks of the purpose which the statesman has for the nation as the "national purpose," and thus suggests that the nation itself is actuated by it, and that the purpose has therefore a collective support which would entitle it to precedence over the claims of individuals. As a matter of fact what one man desires a nation to be, even though he represents his end in the widest collective and historical terms, is still his personal desire, and is entitled to no more weight than his other individual claims.[11]

Such a paternalistic interest in society is to be sharply distinguished from the patriotism of utility, in which the individual desires the prosperity of others as a means to his own; and from the genuinely benevolent patriotism, in which the individual seeks for their own sake the joint and multiple satisfactions of the members of the group. Through such an analysis the ambiguous conception of "the national interest," drops out altogether, and leaves the nation either as a group of human beings for whom some one of its members forms a purpose vicariously; or, as a group of interested individuals having a common object; or, as such a group of interests when one of its members takes a prudent or benevolent interest in the whole.

[11] Cf. Ch. XII, Sect. II.

The interrelation of one and many may be traced through the variations and ascending levels which have already been distinguished more simply in the interrelation of two individuals. The attitude may be cognitive or interested, on the part of either the one or the many, or of both; interest may be dominant or subordinate, positive or negative; it may be directed to the existence of the interest, or to its satisfaction; and the relation may be reciprocal or non-reciprocal.

The full possibilities of this type of relation are realized when there is a reciprocal interest of many and one. Viewed from the side of the many, this is the interest which all have in each. Such interest may reflect that dependence of all on each which is felt with peculiar acuteness in times of common peril, when in order to present a common front it is necessary to leave the flank and rear unprotected. In this case all demand that each shall be governed by the common interest, and desire the good of each for the sake of the common interest. Or the interest of all in each may be a dominant interest, a summation of the kindly interest which each man takes in the satisfaction of another of his kind.

Viewed from the sides of the one, this relation constitutes that over-powering interest which a man takes in the convergent sentiment of those about him, or his supreme regard for collective praise and blame.[12] In the famous myth of Gyges in the Second Book of Plato's Republic Glaucon describes the moral effects of removing this relation. Gyges having possessed himself of a magic ring by which he can render himself invisible at will, straightway embarks upon a career of treason and debauchery. Were he not the object of the scrutiny of others, "then," concludes Glaucon, "the actions of the just would be as the actions of the unjust." Unable thus to hide his deeds in darkness, the individual normally feels himself to be surrounded on every side by a circle of watchful eyes. These eyes not only express attention, which in itself is a potent stimulus, but they intimate an intention to act. Their look contains a virtual threat or promise, a con-

---

[12] For a good analysis of the complex motivation involved in this situation, cf. McDougall's *Social Psychology*, 1910, pp. 199-208.

trol of fortune, and a power over life and death. It is not merely the bright eyes of ladies that "rain influence"; there is an influence in every show of favor or disfavor, which, when it is focussed upon a single individual from the whole circumferential group, is the most constant and inescapable form of pressure to which he is subjected.

The importance of this relation as a deterrent force must not, however, blind us to its positive and auspicious aspect. As a man fears the disfavor of others, so he finds himself confirmed and heartened by their favor. He may bask in the concentrated glow of their well-wishing and approval, or enjoy a sense of security and confidence through being encompassed by friends.

III. COMMUNITY MEDIATED BY MUTUALITY

§ 203. **The Conception of Imitation.** The first mode of union between community and mutuality of interest is that which has just been examined, in which the common object of interest is itself an interest, or in which one and many individuals are interested in one another. The second and third modes of union arise from the fact that community of interest may be mediated by mutuality of interest, or mutuality by community of interest.

To speak of community of interest as mediated by interrelation of interest means that the object of interest is qualified as being the object of a fellow-interest. Here again we meet with a principle which has sometimes been employed as the sole generative and constitutive principle of social unity. It has latterly somewhat declined in scientific repute owing to its being both exaggerated and over-simplified under the name of 'imitation.'

It is evident that community of interest is not exclusively a function of mutuality of interest. Several individuals would be afraid of the same object even if they were unaware of one another's existence. This interrelation accounts only for a certain *increment* of fear, which is in its ·intenser manifestations known as panic. The identity or similarity of environment, together with the constitutional sameness of human nature, would thus of itself conduce to sameness both of primitive reactions and also of habits and other acquired dispositions.[13]

The view that imitation is an hereditary motor pattern can scarcely be maintained in the face of the fact that *anything* can be done imitatively. One can fight imitatively, or one can run away imitatively; one can love or hate one's neighbor imitatively; and one can imitatively believe or disbelieve in God. This consideration has led to the view that imitation is not a specific mode of behavior, but *any* behavior when induced in a specific way; namely, when it is induced in a second individual by its appearance in a first. Imitation, according to this view, is responding *to* a response in such wise as to respond *with* it.

Common-sense associates imitation with the mimicry of the monkey, the 'echolalia' of the feeble-minded, the mocking of the child, or with the process of learning by example. In all of these cases there is an interest *in* the reproduction of the stimulus, a playful, submissive, malicious or rationally motivated effort to repeat a certain effect, a satisfaction taken in its iteration or recurrence. Whether these phenomena signify a congenital trait in man or other higher animals, we need not inquire. The cases that are most primitive are most rare, and the case of deliberate learning from example, which is humanly the most significant, is also the most evidently acquired and the most evidently subordinated to ulterior motives. None of these cases represents a fundamental and far-reaching principle in terms of which to account for the indisputable fact that individuals borrow responses from one another, and thus become similarly disposed, without any judgments of comparison or any interest in sameness as such.

It must be admitted that in view of the importance of

[13] For a criticism of the exaggerated rôle which the school of Tarde assigns to imitation, cf. M. M. Davis, *Psychological Interpretations of Society* (Columbia Studies in History, etc., Vol. XXXIII, 1908-09), pp. 151ff. E. L. Thorndike has emphasized the fact that animals learn by trial and error rather than by imitation. Cf. his *Original Nature of Man*, 1921, Ch. VIII; and *Psychology of Learning*, 1913, Ch. II. Cf. above, § 191.

the subject, the present state of psychological knowledge is highly unsatisfactory. There are, however, two factors of imitation which are unmistakably operative. The manifestation of a response both *communicates* its object and *expresses* its subject, to the observer.

§ 204. Imitation as Communication.

The manifestation of a response by a first subject serves as the stimulus to a similar response in a second individual; as when the manifestation of fear of a mouse in one timorous domestic begets a like fear in a second, or begets a general panic in the household.

Those who magnify the rôle of instinct, explain this phenomenon by supposing that one of the congenital stimuli to each of the major instincts is its outward manifestation in another individual.[14] But the circumstances would seem to be exceptionally favorable to the operation of the principle of the conditioned reflex.[15] The terrifying object is repeatedly given *together with* the manifest terror of others, and it would follow naturally that in the course of time this manifestation should acquire a power to evoke terror in the absence of the terrifying object.

Furthermore, the rôle of the manifestation cannot properly be identified with that of the original stimulus. In the example cited, the visible mouse is at once a stimulus and an object of fear; while the manifestation of terror is a stimulus of fear, but only a sign of its object. The second domestic

---

[14] Thus Professor McDougall, who is largely responsible for emphasizing this principle, says "I think the facts compel us to assume that in the gregarious animals each of the principal instincts has a special perceptual inlet . . . that is adapted to receive and to elaborate the sense-impressions made by the expressions of the same instinct in other animals of the same species—that, e.g., the fear-instinct has, besides others, a special perceptual inlet that renders it excitable by the sound of the cry of fear." *Op. cit., pp.* 93–94. For a criticism of this view, cf. E. L. Thorndike, *Original Nature of Man,* 1913, p. 119. Professor Thorndike's objections seem to me to show, in the first place, that such stimuli are often inoperative, owing to the presence of other stimuli; and that, in the second place, they serve only to confirm an existing predisposition toward the *object* of response. The effect of these objections, although not decisive, is to support the view that such stimuli are acquired rather than original.

[15] Cf. Ch. VIII, Sect. I.

is frightened *by* the other's terror, but is afraid *of* a mouse. It seems clear, then, that the primary function of the imitated manifestation is to signify and communicate its object. The manifestation of terror points to something, more or less specifically located and qualified; and this something, now expected by the observer, becomes the object of his fear. Imitative responses being so construed, the extent to which they are instinctive is thus the question of the extent to which the meaning of signs may be said to be hereditary.[16]   The case of extreme suggestibility is the case in which, through dissociation or a summation of stimuli, the observer's mind is wholly dependent on such manifestations for its expectations. Resistance to suggestion, on the one hand, implies that the individual's expectations are a function of his own independent experience of the situation.

At the same time, it has to be noted that the imitated manifestation not only communicates its object, but also communicates that object's subjective meaning.   The manifestation of terror refers the observer to mouse, but at the same time, to mouse *qualified* as something to be looked for fearfully in a given direction.   It is apparently characteristic of all communication that it both directs attention to an object and also prescribes in some measure the form which the attentive activity shall take.

§ 205. **Imitation as Expression.**   The second factor which is unmistakably present in the phenomena of imitation is the perception of the responding subject, now become the object of a second subject.   In the perception of an object, the sensory response to the datum is associated with anticipatory responses, whose proper objects are ulterior aspects of the objective situation to which the datum belongs.   These supplementary responses "round out" the datum into an object, or constitute the process of *realization.*   Where the object is a responding subject, these ulterior aspects are largely kinaesthetic.   As in the perception of a solid the anticipatory responses involve an imaginary circumambulation, so

16 Cf. § 89.

in this case they involve an imaginary translation or projection to the centre of the object. In the former case one supplements the datum with anticipatory circumspection, whereas in this case one supplements the datum with anticipatory introspection, in the sense of experience from within.[17] It is in this way that a first subject *expresses* himself to a second, and self-expression so construed is essentially a social relation.

Kinaesthetic realization in this sense lies at the basis of the histrionic impulse. Under the name of 'empathy' it is recognized as playing a central part in the aesthetic experience.[18] Whatever doubts may attach to the account here offered, the broad fact is indisputable. When the response of a first organism is the object of a second, this will involve in some measure an enactment of the response by the second. So much of truth is there in the view that one cannot understand an interest without feeling it.

§ 206. **The Mediating Subject as Datum.** The visible presence of the associated and expressive subject gives rise to transports of collective enjoyment, the *élan* of battle, the frenzies of religious worship, or the excesses of the mob. There is no human interest that may not be thus intensified by its collective manifestation, from the lust of those who pillage and sack a conquered city, to the most quixotic enthusiasm, such as that which moved the French nobles, on August 4, 1789, to surrender their hereditary privileges; "an act of self sacrifice which each of its members had refused the day before, and at which they were all surprised the day after."[19] In such cases the expressive stimuli, through their summation and circular confirmation, mount to such levels of

---

[17] It is not, I think, strictly correct to speak of this phenomenon as "ideo-motor action," in the sense of movement induced by the "representation" of movement (W. McDougall, *op. cit.*, pp. 104-105). The fact seems rather to be that bodily movement constitutes a part of the representation of movement.

[18] For an excellent introduction to this topic, together with bibliographical references, cf. H. S. Langfeld, *The Aesthetic Attitude*, 1920, Ch. V.

[19] Durkheim, *op. cit.*, p. 210.

intensity as to over-ride altogether both the residual stimuli from the environment and also the habits, scruples, prejudices and personal control of the participating individuals.[20]

Such phenomena increase in geometrical ratio not only because of the fact that each intensified response becomes in turn an intensified stimulus, but because the induced activities acquire a value and inertia of their own. In the dance or march or other rhythmic responses the vivid realization of movement assumes a playful or aesthetic value, and the activity tends to renew and prolong itself, that is, to assume the recurrent rather than the progressive form. At the same time, in so far as the major emotions are aroused there is an internal augmentation of energy which diminishes fatigue, and not only renders extraordinary exertion possible, but adds a relish to it.[21]

These extreme and abnormal cases only illustrate a type of social relation which is common and normal. The satisfactions of work and play are enhanced by a sense of participation. Common memories are endeared by their mutual recall,[22] and from the same source men derive an increased devotion to a common end.

[20] The classic description of these phenomena is to be found in G. Le Bon, *The Crowd*, 1917, and *The Psychology of Revolution*, trans. by B. Miall, 1913. Good illustrations of religious frenzy are to be found in Durkheim, *Elementary Forms of the Religious Life*, trans, by J. W. Swain, 1915, pp. 215-219, etc. Describing the "corrobbori," a religious ceremony of the Australian aborigines, Durkheim says, "When they are once come together, a sort of electricity is formed by their collecting which quickly transports them to an extraordinary degree of exaltation. Every sentiment expressed finds a place without resistance in all the minds . . .; each re-echoes the others, and is re-echoed by the others. The initial impulse thus proceeds, growing as it goes, as an avalanche grows in its advance. . . . On every side one sees nothing but violent gestures, cries, veritable howls, and deafening noises of every sort, which aid in intensifying still more the state of mind which they manifest." (*Op. cit.,* pp. 215-216.) If one is to employ figures of speech one might say that a major stream of emotional excitement being set flowing in a certain direction, the result is to drain off, or draw into its channel and current, the entire emotionality of the adjacent field. But such figures of speech must not be allowed to obscure the fact that response on the part of one organism to the expressive stimulus presented by another is the elementary and essential process of which the whole is constituted.

[21] Cf. § 126.

[22] Royce attaches special importance, in his theory of the "community," to this participation in a common retrospect. Cf. his *Problem of Christianity*, 1913, Vol. II, pp. 40-50.

§ 207. **The Mediating Subject as Objective.** Community of interest may also be mediated by mutuality of interest when the other-interest is an objective, and not a datum. The other-response, instead of being an expressive sign, as in the case of its sensible presence, may be an object of judgment or belief. It is this which distinguishes the "public" from the "crowd." [23] Modern facilities for transportation and communication have made it possible for vast aggregations to live and act in one another's physical presence. The range of expressive stimuli is now extended over crowds of a hundred thousand and cities of five million. Modern means of publicity, on the other hand have vastly extended the knowledge which each man has of the sentiments and opinions of his fellows, and has rendered it possible for a man to think and feel with a hundred million fellow-nationals, or with the fellow-members of one world-wide empire or language-group, or with the whole of civilized mankind. The increased knowledge of history has at the same time extended the range of contact with the past, and has rendered it possible for the living to associate themselves with the numberless dead in the perpetuation of a common culture.

The public is both wider and more permanent than the crowd. The crowd is related to the public as a mood to a disposition, or as an impulse to the set purposes of character and personality. In crowds, community of interest is mediated by the momentary presence of transient expressions, in the public, by persistent beliefs regarding the profounder and more constant attitudes. The first is illustrated by the audience whose enjoyment of the spectacle is enhanced by the evidence of its enjoyment in others, thus generating by reciprocal stimulation a sharply ascending intensity and volume of laughter or applause; or by the spread of conviction in a mass-meeting; or by the contagious emotionality of religious worship. The second is illustrated by the admiration of the classical in art, or the acceptance of that which is authoritative in science, or reverence for the sacred in religion. In cases of the latter type the object is invested with a dignity that transcends the

[23] Cf. Tarde, *L'Opinion et la Foule*, 1904, p. 3.

passing states and accidental contacts of life. It is charged
with a power proportional to the great company of its silent
and unseen partisans. To each individual in turn it wears
an aspect of collective support in which he participates, but
which over-rules, in the name of all, the private whims or
calculations that might otherwise govern him.[24]

§ 208. **Society as Confirmation.** The crowd and the
public, despite their important differences, both represent the
operation of the same principle, namely, the mediation of common interests by their mutuality or interrelation. The essential
fact in a society so constituted is the fact of confirmation. The
convictions and interests of the several members, being both
convergent and communicative, convey to each member a sustaining sense of agreement. The object of his belief or interest adds to its own intrinsic appeal the borrowed force
of his regard for the sentiment and opinion of his fellows.
The "social mind" in this sense is "common mental content,
common mental qualities and characteristics, *which are realized by these individual members to be common*," and which
when so realized operate as "dynamic social agents upon individuals during childhood and maturity." [25]

A further development of this principle would bring to
light important differences between the mediating influence
of different sets of associates. The attitude of one's inferiors,
superiors or peers, of friends or foes, of the family circle
or of outsiders, of the élite or the vulgar, each operates
specifically and in a manner which has yet to be adequately

[24] For a clear and compact presentation of Durkheim's social explanation of the "sacred," cf. *Bulletin de la Société Française de Philosophie,*
Vol. VI, 1906, p. 125. Durkheim's account is open to objection only in so
far as he does not consistently adhere to the view, which he here implies, that the recognition of the sacred is "un double sentiment"; which,
though mediated by judgments regarding others, has its psychological
being, its duality and its tension, in the breast of the awe-inspired individual.

[25] M. M. Davis, *op. cit.,* p. 68 (italics mine). Cf. also, his statement
that "the dynamic agent of the psycho-social unity is the social mind, a
mass of common beliefs, sentiments, and determinations, possessed by the
individuals of a group with the added consciousness that the other members simultaneously cherish them" (*ibid.,* p. 73). But why "simultaneously"?

studied.[26] In other words, not only does the presence of
one's fellows make a great deal of difference, but it makes a
great deal of difference who is present. Indeed the assent
or approval of *certain* others will sometimes have the effect
of raising doubts or of chilling one's ardor.

It has further to be remarked that the principle of confirmation operates with equal effect whether the associated
interests are competing or non-competing. Emulation may or
may not assume the form of rivalry. It may signify simply
the enhancement of desire through the mutual recognition
of a common goal, when there is no preëmption either of the
path traversed by the desire or of the object in which it is
consummated. When the object is a prize which only one
can possess, emulation implies exclusion and may arouse a
combative as well as an imitative response. The desire for
wealth and for what wealth will bring, is largely a desire
for what is coveted by others, or an interest enhanced by a
sense of exclusive possession and the superiority which this
implies; but intellectual and aesthetic activities, or any common interest which has assumed the form of cooperation, is
enhanced by a sense of harmony.

IV. MUTUALITY MEDIATED BY COMMUNITY

§ 209. As common interests are enhanced by a sense of
participation among the associated subjects, so the interest of
associates in one another is enhanced by a sense of their community of interest.

An interest of mine which I express by the pronoun 'we'
is an interest which I recognize as common. I do not say
"we love or desire" this or that, simply when as a matter of
fact I am one of many who love or desire the same. 'We'
is not a pronoun which a plurality of individuals uses in a
sense analogous to that in which a single individual uses the
pronoun 'I.'[27] It is not an expression of plural self-con-

[26] Cf. E. A. Ross, *Foundations of Sociology*, 1905, pp. 116 ff.

[27] Thus C. H. Cooley argues that "Descartes might have said 'we think,'
cogitamus, on as good grounds as he said *cogito*." (*Social Organization*,
1909, p. 9.) The two terms are, however, not logically equivalent, what-

sciousness. It signifies the recognition by one individual of another individual associated in some common activity, and conduces not only to a greater interest in that in which my fellow is also interested, but also to a greater interest in my fellow by virtue of the fact that his interest and mine are directed to the same object.

This mediation of inter-interest by common interest may take a negative or positive form. Where our common interest is competitive, I view my fellow-subject as a rival or competitor, and this may convert him from a friend into an enemy, or intensify any negative attitude which may already exist. When, on the other hand, the common interest is non-competing or cooperative an enemy may be converted into an ally; while a primitive fellow-feeling may be developed into the strong bond of comradeship, or elevated to the level of Aristotle's "friendship of virtue," in which two individuals are united to one another through their devotion to the same ideal.

The most striking manifestations of this relation are afforded by the devotion of the soldier to his comrades in arms, as illustrated by the following description of the behavior of Indian troops at the battle of the Wadi, in January, 1916:

"The major commanding the battalion I have mentioned was shot in the side as he left the water-cut; he was heard calling out to his men in Hindustani, 'Forward, brave fellows! Go ahead. I am down. But to-day the regiment will win honour. Let none hold back!' The subaltern by his side had been killed trying to get his machine guns up; two of these were now out of action, their squads shot down. Lieutenant ———, wounded twice in the arm, would not stop; wounded again twice in the chest, he fell. His orderly, Ghulab Khan, implored the Sahib to allow him to carry him back, but he insisted that every man should go on. He died of his wounds the next morning. Sepoy Boota Singh brought in man after man under heavy fire. Of enormous physique himself and devoid of fear, he went out five times, lifted the wounded man on his back and carried him in. On his sixth journey he was shot dead. A lance-havildar put up a

ever be their order of genesis, because the one signifies the self-consciousness of one individual, whereas the other signifies the consciousness of *another* individual.

screen of earth around his British officer and stayed with him till dusk, when he carried him back to better cover. Akbar Khan, bugle· major, died of exhaustion. No wounds were found on him, or blood; he had had fever for three days, but would not be left behind. Others went on wounded until they were shot down." [28]

In such cases, which are of common occurrence in time of war, one may observe the operation of both of the modes of mediation to which attention has been called. On the one hand, the devotion of each soldier to the common end is augmented by a recognition of its community, and by the vivid manifestation of this devotion in the shock of battle; while, on the other hand, this increased community of interest increases in turn the interest of each in his fellows, and induces acts of tenderness and self-forgetful service, of which, save for such facts, one would suppose human nature to be incapable.

An interesting variant of this type of relationship is to be found in compensatory satisfactions afforded by social intercourse in times of common adversity. Thus Professor Paul Sabatier says of the French after 1871:

"They went to church because social disturbance creates among men an irresistible need to draw nearer, to take one another by the hand, to mingle their joy and their tears together. Without exactly realizing it, deep down in their hearts they were grateful to Catholicism for its churches always open to all comers, and its tendency to wish to share in the life of City and Fatherland. In truth, for some months in 1871, the vast majority of Frenchmen drew instinctively toward the church of their birth." [29]

In other words, a common negative interest, or a common defeat or disappointment, so heightens the natural human affections that the very mingling of tears begets a sort of compensatory joy.

Another variant of the same type, of fundamental importance for moral motivation, is the interest taken by each in the loyalty of his associates. This is an interest not in

[28] E. Candler, *The Long Road to Bagdad*, 1919, Vol. I, pp. 79-80.
[29] *France To-day*, 1913, p. 45.

the satisfaction, but in the act, of interest.   The soldier *demands* of his comrades that very devotion to the common end which, when it manifests itself, endears them to him.   His hatred of treason is as passionate as his love of loyalty. Less intensely, but more steadily, we hold one another to the same ideals, or insist on the acknowledgment of the common code.   The interest in one's associates may take the form of indulgence, but if there be any suspicion of their abandoning the common cause, or even of a waning enthusiasm, indulgence is swiftly superseded by a sharp censoriousness or by coercive violence.

V. THE SOCIETY OF BENEVOLENT COOPERATION

§ 210. **The Problem of Constructive Social Integration.** It has already been pointed out, both in general terms [30] and in the special application to society, that the several principles by which interests are integrated may have negative as well as positive consequences.   Interests may, in other words, be divided by the very relation which unites them.

Hence the problem of constructive or methodical social integration is not the problem of establishing contacts between men, but is rather the problem of making these contacts as innocuous and fruitful as possible.   It is not a question of creating society, but of saving men from it.   Society is in part an effect of circumstance, or a natural product, and in part an artefact deliberately organized and conserved.   It is inevitable in both senses, as forced upon men by biological and physiographic conditions, and as adopted by them in the elaboration of their interests.   It is the task of constructive social integration to make a virtue of this social necessity, or to make as profitable as possible a mode of life that is both inescapable and indispensable.

In the performance of this task the burden falls upon man's reflective faculties.   Whatever the form of conflict or weakness from which life suffers, the solution lies in developing new threads of mediation by which interests are directed

[30] Cf. § 156.

in new ways upon common objects or upon one another. In this sense the process of constructive integration is always a process of rationalization.[31]

In other words, the escape from the evils incident to organization lies in an improved organization, or in a more thorough and conscious consideration of all the interests concerned, rather than in disorganization or a lapse into blindness and forgetfulness. Assuming, for example, that it is socially healthful and profitable that there should be free competition in the economic sphere, this can be accomplished only by an elaborate system of laws governing private property. *Laissez-faire* is a system of social order as truly as is communism. The personal liberty on which Anglo-Saxon communities pride themselves has to be created and protected by a rational plan. Tolerance does not exist effectively until it is consciously adopted as a regulative principle and embodied in constitutional forms. The values of solitude can be realized only by agreement or by guaranties against the invasion of privacy.

The rationalization or constructive integration of society is not only a corrective process by which the benefits of social life are augmented and the cost reduced; but it constitutes, in the degree in which it is attained, a form of human life with a definite structure of its own. In this respect it is analogous to personality, although, as we have seen, by no means identical with it. It is the social form of the good life represented by Plato's "Republic," and in modern times by Kant's "Kingdom of Ends," Hegel's "State," and Spencer's "Evolved Society." These and kindred philosophical conceptions possess a certain basic agreement in that they define a condition of society in which the good of all and the good of each shall be harmonious, both in the negative sense of compatibility, and in the positive sense of mutual reinforcement. Where the good is conceived in terms of the satisfaction of interests, this condition of society implies a favorable adjustments of particular interests under the regulation of common purposes. Where personality is conceived as the

[31] Cf. Ch. XIII, Sect. V.

peculiar prerogative of individuals such a society will be an association and mutual regard of autonomous persons, of whom each voluntarily adopts a plan of life that provides for all.[32]

§ 211. **The Principle of Cooperation.** The basis of such a social order is *cooperation,* which is the division of labor mediated by a common purpose. The division of labor does not in itself imply a common purpose, nor does community of purpose imply division of labor.

Taken by itself the division of labor means only that a certain specific effect results from the combined efforts of different individuals. This effect itself may not be an object of interest to any of the participants, but may be an accidental by-product; as when a path is worn by successive travellers each bent on his own errand, or a city created by the aggregation of many individuals attracted to the same centre by different ends.[33] The division of labor does not assume the form of cooperation until the associated activities are regulated and inter-adjusted by a purpose to produce the result. But we have now to note that such a governing purpose may preside over a division of labor without assuming the form of a *common* purpose. Thus, for example, the principle of the division of labor is admirably illustrated by a modern industrial plant, in which the finished commodity results from the elaborate inter-adjustment of special processes, to each of which a separate worker or group of workers is assigned. To make this possible, the participants must perform assigned tasks rationally coördinated by a controlling purpose. But it is quite possible, and of common occurrence, that this controlling purpose should be the purpose of the manager and of the manager alone. He has it *for* the rest, but they do not have it for themselves. They may be said to serve his purpose, but his purpose is not their purpose. He induces

---

[32] Cf. Ch. XV, Sect. III. The "superiority" of such a form of life in the scale of values will be investigated below, Ch. XXII, Sect. II.

[33] Such unconscious complicity in historical achievement has led, as we have seen, to the invention of fictitious "social causes." Cf. Ch. XIV, Sect. III.

their services not by revealing his purpose and persuading them to adopt it, but by giving or withholding the means of livelihood. They may be entirely indifferent to, or even wholly ignorant of, the result of their combined efforts.

Such a *vicarious* purpose does not become a common purpose merely through becoming paternalistic or benevolent. A national destiny conceived by the ruler alone, and executed by him through the collective support which his power and sagacity enable him to mobilize, is still his own private and exclusive purpose, even though he should conceive it to be for the good of those whom he uses. Thus in the Thomist view the ruler is "the guardian of right," "the living embodiment of justice," "the architectonic chief."

"Just as the master builder of the cathedral supervises the stonecutters, the carpenters, the sculptors, the painters, so that they may be ready at the proper time and place, so the master builder of social justice oversees all the diverse social activities, and takes account of their relative importance in the community." [34]

But unless those who build know what they are building and are motivated by that rather than by their wage, the unifying purpose is the exclusive prerogative of the master builder.

A confused philosophy sometimes imputes to men a purpose they unwittingly serve, especially if it be a benevolent purpose. The face of tyranny is saved by construing a purpose imposed from without as the 'virtual' purpose of those on whom it is imposed; as what they 'really' seek, although they do not know it, or even stoutly deny it.[35] But the only purpose which we are permitted to recognize is a purpose which is psychologically existent and psychologically operative. The purpose of an activity is that which induces it, and if interested activity having a certain result, M, has to be induced by the promise of a different result, N, or if it is induced in ignorance of the result M, then such an activity cannot be said to have M as its purpose.

[34] M. De Wulf, *Mediaeval Philosophy*, 1922, p. 126.
[35] Cf. § 38.

As there may be division of labor without community of purpose, so there may be community of purpose without division of labor. Two or more subjects of interest may subordinate their several interests to the same end and the induced activities may be both convergent and complementary, yet without any mutual adjustment of interest to interest. This would be illustrated, for example, by an attack *en masse* in time of war, or by a love of country shared by all nationals but without any concerted national policy.

We are now in a position to understand all that is implied in genuine cooperation. This, as has been stated, consists in a division of labor mediated by a common purpose. There must be not only a convergence of interested effort toward the same end, but each participant must for the sake of this common end both accept his own assignment and approve that of others. This form of social integration can be abstractly represented as follows. Suppose the effects, a, b, c, of the activities of interests, I^1, I^2, I^3, so to combine as to produce M. In a cooperative or concerted endeavor I^1 will perform a in order through combination with b and c to produce M. He will, in other words desire not only a, but the performance of b by I^2, and of c by I^3, as complementary means to the end M. At the same time I^2, while performing b, will favor the performance of a by I^1, and of c by I^3; and I^3, while performing c, will favor the performance of a by I^1 and of b by I^2. This situation will differ from a situation in which, for example, I^1 performs a for the sake of N, though unwittingly or indifferently contributing to M; or a situation in which I^1, I^2, I^3, contribute their several services for the sake of M, but without being guided by any mutual recognition of their complementary relations.[36]

Such joint or cooperative activities are, of course, learned by experience, and are learned collectively. This means, how-

[36] Cooperative interests will thus be compatible, friendly and allied. Cf. above, § 166. The view here set forth is close to that developed by F. H. Giddings (*Principles of Sociology*, 1896, and *Elements of Sociology*, 1898); and by C. A. Ellwood, who emphasizes what he calls "social coördination" or "coadaptation" (*Sociology in its Psychological Aspects*, 1915, pp. 143 ff.).

ever, not that the art of organization is learned by the collectivity as such, but by each of its components through interaction with the rest, under the motivation of a common end.
In other words, cooperation does not imply the creation of
a new or corporate personality. It is an inter-personal integration the very essence of which is to preserve intact the
integrity of its component persons. Its control lies not in
any one of its members, nor in any supervening will or judgment, but in its members severally. This is possible through
agreement of judgment and concord of will arrived at by discussion and persuasion. It is, in other words, an impersonal
association, or a federation of persons.[37]

§ 212. **Cooperation and Benevolence.** Cooperation may
or may not be benevolent in its ultimate intent. The common
end which mediates the division of labor, or the investment
of capital, may, as in the industrial corporation, be itself
mediated by the end of personal profit. The individual combines his act with those of his associates for the sake of his
share of the joint product. His interest in his associates is
subordinated to his interest in that which, through their
cooperation, he is enabled to gain for himself. The same is
true of the state, so far as this represents a group of public
utilities. The citizen cooperates with his fellow-citizens for
the sake of that "law and order," or territorial aggrandizement, or defence against external enemies, which he interprets
in terms of his own security and gain.

Without disparagement of this motive, or neglect of its
importance in public and private affairs, one must, nevertheless, distinguish it from another and ultimately benevolent
type of cooperation, in which each partner in the common
enterprise is governed by a desire for the common good. In
this case each person affirms the interest of every other for
that other's sake, and not merely for his own. It is entirely
possible that a man's participation even in industrial cooperation should justify itself to him in terms of its benefits to
all concerned. The disposition of the business man to rational-

[37] Cf. Ch. XV, Sect. III.

ize his activity in terms of "opportunity of employment" or "public service," implies, whatever the degree of its sincerity in any given case, the psychological possibility of doing business with good will.[38] In any case, there can be no doubt of the benevolence of more personal and intimate forms of associated endeavor, such as the friendly partnership or the family. Partners may cooperate out of regard for one another, or for the sake of the ultimate benefits accruing to both. Parental, marital, filial and fraternal affection, or the love of each for all with whom he stands in familial relations, may govern a division of labor within an organized domestic life.

The same principle of benevolence may govern political relations, and distinguish the love of one's country from the love of what one's country has to give. Patriotism in this sense expresses not the need which each citizen has of the complementary services of his fellows, but the affection which he feels towards others of his kind, whom propinquity, familiarity and community of interest have endeared to him.

The principle of benevolence does not imply the *elimination* of struggle and competition, but only their subordination. I do not always serve my opponent best by yielding to him. The values of competitive sport would evidently be wholly destroyed if the participants did not oppose one another. I serve my opponent in this case by offering him the resistance which is the correlate of his effort,—the anvil to his hammer. I do not, like the stern parent, resist him for his own good as *I* conceive it, but for his own good as *he* conceives it. I promote his *interest* by resisting his *activities*. Similarly on the larger social scale, a competitive method, or contest under rules, may be willingly adopted by all participants, each accepting the opposition of the other and the hazard of failure, for the sake of the greater zest or efficiency which is thus imparted to the common life. In the case of sport the desire for victory is sometimes subordinated to a love of the game; and in a competitive economic life the individual's desire for

[38] Cf. § 157.

gain may be subordinated to his regard for the general benefits which the system yields.

On the possibility of benevolent cooperation repose whatever justifiable hopes there are of a constructive integration of mankind, and of reconciling the full advantages of united action with the prerogatives of personality.

CHAPTER XVIII

THE GENESIS AND MUTATION OF INTEREST

I. INTRODUCTION

§ 213. **Limitation of the Topic.** The field of human interests is a scene of perpetual and interdependent change, in which minor fluctuations as well as broader changes of current are transmitted far and wide through the contacts of personal and social life. There is reason to believe that this mobility of interest increases with civilization, and that it promises to be even more characteristic of the future than it is of the present.

We have thus far subordinated the dynamic to the structural question. In our examination of the personal and social integrations of interest we have both implied change and described it; in particular, attention has been called to the modification of interest through alterations of its cognitive presuppositions or mediating judgments. But hitherto our object has been to examine the various forms which interested activity assumes, rather than to isolate and classify its modifying causes. While, therefore, we shall find it necessary to repeat much that has already been affirmed, our attention will be differently focussed. We shall bring together whatever items, whether old or new, throw light upon the mutation of interests,—their waxing or waning, their genesis, redirection or extinction. Since value is a function of interests, we shall at the same time be indicating the causes by which objects become or cease to be valuable.

Granting that all the elements of the interested life of man act and react upon one another, so that the change of one involves the change of all the rest, there are only two alternatives open to the investigator.   He may simply affirm and reaffirm this general fact, varying his language to drive it home, but without advancing its understanding and control; or he may employ the method of abstraction for the purpose of isolating each factor in turn, in the hope of learning how much of the complex and circular effect is chargeable to it. Since both interest and its mediating cognition are functions of the behaving organism, we must take this as our microcosm and examine what happens *there*.   This does not imply any denial or disregard of broader social and historical changes, but only that such sweeping changes are summations of changes in the behavior of organic individuals, and that their explanation and control is to be sought in the intensive analysis of the human units of which they are compounded.

There is a further rule of procedure to be observed if we are to avoid an interminable inquiry into ulterior causes.   We must limit ourselves to the immediate context of interest, or investigate causes only when their direct effects appear upon this plane.   There is an objective background and a subjective foreground which belong to other fields of inquiry. We do not deny these ulterior causes, nor do we belittle them; but we presuppose and omit them.   Interest is a peculiar intercourse between two systems which we call the organism and its environment.   This peculiar intercourse or rapport is in fact a function of all that affects either of these systems.   A given individual's present interest is on the side of its environment a function of the condition of the earth's surface, and of the earth's distance from the sun, and of the structure of the atom.   On the subjective side it is a function of the physico-chemical constitution of the organism, and of innumerable remote biological causes.   Man's interest in his world is a function both of man and of his world, and of all of which either man or his world is in turn a function.   This has only to be remarked in order to be admitted, and being admitted it can henceforth be ignored.   It is evident that no inquiry can be fruitful that does not limit itself to proximate causes.   We shall, therefore, deal primarily with the interaction of interests themselves, introducing outlying causes and conditions only when they are in direct conjunction with interest.

§ 214. **The Question of Control.** The limits of our inquiry may be otherwise defined in terms of *control.* There is no better check upon unfruitful digression. We are concerned to know by what means interests may be generated, excited, modified, limited or negated. Admitting the endless regress of the causal chain itself, we shall search for those crucial points at which human agency may intervene, and through altering the cause predetermine the effect. Our problem is essentially the same as that of moral education or moral hygiene. Assuming a certain disposition of will to be desirable, how may such a disposition be implanted? Such a question arises in the midst of life, with its wider physical and historical background already irrevocably given. It is now a question of adding or subtracting some decisive factor at the eleventh hour. This does not imply that one may not set out to create a new heaven and a new earth, but only that the enterprise does not become one of moral education until it reaches that point at which the moral result is imminent.

§ 215. **The Origin of Interest.** It is possible to investigate the genesis and mutation of interests in any given subject, without solving the problem of absolute beginnings. Just as in biology it is possible to study the birth, growth and death of units of life within the general field of life, without understanding the transition from the pre-organic to the organic level of nature, so it is possible to study the birth, growth and death of units of interest in the field of interests without understanding how interest in general arises in a world that has not known it before. This is as fortunate in the one case as in the other, since questions of absolute beginnings are both obscure and ambiguous.

We shall, therefore, be concerned with the way in which new interests arise in a subject that is already possessed of interests, or the way in which new interests are begotten of old. Inasmuch as the question of absolute beginnings will hereafter be ignored, some brief comment on it is here in order.

The analogy between life and interest is imperfect in one very important respect. The question of the beginnings of life is a phylogenetic and not an ontogenetic question; it arises in connection with the race of living things, but it does not arise in connection with the individual member of the race. The individual is born alive; whatever else it may or may not inherit, it unquestionably inherits life. In the case of interest, however, the question of inheritance is an open and highly controversial question. Is the individual born with a stock of primitive interests which, interacting with his environment, generate his acquired interests? Or is the individual born as a reflex mechanism, the transition to the level of interest being itself a product of experience?

This question is, as we have seen, the question of instinct.[1] There is as yet no authoritative answer from the psychologists, nor is there likely to be in the present state of our knowledge of heredity. But it is worth while to recall what an inherited interest would be if there were one. Interest means, as we have seen, response governed by an accompanying expectation. The existence of interest in any given subject consists in a disposition on the part of the subject to behave in a manner that is constant with respect to its meaning. It implies a variability of acts within limits defined by their common anticipated sequel. It is of the very nature of an interest that it should reflect the meanings which objects and acts acquire under the special circumstances of the individual's experience. The biological utility of interest, as a condition favorable to survival, lies in its providing a means of acquiring specific differential adaptations to those unique circumstances of individual life to which no set of uniform racial mechanisms would be applicable.

To inherit an interest would imply, therefore, either one of three things. It might imply an inborn disposition so to respond to stimuli as to invest them with a certain specific meaning. Such a disposition would then *become* an actual

[1] Ch. VIII, Sect. I.

interest only as a result of experience, but the organism could be credited with the possession at birth of a variety of specific teleological capacities.

Or it might imply, secondly, that over and above these specific capacities for interest the organism possesses at birth specific perceptual or cognitive capacities, determining specific *expectations,* or anticipatory adjustments, in the presence of certain stimuli. In this case, the first presentation of a qualified stimulus would at once possess meaning, and by virtue thereof would at once evoke an interested response.

Or it might imply, thirdly, that the organism is so constituted at birth that its ready-made reflex activities, being imperfectly adjusted to the special exigencies of its individual life, are at once transformed, as a result of failure, into efforts or persistent trials. In this last case, the organism would be credited with a general capacity to form interests when its activities were thwarted.[2]

We shall not, however, be seriously embarrassed in our study of the mutation of interests by the necessity of leaving open the question of their inheritance. If interests are inherited, they are, in any case, essentially modifiable. If they are not inherited we must assume a capacity for their formation. The processes by which a given interest is modified, and the processes by which a capacity for interest, whether specific or general, is realized, are essentially the same processes.

§ 216. **The Four Methods of Control.** It would be possible to divide the topic according to the type of interest which is generated. Having first classified interests as positive and negative, or as independent and dependent, we might then consider the development of positive interests out of negative, or the development of independent out of dependent interests. Such a procedure would, however, be excessively schematic. It would obscure the causes by which such changes are induced, and by which they may be controlled.

[2] Although the question must for the present remain an open one, there are, as we have seen, strong reasons for adopting all three alternatives. Cf. § 89.

The importance of the topic lies in its bearing upon moral education. By this is meant not merely the deliberate effort on the part of parents or teachers to inculcate certain recognized moral sentiments, but the unceasing process by which whether consciously or unconsciously the motor-affective dispositions of an individual, his attachment to this or his repugnance to that, are generated and altered by the play of his natural and social environment. The merchant who advertises his wares is seeking to generate in interested subjects a desire to obtain these wares. The political orator who appeals successfully for votes is creating among his hearers a fondness for the cause which he represents. Both the merchant and the orator are seeking to *endear* an object to a subject. The effect, in so far as successful, is at one and the same time to confer value on the object, and to implant interest in the subject.

Viewing our topic under the aspect of control, let us take any normal individual and ask what influences affect him, or can be brought to bear upon him, in such wise as to beget in him a state of interest which he did not have before. To make the hypothetical case both simple and specific let us ask how he can be brought to desire the apple which I hold in my hand. There are four methods of appeal or inducement of which all may be jointly effective, or of which some may succeed where others fail.

The simplest method is to present the apple to the subject's sensory experience, so that he may feel and smell it, and thus receive effective stimuli to an interested response for which he is already predisposed. I present the apple in such wise as to excite an appetite and at the same time direct the appetite upon this particular object. I may use less rudimentary methods, and *describe* the apple in such terms as to attract him to it. In either case the procedure is fundamentally the same, in that I provide a suitable occasion for the arousal of an interest which he already has, and in so doing relate that interest to the special circumstances under which it is aroused.

A second method is to manifest or simulate an interest

in the apple on my own part. I may gloat over it, express pleasure in it, or taste it, with unmistakable symptoms of satisfaction. In this case, I seek to arouse the interest not simply by affording it a suitable occasion, but by exhibiting the interest itself.

Should these methods fail I may resort to starvation. I may, assuming a control of the circumstances, see to it that the appetite which I hope to excite is deprived of eligible objects other than that which I have to offer. I may remove the apple to a distance, or threaten to throw it away, or describe a prospective dearth of apples. Such procedure is based upon the assumption that the state of an interest at any given moment is a function of the degree of its satisfaction, or the remoteness of its consummation.

Finally, should my subject still manifest indifference, I may seek to gain my end indirectly through dealing with his other interests. He may be in a state of sullen despair, or of distraction, or of fear. Through satisfying, or thwarting, or deadening his other interests by any of the first three methods, I may so affect his general state as to render him more susceptible to the interest which I am seeking to implant.

All of these methods are employed in everyday life—in the way of a man with a maid or of a maid with a man, in parental exhortation, in religious edification, in efforts to extend personal influence, to obtain public support, or to create a public demand. In all of these cases the accepted maxims are the same: "Give people what they want," that is, present your case so that it will appeal to the object's existing interests; "Show that you mean it," that is, manifest in your own person the interest which you desire to awaken in another; "People value only what they have to work for," therefore, hold the object at a distance, so that an effort is necessary in order to obtain it; "See him just after dinner," in other words, cultivate or seize upon a receptive mood when the subject is favorably inclined either through his general well-being, or through the absence of more attractive alternatives.

II. THE PRESENTATION OR REPRESENTATION OF ELIGIBLE OBJECTS

§ 217. **Changes of Cognitive Environment.** Natural or historical changes directly touch an individual's interest only in so far as they alter his cognitive environment, that is to say, in so far as they enter into his system of objects. The Japanese earthquake of 1923 altered the real environment of all mankind. It had the effect of destroying both objects and subjects of interest, such as Japanese treasures of art, and Japanese men and women who treasured them. Indirectly this natural catastrophe had far-reaching effects upon the lives and surroundings of other human beings in distant places, and such effects will continue to radiate and multiply in the ages to come. These facts illustrate the dependence of life, with its freight of interests and values, upon the underlying forces of nature. But having acknowledged these facts, we confine ourselves to certain of their consequences; namely, the new experiences, new beliefs, new expectations, and altered prospects which were acquired and disseminated among contemporary subjects.

It is true that many of these phenomena would have occurred without the earthquake, provided the report of it had gained credence. But in the long run, beliefs reflect the character of the world we live in, and changes of fact, such as the seasonal shortening of the day, or the subsidence of an island, or the recession of a shore-line, are likely, if within the range of human faculties, to be reported and taken account of.

Besides those novelties which arise in the course of nature, there are the novelties which man himself creates; the artefacts with which he has refurnished the earth. These by the circumstances of their origin as well as by their proximity, cannot escape his knowledge, though they may be buried and forgotten when he dies. Their multiplication, in the form of institutions or of physical monuments and utilities, is eminently characteristic of civilization; and may have the effect of eclipsing the natural environment, and thus of confining man to the interior of his own domicile. Here again we are concerned not with the difference which these things themselves make, but with the difference which is made by the knowledge of them.

While man's cognitive environment changes with his real environment it may also change without it. Discovery brings within the field of human response facts which were already a part of nature. The substitution of Einstein's theory for that of Newton does not reflect the changes, such as the sun's loss of heat, which nature has undergone in the interval. The difference between the two theories is not like the difference between a census of England for 1700 and a census of England for 1900.[3] It is a change of belief about the same facts. To such changes of accepted doctrine must be added also the creations of the imagination and of speculative thought, the fancies and conjectures which reflect the range of human inventiveness and increase intellectual resources.

There is not only new knowledge of old facts, but also a new acquisition of old knowledge. In other words, objects already belonging to the cognitive environment of a given individual may by communication be introduced into the cognitive environment of a second, without any change either in the facts or in what is believed about them. In this way the accumulated objects of human knowledge constitute a common fund for all contemporaries and a heritage for future generations.

We have thus far described alterations of the cognitive environment as though they were induced in the subject from without, by the occurrence of events or by acts of communication which thrust them upon his attention. We must now recognize the fact that such changes are also due to the subject's own initiative, whether to his cognitive exploration, or to the experiences arising incidentally in the course of the fulfilment of his existing interests. The subject goes forth to meet his environment and does not wait passively for it to act upon him. His contacts are largely of his own making.

[3] The parallel to the change of mechanical theory would be a *revision* of the census for 1700, made in 1900.

Thus the subject's present interests exercise a selective determination upon that course of his cognitive life which in turn reacts upon his subsequent interests. What he learns depends in large measure on where his interests take him. He meets with novel aspects of his environment while *on his way,* in pursuit of this or that adventure. But while admitting this fact as a contributory condition of cognitive changes we need not further develop it at this point, because it does not affect the way in which such cognitive changes, once they occur, alter the agent's interests.

If, then, we consider the changes in the field of any given individual's response, we see that they may arise from his experience of factual novelties, or from his new discovery of old fact, or from his new acquaintance with old discoveries. His effective environment, or the world he lives in, is thus subject to constant modification.

All of the factors which have been enumerated as enriching the cognitive environment, appear to be increasingly operative in modern life. Though it cannot be said that nature has become more various and changeable, such is the case with human affairs. There is an actual multiplication of human events and of human artefacts, and an acceleration of historical change. Even more pronounced is the increase of discovery, and of the developments or revisions of theory. Most pronounced of all is the improvement of those means of record, communication and education by which discoveries and theories are circulated. The result is that the average man lives in a vastly complicated and rapidly fluctuating world. He finds himself distracted and oppressed by the number of objects, of which, in terms of his existing interests, he is moved to take account.

§ 218. **Their Effects upon Existing Interests.** Let us suppose, then, that in one or another of these ways a new object, such as the Japanese earthquake, swims into an individual's ken. What is its immediate effect upon the interests of him to whom it becomes known? How does the cognitive response to it alter the play of his interests?

It may be received with apathy. One may simply accept it, and assimilate it to one's system of beliefs; or make note of it, and set it aside for future reference. But such an indifferent response is unlikely. There will be few individuals who will not "care," or be moved by some aspect of so many-sided and so vivid an event. That it should be published as "news" rather than filed away in some statistician's cabinet, testifies to this fact. It is an *interesting* event, that is to say, it is a *qualified object of existing interests.*

To those immediately on the ground, the earthquake is a qualified object of fear, or *something to be afraid of.* The expectations which it arouses (such as those of pain or death) are such as these subjects are disposed to avoid. Or one may have already acquired a fear of earthquakes, in which case this particular earthquake qualifies as a case of the eligible kind.

A person at a distance is not afraid of the earthquake, but he may be eager to know more about it. It may awaken his curiosity, because of its novelty or dramatic quality. If he be a seismologist, it may be an object suited to an organized intellectual interest. As an instance of suffering humanity, it may awaken his compassion and afford an outlet for his charitable impulse. If he be engaged in the business of fire-insurance, he will deplore his losses; while if he be a dealer in food-supplies or in building materials, he will count his profits.

Let us suppose that in one or another of these different ways a subject's interests have been called into play by the cognitive assimilation of an event such as the Japanese earthquake. What, then, is the *effect* upon his interests? That an interest should be called into play does not in itself signify a "change of heart,"—to respond to objects already eligible is merely symptomatic of the subject's present state. But one who *has* so acted is differently constituted as regards what will appeal to him in the future.

There are three such modes of change that merit special attention. In the first place, the end is *specified* by assimilating to itself the particular circumstances and activities in which

the interest is consummated. In the second place, an interest
awakened in a particular situation is *diffused* among con-
tiguous objects and activities. In the third place, the particular means which are chosen for the sake of the end, become
themselves *interpolated* or intermediate ends. These are all
positive changes, or accessions of interest. But the readjustment in which they occur has also its *negative* implications,
and results in loss as well as gain.

Let us now consider briefly each of these four forms of
mutation that are directly induced by the presentation or representation of eligible objects.

§ 219. **Specification and Multiplication of Existing Interests.** The effect of specification depends, in the first place,
upon the fact that an interest is essentially variable. This
may be expressed more exactly if we say that the governing
propensity which provides the moving spring of interested
action, may be completed in any one of a number of ways.
This is clearly manifested on the simplest level of interested
action. Hunger may be consummated in food-taking activities, which form a limited class, but which within their prescribed limits vary widely according to the bulk, quality, place,
time and other characters of the particular food consumed.
Maternal love means the existence of a propensity to nourish
or caress objects, which, provided they possess certain general characteristics such as humanity, dependence and con-
sanguinity, may otherwise vary widely, in age, sex, complexion,
temperament, and other marks of individuality. Mother love,
in other words, implies a tendency on the part of the mother
to respond lovingly to her child *whoever* or *whatever* he be.

The enactment of the interest, its peripheral contact with
its object, particularizes it at the same time that it completes
it. The specification of the original propensity becomes a
propensity on its own account. The object which was first
eligible because it was a case of a general kind, now becomes
itself a kind, which renders eligible any of its own varying
phases and aspects. The former interest was mediated by the
mother's recognition of an object as her child, the new in-

terest by her identification of the object as this or that particular child. That which was variable and peripheral in the
first interest has become the constant and central component
in the second. There has been a translation of activities from
lower to higher arcs of integration.

In the case of the Japanese earthquake, fear of danger
has been transformed into a fear of earthquakes, or a fear
of earthquakes into a fear of *this* earthquake. Curiosity in
general has been transformed into a curiosity about something in particular. A general sentiment of humanity has
been translated into a tender regard for suffering Japanese,
and the business of selling goods to any buyer into the business of exporting them to Tokio. By the same process the
appetite for food becomes a fondness for the familiar food
with which hunger has been satisfied, a partiality for the
national dish, or the product of the domestic cuisine. The
instinct of pugnacity becomes an interest in howitzers and
poison gases. Positive self-feeling assumes the form of wear-
ing bright colors before an admiring throng, or of enjoying
the invisible power of a political boss. These changes are
genuine accessions of interest. Whereas the subject did formerly possess the general interest, or the interest in a class or
variable, he did not possess an interest in the particular member of the class or value of the variable.

The effect of such alterations is to multiply interests of
a given type. The general interest continues to breed further
specific interests, as qualified objects present themselves; this
tendency to multiplication being peculiarly marked in modern
life, because of the increase in the variety and range of the
objects presented.

This mode of multiplication also takes another form.
While old interests acquire an increasing variety of new objects, it is at the same time also true that old objects excite
new interests, and thus become multiple sources of satisfaction.[4] Objects cease to be uniquely associated with a single
interest. Fields of interest overlap and their area of inter-

---

[4] Cf. C. Bouglé, *L'Évolution des Valeurs,* 1922, pp. 85-92.

section thus acquires an augmented value.[5]   Objects common
to two or more interests become in this sense objects of the
interest of a total person or of a social group.[6]   Thus man
is disposed, with the enlargement of the range of his cognitive
environment, both to be interested in more objects, and to be
more interested in each object.

**§ 220. Diffusion and Generalization of Existing Inter-
ests.**   When an existing interest is called into play by a
properly qualified object, the first effect, as we have seen, is
to generate an interest in this object itself, in respect of what
is peculiar to it, as well as in respect of the more general
character that rendered it eligible.   This mode of change is
in the direction of a narrowing of the original interest.   We
have now to consider the reverse or broadening effect which
arises from the fact that when an interest is aroused it tends
to be transferred or extended to objects which are presented
or represented simultaneously with the eligible object.   The
result is to broaden the original interest because it is applicable to the associated object only in respect of its more general features.   In the former case the new interest is par-
ticularized by assimilating to itself the peripheral acts by
which it was consummated.   In the present case it is generalized through being reduced to those relatively central responses which admit of a wider range of consummatory
activities.

The facts are exceedingly familiar.   The name, the clothes,
the circumstances which have been presented to the lover
together with the person of the loved one, acquire thereby
a similar appeal to his affections.   The most trivial possessions
of a great man are impregnated with his prestige.   The cry
of a raven heard at twilight becomes permanently charged

[5] Cf. § 257.
[6] Cf. Ch. XVI, Sect. II.   The manner in which varied activities and
interests of a group may be bound together by their connections with
the same central and familiar object or situation, such as a staple food
or the family, is suggestively developed by Clark Wissler, in his *Man and
Culture*, 1923   This and similar works in anthropology contain important
material for the student of the genesis and mutation of values,—material
which, I regret to say, I have been unable to utilize.

with the peculiar emotion of its original setting,[7] or the scene of tragic events is "haunted."

The explanation of these phenomena is suggested by the theory of the associative or conditioned reflex.[8] This theory has been experimentally demonstrated only in its application to simple motor responses, but there are phenomena of feeling and emotion that are clearly analogous. What is called "affective transference" or the "conditioned emotional response," is now scarcely less orthodox among psychologists than the conditioned reflex in the earlier and narrower sense. In affective transference, "the affect originally attaching to some special experience is *loaded* upon another perception or idea." [9] Through the principle of the conditioned emotional response, "particular melodies become associated with the words of songs and with emotional expressions which have been called out by these words."

"Although at first only the words may have had the power to arouse the emotions in question, the music itself, in the absence of the words, will later have the same effect . . . and will long after revive the emotional expression of which they were at first the incidental accompaniment. Conversely, music itself may directly arouse emotional responses, and this fact is made use of to reenforce the conviction which the attending words but partly establish. The stirring airs of the camp meeting or the patriotic rally will bring many to the mourner's bench or the recruiting office who would remain sinners or slackers if appealed to by words alone." [10]

There are several features of this mode of mutation that merit special emphasis.

In the first place, it is almost incessantly operative and affords a ready means of control. Interested response always occurs in a context of circumstances with which the response

---

[7] C. Bouglé, *L'Evolution des Valeurs,* 1922, p. 83. For the compounding of this effect in the case of patriotism, cf. *ibid.,* p. 25. It is customary to speak of objects as being endeared by familiarity, when it is not the familiarity that endears them, but the nature of that *with* which they are familiarly associated.

[8] Cf. above, §§ 85, 134.

[9] F. L. Wells, *Jour. of Philos.,* Vol. XIII, 1916, p. 355.

[10] S. Smith and E. Guthrie, *Chapters in General Psychology,* 1921, p. 60.

is not concerned. Its selective character implies a threading of the way among rival stimuli. While the effect of the control of attention by interest is to exclude these rival stimuli from consciousness, some of them are invariably noticed even though they are forced into the background. There is thus a constant tendency of interest to spread beyond its focus or to cast oblique glances upon those very elements from which it is turning away. He who would influence any given subject of interest can take advantage of this fact. He can not only supply the subject with eligible objects, and thus excite and specify his interest, but he can at the same time bring other and indifferent objects into the field in the confident expectation that the interest which he excites will extend itself to them.

But, in the second place, this method of mutation is limited to the extension or re-direction of an interest of which the subject is already possessed. It differs from the first method, in that interest is created in objects originally without appeal; but it resembles the first method in that it not only depends on evoking an already existing interest, but results in nothing more than a reshaping of it. In the former case an original interest has been directed to one of a class of eligible objects, while in the present case it has been directed to an object not formerly eligible at all. But it is the *old interest* which has acquired a *new object*. Hunger, fear, love or disgust are now alive to objects which were once powerless to excite them, but they still retain enough of their original character to warrant their being called by the same name.

In the third place, it is important to note that the new objects bear a wholly arbitrary relation to the old, that is, their relations are spacial and temporal rather than logical. The subject who has become afraid of the dark because of being told of fearful objects *in* the dark, or afraid of a room in which a crime has been committed, has no *reason* to be afraid of either.[11] This fact has several consequences. It

[11] These examples are cited by Locke, in his *Essay Concerning Human Understanding*, Book II, Ch. XXXIII, q. v. *passim*. Some doubt attaches to the interpretation of all such cases inasmuch as the original stimulus may linger in the form of meaning, so that one is afraid not of the new

greatly broadens the scope of the principle, since *any* object, however irrelevant, may be presented or represented in spacio-temporal conjunction with an exciting object. It tends to the creation of inappropriate interests, through the accidental contiguity of objects, and because the ghost of the exciting object may thereafter haunt any premises which it has once invaded, whether in perception or in imagination. It lends itself readily to the propagation of error, whether through the unconscious play of circumstance or the deliberate malice of those who have something to gain by promoting superstition. It creates emotional displacements which are difficult to correct because they may owe their origin to obscure causes in the individual's forgotten past.[12]

In the fourth place, the effect of this type of mutation is to rarefy the interest which is transferred. It is diluted at the same time that it is diffused. It is quite evident that motor-affective responses cannot be transferred indiscriminately from one object to another, since they require certain determinate objective conditions for their consummation. The dog cannot eat the flash of light which is substituted for the appetizing food, or bite the word 'cat' which is substituted for the animal. The objects which are associated with the mistress cannot be regarded as affording an equivalent satisfaction of romantic love. The haunted room is not a thing to be afraid of in the same way that is appropriate to the deeds which were perpetrated there. There is, therefore, a certain maladjustment which may be corrected in the course of the individual's later experience, or which may be instantly corrected through the modifying expectations which the new object brings with it. The dog may attempt to eat the ray of light, and learn better; but the lover knows enough of faded flowers and "the silent shore of memory" not to expect a response to his caresses. When, therefore, the interest is

stimulus, but of what it means. It is always possible that the conditioned response may depend on this meaning, and disappear when this fades away. Cf. above, § 134.

[12] For the importance of this principle in accounting for and curing phobias, aversions and other psycho-neuroses, cf. Smith and Guthrie, *op. cit.*, p. 61; and Wells, *op. cit.*, p. 335.

transferred to these new and inadequate objects, it is curtailed. It limits itself to those central attitudes, or free expressions, which still remain applicable. The dog may respond to the ray of light with his glands, though not with his jaws and esophagus; and he can bark at the word 'cat,' though he cannot bite it. The lover may contemplate, cherish and caress the souvenirs of his mistress, even though he cannot embrace them.

Thus the general effect of the transfer of interests by association is to reduce them to terms which are objectively indeterminate, or which are applicable to many objects. Such interests tend to take the form of a vague favor or repugnance, or the effort to possess and keep, or the act of curiosity, or such other acts as require no specific structure on the part of their objects.

§ 221. Interpolation of New Interests.

In a mutation of the type just considered an interest is transferred to an activity which occurs simultaneously, but which is evoked independently. We suppose the new condition to intrude upon the scene by accident or by intervention, and then to be swept into the current of the existing interest. In the type of mutation to which we now turn, we suppose an activity to be induced by an interest, and then as a consequence of its interested exercise to become an interest on its own account.

This type of mutation may be most simply described in terms of means and end.[13] Interest is essentially teleological. A certain response occurs because it promises an ulterior response in which a governing propensity is consummated. The object of the subordinate response is the means, and the object of the ulterior response is the end. Accepting this analysis, it would be improper to speak of the subordinate response as an interest, or of its object as an end, unless it functioned itself as a governing propensity selecting anterior subordinate responses in their turn. The fact is, however, that subordinate responses *tend* to *become* governing propensities, and means to become ends.

[13] Cf. § 152.

All interested performance, whether recurrent or progressive, looks forward to the more or less remote future, and develops through intermediate stages. Ordinarily these intermediate stages will play a double rôle. They will figure as expectations attending antecedent stages, and will arouse expectations of ulterior stages; they will be expected of what precedes, and what follows will be expected of them. This is commonly expressed by saying that the successive phases of interested performance are both ends and means. A man who is travelling to California must traverse certain intermediate points, and will in the early stages of his journey be on his way to Chicago. He has, in other words, not only an ultimate destination but also a progressive series of immediate destinations.

A subordinate or intermediate end *is* an end, inasmuch as the expectation of it exercises a guiding and selective function upon antecedent activities, but it is subordinate inasmuch as it owes its force to ulterior ends. The traveller is interested in reaching Chicago, but would not be so interested if Chicago did not mean San Francisco. We have now to note the further fact that subordinate ends tend to become dominant ends. They acquire, in other words, an independent force of their own, which is proved by the fact that they will still determine acts which promise them, even when the ulterior expectations have been lost to view. An intermediate destination becomes a final destination, or a way-station a terminal. Partial phases of former interests thus grow by interpolation and complication to assume the rôle of total interests. There is, in short, a sort of reproduction and multiplication by division.[14]

[14] Ehrenfels describes this type of mutation (*Wertveränderung*) as a sort of directional movement of value (*Wertbewegung*) along the chain of means, ends, and after-effects, which he calls *Zielfolge*. There are movements *nach abwärts, nach aufwärts, nach seitwärts* and *nach innen.* (Ch. V. Ehrenfels, *System der Werttheorie,* 1897, Vol. I, pp. 132–146.) This view is summarized together with his own view, and H. Schwartz's *Motiv-Wandel,* by W. M. Urban, in his *Valuation,* 1909, pp. 194-204. The interpolation of interests is the movement *nach abwärts,* that is, the movement of the end in the direction of the means, or towards the foreground of interest. This view seems to me by its *directional* schematism to obscure the nature of the psychological causes at work. The upward and transverse movements differ ·from the downward movement in more than

This principle of mutation has to be distinguished carefully from others with which it may be allied, and with which it is commonly confused. Thus, it is not an effect of *habit*, in the sense of repetition and uniformity. Custom "stales," and familiarity breeds a contemptuous indifference. The result of repeating the same response to the same object is to automatize and dissociate it.[15] The result of having a number of ready responses available whenever a given interest is excited, is to reduce interest to the simplest form, in which there are only two levels, an end and a variety of alternative means. In so far as one of these means is repeatedly adopted the tendency is to eliminate even this element of selection, and to reduce the interest to a reflex.

Nor is the present type of mutation to be explained like the last in terms of association.[16] There *is* an effect of association by which means, being presented together with ends, tend to be colored by them. In other words, a dominant or controlling interest may be diffused or transferred to its means, which form a part of its context. This effect may be added to that of learning in the case of successful means, or it may tend to counteract that effect in the case of unsuccessful means, leading the agent to repeat mistaken or ir-

direction. After-effects do not tend of themselves to become ends. One does not tend to take food for one's health, rather than for its own sake, simply because health is a consequence of taking food. Health comes to be prized because it is a means, and having thus acquired value it may come to dominate activities which were first independent of it. The transverse movement is the diffusive effect which we have found to be due to association. The inward movement—the tendency for dispositions to become ends in place of their objects, or the subjectifying tendency, is only a special case of the interpolation of interests.

W. Wundt (*Ethics*, Vol. I, *Facts of the Moral Life*, trans. by Gulliver and Titchener, 1897, p. 330) introduces a "law of the *heterogony of ends*," according to which "the effects of . . . actions extend more or less widely beyond the original motives of volition," these unanticipated results being "eminently fitted to become new motives." But in what sense "eminently fitted"?

[15] Cf. §§ 84, 85.

[16] Mutation by specification and interpolation might be said to be due to "association by similarity," as distinguished from "association by contiguity," inasmuch as the two former as distinguished from the last involve an act of recognition, or a judgment of identity or causality. The tendency in psychology, however, is to limit the principle of association to the effects of contiguity, or to connections arising from bare spaciotemporal conjunction.

relevant means simply because of being temporally and spacially conjoined with the excitation of the interest. In either case, the effect of association is to transfer the given interest to associated activities, whereas the effect of interpolation is to create a *new* interest out of an auxiliary activity.

The specific effect here in question arises from the fact that a given end may be effective through a series of levels. A governing propensity not only induces means of the first order, or proximate means, which promises its consummation, but it induces means of a secondary order which promise its consummation through the proximate means. Acting under the control of a governing propensity one does that which promises the propensity's consummation. In this way a means becomes an intermediate or subordinate end. The tentative effort is transposed from the end to the means, and gives to the subordinate acts the character of interest. Instead of opening the box in order to eat, I struggle with the lock in order to open the box in order to eat; or look for the key, in order to release the lock, in order to open the box, in order to eat. Each subordinate act thus becomes in turn a problem or set, defining its own eligible acts and its own consummation. There is a limit in human capacity to the range of such series, but ability to keep in view, and hence to be governed by, such a series of unfolding prospects, is a characteristic of advanced human intelligence. So far the interpolated interest is dependent and temporary. We have next to recognize that such subordinate propensities, organized under the stress of a dominant propensity, tend to persist, or to become permanent dispositions, ingrained in the higher neural centres. The very tentative character which they assume implies that higher centres are engaged, and their pattern persists as a mode of activity that may in future come into control of the organism. In proportion as they engross the subject the ulterior control which gave rise to them tends to be relaxed and they acquire relative independence. In the cases cited, one may come to acquire the special interests of the money-maker or the locksmith as *interests in themselves,* which require no ulterior motivation from love or hunger.

The great importance of this type of mutation lies in the fact that it may give the character of interest to *any activity* or organization of activities of which the agent is capable. Its distinctive character lies in the fact that instead of merely narrowing or broadening interests already in existence, it creates entirely new interests. It does, it is true, draw upon old interests, but it derives from them only their general character of interest and not the particular features which distinguish them from other interests.

Because of its constructive possibilities this method is superlatively useful in moral education. To associate a painful penalty or a pleasant reward with certain acts may serve to inhibit or induce them. But the effect is only to confirm and extend the fear of pain or the desire for pleasure. In order that a new interest shall be created by such measures it is necessary that the individual should, under the pressure of such initial motivation, contrive a means of escaping the penalty or of earning the reward. It is the effort or experimental process so induced which may rise to the level of an interest on its own account. There is no contradiction, as is sometimes supposed, between learning by experience and the use of artificial rewards and punishments, since the latter may be used to call the learning process into play. One acquires interest by trying, but one must first be induced to try, and the greatest possibilities of moral reconstruction lie in the fact that one may by intervention in the course of the individual's life give to any activity the form of a problem.

§ 222. **Negation of Existing Interests.** The several modes of mutation already considered have their negative as well as their positive effects.[17] While these are for the most part evidently implied, it will be instructive to summarize them briefly.

Changes of cognitive environment not only introduce new eligible objects but remove old ones, or render ineligible ob-

[17] The ultimate effects of the negation of interest will be considered below, §§ 226, 228. We are here concerned only to recognize that there *are* such negative effects immediately incidental to the mutations considered.

jects that were once eligible. Altered expectations rob interests as well as cater to them. Natural or historical events, like the Japanese earthquake, have the effect of eliminating many objects of fear, love or ambition, leaving these interests without objects of consummation, or forcing them to seek them elsewhere. Changes of belief, induced by experience, will alter the meaning of responses and destroy their congruence with governing propensities. Thus a young dog will chase moving shadows, hunt them down and attempt to dig them out of the ground, at the same time growling and manifesting great excitement. But the situation does not develop in such wise as to fit the dog's series of anticipatory responses,—his precautionary counter-movements and postures of combat. The shadows do not do what is expected of them. The original meanings being effaced by experience, the shadows presently lose their appeal and the dog views them with indifference or ceases to notice them at all. Similarly, the cult of naturalism, undermining belief in spirits and the life after death, removes from the field of interest both objects of hope and objects of fear. Death, conceived as opening a new chapter of sentient existence, in which one feels the pangs of annihilation or of retribution, is an appropriate object of dread; but conceived as a mere termination of sentient existence, it "loses its terrors." The teaching of Epicurus is thus calculated to destroy a specific interest through reconstituting its object.

"Accustom thyself to reflect that death is nothing to us, since good and bad depend entirely on sensation, and death is privation of sensation. . . . It is but an idle pain that comes of anticipating a thing which will give us no uneasiness when it has come. Death, then, that most dreaded of ills, is nothing to us. For while we are, death is not; and when death has come, we are not." [18]

On the other hand, the presentation or reproduction of eligible objects, and the consequent *specification* of interests

[18] *Epicurea,* edited by H. Usener, 1887, p. 60; quoted by A. E. Taylor, *Epicurus,* 1910, p. 75. This removal of the fear of death is effective only in so far as the fear is based on an expectation of pain; it does not effect the desire to *continue living.*

which results, may itself have a negative effect. According to James, the specification of an interest tends to diminish the strength of the general interest from which it was derived.

"The original impulse which got us homes, wives, dietaries, and friends at all, seems to exhaust itself in its first achievements and to leave no surplus energy for reacting on new cases. . . . It existed *miscellaneously*, or as an instinct pure and simple, only before habit was formed. A habit, once grafted on an instinctive tendency, restricts the range of the tendency itself, and keeps us from reacting on any but the habitual object, although other objects might just as well have been chosen had they been the first-comers.[19]

In other words, the effect of the specification of interests is not merely one of multiplication, but also one of limitation. So far as this principle is operative, appetite, having given rise to a fondness for this or that familiar dish, is thereafter less tempted by *any* food; and a mother having come to love her actual children is less promiscuously loving of all children.

There appears to be an opposite negative effect produced by diffusion. The interest being so abbreviated or generalized as to enable it to be directed to associated objects not originally eligible, tends to supersede the more specific interest from which it was begotten. In so far as this is the case the object originally eligible evokes not the specific response but the generalized response. Thus the lover may come to take towards his mistress only such attitudes as are appropriate to associated circumstances, and sexual love may be superseded by a vague glow of tender affection. Similarly the impulse to minister to a neighbor in distress, having been extended in a generalized, impersonal form to sufferers from famine in China, may be permanently superseded by contributions to organized charity. He who learns to regard all mankind as his brother may come to treat his brother as he treats all mankind.

---

[19] *Op. cit.*, Vol. II, p. 395. What psycho-pathologists call "fixation" is a phenomenon of the same type, as when the natural affections are preëmpted by the objects first and most familiarly presented to them within the family circle. Cf. B. M. Hinkle, *The Re-creating of the Individual*, 1923, p. 14.

The negative effects of interpolation seem to depend on the limits of human foresight. The multiplication of means drives the end from the foreground into the background. Its control of present action depends on a thread of interrelated judgments which grows more attenuated and more fragile in proportion as it is elongated. The tree of interest thus dies off at the top through the absorption of its energies by the laterals and suckers that multiply at the base: life being stifled by its own luxuriance, and man walled in by the products of his own invention.

III. THE PRESENTATION OR REPRESENTATION OF THE ACT OF INTEREST

§ 223. The second means of exciting or augmenting interest on the part of any given subject is by the manifestation of interest on the part of a second subject. We have to note, in the first place, that the behavior of a second subject of the species possesses a peculiar prepotence over other stimuli. To a man there is nothing so interesting as a fellow-man. Granting this, we have to note three types of response which such a stimulus may arouse. In the first place, the behavior of a fellow-man may serve as a sign of *its* object, or as a medium of communication; in the second place, it may serve as a sign or expression of the state of the subject; in the third place, it may serve as a sign of the subject's future action. Thus A's manifestation of anger may excite in B, either a direction of attention to the object of A's anger; or a perception of A's emotion; or an adaptive anticipation of A's impending train of violent action.

In the third of these cases the response of the second subject does not necessarily reproduce that of the first. B may respond to A's anger by seeking to combat it, or by seeking to escape; he may seek to restrain A, and teach him self-control; or he may seek to exploit the effects of A's anger, as when in bayonet drill or warfare the soldier's anger is deliberately excited for the sake of its effect upon the enemy. This case presents no novelty. The behavior of a second subject is simply an object which is eligible in terms of the first subject's existing interests, and serves to alter these interests in one or another of the ways which have already been considered.

In the first and second cases, on the other hand, a connection of object and interested response is established in accordance with a new and independent principle. Whatever be the difficulties of explanation there is no doubt of the occurrence of the phenomenon. An object having no power to excite rage or fear or self-abasement or covetousness in the isolated individual, may arouse such responses with irresistible force when the same individual is in the presence of others who are manifesting them; the degree of the effect being proportional to the intensity, propinquity and volume of such manifestation. Indifference may give way to the liveliest interest, or the complexion of existing interests may be entirely altered. It is unquestionably true, as Le Bon and other social psychologists are agreed in affirming, that "man, as part of a multitude, is a very different being from the same man as an isolated individual." [20]

Some light on the causes of such mutations is to be obtained from our analysis of imitation,[21] and the distinction between its functions of *communication* and *expression*. In the first case, or the case of communication, the sign both points to the object and at the same time determines the mode of response to it. The simplest example is afforded by the well-known effect upon a passer-by of a crowd gazing expectantly in a certain direction. That which is suggested is not merely something-to-be-expected in a certain quarter, but something to be *seen*. The new comer not only attends but gazes in the indicated direction. A sign-post with an arrow or index finger causes such movements of his eyes or orientation of his body as convert the observer himself into a sort of sign-post. Similarly a posture of listening begets a like posture, or adaptation of the auditory mechanisms. A spoken

[20] G. Le Bon, *Psychology of Revolution*, trans. by B. Miall, 1913, p. 102, and *passim*. This volume together with the author's other writings abound in examples of the effects of emotional contagion.
[21] Cf. Ch. XVIII, Sect. III.

word not merely introduces the object to the hearer but establishes a verbal response to it.

The same is true of interested or emotional responses. A's
fear of M does not merely call B's attention to M, thus
presenting M as an object to B, and enabling it to evoke on
the part of B the interested responses for which it is eligible.
This would be the case, for example, if B were already afraid
of fire, and A's cry of alarm merely served to bring it within
his cognitive environment. This in itself would argue no
change in B's interests, though it would be followed by the
change in the direction of specification which we have already
considered. The uniqueness of the present phenomenon lies
in the fact that communication not only ushers in an object
but predetermines the activities by which the second subject
shall respond to it.

This differential effect may be simply added to the first,
as when B is already afraid of fire, but has his terror augmented by the circumstances of its communication. If, however, this differential effect can augment a preëxisting interest, it may also oppose a preëxisting interest, or occur independently. If a child's attention is called to a dog by an
adult's patting it or saying "nice doggie!", this introduction
of a dog as something to be trusted and caressed may serve
to overcome the child's preëxisting fear of dogs. Or a sound
occasioned by a rustle in the trees or a whistling of the wind,
may become an object of fear, rather than of indifference,
if the expression of fear happens to be the means by which
attention is directed to it.

It is doubtful if there are, strictly speaking, any colorless signs, that is to say, signs which wholly efface themselves
in the presence of their objects. In any case, what commonly
occurs is that the sign not only points, but, through the
mechanism of communication, induces a similar posture or
attitude in the subject to whom it is significant. Certain it
is that anger and fear not only communicate their objects,
but at the same time qualify them as things to be hated or
feared. Whatever further characters their object may possess
it can scarcely fail to derive a meaning from the manner of

its communication. Indeed this motor-affective meaning, which consists in the response of the first subject, may indeed be all that there is to show for the object—as in the suggestion of 'something' terrible, hateful or auspicious.[22]

In the second case, which coincides with the process previously discussed as *expression*,[23] the response of a first subject is a sign of that subject's state. The second subject responds, in other words, not by turning towards the first subject's object, but by turning toward the ulterior aspects of that subject himself. He elaborates the perception of him, supplementing the overt and visible aspect by inward kinaesthetic aspects which he can imagine only in terms of his own organic sensations, or by those perspectives which he can grasp only by participation. He tries, as we say, to "enter into the other man's point of view," and to "realize" his subjectivity.

We need no special impulse of sympathy to account for this. It is only a peculiarly elaborate process of the kind which is exhibited in all perception. But the peculiarity lies in the fact that since another person has experiences, and is in part at least constituted by them, the knowledge of another person will imply the knowledge of these experiences. The effect of the knowledge of another subject is to reproduce that subject.

If we suppose that in this case the first subject's object is already given to the second subject, we may say that the latter finds the first subject through his object, whereas in the case of communication he finds the object through the subject. Whereas in the first case an attitude is first aroused and then linked with a new object, in this case a new attitude is linked with an old object. The second case is less dependent than the first on the predisposition of the observing subject, and thus provides a method by which new attitudes,

[22] This is perhaps the essential truth in Tarde's contention that ends are communicated before their means, or that internal imitation precedes external. It is the general motor-affective interpretation or meaning of the object which is most effectively communicated and in which a crowd is united. Beyond this there is a considerable amount of individual variability. Cf. *Les Lois de l'Imitation*, 1905, pp. 216-232.

[23] Cf. above, § 205.

or new motor-affective postures, may be acquired. It passes readily over into 'conscious imitation,' in which the observing subject compares himself with his model and seeks by trial and effort to reproduce him. It is reinforced by whatever social interests make conformity and agreement useful or satisfying.[24]

It is commonly recognized that mutations of this type tend to the disintegration of personality, or that a high degree of suggestibility argues a low degree of rational autonomy. We may now understand more precisely what this means.[25]

In so far as interests arise in any given subject through their being presented or represented in another subject they are independent of the given subject's own personal history. He has not *found* an object to be fearful, hopeful or auspicious as a result of his dealings with it,—it has *not* proved so to be, but the object and the attitude are conjoined in a way that is to him quite arbitrary. An interest so acquired or so strengthened is likewise relatively independent of the agent's other interests or beyond his personal control. It is a function of conditions external to himself.

There is a further disintegrating effect when this mode of mutation occurs in a group or crowd. Interests tend to assume a primitive or atavistic form, or to exhibit the "ancestral soul." [26] This means that behavior is reduced to a highest common denominator, which will be something less than the integrated product of each unique personality. Or, the conduct of the crowd as a whole will be reduced to a form in which all can participate, that is, to the level of the marginal man. There is a further reason for this in the fact that social repressions are removed. The group which is "letting itself go" cannot, in the nature of the case, be censorious in respect of that passion which it is indulging, and ceases, therefore, to exercise a restraining influence upon its members. But the central fact is that interests which are communicated through a group must be such as through inheritance, or common experience, or general capacity, are racial rather than personal in character.

[24] Cf. Ch. XVII, *passim.*   [25] Cf. § 182.   [26] Cf. Le Bon, *op. cit.,* p. 105.

CHAPTER XIX

THE GENESIS AND MUTATION OF INTEREST *(continued)*

I. THE INTRINSIC EFFECTS OF SUCCESS AND FAILURE

§ 224. **Definition of the Question.** There are, as we have seen, four types of control by which interests may be generated and modified.[1] Two of these, which formed the theme of the last chapter, were based upon the intimate relation between the cognitive and the motor-affective life, which makes any given individual's interests susceptible to change through the objects presented or represented to him, whether these objects be ends or means appropriate to his existing interests, or manifestations of interest on the part of other individuals. The two types of control which we have yet to examine are conditioned by the action of interest on interest within the subject. The first and second types of control reflected the fact that the subject's interests are functions of his effective or cognitive environment; the third and fourth reflect the fact that the subject's interests are a function of his internal state and past history. These two broad divisions no doubt overlap one another, since the subject's internal state and past history are themselves functions of his effective environment. There is, however, an abstract or analytical difference between the alterations of interest induced directly by cognition, and those induced by outlying changes of interest itself.

While the third and fourth types of control have in common the broad principle that interest makes a difference to interest within the same subject, these two types are distinguishable from one another at least in emphasis. The third relates to the interdependence of the phases of the *same*

[1] Cf. § 216.

interest. It reflects the fact that each interest possesses a sort of organic unity of its own, so that alterations of one part induce compensatory alterations elsewhere. The fourth type of control, on the other hand, is based on the interdependence or solidarity of the several *different* interests of one subject. Since one of the most notable compensatory changes which any given interest may undergo consists in the generation or conscription of auxiliary interests, it is evident that these two types of control overlap.

The changes of the third type, which may be termed 'intrinsic' as being internal to a single interest, have to do primarily with success and failure. The unity of the interest, its being bent "by hook or crook," or "cost what it may," upon a certain end, means that its facilitation or thwarting at any given moment will induce corresponding changes of intensity.[2] The experimenter controls an animal's appetite not only in that he can excite it, but also in that he can prevent, retard, permit or accelerate its satisfaction. What, we now ask, is the effect upon the awakened interest of its success or failure, of the ease or difficulty with which it is consummated, whether this is controlled by the agency of an experimenter or educator, or is governed by the uncontrolled circumstances of the environment?

The common maxims of motivation and moral education define no simple and unambiguous principle governing this aspect of mutation. On the one hand, we are accustomed to believe that men appreciate only that for which they are compelled to exert themselves, that desire weakens in proportion as it is satisfied, and that perfectly facile action, assuming the form of habit, sinks below the threshold of interest or even disappears from consciousness altogether. On the other hand, there is a greediness in interests by which they acquire strength in proportion to their indulgence, "as if increase of appetite had grown by what it fed on." Interest, furthermore, needs encouragement or hope; repeated failure, or excessive difficulty, breeds a despair by which interests may sink into apathy.

[2] For.an examination of the meaning of intensity, cf. Ch. XXI, Sect. I.

It is clearly evident, therefore, that there is no single formula which will cover these facts. We cannot say that interest is directly or inversely proportional to ease and success, or to difficulty and failure. The effect of these factors is in part a question of their degree, and in part a question of the type of interest which is being affected. There is also a difference between the effect upon the present activity of the interest, and the effect upon its permanent or dispositional state, or its liability to future reawakening. In our attempt to analyze and formulate the principles which govern these changes we shall find it convenient to take as our point of departure the distinction between progressive and recurrent interests.[3]

§ 225. Effects of Success in Progressive Interests.

There is no simple correlation of success and failure in progressive interests with either positive or negative effects. It is evidently not the case that success always quickens interest, or that failure always deadens it; nor is it invariably true that failure quickens a progressive interest, and that success deadens it. We must, therefore, consider both positive and negative effects, in the cases both of success and of failure.

It is evident that it is essential to the nature of a progressive interest that it should *terminate* in success. Strictly speaking a progressive interest is operative until and *only until* its end is achieved, or until that which was expected is believed to be. A politician who is interested in being elected a United States senator ceases to be so interested when having heard the returns he believes himself to be elected. But notwithstanding this primary negative effect of success, there are secondary and indirect positive effects. Two of those are especially noteworthy.

In the first place, the successful issue of a particular progressive interest tends to beget or to strengthen a general interest of which it is a special case. The politician who succeeds in being elected senator will have his general ambition for office strengthened, and will be disposed to aspire to

[3] Ch. IX, Sect. I.

the presidency. His first success will alter his prospects, and present itself in the aspect of a means to an ulterior end of the same type. The means by which the initial success has been gained will have been proved and confirmed, and will offer promise of new successes. In other words, while success terminates the present interested performance, it strengthens the disposition to this or to similar performances in the future, inasmuch as it renders the effective environment more *auspicious* with respect to such performance. There is also a tendency to the development of recurrent interests. Successful activities acquire an inherent agreeableness, both as regards the means and as regards the results. The successful politician tends in other words, to enjoy both the game and its rewards, and is disposed to undertake new campaigns in order that these may be prolonged.

In the second place, there is a positive effect of the success attending the subordinate phases of a complex progressive interest. A successful step in the direction of an end quickens the interest directed to that end, or the pursuit grows hotter as it nears its goal. This is due primarily to the strengthening and consolidation of the governing expectation, through its becoming more immediate. When "the end is in sight," or when victory is within one's grasp, the mediating judgment is less qualified or conditional. The assembling of means and the removal of obstacles tend also to render the general situation more auspicious. In the case of the politician who has succeeded in acquiring the support of this or that group, or who has overcome the apathy or hostility of the electorate, victory is progressively imminent, or less dubitable, and "everything points to victory." The effect is both to enhance the ardor of the pursuit, and to increase the absorption of the subject in this particular interest. There is an increase of hope and of zest, together with a heightened control by the governing propensity.

As regards the negative effects of success, we have already noted that the success of a dominant progressive interest must in the nature of the case bring that particular interest to a close. We must recognize also a negative effect of success upon subordinate progressive interests. The empirical fact is familiar. In so far as the means to any end is completely mastered, it requires little or no attention on its own account.[4] The dominant interest no longer requires tentative intermediaries short of that response which directly produces the desired result. The animal who "knows how" to open a box in order to get food, is no longer, in order to get food, required to solve the problem of opening of the box. This part of the performance is itself no longer interested. It remains a means, but is not an end.

This lapse of a subordinate or interpolated end to the rôle of a mere means is but one of the principles which are loosely grouped under the popular notion of "the dulling effect of habit." There are at least two other and quite distinct principles that produce the same general effect. One of these is fatigue, which diminishes a recurrent interest or tends to give it a cyclical form.[5] Another is the disappearance of that positive augmentation of interest that arises from failure, and to which we now turn.

§ 226. Effects of Failure in Progressive Interests.

The positive effect of failure is seen in its most elementary form in the "rebound to superactivity" which results from inhibition. This is not, as Professor Sherrington has pointed out, a mere effect of quiescence and recuperation. The inhibited activity gathers strength not from its mere disuse but from antagonism. It is as though there were an accumulation of energy in the form of resistance, which takes the form of heightened activity when the inhibition is removed or overcome.[6] Thwarted interests acquire a superadded force from being "pent up," and tend when the pressure is removed or reduced, to *react* with a correspondingly greater intensity. Wounded self-pride will turn, as in the case of the freshman who having been hazed "takes it out" on the new freshman

[4] Cf. *e.g.,* James's famous chapter on "Habit" in his *Principles of Psychology,* 1890.
[5] Cf. § 237.
[6] C. S. Sherrington, *The Integrative Action of the Nervous System,* 1906, p. 212.

in the following year. The man who has been terrorized makes the fittest instrument of terror; the man who has been forced to submission is well qualified for tyranny; [7] humiliation begets arrogance. In these cases the obstructed interest bides its time, and in its permanent or dispositional form gathers strength from its momentary defeats.

In a certain basic sense all interest reflects a condition of failure, namely, the non-existence of that which is desired, or the non-possession of that which is coveted, or, in brief, the non-consummation of a governing propensity. Even reflex activities, such as breathing, may be transformed into interests through being thwarted, or through the removal of their objective component. There are evidently prior conditions which limit the intensification of interest through failure. The fact that an animal will struggle desperately to breathe when he will submit tamely to the interruption of other activities, reflects the latent strength of certain vital interests. [8] The intensity of an interest, or the extent to which the individual as a whole embarks upon it, is also relative to the other interests of the same individual and his scale of personal preference. [9] It is quite true that "blessings brighten as they take their flight," but there is in each case a specific limit to the brightness so acquired. Their flight may be viewed even with relief, or with indifference, or with only a mild concern. The primary effect of failure is not to add new interest, but rather to *realize* interest within preëxisting bounds. Through obstacles we are brought to manifest, and sometimes to our own surprise, the degree of the effort which our interests are capable of inducing.

> "For it so falls out,
> That what we have we prize not to the worth
> Whiles we enjoy it, but being lack'd and lost,
> Why, then we rack the value, then we find
> The virtue, that possession would not show us,
> Whiles it was ours." [10]

[7] Cf. G. Le Bon, *Psychology of Revolution,* trans. by B. Miall, 1913, p. 220; *Psychology of the Great War,* trans. by E. Andrews, 1916, pp. 68-69.
[8] Cf. § 262.
[9] Cf. § 273.
[10] *Much Ado about Nothing,* Act IV, Sc. 1. To "rack the value" is not to create it, but to strain it to its own preëxisting limit.

But failure and obstacles do also generate new interest. Halt an interested activity mid-way in its course, and a pressure is produced at that point, which is not only a measure of the strength of the primary interest, but which acquires augmented strength through exciting auxiliary interests. This is true whether the obstacle is circumvented by trial and error or made the object of a direct frontal attack. The former case has already been considered.[11]   Where the means to the end are not instantly available, these means themselves become ends, and the instrumental activity itself assumes the form of an interest.   Thus the absence or remoteness of food begets the interest of the chase.   Were the chase wholly subordinated to the desire for food, its interest would be directly proportional to hunger.   It is evident, however, that this is not the case.   The blocking of the primary interest has provided a suitable occasion for the appearance of a *new* interest.

There is, in fact, an interest in novelty itself.   The tentative efforts begotten by momentary failure are responses whose sequel is as yet unexpected.   The subject that is trying or performing experiments, is in an undetermined state of expectancy with reference to his environment.   But this is precisely the situation which awakens curiosity.   The organism cannot respond to objects in ways of which it is not already capable, but the interest motivating the response may be a problematic future, a 'something-I-know-not-what' which lies just ahead.[12]   The thwarting of interest throws the subject into an experimental attitude, in which all stimuli possess a certain general promise, or possibility of success, for anything that experience has yet proved to the contrary.   In this attitude the subject is favorably disposed to the impulse to explore, which, having been evoked, operates as an independent and augmenting factor, lending additional zest to the effects induced by the original interest.

[11] § 221.

[12] There is an interesting discussion of this point by H. W. Stuart, in *Creative Intelligence,* 1917, pp. 299-304.   This writer argues that unless there were an interest in the novel as such, life would be simply repetitive.   There is, I think, no inherent paradox in this view.   One may explain it negatively, in terms of the uneasiness begotten by the absence of specific expectations, or positively in terms of a *general* readiness to cope with contingencies.

A similar augmentation of interest occurs in the form of negative interest. The removal of the obstacle is at first a merely subordinate end, but it is speedily augmented by independent interests, such as aversion to pain, or the zest of combativeness. Any of these auxiliary impulses, positive or negative, may reach the degree of intensity at which it passes over into one of the major emotions and rallies to its support all of the energies of the organism.[13]

Where success is achieved by the conquest of difficulty, or as a result of great exertion, its object is permanently associated with these auxiliary interests. An object so attained is "highly prized"; which means that the efforts which have been made to attain it are reawakened when its existence or possession is threatened. What one has fought to achieve one will fight to keep. Hard-won gains are not willingly parted with. The value of money is appreciated by the man who has earned it, while money which comes easily is lightly spent. To the patriot the value of the fatherland is "impregnated" with the "sweat and tears and blood" which it has cost to create and defend it.[14]

Finally, there is a negative as well as a positive effect of failure. This mutation depends on the principle that interest implies hope as well as non-consummation. There can be no interest if there is no promise of success. This indispensable character of auspiciousness may attach to untried possibilities, and may reflect either youth and inexperience, or a wide and fertile imagination. It may reflect past successes, either the proved fruitfulness of certain specific means, or a general confidence begotten by the habit of success. It may reflect a condition of abounding vitality which may be temperamental or vary with health and emotional state. There is, in any case, a limiting point at which baffled interest passes over into despair and apathy. At this point the interest must decline or disappear because there is no aspect of the situation which suggests its consummation. The end must cease to motivate because there is nothing which presents itself as

[13] Cf. §§ 111, 126.
[14] C. Bouglé, *L'Evolution des Valeurs*, 1922, p. 25.

means. There is no interest-judgment [15] which carries conviction, the only objects of response being irrelevant, useless
or insuperable. As "hope deferred maketh the heart sick,"
so hope extinguished deadens the heart altogether.

In the light of such considerations as these it is not difficult to understand the subjectivity of optimism and pessimism.
To be an optimist, or to be happy, it is necessary that there
should be "something to live for," some end as yet unattained.
But it is equally necessary, on the other hand, that this end
should seem attainable: the given situation must be both imperfect and auspicious. Whether this is the case or not depends on the boldness of a man's aspiration, whether he is
animated by a divine discontent, or is "thankful for small
favors." Above all it depends on the strength of those impulses which derive joy from resistance, whether it be a
problem to solve or an obstacle to overcome. Some men are
pessimists because in order to reap it is necessary to plough
and to sow, other men are optimists because they find nature
plastic and fertile. The supreme aim of moral and religious
culture is to stretch effort to the limit which is compatible
with hope and buoyancy.

§ 227. Effects of Success in Recurrent Interests. In
the case of recurrent interests we shall again take as our
point of departure the positive effects of success. A recurrent
interest is essentially self-confirming. It is naturally greedy,
because each successive phase derives motive-power from the
immediate memory of the last. We mean by a recurrent interest an activity that aims to renew or prolong a present
response, each pulse of such an activity being both a consummation and also a promise of more to come. This promise
is freshly and cumulatively verified, so that the activity
gathers momentum as it goes.

But there is evidently a counter-effect, a decline of interest
that results from successful prolongation or repetition. These
negative effects of success are recognized in the principle of
'diminishing returns,' or 'diminishing utility,' which applies

[15] Cf. § 140.

to all consummatory activities. This principle is commonly expressed in terms of the decreasing value of successive increments of the same object when, as in the case of food, it is consumed piece-meal; or of successive uses of the same object, when, as in the case of social or aesthetic satisfactions, it is enjoyed as a whole.[16] In both cases, however, the declining value of the object is correlated with the later phases of successful activity, and it is implied that there is in the activity itself some principle of declining intensity. This principle is based in turn upon two principles which are still more fundamental, the principles, namely, of *fatigue* and of *satiation*.

The physiology of fatigue is both complicated and obscure.[17] "The waning of a reflex under long-maintained excitation" is a familiar and experimentally measurable fact, but its causes are doubtful. It is not necessarily muscular, nor is it confined to muscular innervation. A visual stimulus tends to lose its hold upon the attention, and to be superseded by fresh stimuli in the adjoining field. Professor Sherrington suggests that this may be due to a "negative induction," that is, to a specific tendency of any continued discharge to spread not to allied reflexes, but to the very reflexes which it is temporarily excluding. When the effect reached a sufficient degree the inhibited responses would then supersede the original response. There would, in other words, be an oscillation in which an excluded response would periodically take its turn. Such an effect would be useful to the organism and might be conceived as an evolved qualification for survival, because of insuring a varied activity on the part of the organism.[18]

Over and above such a negative induction, there would in any case be an effect of progressive physico-chemical ex-

---

[16] Cf. B. M. Anderson, *Social Value*, 1911, pp. 108-109. This formula is also used to cover the case of progressive interests, in which means lose their value because through the successful use of other means they are no longer "needed." For discussions of this principle of diminishing utility in its application to general theory of value, cf. W. M. Urban, *Valuation*, 1909, Ch. VI; and Ch. Ehrenfels, *System der Werttheorie*, 1898, Vol. II, Ch. III, § 18.

[17] Cf. C. S. Sherrington, *op. cit.*, pp. 214-223.

[18] *Ibid.*, p. 222.

haustion that would work against the increased facility arising from exercise. Such exhaustion occurs upon different levels, differing in the rapidity both of the effect and of the recovery from it. There is the superficial fatigue quickly induced and quickly dispelled, and the deeper fatigue with its longer rhythms. In the game of foot-ball, for example, there is a series of such rhythms, a fatigue of each play, quarter, half, game and season, with correspondingly longer intervals of recuperation. There is perhaps a deeper weariness of life itself from which there is no recuperation save in the long sleep of death. The greater undulations carry the small, as waves may carry ripples, and each unit, great or small, possesses the same form, being highest at the point of novelty or freshness, and declining steadily to the point of disappearance. In so far as this principle operates, the result is to give to all activities of the recurrent type a certain intermittence. They are not simply persistent, but move in cycles possessing both change and sameness. If the lover's fond contemplation is not to grow dull, its object must have something of that savory novelty to which the poet referred when he said, "Age cannot wither her, nor custom stale her infinite variety." [19]

That there is a waning tendency in successful interest quite distinct from the effect of fatigue, is commonly recognized in the conception of *satiety*. It has long been remarked by moralists that certain interests, such as the aesthetic interests, are comparatively free from the influence of this factor, while other interests, such as the bodily appetites, are comparatively susceptible to it. It is also generally agreed that this influence reflects the presence of a negative, intra-organic factor in interest. We have already noted the presence of such a factor in the case of hunger and appetite. [20] It is characteristic of an appetite that its non-consummation, or

[19] "The pleasure of music fades with familiarity, and requires either to be revived by intermittence, or fed by continual novelty" (Mill's *Autobiography*, 1873, p. 145).

[20] Cf., §§ 110, 111. Urban's contention that "the law of satiety does not apply to feelings of value" (*op. cit.*, p. 164) appears to me to reduce to the fact that satiety does not attach to the positive component of interest, but only to its negative correlate.

its limited consummation, gives rise to a bodily state which is the object of a negative interest varying from pain (as in the case of acute hunger) to a vague distress; or, conversely, that its consummation should be accompanied by the relief or appeasement of such pain or distress. Appetitive interest is thus doubly motivated, and the cycle of satiation is a function of the negative rather than of the positive component.[21]

The interest of eating or drinking is on its positive side of the recurrent type, tending to prolong itself indefinitely, except so far as affected by fatigue. On their positive side such activities even tend to be augmented by their consummation, and to acquire that steadily increasing momentum or greediness to which reference has already been made. On the negative side, however, the motivation of these activities is progressively weakened by the declining intensity of the internal stimulus. At a certain crucial phase this negative motive disappears altogether and the interest is robbed of so much reinforcement. At this moment the interest is purely positive. If continued beyond this point the interest now enters upon the phase of surfeit, in which a new disturbing stimulus appears which can be prevented or removed only by the cessation or reversal of the activity. In the first phase, the positive interest is reinforced; in the second phase it is abandoned, and in the third phase it is antagonized, by the negative interest. In the phase of surfeit the duality of these two factors is unmistakable, manifesting itself in a wavering between the attraction exercised by the external object and the aversion excited by the physiological state.

That aesthetic and like interests are comparatively immune from satiety is due to the fact that this negative component is absent; which, in turn, is explicable by the fact that their consummation involves no such profound physical and chemical changes in the body as those involved, for example, in the taking of food. If the gods enjoy "a perpetual feast of nectar'd sweets, where no crude surfeit reigns," it must

[21] This cycle has been clearly stated and illustrated by Professor Wallace Craig in his article, "Appetites and Aversions," *Biological Bulletin,* Vol. XXXIV, 1918, pp. 101 ff.

be because, being exponents of "divine philosophy," they are satisfied to contemplate their aliment without ingesting it.

That the principles of fatigue and satiety do not account for all cases of the dulling effect of continued or repeated success, has been clearly shown by Professor S. C. Pepper.[22] Aesthetic taste exhibits rhythms of too long a span to be explicable in terms either of exhaustion and recuperation, or of physico-chemical alterations in the individual organism. The best example is afforded by periodic changes in the feeling of consonance.

"The Greeks recognized only the octave as a consonance; in the fourth century the fifth and fourth were accepted; in the eleventh the major third; in the twelfth the major and minor sixths; and to-day we seem to be on the verge of approaching the sevenths." [23]

There are similar changes on a historic scale in the enjoyment of combinations of colors, linear proportions and metrical forms. These facts suggest what Professor Pepper calls "the law of habituation." There is, he thinks, in all these aesthetic activities, a natural "affective sequence," or scale of liking and disliking, depending usually on relative simplicity. Taste tends to move along this scale in the direction of increasing complexity, and owing to the "limited capacity for appreciation," the old combinations lose their attractiveness as the new come to be liked.

Professor Pepper does not pretend to offer a final explanation of these phenomena, but it is suggested, both by the author and by the facts which he assembles, that there is an element of invention in aesthetic interest both on its creative and on its appreciative side. In order that novel combinations of color, tone or line shall be presented to the observer often enough for him to learn to like them, there must first be artists who are interested in trying them, and in order to learn to like them the observer himself must first be induced to try. In both cases there must be that appeal of the novel, that impulse to deal with the unfamiliar, which we have al-

[22] "The Law of Habituation," *Psychol. Rev.*, Vol. XXVIII, 1921.
[23] *Op. cit.*, p. 61.

ready noted and which is commonly known as curiosity. The
mutations to which Professor Pepper calls attention further
imply that aesthetic enjoyment depends not only on the tang
of novelty, but also on the zest of experimental effort. Perfect
ease of adjustment renders the object banal, and taste, like
ambition, craves new worlds to conquer. There appears to
be a unique interest in that which has been *just* mastered,
or in the barely successful activity which still retains something of the quality of an adventure. This same mean between
excessive incapacity and excessive facility seems to characterize intellectual enjoyment, so that a God or Absolute conceived as deriving perfect happiness from contemplation must
first alienate the truth and then learn it. We are thus again
brought back to the basic nature of all interest as inherently
tentative and selective, implying some slight risk of failure
however great the prospect of success.

The principles which explain the negative effects of success
in recurrent interests all imply a positive effect of failure.
Both fatigue and satiety may be carried to a breaking-point
beyond which their effect is wholly negative. But short of
that point, the decline of interest through fatigue induces
rest and recuperation; its decline through satiety induces abstinence and recovery of appetite; while the disuse of habitu-
ated activities enables them to acquire novelty and freshness.
All of these principles are employed as instruments of control.
One *prepares* for enjoyment by periods of rest, or *cultivates*
appetite by abstinence, or seeks deliberately to refresh the joys
of home and friends by voyages among strangers abroad.

These restorative changes prove that the negative effects
of success in recurrent activities relate not to the underlying
disposition, but to the particular manifestation of it. The
persistent disposition reflects itself in *judgments* of value. The
tired foot-ball player would still "like" foot-ball, and the sated
gourmand would still "be fond of" *paté de fois gras*.[24] Despite
the historic cycles of taste, every new-born infant, unlearning
the lessons of the past, begins again with that "natural af-

[24] It is this distinction which appears to underlie Urban's restriction
of the application of the principle of fatigue. Cf. *op. cit.*, p. 159.

fective sequence" that governed the taste of his remote ancestors. It is the individual and not the race that is bored. The mutations which we have just considered thus determine the waxing and waning, or the discontinuity, of values, rather than their permanance.

§ 228. **Effects of Failure in Recurrent Interests.** We have to note, as a positive effect of failure, the rise of progressive subordinate interests from the blocking of recurrent interests. The interruption of the food-taking activity induces a struggle to obtain food; the interruption of aesthetic contemplation induces an effort to restore the situation in which it may be resumed. In time of war a whole nation is thrown into a posture of effort and struggle through hostile interference with its normal consummatory activities.

There is, finally, in recurrent as well as in progressive interests, a negative effect of failure. Starvation carried beyond a certain point will produce, not quickened appetite, but nausea, apathy, coma and death. Rest if carried beyond a certain point will produce decay rather than refreshment. Interests acquired by use may be lost through disuse. Darwin, as is well known, refers to his "lamentable loss of the higher aesthetic tastes," and ascribes it to the atrophy of parts of his brain which might have been "kept active through use." [25] In short, the need of exercise is as imperative as the need of rest.

Some primitive interests appear to atrophy from disuse, as illustrated by the instincts which James describes as "transitory." They exist as capacities in certain phases of the individual's development, and especially in youth:

"In all pedagogy, the great thing is to strike the iron while hot, and to seize the wave of the pupil's interest in each successive subject before its ebb has come, so that knowledge may be got and a habit of skill acquired—a headway of interest, in short, secured, on which afterward the individual may float." [26]

[25] F. Darwin, *Life and Letters of Charles Darwin,* 1887, Vol. I, pp. 81-82. J. S. Mill records a similar experience, and says, "I had now learnt by experience that the passive susceptibilities needed to be cultivated as well as the active capacities" (*Autobiography,* 1873, pp. 143 ff.).
[26] *Principles of Psychology,* 1890, Vol. II, p. 401.

There is, it would appear, a peculiar fragility in interests in proportion as they are of the recurrent type. The thwarting of a progressive interest readily induces a vigorous and aggressive resistance, or a resourceful circumventiveness. The thwarting of an appetite strengthens its negative component. But the disturbance of a contemplative activity may easily be fatal. The mood is destroyed; and the conditions of its restoration are too complicated to appear probable. There are no unappeased pangs to reawaken it. Above all, there is a profound difference of attitude between the contemplative activity itself, and such efforts as would be required to renew it; so that to a person who enjoys contemplation, the struggle to obtain the necessary conditions of contemplation is likely to be uncongenial. If such a person is thwarted he is more likely to desist or complain than to fight or circumvent. He needs "patrons" to protect him. Where, as in cases of war, the more primitive auxiliary interests are called into play, these are likely to supersede rather than to restore the interests which they were called on to save. In short the "higher" recurrent interests are less resilient and less hardy than progressive interests.

II. INTERACTION OF INTERESTS IN THE SAME SUBJECT

§ 229. **Mutations on the Physiological and Biological Level.** In the present division of our topic we are concerned with changes of personality, or of the subject as a whole. But we are concerned with this problem only in a very limited sense, namely, in so far as such changes can be brought under the category of interest. There are other aspects of the problem which cannot be ignored, and they should be mentioned here lest it be thought that their omission implies either their denial or the disparagement of their importance.

The instrument or mechanism of personality is the body, and pervasive bodily changes will be reflected in the personal life and in all of its component interests. Interest is as dependent on the physico-chemical state of the body as is sensation or cerebration. There are many such changes of bodily state whose effects upon the motor-affective life are proverbial and indisputable, obscure as may be their *modus operandi*.

The French physician and physiologist La Mettrie was fond of pointing out how completely the moral dispositions of man were dependent on the state of his bodily mechanism.

"What was needed to change the bravery of Caius Julius, Seneca or Petronius into cowardice or faintheartedness? Merely an obstruction in the spleen, in the liver, and impediment in the portal vein. In Switzerland we had a bailiff by the name of M. Steigner de Wittighofen. When he fasted he was a most upright and even a most indulgent judge, but woe to the unfortunate man whom he found on the culprit's bench after he had had a large dinner! He was capable of sending the innocent like the guilty to the galleys. We think we are, and in fact we are, good men, only as we are gay or brave; [but] everything depends on the way our machine is running. . . . History provides us with a noteworthy example of the power of temperature. The famous Duke of Guise was so strongly convinced that Henry the Third, in whose power he had so often been, would never dare assassinate him, that he went to Blois. When the Chancellor Chiverny learned of the duke's departure, he cried, 'He is lost.' After this fatal prediction had been fulfilled by the event, Chiverny was asked why he had made it. 'I have known the king for twenty years,' said he; 'he is naturally kind and even weakly indulgent, but I have noticed that when it is cold, it takes nothing at all to provoke him and send him into a passion.' " [27]

"The great divisions between men and men," says Jean Christophe, "are into those who are healthy and those who are not." [28] The radical and all-pervasive effect of this factor, and especially of the condition of the alimentary tract, upon the emotional life is difficult to exaggerate, though it is ordinarily thought unworthy of mention in moral treatises. To a strong stomach in the physical as well as in the metaphorical sense, there is very little that life brings that is not palatable.

Not less profound are the differences due to sex,[29] and the mutations of youth and age. The latter are in part due

[27] *L'Homme Machine*, 1748, trans. by C. C. Bussey, 1912, pp. 91, 94-95, 96.
[28] Rolland, *Jean Christophe*, trans. by G. Cannon, 1910, Vol. I, p. 224.
[29] Cf. Havelock Ellis, *Man and Woman*, 1904.

to factors within the purview of a theory of value, factors such as disillusionment, increased knowledge, and the prospect of death. But over and above these there is a factor which experience and education cannot affect, a profound organic alteration which robs life of its relish and elasticity. Age, according to the poet, is the time "when I shall know most, and yet least enjoy." "Youth and extravagant opinions naturally go together," says Bulwer Lytton, in commenting on Southey's remark that "a man should be no more ashamed of having been a republican than of having been young." [30] Extravagance of opinion is not merely an effect of inexperience, but also of ardor, exuberance and courage. The recurrence of this essential youthfulness in successive generations, and hence the continuous rejuvenescence of the race, is one of the prime factors in human development.[31]

That values are a function of 'temperament' is self-evident. In the present state of knowledge this means only that there are motor-affective types to which individuals may be somewhat loosely assigned by virtue of their innate peculiarities. There is a reference to feeling and will in most of these types, such as: 'sanguine,' 'melancholic,' 'choleric' and 'phlegmatic'; 'sensitive,' 'active' and 'apathetic'; 'introversive' and 'extroversive'; 'centripetal' and 'centrifugal'; 'tough-minded' and 'tender-minded'; 'herbivorous' and 'carnivorous'; 'abdominal,' 'respiratory,' 'muscular' and 'cerebral'; 'Apollonian' and 'Dionysian'; 'passive' and 'active'; 'classic' and 'romantic.' [32] The persistence of the category of temperament despite the extreme obscurity both of the facts and of their causes,[33]

---

[30] *My Novel,* 1874, Vol. I, p. 59. When Anatole France says, "J'aurais mis la jeunesse à la fin de l'existence humaine," it is in order that life may reach its climax of poetry and ecstasy at the end; cf. *Le Jardin d'Épicure,* 41 ed., p. 51. For a discussion of this question in its bearings on immortality, cf. G. L. Dickinson, *The Meaning of the Good,* 1907, pp. 199 ff. In this connection, cf. also S. Hall, *Adolescence,* 1904.

[31] "L'humanité ne risquerait-elle pas de s'endormir et comme de se pétrifier, si elle était composée des mêmes hommes prolongeant indéfinimente leur vie?" (C. Bouglé, *Evolution des Valeurs,* 1922, pp. 40-41).

[32] Cf. Lotze, *Microcosm,* trans. by E. E. Hamilton and E. E. C. Jones, 1887, Bk. VI, Ch. II; Ribot, *Psychology of the Emotions,* 1897, pp. 393 ff; G. Stanley Hall, "Psychology as Developed by the War," *Pedagogical Seminary,* Vol. XXVI, 1919.

[33] In its modern form the problem of temperament turns upon two

may be taken to indicate that here also, in the native cast of mind, there is a dynamic factor in values which lies beyond the reach of experience and education, and which is in this case subject to control only through selective breeding.

§ 230. **The Pathology of Interest.** It is evident that values will be dependent in a peculiar degree, and with a peculiar directness, on those mental abnormalities which culminate in insanity. All forms of mental abnormality will affect the individual's valuations through the intimate relation of cognition and interest. An individual who is intellectually defective will fail to suit the emotion to the occasion, as in the "loud laugh that spoke the vacant mind." He will respond inappropriately, and will be unable to rectify his maladjustment by experience. But psychiatrists no longer conceive mental disorder exclusively in terms of "loss of reason" or lack of cognitive capacity. Disease may attack the motor-affective life more directly. There is no classification of motor-affective disorders which the layman may cite as authoritative. The psychiatrist is at present more sure of his symptoms than he is of their causes or underlying unities. But without prejudging their ultimate explanation, these pathological symptoms may be so grouped as to illustrate certain normal characteristics which our analysis has already yielded.[34]

Interest depends fundamentally, as we have seen, upon the existence of certain governing propensities, or drives, which draw upon the energies of the organism and direct

unsettled questions: first, the general psychological question of 'individual differences,' or the range and categories of mental variation, which depend on the method of approach; second, the biological question of heredity, with special reference to 'unit-characters' in man. For a good introduction to the subject, cf. J. Jastrow, *Character and Temperament*, 1915, Ch. V, IX.

[34] For an approach to a study of this question the following works are recommended: W. James, "What is an Emotion?" *Collective Essays and Reviews*, 1920; P. Janet, *The Mental State of Hystericals*, trans. by C. R. Corson, 1901; E. Kraepelin, *Manic-Depressive Insanity and Paranoia*, trans. by R. M. Barclay, 1921; A. Hoch, *Benign Stupors*, 1921; J. R. de Fursac, *Manual of Psychiatry*, trans. by A. J. Rosanoff, 1913; C. A. Mercier, *Psychology, Normal and Morbid*, 1901; W. F. Menzies, "The Mechanism of Involuntary Melancholia," *Journal of Mental Science*, Vol. LXVI, 1920.

them through effort to certain ends. From the stand-point
of interest, therefore, the most fatal disease is that general
listlessness or apathy which marks the absence of such propensities. Such a condition is observed in what is called
'abulia' (or will-lessness), and in so-called 'benign stupors,'
in which the subject manifests lethargy, vacancy and pla-
cidity.[35]

A second and quite distinct group of symptoms appears
to consist in the absence of somatic sensations of the type
that is normally agreeable. The subject is not indifferent,
but suffers acutely from their absence.

"Every function, every action of my life remains, but deprived of the feeling that belongs to it, of the enjoyment that
should follow it. My feet are cold, I warm them, but gain no
pleasure from the warmth. I recognize the taste of all I eat,
without getting any pleasure from it. . . . That lively interest
which a year ago made me hear a delicious concert in the smallest
air their [my children's] fingers played,—that thrill, that general
vibration which made me shed such tender tears,—all that exists
no more." [36]

Such a subject is relatively incapable of 'feeling,' not through
lack of interests, but through the lack of their organic content or object.[37]

In the third place, one finds, as in the case of manic-
depressive insanity, a motor-affective disproportionality. A
subject having no general indifference, nor any incapacity for
feeling, may exhibit some special interest such as fear, or
some class of interests, such as negative interests, in a measure
that is either exaggerated or subnormal. He may suffer from
seizures or obsessions; or he may, as in chronic melancholia,
dwell excessively upon his doubts and failures; or he may,
as in certain criminal types, be abnormally lacking in social
impulses.[38]

[35] Cf. A. Hoch, op. cit., p. 30; C. A. Mercier, op. cit., p. 483.
[36] Quoted in W. James, op. cit., p. 266.
[37] In other words, the subject is defective in those proprioceptive and
interoceptive sensations, which constitute pleasures in the substantive
sense, and which in the attributive sense augment the satisfactions of
objective interests. Cf. §§ 122-126.
[38] Cf. de Fursac, op. cit., p. 91, and passim.

So far as such lack or disproportionality of will and feeling is due to physico-chemical changes, and subject to control only, if at all, through physical or chemical therapy, it must fall outside the scope of the present study. In so far, on the other hand, as it can be construed in terms of an interaction of interests, and is subject to control by the blocking or facilitation of interests through the offering or withholding of their objects, it may be said to lie upon that level of complexity with which a theory of value is concerned. The pathology of value is circumscribed by that same uncertain line which divides surgery, medicine and physical hygiene from 'mental hygiene,' or 'psychotherapy.' Thus, for example, a Swiss psychiatrist describes "a case of psychasthenia with grave alterations of affectivity." The patient, Albertine,

"declares that she has no feeling, but only neutral (*décolorées*) sensations. She speaks of a numbness or torpor of her entire moral being. She does not feel herself to be alive either physically or morally. . . . She is, furthermore, perfectly conscious of the defectiveness of her sensibility. . . . She has visual, auditory, olfactory, gustatory and tactual sensations of normal clearness, but these sensations are not accompanied by any affective tone. . . . She recognizes intellectually that an event ought to be gay or sad. In receiving news of some one's death, she tells herself that it is obviously a sad event, but she experiences no emotion." [39]

It is evident that Albertine's world is in large part a valueless world, and that if there were no sentient beings but Albertines, the greater part of the realm of values would disappear altogether. The author, furthermore, attributes the patient's state to her failure to consummate her interests. Because her interests are unsuccessful she abandons them, whereas a hysteric patient, on the other hand, may take refuge in their fanciful or symbolic realization.[40] In both cases the condition of interest is construed as a result of experience, rather than of merely physico-chemical causes. What failure has induced, success might remedy. A change of affective

[39] L. Schnyder, *Archives Suisses de Neurologie et de Psychiatrie*, Vol. VII, 1920, pp. 92, 93.
[40] *Ibid.*, pp. 100, 101.

environment, a provision of auspicious objects by which interests might be facilitated rather than thwarted, would render unnecessary those compensatory readjustments to which the patient's symptoms are due. Like cause, like cure.[41]

§ 231. **Circumscription and Division of the Topic.** The broad fact with which we are here concerned is the fact that each interest of a given person is a function of his other interests. This equilibrium of interests, such that each is a modifying condition of the exercise of the rest, and such that a change anywhere induces compensatory changes throughout, is, in fact, what we have meant by personality.[42]

In dividing this topic we shall find it convenient to employ the distinction already made between [43] the interactive relation by which interests are compatible, incompatible or reinforcing; and the inter-objective relation by which they are consistent, opposed, allied, antagonistic or friendly. According to the first relation, interests thwart or facilitate one another through employing the same bodily mechanisms and store of energy. Each interest in its exercise draws away from the others, or in its arrest paves the way for them; if Peter is not to be robbed to pay Paul, then Peter and Paul must moderate their respective claims. But if interests may in this way be rivals, it is no less true, on the other hand, that they may reinforce one another, or so function that the success or failure of one is diffused to the rest. The interactive relations of a subject's several interests thus give rise to two types of mutation, that of *compensation* or inverse proportionality, and that of *mood* or direct proportionality.

The second, or inter-objective relation, tends to develop from the first, but this fact must not blind us to the distinction.

[41] Albertine's tubercular heredity is a cause of the type that lies beyond the range of moral control. But the strongly developed affective tendencies of her childhood "encounter, on the one hand, the obstacle of her own scrupulous constitution of mind, and, on the other hand, an unsympathetic and disparaging family *milieu*." She shows marked, though temporary, improvement in a more favorable social environment. *Op. cit.,* pp. 105, 106.
[42] Cf. Ch. XV, Sect. I.
[43] Cf. Ch. XIII. The intimate relation between the present topic and the problem of personal integration is evident.

It is clear that the one principle may operate in the absence of the other. Thus my interest in sport may be incompatible with my vocational interest owing to limits of time or strength, though the objects of these interests may be consistent or wholly irrelevant; if I had time enough, I would engage in both. On the other hand, the love and hate of the same person are opposed attitudes, in the sense that their objects (the well-being or the injury of the person in question) are contradictories; and this is none the less the case even though there be room and time for both. The effect of this principle is either the concerted purpose of a unified personality, usually involving either the repression or the 'sublimation' of one of the opposed interests; or, in the event of the failure of such harmonious integration, the state of self-defeating conflict or dissociation.

§ 232. **Incompatibility and Compensation.** In examining the effects of the principle of compatibility, we shall consider first the compensatory effects, and second those diffused effects which are characteristic of moods.

The simplest case of compensation is that in which the exercise of one interest precludes the exercise of another, and this is most simply exhibited in the physiological conception of the "final common path":

"At the termination of every reflex-arc we find a final neurone, the ultimate conductive link to an effector organ (muscle or gland). . . . The last link in the chain . . . receives impulses . . . from many receptive sources, . . . [and] is the *sole* path which all impulses, no matter whence they come, must travel if they are to act on the muscle-fibres to which it leads."

This necessitates successive and not simultaneous use of the common path by various receptors using it "to *different or opposed effect,*" as in the case of the extensor and flexor reflexes. "The result is *this* reflex or *that* reflex, but not the two together." [44] The relation of rivalry between simple reflexes will extend to any pair of interests of which they are components. It is broadly true of life on every level

[44] C. S. Sherrington, *op. cit.,* pp. 115-117, and Lect. IV, *passim.*

of complexity that relatively many responses converge in relatively few neuro-muscular mechanisms, and that they are therefore mutually inhibitory or allied. In his contention that man is richly endowed with instincts, James affirmed that man "appears to lead a life of hesitation and choice" rather than of instinct, "not . . . because he has no instincts—rather because he has so many that they block each other's path." [45]

The principle of counter-attraction, or of counter-irritation, is on its more complex levels a commonplace of politics and of education.

"A change of opinion usually takes place by diverting attention into a new channel, which has the effect of drawing a red herring across the trail. Laski remarked that people do not disprove miracles; they outgrow them. In fact few opinions are changed by being disproved. Attention is turned to something fresh, and an opinion is formed thereon which proves to have an unsuspected inconsistency with older ideas, and eventually, cuckoo-like, expels those ideas. Opinions have this in common with intrenchments, that they offer an obstinate resistance to frontal attack, but not to a turning movement." [46]

This is equivalent to saying that the principle of incompatibility affords a more prompt and efficacious means of arresting a given interest, than the principle of consistency. An interest, whether successful or unsuccessful, positive or negative, may, regardless of all rational considerations, be simply superseded by the excitement of some inhibitory interest.

The operation of this principle does not in itself imply anything as to the permanent effect upon the interest thus inhibited. This will depend upon those intrinsic effects of success and failure which have been considered above. The law of habit will operate in favor of the inhibiting interest, and tend to confirm its possession of the field to the permanent exclusion of its rival. Where this inhibition is maintained throughout the plastic period of youth, the rival interest may, as we have seen, lose its opportunity. It is none the less true, on the other hand, that interests momentarily

[45] W. James, *Principles of Psychology*, 1890, Vol. II, p. 393.
[46] A. L. Lowell, *Public Opinion in War and Peace*, 1923, pp. 29-30.

dispossessed may gather strength in the interval of disuse and reassert themselves with augmented vigor.

The reverse compensatory effect is not less familiar, though its explanation is more obscure.   In the first case the facilitation of a given interest indirectly blocks other interests, while in the reverse case the blocking of a given interest indirectly facilitates other interests.   This effect is less likely than the first to be used for purposes of control, but it is not less wide-spread and familiar.   Perhaps the only case which is plainly intelligible, is that in which the cessation of a given interested activity makes room for, or paves the way for, or releases, those interests which it has hitherto obstructed, as when the departure of one's friends "leaves one free" to revert to other pastimes.   It is clear that another cause must be assumed to account for the very different instance in which owing to the absence of one's friends one is "driven to take refuge" in other pastimes.   It is as though there were a constant current of interested activity, which, finding one channel blocked, must of necessity flow in other channels.   This is illustrated by the mutations of old age.   The proximity of death cuts off the prospect of long-range future personal attainment in this world; and the effect is to strengthen interests of another type, such as short-range interests in bodily comfort and the affection of children, or interests in the past, or impersonal interests, or interests in another world.

The most important cases of compensation, however, are those in which negative value is converted into positive, or failure into success.   Not only does the failure of one interest generate or strengthen another, but this compensatory interest somehow redeems the failure or "makes a virtue" of it.   This phenomenon is a familiar incident of daily life as well as a deeply significant aspect of religion and of creative art.   What we begin by coveting we end by despising.   A low-born man is easily persuaded that high birth is a stigma, and that there is a peculiar merit in being one of the people; a poor man eagerly adopts that scale of values which excludes the rich man from the kingdom of heaven; the ignorant man makes a gospel of labor, and prides himself upon his calloused hands.

Thus the Franciscans were accused, not wholly without justice, of despising the learning which they lacked, *because* they lacked it, as "an ass would fain make asses of all that he seeth." [47] Similarly, standards in a social democracy tend to reflect what lies within the range of average attainment. Viewed as a social revolution the success of Christianity was due in no small measure to the fact that it blessed poverty, sorrow, oppression and persecution, and conceived them as a means to the kingdom of heaven.

In all of these cases there is an initial desire which, being hopelessly thwarted, is superseded by a new desire, such that what is evil as judged by the first is good as judged by the second. [48] This proves possible because the failure of one interest, such as the desire for material gain, may be the means to the success of a second, such as the desire for social esteem or for a heavenly reward. The compensatory principle here appears as the tendency of failure to breed or accentuate interests of this second type, having the character of attaching positive instrumental value to that which was in the first instance wholly negative.

But such a conversion of evil into good is also possible because the failure of objective interest may provide the consummation of a subjective interest. Thus an insuperable obstacle which in "real life" is an unmitigated evil may be converted into a foil for the playful activity. [49] Or that which in action is evil may in contemplation be an immediate good. Spinoza, having learned from experience "that all the usual surroundings of life are vain and futile," "resolved to inquire whether there might be some real good . . . which would affect the mind singly, to the exclusion of all else," and the discovery of which would enable him to "enjoy continuous, supreme and unending happiness." [50] He sought, in other words,

[47] G. G. Coulton, *From St. Francis to Dante,* 1906, pp. 78-79.

[48] It is, of course, true that this alteration of values may never pass beyond an *affectation* to despise what one first desired, and that such affectation may through dissociation of conflicting interests, deceive even the individual himself. In this case, however, the affectation itself would still illustrate the operation of the compensatory principle.

[49] Cf. Ch. IX, Sect. II.

[50] *On the Improvement of the Understanding,* trans. by R. H. M. Elwes, 1901, p. 3.

an interest which might be consummated even by that which defeated his other interests, and be believed that he found this in that "intellectual love of God" which delights in truth, however painful.

The poetic fecundity of suffering illustrates this same subjective type of compensation. The sufferings of the poet serve the double purpose of revealing life and of stimulating the exercise of the imagination.

"It is better that poets should be

'Cradled into poesy by wrong,
And learn in suffering what they teach in song,'

than that a door should be opened to those who are the shadow of that of which the poet is the reality,—who are only sentimental, only revolutionary, only uncontrolled. It is better that the world should persecute a Shelley than that it should endure a Saint-Just." [51]

The reference here is to the richness of Shelley's experience, as contrasted with the superficial experience of a spoiled child of fortune, such as Saint-Just. But for the effect of compensation it is not sufficient that one should "learn in suffering,"—one must also sing. It is not even sufficient that the imagination should be stirred. Without the creative impulse or the enjoyment of beauty the imagination serves only to amplify the experience of failure, or intensify it by contrast.

"O, who can hold a fire in his hand
By thinking on the frosty Caucasus?
Or cloy the hungry edge of appetite
By bare imagination of a feast?
Or wallow naked in December snow,
By thinking on fantastic Summer's heat?
O, no! the apprehension of the good
Gives but the greater feeling to the worse."

So long as the only interest is that which is defeated, the imaginary success only seems to heighten real failure. There must be an interest associated with the activity of the imagination itself. This may take the form of a sort of

[51] Fred. W. H. Myers, Essay on Shelley, in T. H. Ward, *English Poets,* 1888, Vol. IV, p. 350.

vicarious satisfaction of the defeated interest, which is possible only when the real situation is forgotten or ignored.[52] Or it may take the form of aesthetic satisfaction. This alone is capable of nourishing itself on the very content of failure.

"Why indeed," asks Francis Thomson, "should it be that the poets who have written for us the poetry richest in skiey grain, most free from admixture with the duller things of earth—the Shelleys, the Coleridges, the Keatses—are the very poets whose lives are among the saddest records in literature? Is it that (by some subtile mystery of analogy) sorrow, passion, and fantasy are indissolubly connected, like water, fire, and cloud; that as from the sun and dew are born the vapours, so from fire and tears ascend the 'visions of aërial joy' . . . ? Such a poet, it may be, mists with sighs the window of his life until the tears run down it; then some air of searching poetry, like an air of searching frost, turns it to a crystal wonder."[53]

In other words, sighs and tears do not suffice, even when they are imaginatively projected, without "some air of searching poetry."

§ 233. **Compatibility and Mood.** While at times, through the principle of compensation, the several interests of a subject manifest a sort of inverse proportionality, so at other times they appear to rise or fall together. Compensation suggests a constant quantity of energy which can be drawn into one interest only by being withdrawn from others, or which driven from one interest seeks an outlet in others. The diffusive effect which appears in moodiness, on the other hand, suggests that the total energy somehow varies with the success or failure of any interest.

There is, for example, the buoyant mood, or self-confidence, indicated in the aphorism "nothing succeeds like success." The conviction begotten by one verified expectation seems somehow to be transferable to other as yet unverified

---

[52] Cf. § 103. Such vicarious satisfaction tends to become illusory, through habitual neglect of the painful reality, or through dissociation. A special case of vicarious satisfaction is afforded by parasitic satisfaction, as exemplified by the hanger-on or toady, who, for lack of success of his own, lives in the reflected success of others.

[53] *Works,* 1913, Vol. III, pp. 35-36.

expectations, and so to assume the form of a general auspiciousness attaching to all the circumstances of life. This
effect is constantly assumed in education and in the cultivation
of morale.[54] The child is encouraged to attack more difficult
tasks by the preliminary experience of minor successes.
Soldiers are prepared for battle not only by the memory of
former victories in battle, but by such attention to their
bodily comforts or social needs as shall beget a general hopefulness of the outcome of anything they may undertake. Indeed, so specific and so potent is this factor that it is necessary
in both cases to guard against over-confidence, which is the
divorce of expectation from specific experience, or the careless
assumption that success in one thing guarantees success in
another. Just enough success will act as a tonic, but too
much will act as an opiate or intoxicant.

The opposite effect is not less familiar. The loss of confidence in one thing may lead to the loss of confidence in every
thing. A child should not be allowed to fail repeatedly, but
should be given some other task that he can successfully perform. Troops repeatedly defeated become demoralized and
have to be withdrawn from the line until their confidence
is restored. Repeated failure may generate a superstitious
belief in some malign agency or "jinx," which casts its
shadow of doubt upon a wholly new and different enterprise.
This phenomenon is in part the converse of that general
hopefulness or buoyancy which is generated by success. But
there is also another factor. Failure tends to·become an
obsession. The unsuccessful effort is never completed, and
exerts an evil fascination; one nurses grievances or broods
upon futility. Instead of a spread of despair from one field
to the whole of life, there is a concentration of life in some
sphere of failure where despair is aggravated by a sort of
obstinate renewal of impotent effort.

§ 234. **Consistency, Alliance and Objective Conflict.**
We have been thus far dealing with those interactive rela-

[54] Morale has to do more specifically with the relation of an integral
or higher interest, to a lower or constituent interest.

tions of the interests of one subject, which lie below the rational level. Their compatibility, incompatibility or reinforcement, and the compensatory or diffusive changes resulting therefrom, are independent of their objects. We turn next to those mutations which result from the inter-objective relations of interests, including the case in which one interest is the object of another.

Agreement of interest within the same subject does not mean the identity of their objects, for this would destroy their diversity altogether. But the objects of two interests of the same subject may be consistent with one another, either in the negative sense of being free from contradiction; or allied with one another, in the positive, implicative sense of being related as means and end. Thus an agent's desire for gain may be consistent with an amiable interest in the prosperity of others. The agent, seeing that the two objects do not contradict one another, judges that he can "afford" to indulge his benevolence. There is in this case no augmentation of either interest, but merely a recognized absence of conflict arising from the judgment of the one in terms of the other. This is different from the case in which the agent judges that the prosperity of others will indirectly redound to his own advantage. Assuming that the amiable or humane interest exists in this as in the former case, its gratification is now seen to imply the promotion of the vocational interest. The result is that each of the subject's interests supports the other. He may go about his business with good will, and help others with an eagerness partially borrowed from personal ambition.

Similarly, the acquisitive interest in the possession of precious objects, and the pride in the exclusive control of coveted objects, may ally themselves with the aesthetic interest in their contemplation. Here the various relations of the same physical thing, its possession, its accessibility to observation, and the exclusion of others from its control, all imply one another. The same situation obtains in the case of the sentiment of love towards a person. The fears, the tenderness, the appetites and the ambitions of the lover are all satisfied by states of the beloved which imply one another, so that all of the interests in question are capable reciprocally of providing dominant or subordinate motives. Whichever takes the lead is supported by the rest.

Interests conflict in so far as their objects are contradictory. This contradiction may be direct or indirect, according as the object of one is the contradictory of the other, or only implies the contradictory of the other through a more or less extended series of intermediate steps. Where ends are remote, such contradictions may be concealed and are brought to light, if at all, only by a thorough-going process of reflection. In such cases conflicting interests are entirely compatible,—one may enlist in the service of both God and Mammon. If the preservation of the two interests were the desideratum, it might be argued that in such cases ignorance is bliss.

Where the interests of one subject are known by that subject to be contradictory, each becomes the object of a negative interest generated by the other. Suppose, for example, that one has both an aesthetic or sentimental, and an economic interest, in the same region of nature. The first interest takes the form of a desire that the landscape shall remain untouched, and the second takes the form of a desire that the soil shall be exposed to the sun and cultivated. The first interest is consummated by the preservation, and the second by the demolition, of the same forest. Where this is recognized, the aesthetic or sentimental interest inspires a subordinate negative interest in the satisfaction of the economic interest, and *vice versa*. When reduced to this form, the conflict is inescapable and irreconcilable. The one wishes the defeat of the other, as a means to its own success. Borrowing a term which is ordinarily applied to the social relation, we may say that the one interest is maliciously disposed to the other. So long as malice remains, reconciliation is impossible.

The effects of objective conflict are of three types. One interest may yield and eventually succumb to the other. Thus in the case just supposed the economic interest may have its way, and the aesthetic or sentimental interest may atrophy and disappear as a result of repeated failure. Or, secondly, the interests may continue in a state of conflict. The attempt to eradicate the physical appetites assumes this form, as when the ascetic hates his own bodily pleasures without extinguishing them, while these in their turn resent the religious ideal which antagonizes them. The personality is divided against itself and cannot succeed without failing. Or, thirdly, the result may be one of personal disintegration. The bodily pleasures being intolerable from the stand-point of the religious ideal, and the religious ideal intolerable from the stand-point of the bodily pleasures, each may forget the other, and be indulged in turn. But this disintegrating effect of failure is peculiarly characteristic of the reconstructed forms of personality to which we now turn.

§ 235. **Reconstructive Integration.** Up to this point we have considered integration as involving no more than the mediation of interest by interest. One interest being judged in the light of another interest as consistent or contradictory, is welcomed as an ally, or opposed as an enemy. We have assumed that the interests are unalterable, and that the integration of personality does no more than bring to light and render effective the consistencies and contradictions that already exist. In so far as there are such consistencies and implications the effect of integration is to provide each interest with an augmented motivation, and to enable the subject, now become a person, to do with an easy mind or a whole heart each thing that he is independently disposed to do. But, in so far, on the other hand, as there are contradictions, personal integration in this limited sense serves only to aggravate them, or to convert blind conflict into conscious and malicious discord. In this first and limited sense personality may be a source of division as truly as of union.

In a second sense, which we have now to consider, personal integration means the mitigation or removal of conflict and the substitution of harmony. It is only through the successful achievement of integration in this second sense that personality can be guaranteed against the divisive effect of integration in the first sense.

The mitigation or removal of conflict presupposes that contradictory interests may somehow be altered without losing their identity. Malice must, as we have seen, be irreconcilable, but it is always possible that malice is a specific form assumed by an interest which may be otherwise expressed. The case here rests upon the fact that all interests are modifiable. The interest is more general than its consummation, and the further one rises towards the source of interest the wider the range of its possible satisfactions. The general interest becomes specified through the environment, and tends in this specified form to be fixated by habit, but such specifications need never be regarded as fatalities. The same modifiability which permits of specification permits of alternative specification, and of reëducation through the substitution of another eligible object for that which has proved discordant. The hope of human regeneration may be said to rest on the broad fact that the several interests of man are not *necessarily* contradictory. Their existing contradictions lie upon some superficial level of circumstance and habit,—by going back to their deeper roots it is possible to find objects which are both eligible and mutually consistent. The relatively ineradicable interests, such as sex, hunger, fear, pugnacity or acquisitiveness, are relatively plastic, so that even though they be absolutely ineradicable (as the exponents of instinct would have it) they present no insuperable difficulty. Not even the extremest or most cynical advocate of instincts would hold that asceticism, jealousy, malice, hate, robbery and killing are innate and immutable human traits; and anything short of that justifies the hope, born of necessity, that they may be superseded.

Reconstructive integration means, then, the attempt to find equivalent values that shall be mutually consistent. Their equivalence is qualified by their consistency. They possess what James has termed *"moral* equivalence." [55] This does

---

[55] Cf. "The Moral Equivalent of War," *Memories and Studies,* 1911, p. 267.

not imply, for example, that the subjugation of inanimate
nature affords as adequate a satisfaction of pugnacity itself
as does war, but that it does satisfy pugnacity and satisfies it
as adequately as is consistent with the satisfaction of other
interests.[56] On the other hand, the constructive ideal embraces
the original interests and derives its motivation from them.
For two contradictory objects there is substituted a single
self-consistent object, which is eligible to both interests and
permits of their harmonious exercise.   On the other hand,
however, the constructive ideal does not give free rein to
its constituent interests.   Where conditions are favorable the
original interest may reassert itself blindly, or return to its
old and contradictory objects.   The most notable example of
this is afforded by the behavior of crowds, in which the contagious appeal to elemental impulses breaks down the control
of personal integration.[57]   Personality, in other words, is always threatened with internal rebellion fomented and supported abroad.   A constructive ideal once formed is thus
afflicted with its own characteristic vicissitudes.   To some of
these we now turn.

§ 236. **The Failure of Integration.**   The term 'morale'
applies properly to the state of a constructive ideal, and refers
to the conviction and hopefulness with which such an ideal is
pursued despite the cost which it entails.   The problem arises
from the fact that the ideal does not fully satisfy the original
demands of the constituent interests.   These constituent interests have a sort of inertia, as well as the strategic advantage
of being first in possession of the field.   Their native strength
is perpetually renewed by exciting stimuli and suggestive examples.   Over against them stand principles, purposes, ideals,
and duties;—cold, spectral things with no elemental appeal,
and yet claiming authority over the impulses.   The man who
serves them grudgingly, half-heartedly, intermittently, or pain-
fully,—who is embittered or thrown into inner conflict and
disorder by them—is said to have a low morale.   The man

---

[56] For a further consideration of this problem, cf. § 261.
[57] Cf. § 182.

with a high morale, on the other hand, is he whose emotional life runs with his duty; who loves his ideal, hungers and thirsts after righteousness, and is not only unwearied, but positively happy, in well-doing.

The methods of cultivating and sustaining morale have received special attention in modern war, though they are applicable to every phase and level of life.[58]   Such methods are founded on two principles.   In the first place, the constituent interests must be drafted to the support of the ideal, or the ideal so construed as to appeal to them and enlist their ungrudging support.   In the second place, the individual's idealism must be strengthened by collective *esprit;* the ideal must be represented by symbols, and contagiously manifested in the behavior of others.[59]   It is evident that of these two principles the former is the more fundamental.   A morale which is based on collective enthusiasm is unstable and subject to sharp fluctuations.   Morale is permanently achieved only when the several interests of the person are so completely absorbed as to have no object save that which is contained in or permitted by the ideal.

We are now in a position to understand those mutations of interest and value which arise from the failure of integration.   All such failure may properly be termed 'disintegration,' or (since morale and integration are the same thing) 'demoralization.'   There is conflict between "the earlier, primitively dominant centres of control and the imposed rule of the later, more highly developed but less securely evolved regulations . . . a shift of control inadequately established in nature and nurture." [60]   But there are two quite distinct forms of disintegration.   The simplest and most obvious form is *moral reaction.*   This signifies the reassertion of elementary constituent interests, which having been checked without being assimilated, at length break through the limits imposed on

---

[58] Cf. the author's "Morale in Peace Time," *Connecticut College Bulletin,* 1919, pp. 14-31.   Cf. also W. E. Hocking, *Morale and its Enemies,* 1918; G. Stanley Hall, *Morale, the Supreme Standard of Life and Conduct,* 1920.

[59] Cf. § 188, and Ch. XVII, Sect. III.

[60] J. Jastrow, *Character and Temperament,* 1915, p. 334.

them. This phenomenon is in principle the same as that positive effect of failure which we have already considered, in which a thwarted interest accumulates force during its period of latency, and manifests augmented vigor when it is released.[61] The only difference is that in this case the reaction involves two different levels of interest, and is due not to total repression but to incomplete expression.

The best examples of moral reaction are afforded by cases in which the integration arises from peculiar external conditions without a genuine transformation of character. Moral exaltation which is produced by religious revivals, or in time of war or revolution, when all circumstances conspire to strengthen the emotional appeal of the ideal and to check the original impulses, is commonly followed, when these circumstances are altered, by a period of moral depression. Interests which have been willingly and enthusiastically curtailed now demand indulgence and tend to excess. The same phenomenon may occur, independently of social relations, as a result of continued failure and discouragement. When the situation becomes wholly inauspicious relatively to the ideal, or arouses only a sense of futility and impotence, the individual seeks a line of less resistance and finds consolation in the easier task of satisfying his elementary interests, such as those of food or sex.

§ 237. **Specious Integration and Self-Deception.** Moral reaction may be perfectly candid and truthful. Indeed such terms as 'disillusionment' and 'cynicism' suggest that the abandonment of ideals is accompanied by a relative clearness of vision. It implies moral failure and degradation, but not intellectual disability. It is this latter factor which distinguishes the second form of disintegration, and gives it its pathological character. The first form of disintegration was recognized failure; the second form is specious success, or success founded on self-deception. Integration involves as we have seen, the sublimation of original interests, or their recasting in such shape as shall render them consistent. But the mediating

[61] Cf. § 226.

judgment through which this contradiction or consistency comes to light, may be mistaken. Interests which are really contradictory may seem not to be so owing to ignorance or error. Over and above the error to which mortal mind is proverbially liable, but which experience reduces and corrects, there is a pathological error which is due to an unwillingness to face the facts. This type of error may be said to be universal and chronic, inasmuch as an interest always tends to color its mediating judgments.[62] But it may exist in a degree that is more or less abnormal and incurable. Where such error affects the inter-mediation of interests, and is the basis of a specious integration, there arises that sort of soul-sickness to which psycho-analysis has recently given prominence.

Let us consider, for example, the statement that "the real conflicts of the soul are not between good and evil, but between rationalized good, and what is truly right." [63] That which is "truly right" is that form of any given interest which, being consistent with other interests, enters harmoniously into the personal ideal. The "rationalized good," on the other hand, is that false interpretation of the present form of the interest, which makes it *seem* so consistent when it really is not. The subject obtains a specious solution of conflict by leaving the interest as it was, while rendering it palatable to the ideal by attributing to it relations and consequences which it really does not possess. In this way the individual defeats himself by deceiving himself.[64] His failure is irretrievable in so far as he is incapable of "facing" the truth about his own interests, and therefore of really and successfully sublimating them. Suppose, for example, a conflict between avarice and a general benevolent purpose. The conflict is soluble only when the individual, judging his avarice to contradict his benevolence, so alters his desire for this world's goods as to fit it into a general plan of human amelioration. But his benevolence may have the effect of making his avarice so repugnant to him that he ignores it, refuses to acknowledge

[62] Cf. § 142.
[63] F. L. Wells, *Mental Adjustments*, 1917, p. 14.
[64] That which is vicious in such a process is not rationalization, but *false* rationalization. Cf. Ch. XIII, Sect. V.

it, or misrepresents it. The result is to leave his avarice undisturbed and so to perpetuate the conflict.

§ 238. **Illustrations from Psycho-analysis.** It is customary among psycho-analysts to speak of the interest which is repressed, without being either extinguished or absorbed, as 'unconscious.' This can scarcely mean to refer to that state of latency in which all interests exist during the greater part of their history. A repressed interest or complex is not simply an inactive interest. The very term 'repression' implies conflict and interaction,—not the mere superseding of one interest by another. But if the repressed interest is excited, it must be conscious. That effective anticipation in which interest consists is the very essence of consciousness. The difficulty arises from ambiguity. Conscious interest may mean either one of two things: it may mean that the interest itself is conscious of its object, or it may mean that there is a consciousness of the interest. Active interest must, by definition, be conscious in the first sense, but it need not be conscious in the second. It is precisely this which is meant when it is said that one fails to acknowledge one's interests even to oneself. The unconsciousness of interest refers here not to the absence of the internal interest-judgment (without which interest is impossible), but either to the absence of a judgment of interest, or to the presence of a judgment which misrepresents the interest. The interest *of* which the subject is unconscious, in this second sense, may be wholly dissociated from the dominant system of interests, and assume the form of an unremembered secondary personality; or it may be partially dissociated, as in the case of the remembered dream; or it may be present in disguise. The psycho-analyst is chiefly interested in cases of this third type, and finds even dreams to be disguised, despite the fact that they occur when the censorious personality is off-guard.[65] The psycho-analytical unconscious becomes essentially that which is present in such a form as to disguise its true inwardness to the personal con-

[65] How far memory reëdits dreams to satisfy the demands of waking consciousness is, of course, never perfectly clear.

sciousness, while betraying it to the psycho-analyst. It employs symbols which both falsify and reveal it.

Thus Nebuchadnezzar, suffering from illusions of grandeur, dreams of his downfall. His fears, intolerable to his conscious almightiness, assert themselves symbolically in his sleep.[66] The self-righteous man unconsciously betrays a sense of guilt, and the philanthropist his misanthropy. The alcoholic paranoiac who has ceased to love his wife, but refuses to acknowledge the fact because it contradicts his moral purpose, manifests jealousy. By believing in his wife's infidelity he may treat her with real aversion, and yet in a manner consistent with the assumption that he still loves her. His jealousy (which is also real) is mediated by a false judgment which reconciles his aversion with his standard of loyalty. His dislike of his wife is not intrinsically unconscious, for his behavior is actually induced by the anticipation of the evils which he inflicts upon her; but his jealousy obscures this fact, enabling him to view his conduct as a manifestation of love. This same analysis will apply to those cases of shell-shock in which the subject, ashamed of his fear, and unwilling to acknowledge it even to himself, develops 'symptoms' which enable him to act on his fear and escape its object, without violation of his duty; or to the excessively self-reliant inventor who, by believing himself to be the victim of persecution, can account for his failure without recognizing his incompetence; or to the fanatic who hides his doubts by projecting them, and escapes self-reproach by a furious persecution of others.

In all of these cases the pathological state consists in the fact that the subject possesses a false belief generated by conflict, and so useful as a means of escaping conflict that it is abnormally impervious to the facts. He has obtained a specious solution of his conflict, or a solution founded on error, which stands in the way of his obtaining a genuine solution, founded on truth.[67]

---

[66] This and the following examples are taken for the most part from C. G. Jung, *Collected Papers on Analytical Psychology*, trans. by C. E. Long, 1916, pp. 280-285. For an examination of the neurasthenic and hysteric effects of imperfect integration, cf. J. Jastrow, *op. cit.*, Ch. VI.

[67] Furthermore, the incorrigibility of his basic error is readily extended

The mighty controversy that has divided the camp of the
psycho-analysts throws additional light on this type of disintegration. Professor Freud and Dr. Alfred Adler tend to
identify interest in general with that type of interest which
in personal or moral integration is *subordinated,* while Dr.
Jung identifies it with that type of interest which is *dominant.*[68] It follows that while all three interpret the same
phenomena as failure to secure a genuine solution of conflict,
they tend to construe this failure in different terms. The
same conflict which Freud will construe as a frustration of
sex, or Adler as a frustration of primal selfishness, Jung
will construe as a frustration of personality, and of that
more adequate adaptation to which the individual is attempting
to rise. What with Freud receives a retrospective, causal and
atavistic interpretation, receives from Jung a prospective,
teleological and ideal interpretation. There is, however, no
necessary contradiction between these views. Jung is correct in insisting that the problem of the harmonious unification
of manifold activities through discipline and organization, is
an inescapable problem. Freud is correct, on the other hand,
in affirming that these higher ideals can succeed in accomplish-
ing their integrative function only in so far as they reconcile
and assimilate the original impulses on which they are imposed. The solution lies neither in harsh repression, nor in
loose decentralization; but in the creation of comprehensive
purposes, which enjoy the support of their constituent interests
because they make the most liberal possible provision for
them all.

to whatever further judgments may be necessary to support it. His
whole cognitive field is distorted, and he is so far inaccessible to facts
as to make him incapable of adaptation to his natural or social environment.
    [68] For a comparative statement of these three views, cf. B. M. Hinkle,
The Re-creating of the Individual, 1923, Introduction; C. G. Jung, *Collected Papers on Analytical Psychology,* trans. by C. E. Long, 1916,
pp. 220 ff. Both accounts are favorable to Jung. I do not attempt to
settle this controversy, but only to use it for purposes of illustration.
Still less do I intend any general or unqualified acceptance of the teach-
ings of psycho-analysis.

III. LARGE-SCALE MUTATIONS

§ 239. **Revolutionary Mutations.** The detailed examination of the several causes of mutation has obscured certain broad aspects of the question which deserve at least a brief mention, both for the purpose of summarizing results already obtained, and for the purpose of suggesting their further extension. Changes of value sometimes occur on a grand scale. They may be profound, far-reaching and catastrophic; or they may be epoch-making, and appear as stages in a cyclical or progressive movement which embraces the whole of human history. Such changes serve both as a test of the adequacy of any theory of mutation, and as a field for its application.

Changes are said to be revolutionary when they are all-pervasive, or sudden, or contrary, or when they combine these characteristics. Any of the four principles of mutation which we have considered may play the leading part in revolutionary change thus defined.

Any cognitive change which alters the presuppositions or mediating judgments *common* to a multitude of interests will induce changes in *all* of these interests. The most notable cases of such changes that European history affords are the Copernican theory of the cosmos, and the theory of the natural evolution of man. The older theory of the cosmos taught man to regard himself as the focal point of creation, and the earth as the stage on which God directed the drama of salvation from his place in the heavens. The older theory of human origins taught man to believe in his supernatural creation, nature and destiny. On these two premises the Christian believer based his total plan of life, both his individual projects, and his organized institutions. All that was built on these foundations had to be rebuilt when these foundations were shaken, and there has resulted the revolutionary change from mediaeval to modern Christendom.

The far-reaching change in European civilization ascribed to economic causes may also be interpreted in terms of the cognitive factor, as an effect of interpolation on a wide scale. Scientific discovery invented new tools and opened new channels by which man might satisfy his needs. These instrumentalities became ends in their turn, and the fecundity of science has led both to their vast accumulation and to man's greater preoccupation with them. What was once but the means of satisfying hunger or of securing shelter has become to the individual a career and to the community an enterprise. As compared with antiquity or with the thirteenth century, this change also, is sufficiently massive and radical to deserve the name of revolution.

The effect of *contagion* may also be revolutionary. It is of the very essence of this principle that its effects should be widely diffused. The development of communication has in modern times greatly enlarged its radius of action. By virtue of the high and far-reaching conductivity of modern society, both within and across the lines of nationality, a change once inaugurated is likely to sweep the field. There is also in this principle a source of sudden change. There is a crucial point in the emotion of a crowd or in the milder sentiment of the public, when it has gathered force enough to be irresistible. Its effects are then so swift as to seem even to outstrip the agencies by which they are communicated, as though the change were simultaneously and independently generated in each part.

Failure and success may, as we have seen, have the effect of inducing abrupt changes and reversals. Where interests are similar or common throughout a social group the reactions due to fatigue, satiety and excessive familiarity, or the emotional excitement aroused by resistance, may occur on the same grand scale.

Especially profound and far-reaching are the changes due to the *interaction* of interests. The physical changes occurring below the threshold of interest may have wholesale as well as local effects. As changes of health or age may alter the whole cast of an individual life, so pestilence, exhaustion of natural resources or the ravages of war may revolutionize the interests of a society great or small.[69] Such mutations, like

[69] For a statement of the doubtful thesis that entire civilizations pass through the cycles of *youth* and *age*, cf. O. Spengler, *Der Untergang des Abendlandes,* 1919.

their lesser counterparts, lie outside the limits of a theory of value. But through the existence of common and mutual interests, a society, or even the total system of contemporaneous mankind, may exhibit the operation of the principle of compensation. Interest focussed at one point is withdrawn from others; and a frustrated interest vents itself by indirection, sublimation or substitution. This is illustrated, for example, by the general redistribution of interest occasioned by war. Just as travel and hardships may alter the whole scale of an individual's values, and by evoking new objective or social interests draw his energies away from those petty indulgences for which he once lived,[70] so in war, the intense concentration of a whole community upon the vital and common interests which are at stake, reduces to tepid insignificance the burning ambitions and anxieties of every-day life. Emergencies change the total perspective and alter every detail of the picture, as does that philosophical imagination, of which Plato asks, "Then how can he who has magnificence of mind and is the spectator of all time and all existence, think much of human life?" [71]

The mutations incidental to *integration* may also assume a revolutionary form. The underlying fact is one of a conflict of opposites, so that a change is likely to be a general change of direction and not merely a change of quality or of emphasis. What was denied is now affirmed, and what was affirmed denied. Since the issue is one of control the change is, furthermore, likely to be abrupt rather than continuous. The conditions which pave the way for an insurrection or *coup d'état* may accumulate gradually, but the breach or assumption of authority will commonly occur at a crucial moment when these conditions are ripe.[72]

---

[70] Cf., *e.g.*, the transformation of the character of the young Martin, in Dickens, *Martin Chuzzlewit.*

[71] Emergencies so alter the proportions of things as to reduce *differences* of value to *equality.* "Nobody does shout out at sea, 'Bad citizen overboard.'" (G. K. Chesterton, *George Bernard Shaw*, 1909, pp. 214-215.)

[72] For sudden reversals of this type in the personal life, cf. James's discussion of "conversion" and "counter-conversion" in his *Varieties of Religious Experience*, Lect. IX, X. The crisis is sudden though the way may be prepared by "subconscious incubation" (p. 25).

But the process of integration may give rise to changes which are revolutionary in the sense of being radical and far-reaching, but which are epochal rather than sudden. Nietzsche has shown that the moral code of Christendom is revolutionary in this sense. The system of values which reigned in antiquity was founded on "the privilege of the fewest." It was the "chivalric-aristocratic" code: "good = noble = powerful = beautiful = happy = beloved of God." It implied pride and *noblesse oblige* on the part of the ruling caste, with submissive admiration on the part of inferiors. The Jewish-Christian "slave-insurrection," on the other hand, asserted "the right of the most." Interests hitherto subordinated or repressed "resentfully" conspired to introduce a new régime in which their claims should be more fully allowed at the expense of their priveleged superiors. Since the two systems are essentially orders or hierarchies of value, in which control and subordination are all-important, and since they are "antithetical," the change from one to another involves a *de*-valuing and a *re*-valuing of old values. What was noble under the one system becomes wicked under the other, and what was ignoble becomes saintly and blessed. There is a *reversal* or transvaluation of all values (*"Umwerthung alle Werthe"*).[73]

§ 240. **Mutation and Progress.** In order that a mutation of value may be said to be progressive in the complete sense, it must exhibit two characteristics. In the first place, it must be a mutation whose direction is constant throughout history, and which therefore makes it possible to subsume all history, or some considerable portion of it, under one formula.[74] In the second place, it must be a change which rises in the scale of values; a change, in other words, *for the better.*[75] It is evident that this second factor of progress can be ex-

---

[73] *Genealogy of Morals*, trans. by W. A. Haussmann, 1897, pp. 58, 29, 31, 35, 55 and *passim; Will to Power*, trans. by M. Ludovici, 1909, sub-title.

[74] Even a cyclical theory of history implies that life moves around the circle in a constant direction.

[75] Cf. the author's *Moral Economy*, 1905, Ch. IV.

amined only in the light of that question of *comparative* value to which we turn in the next chapter. But it will be instructive to ask at this point whether any of the principles of mutation which have been brought to light suggest any constant or irreversible change which pervades human life as a whole.

There appears to be at least one principle on which philosophers of history of all schools are agreed, namely, the increase of knowledge. There are, no doubt, losses of knowledge; but, on the whole, the gain is greater than the loss. Assuming that there is no world-wide disaster or cataclysm which destroys the racial memory or the records of the past, the sum of human knowledge both increases in amount and becomes more readily accessible to individuals. Such changes of value as are conditioned by this increase of knowledge will have that historical constancy of which we are in search.

It is true, for example, that all values tend to be more elaborately mediated. Interests operate in an effective environment which is being steadily expanded and complicated; the horizon recedes at the same time that the foreground is more congested. It does not follow that there is an increased hopefulness or sense of power, for there are more objects to be feared as well as more objects to be used or enjoyed. Every new annexation enlarges the boundary to be defended as well as the resources to be exploited. And the sense of ignorance may grow rather than diminish as knowledge increases. It is true that knowledge is fecund, and that the solution of one problem paves the way for the solution of others; but it also raises new problems, so that the work done does not appear to reduce the work to *be* done. There is, however, an increase in the conscious bearings of all interested activity, a multiplication of alternatives and of relevant considerations. All interests tend, for better or for worse, to become more thoughtful and more calculating.

In the second place, the increase of knowledge, and in particular its accessibility to the individual, tends to weaken the effect of habit, custom, authority and other conservative influences, and so to increase the rate of change. The most striking thing, for example, about the "new physics" [76] is not its revolutionary character, but the rapidity with which the revolution has permeated the mind of mankind. The difference between the stubbornness with which in the sixteenth and seventeenth centuries men clung to the belief in the centrality and immobility of the earth, and the readiness with which in the twentieth century they abandon the no less popular belief in the absoluteness of space and time, is of the highest historical significance. But this principle of acceleration has also its compensatory effect. As the rate of change increases there is also a growing recognition of the fact, so that change is anticipated and discounted. The unexpected is expected, and the surprising no longer surprises. At the same time that change is accelerated it can more readily be assimilated to constant and far-reaching purposes.[77]

Finally, there is a tendency to the diversification of interests.[78] The multiplication of their objects tends to their diverse specification, and the multiplication of their means tends by interpolation to the generation of new ends. The saving effect is the greater integration which comes from the knowledge of their interrelations. There is an increase of unity that offsets, and renders humanly possible, the increase of complexity.[79]

A philosophy of history would, then, seek first to formulate those principles, such as increasing mediation, acceleration and diversification, which define the general course of events. This would be its descriptive task. Then, in the second place, it would seek by some critical standard of comparative value, to determine whether or how far the direction of this trend coincides with an upward movement in the scale of values.

[76] The theory of relativity and the quantum theory.

[77] This is not inconsistent with the fact that the power of prediction renders the future less predictable. It is less predictable to a second observer, but the primary effect of prediction is to permit of a certain steadiness and consecutiveness of life.

[78] Cf. § 219.

[79] This is the Spencerian principle of the concomitant increase of heterogeneity and coherence.

CHAPTER XX

THE CRITIQUE OF VALUE

I. INTRODUCTION

§ 241. **Generic and Comparative Value.** The problem to which we now turn is one which has been often encountered in the course of our previous discussions and as often postponed to a more convenient occasion. There is, however, something more than mere convenience in this postponement. Values do not have to be *evaluated* in order to be values. Furthermore, the solution of the relatively complex problem of evaluation or comparative valuation depends on the solution of the relatively simple problem of valuation. The meaning of 'better' and 'best' can properly be examined only after, and in the light of, some conclusion regarding the meaning of 'good.'

There are tendencies both in common-sense and in philosophy to confuse these two problems.[1] When confronted with the opinion that anything desired is *ipso facto* good, moral common-sense appeals to the fact that desires are overruled and condemned by conscience. Inclination, it is said, can scarcely be trusted to define the good, since it so frequently runs counter to duty. This argument virtually implies that what is in any sense evil, or what is less than the best, cannot be good at all.

Another familiar and instructive source of confusion is that type of theory which defines value in terms of a qualified interest, such as persistent disposition, or personal will, or social will, or universal will, or love of God.[2] The confusion

[1] Cf. § 8.
[2] Cf. Ch. IV.

arises from arguing that such a will is the *only* will, and therefore the unique source of value, when it is plainly a special form of will distinguished from or analyzable into other forms of will. That these other forms of will are in some sense lower or inferior does not disqualify them from defining values, even though these values will also be lower or inferior. To assert that a value begins at a certain level of value is as though one were to say that temperature begins at the freezing point or at the boiling point.[3]

While the problem of comparative value is a distinct problem over and above that of generic value, it has to be guarded against the same sort of misunderstanding. It is, for example, a problem of definition rather than of attribution. Just as the problem of generic value is to determine the meaning of 'good,' 'evil' or 'valuable,' rather than to discover cases of them, so the problem of comparative value is to determine the meaning of 'better,' 'best,' 'worse,' 'worst' or 'more' and 'less' valuable, rather than to discover what, if anything, has these characters.[4] It would not be proper, therefore, to state our problem in the form of the question, "What is most worth while?", for ours is the preliminary task of determining what it means to say that one thing is worth more than another. Still less is it proper to ask, "What is that which we all most desire?", inasmuch as this question makes two preliminary assumptions: first, that there is a preference which is both universal and supreme; second, that the object of such a preference would be the best. The first of these assumptions is contrary to fact,[5] while the second, whether true or false, begs the very question which constitutes our problem.

The problem of comparative value, like the problem of generic value, is not to be solved by an expression of personal

---

[3] Mill has been the butt of philosophical critics for introducing an undefined principle of value for the purpose of grading values, but many of these same critics have committed the equal and converse error of presupposing an undefined principle of value in that which is graded. For an example of this illegitimate reduction of generic to comparative value, cf. C. Berguer, *La Notion de Valeur*, 1908, pp. 353-354.

[4] Cf. § 7. For a discussion of the view that 'better' is indefinable, cf. § 18.

[5] Cf. Ch. IV, Sect. III.

bias.[6] If, upon being asked what goodness' is, I give expression to my own likings or desires, either my reply is irrelevant, or it begs the question. Similarly, if, upon being asked what 'better' is, I manifest my personal preference, I assume that the better is the preferred, which is the fundamental point at issue; and I assume that there is something authoritative about *my* preference, which is also open to question. Impressionistic criticism thus presupposes standardized criticism, or the application of principles, and it is with the latter rather than with the former that theory of value is primarily concerned.

The confusion arising from a failure to determine the relations between interest and judgment [7] also arises in connection with comparative value, and especially in relation to the conception of *preference*. This term, like 'appreciation' and 'valuation,' is frequently so employed as to obscure the difference between judgment and interest, thus embodying a claim to truth without liability to error. But if 'I prefer *a* to *b*' means '*a* is better than *b*' then it is a judgment, whose truth is subject to evidence depending on the meaning of 'better'; while if it means 'I like *a* rather than *b*,' then it is a motor-affective fact which *constitutes* such evidence, on the assumption that such comparative liking constitutes what is meant by 'better.' Preference in the former sense is a comparative rating or estimate of values, and it may be as apathetic as the judgment "3 is greater than 2"; preference in the second sense is a state or relation of comparative interest, which, as such, has no judicial status whatsoever. With a view to the avoidance of this ambiguity the term 'preference' will hereinafter be used in the second of these senses, to refer to the fact that a subject is in some sense more interested; while the expression 'judgment of comparative value' will be used, wherever necessary, to indicate the predication of such terms as 'better' and 'best,' including the case in which these are supposed to consist in the motor-affective fact of preference.

[6] Cf. § 6.
[7] Cf. Ch. XI, XII.

Although the fact of preference is thus distinguished from the judgment of 'better,' it does none the less have its factor of *mediation*. Preference, like interest of the simpler type, is always founded on cognition, and in this case it would appear that at least two objects must be presented or represented. That *a* should be preferred to *b* implies a cognition both of *a* and of *b*. That *a* and *b* must be *compared*, or that preference must be mediated by a judgment of comparison, does not follow, though it is evident that this will often be the case. In any case preference, like interest, is fallible in so far as the objects among which the preference selects may or may not be what they are *taken to be*. In this sense there may be said to be a 'preference-judgment,' just as there is an interest-judgment.

The expression 'evaluation' [8] requires a similar clarification. It is commonly used in four quite distinct senses. Sometimes 'evaluation' means a judgment of comparative value, to the effect that *a* is better than *b*. Sometimes it means an interest or preference that is highly mediated, as contrasted with one that is relatively thoughtless; as when I prefer *a* to *b* with circumspection, having considered both objects carefully in relation to other objects, or having considered the bearing of the interests immediately concerned on those more remotely concerned. Sometimes it means the testing of such mediating judgments as are already made, with a view to securing an interest founded on truth rather than on error. This we shall speak of as 'the correction of interest.' Such correction may equally well be applied to preference. Finally, 'evaluation' may mean 'cross-valuation,' or a judgment of value applied to an object which already has value of another type; as when a pleasure is judged to be ignoble, or virtue to be cheap.

§ 242. **Formulation of the Problem.** These preliminary ambiguities being removed we are now in a position to define

---

[8] W. M. Urban and others use the term "axiology" (from the Greek ἀξιόλογος) to denote this topic (cf. his *Valuation*, 1909, pp. 16 ff.) ; and hold that a value is not a value at all until it is validated, as knowledge is not knowledge unless it is true.

our problem. What is that condition of an object in virtue of which it may be said to be better (or worse) than another object, or the best (or worst) among several objects, and which would therefore render true a judgment of comparative or superlative value? There are several facts which may be affirmed at once, subject to a further clarification.

In the first place, the condition in question must be in some sense quantitative, and must render the several objects in question in some sense commensurable. "The comparative form in grammar," says Mr. Bertrand Russell, "is *prima facie* evidence of quantity." [9] The quantitative method is regarded by many writers as unworthy of the subject of values, and a special odium attaches to Bentham's attempted measurement of pleasures and pains. Nevertheless, the very writers who scorn the hedonic calculus do not hesitate on their own account to speak of 'higher' and 'lower,' or of 'degrees,' terms which are not less quantitative than Bentham's, but only less precise.

In the second place, if one object is better than another it must be better in respect of the same condition that renders it good, or worse in the same respect that renders it evil. It must be not only more or less, but more or less *valuable*. Some confusion has arisen from the use of such terms as 'perfect,' 'ideal,' 'norm' or 'standard' for any form or quantity taken as the limit of a series of approximations: "the perfect circle," for example, when taken as that which is serially approximated by the more or less round objects of existent nature. But whatever be the propriety of such verbal usage, we are here concerned with such orders only when the limit and other terms of the series are already values in the generic sense. Now value consists, as we have seen, in the relation which an object sustains to favorable or unfavorable interest, and if an object can be said to be better or worse this must be because the relation in question determines these differences. It is the interest which confers value on the object, and it must also be interest which confers the amount of the value. This would hold whatever the definition of generic

[9] *Principles of Mathematics*, 1903, p. 170.

value. If good is pleasure and evil pain, then the more pleasure the better, and the more pain the worse; if good is wholeness and evil partiality, then the more whole the better, and the more partial the worse; if good is union with God and evil the fall from God, then the nearer God the better, and the remoter the worse; so, if good is favor and evil disfavor, then the more favorable the better, and the more unfavorable the worse. The whole question turns, therefore, upon the measure of favorable and unfavorable interest.

In the third place, if interest is a quantity, then every interest is commensurable; that is, it must be greater or less in *some* respect than *some* interest. But it does not follow that two interests which are commensurable in some respect are commensurable in all respects, or that all interests are commensurable in any respect. Thus two interests might, as is commonly supposed to be the case with two sensations, be commensurable in duration without being commensurable in intensity; or an interest *a* might be commensurable with another interest *b*, and incommensurable with a third interest *c,* as a distance from one point is commensurable with a second distance from the same point, but incommensurable with a third distance from a different point. The range of commensurability is a question of fact to be ascertained by an examination of the kinds of magnitude which interests possess.

Similarly, whether these kinds of magnitude are reducible to one by summation or multiplication is not predetermined by the general assumption that interests are quantities. Units of potatoes are comparable in respect of volume, weight, number and age, but it does not follow that these can be compounded so as to yield a general magnitude in terms of which one such unit may be said, all things considered, to be greater than another. In any case, there will certainly be *some* magnitudes of interest, such as those of private satisfaction, or price, which have a limited range.

Finally, it does not follow from the general fact of comparative value, that there is any absolutely best, or absolutely worst. The only sense of 'best' which can confidently be asserted is the sense in which it is applied to one of three or more terms. If c is better than a, and also better than b, then c is the best of a, b, c. That c is the 'best possible' in the sense that there can be nothing better, does not follow; nor does it follow that because there is a definable sense in which c is the best of the group a, b, c, this sense will yield a term n, than which no other term is better. There is a sense in which unity may be said to be the maximum of the series of fractions, inasmuch as no fraction in the strict sense can be greater than unity.[10] But it does not follow that there is any such limit to the increase of value, any more than there is any greatest number. It would be quite unsafe to assume that there is any perfect object, than which nothing can be better, or even to assume that perfection in this sense means anything at all.

For the further development of our theme we shall, therefore, examine the nature of interest with a view to discovering the respects in which interests are quantitatively variable and comparable. What we can discover about the nature of interest will determine what we can truly say about the better and the best, the worse and the worst. We have but one category of value and we must attach ourselves firmly to that, rigorously avoiding the estimate of values in any other terms than the quantitative comparison of value as already explicitly defined. At the same time we may legitimately expect, in so far as our description of better and best is correct, that the things commonly deemed better and best, such as beauty and love, answer the description.

II. EXAMINATION OF TRADITIONAL VIEWS

§ 243. **Reality and Truth.** Before proceeding further with our positive program in the terms just formulated, it is desirable to reduce to these terms, or eliminate altogether, certain notions of comparative value that have played an im-

---

[10] Waiving the difficulty that unity is not in this sense a fraction at all, but a limit to the series of fractions. This difficulty, also, appears in the philosophical conception of a perfection that transcends the quality perfected.

portant part in the traditional discussions of the subject. Their criticism will serve the double purpose of clearing the field, and of suggesting the constructive principles with which these traditional notions are to be replaced.

First, there is the view which would determine comparative value by the criterion of 'reality.' This may mean any one of several things.[11] Thus it may mean that since reality is good, the more of it the better. But this presupposes some sense in which reality is 'good,' such as harmonious totality, or the will of God, or the happiness of sentient creatures; and the comparative 'better' should, therefore, be formulated in the same terms, as greater harmony, or nearer conformity to God's will, or completer happiness, and not in terms of degrees of reality.

It may, however, be held that since value and reality are the same principle, the more real the better. But such a view either accepts as valuable whatever commends itself to cognition as real, and thus reduces value to fact; or it employs some preconceived principle of value as a criterion of metaphysical knowledge, and hence of metaphysical reality, as in the Platonic insistence that to know what anything really is, is to see the good of it. In the former case, the predicate of value retains no distinctive meaning whatever. In the latter case, we should look for the meaning of better, not in the conception of reality, but in the prior conception of 'good'; the conception of reality and of its degrees being *derived* from that of value, adds nothing to our understanding of it.

There are several further senses in which the notion of reality may be employed in this context. One may affirm that what is 'really valuable' is better than what is not really valuable. If this means that what is valuable is better than what is not valuable, or that any good is better than none, it will be generally admitted; but we have still to formulate the principle of comparison which is employed in such statements, and to which, in our later discussions of it, we shall refer as the principle of 'inclusiveness.' Or, one may affirm

[11] The issues involved in this notion have been reviewed at greater length in Ch. II-IV.

that what is 'really better' is better than what is not really better. If this means that what is in fact better, is better than what is not better, it reduces either to the statement that some value is better than none; or to the principle, applicable to all orders of magnitude, that whatever is greater than any given quantity b is greater than any second quantity a whose magnitude is either less than, or the same as, that of b. The use of the term 'reality' in this connection only obscures the principles really involved.

The terms 'real' and 'really' may, however, be used to mean 'true' or 'truly,' and so construed they introduce a new consideration. The statement that the true good is better than the apparent or false good, or that the 'truly better' is better than the seemingly better, involves a reference to the rôle of judgment in value, and has to be interpreted in the light of the duality of this rôle. The truly good or better may mean that which is judged truly to be good or better. In this case the truth or falsity in question qualifies a judgment *of* value, absolute or comparative. But since the judgment that b is good, or better than a, is true when b *is* good or *is* better than a, the truth of value in this sense reduces to reality as considered above. The truly, as distinguished from the seemingly, good or better may, however, mean that which is liked, desired or preferred in the light of knowledge, as distinguished from what is liked, desired or preferred in the darkness of ignorance and error; where the truth or falsity in question qualifies the mediating judgments on which the interest or preference is founded. An object which is good because of the favorable interest taken in it, may thus be said to be 'truly good' when this interest is founded on true judgments, or 'falsely good' when founded on false judgments;[12] and the same analysis will apply to the truly or falsely bad, or the truly or falsely better and worse. Whether the truly good in this sense can properly be said to be better than the falsely good, depends on whether judging an object truly does in itself confer value on that object, and the distinction made

[12] Cf. § 41. Such language is unfortunate, as certain to be misunderstood.

in an earlier chapter between judgment and interest implies a negative answer to this question.[13] In any case, however, values may be critically compared by an examination of their mediating judgments, and as this is one of the things commonly meant by evaluation we shall provide for it in the present chapter under the name of the 'correction' of value.

The term 'rational' as used to distinguish higher values may signify the same as the term 'true.' But there is another sense of the term, in which it refers to the occurrence of mediating judgments regardless of their truth. A rational interest in this sense, is one that proceeds with circumspection and deliberation, or relates itself in thought to other interests, as contrasted with a blind impulse or head-long passion. It is obvious that an interest may be "calculating" even though all its calculations be false. Such superiority as it then possessed would be due to its securing, whether legitimately or illegitimately, the support of a wider circle of interests,[14] and such a superiority would be measurable only in terms of the principle which has been designated 'inclusiveness.'

An allied term commonly employed in the comparative estimate of values is 'objectivity.'[15] In so far as the meaning of this term coincides with that of the terms 'real' and 'true,' it requires no further examination; but there are further and supplementary considerations which it is sometimes used to suggest. It may, for example, mean that all or some values are independent of any interested subject, and in the latter case it may suggest that the independent values are superior to the dependent. This distinction disappears, however, when value is defined in terms of interest.[16] Or it may mean that some values (deemed on that account superior) are independent of judgments about them and thus free from the discrediting effects of epistemological relativism. But it has been shown that *all* values, while dependent on interest and on

---

[13] Cf. above, Ch. XI, Sect. I, II. Value is conditioned by the occurrence of an interest-judgment, but not by the truth of that judgment. It is a function of belief rather than of knowledge.

[14] Cf. the discussion of rationalization, § 157.

[15] Cf. W. M. Urban, *Valuation,* 1909. (Consult index.)

[16] For the rejection of the objective view in this sense, cf. Ch. II.

interest-judgments, are independent of value-judgments or judgments of interest,[17] so that this principle cannot serve to discriminate grades of value.

While all values are thus subjective in the sense of being functions of interest, and objective in the sense of being independent of judgments about them, it is true, nevertheless, that some values, being antecedently determined by a prior interest, may be said to be independent of an added interest. Thus an object of art already beautiful because enjoyed by others, may be so represented or judged by a second subject, and thus enjoyed by this second subject as beautiful independently of himself. This is the phenomenon of participation and confirmation which has already been considered in detail.[18] It is germane to the present topic in so far as additional interest in an object may be said to confer additional value upon it, or in so far as an object may be said to be better for being the object of multiple interest. But this depends upon the principle of 'inclusiveness' to which allusion has already been made.[19]

The notion of 'universality' adds nothing new, to that of 'objectivity,' [20] and possesses the same ambiguity. A universal value may be an object whose value is grounded upon judgments which, as being true, possess a claim upon the acceptance of all cognitive subjects; or a universal value may be a common value,—an object of universal (that is, of everybody's) interest, in which case its alleged superiority depends on the principle of inclusiveness.

§ 244. **Finality and Self-Sufficiency.** In his famous analysis of the conception of the supreme good in the First Book of the *Ethics,* Aristotle places the chief emphasis on

---

[17] Cf. § 54.

[18] Cf. §§ 154, 208.

[19] There is a further application of the terms 'objective' and 'subjective' to value, according as the interest is directed beyond the body or to the body's own states. Cf. § 118. This distinction affords a useful principle of classification, but as it does not imply a *gradation* of values, further consideration of it will be omitted here.

[20] The same may be said of the notion of 'eternal' as employed in H. Münsterberg's *Eternal Values.*

its aspect of *finality* or *self-sufficiency*. The supreme good is the "end which we wish for its own sake, and for the sake of which we wish everything else." [21]   Translated into the terms which have been employed in the present discussion, this means that the object of a dominant interest is better than the object of any of its subordinate or dependent interests. Relatively to any given interest, the end is better than the means, or the consummatory object is better than its instruments and conditions.   Suppose c to be the object of a dominant interest and a, b, the objects of subordinate interests. I then desire a and b because, and only because, I desire c. Or, having a and b, I still desire $c;$ whereas, having c, I no longer desire a and b.   If all interests were in fact subordinate to one,[22] namely, the interest in M, then M would be said to be self-sufficient, in the sense that its possession would leave nothing to be desired.[23]   But this is a special application of the more general principle of *preference*.   Each interest finds objects more or less to its liking, that is, differing in the degree of their eligibility or accord with the governing propensity. An interest may prefer one means to another, or one consummatory object to another, and will always prefer a consummatory object to its means.

§ 245. **The Hedonic Scale.** This same principle of preference emerges in Mill's famous distinction between the quantity and the quality of pleasure, or between those pleasures which are more intense and those which are "higher" or "best worth having."   The criterion of superiority in the second of these two senses is the choice of the experienced human subject, governed by his peculiar faculties, his pride, his love of liberty, independence and power, and his native "sense of dignity." [24]   When such a subject knowing two pleasures takes the one and foregoes the other, he establishes between them

[21] Trans. by J. E. C. Welldon, 1897, p. 2.
[22] Which, Aristotle to the contrary notwithstanding, is not empirically the case.   Cf. Ch. IV, Sect. II, III.
[23] "We define the self-sufficient as that which, taken by itself, makes life desirable, and wholly free from want" (Aristotle, *op. cit.*, p. 14).
[24] J. S. Mill, *Utilitarianism*, 1863, Ch. II.

the relation of 'preferred to,' or 'better than'; and by extending the range of comparison he may create among all the pleasures which he knows a comprehensive *order of preference* within which each pleasure has its determinate relations and intervals of superiority and inferiority to all the rest.

Mill's candor and clarity of style have prevented his clothing his difficulties in a decent obscurity, so that he has become a favorite class-room example of philosophical fallacies. He is supposed in the present argument unwittingly to have introduced a standard of value inconsistent with his fundamental profession of hedonism. It is objected that he should, in sound logic, have adhered exclusively to the Benthamite dictum that "quantity of pleasure being equal, push-pin is as good as poetry." But, in the first place, the order of preference is in its way as truly quantitative as the order of intensities or of durations which Bentham proposed; and, in the second place, as Mill points out, the whole case for hedonism rests, in the last analysis, upon the evidence of desire, and therefore of preference. If it is the desire of it that makes pleasure good, then the preference of one pleasure to another will make that pleasure better, regardless of its intensity or duration.[25]

The fundamental error of hedonism lies, as has been pointed out,[26] in its failure to distinguish between the *concept* of goodness, namely, the desired, and that *object,* namely, pleasure, to which this concept is supposed uniquely to apply. The hedonistic argument is to the effect that only pleasure is good (and pain, evil), good and evil being implicitly defined in terms of desire. What is charged against Mill as an apostasy to the hedonistic creed is in fact only a comparatively clear recognition of this implicit premise; and it is in terms

[25] "Neither pains nor pleasures are homogeneous, and pain is always heterogeneous with pleasure. What is there to decide whether a particular pleasure is worth purchasing at the cost of a particular pain, except the feelings and judgment of the experienced? When, therefore, those feelings and judgment declare the pleasures derived from the higher faculties to be preferable in *kind,* apart from the question of intensity, to those of which animal nature, disjoined from the higher faculties, is susceptible, they are entitled on this subject to the same regard." (J. S. Mill, *op. cit.,* p. 16.)

[26] § 50.

of this implicit premise that he finds the criterion of comparative value not in amounts of pleasure and pain, but in comparative desire, or preference.

The real defect in Bentham's hedonic calculus lies not where the critics of utilitarianism are accustomed to locate it, but in the direction implied by Mill's revision. Much good ammunition has been wasted in arguing that the program which Bentham formulated was impractical and illogical.[27] The practical difficulty of comparing pleasures as regards their intensity and duration,[28] is, as has often been shown, beside the point. That 'better' means more intense and durable pleasure, is not disproved by showing that it is extremely difficult to determine which of two pleasures is the more intense and durable, for it may well be that it is extremely difficult to discover which of two objects is the better.

There is a failure to recognize that the logical difficulties are also beside the point. Not that these difficulties are insuperable; it has, as a matter of fact, never been proved by an application of refined logical methods, that intensities and durations of pleasure and pain are theoretically incommensurable. Bentham's error lay, however, not in proposing to measure the immeasurable, but in proposing to measure the wrong thing. The rejection of the thesis that value is an object, or a quality of objects, or a potentiality of objects, taken as independent of interest, implies the rejection of a similar thesis regarding comparative value; and the interpretation of pleasures and pains as objects having value only in so far as viewed with favor and aversion, implies that their purely objective measure can no longer be accepted as a meas-

[27] The best summary and examination of such arguments is to be found in E. Albee, *History of Utilitarianism*, 1902, and H. Sidgwick, *Methods of Ethics*, 1893 (consult index). Cf. also F. H. Bradley, *Ethical Studies*, 1876, Essay III, and H. Rashdall, *Theory of Good and Evil*, 1897, Vol. II, Ch. I.

[28] Bentham enumerated seven magnitudes of pleasure and pain, namely, intensity, duration, certainty, propinquity, fecundity, purity and extent. *Principles of Morals and Legislation*, 1823, Vol. I, p. 54. The last is clearly the same as our principle of relative inclusiveness. Of the others all save intensity and duration have to do with the relation of one pleasure or pain to another, rather than with their quantity. In the interest of simplicity they will be omitted here, but they will all, either expressly or by implication, be provided for in the sequel.

ure.[29] The Stoic is right in contending that pleasure is no good, and pain no evil, if and in so far as one succeeds in cultivating indifference to them. If pleasure is good because it is desired, then one pleasure is better than another not because it is more pleasure, but because it is more desired. That a thing is good does not imply "the more the better," since it is quite possible to have "too much of a good thing." If one hundred men are far from home, it does not follow that two hundred men are twice as far from home; or that if sky is blue, more sky is bluer. Favorable interest in an object does not imply more favorable interest in more of the object, for as the object increases the favor may change to apathy or disfavor.[30] We conclude, therefore, not that comparisons of intensity and duration should be rejected as irrelevant, but that they should be transferred from pleasure and pain to interest. Comparative durations of interest suggest again our principle of relative inclusiveness. Whether intensity of interest does or does not reduce to preference has yet to be considered. Provisionally, at least, it may be allowed to stand as an independent principle.

§ 246. **Importance and Attainability.** Values are commonly compared as more or less *important*. Fundamentally, this has to do with causal relations rather than with values. A cause is said to be important either when it is indispensable to a certain effect, or when its effects are multiple and far-reaching. Thus, for example, the mechanic in a laboratory is sometimes more important than the director, in that he is more difficult to replace and more generally useful. This

[29] Cf. Ch. II, III, X (Sect. II).

[30] The argument here formulated comes to the same thing as G. E. Moore's "naturalistic fallacy." Cf. that writer's *Principia Ethica*, 1903, §§ 10-14. Mr. Moore, however, denies that there is *any* factor other than abstract and indefinable goodness itself, by which degrees of goodness are determinable and measurable. Cf. his *Ethics* (Home University Library), pp. 246-249. The criticism of this view is to be found above, Ch. V, Sect. II. Whereas Mr. Moore argues that there is *nothing* which, if added to a good object, will necessarily make it better, our view would be that there is nothing which, if added to an object, will necessarily make it the object of increased interest; or nothing which, if added to a good object, will necessarily make it better, except more interest.

principle applies in the field of interest both to instruments
or means, and also to consummatory objects and to interests
themselves.   The importance of food may be construed in all
of these senses.   Thus a job may be important as being the
only means of securing food; or a given supply of food may
happen to be the only supply available, and thus the unique
object in which the food-taking impulse may be consummated;
or the satisfaction of the food-taking interest may be important as having multiple and indispensable effects upon other
interests; or, as being an ineradicable or biologically necessary
interest, it may compel the individual to provide for it as
a condition of personal happiness.   The *recognized* (as distinguished from the *neglected*) importance of an object in either
of these senses will then affect its place in the order of preference, or the intensity of the interest which is taken in it, or
the number of interests which will be concerned.   The fact
of importance thus determines comparative value only in so
far as the judgment of it mediates interest.   Relative importance is not in itself a criterion of comparative value, but a
relatively important object tends to become more valuable
through being the object of a greater interest in some one
of the senses already enumerated.[31]

Finally, we have to dispose of the criterion of attainability
or security.   An object by which the object of interest is
attained is, of course, better, in the sense of being a preferred
means; as when religion is thought better than wealth or
power, as a means to happiness.   But it has also been supposed
that an object of interest is better for being itself attainable.
This criterion has played a notable part in turning men from
so-called worldly values, to the values of another world, as
in the case of Christianity; or to the subjective values of the
will and the intellect, as in the case of the Stoics and Spinoza.
Is an object of interest more valuable for lying within the
range of capacity, or for being impregnable to the vicissitudes
of fortune?   The consistent acceptance of this principle would

---

[31] In the economic field where importance plays a leading rôle it affects
prices only in so far as it is translated into felt need, and into a willingness to exchange which expresses an order of preference.

imply the supreme value of such objects as are most easily and surely attainable, which would imply that reduction of life to its primitive appetites,—that scorn of culture and arrogant defiance of mankind, that earned the ancient cynics their evil reputation. It is not to be forgotten that Spinoza, who sought refuge from the vanity and futility of worldly success, ended his *Ethics* with the words, "all things excellent are as difficult as they are rare." The fact is that attainability and security in and of themselves have nothing to do with value. The greatest goods may be those which are most remote, most uncertain and most precarious.

It is true that the interest which is directed to objects and confers their goodness on them, is sustained only by hopefulness. To be interested in an object implies the adoption of means and of subordinate interests which are believed to lead in its direction. Hence the belief that an object is absolutely unattainable will reduce the interest in it to a pious wish and eventually to apathy. But degrees of hopefulness bear no fixed relation to quantity of interest in any of the ways in which this can be measured; and in any case attainability, like importance, is related to value only indirectly through the effects which a *belief* in attainability have upon the intensity, preference or inclusiveness of an interest.

III. THE CORRECTION OF VALUE

§ 247. Our survey of the various notions which have been employed for the critical comparison of values has led to the elimination or reduction of truth, reality, rationality, objectivity, universality, finality, quality, quantity of pleasure and pain, attainability and importance. We are left with four notions which we shall now seek to clarify and which we shall hereinafter employ as principles for the systematic gradation of values. These four notions are *correctness, intensity, preference* and *inclusiveness*.

All four of these notions satisfy the general requirements which have been formulated in our preliminary examination of the topic. They may properly be employed for the comparison of values because, in the first place, they all qualify interest, which is constitutive of value; and because, in the second place, they compare values in such wise as both to preserve the generic character of value among the elements so compared, and at the same time, avoid the introduction of any new conception of value not comprehended within that generic character.

Let us now turn to an examination of the principle of correctness, first noting its important difference from the other three. Whereas all four principles agree in that they enable us to judge value without compromising it, the first, being a non-quantitative principle, does not yield a judgment of comparative value, or of better and worse. To judge an interest to be correct or incorrect does not in any sense predicate more or less of the interest, and thus does not in any sense predicate better or worse of its object. To judge an interest in terms of intensity, preference or inclusiveness, on the other hand, does introduce comparisons of magnitude, both in the interest and in the value which the interest confers on its object. In other words, there are two fundamental methods of criticism, the corrective method, and the quantitative method; the first expressed in the judgment, "this value is founded on truth or error," and the second expressed in the judgment, "this value is greater or less."

The proper understanding of the principle of correctness depends, as we have seen, on distinguishing sharply and tenaciously between judgments of value, and interest-judgments. Strictly speaking, only judgments can be true or false. Values themselves, taken as relations of objects to interest, either are or are not, and judgments about them, or judgments of value, are true or false accordingly. Interest-judgments, on the other hand, are those judgments about the object which mediate the interest; and these judgments, also, may be true or false. Thus a value may be either the *object* of a true or false judgment, or *founded* on a true or false judgment. This important distinction is easily blurred, as in the case of the Stoic interpretation of the passions, in which it is not clear whether passion falsely ascribes value to its object, or is based on a false opinion of the nature of the object.[32] Both principles appear in Plato's examination of pleasure in the *Philebus,* where it is held that men are mistaken not only in thinking pleasure alone to be desired, but also in the notions of pleasure which underlie their desire for it.[33]

The same distinction must be observed also in the case of preference. A subject may judge truly or falsely that one object is preferred to another (whether by himself or another subject), or he may prefer one object to another on true or false grounds. The man who leaps from the frying pan into the fire may judge falsely that he will like fire better, or (more probably) he may choose the fire on the basis of a mistaken opinion of its properties. The former is a mistaken judgment of comparative value, the latter is an act of preference founded on erroneous interest-judgment.

Value is more intimately concerned with the interest-judgment than with the judgment of value. The falsity of the judgment of value makes no difference to the value, even when the subject recognizes its falsity; whereas the falsity of the interest-judgment, if the interested subject be convinced of it, alters the value. Because of the fact that the interest *depends* on the interest-judgment, and is confirmed or altered by its proof or disproof, it is customary to speak elliptically of the values themselves as, in this respect, true or false. Thus a man who courts a woman whom he supposes to be an heiress, and becomes indifferent to her when he learns that she has been disinherited, reveals by his loss of interest the fact that this interest was founded on an erroneous judgment. Similarly, one may prize a painting on the false supposition that it is the work of Titian, or admire a gown on the false supposition that it is made of real lace. Because of this

---

[32] Cf. references in St. G. Stock, *Stoicism* (Philosophies Ancient and Modern), p. 42.

[33] Plato speaks of "true pleasure" and of "true knowledge" as eminently good, and seems to mean two things: first, what is truly taken to be pleasure or knowledge; second, what is truly judged about pleasure or knowledge. The pursuit of pleasure is then correct, in so far as one knows real (genuine, pure) pleasure from its false appearances, and knows what may be expected of pleasure. Cf. R. G. Bury, *Philebus of Plato,* 1897, pp. xxii, xxix, etc.

peculiar relation between the value and the error, it is customary
to speak of such errors as "value-errors," and to impute them
to the value itself; without clearly recognizing that they attach
primarily to the underlying judgment rather than to the interest, and qualify the value only in so far as the judgment
is a condition of the interest.[34]

The object of a correct interest is not *ipso facto* better
than the object of an incorrect interest. For better, like good,
depends upon what happens to the interest itself; since it is.
from this, and not from the mediating judgments, that the
object derives its value. That immediate value of God which
arises from the love and admiration of man, is founded on
the belief in his existence, but it makes no difference to this
value whether the belief be true or not, and whether, therefore, God exists or not.[35] Good will is not the less good will,
because blind mortals know so little of the remote effects of
their acts and of the efficacious means to human happiness.[36]
The foolish fears of death which Epicurus scorned were none
the less fears for being foolish. If a subject fears death
because of a mistaken supposition of something after death,
he fears it none the less, and death will be an evil until,
through being persuaded of its groundlessness, the subject
loses his fear. One who is in error does not know it, and
therefore persists in interests which are mistaken. The error
does not diminish the value until it weakens the interest
through being found out by the interested subject himself.

If we are to adhere consistently to our definition we must,
then, be prepared to say that the objects of such interests are
none the less valuable because the interest is mistaken, while
admitting that a mistaken interest is relatively unstable because of the likelihood that the subject will sooner or later
be convinced of his error. This last consideration gives a
double meaning to the expression 'well-founded,' as applied

[34] Cf. Ch. Ehrenfels's discussion of "Wertirrthümer," *op. cit.*, Vol. I,
Part I, Ch. IX; and A. Meinong, *Untersuchungen der Werttheorie*, 1894,
pp. 75-81.
[35] Herein lies the justification of the Ritschlian theology. For an introduction to this topic with bibliography, cf. E. C. Moore, *Christian
Thought since Kant*, 1912, Ch. III.
[36] Cf. H. Sidgwick, *Ethics of Green, Spencer and Martineau*, 1902, p. 46.

to values. A value founded on truth is not only wisely and rightly founded, as judged by cognitive standards, but is *securely* founded. It will be unshaken by complete knowledge, whereas a value founded on error is precarious and unstable, owing to danger of detection. This instability will vary with the spread of enlightenment, and with the degree to which the mediating judgment is verifiable in human experience. Within the narrower range of observable fact a mistaken interest is highly transitory, while the more far-flung interests of politics and religion repose on error undisturbed for centuries and epochs.

This mode of criticism is widely employed,—more widely, perhaps, than any other. Each group of interests has its own characteristic mediating judgments: as, for example, the judgments regarding the means of human and social welfare, which underlie moral sentiments; the judgments of physical cause and effect, which underlie economic demand; the judgments of form or authorship, which underlie aesthetic appreciation; and the metaphysical judgments, which underlie the religious emotions. Criticism in each of these fields means ordinarily the testing and revision of these judgments, the discrediting of old interests based on obsolete belief, and the formation of new interests based on advancing knowledge.

IV. THE MEASUREMENT OF COMPARATIVE VALUE

§ 248. **The Three Standards of Measurement.** The principle of correctness being assigned a peculiar status, there remain three principles all of which, because they define quantities of interest, may be said to provide standards of comparative value, by which to distinguish good, better and best, or bad, worse and worst.[37] These three principles are *inten-*

[37] As regards the quantitative method, I have been most aided by the chapter on "The Different Kinds of Magnitude" in W. E. Johnson, *Logic* (Part II, 1922, Ch. VII). My three quantitative principles of intensity, preference and inclusiveness correspond closely to this writer's "intensive," "distensive" and "extensive" magnitudes, respectively. For a more fundamental discussion of these questions the reader is referred to B. Russell, *Principles of Mathematics,* 1903, Part III (pp. 170, 175, 178, 182, etc.). For discussions of the measurement of interest and value, cf. Ch. Ehrenfels, *System der Werttheorie,* 1897, Vol. I, pp. 78-92, 146-157; E. Mally,

sity, preference and *inclusiveness*, and they may be summarily stated as follows. An object, wine, is better than an object, water: (1) if the interest in the wine is more intense than the interest in the water; (2) if the wine is preferred to the water; and (3) if the interest in the wine is more inclusive than the interest in the water. Deferring for the present the special question of commensurability, let us seek a preliminary understanding of these three principles, and assurance of their irreducibility.

Any given concrete interest, such as Robinson's thirst for water, may wax or wane, or vary in degree of excitement. Let us speak of this variable magnitude as the intensity of the thirst. Now suppose Robinson, still governed by thirst, to be solicited by several alternatives, such as wine, cold water and tepid water, all of which are eligible, that is, promise the satisfaction of his thirst. Robinson then prefers wine to cold water, and cold to tepid water. He does not, strictly speaking, desire one *more* than another, but one *rather than* another. Preference expresses itself in the form, "this is more to my taste than that," rather than the form, "my taste for this is stronger than my taste for that."

That such an order of preference is distinguished from the scale of intensities seems to follow from several generally recognized facts. In the first place, the minimal point of the one series is not the same as the minimal point of the other. The minimal intensity in interest is the point at which the interest rises above the threshold of apathy. Thus, for example, the interest of the thirsty man in tepid water diminishes in intensity, as he drinks it, until, beyond a certain point, it ceases to appeal to him at all. When, on the other hand, we speak of his interest in tepid water as least in the order of preference, we mean that he drinks it only in default of cold water or wine. It represents a minimum of interest in the sense

"Untersuchungen zur Gegenstandstheorie des Messens," in A. Meinong's *Untersuchungen zur Gegenstandstheorie u. Psychol.,* 1904; and H. Bergson, *Time and Free Will,* trans. by F. L. Pogson, 1910, Ch. I.   The difficulty of obtaining definitive conclusions as regards the measurement of interest is complicated by the fact that mathematical and logical experts are as a rule unacquainted with the *minutiae* of psychology and physiology, and *vice versa.*

that while tepid water displaces none of the class of eligible objects, it is itself displaced by all of the others.

This difference between 'intenser than' and 'preferred to' is further confirmed by their independent variability. As the interest in tepid water rises in the scale of intensity, it does not rise in the order of preference and take the place of cold water or wine. The interest of the very thirsty man in tepid water may reach any degree of intensity, and still remain least in the order of preference. Furthermore, in order to determine the place of an object in the order of preference one attempts to equalize and discount the intensity of their appeal. When finely discriminating preferences are made the alternatives are "considered," so as to hold them at the same distance; or only nascently adopted, so that there may be a rapid oscillation among them.

Now, in order to introduce our third quantitative principle, let us suppose that our subject Robinson is a person having the two interests, thirst and a fondness for bathing. These two interests are distinct in the sense that they are functionally independent. The decline of the intensity of thirst does not weaken the appeal of water to the bathing proclivity, and hence does not diminish the value which water derives from that interest; and *vice versa*. Furthermore, the place of water in the order of potation differs from its place in the order of ablution. We may easily suppose Robinson to prefer tepid to cold water and water to wine for purposes of bathing, while preferring these same objects in the inverse order for purposes of drinking. The two interests being thus conceived as independent, and as conferring value on their objects each independently of the other, it follows that an object of one of these interests, such as water, derives *additional* value from being *also* the object of the other. A supply of water desired both for drinking and for bathing, is better than the same supply of water desired only for drinking, or only for bathing,—not in the sense of being preferred, nor in the sense of being more intensely desired, but in the sense of being more inclusively desired.

The quantitative principle here employed is that of extensional wholes,[38] the class of interests, thirst and a fondness for bathing, being greater than the members which it comprises or *includes*. This principle does not require that the two interests should be the interests of one subject, or that their object should be the same, as in the case just supposed. It does not appeal the question to the higher court of personal choice, or social will, and thus *beg* the question. It may, therefore, be used to explain *why* a complex personal interest confers greater value on its objects than does one of its constituent appetites, or why a group of subjects confers greater value on its objects than does one of its constituent members, or why a common object is better than a private object. In other words, instead of taking the integration of personal and social life as *ipso facto* and inexplicably 'higher,' it analyzes and exhibits the ground of their claims.[39]

All three of these principles are recognized both by philosophy and by common-sense. The intensive principle is that which is most emphasized in the hedonistic school and in the cult of feeling. The preferential principle is that which is most emphasized in humanism, or in the cult of rationality and taste, where the level or quality of interests is accounted more significant than either their intensity or their number. The principle of inclusiveness is most emphasized in moral rigorism, whether in the exaltation of the self above its fleeting and partial appetites, or in the exaltation of the group above its members, or in the exaltation of humanity at large above any lesser group.

These three principles are independent, and must all be embraced by any theory which attempts to define the compara-

---

[38] As distinguished from "extensive wholes." Cf. W. E. Johnson, *op. cit.*, p. 168. The interests in drinking and in bathing are not related as parts of space having contiguity and a common boundary, but merely as members of the same class.

[39] W. M. Urban, for example, speaks of "synthetic preference," as characterizing "personal" in contradistinction to "condition" values, and "over-individual" values in contradistinction to personal. The principle of extent has reference not to preferences *on* these higher levels, but to comparative value as *between* these levels. In this sense what is preferred on the "higher" level is better than what is preferred on the lower, even though no one prefers the one level to the other. Cf. also A. Meinong, *Grundlegung der allgemeinen Werttheorie*, 1923, pp. 142-167.

tive value of all objects in all respects. They are independent in the sense that they are irreducible one to another, both in their meaning and in their causal variations. Intensity is not a function of preference, nor preference of intensity. A more inclusive interest may be more or less intense than a less inclusive interest. Similarly the preferences of a more intense or inclusive interest may or may not confirm those of one that is less intense or less inclusive. Our plan is to retain all three principles, and so provide for that modicum of truth in the different and opposing theories of value which have emphasized some one at the expense of the other two. We are confronted, therefore, with the problem of the interrelation and commensurability of these three principles as complementary methods of determining comparative value *on the whole*. To this problem we shall turn in the next chapter.

§ 249. **The Comparison of Good and Evil.** In order to simplify and isolate the principles or standards by which interests may be measured, and their objects brought into systematic relations of comparative value, we have thus far confined ourselves to positive interest, and to the positive value, or good, which this confers on its objects. We have now to introduce the case of evil in order to see how this may be brought into relations of comparative value with good. This comparative estimate of good and evil is involved whenever one "counts the cost," or reckons the gain greater than the loss.

The meaning of evil, turns, as we have seen, on the meaning of *negative interest,* as distinguished from the mere absence of interest, and as distinguished from mere negative results.[40] Evil is not absence of value, but value having the character of polar opposition to good. Nor does evil consist in a mere thwarting of interest, any more than good consists in its mere facilitation. We have noted that means or instruments of good are themselves good only when they are objects of favorable interest on their own account, though they may be said to be *potentially* good in the sense that the

[40] Cf. Ch. VIII, Sect. II.

knowledge of their good effects tends to generate a subordinate interest in them.[41] Similarly, that which baffles interest and destroys good is actually evil only in so far as the knowledge of this effect arouses the disfavor of the subject,—though the tendency to this disfavor may be said to constitute a potentiality of evil.

It follows that magnitudes of evil will be relative to magnitudes of negative interest. Being structurally similar to positive interest, negative interest may be measured by the same standards. Thus, first, one object is worse than another when the negative interest in it is more *intense,* or more highly excited. Second, *b* will be worse than *a* when any interest prefers *non-b* to *non-a.* The immediate practical effect may be the same as though one preferred *a* to *b,* but there is a profound difference none the less, inasmuch as in the latter case *a* is favorably regarded, or good, whereas in the former case *a* is unfavorably regarded, or evil. Thus he who "prefers the lesser pain" does not desire pain at all, whether little or great; and his preference can be accurately described only by saying that he prefers the negation of great pain to the negation of little.

Where there is a subordination of interests, objects take the sign and degree of their value from the interest directly addressed to them. Where the dominant interest is negative the subordinate interest may be either positive or negative; and there is the same alternative possibility when the dominant interest is positive. Thus one may seek an instrument by which to alleviate pain. The seeking of the instrument is a positive interest, and where preference is called into play its objects assume an order of good, better and best. In this case good is good none the less for being conditioned by evil. Or, one may avoid the fire in order to avert pain, and in this case the preferences exhibited in the avoidance and in the aversion are both negative, evil being conditioned by evil. Or, one may avoid an acquaintance for the sake of keeping a rendezvous with a friend; in which case the preferences of

[41] Cf. § 152.

avoidance are again negative, while the dominant interest is positive, good being conditioned by evil.

Third, *b* is worse than *a* when the negative interest in *b* is more *inclusive* than the negative interest in *a*. An object which is loathed by *L* and *M* is worse, other things being equal, than an object which is loathed only by *L*, or only by *M*. The object of a personal antipathy is worse than the object of appetitive distaste, and the enemy of society is worse than the enemy of any of its constituent members.

An object is worse than another *on the whole*, in so far as these three standards are jointly and commensurably applicable to negative interest, and the problem of their commensurability is precisely the same as in the case of positive interest.

Similarly, positive and negative interests may be compared with one another. A positive interest may be said to be more or less *intense* than a negative interest, and when their intensities are the same, amounts of good and evil are, in this respect, the same. Similarly, good may be compared with evil in respect of *preference*, as when *a* is preferred to *non-b*, or *non-a* to *b*. A good illustration of this is afforded by the cases of complex interests in which the dominant and subordinate components are of opposite signs. When an anaesthetic is sought in order to avert pain, freedom from pain is preferred to the possession of the anaesthetic, as the consummatory object is preferred to its means. The evil is in this case greater, in respect of preference, than the good. In the converse case, in which an interruption is avoided for the sake of friendly intercourse, the consummatory good is greater than the instrumental evil, or one prefers the presence of the friend to the absence of the intruder. Finally, the inclusiveness of a positive interest may be compared with that of a negative interest, and a personal and social evil, or an evil of longer duration, may be said to be greater than the good of a constituent appetite, or a good of fractional duration.

Equal positive and negative interests in the same object do not cancel one another. Assuming that *a* is the object of a positive and a negative interest of the same magnitude, the effect is not as though there were no interest at all, but is analogous to a balance of opposing forces. There is both good and evil, in equal amounts. It follows that in comparing two magnitudes of value of which each has a positive and a negative component, one might adopt one of four different methods. An advocate of the adventurous life might compare them in respect of total value, ignoring the signs. A pleasure-lover might compare them in respect of gross goodness, without "counting the cost," or the evil. A purist, on the other hand, might compare them in respect of gross evil, placing higher that which was freest from contamination. All these modes of comparison either ignore good or ignore evil, or ignore the relation of opposition between them. There remains the method of comparison in terms of net good or evil, or in terms of the algebraic sum of the two components.[42] While this method would assign to the same place on the scale a pure good whose magnitude was m, and a mixed good in which the margin of good over evil was m, it would not identify them, or deny their important differences. It would mean simply and solely that their value was equal as measured by the joint scale of *good-and-evil*. Whether such a comparison is possible, has yet to be seen.[43]

§ 250. **The Alleged Primacy of Good.** It has sometimes been argued that a sort of primacy naturally attaches to good, and furnishes a guarantee of its supremacy. It has been supposed, for example, that there is no evil which is not the offspring of good. Does our analysis lend support to such a view?

In the first place, it may be contended that good is prior to evil in that evil is definable only as the negation of the good. But this, as we have seen, is not true. The negation of good is not *ipso facto* evil, and there are evils, such, for example, as pain, which are not the negation of good.

[42] It would be theoretically possible to establish a scale in terms of the ratio of good to evil or to their sum. But in this case we should have to admit the equal value of all pure goods, where this ratio would in all cases be infinity or one.

[43] Cf. § 259.

In the second place, it may be contended that evil is always reducible to good, when defined as that the negation of which is good. But that a mere negation should be good contradicts our definition of good. If the object of interest is expressible only as *not-a,* the interest is by hypothesis negative, and *a* is evil. In order that there should be good it would be necessary that *b* or *c,* cases of *not-a,* should be objects of positive interest.

Or one may attempt to reason from the fact that good generates evil. It is true, as we have seen, that final good may give rise to instrumental evil; as when, through solicitude, our loves are turned to fears. But this, while it might assure to good the dominion of the past, would appear to consign the future to evil. Furthermore, the reverse process is no less native to good and evil, since final evil may generate instrumental good, and that which was sought as a remedy may be enjoyed as a sweet. The fact is that, so far as one can see, nature is equally prone to positive and to negative interests, and life equally as well qualified to people the earth with goods, the objects of the one, as with evils, the objects of the other. At any rate there is nothing in the nature and structure of a negative interest that prevents its being a dominant interest, or that prevents the existence of a world in which all interests are negative. A world containing no interests but fears, hates and disgusts, is not *inconceivable,* and there are times when the world of each one of us assumes such a form.[44] Such a world would have no value but evil. The actual world in which we live our several lives of varied and conflicting interests, is not such a world, but there is nothing in theory of value to forbid its becoming such in the future. Similarly, a world in which the only interests were hopeful and joyful is also possible, both as a hypothetical alternative and as a purpose for the future.

It is argued, however, that all action is "for the best,"

---

[44] I do not, of course, deny, that the conception of an organism implies adaptation to environment, or some large measure of agreement between its needs and surrounding objects. But it is quite thinkable that food-taking, sex, parental care, etc., should all remain, like breathing, below the level of interest; or that needs should be felt only when, being denied, they have given rise to fear or avoidance of pain.

and that so far at any rate as conscious life is concerned, forward movement must incline upward in the order of values.[45]   It is true that interested action tends to the realization of its object, to the existence and continued existence of what is regarded with favor, or to the non-existence and continued non-existence of what is viewed with disfavor.   But when this is said there is nothing more to say.   The object is not necessarily better for being realized.   It is true that when a progressive interest is consummated it comes to an end, and that, therefore, when fear is consummated in escape [46] fear ceases to be, and its fearful object with it.   In this case there is a loss of evil.   But precisely the same thing happens in the case of positive interests of the progressive type, where consummation brings a loss of good.   Similarly, a consummatory object is preferable to the instrumental object, and thus not only implies a change for the better in the case of complex positive interests, but a change for the worse in complex negative interests.

If, on the other hand, one supposes the case in which varying quantities of the object are correlated with degrees of preference, as when "the more the better," or "the more the worse"—then as the object diminishes there is less and less to fear; but, by the same token, as the object increases there is less and less to desire.

Negative interests of the recurrent type, as exemplified in continuous avoidance or prevention, may be said to add equal units of evil in equal units of time; while positive interests of the recurrent type, are similarly cumulative in respect of good.   But there is no implication that the situation after consummation is either in the one case worse or in the other case better than the situation before.   Therefore the possibilities which are definable merely in terms of the forms and variations of interest, cannot be said to prove that life

[45] Cf. the "Gesezt der relative steigenden Wertgrösse," a law of relatively increasing value, formulated by R. Eisler in his *Studien der Werttheorie,* 1907, p. 24.

[46] A fear, as a negative interest, is realized by the occurrence of the negative event, such as escape, which was desired.   It is misleading to speak, as is often done, of fear's being realized by the fulfilment of the expectation which provoked it.

will necessarily move in a direction of increasing good or of diminishing evil.

To this conclusion we have to add the fact that the change resulting from the activity of one interest may create a situation which is either good or evil in relation to ulterior or subsequent interests, whether of the same or of other subjects. There is, as we have seen, no contradiction in the supposition of conflicting interests, or any ground for assuming in advance the existence of a single harmonious system in which what is best for one shall be best for all. We can define such a system hypothetically, but its existence is a question of empirical fact or of historical achievement.

There is thus no *a priori* ground for optimism, that can be deduced from the structure of interest, or from the meaning of good and evil. It is entirely thinkable that a world should exist in which there should be a margin of evil over good, or in which there should be no good at all, but only evil. In the latter case there would be no positive interest, but only negative interests, which would justify a summary purpose to annihilate the universe or to cultivate insensibility. From the standpoint of the general theory and principles of value, in other words, pessimism is as rational as optimism. If Hegesias, the "death-counselling" Cyrenaic of ancient times, was mistaken in proclaiming the gospel of suicide it was not because of self-contradiction, but because of a failure to recognize the positive interests abounding in himself and in the world about him.

CHAPTER XXI

THE COMMENSURABILITY OF VALUES

I. THE STANDARD OF INTENSITY

§ 251. The Arousal or Excitement of Interest. The time-honored topic of the *summum bonum* suggests that all values can be arranged in a single, all-comprehensive and systematic hierarchy, in which every object which is good or bad occupies a unique place determined by its relations of better and worse to all the rest. The extent to which this is true, and the precise sense in which it is true, is the topic of our present chapter. In order to find a solution it will be necessary to examine more carefully those principles of quantitative comparison which have already been summarily expounded, and to examine them with special reference to their commensurability.

Such terms as 'better' and 'best,' 'worse' and 'worst,' 'higher' and 'lower,' 'superior' and 'supreme,' clearly imply 'more' and 'most,' 'less' and 'least,' *in some sense.* Many philosophers, having discovered that certain familiar principles of comparative magnitude which are applicable in arithmetic and physics are not applicable to values, have been content to dismiss the matter by simply denying that value is 'quantitative.' Meanwhile these philosophers themselves, in agreement with common-sense, continue to employ a vocabulary which means comparative magnitude if it means anything. It does not much matter whether that which is quantitative in a qualified sense is *called* 'quantitative,' or 'quasi-quantitative' or 'non-quantitative' or 'qualitative'; but it is highly important to discover precisely what it is, and how it justifies the use of at least some of the terms of the quantitative vocabulary, such as 'more' and 'less.' It appears to be the case, for example, that one value is greater than another in the sense that some terms lie beyond other terms in a serial order, and also in the sense that a whole exceeds any one of the parts which compose it. Relations of this sort give a meaning to the comparative and superlative forms of adjectives, whether or not it is possible to add or multiply such differences. Instead, therefore, of disputing the question whether values are quantitative and measurable in some familiar or technical sense, we shall seek to discover the specific sense in which values *are* quantitative and measurable, hoping in this way not only to learn something about values but also, perhaps, to enlarge the meaning of 'quantity' and 'measure.'

Appeal to the principle of intensity is, as we have seen, characteristic of the cult of feeling, as illustrated, for example, by the famous Conclusion of Pater's *Renaissance:*

"How shall we pass most swiftly from point to point, and be present always at the focus where the greatest number of vital forces unite in their purest energy? . . . We have an interval, and then our place knows us no more. Some spend this interval in listlessness, some in high passions, the wisest, at least among the 'children of this world,' in art and song. For our one chance lies in expanding that interval, in getting as many pulsations into the given time. Great passions may give us this quickened sense of life, ecstasy and sorrow of love, the various forms of enthusiastic activity, disinterested and otherwise, which come naturally to many of us. Only be sure it is passion—that it does yield you this fruit of a quickened multiplied consciousness." [1]

In what terms shall we conceive the measure of this "listlessness," this "ecstasy" and "quickened sense of life," this "high passion" and "enthusiastic activity"?

When sensory pleasures and pains, or substantive feelings, are conceived as *objects* of interest [2] then their intensity can no longer be identified with the intensity of interest. It may be, and doubtless is, true that the intensity of liking and disliking is proportional to the intensity of the pleasure liked and the pain disliked, but it is a different intensity, and the

---

[1] W. Pater, *Renaissance*, 1903, pp. 249-252.
[2] Cf. §§ 113-115.

proportionality which is characteristic of the case of pleasures and pains does not hold generally. Even in the case of pleasure and pain it is proper to inquire what is meant by saying of the greater pleasure that one *likes it more,* or of the greater pain that one *dislikes it more.*

Having adopted a motor view of liking and disliking we must look for a motor view of the measure of their intensity. The view of this type which is most ready to hand is that which would measure the intensity of interest by its overt manifestations. Thus one may propose to judge an interest by the external changes which it induces, and measure these in terms of work done, or foot-pounds. But it is evident that it is possible to lift one pound with eagerness and ten pounds with apathy. There is no fixed ratio between the amount that one does and the degree of one's interest in doing it. A less external standard is that which charts the amplitude or rate of bodily movements, as in measurements of the intensity of the kick of the spinal frog. But it is evident that the interest of the professional dancer (in spite of certain vulgar prepossessions to the contrary) could not be gauged in this way. Nor would one seriously propose to measure the degree of a man's fear by the rapidity or distance of his retreat. Standards such as these measure only activities, or the effects of activities, of the skeletal muscles, and even here take no account of the extent to which these activities are interested.

Can the intensity of interest be measured by exertion, or by the amount of effort expended, as judged by the amount of physical energy consumed? This is a more plausible suggestion. But some interests *call for* more exertion than others, or the same interest calls for more exertion at one time than at another; and this factor is clearly distinguishable from the factor of intensity. The man who sits in a comfortable stall and listens to the concert is not *on that account* less interested than a man who has to stand in the rear of the house and strain his muscles to see and hear. The necessity of putting forth effort may, as we have seen,[3] *cause* a greater intensity of interest, but it does not constitute such intensity. The in-

[3] §§ 226, 228.

terest of the less fortunate as well as of the more fortunate
auditor would be said to lapse when his attention wandered,
whether, as in the one case, owing to a muscular cramp, or,
as in the other case, owing to the seductive charm of the lady
in the adjoining box. Interests such as aesthetic interests,
which are relatively effortless, or which consume a relatively
slight amount of physical energy, are not on that account
characteristically lacking in intensity. "With all my heart"
does not mean the same as "with might and main"; nor does
easy success constitute indifference, though it may lead to it.

It is evident that the dynamic demands which an interest
makes upon the body will vary independently of its intensity.
The body may serve an interest by a state of quiescence as
well as by a state of activity. The interest of the hunter
watching for his game is at the moment best served by immobility.[4] The important thing is that the body or any part
of it should acquire that state, whatever the degree of its
activity, which *serves* the interest. We may then say that
the degree of an interest's arousal is the degree in which it
has acquired command of the body as a whole; or, the extent
to which the several parts of the body are determined, whether
in their functioning or in their inhibition, by the requirements
of the interest. Different interests of the same organism employ the same mechanisms and energies. An interest is
aroused in the degree to which it has taken possession of
these mechanisms and energies, or the degree in which the
body as a whole is attuned to it. In the case of a fully aroused
interest the whole posture of the body and organization of
its activities would express the interest and be focussed upon
its object. The organism could be said to live and move and
have its being in the interest. Mr. Bergson, in the course
of his proof that rising psychical intensities are qualitative
rather than quantitative changes, describes the manner in
which "an obscure desire gradually becomes a deep passion."

"Now, you will see that the feeble intensity of this desire

[4] There is, no doubt, a considerable expenditure of nervous and muscular energy in inhibition; but it is not, I think, comparable in amount
with that of pursuit.

consisted at first in its appearing to be isolated and, as it were, foreign to the remainder of your inner life. But little by little it permeates a larger number of psychical elements, tingeing them, so to speak, with its own color: and lo! your outlook on the whole of your surroundings seems now to have changed radically." [5]

It is, as Mr. Bergson points out, a question of the "pervasiveness" or "permeation" of the desire,—the degree to which a specific concentration of activities or direction of intention governs the mind as a whole.

Despite our ignorance of the physiological terms in which intensity of interest should be expressed, we can conceive it in abstract terms as a quantity of a certain type. It is a ratio of the elements which are acting under the control of the interest, to the totality of the elements of the organism. [6] A low degree of intensity might be due either to a reduction of interested activity in the organism as a whole, or to a division of interest. Thus a failure to put one's whole mind to a task sometimes means that a part of one's mind is occupied elsewhere, and sometimes that a part of one's mind is unoccupied altogether. Intensity being so conceived as a ratio, it becomes possible to pass from one interest to another not only within the same organism but among different organisms. Intensity, in other words, is measured by the magnitude of the fraction rather than by that of its denominator. By this method it is possible to provide for the obvious fact that the biting fly is more intense than the languid elephant; or that the "little man" may be "hotter" than the big man, who views him with luke-warm condescension; or that the whole-hearted play of the child is more intense than the half-hearted coöperation of his nurse, even though the one is the heart of an infant and the other the heart of an adult.

§ 252. **Inhibition and Strength of Interest.** It might be supposed that the relative intensity of two interests of the

---

[5] *Time and Free Will*, English trans., 1920, pp. 8 ff.

[6] Including all of the functions of the organism which are capable of being controlled by interest either *directly*, or *indirectly* (as when digestive, circulatory, glandular and other physiological processes are governed by certain emotional states which themselves are subject to voluntary control; cf. § 77).

same organism was measured by the outcome of their mutual antagonism.   Since they make use of the same mechanisms and energies, are they not matched against one another in competition for these?   Does not the triumph (by inhibition) of one interest over another prove its greater intensity? Our contention has been rather that inhibition, or exclusive possession of the organism *constitutes* intensity.   An inhibiting interest is *eo ipso* in a state of activity, and an inhibited interest in a state of inactivity.   Inhibition is an effect of activity, and the more intensely active the interest, that is, the higher the ratio of its active elements, the wider is this effect.   Intense interest tends, in other words, to a total inhibition of rival interests, or to total preoccupation of the organism.

But can one go behind this fact of possession and dispossession and say of a certain interest that it has a certain ascendancy over its rivals whenever it cares to assert itself? Does one interest have a greater inhibitory *power* than another?   Apropos of sexual and pain reflexes, Professor Sherrington says:

"It would seem a general rule that *reflexes arising in species of receptors which considered as sense-organs provoke strongly affective sensation caeteris paribus prevail over reflexes of other species when in competition with them for the use of the 'final common path.'*   Such reflexes override and set aside with peculiar facility reflexes belonging to touch organs, muscular sense-organs, etc.   As the sensations evoked by these arcs, *e.g.*, 'pains,' exclude and dominate concurrent sensations, so do the reflexes of these arcs prevail in the competition for possession of the common paths.   They seem capable of *pre-eminent intensity* of action. . . . Those species of reflexes which are habitually prepotent in interaction with others are those which are habitually intense." [7]

The "habitual intensity" in terms of which Professor Sherrington accounts for "prepotence in interaction," apparently refers to the presence of substantive feeling; [8] and his view may be construed to mean that interests excited by or-

---

[7] C. S. Sherrington, *Integrative Action of the Nervous System,* 1906, pp. 231-232.   Cf. above, § 116.

[8] Cf. above, § 126.

ganic sensations are prepotent over interests peripherally excited. Such interests are not, however, more intense in the sense of degree of arousal. An interest having a somatic object is not, simply *on that account,* more aroused than an interest having any other object; and when such an interest *is* fully aroused, it is not more aroused than any other interest when *that* is fully aroused. We cannot say that it is peculiar to such an interest to *be* fully aroused, since it exhibits its power through displacing fully aroused interests when it is itself as yet only partially aroused. It possesses its "prepotence" before it is aroused at all. We have, therefore, to admit a distinct factor, which we may call the latent 'strength' of an interest, and which signifies its tendency to become aroused. A stronger interest is one which more readily acquires control of bodily mechanisms, or whose required integrations coincide with what is in some sense a line of less resistance. A stronger interest short-circuits a weaker interest. It is this factor which is referred to when one speaks of an interest as 'deeply-rooted,' or relatively 'ingrained.' This factor does not, however, provide an independent standard for the measurement of value, because strength of interest *manifests* itself only in intensity. A stronger interest tends to become more intense, but its object possesses greater value only when and in so far as it *is* more intense.

Interests supposed to be innate, and having the somatic reference of which Professor Sherrington speaks, make up what is sometimes loosely described as an instinct of self-preservation. No doubt interests in the body's own state, such as aversion to pain and liking for erotic and other varieties of organic pleasure, are both strong, primitive and, in their effects, preservative of the individual and of the race. In this primitive and unreflective form, however, they are not interests *in* preservation, but only in the particular bodily states to which they address themselves. Nor do they, owing merely to their *strength,* invest their objects with greater value; although for purposes of education and social control, it is important to recognize them as forces to be reckoned with. It is not less important to note that interests may pos-

sess strength by virtue of habit as well as by virtue of in-
nateness. In order that interests which are greater in respect
of preference or inclusiveness shall be capable of maximum
intensity, it may be necessary that through training and discipline they should *acquire* latent strength.

II THE STANDARD OF PREFERENCE

§ 253. **The Order of Preference.** There is, it would
appear, a sense in which the interest in a given object may
be said to be more or less intense at different times, and which
may be extended to cover the case in which one of two interests (differing either subjectively or objectively) is more
intense than the other. In this sense intensity means degree
of arousal, or the extent to which the organism as a whole
is acting under the control of the interest. It is implied in
this view that all fully aroused interests are of equal intensity.
In other words, comparing interests as wholes embracing all the
phases of their arousal, there is no difference between the intensity of the one and that of the other. There is no intrinsic intensity attaching to a particular interest, but each interest
is capable of all fractional intensities from zero to unity.

What is the sense in which one of two objects is better
than the other when they are objects of the same interest?
Assuming that the interest is capable of being fully aroused
by either of the two, does it mean anything to say that the
direction of the interest to another object *would* be better
than its direction to the present object? The factor of intensity is here eliminated, and the answer must be looked for
in terms of our standard of *preference*.

Preference, like intensity, is one of the persistent standards
of common-sense and philosophy. It is the standard which
distinguishes the cult of humanism, and which refuses to
measure the "nobler" joys of man in terms of the "base"
satisfactions of the brute. It is this principle which Mill
invoked when he seceded from orthodox utilitarianism, and
which is implied in Pater's reference to that "highest quality"
which art may give, and which in his view evidently outweighs

the "quickened sense of life" and "enthusiastic activity" which characterize "high passion." Not only is this principle invoked in all questions of taste and of standardized appreciation, but it is the chief means of social control. Even what is commonly called 'coercion' consists in presenting the agent with alternatives, such as "your money or your life," and thus assumes that the agent may discriminate and choose between them. 'Liberty' in the social and political sense, as distinguished from 'freedom of the will,' in the psychological and metaphysical sense, consists in the range of effective preference, or the extent to which the social organization leaves original personal preferences unaltered.

Before analyzing the meaning of preference we have first to remove an ambiguity. It might be supposed that when one interest inhibits another, the object of the one has somehow been preferred to the object of the other. But preference implies a preferring interest. What interest, then, has in this case preferred the one object to the other? Not the inhibiting interest, for that is bent exclusively upon its own object; not the inhibited interest, for that is not allowed to manifest itself at all. Nor does inhibition imply an act of preference on the part of the total self. The first interest *excludes* the second, but there is no preference between the object of the one and the object of the other, such as occurs in personal choice. Inhibition, instead of providing for such choice, renders it impossible by silencing one of the interests which is an indispensable party to its occurrence. If the plaintiff expels the defendant from the court this does not bring a decision but simply prevents the trial.[9]

That an interest exhibits preference among its eligible objects,[10] or that these objects are more or less eligible, appears

---

[9] What does constitute personal choice we shall inquire later (§ 263). We do not deal with it here because it is obviously a *complex* case of preference.

[10] In order that there shall be preference it will not suffice that the relatively ineligible shall be merely possible, in the Leibnitzian sense. Any existential system whatsoever may be said to exhibit 'selection' in the sense that it does not exhaust the possibilities which some more abstract system, such as that of all consistent propositions, provides. But with selection in this abstract sense we are not here concerned. There is no

to be as fundamental a feature of interest as its having objects at all. Interest not only selects *its* objects from among
the objects of the environment, but selects *among* its objects.
There is such a selection not only among objects of a consummatory interest, as in the scale of taste, but also among
means and objects of subordinate interests, as in the scale
of utility. Furthermore, as we have seen, every interest prefers its dominant to its subordinate end, or its final to its
instrumental good,[11] as the hungry man prefers the food to
the bill of fare.

The physiology of preference is wholly speculative. The
preference of the final object to the instrument suggests that
the preferred object advances the governing propensity further
towards fulfilment. The preference of one final object to
another, or of one instrument to another, suggests that the
preferred object fulfils the governing propensity more adequately. Both suggestions may perhaps be subsumed under
the idea of completeness of satisfaction, or of *fitness* between
the object and the subjective demand.

But the important feature of preference is that it arranges
the objects of any given interest in an order, relatively to one
another, and in a manner that cannot be reduced either to the
intensity or to the inclusiveness of the interest. This order
of preference has its own characteristic magnitudes, which
determine comparative values.

An order of preference is a case of what Mr. W. E. Johnson calls a "distensive magnitude," or magnitude of "qualitative difference";[12] or "degree of difference" among "qualities
ranged under the same determinables," as when qualitatively
different hues are ranged under the determinable or generic

proof of favorable or unfavorable bias unless an opportunity is afforded
of displaying it. The Leibnitzian existent world cannot strictly be said to
exhibit selection, for the simple reason that it does not do any selecting.
There is no case of its actually disregarding or manifesting indifference
to some of the logical possibilities that it does not realize.
  [11] Cf. § 244.
  [12] *Op. cit.*, pp. 162 ff. The terms of such an order may or may not be
quantities in some other order of magnitude, but their place in the preference scale is not determined by such other magnitude, being a function
solely of the relation of preference. Thus less pleasure may be preferred
to more, or reputation may be preferred to pleasure.

character of color. This would be illustrated by the scale of differences from blue to green through the intervening blue-greens and green-blues. Each term in this series would be related to its antecedents as less blue and more green, irrespective of any other quantitative differences, such as those of brightness or intensity. Preference generates a similar *transitive, asymmetrical* relation among its terms. It is transitive because if *b* is preferred to *a*, and *c* to *b*, then *c* is preferred to *a;* and asymmetrical because if *b* is preferred to *a*, then *a* is not preferred to *b*, but stands in a converse relation which is different from the original relation.[13] The three terms in order of preference may be said to constitute a "stretch," which is greater than any of its included stretches. Thus the stretch *a — c* is greater than the stretch *a — b*, or we may say that *c* lies beyond *b*. It is customary where values are in question to conceive a stretch as extending in the vertical rather than in the horizontal direction, and to speak of *c* as 'above' or 'higher' rather than as beyond *b;* but this is purely figurative difference, as nothing is meant in either case except magnitude of stretch from a common point of origin.

We may now understand the senses in which two objects may be of equal value as judged by their place in the same subjective order of preference. *c'* is in this sense equal to *c:* when *c'* and *c* are both objects of the preferring interest; when neither *c'* is preferred to *c*, nor *c* to *c';* when *c* is preferred to all objects to which *c'* is preferred; and when all objects that are preferred to *c'* are also preferred to *c*. It is important to note that in this case it would not be proper to say that there was indifference to either *c'* or *c*, in the sense of lack of interest, or in the sense of zero intensity; but only that the preferential interest did not care *which* object, whether *c'* or *c*. Both objects may stand high or low in the order of preference, although both must stand at the same level; while the intensities may be of any degree, and may even vary in relation to one another.

§ 254. A Common Order of Preference. The most im-

13 Cf. B. Russell, *op. cit.*, p. 218.

portant conclusion which follows from this analysis is the impossibility of a preferential comparison of the values which objects derive from different orders of preference. Such comparison would depend upon establishing a term of equality, but this in turn would require a through and through coincidence between the two orders. It follows that two orders of preference are commensurable only when two interests prefer the same objects in the same order.

There are two interesting cases which seem to contradict this conclusion. In the first place, there is the case in which two preferring subjects differ only in their threshold of preference. Let us suppose, for example, that M prefers b to a, c to b, d to c, and e to d; while N prefers c to a, d to b, e to c, but has no preference as between a and b, b and c, c and d, or d and e. These two orders are readily resolved into one if we employ the method of indirect preference. N may be said to prefer c to b *indirectly*, in the sense that he prefers c to that, namely a, to which he does not directly prefer b; and his order of preference coincides with that of M in the sense that his indirect preferences all coincide with the latter's direct preferences. Thus though M's taste is more refined and N's more coarse, they agree none the less. In accordance with this principle it is possible to suppose a limitless series of preferring subjects, having the same preferential standard, but differing among themselves in their refinement of taste.

This principle being accepted, it is necessary to modify the statement of preferential equality which was made above. Where N's preferential threshold is higher than M's, it is evident that the preferential value of c is the same although c is preferred by M to an object, namely b, to which c is not preferred by N. We provide for this case by stating that M's c and N's c are equal when c is preferred by N *directly or indirectly* to every object to which c is preferred by M; or (letting 'greater than' represent the preferred and 'less than' the preferred-to), by stating that every object less than c in M's preference, must in N's preference be either less than c, or less than some object (d) which is not greater than c.

A second alternative is presented by the case in which M prefers b to a, c to b, d to c, e to d, and f to $e;$ while N prefers c or d to a or b, and e or f to c or $d;$ and O prefers d or e or f to a or b or c. Between such preferential orders there would be only a "rough" correspondence. It is not necessarily a matter of threshold, for N might discriminate between a and b, c and d, etc., but give them an order of precedence different from that of M. The preferences of M and N are then incommensurable as regards a, b, c, d, e, f, but commensurable as respects the groups of objects (a, b), (c, d), and (e, f); while the preferences of M, N and O are commensurable only as respects the groups (a, b, c) and (d, e, f).

§ 255. **The Standardization of Preference.** Let us consider the bearing of these results on the dictum *"de gustibus non disputandum est."*

We have first to distinguish a difference between two judgments of comparative value, from a difference of preference. The former case is represented by my judgment that *"b* is better than *a,"* as opposed to your judgment that *"a* is better than *b."* This is a difference of opinion, which assumes a common meaning for the predicate 'better,' and which has ultimately to be appealed to some one of the three principles which have been formulated. Preference would here enter into the discussion only so far as it was agreed to construe 'better' as 'preferred,' there being a difference of opinion as to what was in fact preferred. This possible confusion being avoided, we may ask in what senses differences of taste are debatable, when these are construed as *differences of preference.*[14]

In the first place, in so far as they are mediated by contrary judgments of fact. If you prefer a Raphael Madonna to a newspaper cartoon because you believe its composition

---

[14] In the interest of theoretical completeness one should, no doubt, provide for the case in which differences of opinion regarding preference may be argued on *a priori* grounds from the principle of order; as when, in order to prove to you that you prefer c to a (as I do) I argue that you admit preferring c to b and b to a, and *therefore*, etc.

to be superior, and I prefer the cartoon on the same ground, we can fall to debating the question of their composition, provided this in turn is not a matter of preference but of design.   Or we may hold different views as to the conception and intent of the artist, on the assumption that these actually occurred and are somehow ascertainable.   In both cases we virtually appeal to the same set of facts to arbitrate our disagreement, and in so far as the difference of taste is really grounded on this difference of opinion it will be resolved by the correction of the opinion.   In the case of progressive interests, where there is a choice of means by which to obtain a desired result, the mediating judgment is one of cause and effect, and this, being liable to error, may be debated and resolved by appeal to the facts.   Thus my preference of a certain route to a given destination may be argued against yours on the ground of direction, distance, or facility; and my preferred remedy may be compared with yours as regards its efficacy.   In so far, in other words, as differences of preference are due to differences of opinion, they may be discussed with the justifiable hope of their being resolved.

In the second place, differences of preference may properly be discussed when they are due in any degree to the relative ignorance of one party.   If my preference of b to all other eligible objects is due to the fact that I am ignorant of c, you may properly make me cognizant of c and of its claims; or if my preference of b to a is due to the meagreness of my knowledge of either or both objects, you may present them to me more vividly, or represent them more adequately, or by demonstration enable me to compare them more fully and with a more refined discrimination.   You may present the Raphael Madonna to me in a new light, and persuade me to look at it more closely, while at the same time keeping my interest alive by the contagious effect of your own admiration.   If it be a question of a route or a remedy you may exhort me to try it, arguing that I would *like* it better if I *knew* it better.

Or, thirdly, a discussion of taste may take the form of a mere comparison of preferences, in which a common object

is measured by both of us, each according to his own interest. This may lead either to our agreement, that is to our
assigning the object to the same place in a common order of
preference, in which case we learn that our standards are the
same, and value the object with a new sense of confirmation
and joint participation; or it may lead to the discovery that
our standards are different, as when we "agree to disagree."
In the latter case argument is either terminated and superseded by a non-contentious interchange of views; or it degen-
erates into a meaningless wrangle in which each of us
reiterates a different affirmation, and in which each party
seeks to prevail by endurance, or by the power of his voice,
or by personal prestige, rather than by reason. When, in other
words, all cognitive differences have been eliminated or discounted, and two preferences still conflict, we are confronted
with two undebatable facts both of which have to be accepted
by both parties, the facts, namely, that whereas in the last
analysis I prefer b to a, you prefer a to b. Such a conflict
of preference, like conflict of interest, is a datum of value
and an instance of its ultimate and irreducible relativity.

When we speak of 'standardizing' interests, whether dominant or subordinate, any one of several things may be meant.
In the first place, it may mean the formation and completion
of an order of preference. To achieve this the interest must
be introduced to a wide variety of eligible objects and arrange
them in rank. The lack of a standard may be due either to
ignorance of objects or to a failure to compare them. The
connoisseur such as the expert judge of good wines, must
taste many wines and must also refine his discrimination, or
lower his threshold of preference. Similarly, the expert in
the technical arts will be one to whom a wide range of alternative instrumentalities is known, and who is enabled by
his experience and discrimination to grade them in an order
of utility. In this sense an interest is standardized in so far
as its eligible objects or means are all known and tried, and
in which an order of relative superiority is established among
them. The cultivation of the interest is the extension and

completion of this order in the direction of superiority, or the effort to find better-qualified objects.

Similarly, the social standardization of interests of the same type renders explicit the agreement of these interests, both their common objects and their common order, so that they may become commensurable. A special case is afforded by the method of indirect preference, by which two standards are shown to be the same despite a difference of threshold. In so far as the standard of the expert represents the completest and most discriminating preference of any type of interest, it assumes the form of a social standard, on the assumption that other subjects governed by the same interest *would* adopt the same order of preference were they as "knowing" as the expert. The expert's standard is a social standard, in other words, in the sense that it is the *implicit* or *potential* standard of all interests of the same type; or, as representing the standard to which all interests of the type converge in proportion as they are educated.

In the third place, the standardization of an interest may mean the raising of its activities to the highest point in its order of preference, or the bringing of its activities "up to standard." For an interest standardized in the first sense may still in execution fall short of its best, or be content by accident or inertia with an object that occupies a relatively low place in its own scale.

Finally, standardization is sometimes taken to mean the bringing of different orders of preference into agreement, thus *making* them commensurable. Recognizing the psychological possibility of the conversion of one subject to the preferences of the other, or of both to some third order, it is interesting to inquire whether such a condition of agreement can be said to be better than the previous state of disagreement. Suppose that James prefers Bach, and John prefers Strauss. Would it be better or worse if both James and John preferred Bach? Judged by James's standard it would be better, and judged by John's standard it would be worse. Assuming these to be the only standards, there is clearly no answer to the question in terms of preference. To introduce the preferences of Thomas only aggravates the difficulty. If he prefers agreement to disagreement, his preference as it stands is irrelevant to the preferences of James and John, since these have no interest in the question of agreement. If Thomas's interest in agreement leads him to accept the order of James or of John, he falls into disagreement with the other. It is scarcely necessary to labor the point further. If the preferential agreement of two or more interests *is* better than their disagreement, then 'better' cannot here be determined in terms of preference.

§ 256. **Preference and Intensity.** Since we may compare two different objects of interest either in respect of intensity or in respect of preference, we may now proceed to speak of one object as better than another in respect of intensity and preference combined.

The possibility of such comparison is, however, strictly limited. It is evident that where objects are equal in respect of preference, the object of more intense interest is better on the whole; and that the same is the case with the preferred object when intensities are equal. When, however, we attempt to compare two objects whose correlative interests are unequal both in intensity and in preference we meet with a prohibitive difficulty. It might be supposed that we could construct a two-dimensional scale, whose vertical steps represented the order of preference and whose horizontal steps represented degrees of intensity. In the case of the foot-pound measure of work, or the wages-per-hour measure of earning capacity, there is no difficulty in defining such a complex magnitude even when the component magnitudes are of different kinds.[15] It is represented by a product of the component magnitudes; or, when plotted on a graph, by the area of the rectangle the lengths of whose sides are equal to these magnitudes.

But while it is possible in this way to define complex magnitudes whose components are of different kinds, it is evident that the component magnitudes must themselves be of the

[15] W. E. Johnson speaks of these as "rate-magnitudes." Cf. *op. cit.*, pp. 180 ff.

extensive type, or that they must be divisible into equal units. We can say that the work done in lifting twelve pounds one foot is equal to that done in lifting six pounds two feet, only because twelve pounds are twice six pounds and two feet are twice one foot; because, in other words, a foot is a foot, and a pound a pound, whatever the existing magnitude to which it is added or from which it is subtracted. It is assumed not only that the two magnitudes can be multiplied by one another, but that the reduction of the one can be offset by the increase of the other in some constant ratio throughout the scale, so that, for example, $18 \times 1 = 1 \times 18 = 9 \times 2 = 2 \times 9 = 6 \times 3 = 3 \times 6$. Similarly, when such complex magnitudes are plotted on a graph it is necessary that each kind of magnitude should be divisible into units which preserve their equal magnitude however far they may lie from the origin. It is only through such fixed and equal units *within* each magnitude that a unit of one can be correlated with a unit of the other, and so be represented as equal steps in either the horizontal or vertical direction.

But this condition is not fulfilled in the case of the magnitudes of intensity and preference. We can say that one interest is more intense than another, and that one object is preferred to another; but we cannot say, in either case, that the successive increments are equal, or that one interest is more intense or preferred *by so much,* or that one interest is twice or one-half as intense or preferred as the other. It appears to be meaningless, in other words, to say that what an object loses by a decline in intensity can be offset by a rise in the order of preference. This conclusion as regards two-dimensional value, in terms of intensity and preference, follows from the fact that the dimensions in question are quantitative in the limited sense which holds of all orderly or progressive series. This fact permits us to say only that where there is equality in respect of one dimension, increase in the other dimension yields an increase of the total.

It remains significantly true that an object that is high in the preferential scale and of intense interest is better than an object that is lacking in either respect. How shall this maximum be attained? There appears to be a specific order of precedence which is prescribed by the peculiarities of the factors concerned. It is necessary first to exercise preference and then to intensify the interest. This order of procedure is prescribed, in the first place, by the fact that all interests in all objects are capable of the same intensity. It is also prescribed, because, on the one hand, the raising of the intensity of a given interest tends by inhibiting rival objects to preclude preference, and so to cut off better possibilities, as measured by that standard; while, on the other hand, the act of preference in no way interferes with a subsequent increase of intensity. This relation of intensity and preference may be illustrated by the aphorism that "a bird in the hand is worth two in the bush." This may mean that an interest will prefer a more certain means of fulfilment to a means that is more doubtful. Preference would then be mediated by a judgment of probability regarding certain causal relations. Or, the dictum may mean that the interest in the near is more intense than the interest in the remote, and that this relative intensity tends to obscure rather than assist the act of preference based on the calculation of probabilities. Propinquity may, in other words, count doubly in favor of an object's value, as exciting the interest more intensely, or as raising it in the order of preference, but there is a tendency of the first of these effects to interfere with the second.

The characteristically intense interests are disparaged, not for their intensity, which should rather be urged in their favor, but for their inertia, or their tendency to remain upon a comparatively low level of preference. They have a like tendency, through insistence on themselves, to prevent the formation or the expression of an integral personality, and for these two reasons together are commonly held to be degrading.[16]

[16] Those who, like Ehrenfels (*op. cit.*, Vol. I, pp. 214-249), profess to identify intensity and preference, or explain preference in terms of relative intensity, ignore the fact that in order to obtain evidence of preference it is necessary to discount differences of intensity, or to remove them.

III. THE STANDARD OF INCLUSIVENESS

§ 257. The Overlapping of Interests. Preference can be standardized only by a common order, but such community of preference already creates a situation to which the standard of inclusiveness is applicable. Interest is added to interest in the same objects, and these objects derive augmented value from the summation of the interests taken in them.[17]

The principle of inclusiveness, like those of intensity and preference, is a widely recognized standard, and has from time to time been urged against the other two. Even Pater tacitly recognized this principle when he praised the "variegated, dramatic life" as distinguished from the life of habit by the richness and fulness of its content.[18] It is commonly employed in arguing for the realization of the total self, as distinguished from its constituent parts; or for the good of the nation, as distinguished from that of its individual member. It is this principle to which humanitarian moralists have appealed in insisting upon "the greatest happiness of the *greatest number*," or a government for the people, or a universal way of salvation.

The explicit acceptance of this standard by recent philosophers, is best illustrated by the following passage from William James:

"That act must be the best act, accordingly, which makes for the *best whole,* in the sense of awakening the least sum of dissatisfactions. In the casuistic scale, therefore, those ideals must be written highest which *prevail at the least cost,* or by whose realization the least possible number of other ideals are destroyed. Since victory and defeat there must be, the victory to be philosophically prayed for is that of the more inclusive side,— of the side which even in the hour of triumph will to some degree do justice to the ideals in which the vanquished party's interests lay. The course of history is nothing but the story of men's struggles from generation to generation to find the more and

---

[17] It need scarcely be said that the terms 'add' and 'sum' are here used only as first approximations to meanings that will be progressively refined in the sequel. They are not to be thought of as having any precise arithmetical or extensive significance.

[18] *Op. cit.,* p. 249.

more inclusive order. *Invent some manner* of realizing your own ideals which will also satisfy the alien demands,—that and that only is the path of peace." [19]

What, more exactly, does such a standard mean and imply?

There is a fundamental characteristic of the principle of inclusiveness which must be held clearly in mind, and whose full implications will appear later. This principle is applicable only to interests or aggregates of interests that are related as *whole and part*. The whole is greater than its part because it contains the part, *and* something besides; thus exceeding the part, *whatever otherwise be the magnitude of either whole or part*. The determination of comparative inclusiveness depends on the possibility of superimposition and overlapping. To compare two "co-exclusive" interests or aggregates of interest it would be necessary to establish some unit which could be transposed from the one to the other,[20] and which would have some inherent magnitude of extent that remained unaltered in the process. How this is possible or conceivable in the case of interests, does not appear.

This principle has an important application to the question of the summation of positive and negative values. The object which James and John both like is better than the object which either or both dislike, because the latter contains no more good than the former and *some* evil. Similarly, what James and John both dislike is worse than what either or both like. But whether what James likes and John dislikes is better or worse than what James dislikes and John likes, is indeterminable, for it would imply the possibility of comparing the extent of the liking of James with the disliking of John, these being co-exclusive. It is impossible for the same reason to judge by the method of inclusiveness between the objects of two *conflicting* interests, because in this case each object would be both good and evil. A whole of good or a whole of evil may be judged better or worse than its included part, but two mixed wholes cannot be so compared because this

---

[19] W. James, *Will to Believe*, etc., 1898, p. 205. The same principle is employed in W. G. Everett, *Moral Value*, 1918.

[20] Cf. W. E. Johnson, *op. cit.*, pp. 167, 168, 175.

would involve comparing the good with the evil in each whole, or the comparing of part with part.

The standard of inclusiveness may also be expressed as follows. If an interest M confers value on its object a, and if a second interest N confers value on the same object, the interest M persisting,[21] it follows that a derives augmented value from this fact. Or if a *is* the object of the favorable regard of both M and N, and if either of these interests be withdrawn leaving the other, there will then be a loss of value, although a will still retain value owing to the remaining interest.

This is the same principle which is implied in the fact that a universe with an interest in it, contains more value than a universe devoid of interest;[22] which does not mean that there is any interest which prefers the one universe to the other, but that the two universes differ in respect of the absence and the presence of value. If we conceive life to arise within a universe previously lifeless, then we may say that value has been introduced into a situation in which previously there was none. Further increments of interest will then have the effect of introducing more value, provided they do not destroy the interest already existing. Similarly value may be diminished or destroyed by the reduction or annihilation of life. It is in this sense alone that a second object can be better than a first when the first has no value at all. If b is preferred to a, both a and b must be objects of interest, and therefore good; and there is a similar implication when the interest in b is more intense than that in a; but by the principle of extent b is better than a, when there is an interest in b and none in a. There is no other principle which will give meaning to the dictum that " 'tis better to have loved and lost than never to have loved at all."

There is an effect of overlapping when two interests have the same object, whether or not the interests are similar, and this overlapping is implied when a class of objects assumed to be valuable in relation to one type of interest, is found

---

[21] For the sense in which a component interest persists, cf. § 261.
[22] Cf. § 55.

to be valuable also in terms of another. Such *cross*-valuation is one of the meanings of *e*valuation, as when objects having beauty in relation to the aesthetic interest are deemed to have a superadded value by virtue of their relation to economic or moral interests. Evaluation in this sense is the application of a new standard to objects already judged good by an old, and it implies, for example, that an act which is virtuous and priceless, as well as beautiful, is better than an act which is merely beautiful.

This effect of overlapping is equally well illustrated by the case of the object of consummatory interest, as when the same music is enjoyed by two or more listeners; and by the case of the object of a subordinate interest, as when two or more subjects seek the same means for diverse ends. The summation of value which results from the community of intermediate interests governed by different ulterior purposes, is notably characteristic of the material and social interconnections of modern civilization. There is, as a matter of fact, more unanimity as regards what is wanted than as regards what it is wanted for, so that the common instrumentalities of life often assume an aspect of more solid worth than the more private and remote values which they subserve.

The principle of inclusiveness also holds when the added interests have different objects. Let us suppose that pushpin is an object of favorable interest to James, and poetry to John. Then if to James's interest in pushpin there is added John's interest in poetry, there is more value in the world than there was before; pushpin *and* poetry are more valuable than pushpin *or* poetry. This does not mean either that pushpin-and-poetry is desired as one object, or that James-and-John desire as one subject; and cannot be argued to prove that either James or John desires both pushpin and poetry, or that either pushpin or poetry is desired by both James and John.[23] Pushpin and poetry constitute a more inclusive aggre-

---

[23] On the assumption that he is guilty of this confusion in arguing that the general happiness is desirable (in the sense of being desired), J. S. Mill is accused of committing the fallacy of "composition and division." The crucial passage is the following: "No reason can be given why the general happiness is desirable, except that each person, so far

gate of goods, but it does not follow that they constitute *a* good, any more than a quart of peas constitutes a pea. One aggregate of objects may be said thus to *contain* more value than another, even when, as an aggregate, it possesses no value at all.

The measurement of value by the duration of interest employs the same principle.[24] If the interest M confers value on its object a, at the moment t^1, and continues to confer value on its object at the succeeding moments t^2, t^3 etc., then the object possesses greater value in the interval $t^1 - t^3$ than in the shorter interval $t^1 - t^2$. This does not mean that if an hour's worth of an object is good, a day's worth is better, since the interest may lapse after an hour, or change from favor to disfavor; but only that a day of goodness is better than an hour of goodness, the interest which confers the goodness being assumed to persist. If the good conferred in the interval $t^1 - t^2$ is not cancelled by that conferred in $t^2 - t^3$, the good conferred in $t^1 - t^3$ contains that in $t^1 - t^2$, together with other good besides.

§ 258. Inclusiveness, Intensity and Preference. Such is the standard of inclusiveness, as applied to value. Now let us consider the commensurability of magnitudes so determined with those determined by the other standards already considered. If one may speak of interests as more or less intense, and of aggregates of interests as more or less inclusive, then one can speak of one aggregate of interests as being both more inclusive and more intense than another. The

---

as he believes it to be attainable, desires his own happiness. This, however, being a fact, we have not only all the proof which the case admits of, but all which it is possible to require, that happiness is a good: that each person's happiness is a good to that person, and the general happiness, therefore, a good to the aggregate of all persons" (*Utilitarianism*, 1863, p. 52).

[24] There must be some duration in order that there shall be any value, but this minimal duration will be what is required for the occurrence of interest. To require, as a condition of there being any value at all, a degree of dispositional constancy greater than this minimum (as when one contrasts a disposition with a fleeting or momentary desire) is, again, to confuse comparative with generic value. (Cf. W. M. Urban's discussion of the view of F. Krüger, in the former's *Valuation*, 1909, p. 50.)

greater joy in heaven over one sinner that repenteth than over ninety and nine righteous persons, would seem to refer both to the greater number of those who rejoice and to the greater degree of their rejoicing. But can a lesser inclusiveness of interest be offset by a greater intensity and *vice versa?* Can we conceive a product of inclusiveness and intensity which would remain constant, despite variations of its components; and which would signify that a more intense but less inclusive interest might confer as great or even greater value on its object, than an interest that was less intense but more inclusive?

It is evident that the same condition which precluded the multiplication of intensity and preference will preclude the multiplication of intensity and inclusiveness. This last dimension of value is also of the type of order. That the including interest is greater than the included is clear, but that it is greater by so much, or so many times as great, is meaningless; for this would imply the divisibility of interests into equal extensive units, and the direct comparison of co-exclusive interests. We are limited, as in the previous case, to the conclusion that where interests are equally inclusive, the more intense the better; and where they are equally intense, the more inclusive the better.

There is here also a prescribed order of procedure. Since all interests are capable of the same intensity, the prior concern of one who wishes to secure the greatest total good, will be with their inclusiveness. Furthermore, while there is nothing to prevent a long life's being as merry as a short one, an excess of present merriness may cut off the possibility of long life. The art of happiness would therefore seem to require that the expanse of life should be considered in advance of its intensity, or that one should secure the maximum interval of life, before "getting as many pulsations as possible into the given time."

What is to be said of the commensurability of inclusiveness and preference? Comparisons which employ both standards are commonly made. "Better fifty years of Europe than a cycle of Cathay," appears to mean that there is more value in a little living, providing it be Christian and "in the foremost files of time," than in a life of greater extent which is "vacant" and "barbarian," "like a beast with lower pleasures, like a beast with lower pains." [25]

We have seen that the objects of two interests are comparable as regards preference only when the interests have the same order of preference. It is possible to give a meaning to this if we suppose that two interests whose preferences coincide may at any given time be dealing with different objects having different places on the common scale. Thus two lovers of music, agreeing in their preference of Bach to Strauss may at any given time be differently occupied, the one enjoying Bach and the other Strauss. One could then properly say that the Bach of the one was better than the Strauss of the other, in terms of the common standard of preference. Such being the case, could one also say (introducing the standard of inclusiveness) that Strauss enjoyed by both might be as good or better than Bach enjoyed by one, supposing the magnitude of inclusiveness to offset inferiority in the scale of preference? This is clearly impossible for the same reason that stands in the way of the multiplication of intensity and preference, or of intensity and inclusiveness. It is, nevertheless, possible to say that the object of their common preference is better when enjoyed by both than when enjoyed by one; and that there is more value in their aggregate enjoyment at higher than at lower points on their preferential scale. Bach enjoyed by both is better than Bach or Strauss enjoyed by either, or than Bach enjoyed by one and Strauss by the other, or than Strauss enjoyed by both.

The application of such a joint standard would mean simply that, given objects of equal beauty, the more that enjoy them the better. Assuming, as appears to be the case with most interests, that the preferred objects are comparatively rare, and the interest in them comparatively difficult ("difficilia quae pulchra"), it is intelligible that there should arise a massing of interests at the lower end of the scale, thus generating 'vulgar' goods in the sense both of community

[25] Tennyson's *Locksley Hall.*

and of inferiority. Of such a good it must not be said that it is on the whole better than a private and more eminent good; or that, in terms of the double standard, its wide appeal offsets its baseness. This judgment is involved in such errors as: (1) the opinion that the vulgar good is superior (in the sense of the preferential scale) to the private good; (2) the supposition that the total value would be augmented by an individual's descending to the average level; (3) the failure to recognize clearly that everything short of a massing of interests on the highest level of preference is something less than the best. Confusion of some such form constitutes that loss of cultural standards, or of taste, which is likely to result from a blind emphasis on the standard of inclusiveness.

It is of highest importance to recognize that, while preference and inclusiveness both measure value, they do not measure it in the same way. Increase, in the sense of inclusiveness, does not imply increase, in the order of preference. Strauss is no better than Bach in the preferential scale for being twice preferred, than is a length any longer for being twice measured. The standards of inclusiveness and preference are independent. He who says that bread is better than cake, meaning that bread is a staple, and he who says that cake is better than bread, meaning that cake is a delicacy, may both be entirely correct in their judgments; and no contradiction arises between them unless the difference of standard is ignored. He who says that one table is bigger than a second table, measuring only its length, and he who says that the second is bigger, measuring only its width, cease to contradict one another as soon as they realize precisely what they are measuring. Similarly the exponent of democracy who praises the common goods, and the exponent of aristocracy who praises the choicer goods, engage in a blind and fruitless altercation until they recognize that they are both correctly measuring different dimensions of value; or until they understand that the best life is that in which the choicer goods are also the common goods.

§ 259. **Conflict, and the Priority of Inclusiveness.** We

have seen that the standard of preference takes precedence of the standard of intensity, meaning that in order to create values that may be said to be roundly better, in terms of both preference and intensity, it is necessary to proceed from preference to intensity rather than in the reverse direction. This is because, while intensification precludes preference, preference may always be intensified. There is a similar order of precedence as between preference and inclusiveness. This results from the fact that the principle of inclusiveness requires that interests shall be rendered harmonious. Their prior exercise of preference tends to preclude this reconciliation, while, on the other hand, reconciliation permits the subsequent exercise of preference.[26] The question hinges on the application of judgments of comparative value to conflicting interests, that is, to interests that are incompatible, opposed or antagonistic.[27]

It is the conflict of interest which most commonly provokes a judgment of comparative value, and provides the most important occasions for the application of such a judgment. The gravest choices of life are not those in which good is balanced against evil, or more good against less good, or less evil against more evil, but those in which one mixture of good and evil is balanced against another. There is good and evil in both alternatives, but there is held to be a larger net gain or a smaller net loss in the one than in the other. This occurs both in personal judgments in which a lesser interest is sacrificed to a greater, and in social judgments where one man's suffering is held to be less than the happiness of the community. What judgment of better and worse is strictly applicable in situations of this type?[28]

Of two conflicting interests, L and M, is it better that L should prevail at the expense of M, or that M should prevail at the expense of L? Or, supposing L to desire a, and

[26] This does not mean that such subsequent preferences agree with those which the same interests made, or would have made, prior to their reconciliation. Cf. § 261.

[27] Cf. § 156.

[28] In my *Moral Economy*, 1909, I have taken this problem to be typical of morality, and have used the term "economy" to designate that principle of *provident organization* by which the problem is solved.

M to desire b, and supposing L to have an aversion for b, and M for a, which is better, a or b? [29] So formulated, the solution would depend on a quantitative comparison of L and M. For the good of a is derived from L, the good of b from M, the evil of a from M, and the evil of b from L; so that whether we compare a and b in respect of their gross good, gross evil, net good or net evil, in any case we are compelled to weigh the claims of L and M. But this, it seems, cannot be done. L may at any given time be more intense than M, but this standard is of negligible significance because all interests are capable of unit intensity, and are peculiarly liable in cases of conflict to be raised to this maximum. The typical situation in which a resolution is required is that in which the conflicting interests are of equal intensity. The standard of preference will not apply, because L and M have no common order of preference, while to invoke the preference of a third subject would measure the new values of a and b relatively to this third subject. The principle of inclusiveness does not apply except as regards gross value. There is more of good *and* evil (or of value in the generic sense), in a and b than in either a or b. But this does not throw any light on the comparative amounts of net good or evil ascribable to a and b respectively. Such a judgment would require a comparative estimate of the good of a determined by the favor of L, and the evil of a determined by the disfavor of M, and similarly with b; and this would necessitate a direct comparison of L and M, which cannot be made by the method of inclusion because L and M are co-exclusive.

We seem forced to conclude, therefore, that the problem of the comparative magnitude of two conflicting interests of equal intensity is insoluble, and that it is impossible to judge that one of their objects is better or worse than the other. To the question, "Is it better absolutely, or objectively, that this interest should prosper at the expense of that, or that at the expense of this?" there is, strictly speaking, no answer. One alternative is better relatively to the first interest, an-

[29] This would be the case of opposition.

other alternative relatively to the second interest; neither can be judged to be better on the whole.

There remains only one comparative judgment of better or worse which is free from this relativity, and which points the way to a resolution of the conflict, namely, the judgment that the satisfaction of both interests *would be* better than the defeat of either. This is a hypothetical application of the standard of inclusiveness. To employ the language of whole and part, that which contains the good relative to both interests contains the good relative to each, together with some increment from the other; and is therefore better than that which contains the good of one to the exclusion of the good of the other.

We may now understand the limited sense in which preferential agreement may be said (in accordance with the principle of inclusiveness) to be better than preferential disagreement; or the sense in which a universal standardization is commendable.[30] Preferential agreement cannot be said to be better in principle than preferential disagreement, even as judged by the standard of inclusiveness. If James prefers Bach and John prefers Strauss, there is nothing in the situation as so far defined to imply that the one object negates the other. The enjoyments based on these different preferences may be quite compatible and consistent with one another; and if so, then their sum is as great as it would be if they were both preferring and enjoying the same object. Bach *and* Strauss singly enjoyed are as good as either Bach *or* Strauss doubly enjoyed. The case of Jack Sprat and his wife affords an illustration which shows that preferential disagreement may yield a sum of goods, while preferential agreements often lead to conflict. Where Jack Sprats and their wives both prefer fat, or both prefer lean, situations often develop in which one interest is served only at the expense of the other. Preferential agreement is better than preferential disagreement, then, only so far as the former escapes, while the latter causes, a conflict of interest. But may not preferential disagreement be better than preferential agreement, on the same

[30] Cf. § 255.

ground? The answer lies in the fact that preferential disagreement is harmonious either through the happy accident
of compatibility, or through a more fundamental *agreement*.
The only way in which interests can be so determined as to
guarantee their harmony, is to be governed by some comprehensive order of preference within which their disagreements
may be provided for and rendered innocuous.

Since it is only in so far as all interests are brought within
one harmonious system under a universal order of preference
that they can be rendered all-commensurable, it follows that
such all-commensurability is best only as judged by the standard of inclusiveness. This standard thus takes precedence
of the others as being the only standard by which the standardization of values can itself be justified. The structure of
such an all-commensurable system may now be briefly summarized.

§ 260. **The Three Standards and Their Order of Application.** We conclude, then, that values are comparable by
the application of three different standards, which can be applied jointly only when applied in a certain order.

The identity of an interest depends on two factors, the
objective and the subjective. If we speak of an interest as
a disposition of an organism relatively to a certain object b,
we can compare this disposition at the various stages of its
actualization, and speak of it as more or less *intense*, or completely aroused. In this case we suppose the expectation to
remain the same, and the degree to which the organism is
governed by it to vary. When we say that all maximum
intensities are equal we mean that there is an adjustment, or
alignment, or posture of the total organism which is appropriate to the realization of that particular object, or which is
explicable by reference to it; as when a man's total behavior
is describable as an enjoyment or pursuit of b. The state
of the organism is the perfect complement of b, and b is in
complete control of the organism; or, all of the activities of
the organism are explicable as functions of the expectation
of b.

When we turn to *preference*, we suppose a state of the organism describable in terms of a class of objects, *a, b, c,* as follows: the organism is excited by *a,* but only in the absence of *b* and *c;* it is excited by *b* in the presence of *a,* but only in the absence of *c;* it is excited by *c* unqualifiedly. Or, when *a, b,* and *c,* or *b* and *c,* are promised, it responds to *c;* when *a* and *b* are promised, it responds to *b;* while it responds to *a* or *b* or *c* if promised alone. This interest in *a, b, c,* may be latent, meaning that the organism is capable of assuming that state in which *a, b* and *c* will appeal to it in this peculiar way. *a, b,* and *c* then constitute an order of which it can be said that $b > a, c > b$ and $c > a$.

The standard of *inclusiveness* refers to the fact that several interests may be taken together as a whole, which is greater than its parts. As will appear more clearly in the sequel, the most important case of this is the integration of the interests of one subject so as to form a composite, or resultant interest, which contains the component interests in the peculiar sense that it is compounded *of* them and may be analyzed *into* them. The special case of integration in which other interests are subordinated to the interest of universal benevolence, and in which some integration of this type is adopted by all interested subjects, will be seen to define the greatest possible interest, as judged by the standard of inclusiveness.[31]

Finally, these three standards bear a peculiar relation to one another. They cannot be multiplied or divided into one another, for lack of the equal units which would be necessary to render them commensurable. A maximum of interest judged by all three standards, or a best on the whole, can be defined only by raising interests to each maximum in turn, and in a certain order. Intensification precludes the exercise of preference, and the exercise of preference precludes integration. A system of interests which shall be the greatest in all three senses can be achieved only by first achieving a harmonious integration of all interests. Component interests being so compounded as to realize the greatest inclusiveness,

[31] Cf. §§ 271, 279.

the resultant interests may then exercise preference, each choosing its best; and having so chosen, each interest may then be brought to its maximum of intensity.

This same order of precedence among the three standards of comparative value may be otherwise expressed as follows. Any interest in any object is capable of being fully aroused, so differences of intensity are significant only relatively to a particular interest in a particular object. Preference, on the other hand, establishes an order among objects relatively to a given interest. The standard of inclusiveness, finally, is relative neither to interests nor to objects, but may be applied absolutely. The first standard, intensity, makes possible the comparison of the several phases of the same interest in the same object; the second, preference, makes possible the comparison of the several objects of the same interest; the third, inclusiveness, makes possible the comparison of the objects of one interest with the objects of another without the introduction of a third interest, and is therefore the only standard by which all interests can be brought into one system having a maximum in all three respects, or on the whole.

CHAPTER XXII

THE HIGHEST GOOD

I. THE SUPERIORITY OF THE PERSONAL WILL

§ 261. **The Composition of the Personal Will.** It is commonly assumed that a harmonious personality or society is better than a conflicting personality or society. We have been led to conclude that this is true as judged by, and only as judged by, the standard of inclusiveness hypothetically applied. This standard thus plays a peculiar rôle in the definition of the hierarchy of values, as the only standard by which a greatest good can be comprehensively defined, or placed above *all other* values, whether good, evil, or a mixture of the two. This greatest good will be the object of an all-inclusive and harmonious system of interests. To the principles of personal and social integration on which the realization of such a situation depends, we now turn. Conflict of interest occurs between the interests of the same person, and between the interests of different persons. Let us examine the first of these cases with a view to the amplification and confirmation of the principle that harmony is better than conflict.[1]

[1] Cf. § 44, and especially Santayana's admirable statement there quoted. Except for an explicit recognition on my part of the quantitative implications of the whole-part relation, the view herein set forth does not appear to me to differ essentially from Santayana's account of the formation of ideals, in his *Reason in Common Sense,* 1905, Ch. X, XI. Cf., *e.g.,* the following:

"Here we have, then, one condition which the ideal must fulfil: it must be a resultant or synthesis of impulses already afoot" (p. 260); "When two interests are simultaneous and fall within one act of apprehension the desirability of harmonizing them is involved in the very effort to realize them together" (p. 267). E. B. Holt speaks of a reconciliation of conflict, which "consists in a free play of *both* the involved sets of tendencies, whereby they *meet* each other, and a line of conduct emerges

Suppose two constituent interests of the same person to be opposed or antagonistic, so that the good relative to one constitutes or implies evil relative to the other. A state of things in which these identical interests were harmonious, or in which the sum of their objects was an addition of good to good without loss, would be better than the given state of conflict. A transition from the present to the hypothetical state would be a change for the better, or a process of improvement. But how may such a change be brought about?

We ordinarily describe the method as a curtailing of one or each of the interests, so as to make room for the other; as when a man who loves both sport and business, limits his sport to the week-end and his business to the other five days. This description suggests an operation from without by which both interests suffer loss. Such an operation is no doubt possible, in the moral as well as in the surgical sense. The person in question might be locked out of his office on Saturdays and Sundays, and the golf-links might be closed on the other five days. In this case both interests would obtain satisfaction, but both would be defeated; and whether there would be a net gain or a net loss would be impossible to ascertain without measuring the two interests against one another, which, as we have seen, is impossible.

Let us now suppose, on the other hand, that the adjustment is effected internally by the person himself,—through his attempt to satisfy both interests, and through his thinking out and adoption of a plan. In this case no factor operates

which is dictated by *both* sets of motives together, and which embodies all that was not downright antagonistic in the two. This sounds like compromise, whereas its mechanism is utterly different. And it were best called reconciliation or resolution." (*The Freudian Wish*, 1915, p. 122.) The author emphasizes the importance of having the subject discover and resolve the contradiction for himself, so that the integrated activity may be based on his own understanding of the object, or on his own mediating judgments. The context contains an admirable statement of the moral and educational applications of this thesis.

For a similar account of personality as an achievement rather than a presupposition, cf. L. T. Hobhouse, *The Rational Good*, 1921, Ch. II. According to this writer, will is "a gathering of much, ideally of the whole, conational energy of our nature canalized into a deep and steady stream flowing within determinate limits in ordered activity to foreseen ends" (p. 52).

save the two interests themselves, each in turn taking account of the other, and both contributing dynamically to the outcome. The plan or course of action so generated may be said to embrace both interests, because both have gone into the making of it. They have, furthermore, gone into it without any residuum, so that both interests may be said to be wholly satisfied.

That which occurs is comparable to chemical synthesis or to a resultant of forces. When two elements unite to form a compound the elements are said identically to compose the compound. The properties of the constituent elements are superseded by the properties of the compound, as when two gases compose a liquid. Nevertheless the compound is said to contain the elements, and nothing but the elements, in a sense peculiar to the reversible process of composition and decomposition. In the first place, the elements enter into the compound, or generate it by their co-presence and reciprocal action; in the second place, the compound conserves the elements, since it may again be resolved into them, their original properties being restored; in the third place, it comprises only the elements, since they are sufficient to compose it, and since if one of the elements be withdrawn the residuum consists of the other element.

A resultant of forces exhibits the same type of structure. The body does not move in accordance with the nature of either the centrifugal or the centripetal force in isolation, but does move strictly in accordance with the nature of both forces operating jointly. Its motion can be produced wholly by the application of the two forces in question without the application of any additional force, and its behavior can be resolved into them without any residuum. Although the component forces may not be recognizable in their joint operation, their presence and persistence is revealed by the fact that when the centripetal force is removed the body moves centrifugally and *vice versa*.[2]

_____

[2] "Composition is not truly addition," says B. Russell (*Principles of Mathematics*, 1903, p. 477). Similarly, C. D. Broad remarks that "a vector-sum is not a sum in the ordinary sense of the word" (*The Mind*

Similarly, let us suppose that two interests seated in the same organic individual, are capable by reflection of entering into one field of motivation, so that each is modified by the presence of the other.[3] Then there occurs a process which may by analogy be described as a process of moral or personal composition, or as a sort of "vector-sum." The behavior of the individual cannot be described as that of a man who loves his business or as that of a man who loves sport, but only as that of a man who is governed by both inclinations operating jointly. We express this ordinarily by saying that the integral purpose is the person's 'real' purpose. It is not what sport demands, or what business demands, but what *he* demands; the adjective 'real' meaning that only in this purpose, as distinguished from the isolated interests, the person as such emerges and becomes effective.[4]

The two interests, taken in conjunction, account sufficiently for the person's behavior, without the necessity of imputing any other interest to him. His conduct can be exhaustively resolved or decomposed into these interests, and each of them is present and persistent, since if one of the interests is removed he behaves wholly in accordance with the other. We may then say that his plan or course of action is a composite whole or resultant, of which the parts are the several interests by which the plan or course of action is generated and into which it can be analyzed; notwithstanding the fact that the individual does not act either like a man who loves business or like a man who loves sport. He differs from a man who likes business in the respect that he also likes sport, and he differs from the man who likes sport in the respect that he also likes business. The effect of the joint operation of both inclinations is a form of behavior which is characterized by

and its Place in Nature, 1925, p. 62). My only contention is that a vector-sum is a sum in *some* sense, justifying a use of the terms 'greater' and 'less' as applied to whole and part.

[3] Each is "mediated" by the other, and the integrating process is that which has been described as "rationalization." Cf. §§ 166, 167.

[4] It is in this sense that I may speak of an actual desire as not what I "really desire." This does not mean that the desire is unreal, but only that it is not really 'I' that desires it. It is not, in other words, an expression of my integral personality, though its occurrence is indisputable, and though it belongs to my psychological history.

the absence of some of the properties of each inclination and the presence of certain new properties, which are the properties of his integral personality. The system of the objects of this synthetic or composite personal interest, since it satisfies both interests, may be said to be better than the original pair of objects which satisfied one interest and defeated the other.[5]

It may be objected that the satisfaction of the personal interest does defeat the constituent personal interests, inasmuch as these are limited by one another, or do not operate jointly as they *would* operate severally. But let us again return to our chemical and mechanical analogies. The properties of the compound are determined by the properties of the elements. If the elements were deprived of their elementary properties the compound would not possess its composite properties. The elements with their properties do not merely go into the compound and emerge from it again, but participate in it. Similarly, if the one force were not operating centrifugally and the other centripetally the body would not move as it does, even though its motion be neither centrifugal nor centripetal. The compound does not violate or negate the properties of its elements, but absorbs and transcends them; there is an effect of having neither set of properties because of the presence of both; but if either element lacked any of its own specific properties, then the compound would lose its characteristic identity. The body which is moving along the diagonal of the parallelogram would not so move unless it were acting under two divergent impulsions. Neither of these component forces is ineffective, neither is thwarted; the behavior of the body is describable only in terms of their joint effectiveness and control. We may not say that in the course of their composition and decomposition the original elements or forces first lose and then resume their identity, or that at any stage they cease to be operative. They enter fully into the whole, and when the whole comes into being they constitute it and it obeys them.

Similarly the behavior of the integral person does not

[5] Though it cannot be said to be better than a pair of objects satisfying both interests independently.

involve the negation of either constituent interest. On the contrary were both interests not fully operative the total behavior would be altered. Were either interest abated in the least the person would act differently. To suppose that the interests were defeated would imply either that they ceased to operate, which contradicts the supposition that they exhaustively determine the person's integral behavior; or it would imply that each constituent interest was counted twice, as moving the individual in isolation, and as moving the individual in conjunction with the other. This double rôle would contradict the assumption that in perfect integration the constituent interests have been completely absorbed in the whole, or operate only in so far as they participate.[6]

§ 262. **Subordination and Self-Love.** A well-integrated personality implies something more than the mere absence of conflict. In so far as such personality is achieved, harmony is not an accident but is guaranteed.[7] We must not be led by the analogy of the parallelogram of forces to suppose that such a personal or moral system is the result of the mere juxtaposition of the constituent interests. There is a factor which conditions their union, namely, that process of mediation which has already been examined.[8] It is this process which Professor L. T. Hobhouse thinks deserving of the name of "practical reason":

"The problem of the practical reason is to develop the elements of a working consistency, mutual support, or, as I call it, Harmony, within the entire sphere of impulsive feeling, and the 'force' of the rational is the summed energy of the felt needs acting as an organized whole. Rational aims focus the felt wants of man so far as they are consistent. Reason operates on the primary impulses by purging them of mutual inconsistency and shaping them into contributory elements in a system of life by

---

[6] For *imperfect* integration, in which the constituent interest retains something of its original independence, cf. §§ 236-238.

[7] It must not be forgotten that harmonious integration justifies itself *only* by the avoidance of conflict. Such integration would be no better than non-integration were the interests so irrelevant as not to cross one another. Contact of interests as a source of conflict is a breeder of evil, and a well-recognized mode of achieving harmony is the adoption of a plan by whch isolation is secured. Cf. § 156.

[8] Cf. Ch. XIII, XV, Sect. I.

which in turn they are in their modified form sustained and furthered."[9]

The achievement of harmonious personality depends in particular upon two modes of mediation, the mode in which one interest is mediated by another interest, and the mode in which an interest is mediated by a judgment of interest. The former mode gives rise to subordination, and the latter to inter-interest, or mutuality, of which love is a special case.[10]

When one interest is subordinate to another, conflict is impossible, because the subordinate interest ceases to exist at the moment when conflict arises. There are two varieties of subordination, which it has now for the first time become useful to distinguish, and which it will be convenient to designate respectively as 'positive' and 'negative.' Positive subordination is the familiar case in which a subordinate interest, deriving its motivation wholly from an ulterior dominant interest, exists only so far as its object promises the fulfilment of that ulterior interest. Negative subordination, on the other hand, is the case in which the subordinate interest exists only so long as its object does not threaten the defeat of the dominant interest. In the latter case the dominant interest exercises a censorship over the subordinate interest, but does not supply its motivation. If a be the object of the subordinate, and b of the dominant interest, then the case of negative subordination is that in which the interest in a is independent of b up to the point at which a implies *not-b*, when it lapses; as when an avaricious person ceases to desire money at the moment when he judges that his gain will be at the expense of his friend.

The mediation of an interest by a judgment of interest constitutes love or benevolence (as distinguished from malice), when the fulfilment of a second interest is the object of the desire or liking of a first. Where such a benevolent interest and its object are constituents of the same subject it is customary to speak of the former as self-love, or self-interest.[11]

[9] In *Contemporary British Philosophy*, 1924, edited by J. H. Muirhead, p. 157.
[10] Cf. §§ 152-154.
[11] This is, I believe, the correct usage; although these and like ex-

In so far as self-consciousness is possible, self-love is possible; that much seems clear. It follows that there are as many forms of self-interest as there are ideas of the self, and as the self is a many-sided entity, it may be viewed by itself as well as by others in various aspects.[12] The self as an aggregate of interests seated in one organism and capable of personal integration,[13] may be conscious of itself either piece-meal or as a whole. Thus self-love may mean an interest on the part of a self in the fulfilment of any one of its own constituent interests, as when, for example, a man consciously cultivates and measures his success in politics or in creative art. Or self-love, in a more complete sense, may mean the emergence within a self of an interest which passes in review the entire aggregate of the self's interests and takes such measures as may insure their joint success. Where such an interest becomes a dominant interest it evidently eliminates conflict, since each interest is then subordinated to all interests, or ceases to assert itself at the point where it violates another. How far a harmonious personality shall assume this form seems to be an arbitrary matter, since harmony may be achieved equally well by an absorbing passion and by a circumspect self-regulation.

§ 263. **The Scale of Personal Preference.** We may now understand something of the structure of a harmonious personality. There will be a dominant interest emerging from the synthesis of the primary constituent interests, and which may be self-forgetfully bent on its own end, or take the form of a new interest in the aggregate fulfilment of the old. To this dominant interest all other interests will be subordinated. This subordinatio. may be either positive or negative, but since the dominant interest commonly arises from the reciprocal modification of preëxisting interests, when these operate jointly and are made aware of one another through reflection,

pressions are often used to imply "selfishness," that is, the *absence* of interest in the interests of other agents.

[12] Cf. James's description of "the material self," "the social self," "the spiritual self," etc., in *Principles of Psychology,* 1890, Ch. X.

[13] Cf. Ch. XV, Sect. I.

their subordination will tend to assume the negative form. In other words, each interest will occupy as much room as the rest permit. The control of one interest by another will not be that of a source over its tributary, but rather that of the limitation of one independently originating force by another. Nevertheless when the organization is effected there will be a hierarchical arrangement of interests, such that an interest lower in the scale withdraws its claim at the point where this conflicts with the claim of an interest higher in the scale.

This scale may be said to constitute the scale of personal preference. It is important to distinguish between an interest's 'strength,' [14] and its place in this preferential scale, though the one may be causally related to the other. That an interest is headstrong, intractable and more or less dissociated does not mean that it is preferred; any more than a runner's unwillingness to enter the race is evidence of his speed. An interest finds its place in the scale of personal preference only in so far as it participates through reflection in the synthetic choice by which its own place is allocated. Where its strength tends to prevent or interrupt deliberation, this strength is not evidence of personal favor but rather of personal disintegration.

As representing all of the interests from which the person is integrated, the personal scale is a common scale in which all of the constituent interests concur, or which they all endorse. At the same time it is important to note that up to a certain point the personal purpose and its scale of preference leaves constituent interests unaltered. Each interest will possess a certain 'liberty,' or a range within which its particular preferences are not determined by the dominant purpose. Thus a man who having reviewed and organized his interests and given political ambition precedence among them, need consult only his palate in choosing between green and ripe olives, or his aesthetic taste in choosing between etchings and water-colors. Each interest preserves in the economy of the

[14] Cf. § 252.

whole a certain domestic life of its own,—a neutral sphere within which it is permitted to do as *it* pleases.

The organization of a harmonious personality may be said to define a system of objects which are better than the aggregate of the objects of the conflicting interests which it superseded, since the former enjoy the favor of all of the given group of interests, whereas the latter were favored only by a fraction of this group. It also defines a system of objects which are commensurable one with another in respect both of preference and of inclusiveness. It is true that there are orders of preference relative to each constituent interest which remain incommensurable with one another, but relatively to the choice of the person as a whole, all objects now find a place in one order. This order of personal preference is of a coarser scale [15] than those of the subordinate interests, and that which is better relatively to one of the latter will be of equal value relatively to the former. Altitudes of aesthetic preference may be represented simply by their points of intersection on the scale of personal preference. Thus, for example, the superiority of water-colors to etchings in the aesthetic scale may not appear at all in the personal scale, the dominant purpose having no preference between the two, but distinguishing them only as a class from the objects of other interests.

It is now possible to define a best object, as that preferred to all other objects by the interest which is given precedence over all other interests. But such a supreme object will be less good than the total system of objects, since the latter contains not only this object but all other objects favorably regarded by the constituent interests of the total person.

Our conclusions may be summarily stated in terms of a personal *standard* of value, which renders a person subject to one or more of the following critical judgments:

First, a person may be criticized as having succeeded or failed in that achievement of a harmonious personality which is in principle better than a disordered and conflicting aggregate of interests.

[15] Cf. § 254.

Second, the several objects of a person's integral interest may be compared as regards their place, high or low, in the personal scale.

Third, the person may be criticized as having committed error in the mediating judgments by which his personality is integrated, or as having failed to see clearly and truly the relations of means to ends, and of one of his interests to another.

Finally, a person may be criticized as selfish, that is, as lacking benevolent interest in the interests of other persons. Having achieved personal harmony a self may yet be open to the charge of social conflict, or of having fallen short of that best which consists in universal harmony. It is not to be supposed that personal integration or even self-love is necessarily selfish. The several interests of the same subject may be interests in the interests of another subject. Thus the mother, for example, may enjoy the pleasures of her child, and at the same time be ambitious for his worldly success. Both are interests *of* the mother, *in* the child. So far as the mother integrates these two interests, by viewing one in the light of the other or seeking to realize them jointly, she exhibits self-love; but inasmuch as the interests which thus mediate one another are both interests in the child, her sentiment is also altruistic. Whether a person be highly or loosely integrated, whether he be self-conscious or self-forgetful, he may yet be either selfish or humane. While one perfect in self-love is not necessarily selfish, it is thus equally true that such a personal achievement has yet to be judged in the light of that ulterior standard to which we now turn.

II. THE SUPREMACY OF THE ALL-BENEVOLENT WILL [16]

§ 264. **Conflict between Persons.** Having defined the sense in which a harmonious personality is superior to a state of inner conflict, we have now to consider the more notable case of the superiority of a harmonious society to a state of conflict between persons. The problem is vividly presented

[16] Cf. also Ch. XV, Sect. III; and Ch. XVII, Sect. V.

by a striking passage in James's essay on "The Moral Philosopher and the Moral Life":

"If the hypothesis were offered us of a world in which Messrs. Fourier's and Bellamy's and Morris's utopias should be all outdone, and millions kept permanently happy on the one simple condition that a certain lost soul on the far-off edge of things should lead a life of lonely torture, what except a specific and independent sort of emotion can it be which would make us immediately feel, even though an impulse arose within us to clutch at the happiness so offered, how hideous a thing would be its enjoyment when deliberately accepted as the fruit of such a bargain?" [17]

The "specifical and independent emotion" which inspired the writer of this paragraph, and which affects us so poignantly when we read it, is a distinctly modern and occidental sentiment,—the legitimate offspring of Christianity and democracy. There was a time when the European conscience would not even have been disturbed by the thought that a single favored individual, or a small caste of the *élite*, should enjoy happiness through the misery of millions of lost souls. The new conscience not only requires that the majority shall be admitted to happiness, but that no man shall be excluded from it. It is as though one were to feel that the feast cannot begin until every one is seated at the table, or that joy cannot be unalloyed without a sense of universal participation.

In creating this fictitious case the author was for the moment concerned to show that there is a moral sentiment *sui generis*, which cannot be reduced to the memory or expectation of private pleasures. A historian of the age in which we live would doubtless record the fact that there are persons with consciences so tender that they cannot be happy unless they believe that everybody is happy. Is this the end of the matter? Have we here to do only with a peculiar hypersensitiveness, like the fear of cats or the vertigo felt in high places? Shall we merely enter it in our clinical catalogue of human experience? Or shall we *credit* this species of conscience as possessed of moral insight? Does it contain some

[17] *Will to Believe, and other Essays,* 1898, p. 188.

judgment of comparative value that is *true*, in the light of fact and reason?

We have first to note the unmistakable presence of judgment. When I imagine the situation, I not only feel pity for the lost soul and disgust at the millions who are willing to be happy at his expense, but I experience the firm conviction that the happiness of a million somehow fails utterly to compensate or even to mitigate the torture of one. I feel that my feeling has nothing to do with it, and that the situation would not be materially altered if I were to become careless about lost souls and less squeamish about tainted happiness. The conviction is all the more explicit because it involves the rejection of a plausible alternative. It would seem that the happiness of the millions *ought* so far to outweigh the torture of the lost soul as to reduce the latter to a negligible quantity. One *ought* to comment favorably on the thrifty expedient by which so much good is purchased at so small a price. But no such judgment occurs. On the contrary, the evil of the one seems unrelieved, and even aggravated, by the fact that it is a cause of the good of the many.

That this judgment is justified, there is, in the light of the foregoing analysis of comparative value, good reason to believe. As co-exclusive, the claims of the lost soul and of the happy millions are incommensurable. They may be assumed to be of equal intensity,—their preferences are opposed and therefore incomparable. To declare the good of the millions to be greater than the evil of the one would ignore this incomparability, and would assume on the part of unit-persons an equality of extensive magnitude to which it is impossible to give any meaning. We must not be misled into supposing that because the good of the millions is neither greater than nor less than the good of the one, the two goods are therefore equal. The supposition of the equal extensive magnitude of persons may arise from this confusion, since conflict most commonly occurs between two unit-persons, each of whose claims is deemed to be 'as good as' that of the other. But since the situation is not affected by adding persons to either side of the equation, it is evident that the relation is not one of equality at all, but of incomparability. The evil of the lost soul is pure, stark, unmitigated and unrelieved.

§ 265. **The Postulate of Concurrence.** There is, then, no solution of the problem through a comparative judgment *between* the lost soul and the happy millions. Is there *no* comparative judgment which will point a solution? The sentiment which James describes suggests, if it does not embody, such a judgment. What is the active impulse that the situation arouses in us? The answer seems clear. We are impelled to go out to that lonely sufferer and *bring him in.* We ask those seated at the table to move up so that the uninvited guest may find a place at the table, or appeal to the fortunate so to alter or moderate their claims as to make them consistent with those of the unfortunate. At the same time we appeal to the newcomer to adjust his claims to those of the group with whom he is now associated. In order that all may be seated it may be necessary that some one shall take the foot of the table or accept a smaller portion than the rest. We find no injustice provided this less privileged person accepts his share of his own volition. We persuade him to *concur,* pointing out that unless he or some one in his place will accept some abatement of his original claims there cannot be room for all. We have found a solution when, and only when, the wills of all are so attuned that each is content with a situation in which provision is made for all.

Whatever may be true of the decision of war, a *solution* of conflict is to be found only in a "peace without victory"; that is, when those who formerly protested now concur. The most familiar application of this principle is to the political conflict between a majority and a minority. So long as there is disagreement in respect of preference, the conflict can never be resolved by a measurement of numbers; or, if the conflict is so resolved, the outcome is the triumph of the stronger but not of the better cause. The *justification* of the majority lies not in its numerical superiority, but in a *general willingness to abide by* the will of the majority. If it were so agreed in advance, the will of two-thirds, or of a plurality (even when a minority) would be just as sacred.[18]   It is becoming more and more apparent that the settlement of international differences appeals to the same principle.   The innumerable conferences which have followed the war are evidently based on the assumption that by discussion the interests of all parties can somehow be satisfied, the only guarantee of peace being a constructive plan which provides for all, and in the support of which all are positively united.

The practical recognition of the same principle in every-day life appears in the appeal to some existing agreement, or in the effort to obtain concurrence, whenever it is desired to settle an issue on the basis of right rather than of force.   Indeed, to raise between man and man the question, "What is the good way?" is to invite attention to common facts in the expectation of seeing alike; or is a joint undertaking by agreement, to find something that can be agreed on.

In all spheres there is a sense of guilt in the presence of discord.   Even the most chauvinistic nation wants to be generally accepted in the rôle to which it assigns itself, as the champion of culture or civilization.   Even a policy of isolation seeks (for example, in the United States) to justify itself as an experiment in free institutions, a refuge for the oppressed, or a model for the political regeneration of the world.   There is scarcely any form of individual or party self-assertion that does not excuse itself as for the general good, and so make at least some slight effort to obtain the willing consent even of those whom it injures.   All of these rationalizations, even when they are uncandid or little more than conciliatory gestures, nevertheless testify to an admission in principle that a conflict of interest can be *solved* only when the conflicting parties are brought into agreement.

In seeking such a solution we virtually employ the principle of inclusiveness, as that has already been applied to the case of personal conflict, and as it is more or less consciously

[18] It is this recognition of the need of agreement that underlies the theory of popular sovereignty, and that has led to the introduction of fictions such as Rousseau's "general will" (*Contrat Social*, Bk. I, Ch. 1-3), to provide for such agreement when actual wills disagree.

adopted in all moral reasoning. It is evident that a situation
in which both the one and the millions were happy *would be*
better. We do not attempt to compare the weight of the
majority and minority interests with one another, or balance
one man's loss against a million's gain. We acknowledge
that there are amounts or degrees of value associated with
each party, between which it is impossible to discriminate because they are incommensurable. We fall back on the principle
that just as the fulfilment of an interest is better than its
defeat, whatever the intensity or grade of the interest, so a
situation which fulfils that interest will, other things being
equal, be better than a situation which defeats it. By the same
token, the fulfilment of any given interest together with the
fulfilment of a second interest, will be better than the fulfilment of either interest together with the defeat of the other.

§ 266. **The Independence of Persons.** Just how does
such a harmonious integration take place? What relation
between the constituent persons does it involve? When we
raise this question we meet at once with the fundamental
difference between personal and social integration, which consists in the fact that the principle of subordination is operative
in the one and inoperative in the other. The relation of dependence in which one interest derives its motive power from
another, or loses its motive power when opposed by another,
is a relation which is internal to a person, and does not obtain
between persons.[19]

In order that we may view the matter as precisely as
possible, let us put ourselves successively in the place of the
millions, of the lost soul and of a disinterested observer.
As one of the millions, I justify the defeat of the lost soul
on the ground that it is a means to my own success. In

---

[19] For a fuller statement of the argument, cf. §§ 188 ff. This is
what Professor Goblot has in mind when he says that two ends, in order
to be compared, must be subsumed under an "ulterior and superior end."—
E. Goblot, *Traité de la Logique*, 1922, pp. 370-371. Cf. Ch. XVII, *passim*,
on "Les Jugements de Valeur." Such a verdict cannot be rendered by *any*
third or ulterior interest, but only by a third interest which is related
to the others as end to means, and which must, therefore, be an end of
the same person.

this way evil seems to have been transmuted into good. I may positively delight in the lost soul's pain,—and not from malice, but from the enthusiastic anticipation of my own pleasure. I prudently subordinate my natural sympathies, and contrive that my feelings towards the sufferer shall be dictated entirely by my ulterior desire.[20] But if I now transfer myself to the position of the lost soul, I find that in fact the evil has not been removed at all. As lost soul I dislike my pain with a heartiness that is not in the least diminished by the fact that it ministers to the pleasure of millions of mankind. On the contrary, I now desire such limitation of the pleasures of the balance of mankind as shall relieve my pain. I see their loss as my gain.

If now I ascend to the judge's bench and review my previous partisanship I see that in each case I made the same rather stupid blunder of supposing that I could subordinate the interest of another person simply by subordinating my *own* interest *in* that interest. I enjoyed the illusion of converting evil into good because I took it for granted that when I had ceased to shrink from the other man's pain, he had ceased also; or that when I *treated* his interest as a means to my end, his interest had *become* a means to my end. I now see from my neutral vantage-point that the other man's interest is not in the slightest degree affected by the subordination of my interest in it. I can subordinate one of my interests to another, and so can he; but neither of us can by so doing in the least diminish the independence of the other's interest. I may be tempted as a neutral observer to commit the same error from my new station. I may find the triumph of one of the rival parties more to *my* liking, or I may even find their very rivalry a means of satisfying my dramatic interest, and thus seem to achieve a condition of pure goodness. But, here again, all that I have done is to reduce my interests one to another without in the least altering the rival interests themselves.

The Kantian dictum, "So act as to treat humanity, whether

[20] I adopt Nietzsche's counsel of "hardness," not from a desire to hurt, but lest I be diverted from my main purpose.

in thine own person or in that of any other, in every case
as an end withal, never as a means only," [21] may be interpreted
as an appeal to empirical fact. The ultimate purposes of
persons remain ultimate regardless of how other persons treat
them. By supposing that the interests of other persons are
no more than the uses which they have for us, we are led
to *ignore* their independence, but we do not in any way negate
it. All independent personal ends are *absolutely* independent.

It is the absence of this relation of dependence or subordination between persons that prevents their fusion or synthesis in a person of a higher order. The essential error of
Durkheim's and other like philosophies is, as we have seen,
the transposition to the social relation of a mode of composition that applies only to the several interests of one and
the same organic subject.[22] It is impossible by the direct
application of the method of subordination to secure a harmonious society. We must, therefore, in this case place our
whole reliance on that second method of integration, the
method of love or benevolence, whose application in a limited
sense we have already noted in the case of personal integration.

What we require is a *personal* integration that shall be
socially qualified, or that shall guarantee a harmonious fulfilment of all interests. The first step towards such a solution
is to suppose any given person M to be governed by the purpose of universal benevolence within a community of two
persons, M and N. Such a will effects an adjustment between the two persons in so far as M's love of N, being
benevolent, is mediated by a judgment regarding N's interest.
But N's interest itself still remains outside the unity, and
cannot be said to have been absorbed by the new integration.[23]

[21] *Metaphysic of Morals,* trans. by T. K. Abbott, *Kant's Theory of
Ethics,* 1883, p. 47.
[22] Cf., Ch. XVI, Sect. I. Durkheim speaks of a "synthesis" of
individual persons comprised within a qualitatively distinct social person.
Cf. *Bulletin de la Soc. Française de la Philos.,* 1906, pp. 128-129.
[23] Even the most sympathetic spectator could not supersede the interests of those to whom his sympathy was addressed, because of the fallibility of his judgment. A pure lover of mankind might still find himself
in conflict with mankind; and the harmony of his humanity would not
preclude a conflict among the men who were its objects. Nevertheless
such a love, sometimes imputed to parent, ruler or God, prefigures that
harmony which is fully achieved only when it is confirmed by all parties.

The next step is to secure a like purpose in N, and the final step is so to modify the benevolence of M and N as to bring them into agreement. The resulting situation will be freed of all possibility of conflict, since neither M nor now N has any interest contrary to the dominant benevolent purpose which they share. Finally, let us add O, P, Q, etc., until all persons are comprised within one community each member of which wills only what is consistent with the wills of all the rest. Such a will is personal in its seat, and in the mode of its composition; while it is social in its object, and in its distribution. Let us now examine this solution more in detail.

§ 267. **Harmony through Universal Love.** In order to understand the harmonizing effect of love it is necessary to define this attitude strictly. Love means, as we have seen, a favorable interest in the satisfaction of a second interest. In the present context it is assumed that the second interest is the interest of a second person. Love begins and ends abroad. That "charity begins at home" is one of those many proverbs which have been coined by the devil to flatter human weakness. Love is, in the next place, essentially *indulgent;* it coincides with, and supports, the interest which is its object. The success or defeat of the loving interest will be a function of what is judged to be the success or defeat of the loved interest. Other-love, in this sense, may be directed to any one, or to the whole system, of the second person's interests. Where love is directed to the whole person it may oppose one of that person's particular interests, in so far as the person is imperfectly integrated. Where a person suffers from internal conflict, another's love may side with the integral self against the insubordinate element; but if love is to be indulgent, there must already be such an integral self in some form or stage of development. Love, in other words, is an interested support of another's preëxisting and independently existing interest.[24]

---

[24] This does not preclude the possibility that the loved one may be momentarily unaware of his interest, and need to be reminded of it; but

There are several common meanings of love which this definition excludes. In the first place, love is neither approving nor censorious. It does not prescribe the object of the loved interest, but desires that that interest shall have its object *whatever* that object. Suppose a son to desire fame; then the father's desire for the son's fame, if founded on the father's admiration of fame, is not love; nor is it love if the father desires that the son shall substitute for fame some other object, such as knowledge, which he, the father, prefers. Action towards another dictated by the agent's belief that he knows better what is good for the other than does the other himself, may be praiseworthy, but it is not love.[25] The true quality of love is to be found in that sensitive imagination which can find its way into the secret sources of a man's joy and sorrow.[26] Similarly, censoriousness, though it may be just, is not love. Love does not rebuke the sinner, or rejoice in his merited punishment; but grieves for him, and seeks to *bring him in,* as the shepherd seeks his lost sheep. Love, like Thomson's "Hound of Heaven," follows its object relentlessly into every corner of the universe and refuses to be offended or repelled.

The support of another's interest that springs from a sense of plenitude and power, or that looks to bind the other in gratitude, is not love. Nor is it love when an appetite feeds upon another individual, even though the other be of the same species. So-called sex-love may be as unloving as cannibalism. Finally, love must have an object other than itself. To love another's love of oneself, supposing oneself to consist only in love of the other, would be meaningless, even though it occurs in poetry and fiction. The circle must be broken at some point by an interest directed to an object, in order that

only that the interest must really be his, and not merely one felt in his behalf by somebody else.

[25] It was patriotism and not love for the Alsatians which dictated Treitschke's judgment that "we Germans, who know both Germany and France, know better what is for the good of the Alsatians than do those unhappy people themselves" (quoted from H. W. C. Davis, *The Political Thought of Treitschke,* 1915, p. 112).

[26] Cf. W. James, "On a Certain Blindness in Human Beings," *Talks with Teachers,* etc., 1899.

there may be something for love to indulge. What seems to be circular love is the gratification afforded to each of two individuals by the presence of the other. Other-love finds itself most purely embodied in parental love, for the very reason that it is commonly one-sided or unreciprocated. Reciprocity adds to the intensity of love, but tends to impair its purity through introducing an element of sensuous gratification or of self-reference.

Love in the present sense consists essentially, then, in an activity which supports the interested activity of another person; seeking to promote that other person's achievement of what he desires, or enjoyment of what he likes. Universal love would be such a disposition on the part of one person towards all persons. If it is psychologically possible (in the sense of the general capacity of human nature) towards one, it is psychologically possible towards two or more; or towards all members of a class, such as the family, the nation, mankind, or sentient creatures. This attitude of general kindly interest, or of amiability, has its negative form, as in Lincoln's maxim, "with malice toward none, with charity for all"; and its positive form, as in good Samaritanism and humanity. A personal integration dominated by such a purpose is known in the tradition of moral philosophy as 'good will.'

§ 268. **The Conflicts of Benevolence.** Such a universal love, felt by any person for all mankind, including himself, defines a system of objects which is better than any personal system which lacks this benevolent purpose. The man who loves his neighbor as himself loves more inclusively than the neighbor who does not reciprocate. This is true only because the latter is a partial constituent of the former. While in this sense unselfishness takes precedence of selfishness,[27] it is not justified in *overriding* the latter. We cannot say that the triumph of unselfishness and defeat of selfishness, is better than the triumph of selfishness and defeat of unselfishness; because the defeat of selfishness would imply the defeat of that unselfishness which embraces it.

[27] Selfishness meaning not self-love, but the *absence* of other-love.

We can only say that the triumph of both which is implied in the triumph of unselfishness, is better than the triumph of one which is implied in the triumph of selfishness.[28] Love is not satisfied by the suffering of the sinner even when it is merited, but only by his repentance and participation in the general happiness.

Unfortunately, however, the good will of one person does not necessarily accord with the good will of another person. It is doubtless true that a great part of social conflict can be attributed to a difference of ultimate purpose. A will which incorporates interests a, b, and c differs from a will which incorporates a, b, c, and d, and the solution then lies in modifying the first will by the incorporation of d. This situation is commonly obscured by the supposition that d is already incorporated, when the first will has an interest in the subject of d, but not in his interest; as when the father's interest in his son is supposed to embrace the son's interests, when it really embraces only a certain state or condition of the son. Often the situation is candidly recognized, as when a nation may assert itself against the larger interest of mankind and claim on its own behalf a finality which it does not really possess. Different integrations of interests will have different objects, and it is absurd to suppose, as has been claimed in behalf of the doctrine of *laissez-faire*, that there is any preëstablished harmony between self-interest and social-interest. They may partially coincide, or accidentally and momentarily agree, but sooner or later they will differ, *because their premises differ*. The only way in which self-interest and social-interest can be made to agree in principle,

---

[28] This principle has an important bearing on jurisprudence and on the relation of man to lower forms of life. Punishment involves the deliberate inflicting of pain or some other form of evil on the guilty man, and does defeat his interest. This can be rationalized ultimately only provided the guilty man can be said to have agreed to suffer the penalty of his transgression. This would be the correct interpretation of the Socratic maxim that virtue can do no evil, or that it is impossible to justify an act in terms of evil consequences. Where, as in the case of the *use* of animals, or the punishment of the defiant transgressor, the interest of the second party is ignored, the relation becomes one which cannot be moralized, but can be defended only in terms of the interest of the stronger.

or necessarily, is to subsume the interests of the self under an interest in society.

Although social conflict can often, perhaps usually, be resolved by showing that one of the conflicting wills embraces the other and is therefore better, or entitled to precedence, this does not fully meet the difficulties. The supreme tragedy of life is the conflict of good wills, or the opposition of the integral interests of two equally well-intentioned persons. Two men may love mankind equally and yet be brought into antagonism with one another by the very earnestness of their benevolence. How is this possible? It arises obviously from the fact that the same constituent interests, where some are present and others represented, may be differently mediated and integrated. To present the fact in the simplest form, suppose three persons, L, M and N, to love one another in accordance with the Golden Rule. Suppose each to be interested in the interests of the other two as well as in his own, and suppose the complexus of interests in each person to assume the form of a unified purpose or plan of life, with an order of precedence among all the interests involved. It is entirely possible that three different and opposing purposes should emerge, since in L's purpose M and N are represented only through L's benevolence, while L and N are so represented in M, and L and M in N. These differences are likely to involve other differences of angle, of distance, and of judgment as to the causal relations of means to ends. It follows that such differences will be mitigated by the perfecting of sympathy or understanding, and by the substitution of common truth for diverse error. The way to secure a just solution is to seek a benevolent purpose on which all can unite. In such a purpose the effects of bias will neutralize and cancel one another. The purpose of which it can be said that it most perfectly incorporates the interests of all three is the *common plan* adopted by L, M and N, after the discussion of the three benevolent plans initially proposed by L, M and N severally. All parties will be disposed to harmony because of being benevolent, and when agreement is desired the chief obstacle to its attainment is already overcome.

These are, however, questions of moral education and of social reconstruction. The important thing is to recognize not only that an agreement of good wills is possible and may be methodically cultivated, but that such an agreement is better than anything else, and may properly be adopted as a standard and end.

This conclusion is perhaps not far from the meaning of Kant's famous rendering of the 'categorical imperative': "Act on that maxim whereby thou canst at the same time will that it should become a universal law." [29] The defect in this formula as it stands, lies in the term "canst," which seems to appeal to a psychological capacity, and to suggest a subjective criterion of right conduct. There is, as a matter of fact, *no* maxim that *can*not be willed to become universal law. Amended in accordance with the conclusions already reached, Kant's imperative would read, "Cultivate that kind of will that is qualified to bring harmony through its universal adoption." A will meeting this requirement will be first of all a benevolent will; and beyond that a conciliatory will, disposed by experience and discussion to the adoption of a common plan.

§ 269. **The Structure and Scale of the All-Benevolent Will.** The supreme will would thus be both universally benevolent and also *repetitive* or *recurrent*. It would not be a single will except as regards its objects. It would be a common will only as consisting in the willing *of* the same by different persons, but subjectively there would be as many wills as persons. The structure of such an inter-personal system of interests has already been examined. It would be a *federation* [30] rather than a corporate unity, in that it would be composed of a multiplicity of independent wills; none having any superiority over others, although the aggregate would be superior to the components. The system would be unified not by the subordination of one person to others, but by the devo-

---

[29] *Metaphysic of Morals,* trans. by T. K. Abbott, *Kant's Theory of Ethics.* 1889, p. 38.
[30] Cf. Ch. XV, Sect. III.

tion of all to the same ideal; and by the reciprocal relations which this common ideal would involve, and to which all alike, by virtue of holding the same ideal, would subscribe. It would be a system of *cooperation,* since, owing to the bond of love, each person would support all the rest, and each would directly or by indirection will the activities of all his partners in the common plan.[31]

The scale of the preferences of such a perfectly socialized will would not necessarily coincide with that of the same person prior to such an integration, for the aforesaid reason that the same conclusions do not necessarily follow from different premises. The only way to make a personal preference coincide with universal benevolence is to make a person universally benevolent. There would nevertheless be stretches of all-benevolent preference which would coincide with personal preference, or which would incorporate the latter without modifying it. In a perfectly ordered society there would remain a plurality of wills, not only in respect of subjective agency, but also in respect of the interest of each of these wills in uniquely personal objects. As in the organized person, so here also, there would be zones of 'liberty' where the higher social principle would leave personal activities undetermined. The all-benevolent will legislates in terms so general as to leave a large measure of autonomy to self-love. It maintains a sort of protectorate in which it claims jurisdiction only over foreign affairs.

Superior principles do not annul the operation of subordinate principles: to a very considerable extent they permit and endorse them as they stand. International good will leaves innumerable alternatives open to national aspiration, as the sentiment of humanity leaves to each man his own choices of individual perfection. Within the personal life, again, the paramount purposes of benevolence and self-love, leave to each interest its own range of preference. There is an autonomous province of self-interest within the universal realm, and an interior province of taste within that of self-

[31] For illustrations of this type of social integration, cf. Ch. XVII, Sect. V.

interest. Each of these provinces and sub-provinces has its laws, or its rationale of choice. Here it is that one finds that "good" of which Nietzsche speaks, which is opposed, not to "evil" but to "bad"; that good which is equivalent to the "aristocratic," "beautiful," and "loved by the gods." [32] According to Nietzsche, such good is certified by disagreement:

> "One must renounce the bad taste of wishing to agree with many people. 'Good' is no longer good when one's neighbor takes it into his mouth. And how could there be a 'common good'! The expression contradicts itself; that which can be common is always of small value. In the end things must be as they are and have always been—the great things remain for the great, the abysses for the profound, the delicacies and thrills for the refined, everything rare for the rare." [33]

The code of Nietzsche is, however, essentially a provincial code. It is a child's code, which is conditioned on the protective government of the elders; a play-time code, for which provision must be made under the rules of the workaday world. This is entirely consistent with the fact that the irresponsibility of childhood is more agreeable than the apprehensions of adult life, or that play is sweeter than work. It may be argued that the merit of the higher principle lies in its permitting the operation of the lower. But when one so argues one is implying that foresight provides for irresponsibility, and work for play, in a sense in which the reverse is not true. The fact remains that control must be vested in the higher. Only a social system founded on universal benevolence can make it possible that one should do as one likes, or that, within certain limits, one should choose in accordance with the dictates of pride and taste. Having, in short, agreed on their fundamental course of action, and so obtained a guarantee of non-interference, men can then afford to disagree. A survey of human history makes it fairly evident that when men are in conflict they are very much alike, while when they have achieved a durable peace through having adopted a common plan of life, their individual differences

[32] *Genealogy of Morals,* I, §§ 2, 7, 16.
[33] *Beyond Good and Evil,* Aphorism 43, English trans., by H. Zimmern, 1907.

multiply. Nor is it true that richness and diversity of life are promoted by isolation. Friendship is a better means of liberty than avoidance, for he that is not with me at heart may at any time be against me, and those whose ways are divided may unexpectedly collide in the dark.

An all-benevolent will, or a benevolence of which all persons are the object, and which is each person's controlling purpose, is a unique mode of life—an integration *sui generis*. It is neither a personal integration nor a mere community of interest, but a union of the two. It might be said that the form or quality of this type of will is a personal achievement. It is the characteristic product of a personal life in which all interests are subordinated to the love of the aggregate of persons, a will resulting from the catalytic action of universal benevolence within the chemism of that complexus of appetites and desires that is rooted in one organism. This fact justifies those reformers who insist that there can be no hope of social amelioration save through regenerating the hearts and wills of individuals. But while the perfected will is thus in form and structure a personal will, it is socially qualified in a double sense. On the one hand, it must have all mankind as its preferred object; and, on the other hand, it must be reaffirmed, repeated and reiterated by all individual members of mankind. It is not a social will, but it is a personal will socially directed and socially multiplied. It is a preferred will because it is everybody's good will towards everybody. It is a will in which it is reasonable for all to concur, not because of some occult property or authoritative sanction, but because such general concurrence is reasonable. God is not a glory that justifies the damnation of men, except in so far as men are participants in the glory and are *willing* to be damned for it.

This peculiar accord of persons loses nothing from the fact that it cannot properly be termed a person. The demand that God shall be a person is only the last of the anthropomorphisms by which man has compromised God by the desire to worship him. When persons live in accord the total situation is something greater than a person, as truly as an organism is something greater than a cell. To conceive God as a person is both to confuse the meaning of personality, and to deny to God the right to be himself. It argues an inability or unwillingness to think the novel in its own terms.[34] The apostolic teaching that "God is love," which has been reaffirmed by so many sages of secular inspiration,[35] may well mean something richer than that God is a loving person.

The conception of an all-benevolent will, or of a moral control (to paraphrase Lincoln's famous formula) *of* all persons, *by* all persons, *for all* persons,—defines a system of objects whose values are all-commensurable. Such a supreme or absolute system of preferences may, furthermore, be *corrected,* as respects its mediating judgments. The true best will be the preferred object of such an identical will when it is not only benevolent but also enlightened.

That all persons should be *truly happy,* that they should enjoy and attain what as persons they like and desire, may seem a somewhat banal conclusion of so laborious an argument. But a philosopher should be able to endure the confirmation of the wise, and even derive assurance from agreement with those persistent ideas which have been revealed to the insight of the few and ratified by the common-sense and instinct of the many. It is not to its discredit that an opinion should remove the superficial differences and swell the fundamental unison of human aspiration. Sages have been divided on two questions: Does the supreme good consist in utility and pleasure, or in some deeper well-being, such as virtue, self-perfection or saintliness? Does the supreme good appertain to the human individual, or to some greater social or cosmic whole? These dilemmas disappear, and the demands which underlie them are met, if the supreme good is conceived as the object which satisfies all individuals, when individuals are both personally integrated and harmoniously

---

[34] S. Alexander is, I think, correct in insisting that deity shall be conceived as a type of emergence which is *founded* on personal life, but which cannot be adequately defined in terms of such categories as mind, spirit or personality. Cf. *Space, Time and Deity,* 1920, Bk. IV.

[35] "—that Living Love that wills the blessedness of others" (Lotze, *Microcosmus,* trans. by Hamilton and Jones, 1887, Vol. II, p. 721).

associated; and if this object is interpreted to mean the joint
and inclusive satisfaction of all individuals. In the conception
of a happiness of all which is the condition of the happiness
of each, there is standing-ground alike for Stoics and Epi-
cureans, for Kantians and Utilitarians, for Christians and
Pagans. The highest good is not sheer satisfaction of maximum intensity, but, as Plato taught, an *order* of satisfaction,
whose form is prescribed by reason.[36] The highest happiness
is not that which is most comfortable and easy of attainment,
but, as Christianity has taught, that tragic happiness which
is at once the privilege and the penalty of love.

§ 270. **The Highest Good as an Ideal.** The highest
good is doubly ideal. It is the ideal object of an ideal will.
It is an ideal object in the sense that it is constructed [37] out
of the objects of the original interests which compose the
integral will; and is the project rather than the fulfilment
of that will. But the will itself is likewise a construct. The
highest good, in other words, is that definable ideal which,
if adopted by all as an ideal, *would* be best; and it is the
ideal which is by its nature best qualified to be so adopted.
If, then, one asks, "Does such all-harmonious, all-benevolent
and enlightened unanimity exist?" there can, on empirical
grounds, be only one answer: "Alas! no. The outstanding
fact of life is conflict." But the whole significance of a theory
of value lies in such words as "Alas!" Why "Alas!" unless
it be true that it were best that such a unanimity *should*
exist? The best so defined is a hypothetical and not a historical fact; a hypothesis constructed, however, in accordance
with the meaning of the term 'best,' and therefore having
the force of truth. If I say that another world-war *would be*
a supreme catastrophe, or that a man having a stature of ten
feet *would be taller* than any man now alive, I affirm what
is true despite the non-occurrence of war or the non-existence
of giants. It is a sound inference from established facts and
principles, and a proper answer to one who is curious about

[36] Cf. the *Philebus*, 62, and *passim*.
[37] For 'constructive ideal,' cf. § 167.

such contingencies and possibilities. So if one asks generally what would be best, and is answered in terms of that which neither did, nor does, nor ever will exist, such an answer is not on that account either inapt or untrue.

There is only one ground on which it can be argued that this ideal must, despite appearances on earth, be realized in heaven. It may be argued that if any object has value at all its value must be comparable (as equal, greater or less) with every other value. Granting that objects do have value, and assuming that this implies commensurability or a single all-comprehensive hierarchy, it is argued that an all-harmonious will must therefore be affirmed in some met-empirical and metaphysical sense.

In concluding the essay in which he adopts the principle of inclusiveness, William James says:

"It would seem, too, . . . that the stable and systematic moral universe for which the ethical philosopher asks is fully possible only in a world where there is a divine thinker with all-enveloping demands. If such a thinker existed, his way of subordinating the demands to one another would be the finally valid casuistic scale; his claims would be the most appealing; his ideal universe would be the most inclusive realizable whole. If he now exist, then actualized in his thought already must be that ethical philosophy which we seek as the pattern which our own must evermore approach. In the interest of our own ideal of systematically unified moral truth, therefore, we, as would-be philosophers, must postulate a divine thinker, and pray for the victory of the religious cause." [38]

The force of this passage evidently depends on a theory of knowledge which accepts as true in fact that to which it is reasonable to aspire, or which justifies *believing in* what one *prays for*. Waiving this pragmatic or moral theory of knowledge,[39] there is no ground in fact or reason, why values

---

[38] *Op. cit.,* pp. 213-214. James cites J. Royce's *Religious Aspect of Philosophy* (1885) as affirming that such a "divine thinker" is metaphysically real. Royce's philosophy furnishes the best example of an argument for the reality of a universal community from the assumption of the all-commensurability of values.

[39] Cf. above, Ch. XI. We must also, in the light of the foregoing, reject James's assumption, so contrary to his characteristic individualism,

should not be conflicting and incommensurable, and yet be values. God defined as a will which *would* make all demands harmonious and commensurable *if* it existed, is so defined by combining the *facts* of discord and incommensurability with the *principles* of comparative value. The result is not a statement of historical fact, but a norm of legitimate aspiration. So construed, James's methodological God, conceived in the interest of ethical thought, may be reconciled with his real God, conceived in accordance with the facts of the moral life. God is that being whose nature may be judged highest, in the sense proper to a goal as yet unattained but rationally binding on the will. God is a being far exceeding and surpassing man, and yet dependent on man's moral effort. The world becomes divine through being willed to be divine, and hence its being divine is conditioned by the dynamic faith through which high resolves are carried into effect. God's existence may in this sense result from a belief *in* God, though not from a belief that God already exists.

There are two important demands which an ideal should satisfy: it must be that which it is claimed to be, namely the best; and it must be realizable. Neither of these demands requires that the ideal shall be in fact realized. To affirm this tends, on the contrary, to defeat both demands. When Green, for example, insists that the "moral will" is metaphysically real, he is compelled to judge the moral will by its manifestations in history, and thus to accept the rule of custom or institutional authority.[40] It is inevitable that a will such as history manifests should be less good than Green or any other reflective moralist can *conceive*. There remains only the alternative of judging the historical moral will by its good manifestations, while excusing the rest as inscrutable. Quite apart from the illegitimacy of thus selecting the evidence,[41] the result is to make the ideal empty and indeter-

that God's demands could "envelop" man's, without man's concurrent will; or that any individual's demands could be "subordinated" *for* him by another will, even though it should be the will of God.

[40] The difficulties encountered by such a view are illustrated by the discussions in Green's *Prolegomena to Ethics,* 1890, pp. 350 ff.

[41] Cf. Hume, *Dialogues concerning Natural Religion.*

minate. The same motives are at play in popular piety. Assuming God to be both perfect and the responsible author of history, one is compelled to judge God in the light of history. Even though one judges God only by the good in history and ignores the evil, it is necessary to lean heavily on the limitations of human intelligence. One must either judge God strictly and fairly by the historical evidence, in which case he is less than the best; or one must give him the benefit of the doubt, which puts a premium on doubt and tends to divest the ideal of any content whatever. Simple and humble piety meets the difficulty by extending limitless credit to God, in order to save him from moral bankruptcy; but the effect is to impoverish both man and God, robbing the former of knowledge and the latter of meaning. The persistent danger of religion is that through excess of faith in his existence God should cease in any moral or intelligible sense to be divine.

It is not to be supposed, on the other hand, that the highest good would lose its supremacy if it were realized. James appears to affirm this when he says

"The solid meaning of life is always the same eternal thing,—the marriage, namely, of some unhabitual ideal, however special, with some fidelity, courage, and endurance; with some man's or woman's pains.—And, whatever or wherever life may be, there will always be the chance for that marriage to take place." [42]

If the universal happiness were attained it would not, however, cease to possess value, provided it were enjoyed. Its value may without diminution pass from the progressive to the recurrent form, or from that which is sought by aspiration and struggle, to that which is cherished and perpetuated. So long as it is unattained, the effort to attain it is both rational and heroic; but it is not reasonable on that account to turn away from its consummation to some quixotic enterprise, simply in order to be heroic. This would be true only on the false hypothesis that the supreme end is the heroic performance of anything, no matter what.

In any case, the ideal must present itself as something *to be realized*. Its consummation must in some measure be

[42] *Talks with Teachers,* etc., 1899, p. 299.

imaginatively anticipated, in order that it may operate as a specific expectation. The ideal must be fitted to the nature of the will, and perfection must have a meaning in terms of experience. There must be moments when man at *his* best, catches the color and flavor of *the* best; or, as it is commonly expressed, there must be a spark of God in man. Nor has there ever been any serious disagreement as to what this moment is. It is that moment of melting tenderness felt in the presence of beauty, or of chivalric devotion to a cause, or of compassion for the brave struggle and patient suffering of sentient creatures; when one is drawn into some major current of life, and when the joy that testifies to human interest is mingled with the tears that testify to its unnatural exaltation. If it be objected that such moments are too essentially personal to exemplify an associated and reciprocal life, then let the answer be found in those moments of perfected intercourse in which happiness is founded on generosity, and in which there is a sudden revelation of the meaning of marriage, of friendship, of human fellowship.[43]

The lesson of life is thus not a counsel of unattainable perfection, or the formulation of a definable, but unimaginable and humanly meaningless aspiration. It is rather a question of living on those heights to which one momentarily ascends, or which have been visited and memorably reported by spiritually gifted men.

It may be that any formulation of the highest good will leave men dissatisfied. It must necessarily be rejected by those who through their habitual preoccupation with utilities are unable to conceive of any good thing which is not good *for* something, and who are nevertheless intelligent enough to see that goods of this sort always raise and leave unanswered a question of ulterior good. Present such persons with any good whatsoever, such as beauty or friendship, and their only possible response will be the mechanical reiteration of the query, "To what end?" Others will be dissatisfied

---

[43] For the blend of joy and kindness ("Jubilation is an expansive affection") which is characteristic of religious saintliness, cf. W. James, *Varieties of Religious Experience*, 1902, pp. 279-283, 344, 388.

because they have unconsciously assumed that if the ideal is to be rational it must recommend itself to their preëxisting personal tastes and preferences. They look upon the highest good as a sort of Santa Claus whose claim upon their allegiance may rightly be denied if he does not bring them the particular boon which they crave. Still others, who may have transcended the categories of utility and of self, may yet feel no conviction because of the abstractness of the terms in which a universal end must necessarily be formulated. It is not to be expected that one should warm to the highest good save in certain moments of exaltation that can scarcely be expected to occur when one is reading a philosophical treatise.

And yet those moments in which the perfected will is lived and experienced, and which serve as a clue by which it may be recovered and sustained, are perhaps more often achieved by simple-minded men than by the learned or artful. Of all great gifts the commonest is loving-kindness: and of all great gifts, this is the greatest.

POSTSCRIPT

There are three accepted classifications of values. The most venerable of these, both in antiquity and in repute, is the trinity of canonized values, known as "the True, the Beautiful and the Good"; or the tetrad in which to these three there is added the higher unity of God. This classification employs two principles: a triadic psychology, which divides mind into thought, feeling and will; and an absolutist philosophy, which affirms that these three acts define a convergeant goal of aspiration. The Absolute or God, when thought is Truth, when felt is Beauty, and when willed is Goodness. Or: thought, when universalized, is Truth; feeling, when universalized, is Beauty; will, when universalized, is Goodness; while that harmony in which these three are reconciled is God. This mode of classification, since it turns upon the question of the standards by which values are to be graded and validated, may properly be called an 'axiological' classification.

A second mode of classification is that which, assuming values to be functions of interest, divides them in accordance with the several modalities of interest or the different relations which objects may sustain thereto: Such a classification has been virtually provided in the present work. It remains only to extend to values the distinctions that have already been applied to interests, and hence to classify them as positive and negative, progressive and recurrent, potential and actual, independent and dependent, playful and real, submissive and aggressive, subjective and objective, immediate and mediate, or personal and social. This classification may be termed 'psychological.'

The third mode of classification is that which adopts the divisions already made among the several moral or social sciences, accepting as units those values or groups of values which have acquired an institutional form, such as cognitive, moral, economic, political, aesthetic and religious values.[1] This method of classification might appropriately be termed a 'historical' classification.

The axiological classification is objectionable on several grounds. It is based upon a doubtful psychology; it classifies values in terms of their grades and hierarchical eminence rather than in terms of their actual differences, and includes only values of a certain superlative dignity; it treats truth as a value, and hence assumes a highly questionable view of the relation of cognition and interest. It tends generally to promote a worshipful rather than an observant attitude towards the whole subject.

The psychological classification, standing alone, tends to be excessively detailed and schematic. Interest has so many aspects and ramifications that it is impossible to exhaust its varieties. Classifications of this type are too easy to make, and too likely to prove barren when they are made.

A fruitful theory of value will accept those stable and well-marked unities in which the values of life are already grouped. The great *foci* of interest are science, conscience, art, industry, state and church. Perhaps there is no absolute reason why this should be so, but there is no denying the fact that it is so. Having examined the general nature of value, and elucidated the principles which determine its varieties, its mutations and its grades, the next task is to employ these principles for the rectification of frontiers and the establishment of order among its historically authentic realms. Such would be the proper sequel to the present work.

[1] Cf. § 2.

BIBLIOGRAPHY

The following works deal broadly with the subject of value. They are arranged in order of clearness and accessibility from the stand-point of an English reader who is unacquainted with the field. References on special questions will be found in the foot-notes.

D. W. Prall: "A Study in the Theory of Value," 1921 (Univ. of Calif. Publ. in Philos., Vol. III, No. 2).

M. Picard: Values, Immediate and Contributary, 1920.

J. F. Dashiell: The Philosophical Status of Values, 1913.

W. H. Sheldon: "An Empirical Theory of Value," Jour. of Philos., Vol. LXI, 1914.

J. S. Mackenzie: "Notes on Theory of Value," Mind, N. S. Vol. IV, 1895.

G. E. Moore: "The Conception of Intrinsic Value," in his Philosophical Studies, 1922.

J. Solomon: "Is the Conception of 'Good' Undefinable?" Proc. Arist. Soc., 1905-06.

J. L. McIntyre: "Value-Feelings and Judgments of Value," Proc. Arist. Soc., 1904-05.

A. P. Brogan: "The Fundamental Value Universal," Jour. of Philos., Vol. XVI, 1919.

W. M. Urban: Valuation, its Nature and Laws, 1909.

H. Münsterberg: Eternal Values, 1909.

B. Bosanquet: The Principle of Individuality and Value, 1912.

C. Bouglé: L'Evolution des Valeurs, 1922.

Ch. v. Ehrenfels: System der Werttheorie, 1897.

A. Meinong: Zur Grundlegung der allgemeinen Werttheorie, 1923.

A. Meinong: "Für die Psychologie und gegen den Psychologismus in der allgemeinen Werttheorie," Logos, Vol.
III, 1912.

W. Stern: Wertphilosophie, 1924.

G. Berguer: La Notion de Valeur, 1908.

F. Orestano: I Valori Umani, 1907.

G. Simmel: Philosophie des Geldes, 1900.

R. Eisler: Studien der Werttheorie, 1902.

J. C. Kreibig: Psychologische Grundlegung eines Systems der
Werttheorie, 1902.

F. Krüger: Der Begriff des absolut Wertvollen als Grundbegriff
der Moralphilosophie, 1898.

INDEX